A Companion to Nineteenth-Century Europe

BLACKWELL COMPANIONS TO EUROPEAN HISTORY

This series provides sophisticated and authoritative overviews of the scholarship that has shaped our current understanding of Europe's past. Each volume comprises between twenty-five and forty concise essays written by individual scholars within their area of specialization. The aim of each contribution is to synthesize the current state of scholarship from a variety of historical perspectives and to provide a statement on where the field is heading. The essays are written in a clear, provocative, and lively manner, designed for an international audience of scholars, students, and general readers. The *Blackwell Companions to European History* is a cornerstone of Blackwell's overarching Companions to History series, covering European, American, and World History.

A COMPANION TO NINETEENTH-CENTURY EUROPE

1789–1914

Edited by

Stefan Berger

© 2006 by Blackwell Publishing Ltd

BLACKWELL PUBLISHING
350 Main Street, Malden, MA 02148–5020, USA
9600 Garsington Road, Oxford OX4 2DQ, UK
550 Swanston Street, Carlton, Victoria 3053, Australia

First published 2006 by Blackwell Publishing Ltd

1   2006

Library of Congress Cataloging-in-Publication Data

A companion to nineteenth-century Europe, 1789–1914 / edited by Stefan Berger.
    p.   cm—(Blackwell companions to European history)
Includes bibliographical references and index.
ISBN-13: 978-1-4051-1320-5 (alk. paper)
ISBN-10: 1-4051-1320-0 (alk. paper)
1. Europe—History—1789–1900. 2. Europe—History—20th century. 3. Europe—Social conditions—1789–1900. 4. Europe–Social conditions—20th century. 5. Europe—Civilization—19th century. 6. Europe—Civilization—20th century. I. Berger, Stefan. II. Series.

D299.C623   2006
940.2′8—dc22
2005013073

A catalogue record for this title is available from the British Library.

Set in 9 on 11 pt Gallard
by SNP Best-set Typesetter Ltd, Hong Kong
Printed and bound in India
by Replika Press Ltd

The publisher's policy is to use permanent paper from mills that operate a sustainable forestry policy, and which has been manufactured from pulp processed using acid-free and elementary chlorine-free practices. Furthermore, the publisher ensures that the text paper and cover board used have met acceptable environmental accreditation standards.

For further information on
Blackwell Publishing, visit our website:
www.blackwellpublishing.com

Contents

Figures

Contributors

Stefan Berger is Professor of Modern German and Comparative European History at the University of Manchester. Currently, he directs a five-year European Science Foundation Programme on the theme of "The Writing of National Histories in Europe" (www.uni-leipzig.de/zhs/esf-nhist). He has published widely on comparative labor history, national identity, the history of historiography, and historical theory. His recent books include *Inventing the Nation: Germany* (London, 2004), *The Search for Normality: National Identity and Historical Consciousness in Germany since 1800* (2nd revd. edn., Oxford, 2003), *Social Democracy in Nineteenth and Twentieth Century Germany* (London, 2000), *Writing History* (ed. with Heiko Feldner and Kevin Passmore) (London, 2003), *Historikerdialoge* (ed. with Peter Lambert and Peter Schumann) (Göttingen, 2003), and *Policy Concertation and Social Partnership in Western Europe* (ed. with Hugh Compston) (Oxford, 2002).

Kathleen Canning is Professor of History, Women's Studies, and German Studies at the University of Michigan and former North American co-editor of *Gender and History*. She is the author of *Languages of Labor and Gender: Female Factory Work in Germany, 1850–1914* (Ithaca, 1996), co-editor with Sonya O. Rose of *Gender, Citizenships and Subjectivities* (Blackwell Publishing, 2002), and author of *Gender History in Practice: Bodies, Class and Citizenship* (Ithaca, 2005). She is working on a new book entitled *Embodied Citizenships: Gender and the Crisis of the Nation in Germany, 1916–1930*.

Ivan Crozier is a Lecturer in the Science Studies Unit at the University of Edinburgh. He previously held a research fellowship at the Wellcome Trust Centre for the History of Medicine at University College, London. His research interests include the history of forensic psychiatry, the history of sexology, the sociology of scientific knowledge, and the history of the body. He is editor (with Christopher Forth) of *Body Parts: Critical Explorations of Corporeality* (Lexington, 2005). He has published essays in numerous academic journals.

James R. Farr is Professor of History at Purdue University. He books include *Artisans in Europe, 1300–1914* (Cambridge, 2000), *Authority and Sexuality in Early Modern Burgundy, 1550–1730* (New York, 1995), and *Hands of Honor: Artisans and Their World in Dijon, 1550–1650* (Ithaca, 1988). He edited *The Industrial Era in Europe, 1750–1914*, World Eras, Vol. 9 (Columbia, SC, 2003), and has two books in press: *Murder, Passion and Power in Seventeenth-Century France* (2005) and *Work and Culture in Early Modern France* (2006).

Ute Frevert is Professor of History at Yale University. She is a Fellow at the

Wissenschaftskolleg zu Berlin and at the Center of Advanced Study in Stanford. Her main research areas include the social and gender history of modern Germany, military–civil relations, and European identities. Her major works in English are *Women in German History* (Oxford, 1989), *Men of Honour* (Cambridge, 1995), and *A Nation in Barracks* (Oxford, 2004).

John Garrard is Senior Lecturer in Politics and Contemporary History in the School of English, Sociology, Politics, and Contemporary History, and member of the European Studies Research Institute, at the University of Salford. Although primarily a historian, his research interests lie on the borderlines between history and political science. His publications include *The English and Immigration: A Comparative Study of the Jewish Influx 1880–1910* (Oxford, 1970), *Leadership and Power in Victorian Industrial Towns 1830–80* (Manchester, 1983), *The Great Salford Gas Scandal of 1887* (Manchester, 1988), and *Democratization in Britain: Elites, Civil Society and Reform since 1800* (London, 2002). He is currently editing (with James Newell) *Scandals in Past and Contemporary Politics* and a book on *Heads of the Local State in Past and Present*.

Sharif Gemie is a Reader in History at the University of Glamorgan. He has researched themes such as the interplay between literature and political culture, and the development of anarchist political culture. He became editor of *Anarchist Studies* in 1996. In recent years he has developed an interest in Spanish political culture, and has published on topics such as Orientalism, Brittany, and Galicia.

Hamish Graham teaches early modern European and nineteenth-century history, as well as more specialized courses on the French Revolution and the history of crime, at the University of New South Wales in Sydney. His research is focused on the competing demands for forest resources in eighteenth-century France. Articles on aspects of forest policy and woodland disputes under the Old Regime have recently appeared in *French History*, *European History Quarterly*, and *Rural History*.

Mike Hawkins is Reader in Social and Political Thought in the School of Social Science, Kingston University. He has published *Social Darwinism in European and American Thought, 1860–1945: Nature as Model and Nature as Threat* (Cambridge, 1997), as well as journal articles on nineteenth- and twentieth-century French social and political thought.

Oded Heilbronner is Lecturer at the School of History, Hebrew University, Jerusalem and Shenkar College for Design and Engineering, Tel Aviv, where he teaches European history, popular culture, and British history. His publications include *Catholicism, Political Culture and the Countryside: A Social History of the Nazi Party in South Germany* (Ann Arbor, 1999) and *Populäre Kultur, Populärer Liberalismus und das Bürgertum im ländlichen Deutschland: 1860s–1930s* (forthcoming).

Matthew Jefferies is Senior Lecturer in German History at the University of Manchester. He is the author of *Politics and Culture in Wilhelmine Germany: The Case of Industrial Architecture* (Oxford, 1995) and *Imperial Culture in Germany, 1871–1918* (Basingstoke, 2003), as well as articles on environmental history, lifestyle reform, and naturism. He is currently writing a historiographical study of the German Empire for Blackwell's *Contesting the Past* series.

Robert Lee is Chaddock Professor of Economic and Social History at the University of Liverpool and Co-Director of the Centre for Port and Maritime History. He is the author, editor, and co-editor of ten books on German and European demographic, social, and economic history, including (with Richard Lawton) *Population and Society in Western European Port-Cities c. 1650–1939* (Liverpool, 2002). His current research projects include "Official statistics and demography in Germany, 1872–1939" (funded by the Deutsche Forschungsgemeinschaft) and "Shipping, trade, and mercantile business in Liverpool, 1851–1901" (funded by the Leverhulme Trust and English Heritage).

Jörn Leonhard is Associate Professor at the University of Jena. His publications include analyses of the semantics of liberalism in

European comparison: *Liberalismus. Zur historischen Semantik eines europäischen Deutungsmusters* (Munich, 2001); the emergence of European nationalisms: *Nationalismen in Europa: West- und Osteuropa im Vergleich* (edited with Ulrike von Hirschhausen) (Göttingen, 2001); and *German Unification in Perspective: Ten Years of German Unification: Transfer, Transformation, Incorporation* (edited with Lothar Funk) (Birmingham, 2002). Forthcoming is a comparative study on the relation between war experiences and nation building in France, Germany, Britain, and the United States, 1750–1914: *Bellizismus und Nation. Kriegsdeutung und Nationsbestimmung in Europa und den Vereinigten Staaten 1750–1914.*

Carl Levy is a Reader in European Politics and Head of the Department of Politics at Goldsmiths College, University of London. His major fields of interest are comparative modern and contemporary European history and politics and the history and politics of modern Italy. Recent publications include *Gramsci and the Anarchists* (Oxford, 1999) and *Three Postwar Eras in Comparison: Western Europe 1918–1945–1989* (edited with Mark Roseman) (Basingstoke, 2001).

William Mulligan teaches modern history at the University of Glasgow. He has written on the German army in the interwar period, including *The Creation of the Modern German Army: General Walther Reinhardt and the Weimar Republic, 1914–1930* (Oxford, 2004). He is currently working on British foreign policy in the nineteenth century.

Edmund Neill recently completed a DPhil at Oxford University comparing the political thought of Michael Oakeshott and Hannah Arendt. He is a former lecturer in modern history at both Christ Church and Somerville colleges in Oxford, and has published a number of articles and reviews on the history of nineteenth and twentieth-century British political thought.

Kathryn M. Olesko is Associate Professor and Director of the Master of Arts in German and European Studies at Georgetown University, Washington, DC. Her recent publications are on precision measurement, instrumental errors, science pedagogy, and the role of science and technology in the construction of modernity. She is completing a book on the cultural history of precision measurement in the German states from 1648 to 1989. As editor of *Osiris*, she seeks to bridge history and history of science.

Shane P. O'Rourke lectures in Russian history at the University of York. He is presently completing a history of the Cossacks to be published in 2005/2006.

Pamela Pilbeam is Professor of French History at Royal Holloway, University of London. Her most recent books are *Madame Tussaud and the History of Waxworks* (London, 2003) and *French Socialists before Marx: Workers, Women and the Social Question in France* (Teddington, 2000). She is currently working on two books: *Saint-Simonians: Free Love to Big Business* and *Bourgeois Society and Culture in Nineteenth-Century Europe*.

David Rechter is University Research Lecturer in Oriental Studies at the University of Oxford, Research Fellow of St. Antony's College, Oxford, and Rachel Finkelstein Fellow in Modern Jewish History at the Oxford Centre for Hebrew and Jewish Studies. He is the author of *The Jews of Vienna and the First World War* (London, 2001) and joint editor of *Two Nations: British and German Jews in Comparative Perspective* (Tuebingen, 1999) and *Towards Normality? Acculturation and Modern German Jewry* (Tuebingen, 2003).

Jutta Schwarzkopf has taught modern British history at various German universities, mainly at the University of Hanover. Apart from her most recent book, *Unpicking Gender: The Social Construction of Gender in the Lancashire Cotton Weaving Industry, 1880–1914* (Aldershot, 2004), she has written numerous articles on issues of class and gender in nineteenth-century Britain, focusing on Chartism and waged work.

Anthony J. Steinhoff is Assistant Professor of Modern European History at the University of Tennessee at Chattanooga. A specialist on German and French social and religious history, he is presently completing a monograph on Protestantism and religious culture in the city of Strasbourg between 1870 and 1914. His recent publications include a contribution on religion and German nation building for volume nine of the *Cambridge History of Christianity*.

Bo Stråth is Professor of Contemporary History at the European University Institute in Florence. His research focuses on modernization and democratization processes in Western Europe in a comparative context, in particular on the issue of a European culture and a European modernity in comparison. Among his most recent publications are *States and Citizens: History, Theory, Prospects* (with Quentin Skinner) (Cambridge, 2003) and *The Meaning of Europe: Variety and Contention Within and Among Nations* (with Mikael af Malmborg) (Oxford, 2002).

Trutz von Trotha is Professor of Sociology at the University of Siegen in Germany. For many years he has researched the colonial and postcolonial state, violence, war, the rise and fall of the state, and new forms of political orders, especially in West Africa. Among his recent publications are *Reorganization or Decline of the Rule of Law?* (edited with Jakob Rösel) (Cologne, 2005) and *Healing the Wounds: Essays on the Reconstruction of Societies after War* (edited with Marie-Claire Foblets) (Oxford, 2004).

Daniel M. Vyleta holds a Junior Research Fellowship at Fitzwilliam College, Cambridge, and is currently working as Assistant Professor at the European College of Liberal Arts in Berlin. He is the author of *Crime, News and Jews: Vienna 1890–1914* (Oxford, 2004).

John C. Waller is a Lecturer in the History of Science and Medicine at the University of Melbourne. His research focuses mainly on theories of heredity and hereditary malady in the 1700s and 1800s and their social impli-

cations. He is the author of three recent books: *Leaps in the Dark: The Forging of Scientific Reputations* (Oxford, 2004), *The Discovery of the Germ* (New York, 2003), and *Einstein's Luck* (Oxford, 2002).

Chris A. Williams is a Lecturer in History at the Open University. He researches the history of crime and policing since around 1780. He edited the collection *Giving the Past a Future: Preserving the Heritage of the UK's Criminal Justice System* (London, 2004).

James A. Winders is a modern French cultural historian and Professor of History at Appalachian State University. His books include *European Culture Since 1848: From Modern to Postmodern and Beyond* (New York, 2001), *Gender, Theory, and the Canon* (Madison, WI, 1991), and the forthcoming *Paris africain: Rhythms of the African Diaspora* (New York).

Michael Wintle is Professor of European History at the University of Amsterdam, where he directs the degree programs in European Studies. His current research interests are in European identity and especially the visual representation of Europe, cultural aspects of European integration, European industrialization, and the modern social and economic history of the Low Countries. He has published widely on Dutch and European history, including *Culture and Identity in Europe* (Aldershot, 1996), *Under the Sign of Liberalism* (Zutphen, 1997), *An Economic and Social History of the Netherlands* (Cambridge, 2000), *The Idea of a United Europe: Political, Economic and Cultural Integration since the Fall of the Berlin Wall* (Basingstoke, 2000), and (ed. with M. Spiering) *Ideas of Europe since 1914* (London, 2002).

Map 1 Europe 1740–1789

Map 2 Europe in 1816

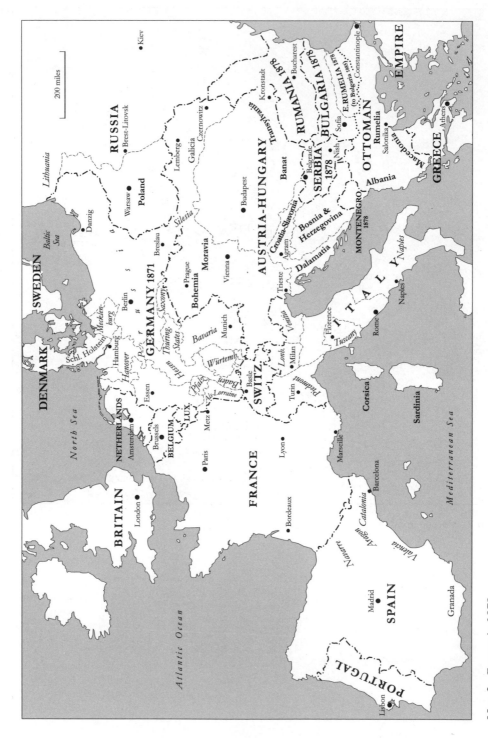

Map 3 Europe in 1878

Introduction

STEFAN BERGER

The nineteenth century started with revolution and ended with the advent of a major war. The year 1789 introduced a new grammar of politics and formulated a new conception of society. The idea of a society of orders, where people were born into a particular class and stayed there, gave way to notions of mobility, where property, ownership, gender, and education defined a meritocracy of deserving citizens. These were bound up with the gradual and uneven emergence of a new grammar of economics, as it was formulated above all in Europe's "first industrial nation," Britain.[1] The spread of market values across Europe meant the commodification of all social relations. The Napoleonic armies spread the new ways of thinking about society and politics across Europe. The inaptly named "restoration period" after 1815 could not turn the historical clocks back to pre 1789 time. The old system had gone for good and Europeans had to learn to accommodate to a new set of social practices. Similarly, when the lights went out in Europe in the autumn of 1914, the curtain fell on the long nineteenth century. The societies that emerged from the experience of the Great War, whether they belonged to the victors or the losers, were qualitatively different from the ones that had entered it.

The aim of this volume is to give students of European history a firm grasp of the many topics and debates which have made "the long nineteenth century" such a rewarding field of study for generations of historians. The oldest historiography, going back to the nineteenth century itself, is the one which deals with political, diplomatic, and international history. It conceptualized the history of Europe as the history of the European state system and the framing of international politics by "great" statesmen. Equally, there is a distinguished tradition of writing European history as the history of ideas.[2] Here, Europe tended to equal progress and civilization. It also meant Christianity and the defense of Christianity against Islam in particular became the staple diet of European history writing. Secular concepts based on Enlightenment ideas about a particularly European rationality, European liberty and the classical heritage came to challenge the identification of Europe with Christianity. And later in the century ethnic and racial concepts became a popular means of defining Europe.

The social and economic history of the nineteenth century can also look back on a very well established literature: while its origins go back to the late nineteenth and early twentieth centuries, it arguably had its heyday in the post-World War II period, when social history seemed, at least for a while, the only show in town.[3] Heavily influenced by Weberian and Marxist concepts, it sought to identify patterns of socioeconomic developments and their reverberations in the fields of politics and culture. Eric Hobsbawm's monumental three volume history of the nineteenth century stands as a lasting monument to this kind of social history.[4] The pluralization of historiographical discourses from the 1970s onwards brought a wide range of new and interesting perspectives, including gender history, history from below and the methodological challenges of poststructuralism and the linguistic turn. The "new cultural history" is, of course, not so new now and it is possible in the subsequent chapters to provide a synthesis of some of the areas where it has been most productive.

The overall structure of the volume falls into six parts, which form distinct but overlapping interpretive axes of European history. The contributions to each part demonstrate that European history today is written from a bewildering multitude of perspectives. Part One seeks to problematize our understanding of European history by asking how notions of Europeanness were constructed in the nineteenth century. What is regarded as European has been and continues to be a matter for debate and cannot be reduced to some notion of fixed geographical and cultural characteristics. Notions of Europeanness have developed gradually in a long and complex process. As Bo Stråth reminds us, Europe is not a straightforward geographical description. Complicated processes of border-setting included or excluded various geographical areas at different times: Eastern Europe, Russia, the Slavs, Islam, the Ottoman Empire, the Orient, North Africa, Asia, and the United States were all defined as Europe's "other" at one time or another and by different constituencies. With the onset of European colonialism and imperialism, Europe expanded to become a truly global category. After all, European heritage could now be found in all parts of the globe. White European settler societies such as the United States, Canada, Australia, or New Zealand are hard to imagine without their European heritage. In the name of Europe different nation-states have also been engaged in staking out claims of regional hegemony. Thus, for example, the concept of "Central Europe" was intimately bound up with the aggrandizement of Germany to the detriment of smaller nations in this region. Equally, the idea of "East Central Europe" was widely used as a means of distancing the nascent nation-states in this region

from the empires of Russia, Prussia, and the Habsburgs. Larger historical regions which transcend nation-states have played a major role in forming our understanding of Europe as a continent.[5]

Constructions of Europe's internal and external borders and the writing of Europe's history were intimately connected to visual representations of Europe, the topic of Michael Wintle's contribution to this volume. Europe was consistently portrayed as superior to her fellow continents. In the era of mass nationalism in the second half of the nineteenth century visual representations of the nation overlaid those of Europe, often using the same arsenal of images. As the idea of a united Europe was replaced by the idea of rivaling nations, an essential Eurocentrism continued to inform Europe's visual culture. But Europe also became the symbol of an international arbiter between the quarrelsome nations. Notions of one European family remained strong even during times of intense nationalist rivalry.

Part Two looks at the economic and social history of Europe. In the nineteenth century Europe underwent a fundamental transformation from a predominantly agricultural society to one based on industrial production and international trade. Gradual and uneven economic change impacted on the make-up and social relations of European societies. First and foremost, historians have increasingly taken leave of the idea of an "industrial revolution."

European societies remained predominantly rural and agricultural during the entire nineteenth century. Hamish Graham emphasizes the extraordinary diversity of rural life and durability of rural traditions. Peasant-worker families and the impact of proto-industrialization added to this diversity. The land made a significant contribution to overall economic output. Changes in agriculture were a major precondition for industrialization, as the provision of more and better food led to a sustained population growth which provided labor and raw materials needed in the industrialization process. The countryside also provided markets for urban produce. State authorities were above all interested in penetrating and ruling over an often unruly countryside. The nationalization of peasants, the standardization of rules in the countryside, the imposition of uniformity as far as legal codes, currencies, and maps were concerned, were all attempts at making rural societies less "foreign" to the urban centers and bringing them into national and state communities. Rural society often resisted such encroachments of the central state, as attachments remained heavily local and regional.

Economic historians have equally urged us to view industrialization as a regional phenomenon. As Robert Lee explains, they have gone beyond the notion of technological innovation and drawn attention to the importance of cultural and political factors, especially the role of the state, education systems, and entrepreneurial identities. A much more long-term view of industrialization emerged, as earlier ideas of an allegedly crucial 30 year period looked increasingly unsustainable. Many economic historians have questioned the appropriateness of the very term "industrial revolution," as it does not capture the far more gradual evolution of market forces and market orientation which came to dominate European social and cultural processes. Yet industrialization did result in significant population growth spawning processes of urbanization. Lee gives us chapter and verse on the massive proportions of population growth in the nineteenth century, yet stresses the diversity of factors producing such an explosion of numbers. Significant attempts to limit families set in only from the 1880s, at about the same time when sanitary reforms and the rise in living standards reduced mortality rates drastically.[6]

Socioeconomic developments were directly related to changes in social relations. As Carl Levy points out, the long decline of serfdom led to the emergence of a whole variety of forms of free labor under different systems of land tenure. Political hegemony in the countryside was highly contested and diverse groups propagated the values of the land in order to pursue very different political strategies. Landed elites were undoubtedly still powerful in 1914, but these elites were not the same as those who dominated the land around 1800. In effect, in most places the traditional landed elites had merged with representatives of the middle classes to modernize the outlook and strategies of landed society and make it ready for both capitalism and mass politics.

But who were the middle classes? Pamela Pilbeam stresses the diversity of groups all claiming to belong to the "middling sort." It was, above all, an aspiring class of people whose markers of belonging were education, property, family, and leisure time. They did not, however, share one political orientation and a previous loose identification of the middle classes with liberalism has by now become very unfashionable among historians.

The rise of the middle classes was accompanied by the decline of the artisanate as an autonomous group. As Jim Farr explains, the new industrial order had a deeply corrosive effect on the artisans' guild system, based on the values of paternalism, hierarchy, and subordination to discipline. As corporate craft traditions were increasingly undermined by new economic strategies, legislation, and commercialized forms of mass culture and consumerism, artisans hung on to the traditional image of independence for as long as they could. They did not want to sink into the mass of proletarians and wholeheartedly embraced the social values of the middle classes. But at the same time their corporate traditions influenced early labor movements across Europe. Ideas of worker collectivism and self-improvement through education, so prominent among the labor movement, had strong roots in the worlds of the nineteenth-century artisan.

The new economic order made an increasing number of people identify themselves as a new social stratum, the working class. Jutta Schwarzkopf delineates its major characteristics. Workplace and home were clearly separated. Working lives were dominated by a new factory discipline symbolized by the clock and the machine. The social distance between those who owned property and those who sold their labor rose immeasurably. The textile mills of Europe were the laboratory in which the new economic order first became apparent. But the new social order also manifested itself outside the factories. Overcrowded housing conditions, poverty, disease, accidents, and the general insecurity of the basic proletarian existence all produced solidarities which were often based on neighborhood networks and kinship ties.

The beginnings of social policies were geared towards alleviating the worst aspects of material deprivation experienced by workers, but they also actively propagated middle-class standards of morality aimed at integrating workers into national societies and fending off the specter of social unrest and revolution.

Part Three examines political developments in nineteenth-century Europe. As Sharif Gemie points out, revolution was in fact a common European experience in the nineteenth century. Starting with the foundational moment of the French Revolution of 1789, a whole succession of revolutionary movements sought to overturn the existing social and political order. "The people" became the rallying cry of those who wanted to erect a new political order on the foundations of citizenship. It soon merged and became overlaid with languages of class, which sought to combine political change with ideas of an altogether different socioeconomic order. The European revolutions of 1848 and the Russian Revolution of 1905 were arguably seminal events with grave consequences for the development of European societies. Those actively participating in revolutions found in them an important moment of self-identification and a strong sense of community. Throughout Europe the emergence of a public sphere was the precondition for the emergence of revolutionary movements. For much of the period revolutionary traditions were tightly linked to ideas of liberty and freedom, challenging the traditional social order. But towards the end of the nineteenth century right-wing movements also began to advocate notions of a revolution which rose to prominence during the first half of the twentieth century.

During the nineteenth century states became the most important bulwark against revolution. Jörn Leonhard reminds us that European states acquired their modern meaning through the increasing power of state bureaucracies, the strong alignment of state power to particular social classes, and the firm distinction between state and society. Centralized state power increased in order to deal with a rising number of challenges such as incorporation of diverse territories into the state, the training of a new professional elite of civil ser-

vants, migration, the threat of revolution, handling the communications revolutions, the diverse consequences of industrialization, and, last but not least, the preparation for war. Leonhard turns the spotlight on education and the welfare state as two key examples of the increasing will of the state actively to shape the lives of its citizens. Both areas also provide ample evidence of the considerable resistance such increased intervention produced among many groups of society.

Revolutions challenged the state to democratize and liberalize state structures and to take seriously the agency of its "people" and aspiring citizens. As John Garrard points out, those states which tended towards liberal forms of government in the eighteenth century were far more successful in democratizing in the nineteenth century than those regimes which were run on more authoritarian or absolutist lines. Yet ultimately the emphasis everywhere was on political control. Where European elites were willing to grant manhood suffrage they did so because they believed that they could manipulate the results and manage mass politics. But the impact of mass politics could be felt even in regimes which did not allow for any widespread formal participation in the political process. Mass meetings, demonstrations, petitions, and street politics more generally became widespread as politics turned into a mass spectacle and public entertainment.

Workers and their organizations increasingly played a prominent role in politics. They championed diverse ideas of a more equal and socially just society. Labor movements, as Stefan Berger emphasizes, were ideologically heterogeneous. Liberal, socialist, anarcho-syndicalist, and Catholic associations developed very different notions of what was in the workers' interests. National movements provided a formidable challenge to labor's internationalism. They promised inclusion but practiced exclusion of both "internal" and "external" enemies. They were champions of often contradictory and competing narratives about the nation which came complete with foundational moments, national heroes, and a whole array of national symbols and myths all attempting to ascertain the long and proud pedigree of the nation. National movements could be participatory movements of people demanding a greater say in the affairs of the state, championing ideas of traditional freedoms and rights of the people which had to be reinstated. But as Berger underlines, they were also highly effective champions of aggressive expansionism, imperialism, and the belief in the superiority of one's own nation.

Both labor and national movements were dominated by men and characterized by a good measure of anti-feminism. And yet both movements gave women considerable scope for developing their public roles. Thus, there were 150 female Chartist organizations in Britain, and the 1848 revolutions on the continent witnessed the proliferation of women's clubs and associations. The French Revolution of 1789 was, as Kathleen Canning argues, the crucial event for reconfiguring the "woman question" for the nineteenth century. It mobilized women around the issue of rights, brought partial advances for women through the French constitution of 1791, and inspired women in other parts of Europe. Neither of the attempts of Napoleon or of Metternich to restore the old pre-revolutionary gender order was successful. The genie was out of the bottle and all recurring attempts to push women back into the private realm after periods of intense politicization could not prevent the flowering of a major pan-European debate about the character of both sexes and how they differed. Some of the most radical ideas about reconstructing the existing gender order were formulated by the utopian socialists. Overall, the "woman question" became increasingly tied up with issues of constitutionalism, individual rights, and the social and the national question. For middle-class women in particular, nationalism and charity work for the poor formed two important areas where they could become active within the public sphere. Maternalism and social reform were in turn closely related to the issue of empire building. For working-class women, the ideologies of "social motherhood" and domesticity made it difficult to negotiate the world of work with the world of family responsibilities, as female employment was widely perceived as bringing social instability to working-class families and having a negative impact on national birth rates and the

health of the nation more generally. Nevertheless, it seems difficult to uphold an older notion that women, during the first half of the nineteenth century, retreated into the private sphere of home and family, while men occupied the public spheres of politics, business, and civic affairs.[7]

Part Four concerns itself with the intellectual history of nineteenth-century Europe, which was characterized by intense competition between liberal, conservative, and socialist ideologies. All three, according to Edmund Neill, were reactions to the European Enlightenment. Liberals were champions of progress, private property, national self-determination, and individual liberty, initially defined as freedom from state interference. Conservatives, by contrast, emphasized stability, continuity, religious bonds, and the importance of heritage and history. During the course of the nineteenth century both conservatism and liberalism diversified into a set of movements only loosely connected. Towards the end of the century socialism provided a fundamental challenge to the way both conservatives and liberals imagined society to work.

If the social and economic theories of Karl Marx provided much inspiration for socialists, the ideas of Charles Darwin formed the starting point of another powerful intellectual current – that of Social Darwinism, explored by Mike Hawkins. Social Darwinists came to believe that biological processes determined human behavior and social processes. The diversity, adaptability, and simplicity of Social Darwinist beliefs explains much of their popular appeal in the second half of the nineteenth century. In the age of imperialism Social Darwinists warned against "interracial breeding" and were obsessed with degeneration and the struggle for racial superiority.

Many key intellectuals of the nineteenth century, like Marx, Darwin, Nietzsche, and Freud, were heavily critical of Christianity and the Christian churches. Given the sustained attacks on the intellectual hegemony of the churches, historians tended to view the nineteenth century as a century of secularization. The French Revolution and the long arm of Napoleon's armies had certainly weakened the power of the church by widely redistributing church property. But more recently historians have discovered the adaptability and resilience of Christian beliefs, and some have even spoken of the nineteenth century as a second confessional age, in which religion played a major role in people's lives. The Catholic church, as Oded Heilbronner outlines, suffered under an onslaught by the liberal-national movements which tended to be hostile to Catholicism as a transnational, Rome-centered movement. Only in Poland and Ireland, stateless nations before 1914, did the Catholic church enter close alliances with national movements intent on overthrowing what were perceived as foreign oppressors. And in Spain the traditionally close alliance between church and state was also maintained. But everywhere the Catholic church sought very successfully to reenforce the Catholic milieu and turn it into a bulwark against the modern influences of liberalism, rationalism, progress, socialism, Darwinism, nihilism, nationalism, and psychoanalysis. It could rely in particular on the appeal of popular piety and on women activists, who were among the most loyal and fervent supporters of the church and contributed to a growing feminization of the Catholic religion.

Protestants had fewer difficulties with nationalism. In fact Protestantism and nationalism merged in a number of states so as to become virtually indistinguishable. Popular pietism and evangelism were the driving forces of a revival of Protestantism in the nineteenth century, as Protestant beliefs became increasingly heterogeneous even within state churches. While there was, as Anthony Steinhoff concedes, undoubtedly a process of "unchurching," which predominantly affected the urban male working classes, the Protestant missionary societies made Protestantism a global force to be reckoned with.

None of the major Christian churches in Europe rejected the challenges of modernity so thoroughly as the Orthodox church. It was, as Shane O'Rourke points out, shaped to a significant extent by the existence of three empires. The Byzantine Empire produced the doctrine of a symphony between church and state which allowed the church considerable autonomy. In the Ottoman Empire the patriarchs of Constantinople wielded considerable religious and worldly powers. Their loyalty to the sultan produced manifold conflicts with local Orthodox churches within the Ottoman Empire, which occasionally put them at the helm of local national movements fighting for independence from the empire. In the Russian Empire the Orthodox church was almost totally subservient to the Russian state.

Both the old Christian Europe and modern intellectual currents were frequently united in their stance against European Jewry. Antisemitism had been a hallmark of European society for a long time, but the nineteenth century held out the promise of emancipation. For the first time it became imaginable that Jews would leave the religious ghetto that they had occupied for centuries. One part of European Jewry reacted enthusiastically to this prospect and preached assimilation. Another part attempted to strike a balance between their traditional ways of life and assimilation. And yet another part rejected Enlightenment values and relied on traditional definitions of Jewishness. But every Jew had to respond to the advent of modernity. As David Rechter points out, Western European Jews on the whole tended toward the first two options, while Eastern European Jews were most likely to favor the last option.

Part Five deals with aspects of cultural history in nineteenth-century Europe. Increasingly diverse forms of popular culture, including mass spectator sports, music halls, café house culture, early cinema, photography, museums, and lending libraries, catered for the growing leisure time of people. James Winders finds in Romanticism the key influence on both popular and high culture. Romanticism had a complex and ambiguous relationship to the traditions of the Enlightenment, which provided both inspiration to the Romantics and provoked their violent rejection. Romanticism's cult of the individual genius, its championing of nature, its cult of youth, its rejection of industrial society, and its emphasis on conveying emotion all shaped European society in a perplexing variety of ways, which were politically contradictory and multipolar. Romantics could be found in the camps of revolution, reform, and reaction. They became champions of subsequent Realist movements with their strong concerns with the social question just as much as they turned towards Symbolism, with its concern with the liminality of human experience. And, of course, Romanticism also underpinned much of the new irrationalism, so popular with the turn-of-the-century avant-garde.

The advances of mass culture would have been unthinkable without the growing literacy rates among a wider population. These were directly related to the introduction of compulsory schooling. As Sharif Gemie argues, schooling and the development of a "schooling program" was a genuinely European project which aimed primarily at instilling a sense of order and responsibility into the masses so as to allow modernization of European society to proceed in an orderly fashion. But schools did not necessarily produce the well-ordered individuals which state bureaucracies desired. They could equally produce dissident identities, as they were often genuinely unpopular. Pupils connected them to physical violence and places of ill-health. And many poorer families, who needed the labor power of children in their quest to survive, resented the state's insistence on sending their offspring to school.

History became a core subject in European schools. A strong sense of the historicity (i.e., of the historical rootedness of all that existed) was, as Matthew Jefferies points out, one of the most distinctive features of the nineteenth century. As knowledge of the past allegedly allowed for the better understanding of the present and the correct prediction of the future, history became instrumentalized for a wide variety of purposes. Only towards the end of the nineteenth century did historism[8] decline in importance, as it was identified more and more with antiquarianism. In the context of the cultural pessimism of the *fin de siècle*, fewer people were willing to believe in the explanatory powers of history and instead shared Nietzsche's indictment of history as a burden on life.

If Nietzsche was instrumental in the demise of historism, he was also scathing about the impact of science on European culture. As Kathryn Olesko argues, conceptions of scientific knowledge changed in a major way during the nineteenth century. Specialist scientific disciplines now emerged, as did the "scientist" as a new persona. European state examination systems for scientists produced upward social mobility for many members of the middle classes, as new sites for scientific research flourished: the university-based laboratory and institute, the industrial and government-sponsored laboratories, and the private research institutes. Many of these developments first happened in Germany, but they were quickly taken up and adapted in other European countries. Science was to be crucial in furthering a new understanding of both self and society in the nineteenth century. Systems of classification and the construction of hierarchies as well as definitions of "normalcy" and "deviance" all rested heavily on scientific methods, in particular methods of measuring. The new scientific culture helped to define bourgeois values such as toleration, openness, and rationality. Furthermore, many scientific inventions revolutionized the everyday life of the people of Europe. They contributed to new ways of seeing the world. Science was also becoming indispensable to European states attempting to provide good government, which was increasingly understood to be a byword for regulating and policing society. Nations and empires needed statisticians, cartographers, and other scientists to define their borders and provide justification for their being, their expansion, and their superiority over neighboring nations and the colonized parts of the globe.

Despite the skepticism and critique of science put forward towards the end of the nineteenth century by Nietzsche and Max Weber, among others, science enthralled the European public, as it seemed to promise solutions to a variety of problems relating to the organization of social life. Chris Williams reminds us that policing methods were transformed through the emergence of criminalistics as a science. The police contributed to the increasing bureaucratic regulation of life and it aimed at stabilizing the existing political and social order by adopting scientific methods. Dan Vyleta stresses both the diversity of scientific constructions of criminality and its change over time. The discourse about criminality became increasingly medicalized, with issues of degeneration and national decline taking center stage.

Medical knowledge more generally had made major advances throughout the nineteenth century, although, as John Waller argues, very little was actually put into practice. Eighteenth-century treatment regimes, geared towards individuals and their physical constitutions and lifestyles, remained the norm. They were based on highly individualized views of illness which failed to take into account considerations of the health of wider populations. Sanitary reform was a major debating point in the nineteenth century, and advances in the field of bacteriology increased the understanding of the origins of major epidemics, but progress was checked time and again by the cost of major public health reform. Overall, medical discourses had a strong moral undertone, as illness was widely perceived as the result of sin, while health was seen as reward for the virtuous.

When Freud, the founding father of the science of the psyche, discovered the unconscious of the individual self he postulated it as the most important driving force of a person's individual development and of the entire historical process. In particular it was sex and death which, he argued, were central to the explanation of human behavior. Sexuality, Ivan Crozier tells us, thus moved from being largely a moral concern dominated by religious teaching to a scientific issue to be explored systematically by a new science with close links to medicine, which called itself sexology. Sexuality and especially sexual deviance became a topic of scientific enquiry resulting in the formulation of specific treatment regimes.

Part Six assesses the development of the international system of great powers in the long nineteenth century. The European state system underwent a period of profound destabilization with the period of the revolutionary and Napoleonic wars. At the end of it, the Congress of Vienna attempted to stabilize an entirely different map of Europe than had existed before 1789. With the exception of the Crimean war in the middle of the century, the post-1815 Concert of Europe was very successful in managing crisis and averting the threat of war. Conflict resolution was achieved through diplomacy, alliance systems, and the ideal of the balance of power. As William Mulligan demon-

strates, the five great powers (Pentrachy) were essentially the same during the entire nineteenth century, but their relative importance changed, as Prussia/Germany rose to prominence, while Austria-Hungary declined and the Ottoman Empire turned into the "sick man of Europe." Britain remained the major European sea power intent on preventing, first France, and later Prussia/ Germany, from dominating continental Europe. After 1848, notions of national prestige came to dominate foreign policies and contributed to aggressive forms of power politics, increasing the risk of military conflict.

Warfare itself had become, as Ute Frevert points out, a very different thing under the impact of the revolutionary and Napoleonic wars. As wars were from now on fought in the name of the nation and the people, warfare became more total and absolute than ever before. Advances in technology ensured that it also became more violent. Conscript armies faced each other, as wars became the affairs of citizens. It was this reference to citizenship which excluded women from military service. Not perceived as being fit to serve, they were in turn regarded as unable to participate in other civic affairs, especially politics.

Yet nineteenth-century Europe by and large fought its wars outside of Europe. Colonial conflicts increased tensions between the European powers, but they also acted as a safety valve, deflecting conflict away from the European continent. Colonialism was in effect, as Trutz von Trotha argues, the central ingredient of globalization in the nineteenth century. Different forms of colonial expansion produced a variety of power relationships between conquerors and conquered. Diverse strategies of providing legitimacy for colonial rule met with strategies of defiance on the part of the colonized.

Colonialism exported Europe to the wider world and, at the same time, it brought the wider world to Europe. It is therefore impossible to write the history of Europe without constantly reflecting the ways in which colonial empires shaped different nation-states in Europe and thus became part and parcel of the self-understanding of Europe.[9] By the end of the nineteenth century the internationalization of trade and economic life had produced a single world market. Globalization brought a wave of processes of cultural transfer which has caught the attention of historians more recently. It has contributed to undermining an older picture of autonomous and internally stable national cultures and instead underlined the extent to which such national cultures depended on the continuous selective appropriation of "foreign" elements. Proper attention to the importance of processes of cultural transfer will make it more difficult in future to write European history as the history of its nation-states and instead invites historians to consider a framework of cultural appropriation and mediation.[10] Thus, for example, the strategies of Irish tenant farmers in their struggles against landlords were copied by Italian peasants. The French gendarmerie system, put into place under Napoleon Bonaparte, was exported to most of Europe in the first half of the nineteenth century. Subsequently, considerable cross-border and transnational cooperation between different national police forces ensured the European-wide surveillance of political revolutionary and dissident movements. The German socialist and Catholic milieus were models for other socialist and Catholic associations across Europe, which attempted to adapt what they perceived as organizational and ideological models. Daniel O'Connell's campaign for Catholic emancipation between 1824 and 1828 employed all the weapons of a developed civil society. It mobilized the press and voluntary associations and used the public meeting to great effect. Once again, many emancipatory movements across Europe looked to Ireland for inspiration. In 1848 issues of communication, assembly, and organization came to the fore across Europe and the revolutions were of major importance in developing civil societies across a wide range of European states.[11] They in turn fostered the breakthrough to constitutional forms of government – a trend which had received a major push in 1848 and which, despite initial defeats, was irreversible. The first half of the nineteenth century had in fact witnessed the proliferation of both public and secret clubs and societies: the Hampden Club in Britain, campaigning for franchise reform, and the Italian Carbonari or the French Charbonnerie, with their concerns of social and political reform. The largest and best-known group of the 1830s was Giuseppe Mazzini's Young Italy, which was feted throughout Europe. In the world of ideas, there were figures of true European standing, such as Herder, Darwin, Nietzsche, Marx, Mill, and Freud, whose writings were translated and whose ideas were received in very different social contexts, where they informed a wide variety of social practices. Experiences of migration and diaspora further increased the receptivity of European societies to "foreign" ideas and made for the adaptation of social and cultural practices in different societal contexts.

Histories of cultural transfer, entangled histories, comparative histories, and transnational histories have sharpened our awareness of European-wide processes and practices.[12] At the beginning of the twenty-first century, historians across Europe are moving away from a concern with national processes and taking into view transnational developments. Future European histories will no longer resemble an assembly of parallel national histories and instead become histories of cultural encounters within the geographical space constructed as Europe. Notions of national peculiarities and exceptionalisms will fade, as historians of Europe strive to answer questions about the European historical experience. Will such histories service the project of the European Union and project its aims back into history, just as their nineteenth-century predecessors serviced the nation-state? From the early 1990s onwards the political project of the EU has actively sought to enlist historians (and other producers of narratives about the past) in an endeavor to construct European cultural identities.[13] The danger here lies in transporting notions of homogeneity and peculiarity from the level of the nation to a transnational entity defined as Europe. Comparative histories of Europe, which pay proper attention to the manifold processes of cultural transfer, will have to insist on the variety and interrelatedness of social, economic, cultural, and political developments across Europe.[14] Furthermore, they will have to take into account the many points of contact and exchange with the non-European world. This Companion to nineteenth-century European history is meant to be one small step on the road to such a future European history.

A good deal of comparative, transnational, and entangled history writing involves Britain. Indeed, in many of the chapters in this volume Britain emerges as a model emulated, misunderstood, and adapted by a whole string of European countries. Yet, equally, Britain makes an appearance as an exceptional case, a country set apart from developments elsewhere in Europe. This peculiar tension between model and exception is worth exploring at somewhat greater depth. Britain was clearly an early developer and experimented with ideas and practices later adapted on the European continent. Thus, visual constructions of national identity appeared in Britain already during the eighteenth century, while most continental countries only developed them during the nineteenth. The British parliamentary system was upheld by liberals throughout continental Europe as a model to follow, and even those who wanted to reject or modify it, still had to deal with it. British civil society was the most developed of its kind in the first half of the nineteenth century, and again served as inspiration for many continental Europeans. The London Metropolitan Police served as a European-wide model for civil police forces, especially as it was widely perceived as having played a crucial role in the defeat of Chartism in 1848. The European-wide prison reform movement also looked to Britain for explanations about the meaning of prisons and ways of imprisonment. In particular the famous Pentonville prison became a model for continental European prison reformers.

The "Norfolk system" of crop rotation had an important impact on continental versions of the agricultural revolution, even if historians more recently have dismissed ideas of a unilinear British model in the economic development of nineteenth-century Europe.[15] There were many diverse paths to industrialization. Thus it has been observed that the organization of financial markets and industry in Britain and Germany provided diametrically opposed models in Europe. In terms of state building the British experience was characterized by the strength of aristocratic self-government, which

delayed state interventionism. If there was a European model of the state, it was the French, or more precisely, the Napoleonic state, which became an export model with its centralized administration and separate educational facilities for technocratic state elites. State bureaucracies in Britain were only significant in one area: that of empire and British overseas expansion. But even allowing for diversity and dismissing ideas of a universal British model, it still remains the case that nineteenth-century Europe was looking towards Britain. It seems therefore all the more incomprehensible that many European histories, up to this very day, should exclude the history of Britain from the history of Europe. Jonathan Sperber's argument about Britain inhabiting the same cultural world but on a "divergent track" from the rest of Europe is intriguing,[16] but ultimately does not do justice to the fact that, first of all, Europe was characterized by a multitude of different tracks, but all of them, including Britain, were part of the same railway system or the same cultural world. Britain needs to be treated at long last as an integral part of the European experience. Any continued exclusion of the British Isles from continental Europe will only prolong the mistaken assumption of an alleged "splendid isolation" of Britain within European history. The continued widespread division of university courses in Britain into British and European history is a most unfortunate one and needs to be challenged. The history of the continent can neither be taught nor written without proper reference to the British Isles. The chapters in this volume therefore all concern themselves with Britain as an integral part of European history.

The impact of the Cold War on historiography meant that much European history after 1945 was concerned essentially with Western Europe. Eastern European history became the preserve of a specialized sub-branch of history with its own distinguished traditions. It remains one of the most important tasks of the post-Cold War Europe to reintegrate the histories of Western and Eastern Europe, and contributions in this volume are meant as a first step in this direction. Where the history of Eastern Europe has not been the poor cousin in the past, it was because the author had special expertise in Eastern Europe. Thus, for example, anyone reading Norman Davies' splendid European history could be forgiven for thinking that Europe's most important power had been Poland.[17] In the circumstances this is in fact a welcome correction to the West European bias that characterized many other European histories, where Eastern Europe featured as the backward "other" of the West. Even a first class European history such as Robert Gildea's can include statements such as: "At the end of the century there was a polarization between the industrial core and backward southern and eastern Europe, which was relegated to the function of providing food and raw materials for the industrial areas."[18] There is a long tradition of orientalizing Eastern Europe and portraying its only mission as being that of constantly trying to catch up with the West but never quite managing it. A civilized and progressive West is basically juxtaposed to a backward East. Although this is, on balance, not the case with Gildea's history, even with a sophisticated contemporary historian like him, notions of such Orientalism can easily creep in. It will need major efforts to portray the more ambivalent and contradictory experiences of both Western and Eastern European countries. Once again, the thematic chapters of this volume have set themselves the task at least to begin addressing this ambition. Nineteenth-century European history, as it is presented in this Companion, moves beyond the perspective of national histories in that it seeks to identify themes which were all-European and impacted on several or most European societies, albeit in different and always interdependent ways.

NOTES

1 Mathias (1969).
2 Woolf (1992).
3 Welskopp (2003).
4 Hobsbawm (1962, 1975a, 1987).
5 On the concept of these transnational European regions, see Troebst (2003).
6 Historians have been quarreling for a long time over the question of whether standards of living increased or decreased in the early phases of industrialization. For a succinct summary of the debate, which has focused on Britain, see Daunton (1995).
7 On the idea of separate gender spheres and its critique, see Downs (2004), especially chapters 5 and 9.
8 The use of the term "historism" rather than the more common "historicism" is deliberate. Whereas historism, as represented by Leopold von Ranke, can be seen as an evolutionary, reformist concept which understands all political order as historically developed and grown, historicism, as defined and rejected by Karl Popper, is based on the notion that history develops according to predetermined laws towards a particular end. The English language, by using only one term (historicism) for those two very different concepts, tends to conflate the two. Hence, we suggest using two separate terms.
9 On the importance of the relationship between core and periphery in the British Empire, see Hall (2002).
10 See, for example, Henk te Velde's introduction to the special issue of the *European Review of History* 12: 2 (2006), which deals with the transfer of political ideas and practices.
11 The connectivity of the European revolutions of 1848 is explored by Körner (2000).
12 Conrad (2004).
13 Shore (2000).
14 Woolf (2003).
15 Pollard (1981).
16 Sperber (2000: 43–6).
17 Davies (1996).
18 Gildea (1996: 275).

Part I

The Idea of "Europeanness" and the Construction of European Identity

CHAPTER ONE

Insiders and Outsiders: Borders in Nineteenth-Century Europe

BO STRÅTH

As a geographical term the borders of Europe are unproblematic. In the East they follow the Ural Mountains and the Ural River from the Ice Sea to the Caspian Sea. The borderline then turns west with the Caucasus, the Black Sea, and the Straits of Bosporus as the divide. Through the Mediterranean the borderline separates Asia Minor, the Near East, and North Africa from Europe. Thereby a term like Near East is labeled from a European perspective. West of Gibraltar the line turns north and includes Ireland and Iceland up to the Ice Sea. The academic debate in geography does not deal with these borderlines but with the question whether Europe is a continent of its own or whether it is more proper to consider it the western corner of a huge Eurasian continent.

In political-historical terms the definition of the borders of Europe becomes much more problematic and contested. Turkey and Russia have both a European and an Asian part, but with what justification has this internal divide been drawn? The two Americas, Australia, and New Zealand were colonized and exploited from Europe to the extent that the original populations were extinguished or extremely marginalized. The culture today has a close connection to their European heritage. What is the difference to Europe?

The political and cultural-historical definition of Europe is complex and contested and it varies over time. The spatial projection takes on a temporal dimension. The point of departure

of this chapter is that borderlines are not only defined in geographical terms or through legal codification, but also that they are in particular culturally constructed. Mental divisions of Us and Them are important.

When the ancient Greeks talked about Ευρπ, it is unclear from where and from what language they derived the term. One theory is that the origin is Semitic and that it meant the land in the sunset. From their position in the archipelago of the East Mediterranean, the land in the sunset was to the North as well as to the South of the sea basin, what today is both Europe and Northern Africa. The meaning of Europe had no political implication, but it was just a geographical term to describe one of the points of the compass from the Greek origo. The Mediterranean became what the name says: the Sea in the Middle of Land, a unifier rather than as today a divide. The antique culture, which over several millennia emerged around the sea basin beginning in Mesopotamia and Egypt and culminating in the Roman Empire, was in the self-interpretation understood as the center of the world in the same way as China was seen from inside: the Middle Kingdom.

The borderline went through the Alps in the North. For the Greeks, *barbaros* was the term for those who did not speak Greek, those who talked gibberish, and since the cultural influence to the Greeks came from the East this became the label for those tribes in the North who did not understand Greek. *Deutschland* comes from the Latin term *theodiscus*, popular language, referring to the *lingua vulgaris* of those who did not speak Latin and of the *lingua gentiles* of the pagan gentiles. The labeling from the outside was incorporated in the self-understanding of the German-speaking tribes.[1] The North of the Alps was the land of the others. The *limes* moved constantly northwards with the expansion of the Roman Empire.

Since then the meanings of Europe have shifted and there have been many various discourses on the concept. Europe was not, and is not, an easily definable term with concrete and essential proportions, but has since antiquity been discursively shaped through constant negotiation of who to include and exclude. In such negotiation the boundaries of Europe have been repeatedly reshaped. Europe cannot be defined, because as Nietzsche argued, what can be defined has no history. And the other way round: what has a history escapes definition. And Europe has a history.

The expansion of Islam changed the ancient situation around the Mediterranean. The emerging divide between the North and the South of the sea basin (and across the Iberian peninsula) was emphasized through the crusades. The non-political Greek concept of Europe lost importance. A politically loaded concept with unifying pretensions emerged: Christianity. The emergence of a cultural distinction between a Christian Self and a Muslim Other accelerated during the Ottoman expansion in the Balkans in the fifteenth and sixteenth centuries. This process had begun with the crusades but it speeded up not least through the use of the new printed media. The Turkish peril was propagated as the main threat against Christianity in the Habsburg Empire and, albeit less intensely, in France and in the city states of what today is Italy. However, on the other side, in a contradictory way, the military and economic power struggle in the Levant between Habsburg, France, Spain, and the city states penetrated the Christian-Islamic/Ottoman divide and went in many respects beyond the religious dichotomy. Economic interaction and military conflicts between Ottoman rulers and European powers in the Mediterranean and in the Balkans were in principal no different from corresponding interactions within Europe, although they were entangled with the discourse on the Turkish peril. In constantly shifting constellations some European powers made pacts with the Ottoman rulers while others made war. In this way the constructed religious/ethnic borderline between Europe and the Turkish Other became a fluid European line of contention.[2]

This fluidity continued also with the Enlightenment. In the nineteenth century the Ottoman Empire was seen as one of the participants in the "European Concert" after the Vienna Congress and at the end of the century, when the power balance established in Vienna seemed ever more fragile, the empire was considered "the sick man of Europe."

From the crusades onwards the (Catholic) church was the carrier of universalism and "trans-statism" in the name of Christianity in opposition to the emerging centralized and territorially organized states. Europe was used as a concept, but with a much smaller value load. This Christian universalism became problematic with the emergence and spread of Reformism/Protestantism in the sixteenth century. Christian universalism was increasingly integrated into and identified with the centralized state regimes and the foundation myths they developed for legitimization. In 1648, after 30 years of religious warfare, the universalistic and state-transgressive pretensions of the Catholic church had become impossible. There was not one church, but many.

It was in that situation that there emerged the concept of Europe as connoting universal values. It was with the discourse of the Enlightenment that Europe emerged to fill the void Christianity had left. The idea of Europe as a community belonged to the Enlightenment project.[3] With the pretension of universalism followed contention about content and shape. The question of insiders and outsiders became crucial. There followed the question of the borderlines of Europe. In this process of cultural construction in particular three borders were identified: Eastern Europe, the USA, and the Orient.

Europe looked at itself in the mirrors of its Others. The construction of Europe in these mirrors contained contradictory feelings of both superiority and inferiority: admiration in the American and Asian mirrors, while in the East European (and African) mirrors superiority undoubtedly dominated. In all these mirrors the Other was absorbed through the European pretension to universalism.

In a contradictory way, and in contrast to Muslim Asia which, during the eighteenth century, was increasingly referred to as the Orient, Christian Europe came to be seen as both the ideal and as the focus for contempt. Schlegel, Schopenhauer, Nietzsche, and others inverted the idea of Europe as a civilization project. As opposed to the image of a despotic Orient in contrast to an enlightened Europe, in their version there emerged the image of a sublime and exotic Orient based on a culture superior to that of a decadent Europe. Different discourses superimposed themselves one upon the other, gradually to form the image of Europe as a specific civilization with clearcut cultural borders.

One of the discursive fields in the Oriental image was that defined by the opposition of the Enlightenment and despotism. However, not every opposition represented a negative stereotype of the Orient in European eyes. The translation of *A Thousand and One Nights* into French at the beginning of the eighteenth century reinforced the image of a miraculous Orient. The recurring enthusiasm for China and India can be seen as either a direct or an indirect criticism which enriched and problematized the European image of itself as a civilizing project. The discursive antinomy in the European view of the Orient was not so much a competition between different schools of thought, as something which characterized individual thinkers. Some, for example, regarded Muhammad as an enlightened philosopher, others as a cheat, while Voltaire admired Muslim tolerance, which he contrasted to Christian intolerance.

Although the demarcation between an enlightened Christianity and a fanatical Islam was a frequent component of the European discourse, there was at the same time not only Voltaire's opposite view, but also the merger of the Enlightenment and despotism into one idea which was applied to both Europe and the East. For Europe, the notion of enlightened absolutism was an expression of this merger. These developments are well documented in Edward Said's *Orientalism* (1978).

Asia and the idea of the Orient was thus one of the mirrors in which a European self-image emerged in a long historical process. It was a mirror in which one could discern many different and competing images, and it was also a mirror where one saw what one wanted to see. There were positive and negative elements of both Europe and the Orient reflected in this mirror, and each one served as a line of demarcation. The cultural borderline between Europe and the Orient was fluid and contradictory.

The American Revolution was experienced as something new in the history of humankind. Writing more than 150 years after the revolution, the German-American philosopher Hannah Arendt referred to it as "the feeling of a new beginning" shared by both Americans and Europeans. Europe was ruled by tradition and habits, whereas the Americans discussed and chose their constitution.[4] Arendt's view was not, of course, new. In the mid-nineteenth century Leopold von Ranke wrote that the American Revolution was more revolutionary than any of the revolutions that had preceded it, and that it had meant a total shift of perspective. Before the American Revolution, the world was governed by kings with God's grace. With the American Revolution, the idea was born that power lay with the people. Ranke discerned two views – two worlds – that stood against each other: one was the Old World, and the other the New. They were seen as the two poles in a moral world order. Earlier, the American Indian, as the elevated noble savage, had been contrasted to the depraved European. From the 1780s, the revolutionary creator of a new social order took the place of the Indian. However, it should be added that what was seen in the American mirror was also an element of the European Enlightenment rhetoric in which Rousseau and others who lauded the natural, primeval state and criticized civilization were advancing the ideas of modernity. Reinhard Koselleck has described this shift of perspective in the American mirror as the emergence of a Manichaean worldview, where the old world of despotism and the new world of freedom were polarized and, simultaneously, became dependent on one another.[5] Europe and America are seen as two connected vessels: when the one is emptied the other is filled. This moral geography takes on historical necessity, a necessity which was intrinsic in the metaphor itself. Being the Old World meant that the days of Europe were numbered. The future belonged to America as the New World. However, the metaphor also contained other possibilities. Europe stood for experience and wisdom which, during the nineteenth century, emerged as an alternative view in the American mirror and could also be related to the white man's burden, which was seen reflected in the Asian and African mirrors. Europe had an educating mission: it stood for science-based classical culture and education and aesthetic values expressed in art, music, and literature. This cultural Europe was contrasted to an America without culture, history, and morality. "Moral" and "immoral" as labels for Europe and America shifted with respect to the image of an Old World, no longer predominantly "depraved," and a New World, no longer predominantly "revolutionary."

Both these interpretive frameworks were underpinned by the frontier myth which emerged in nineteenth-century America as a kind of foundation myth.[6] This was the Puritan myth of New England as God's New Israel, in which "exodus" was the term used for the migration of the Pilgrim Fathers to America. The idea of the North American continent as a new Garden of Eden was cultivated in both the Old and New Worlds. In this mythology, frontier was the *limes* between Euro-American colonization and the wilderness, a wilderness which was not a deterrent, but rather an invitation to cultivate the free land in the West. The metaphor was used to describe both the process of migration and colonization and the form of social organization on this border of civilization. The myth legitimized collective expansion as a Manifest Destiny and promoted the emergence of fundamentalism – as opposed to pragmatism – as a key element in American political culture.[7] In the extension of this Manifest Destiny, the native Indians no longer appeared as the noble savage in contrast to the depraved European, and the violent confrontation with the aboriginal inhabitants was celebrated as a regenerating experience where the white

pioneer emerged strengthened and purified as the New Man. The mythologization of the frontier as the place which gave rise to the unique emancipatory social and political order of America based on a democratic-egalitarian spirit and a confident pioneer individualism, released American democracy from its European connection. Freedom and equality were seen as essentialist American products. The well-known "frontier thesis" of historian Frederick Jackson Turner in 1893 was important for this image.[8] However, this image must be related to the entire ideological embedding of the American dream based on Christianity and ideas of eternal renewal rendered possible by infinite space.

The American–European historical relationship can be described in terms of two plots. First, the Enlightenment philosophers looked upon post-revolutionary America as a kind of better Europe, as a place of an applied Enlightenment. The Enlightenment structures of constitutionalism, tolerance, and citizenship which, in comparison with Asia, were seen as European, were, in the American comparison, regarded as American. Although America had not yet made any great steps in science, art, or literature, these were all areas where something great could be expected from the young republic, the heir of the republican states of antiquity. The second plot, entangled with this first one, concerned the wild, uncultivated, and violent America of the Wild West as opposed to the civilized, dignified, and mature Europe. In the American foundation myth this latter plot was successfully incorporated into the former.

Eastern Europe emerged as a concept of demarcation with respect to the Enlightenment. As Enlightenment philosophers established "Western Europe" as the seat of civilization, so too they invented an "Eastern Europe" as its complementary other half. Eastern Europe exhibited a condition of backwardness on a relative scale of development;[9] however, the philosophers did not bestow on Eastern Europe the radical otherness ascribed to non-European "barbarians." The opposition between civilization and barbarism assigned Eastern Europe to an ambiguous space. Since Tacitus, the old division of Europe had been between the North and the South, between the

Empire and the Barbarians. It was Voltaire who led the way when Enlightenment philosophers shifted their gaze to the contrasts and demarcations between East and West in their construction of Us and the Other. A conceptual reorientation of the European map occurred when the old lands of barbarism and backwardness in the North were displaced to the East.[10]

Territoriality was older than the Enlightenment, but the Enlightenment invented Western and Eastern Europe as complementary concepts, defining each other by opposition and adjacency. Larry Wolff (1994) has shown that travelers were crucial to this work of reorientation. The lands of Eastern Europe were sufficiently unfamiliar in the eighteenth century such that each traveler carried a mental map that could be freely annotated, embellished, refined, or refolded along the way. The instruments of mental mapping were association and comparison. Making associations among the lands of Eastern Europe meant intellectually combining them into a coherent whole. The comparison with the lands of Western Europe then established the division.

The idea of Eastern Europe was entangled with the evolving Orientalism, for while philosophical geography casually excluded Eastern Europe from Europe, implicitly shifting it into Asia, scientific cartography seemed to contradict such a construction. As Wolff has pointed out, there was room for ambiguity. Such uncertainty encouraged the construction of Eastern Europe as a paradox of simultaneous inclusion and exclusion: Europe, but, at the same time, not Europe. The popular perception of Peter the Great is a case in point: enlightened modernizer, prepared to learn from the West, but locked in a more or less hopeless struggle with a barbarian environment.

Friedrich Naumann championed the idea of *Mitteleuropa*, which described a domain marked out for German economic and cultural hegemony. Naumann based his concept on a long debate that went back to the reaction to Napoleon in the early movement for German unification. There the idea of *Mitteleuropa* had emerged as a response to a perceived threat and a feeling of crisis. Novalis and, more especially, Friedrich Schlegel, whose dream of a reconcil-

iation of French and German civilization turned into hostility towards France and the modernity it incarnated, developed an anti-Western idea of *Mitteleuropa*.[11] The "middle" began to take shape as a virtuous location. It was, in Herder's philosophy, a "golden" and "happy" location where extremes were excluded. When he spoke of "well-built" people inhabiting "the central zone of the earth," the concept of "the middle" connected geography to ethnicity. German geographers, however, largely ignored the political idea of *Mitteleuropa*. They continued to operate using an older division of a Northern, a Middle, and a Southern Europe. Their Middle Europe stretched from France to the Black Sea. As long as France had a place in this Middle Europe it was unthinkable in the geographical discussions that any political or ideological value should be attributed to it. It was when France was excluded from the *Mitteleuropa* concept at the end of the nineteenth century and when, at the same time, an expansion in the direction of Austria-Hungary and further to the Southeast occurred, that the concept, supported by geographers, became explosive.[12] This development was regarded by the Czech philosopher and politician T. G. Masaryk – the first president of Czechoslovakia – and R. W. Seton Watson as proof of German imperialist aspirations. Consequently, they developed the concept of "New" rather than "Central" Europe to describe their image of Europe during World War I.

Concepts such as Central Europe and Eastern Europe do not emerge "naturally" out of the subject matter itself. The concepts are matters of choice, and these choices are by no means neutral, for they evoke a cluster of connotations, positive or negative, outside as well as within the region they are imagined to define. As the examples of the three mirrors of Europe demonstrate, the question of what Europe really *is* has no unequivocal answer. Europe is a continuous discourse on unification, and as such is basically a political project. Europe is charged with various meanings synchronically as well as diachronically. This discourse has had the demarcation of the Other in terms of Us and Them as an important point of departure. This demarcation has also been part of the political project, and therefore it has varied over time as well as at specific points in time.

Empires meant the radiation of European power over the world. Should the colonies therefore be seen as part of Europe or not? The ambition was no doubt to spread European culture to the colonies, and in that respect include them in Europe. Colonialism emerged from European expansion in the sixteenth century. The colonial order changed with the cessation of the slave trade and the subsequent dissolution of the Portuguese and Spanish empires in the early nineteenth century. The subsequent phase of industrial capitalism is the era usually referred to by the term "colonialism." During this phase, the goal of finding new sources of raw materials and new markets in an ever more global economy was of paramount importance for the industrializing nations. Britain, France, Germany, Italy, Belgium, and the Netherlands were the main colonial powers. They shared among themselves large parts of Africa and Asia, either by reaching agreements at conferences like that in Berlin in 1885, or through military confrontation. Like America after its discovery by Columbus, black Africa was considered a *terra nullius*, without government, and wide open for the first civilized people who claimed it.

In retrospect, many of the conquered regions were of limited economic value, but in the race among colonizers, colonies were often established simply to prevent their being overtaken by others in this competition; the bid to gain prestige through political power played a considerable role during this expansion. Colonialism was often associated with the idea of white supremacy over other population groups, which in turn occurred under the assumption of the superiority of European civilization and the duty to spread it to other cultures – Kipling's "white man's burden." The idea of the superiority of European civilization functioned as a demarcation of the Other, but all the same, it did not prevent struggles or (civil) wars within this civilization, in a more or less conscious reference to Darwinian evolution theory and to the biological classification of races.

The contradictions in the European process of boundary making reached their height in the opposition between the idea of a universal mission and its confrontation with the values of other civilizations, and in the opposition between the idea of a European global mission and the clash between European nation-states and empires about the division of the world. In the period between 1850 and 1950 the process of boundary setting was not only an issue of Europe's external borderlines, but also of internal demarcation. This was the period of both European global expansion and internal nation building.

The emergence of the nation-states has traditionally been understood in relation to a strong concept of cultural cohesion. This view has employed a concept of culture, shared values and beliefs, which assumes the existence of well-defined and bounded human communities with high cultural homogeneity.[13] By contrast, a more recent view sees the existence of such communities as the result of work aiming at a "cultural construction of community" that sought to produce boundedness and internal coherence.[14] The religious composition and the national cultures of Europe and the European nation-states have indeed been the historical *outcome* of such cultural construction, undertaken in the face of deep political crises. Thus, the idea that modern administrative-political orders needed to be built on *religious* homogeneity under state control was a conclusion drawn from the era of religious wars. The idea that participatory political orders needed to be built on *linguistic* homogeneity was a consequence of the largely aborted "democratic revolutions" beginning in the late eighteenth century.[15]

What does this history of European external and internal border making tell us about the future prospects for Europe? What kind of borderlines will emerge? Will the demarcation of the Other outside Europe be soft or hard, dialogical or clashing? What are the prospects for overcoming national divides within Europe? History does not give us the answers to such questions. History tells us only that boundary setting can go in widely different directions, and that little in the long run is determined by the past.

A "lesson" to be learnt from this historical experience is the relativity in terms of the values used to define boundedness and homogeneity.

Linguistic diversity is less divisive when the focus is on religious homogeneity; religious diversity can be more easily accepted in times of linguistic-cultural homogeneity. This means that within a broad range of cultural markers, some are used as "core values" while others can be more easily contested. The selection of core values and their relative importance among other values varies according to context. Thus, nineteenth-century European polities came to be marked by a profound ambiguity. On the one hand, their internal structures gradually – and not at all steadily – widened the spaces of freedom, while, on the other hand, they developed patterns of integration and exclusion that still mark contemporary Europe based on nation-states.

Any conception of culture that remains bound to strong notions of shared values and homogeneous populations without systematically analyzing the shifting structure of value systems will not, as Peter Wagner convincingly argues, be able to thematize, even less contribute to overcoming, such patterns. While value patterns may have to be considered as a "given" at a particular point in time, they do not persist over time, but are transformed in processes of cultural reinterpretation.[16] The process of building a European society, therefore, need *not* be understood, with *specific* reference to the experiences of nineteenth-century patterns of nation building in European history, as a repetition of cultural homogenization on a larger scale. The process can be analyzed with more *general* reference to European experiences, as a process of cultural construction that, under current conditions, places emphasis on maintaining diversity and relies on dialogical interaction across cultural commitments, rather than on cultural commonality, for the building and maintenance of social and political institutions.

Thus, it is evident that the term "Europe" cannot refer to any stable, common heritage shared by the inhabitants of European territories over long periods of history. In this sense, there are no European borders representing a coherent set of values and beliefs common to all Europeans and stable over time, a heritage that could determine the current cultural outlook of Europe. In contrast, going back to the "eccentric identity" formed in the encounter between Greek and Roman political thought and Jewish and Christian religious beliefs, in particular, European history and the setting of its borders have been marked by continuous reinterpretation of the human condition with the use of the cultural resources at hand.[17]

There is certainly a specificity of European society, compared to other societies and civilizations. However, this specificity is not culturally determined by a common past. Rather, it has emerged in recurrent confrontations with new kinds of problems and attempts to come to terms with these problems. Such problems have often had to do with the relations between various European power centers, or with the position of Europe in the larger world context. Each challenge and each solution has over time developed specific institutions, practices, discourses, and memories. In this sense there is a European specificity and uniqueness.

In this light, a series of problem-driven interpretations of and solutions to political challenges led, on the one hand, to the *internal* cultural diversity of Europe.[18] It began with the fragmentation of Europe into centralized administrative states, which were conceived as religiously rather homogeneous after the Treaty of Westphalia. It continued in the nineteenth century with the fragmentation into nation-states based on the idea of collective self-determination. On the other hand, another series of problem-driven interpretations set *external* boundaries towards that which was conceived as non-European. Links in this chain were the definition of the Southern and the Eastern boundary as a religious divide towards Islam and Orthodox Christianity, and in the East also as a linguistic-ethnic divide towards the Slavic,[19] and the expansion across the world through colonization and the diffusion of European cultural components to the New World. The external boundary setting entailed problematic forms of "Eurocentrism" in cultural-intellectual life, and the rise of other "Western" forms of modernity, such as, most importantly, the North American. European heritage may thus be seen as one of internal cultural division and external boundary setting.[20] The attempted annihilation of European Jewry could be considered as a setting of new internal as well as external boundaries, since European Jews inhabited an ambiguous space between belonging as citizens to the nations in which they had lived since the Middle Ages, and continuous persecution.

The meaning of "internal" and "external" here is certainly nothing given at any point in time, but precisely at the core of cultural interpretation and dispute. The internal and the external dimensions of European history demonstrate how a certain specificity of European modernity emerged, and keeps being transformed, in processes of cultural construction. With the benefit of hindsight, one can see that the *separation* of contentious issues – such as religion, language, degree of social commitment – has often been chosen as a temporary solution to political disputes over cultural diversity. Such separation, however, has never provided a long-term resolution of these issues. Rather, separation has hardened the boundaries between – and often also within – various European societies and polities, leading to the recourse to outright violence and warfare.

NOTES

1   Koselleck (1992).
2   Höfert (2001).
3   For a summary of the historiography on the concept of Europe with references, see Stråth (2000a). See also the review essay by Gerard Delanty (2003).
4   Ambjörnson (1994: 70–1).
5   Koselleck (1988: 148–54).
6   Bischoff and Marino (1991).
7   Eisenstadt (1999).
8   For a discussion of the frontier myth, see Waechter (1997: 30).
9   Bugge (1999).
10 Wolff (1994: 7–8).
11 Le Rider (1994); Droz (1960).
12 Schultz (1989). As Bugge (1999) observes, this normative interpretation of geographical centrality continues with Czech, Slovakian, Polish, Lithuanian, and other claims that the geographical center of Europe is to be found in *their* territories
13 Clifford (1988) and Clifford and Marcus (1986).
14 Stråth (2000b).
15 Benedict Anderson (1983); Hobsbawm and Ranger (1983); Noiriel (1991).
16 Malmborg and Stråth (2002); Spohn and Triandafyllidou (2003); Stråth (2002); Therborn (1995); Wagner (1994; 2006); Wagner and Zimmermann (2004).
17 Brague (1999). See also Cacciari (1994); Wagner (2004).
18 Wagner (2003).
19 Todorova (1997).
20 Stråth (2000a).

GUIDE TO FURTHER READING

An excellent overview of the emergence of a demarcation between Eastern and Western Europe in the Enlightenment discourse is provided by Larry Wolff, *Inventing Eastern Europe*. The classical work on the division between the East and the West is Edward Said, *Orientalism*. Maria Todorova in her *Imagining the Balkans* provides innovative perspectives on the mental maps of the Balkans. Unlike Orientalism in the vein of Said, which describes an imputed opposition between the Orient and the Occident, "balkanism" in the view of Todorova deals with an imputed ambiguity. Orientalism describes the West and the Orient as incompatible entities, as differences between types, while the discourse on the Balkans is seen as having always evoked the image of a bridge or a crossroad between East and West, as a difference within one type.

For a more general discussion of the borders of Europe, see Mabel Berezin and Martin Schain's *Europe without Borders*, which provides the reader with three guiding questions: first, is the territorially bounded nation-state simply a product of eighteenth- and nineteenth-century geopolitics and Western cultural hegemony, whose dominance and utility is receding before new institutional structures? Secondly, is territory an ephemeral and shifting line that may be drawn anywhere or nowhere, depending upon historical context? And thirdly, does the collective experience of living in a territory with a distinct set of cultural and legal norms over time produce thick attachment and shared culture that do not easily dissolve? On all this, see also Bo Stråth, *Europe and the Other and Europe as the Other*. For a discussion of the inner borders between the nation-states of Europe, see Mikael af Malmborg and Bo Stråth, *The Meaning of Europe*.

Chapter Two

Visual Representations of Europe in the Nineteenth Century: The Age of Nationalism and Imperialism

Michael Wintle

An essential element of European history consists of the changing idea of Europe itself. What have people thought Europe is? What has it stood for? And what have been the perceived differences between Europe and the rest of the world? In short, "What is Europe?" The particular approach taken in this chapter to answering these questions concerns the way in which people have envisioned Europe in the past, in the sense of having a *visual* picture of the continent and what it stands for. The idea of Europe can be examined in maps, drawings, engravings, and paintings, in addition to the more conventional textual sources. Such images of Europe, of the other continents, and of the nations are all around us, as they have been for many hundreds of years. The fact that they appear all over our art (high and low), our buildings, our cartoons, our maps, and our public spaces means that they are often hardly noticed; they form an accustomed part of our visual culture. However, their ubiquity and ordinariness in no way diminish their power. As Michael Billig argued cogently about single-state nationalist propaganda in his *Banal Nationalism* (1995), the fact that national flags and other symbols are as common as wallpaper, and are not always waved in one's face, does not mean that their power is diluted, or that they do not form a general frame of reference for almost all the discourse which takes place in their presence. The same is true of the visual

representation of the continents, as will become clear in the ensuing pages. The emphasis here will fall on self-images of Europe in an age of European dominance, when the assertion of Europe's superiority reached its greatest heights, but at the same time began to fragment under the pressures of nationalism.

Traditions of Representing Europe

Before the Renaissance, maps and other visual images of the continents had seldom given Europe any special status. Strands of ancient and medieval thought had occasionally awarded it a certain preeminence because of its climate, its religion, or its association with Noah's son Japheth,[1] but this had not been systematically applied, and certainly not in the visual arts and crafts. The Ancients were far too focused on the Mediterranean Sea as the center of their world to have more than a passing regard for Europe as a continent, and in the medieval period the three continents then known were invariably portrayed as an expression of harmony in God's universe, with no special honors awarded to Europe. The "T and O" maps of the early Middle Ages and the *mappae mundi* of the high and later medieval period all demonstrate this subjection of earthly matters, including the glorification of one's own continent, to the metaphysical assertion of the peace and order of God's whole universe.[2]

All that, however, was to change at the time of the Renaissance. It was the age of European expansion, and maps needed to reflect Europe's pride in its achievements. Matters did not alter overnight in 1492 with Columbus's "discovery" of the Americas: knowledge of a fourth continent had been intermittently percolating European intellectual circles for some time beforehand, and the impact of the "discoveries" themselves took decades if not centuries to sink in.[3] But certainly by the later sixteenth century, a new confidence and self-importance had begun to appear in the portrayal of Europe in its global context. This new kind of visual imagination was associated with the new navigational voyages of European discovery, scientific changes in mathematical cartography, and European commercial extension to new areas of the globe. Although the old cartographic traditions lived on, most European maps of the world would henceforth show Europe as very much the dominant continent in the world.[4]

This major change in the way in which Europe was portrayed vis-à-vis the rest of the world is well illustrated in the books of iconography which circulated among artists and decorators, to help them with the details when they wanted to adorn their work with such subjects as the muses, the elements, the seasons, or the continents. The most famous was Cesare Ripa's widely used Iconologia, first published in 1593, and in an illustrated edition in 1603. The plates of the four continents from the 1644 edition are shown in figure 2.1, and they formed the basis of the imagery and iconography in the portrayal of the continents, in many cases until well into the twentieth century. Ripa shows Europe as the only crowned and seated continent, queen and chief of the world, adorned with horns of plenty, a tempietto symbolizing the true church, crowns to show the power of her princes and popes, weapons and chargers for her military prowess, a palette and musical instruments to symbolize the arts, mason's instruments for architects, and (most importantly perhaps) owls and books to signify knowledge and scholarship.[5] Asia stands beside her, with a camel behind, and swinging a censer, her most characteristic accoutrement. She is fully and richly dressed, carrying a bunch of herbs or precious wood, and she is heavily bejeweled. Africa is naked but for a skirt, and has a dark skin. She is accompanied by a lion and a scorpion, and wears an elephant-scalp headdress, which had been used to signify Africa since ancient times. She has a simple necklace, and carries a huge cornucopia. America is of course the most primitive image of all. She is near-naked, and her headdress is of feathers, some of them from a peacock. She carries only a bow and arrow, with a quiver slung from her shoulder. At her feet are an alligator, and most tellingly, a severed head with an arrow through its forehead: this is the symbol of cannibalism, the ultimate feature of barbarism, savagery, and primitiveness. Compared with the cultured and civilized sophistication of Europe, the exotic, primitive, and even bestial presentation of the other continents is an archetypal example of an "Othering" process. In the myriad editions of Ripa's Iconologia published over the next centuries, the images were developed and refined, evolving with the taste of the day but retaining all the essential symbols and characteristic accoutrements, which became engrained in the representation of the continents. All this was portrayed in a specific and prescribed series of ways, which were instantly recognizable to the viewers. These traits of superiority continued to characterize the portrayal of Europe in the nineteenth century as well.

Civilization and Exoticism

With the advent of the nineteenth century, a good illustration of this Othering by means of exoticism, derived from the Ripa tradition, is a wallpaper screen of the continents and seasons, printed in distemper colors in Paris in about 1820, and now in the Art Institute of Chicago (figure 2.2). Europe is shown standing with a diadem crown, clothed and cloaked, holding a spear and shield with a lion's head boss. At her feet are a globe, musical and mathematical instruments, a white horse, armor, cannon, and

Figure 2.1 Cesare Ripa, The Four Continents (1644: 601–5).

Figure 2.2   Screen showing the four continents and two seasons (summer and winter), French, ca. 1810–30, displaying Europe and Africa. Wallpaper printed in distemper colors from woodblocks. Art Institute of Chicago, Gift of Paul Rosenberg, 1931.4.

banners. The impression intended is one of sophistication and of overwhelming military power, and many of the symbols are still those derived from Cesare Ripa. Asia (not shown here) stands next to a camel, with a feathered turban, holding a branch of an exotic plant, and in her right hand a smoking vessel. Beside her stands a billowing censer. There are many jewels, and a bowl of fruit. Africa (shown in figure 2.2) stands by a lion. She is dark-skinned, and wears a plain headband. She carries a cornucopia out of which a large snake reaches over her head, reminiscent of (though quite different from) the elephant's trunk she wears in many other representations. In her left hand she holds an unbroken chain, which stands for slavery. She is set in a lush mountain landscape, with a bow and arrow at her feet and a quiver in the tree; there is also an ivory tusk. In the distance we spy the sea. America, meanwhile, stands alone in a palm-tree landscape, with an alligator behind and with a parrot and a bow and arrow in her hands. She has a naked torso

and a feather headdress. This is a representation of primitivism, missing only the cannibalism of earlier versions: the "denizen of a halcyon world of exotic nature."[6] The relative portrayal of the continents is employed to enforce the grandeur and civilization of Europe, while the exotic alterity of America, Asia, and Africa is here part of forming the identity of the civilized Europeans.

There was, therefore, a tradition of representing Europe and her sister continents, which started at the time of the Renaissance, and continued right throughout the nineteenth century. Figure 2.3 shows a statue of Europe which adorns the front of the Natural History Museum in the imperial city of Vienna. It was designed by Karl Hasenauer in 1889, as was its partner on the other side of the door, which represents America and Australia. Europe has a crown in the form of a starburst, and a torch of liberty in her left hand. She is fully clothed in Grecian drapes, with sandals. Next to her is a young male, looking adoringly at her, holding

Figure 2.3 Karl Hasenauer, Statue of Europe, outside Natural History Museum, Vienna, 1889. Author's photograph.

a lyre, with a palette at his feet, representing the arts. The other statue unequivocally takes the noble savage route. America is a dignified Indian brave, with a few feathers and a tomahawk, and bracelets on his biceps and ankles. Australia is a bare-breasted aborigine woman at his feet, holding a small child and looking somewhat resentful. This is an intensely Eurocentric image, full of the knowledge of superiority in wealth, arms, and all aspects of culture.[7]

Moreover, such images were widely circulated, and permeated popular culture as well as "high art." Sets of playing cards were issued at the end of the nineteenth and the beginning of the twentieth centuries, based on the four continents (suits) and countries (13 for each continent). Like the cigarette cards of half a century later, they are tacky and tawdry, but the imagery was powerfully spread through this form of "visual culture," just as much as by grand public statuary. One particular set (among several of similar design) held in the Metropolitan Museum of Art in New York shows Europe with a sword and her other traditional attributes (including a large cog to signify industrialization), while urns for incense represent Asia, clubs of war stand for Africa, and medallions recall gold for America.[8]

Alongside general superiority, the continent of Europe was also shown in another traditional role as international arbiter, settling disputes between the unruly nations, whether from Europe or further afield. In a cartoon called "Enough!" which appeared in *Punch* on May 1, 1897, Europa was drawn as a fair but firm young maid in armor, imperiously calling a halt to the war between Greece and Turkey which had broken out in April 1897.[9] The sword was still the symbol of the continent, as was her armor, but it is her role of arbitration and pacification which was being played up. It had grown out of the idea of Europe as the Concert of Powers in the nineteenth century, which would be shattered by World War I; in the 1890s, however, the belief that Europe as a whole could regulate itself and others was still a real one.

However, there could be an element of irony and even self-parody in many of these portrayals, including those of the white man's burden, especially in the press. Figure 2.4 shows a cartoon which appeared in a French magazine of 1896, entitled, "Like a Succubus, Africa weighs on the Repose of Europe." It is an instantly recognizable take-off of the universally known painting of 1781 by J. H. Fuseli, *The Nightmare*.[10] The original shows a small furry demon of hideous visage crouching on the torso of the vulnerable young woman, dramatically posed exactly as she is in the cartoon of 1896. Fuseli's painting is deeply sinister, and doubtless awoke in the contemporary and subsequent Victorian psyche a succession of forbidden thoughts about the "dark angels" which might trouble the defenseless sleep of a seemingly innocent and carefree young woman of the upper classes. The cartoon parody substitutes Africa for the demon, squatting on the damsel's breast, and the sexual frisson of the original has been anything but expunged. However, rather than her own murky fantasies, here it is the reality of political imbroglios in imperial Africa which is playing havoc with the repose of noble but vulnerable Europe. Demonic Africa seems about to violate the sleeping Europe, while in the background various African "hornets' nests" are shown: John Bull is getting his fingers burned in the Transvaal, Italy is receiving more than it bargained for from the natives of Abyssinia, while Germany, Belgium, and France are also shown having to pay the price of their African adventures. This is the white man's burden indeed; at the same time, there is still no mistaking the moral superiority of Europe asserted in the image.[11]

The Rise of Nationalism

One of the most informative phases in which to observe the imagery of Europe is during the time of the rise of nationalism. What effect did the intense visualization of nationalism have on the way in which the *continent* of the European nation-states was graphically portrayed? Since ancient times, there has been a long history of personification and other kinds of geographical imagery used for purposes of shorthand to identify certain towns, regions, provinces, and countries, as well as continents. Such images,

Figure 2.4   Cartoon: "Like a Succubus, Africa weighs on the Repose of Europe," 1896. *Le Rire* (April 18, 1896).

including those on maps, have been widely employed to focus feelings of identity and allegiance.[12]

Since the Renaissance and the rise of the modern state, this personification of the nation has been widely popular. For example, the "Ditchley" portrait of the English Queen Elizabeth I by Marcus Gheeraerts the Younger, now in London's National Portrait Gallery, painted in 1592 and showing the queen firmly planted on a map of England, symbolizes the association of the crown and the nation in a most powerful manner.[13] The Low Countries were continually personified (or "animalified") as a lion, the Leo Belgicus, in their noble struggle for the nation against the tyranny of Philip II and his henchmen.[14] The Netherlands in its Golden Age of the seventeenth century used personification of the provinces and the nation, both as a convenient form of reference and as a vessel for communicating the virtues of the young republic.[15] An international exhibition in 1998 in the Deutsches Historisches Museum in Berlin collected many of these images from most of the nations of Europe, and it is a convention which follows similar rules in most countries.[16]

This use of geographical imagery to laud and glorify a particular location became widespread, not least with major trading ports like Amsterdam. Its Central Railway Station is one of the Dutch temples to modern technology, and there is a set of reliefs carved above the main entrance, shown in figure 2.5. The panels are by Ludwig Jünger and date from the 1880s.[17] The personifications of the continents are bringing their goods to Amsterdam (who resides in the central tympanum, not shown here); in this panel Europe and Africa are presented. Europe has a wine jar, and is accompanied by children bearing a basket of grapes (a traditional emblem of European sophistication in farming and diet) and a large book, signifying wisdom. Behind her, black Africans

Figure 2.5 Europe and Africa, Centraal Station facade, Amsterdam, 1880s. Author's photograph.

represent the exotic Other, with ivory, a parrot, a lion, and a bale of produce. Opposite, in the east tympanum (not shown), Asia and America are depicted as a bearded mandarin, coolies, and a feather-bonneted American Indian girl with an alligator. These tableaux of the imperialist 1880s convincingly recall the panel on the south front of the great City Hall of Amsterdam (now the royal palace on the Dam), built to glorify the city in 1648, in which the four quarters of the world bringing their tribute to the city are personified. In many ways, little had changed since 1648.

Other countries, too, used geographical visual imagery to voice nationalistic feelings in the early modern period. France was often shown as Minerva,[18] and one of the most familiar of such early figures was Britannia. Indeed,

England in the eighteenth century was the source of many seminal developments in the construction of a national identity, as Linda Colley has shown in her book, *Britons* (1992); the visual aspects of the construction were essential. John Bull was also popular as a visually distinctive personification of England, and it is interesting that he changed over time, illustrating how such images can interact with public opinion. In the early eighteenth century his appearances were incidental, but by the mid-century he was regularly portrayed as a gormless, rather inept figure. By the 1790s he was heroic in character, presenting England at its best, while in the early nineteenth century he was used by the cartoonists to signify bellicose jingoism, a role he has more or less retained ever since.[19] But it was Britannia who was really to symbolize the nation, and indeed to take on many of the trappings of Europe the Queen, as modern national feeling unfolded.[20]

In the course of the nineteenth century these sentiments spread through most of the nations of Europe, as state building was joined by nation building, and as the political elite became increasingly aware that it had to win the hearts of the ever-expanding electorate. By the end of the century mass politics had permeated public life, and suitable images were deployed, embodying the romantic nationalism of the age.[21]

In France, the tradition continued of embodying the republic in Minerva-like figures, for example in a painting entitled "La Republique" by Jules Ziegler of 1848, at the launch of the Second Republic.[22] The monuments and public buildings in almost every French village were marshaled in the nineteenth century to promote the nation, as "the civil authority waged the battle for the minds of the people."[23] However, from the time of the French Revolution onwards, popular politics played an ever more important role in France, and rather than the intellectual appeal of the Minerva lady, the French people warmed to the figure of Marianne. This more approachable personification of the republic was painted famously in 1792 in the turmoil of revolution by Antoine Gros, with her bared breast, Phrygian bonnet, helmet, and bunch of staves or *fasces*.[24]

Perhaps the most famous incarnation, though hardly a typical one, is François Rude's extremely dramatic sculpture on the Arc de Triomphe in Paris, called "The Departure of the Volunteers" (and sometimes known – incorrectly – as "The Marseillaise"). It was executed in the early 1830s, and is a highly warlike – even alarming – rendition of Marianne.[25] The tone of the piece is violent and heroic, and the national personification is covered with armor, helmet, a drawn sword, and wings. The ensemble bristles with weaponry. She is held aloft by a phalanx of French heroic warriors through the ages, and the insignia of the Gallic Roman legions are in evidence. Potentially even more stirring was Eugène Delacroix's painting of her, bare-breasted and freedom-bonneted, leading the resistance on the barricades in the July

1830 Revolution; it most readily captured the spirit of militant socialist French republicanism.[26] She, Marianne, was a demi-goddess, but one very definitely of the people, and so thoroughly fitting for the age of democracy. Another version of her by Honoré Daumier in 1848, entitled "La République Nourricière," shows the republic (Marianne) suckling the children of the world, an image of France exporting the revolution, in the first place to Europe. Here, Marianne is an extremely muscular young woman with a huge chest, sitting bare-breasted in a massive stone throne, with vague chiseled features and holding the flag of the republic. Two very solid young male children suckle, one on each breast. Another well built, blond, male child sits at her feet, reading a book.[27] The same conceit was utilized forty years later in a painting of the Netherlands personified by Georg Sturm, entitled "Self-Sacrifice." It was part of the decoration of the new Rijksmuseum in Amsterdam in the 1880s, but was removed and then lost in 1945. It shows a Dutch nun, a white sister, suckling a brown infant at one breast and a white one at the other. It embodied the white (wo)man's burden, and projected the self-image of the Netherlands nurturing both her own (white) people from the Low Countries, as well as the black and brown people of her massive tropical empire in Southeast Asia.[28]

These images, and hundreds like them, were publicly commissioned works of art, in the overt form of being the subject of public competitions; nearly all such work has always been "commissioned" in the sense of needing to be pleasing to its patron, but these examples of national images were directly government sponsored, and the effects are clear to see. In the words of Maurice Agulhon, "Talent and inspiration are necessary for all works of art; but in these circumstances the choice of a policy was also necessary."[29]

We see similar trends in all European countries, for example in the German lands, especially after 1870. "Germania" is perhaps less familiar than Britannia or Marianne. Figure 2.6 shows an extraordinary painting of her by Friedrich von Kaulbach, dated 1914, now in the Deutsches Historisches Museum in Berlin. She is young and blonde, clothed in medieval

Figure 2.6 Friedrich August von Kaulbach, "Germania, 1914." Deutsches Historisches Museum, Berlin.

steel armor, with a suitably contrived breast-plate and with sword in hand. A flowing black skirt covers her leg-armor, but reveals her heavy steel boots. Her golden shield has the imperial crowned eagle on it, and on her head sits a richly jeweled golden crown. The background is vaguely suggestive of burning cities and rivers of blood. The extraordinary feature of the painting, however, is the face: above the pursed lips and flared nostrils of the aquiline nose, the eyes almost literally blaze, with patriotic passion and with fury at anyone who would dare to raise arms against the fatherland. "Germany, August 1914" is inscribed ominously above her head. A similar though less violent image of the German nation is Lorenz Clasen's "Germania auf der Wacht am Rhein," a painting of about 1900, now in the Kaiser Wilhelm Museum in Krefeld. This time she is less aggressive but more watchful in defense of the nation. She has a broadsword and eagle-shield, but is crowned with an oak garland, and otherwise wears medieval women's clothes rather than armor. The background is an idyllic pastoral view of the Rhine, with beautiful castles and villages to be protected.

Other examples abound.[30] For example, there is a painting now in the Carlsberg Glyptotek in Copenhagen by Elisabeth Jerichau-Baumann of 1851, entitled simply "Denmark." The female personification is young, blonde, and Nordic; she wears no armor but carries a sword and is backed by harvested sheaves: a young female peasant-soldier. She shoulders the Danish national flag like a pike-staff; she is not belligerent, but strong and determined, and the sky behind her is darkening. In Sweden, the same romantic or cultural nationalism was reflected in the popularity of paintings glorifying the national hero, such as Gustaf Cederström's "Bringing home the body of King Charles XII," painted around 1900 and now in the National Museum in Stockholm. Solemn-faced, straight-backed, battle-battered soldiers carry their sovereign's corpse down a steep, snow-covered mountain path, somber and proud to bear their heroic burden through the wild elements which mold the national character.

Such personifications could be loaded with all kinds of ideology. A poignant example among many is a great golden statue of Belgium, made in about 1900 by Arsène Matton, who specialized in the portrayal of Africans. Together with three other monuments with a similar message, it has pride of place in the great hall of the Congo Museum at Tervuren near Brussels, and is called "Belgium provides Protection to the Congo." This image carries the entire repertoire of the white man's burden of European imperialism. Belgium is portrayed as a maternal young woman, offering succor and comfort to some children who represent the colony, which was a traditional way of showing the colonial relationship, but an especially ironic one in the case of Belgium. The nation dated only from 1839, and the public was generally uninterested in colonial pretensions. However, its monarch Leopold II had set up in the Belgian Congo the most infamous terror regime; he was publicly indicted in foreign parliaments for his brutal rule of systematic violence and asset stripping. In 1908 the colony would be removed from his control and taken over by a reluctant and embarrassed Belgian state. This statue was commissioned for the great hall of his triumphal Congo Museum at the height of the scandals. It is a heady piece of propaganda, but no less expressive of genuine national sentiment for all that.

The same technique was employed in sub-national groups too, such as the Flemings in Belgium: a highly sentimental sculpture of "Flandria Nostra," as a medieval damsel on a pawing horse, was carved by Jules Lagae in 1901 and now adorns the lobby of the Town Hall in Bruges. Outside Europe very much the same applies: the creation of appropriate visual images has been essential to the making of Canada as a nation-state in the twentieth century,[31] and some exquisite images of Mother India in the shape of a map of the country have filled Indian schoolbooks in recent decades, especially around the time of independence and partition.[32]

The European Family

There has thus been a lively tradition of representing the regions and nations, as well as the continents, by personification and other forms of geographical imagery, especially since the Renaissance. There has also been a tradition, active since the seventeenth century at least, of representing Europe as a "family" of personified nations. For example, in Johan Blaeu's map of Europe from his Grand Atlas published in Amsterdam in 1662, along the top edge are views of nine major European cities illustrated on the map, and down each side are vignettes of couples from various parts of Europe, ranging from Greeks and Poles to Castilians and English. They are upper-class types, dressed in fine clothes. It is a kind of costume parade (indeed, costume geographies in book form were a popular genre), and they all look quite similar to modern eyes, with the ubiquitous long dresses for the ladies, and hose for the men. The Greeks and Hungarians look slightly exotic, but the only discordant note in this "happy family" is the fact that the Venetians are represented by two men, while the other nine nations are fronted by a mixed couple.

It was a genre which remained current. A German painting of the eighteenth century, now in the Austrian Museum for Folklore in Vienna, moved a step further and showed ten European male types in costume, from French and English to "Greek or Turk" (the latter evidently indistinguishable).[33] The costumes were now more differentiated, from the tweedy English country gentleman to the effeminate French courtier. Significantly, there was a great table appended of their characteristics: virtues, vices, likes, dislikes, and religion. Not only were there national costumes portrayed, but national characters as well.

Many of these early images of the European family were generally harmonious. But families are by no means invariably peaceful, and with the advent of the age of nationalism from the later eighteenth century onwards, the nations of Europe were often depicted as being anything but friendly towards each other. The cartoonists in particular were intent on portraying the nations of Europe as more like a pack of bickering dogs, as happy to tear each other's throats out as to act in concert, and often picking on one of their weaker members. One by the famous James Gillray of 1799 was entitled "The State of War, or the Monkey Race in

Danger."[34] The nations were represented in it by animals or monsters: the British lion, the Turkish crescent, the Russian bear, and the Austrian double-headed eagle, all doing their best to slaughter the ragged French monkey. It expressed the victory hopes of the Allies at the start of the Second Coalition War against France, and in this personification of the nations of Europe by their caricature animals, the dominant themes were viciousness and gang warfare.

Another English cartoon from the Napoleonic period called "The Corsican Toad under a Harrow"[35] appeared in 1813, when Europe was finally going about crushing Napoleon, or so it appeared. The coalition powers were shown as national soldiers, except for Holland, who appears as a fat, pipe-smoking peasant. A Russian Cossack was also included, lending a hand to persecute the French, who were being crushed under a large piece of agricultural apparatus to the delight of all present.

In the later nineteenth century, with the increasing strength of nationalism, and in particular the rivalry between the imperial powers, the depiction of the European family became even less harmonious. It is particularly well captured in the satirical cartoon work of Frederick W. Rose, which portrayed the countries on a map of Europe as caricatures of their inhabitants or rulers. He made several versions from the 1870s onwards; they were immensely popular and were translated into many languages. In figure 2.7, his "Novel Carte of Europe, designed for 1870," Germany is shown as a helmeted and whiskered Bismarck, kneeling on Austria, with one heavy hand on the Balkans and the other on Belgium and Holland. France is an incensed Zouave, drawing his sword to resist German pretensions (it was the time of the Franco-Prussian War). Russia and Scandinavia are predatory beasts, and Britain is a fussy old lady with her dog Ireland on a leash. Southern Europe is more or less decadent. There is no unity in Europe here: it is made up of highly differentiated and potentially inimical nations, with aggression and weakness seldom far below the surface. We can see before us the nationalist upsurge which was to carry Europe into imperialist antagonism

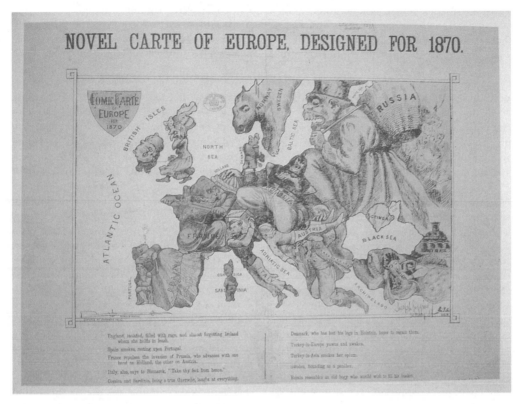

Figure 2.7 F. W. Rose, "Novel carte of Europe, designed for 1870." From Goss (1993: 339).

and World War I. Rose-derived images continued in various versions, languages, and editions right up to World War I. There is another by Rose himself, the famous "Octopus," from 1877, with Russia shown as a tentacled land-grabber.[36] There is a variant from the late 1890s called "Fishing in troubled waters," with John Bull, the tsar, and the French all dangling their rods in the European maelstrom.[37] Indeed, there exists a German version published in 1914, as well as a British version of the same date peopled by dogs (bulldog, poodle, dachshund, etc.); the images had been slightly altered, but 44 years on, the conceit still retained its potency.[38] Other cartoonists took up the theme of a map of Europe peopled by personifications of the nations at each other's throats, and it was evidently a popular genre: William Harvey, using the pen-name "Aleph," compiled a book of prints of the nations of

Europe in the 1870s as caricatures fitted into their own maps, and the public clearly saw the point.[39]

From the 1870s right up to World War I, all the major European periodicals carried such cartoons regularly, with the emphasis on national representation, and on the potential for disagreement between the nations.[40] The question arises of how this new ascendancy of the personification of the nation affected the visual representation of Europe as a continent. Europe continued to be characterized as a noble young woman in a good cause. In a cartoon appearing in the periodical *Fun* on September 24, 1870, entitled "A Word for Peace," Europe personified is shown attempting to restrain the bickering Prussia and Paris (portrayed respectively as a bullying, moustachioed Prussian officer and as a testy, resentful Marianne), who are about to start the Franco-

Prussian War.[41] We have already noted Europe personified as arbitrator between Greece and Turkey in 1897 in a *Punch* cartoon. However, just as frequently the continent tended to be drawn in cartoons in rather disparaging terms. For instance, in French and German periodicals during the 1890s, she was portrayed as a desperate old harridan trying to keep the balance of power in Europe together, or as an equally unattractive and distressed old woman under attack from the rising power of Japan.[42]

Honoré Daumier, whose picture of Marianne suckling was noted above, was also a specialist in the portrayal of the precariousness of Europe's equipoise, and therefore its survival as a political entity. In a series of cartoons for the magazine *Charivari* in the 1860s, he repeatedly demonstrated the vulnerability of the European concert. For the edition of December 1, 1866, in a drawing entitled "L'Equilibre Européen," he showed the globe balanced on the massed bayonets of the European armies, and on April 3, 1867 he presented the crowned personification of Europe teetering barefoot on a globe which was drawn like a stage-anarchist's spherical bomb, about to explode.[43] On February 7, 1867 he produced the illustration shown in figure 2.8, entitled "New Aerial Suspension," which was another study on the fragility of the European balance of power, and of European peace in general. Above the craning heads of the personifications of the European nations, Queen Europe is serenely resting at ease in a languid, relaxed pose, but suspended only by her elbow which in turn is supported only by the point of a single bayonet from below. The rest of her body has been levitated, and is about to collapse and crush all the credulous countries underneath. All these cartoons are from an era of escalating rivalry which was eventually to lead to World War I, and the portrayal of Europe is no longer as a queen of a united continent, no longer triumphant, and no longer at peace with itself.

However, it is not the case that the Eurocentrism of these images was in decline. On the eve of World War I, Eurocentrism was now more often portrayed in national rather than continental form: Britannia, Marianne, and Germania were beginning to take over from the maid Europa and from Europe the Queen. However, the unthinking certainty of European superiority was undiminished.

The Eurocentrism in the image in figure 2.9 is overpowering, despite the fact that it features Britannia, Marianne, Germania, and others taking over from Europe the Queen. This famous drawing by Hermann Knackfuss is of the nations of Europe personified as young warrior maidens; it dates from 1895, and was apparently derived from an original sketch by none other than the German Kaiser Wilhelm II himself. A group of seven or eight of the doughty maids is assembled on a craggy outcrop of rock, high above the river and plain below, which is dotted with picturesque villages and fine, spired towns. Across the valley a holocaust is raging, and in its dense, lightning-riven fumes can be made out an oriental dragon-demon and a statue of the Buddha. An armored male seraph, with a cross on his brow and a multiple-blade sword in his hand, is exhorting the national personifications: "People of Europe – defend your holiest possessions!" (the title of the drawing). A huge crucifix in blinding light hovers in the sky above them, and although Britannia looks somewhat reluctant, the Austrian Empire is taking her by the hand and leading her on, while Marianne in her Phrygian bonnet (and medieval armor) is clearly resigned to conflict, and eagle-helmeted Germania is spoiling for a fight. The Other across the river is extra-European; it is evil and dangerous, and the nations of Europe are being asked to unite in their superiority to resist such predatory forces. It is an intensely Eurocentric and indeed anti-Asian image.

The yielding of Europe personified to the forces of nationalism sometimes meant that the images of Europe which had been so common were "usurped" by nationalistic personification. This implied a certain breakdown in European solidarity, even if not in Eurocentrism, by the time of the age of New Imperialism in the last quarter of the nineteenth century. In the socialist artist Walter Crane's map of the British Empire at the time of the "scramble for Africa" in 1886 (figure 2.10), Britannia now sits as the centerpiece of the marginalia, receiving the tribute of adoring parts of the empire, just as

EUROPE

Nouvelle suspension aérienne

Figure 2.8 Honoré Daumier, cartoon, "Nouvelle suspension aérienne." *Charivari* (February 7, 1867).

Europe had graciously taken the gifts of the other continents in previous incarnations. The "natives" of the world gaze in wonder at her, as the empire builders look on with approval. Her iconographical accoutrements are battle-dress, the Union Jack flag, and Neptune's trident, showing her dominance of the seas. In this immensely powerful image, Britain has taken over the role of Europe in general.[44] This is nationalistic but Eurocentric imperialism. Many such maps were produced and sold in their thousands; for example, Howard Vincent's Map of the British Empire, the twenty-first edition of which was published in 1924. At the top was written "Union is strength," and at the bottom, "God save the King Emperor," who was pictured in person: George V. The map was on the Mercator projection, and thus geographically Eurocentric; it exaggerated the size of the Northern latitudes, making the red expanse of Canada look especially huge. This was "painting the map red," and an inset at the bottom showed how far it had expanded since 1713. A table displayed the empire's vast economic wealth, the world encompassed. And Britain was not alone: all

Figure 2.9 Hermann Knackfuss, "People of Europe – Defend your Holiest Possessions!" 1895. AKG-Images, Berlin.

Figure 2.10 Walter Crane, Map of the World showing the extent of the British Empire, *The Graphic* (July 24, 1886), supplement.

the imperial nations of Western Europe were engaged in comparable triumphalism around the end of the nineteenth century.

Conclusion

These images of Europe and the nations carry considerable significance. First, they are ubiquitous: they have been literally all around us in the modern fabric of life since the Renaissance, in high art, applied art, cartoons, woodcuts, and on buildings. Moreover, it is not the case that they are simply for decoration. Many artists and artisans may have used them for that purpose, but others were quite overt in their cultural assertions about the nature of Europe (usually very positive) and the other continents (always denigratory in one form or another). Even the "innocent" or oblivious examples carried the same cultural message of European superiority.

Furthermore, our attention has been drawn by these images to the period of intense nationalism, especially in the later part of the nineteenth century. Over the centuries, the characterization of the nation was not generally at the expense of the positive portrayal of Europe, and a European identity seems to have sat quite happily alongside national and regional identities. Even when there was intense rivalry between the nation and the continent, in the period of rising nationalistic and imperialist rivalry, the level of Eurocentrism in nearly all these images was not diminished in the least: since the time of the Renaissance, Europe had always been superior, whether it was figure-headed by Queen Europa or by the national champions of Britannia, Marianne, Germania, and their sisters. In the modern age, the image of Europe has been unremittingly Eurocentric, and in many ways that Eurocentrism reached its zenith in the age of imperialism preceding World War I.

NOTES

1 Hay (1968).
2 Wintle (2001: 192–6).
3 Zerubavel (1992).
4 Wintle (1999).
5 Den Boer et al. (1995: 53, 55); Hale (1993: 49); Le Corbeiller (1960: 216–19).
6 Honour (1975: ill. 155).
7 Wintle (2002: 208–9).
8 Metropolitan Museum of Art, New York, Prints and Drawings, James Hazen Hyde gift, 59.654.18.
9 Douglas (1994: 120).
10 See the illustration of the first version of the famous painting in Tomory (1972), color plate I. It was much copied and parodied: see Tomory's six examples, ills. 222–8.
11 See the comments in Nederveen Pieterse (1992: 86).
12 Monmonier (1996).
13 Harley (1983: 33).
14 Tooley (1963); Leerssen and Montfrans (1993: 94–9).
15 See, for example, the work of Raphael Sadelaer the Elder (1555–1628), who made many engravings of the nations of Europe personified; Knipping (1974: 365).
16 Flacke (1998).
17 Vanvugt (1998: 60).
18 For example, in a painting by Giovanni Romanelli of 1655 called "The Glorification of France," now in the Palais des Beaux Arts in Lille.
19 Porter (1988: 198); Langford (2000: 11).
20 In the Fitzwilliam Museum in Cambridge (C.89.1932) there is a fine figurine of her, made of Derby soft-paste porcelain in about 1765, and brimming with insignia. There is a lion, a globe, trumpets, cannon, a helmet, a wreath, cannonballs, a breastplate, and a shield. The nation, eighteenth-century Britain, was visibly emerging, full of all the nationalistic bravado.
21 Jan Bank (1990) has remarked on the importance of the visual image to the nation-building efforts of nineteenth-century governments; he calls this "cultural nationalism."
22 Now in the Palais des Beaux Arts in Lille.
23 Baker (1992: 286).
24 Illustrated, for example, in Agulhon and Bonte (1992: 12).
25 Agulhon (1981: 44–5).
26 Ibid: 42; Agulhon and Bonte (1992: 26–7).
27 Original in the Musée d'Orsay, Paris, RF 1644.

28   Illustrated with notes in Vanvugt (1998: 83).
29   Agulhon (1981: 82).
30   Again, for a good selection, see Flacke (1998).
31   Baker (1992: 250–2).
32   Ramaswamy (2001: 97–114).
33   "Völkertafel," illustrated, for example, as the cover of Leerssen (1999).
34   Duffy (1986: 311).
35   Printed in ibid: 347.
36   Illustrated in Goss (1993: 337–8).
37   Pictured in Barber and Board (1993: 84).
38   The German version, "Humoristische Karte von Europa," is accompanied by an extensive text; a copy is held in the Imperial War Museum, London. The British "dog version" is by George Washington Bacon, entitled "Hark! Hark! The Dogs do Bark!," and a copy is held in the National Library of Scotland, Edinburgh.
39   A collection has been republished in Osborne (1999).
40   For a good crop of examples, see Douglas (1994).
41   Waller (1995: frontispiece).
42   "L'Equilibre Européen" in *Le Grelot* (October 8, 1893) and "Die ostasiatische Frage" in *Kladderadatsch* (May 5, 1895), illustrated in Wintle (1999: 160).
43   Salzmann (1988: 342–5).
44   Wintle (1996: 85–6); Whitfield (1994: 124–5).

GUIDE TO FURTHER READING

The field of the visual representation of Europe was pioneered by the seminal work of Denys Hay, *Europe: The Emergence of an Idea*. Useful insights have more recently been provided by Hale, *The Civilization of Europe*; Pastoreau and Schmitt, *Europe*; and Den Boer et al., *History of the Idea*. On the use of visual evidence in history, see Porter, "Seeing the Past"; and Burke, *Eyewitnessing*. The visual representation of France has been well covered in the work of Maurice Agulhon (*Marianne into Battle* and *Marianne*), while a splendid exhibition in Berlin has recently covered the field of national representation in Europe very thoroughly (the catalogue is available: Flacke, *Mythen der Nationen*). This chapter draws on a larger research project entitled "The Image of Europe." The results will be published in a monograph in due course.

PART II

Agriculture, Industry, and Social Change

CHAPTER THREE

Rural Society and Agricultural Revolution

Hamish Graham

In 1904 officials presented the Spanish Ministry of Agriculture, Commerce, and Public Works with a report about irrigation needs. For the arid south and interior of the country this was obviously a more pressing issue than in well-watered Galicia in the northwest. There, as the experts discovered, their efforts to improve farming methods confronted other difficulties. For one thing, this was a region of very small farms, often scattered across discrete parcels. The report found one in the province of La Coruña which amounted to a "field" (if that is not too grand a term) with an area of only 32 square meters. James Simpson has noted that tiny holdings were not uncommon in Galicia, partly as a result of local tenurial rules. But agricultural officials were further troubled by the complexity of property relations in this region. For the small field in question there was one "owner" who enjoyed the right to till the soil; another harvested the fruit from a chestnut tree that grew there; and a third received rent from this pocket of land, an annual payment of six eggs provided in alternate years by the farmer and the "owner" of the chestnut tree. In the ministry's opinion such complicated "customary" arrangements were more than just a stark demonstration of inefficient land use – they were a positive hindrance to better farming practice.[1]

Extraordinary as it seems that officials would bother with such a minuscule property, the fact that it was documented draws attention to Europeans' interest in rural communities during the nineteenth century. This chapter outlines some of the forms that their interest took, and surveys various efforts by historians to investigate them. The tiny Galician field also illustrates the key themes of this chapter. For one thing, it highlights the diversity of agricultural methods and rural life in nineteenth-century Spain, from the vast estates (*latifundia*) of southern regions like Andalucía to the compact, dispersed properties of the northwest and their tiny herds (which averaged 3.1 cattle in 1865). But if rural communities were so dissimilar even within one country, how can historians identify their shared characteristics across Europe? Furthermore our evidence of that diversity commonly depends on the reports of government officials, agricultural experts, newspaper columnists, and other commentators. Virtually none of those writers was a woman and, unlike the "owners" of the Galician field, they were not small landholders who could appreciate the advantages (whether economic, social, or dietary) of some chestnuts or half-a-dozen eggs. Rather than revealing the realities of rural life, therefore, reports about the "problems" of the countryside were shaped by the assumptions and preoccupations of an educated, urban elite. How do historians deal with the difficulties of analyzing such sources?

At the outset, though, this example reminds us how "traditions" could endure despite the multiplicity of changes that Europeans experienced during the nineteenth century. For this reason a rural and agricultural history of nineteenth-century Europe must address two major issues: profound transformations and the persistence of continuities. This was after all the century of revolutions, not merely political upheavals, from France in 1789 to Russia in 1905, but also the apparently inexorable growth of cities, industrial production, and ever-faster forms of transport and communications. Yet the countryside was home to most of Europe's population in 1914 as it had been during the French Revolution, and the majority were still peasants who tilled the soil and tended their animals in order to survive. Moreover, small-scale farming, workshop manufacturing, and petty trading remained prominent features of a European society which, as Mayer argued, was long dominated by landed aristocracies supported by the "traditional" institutions of church and state.[2]

Equally apparent was the persistence of urban and educated attitudes towards inhabitants of the countryside, who were frequently viewed with a mixture of condescension and disgust. In 1846, for instance, a short story by D. V. Grigorovich described the brief and pathetic existence of a Russian peasant woman: *Derevnia* (The Village) charted its subject's many tribulations, from lonely orphanhood to an arranged and abusive marriage, which ended with her untimely death. While literary men of a "Westernist" bent praised the writer's ability to portray the grim realities of rural life, Slavophile commentators attacked the story as offensive and lacking in moral sensitivity. In France, Jean-François Millet produced impressive paintings of country folk, such as "Les Glaneuses" (The Gleaners), three stooped women gathering up spilled grains after the harvest, or the unsettling sight of an exhausted farm laborer, "L'Homme à la houe" (Man with a Hoe). The images may strike us as stereotypical depictions of poor peasants engaged in backbreaking toil. Yet at the time of their presentation (in the Paris salons of 1857 and 1863, respectively) these works were attacked by critics, some of whom reacted to what they regarded as Millet's realism – he was accused of trying to arouse political sympathies for the oppressed, and labeled a socialist – while others

rejected the vulgarity of artistic claims to represent the brutish existence of peasants. Elite attitudes were in many respects contradictory, in that they emphasized contrasting views of the rural landscape and its inhabitants which derived from the Enlightenment's fundamental ambivalence towards the natural world, torn between admiration for its useful, productive, and decorative features, yet fearful of the untamed, the disruptive, and the harmful. The reactions provoked by Grigorovich's stories or Millet's paintings nonetheless demonstrate how prominently rural people figured in the consciousness of nineteenth-century Europeans.[3]

For many years, however, economic historians and historical geographers glossed over such continuities, focusing instead on transformations and upheavals, especially the trends towards urbanization and industrialization. Particularly when analyzing and explaining the experience of continental Europe (as distinct from the British Isles), questions of landholding, agricultural production, or rural society were often relegated to a secondary role. Some scholars seemed to doubt that the countryside contributed much to the momentous developments of the period. To that extent their histories tended to replicate the dismissive attitudes of elite commentators, especially agricultural observers whose successive reports from many countries expressed frustration at the lack of rural innovation and enterprise. In explaining why peasants in Eastern and Central Europe were slow to cultivate potatoes, for example, Blum condemned their "conservatism and suspicion," blaming their "obduracy and ignorance" of this crop's potential yields for "the injuries that they inflicted upon themselves."[4]

Treatment of the English experience, by contrast, frequently reproduced contemporary claims that an "agricultural revolution" could be identified by certain prescribed changes. Open fields and commons were enclosed, thereby guaranteeing farmers' exclusive rights over farms of a profitable size, and safeguarding their animals from interbreeding with the communal herd. Thus freed from collective constraints, they could plant crops such as clover and turnips in place of unproductive fallow. This not only supplied additional fodder for livestock whose manure added to soil fertility, but also the nitrogen-fixing properties of legumes (though unknown at the time) replenished the soil with the nitrates required for cereal production. Besides being valuable animal feed, turnips facilitated weed control and thus encouraged better grain crops and more nutritious pasture. These changes were associated with the "Norfolk system" of crop rotation, whose effects were described by an enthusiastic Arthur Young in 1768: "Instead of boundless wilds and uncultivated wastes inhabited by scarce anything but sheep, the country is all cut into enclosures, cultivated in a most husbandlike manner, richly manured, well peopled, and yielding a hundred times the produce that it did in its former state."[5] Historians' early accounts of agricultural innovation frequently praised the efforts of a few farsighted individuals such as Jethro Tull or "Turnip" Townshend. The origins of rural transformations were therefore located in the first half of the eighteenth century, where their presumed role was to prepare the way for later and more significant changes.

When scholars gave prominence to agricultural developments in continental Europe, they were usually portrayed as the initial stimulus for economic growth in the nineteenth century. Standard accounts noted that rural society provided the labor, food, raw materials, and accumulated capital which were then invested in industry or infrastructure. In "supply side" formulations, agriculture contributed in two ways to the transformation of Europe's pre-industrial economy. Firstly, changes in agricultural methods were able to increase the overall level of food production, which then supported a larger population that was no longer actively engaged in producing its own food. This represented a crucial mechanism which (along with food imports) allowed Europe to avoid the Malthusian trap. Such changes were achieved through increases in the productivity of agricultural labor, often through more cost-effective employment of rural workers, and the use of better tools and equipment. Secondly, with more food available from fewer farmhands, rural labor was "released" for work in manufacturing and service occupa-

tions, especially in urban centers. The successful adaptations of agricultural production allowed the countryside to become a source of "capital accumulation" which encouraged investment, not only in agriculture itself, but also (via profits, savings, and taxation) in other sectors, such as industry and services. These new opportunities sparked changes in institutions, notably in the law (especially over landownership and tenancies), and the provision of credit and insurance. Agricultural expansion also had ramifications for the "demand side" of industrialization by generating rural demand for consumer goods produced in the urban centers, and subsequently for specialized manufactured products such as agricultural machinery. In these ways, we were told, Europe was transformed.[6]

More recently, however, several historians have been influenced by the Annales school's approach to "total" history, and its focus on climate, landforms, demography, and agriculture. The primacy that Annalistes accorded to food supplies and population levels, and the profound consequences of their long-term changes, have been adopted, adapted, and debated by various schools of thought. Some extended historical geography's traditional interest in "natural resources" to consider broader questions about the environmental factors which offered both constraints and opportunities for agricultural development. Others preferred to emphasize the fundamental role of changing demographic patterns, and the importance of population growth in generating demand, thereby stimulating agrarian and technological innovation. Yet there was general agreement that agricultural and rural history are valuable areas of study, and that the nineteenth century represented a crucial phase in the history of Europe's countryside.[7]

One reason for paying special attention to these matters was the sheer weight of numbers. Even by 1900 most Europeans still lived in the countryside. In 1800 the continent's population was around 180 million; by the first decade of the twentieth century overall numbers passed 400 million, of whom at least 84 million (or 51 percent of the economically active population) were primary producers in agriculture, forestry, and fishing. Most were cultivators, pastoralists, and laborers who were regarded (and regarded themselves) as peasants. Naturally these continent-wide generalizations did not apply everywhere. In countries like Bulgaria, Romania, and Russia, more than three-quarters of the working population were on the land in the decade before World War I, while the figures for Austria, Hungary, Portugal, and Spain were all over 60 percent in 1900. The comparable proportions in the Netherlands and Belgium were less than a third, and in Britain, less than 1 in 10.[8]

Of course, Europe's agricultural populations were not unaffected by the nineteenth century's great currents of change: enclosures, the abolition of commons, emancipation from serfdom, land redistribution schemes, massive emigration (towards cities, colonies, the New World), and economic crises, particularly the great "agricultural depression" of the 1870s–1890s. Rural life was subjected to massive and irrevocable changes during the nineteenth century. Yet the land continued to make a major contribution to overall economic output in many countries. As late as 1913 primary production represented 37 percent of gross national product in Italy, while the comparable figures were 35 percent for France (1908–10), 30 percent for Denmark (1910), and 57 percent for Hungary (1911–13). Admittedly, these "national" figures concealed important regional disparities. Agriculture may have occupied more than half the economically active population across the Austro-Hungarian Empire at this time, but there was much to separate a vine-growing region like Istria (now divided between Slovenia and Croatia) from the arable belts of Moravia and Bohemia, or from Styria, where forests and "wastelands" accounted for over half the land area in 1902. Beyond anonymous demographic and economic data, however, the multiplicity of Europe's rural landscapes and their distinctive characteristics make it difficult to generalize about the continent as a whole.[9]

Peter McPhee's work on political movements in rural France offered a means to resolve this problem. Rather than pursue definitions derived from ever more specialized studies, he proposed some "leading questions" which would allow historians to indicate broad thematic similarities while also highlighting distinctive features. Given the primacy of rural production in our period, a first set of questions concerns the land itself, the uses to which the soil was put, and the differential levels of access available to rural inhabitants. A second set of questions focuses on the nature and consequence of the internal stratification that characterized all rural societies – the pronounced disparities among "peasants," as well as those between peasants and the many non-peasants who lived among them. A third set of questions explores the asymmetrical power relations between rural inhabitants and the various institutions that represented the wider economic, political, and cultural contexts. This approach could be adapted for the more wide-ranging task of examining not only the diversity of Europe's rural communities and their agricultural activities in the nineteenth century, but also the rich variety of historians' interests. In all three lines of enquiry, though, historians confront the issues raised by the nature of their sources and how best to interpret them.[10]

In rural societies, land comes first. Forms of agriculture both arable and pastoral, and the production methods employed (crops, animals, land management, labor, equipment and machinery) have long been the standard topics for economic historians and historical geographers. Most concentrated on the technical aspects of farming: in Mark Overton's self-deprecating phrase, the themes of "cows and ploughs." The nineteenth century received its share of scholarly attention, although there was wide disagreement about precisely when and how agriculture was transformed. As we have observed, British historians tended to look for the origins of their agricultural revolution in the eighteenth century or even earlier, although they reached no consensus. In the first instance, then, Overton and others were keen to be precise about the meaning of "agricultural revolution." The criteria proposed focused on three areas drawn primarily from the English experience. First was historians' traditional concern to identify changes to farming techniques: new crops, particularly for animal fodder; new forms of crop rotation; better pastures and improved breeds of livestock; and the use of agricultural machinery. A second consideration was the overall expansion of agricultural output which was capable of supplying food for a consistently growing population. Third, these changes must be achieved through significant increases in the productivity of agriculture's two main inputs, land and labor. This meant not only sustained growth in overall agricultural output, but also fundamental changes to the ways in which land and labor were employed. Overton emphasized the advantages of trying to estimate productivity advances in English agriculture, especially by identifying increased yields in crops other than wheat, more intensive forms of livestock management, and labor productivity gains. These issues contributed to his analysis of the "agricultural revolution" in England, and underpinned his argument that its most dynamic phase must be reinstated in the century between 1750 and 1850.[11]

This period's "revolutionary" nature was also apparent because of changes to the wider social, institutional, and cultural contexts in which English farming was carried out. They included the rural economy's ability to produce raw materials for manufacturing and industry, the market systems available for agricultural commodities (including land and labor), and the institutional frameworks of law and finance within which rural produce was owned, grown, and traded. Alongside these developments there emerged in England a distinctive form of rural society in which access to land was effectively confined to a tiny elite of owners and substantial tenant-farmers. For Overton, these broader changes emerged intermittently over a long period of time, and they were certainly difficult to analyze quantitatively, but they ensured that England's "agricultural revolution" had huge and irreversible ramifications, not just for the countryside and its inhabitants but for the whole of British society. This wider vision of agricultural transformations represented an important step towards what several historians regard as more comprehensive conceptions of an "agrarian revolution," and more nuanced approaches to rural history in general.

Studies like Overton's raise important issues for scholars of European agriculture and rural society, particularly during the nineteenth century. Were the productivity gains that

Overton associated with England's "agricultural revolution" of 1750–1850 capable of being sustained in the decades that followed? How convincingly could these changes be seen as the successive "stages" of agricultural development? And could the English experience of agricultural revolution be identified in other parts of Europe?

Britain – or rather southeastern England – was long presumed to represent a "model" for changes in agricultural practice and rural society. Such ideas were well publicized at the time, not least by avid agronomists like Arthur Young. His enthusiasm for the advantages of the "Norfolk system" led him to draw invidious comparisons between what he knew in East Anglia and the agricultural practices he observed elsewhere. "In the management of arable ground, the Irish are five centuries behind the best cultivated of the English counties," Young wrote in his *Tour in Ireland* (1780), although he went on to sympathize with a rural population who faced great hardship as a result of poor housing and chronic indebtedness. His subsequent reports of travels in France, Catalonia, and northern Italy applied similar criteria of comparison, and his son continued his work by devoting several decades of his life to advising nineteenth-century Russians on agricultural improvements.[12]

However, the "high farming" approach represented by the Norfolk four-course had its limitations, as Overton pointed out – it was "sustainable" only in the economic and institutional circumstances of England in the period up to about 1870. English farms may have been large by the standards of some other parts of Western Europe, and their farming methods were successful in integrating arable cultivation with stock raising, but this form of agriculture could not compete on global markets, especially with large-scale producers of grain and meat in North and South America, or Australia. British wheat prices were therefore hardest hit during Europe's "agricultural depression" of the late nineteenth century. Overton also suggested that a country-dweller from sixteenth-century England would have encountered many familiar features in the rural world of 1850. It was the subsequent transformations wrought by Britain's "second agricultural revolution," based on massive imports of animal fodder (especially oil-cake) and fertilizers such as guano, and the slow spread of more efficient tools, implements, and farm machinery, which produced more stark comparisons.[13]

On the other hand, historians' studies of economic development in various European (and non-European) settings have questioned the usefulness of earlier assumptions that agricultural/agrarian change was a process which originated in an identifiable set of conditions and then advanced by prescribed "stages." The essays collected by Mathias and Davis led them not only to announce "the demise of the British-based unilinear model of modern economic growth," but also to rejoice in the fact that its passing had revived interest in the distinctive features of agricultural history, by focusing on areas and periods of regional specialization. As a result of such work, scholars appreciated the difficulties and even the unhelpfulness of regarding agriculture as a distinct "sector" of the nineteenth-century European economy. Equally under scrutiny were the expectations that industrial and urban expansion necessarily entailed the widespread dispossession of smallholders and rural depopulation, or that some forms of farming were inherently doomed to block the expansion of commercial agriculture. Contrary to established views, for example, studies suggested that not all *latifundia* remained mired in archaic forms of production and exploitative labor relations. Absenteeism among large landowners was not as prevalent as commonly assumed, while investment strategies were often capable of responding flexibly to market shifts and political circumstances. Examination of business records allowed Petruscewicz and Fonseca to highlight the dynamism and range of interests of specific estates in Calabria (southern Italy) and the Alentejo (Portugal), thereby challenging pervasive assumptions about regional "backwardness."[14]

Attention was similarly paid to the persistence of small-scale rural enterprises with multiple interests, and the diversity of employment patterns in the European countryside, both of which indicated the close integration of agricultural production with artisanal manufacturing, petty trading, and service activities. The peasant households that predominated in many parts of the continent were not necessarily inefficient or unproductive. Indeed, it was their continued commitment to landholding, agricultural polyculture, and a range of "pluri-activities" which made them capable of adapting to changing conditions. Again, studies of regional specialization have helped to demonstrate the diversity of paths towards economic and social development. Silk production in the Alto Milanese of northern Italy, for instance, was an extremely profitable and durable feature of the economy, generating exports worth about a third of the national total in the late nineteenth and early twentieth centuries. The industry's capacity for capital accumulation derived from the value of the product and the low costs of production. In the view of Bull and Corner its durability depended on the emergence of a distinctive "social form," the "peasant–worker family." Involvement in both agriculture and manufacturing allowed for flexibility in work practices and investment choices by household members while ensuring a measure of material security through landholding. It was a social form that became so established that it persisted in this region long after silk production had diminished.[15]

Recent studies also highlight the need to consider broader environmental and ecological issues: how did arable cultivation and livestock rearing intersect with rural people's multiple exploitation of "wastelands," forests, rivers, lakes, and mountainsides? Like agricultural land, these other resources faced pressures from an expanding population during the nineteenth century. Competing interests intensified existing strains in the European countryside, while simultaneously creating new ones. In some areas they also revealed important shifts in land use, from subsistence cropping and extensive pastoralism to more intensive forms of commercial production like dairying, olives, vines, or market gardening (fruit and vegetables). McPhee's microhistory of the drawn-out struggles between noble landowners and poor peasants for control of the scrubby, infertile hillsides (*garrigues*) of the Corbières in southern France highlighted an evolving contest over the demands of sheep herding, charcoal burning, cereal growing, and wine production. The consequences, as McPhee demonstrated, were both economic and environmental. While the region's hillsides were progressively denuded of tree cover in the late eighteenth century, the rural economy was eventually transformed by the development of small-scale but market-oriented viticulture. However, the conflicts were not resolved without violence, as a half-century of aristocratic intimidation and popular resistance culminated in ritualized murder.[16]

The social composition of rural societies and the tensions provoked by inequalities of wealth and status provide a second set of questions. Relations among different kinds of "peasants" were as important as those between peasants and the ever-present groups of rural artisans, laborers, and out-workers, or with the representatives of local authority (merchants, officials, rural notables, clergy, aristocrats). McPhee's work on the Corbières was by no means the only one to confirm that relations between the "rulers" of rural communities and their "dependants" were commonly marked by conflict.

Of primary significance were tensions over access to land, an issue which Josef Mooser examined in western Germany during the first half of the nineteenth century. By focusing on two nearby but contrasting areas of Westphalia, Mooser aimed to illustrate how property relations and land use in different contexts found expression in different forms of social conflict, as gauged by the incidence of wood stealing. One case study was Paderborn, an overwhelmingly agrarian region with limited opportunities for non-agricultural production and employment. Many of the population were "small peasants" who supplemented the produce of their meager lands (whether freehold or leasehold) by exercising their customary rights to gather fodder, fuel, and construction timber from local forests. Landownership was dominated by the aristocracy who – together with the Prussian state – also owned most of the woodlands. In Minden-Ravensberg, by contrast, there were few large estates. Most of this area's inhabitants were either landowning "peasant" cultivators, or *Heuerlinge* (landless laborers and small tenant-farmers whose households survived by spinning and weaving textiles). Here the woodlands were overwhelmingly in the hands of the peasant proprietors, who gained their income from rents as well as agricultural produce. For Mooser, the key distinctions between these two parts of Westphalia were the role of collective property rights (especially over forest resources) and the uneven development of commercial agriculture during the early nineteenth century. Almost all communal lands had been divided by 1800 in Ravensberg, where "middling peasant" landowners took the lead in advancing "agrarian individualism," while the landless *Heuerlinge* were increasingly dependent on industrial labor. However, it was the noble proprietors who promoted "economic modernization" in Paderborn, where customary rights to woodlands persisted well into the 1840s, when their piecemeal removal provoked economic hardship and "bitter struggles."[17]

The main social dimensions of forest "crimes" in these parts of Westphalia reflected the different contexts and conflicts. Mooser identified two primary motivations for the incidence of wood stealing. In most of the Paderborn cases, peasant wood-thieves were "simply defending the old rights of usufruct" which large landowners wanted to abolish, but in Ravensberg it was more "a confrontation between two classes": the marginalized *Heuerlinge* stole wood from peasant proprietors in order to safeguard "their entire economic system – the family economy." However, Mooser then blurred the issue by remarking that a good deal of timber theft seemed to result from outright poverty and sheer desperation. Questions arise moreover, whether historians can identify elements of "social" protest in the records of rural criminality, while some scholars would take issue with Mooser's suggestions that the transformation of social and economic relationships in the countryside was a natural consequence of the expanding "proto-industrial" production of textiles.

Initial formulations by Mendels, Medick, and others since the 1970s identified "proto-industrialization" as a distinctive form of rurally based manufacturing characterized by small-scale domestic production, organized on a regional basis (though directed at "export" markets), and carried out by a labor force that also worked seasonally in agriculture. Textiles produced through artisanal workshops and later the "putting-out" system took pride of place in these studies. In this way their early work envisaged that proto-industrialization prepared the way for urban, factory-based industrial production in the later nineteenth century, not merely as a result of the opportunities it presented for capital accumulation and investment, but also because they equated the development of proto-industrial manufacturing with significant changes in demographic indicators (declining age at first marriage, rising fertility rates, larger family sizes). These shifts led to sustained population growth, thereby stimulating demand, not least from proto-industrial workers who were increasingly purchasers rather than producers of food. The overall consequences were regarded as symptoms of a large-scale transformation of the institutions and mores of "traditional" rural societies (landholding patterns, inheritance practices, commercial agriculture, population mobility) which, between the end of the Middle Ages and the mid-1800s, created the preconditions for the self-sustaining expansion of industrial capitalism in Europe.[18]

Among the essays collected by Ogilvie and Cerman, two offer useful illustrations of the adjustments and criticisms applied to the proto-industrialization model. Since Mendels' foundational study concerned Flanders, the survey of proto-industrial manufacturing in Sweden by Magnusson, and Cerman's contribution on Austria, provided important comparisons. At the outset both Magnusson and Cerman extended their view of proto-industrial production to include some forms of manufacturing that were initially excluded on the grounds that they were capital intensive rather than labor intensive, and not primarily based on domestic labor: both discussed, for example, the proto-industrial features of metal smelting. They also disagreed with standard formulations over the rural location of proto-industrial production (Cerman included urban manufacturing, which for a long time operated under some measure of guild control) and the prerequisite of export-oriented output (in the Swedish case Magnusson saw this as less crucial). Finally, in explaining why there seemed to be no automatic connection between well-established proto-industrialization and the emergence of urban, factory-based forms of manufacturing, Magnusson and Cerman emphasized both the geographical factors (such as the availability of raw materials and transport networks) and the importance of state interventions, especially policy decisions (on customs dues, subsidies, inheritance provisions, and taxation) which affected agriculture, industry, and trade.[19]

In sum, the studies coordinated by Ogilvie and Cerman discovered a variability of demographic indicators where proto-industrial theories had predicted similar patterns: in some proto-industrial regions age at marriage did not decline noticeably, and there were no rises in fertility rates or overall population. This work likewise questioned the emphasis on the putting-out system as an organizational feature of proto-industrial production. Several contributors highlighted the range of strategies that were applied to forms of production, methods of marketing, and the division of labor. Not all types of proto-industrial manufacturing were based on household labor (the "family economy"), since many rural by-employments were pursued, either seasonally or in the short term, by young, single men and women. Domestic production moreover was not necessarily the norm: as Bull and Corner pointed out, silk-making "manufactories" were common in northern Italy in the nineteenth century. Indeed, it was this observation which led these two historians to reinforce the criticism voiced by several others: the notion that proto-industrialization was a "stage" in the development of industrial capitalism ("industrialization before industrialization," as Medick and others put it) was fundamentally challenged by the silk-producing peasant-workers of Lombardy, whose efficiency and adaptability did much to forestall the emergence of an urban, factory-based industry. On the other hand, a theory of proto-industrialization that originally aimed to explore the initial phases of industrial and capitalist development in early modern Europe has had major ramifications for scholars of the nineteenth-century countryside. Not only have they shown how proto-industrial manufacturing existed alongside the expanding factories of the great industrial cities, but they have also been able to demonstrate the flexibility and durability of proto-industrial production which persisted in many parts of the continent well into the nineteenth and even the twentieth century.

Nonetheless, in those times and places where proto-industrialization gave way, the consequences were often profound. Magnusson noted that the handicraft production of textiles (especially linen) declined in Sweden after the 1870s, replaced by mechanized, large-scale manufacturing. Some observers lamented this change at the time, fearing the loss of "female industries." Similar changes occurred in Ireland where sections of the dairying industry were "industrialized" by the development of large creameries in the last decades of the nineteenth century. There, however, Bourke found that the sentiments expressed were often less positive. A few commentators among the clergy worried about the proliferation of factories that deprived rural women of income, but the predominant view believed that men (and machines) would work more skillfully and consistently. Besides, as one Irish "expert" retorted, "the farmer's wife has enough employment to keep her out of mischief without making butter."[20]

In recent years scholars have directed attention to the questions raised by that most pervasive of social distinctions, the sexual division of labor. Issues of gender identity loomed large in the consciousness of nineteenth-century Europeans, but it is less clear how idealized notions of femininity and masculinity were manifested at the "grassroots" of society. As we saw in the case of Grigorovich's short story or Millet's paintings, the analysis of visual and literary representations of rural society has its limitations. Initial forays by historians tended to focus on the gendered nature of rural work. As ever, there was the problem of sources: few laboring folk had the time, literacy skills, or inclination to set down a record of their working lives, while much of the prescriptive literature (often in the form of legislation, newspapers, sermons, manifestos, and petitions) was of dubious value as historical evidence of work practices and family life. Yet a wealth of insights has been generated by studies undertaken in many parts of Europe. Like Bourke's work on the Irish dairy industry,

Sayer's study of women's involvement in English agriculture found many evocative sources among the reports of royal commissions and Poor Law officials, whose varied expressions of sympathy or aversion reinforced the messages from visual images and literary texts. Sayer demonstrated how these representations of women's work in the fields reflected wider issues in the middle-class urban sensibilities of nineteenth-century England.[21]

In an attempt to get closer to the attitudes that prevailed among rural inhabitants themselves, however, Martine Segalen developed an innovative approach to the study of gender relations in the countryside of nineteenth-century France. Among other forms of evidence (folkloric records, family trees, photographs), this historical anthropologist juxtaposed accounts of men's and women's work activities with domestic architecture and the layout of farm buildings; she also examined regional proverbs, which she felt captured "the voice of the peasants." From both aspects of her study Segalen concluded that the rural work of women and men was essentially complementary: a sexual division of labor existed, but it was not necessarily exploitative. Peasant families were not inherently patriarchal, she argued, because country people knew that a household's survival depended on everyone's commitment to hard work and reciprocity. Of course, proverbial expressions often reflected masculine assumptions and anxieties: "Keep the trousers on if you want peace" (Corsica); "A hen crowing like a cock and a cock laying eggs means the devil's in the house" (Brittany). Like visual images and literary texts, folk sayings were commonly normative, and thus posed problems of selectivity and interpretation. As Segalen acknowledged, rural proverbs revealed a range of often contradictory attitudes: "A hardworking woman is worth her skinful of money" (Catalonia); "A man has two good days on [this] earth, when he takes a wife and when he buries her" (Languedoc and other provinces). Yet this study's major contribution was to emphasize the importance of affective relationships between women and men: "Drinking, eating, sleeping together, [that] seems to me to make a marriage" (Anjou); "Man and wife are joined for life" (Gascony).

For all their problems, Segalen's evidence offered insights into the emotional dimensions of family life, an area that was documented only rarely – on intermittent occasions of serious conflict – by those usual sources of historical record-making, state bureaucracies.[22]

Power relations between rural inhabitants and the various institutions representing the wider economic, political, and cultural contexts of the nineteenth century were invariably asymmetrical. Exploring the mechanisms and ramifications of that power imbalance constitutes a third set of questions for historians of the European countryside. Competition for environmental resources arose not only from large landowners and within rural communities themselves, but also from powerful outsiders such as urban consumers and state institutions. The most obvious impacts are well known: the legislative and administrative provisions affecting rural societies (the emancipation of serfs, land redistribution schemes, the abolition of customary and collective rights, "foreign" and/or colonial rule); depopulation or displacement, and economic crises. The countryside's responses are equally familiar, although historians' one-time fascination with the causes and repression of mass uprisings and the "archaic" forms of peasant politics has given way to studies of "everyday forms of protest," and the prevalence of sociocultural maneuvering. A good deal of work drew attention to the profound effects on rural communities brought about by the development of markets (national, continental, and global), the expansion of state authority, and the diffusion of elite cultures dependent on literacy and "national" languages. In the 1970s some scholars characterized these accumulated changes as the advance of "modernization." Judged by those criteria most "Frenchmen" remained "peasants" until at least the 1880s, announced Eugen Weber, since only in the last decades of the century did they relinquish their geographical isolation, subsistence-oriented farming methods, and archaic cultural practices.[23] Weber's views met stern criticisms at the time and subsequently, but his arguments raised interesting questions about the nature of the evidence that historians rely on. If many of our sources seem to demonstrate the importance and resilience of rural life, then scholars have also learned to

appreciate the problems of the documents they use. Information about rural society is patchy, although not primarily because the records have disappeared; many data were simply not recorded in the first place.

Our awareness is therefore constrained by the limitations of official knowledge. Estimating the size of the agricultural labor force is particularly uncertain, for instance. In several countries, especially in Eastern Europe, there was no record of reliable occupational data until the very end of the century. Even then there were problems of classification, particularly in Russia and Poland where millions of domestic servants working in agriculture were counted in the "service" sector. Nineteenth-century surveys of farming practice and official data about agricultural production were notoriously incomplete. Although many governments set out to gather statistics on the inputs and the outputs of agriculture, the resulting reports and recommendations make life difficult for historians. Only after about 1870, for example, did most governments collect systematic data about the area of land under cultivation, the production of cereals and other crops, and the numbers of livestock. Even then statistics were not regularly available for some parts of Europe (the Iberian peninsula, the Balkans, and Britain) until the 1880s or even later. In Spain the most complete and consistent sets of agricultural data, which have been extensively analyzed in the past two decades by historians of the GEHR (Grupo de Estudios de Historia Rural), exist only from the 1890s.[24]

How could we explain this lack of information? Recall for a moment the Galician field that covered a mere 32 square meters and apparently had three different "owners." Quite apart from its size, which represented a nightmare for promoters of agricultural improvement, this field's complex property arrangements would have made it troublesome to assess for taxation purposes. From the perspective of government officials in the nineteenth century, rural communities were preternaturally opaque.

James Scott preferred to describe the authorities' difficulties in such cases as a product of the pervasive "illegibility" of rural society. Before the eighteenth-century Enlightenment, European rulers had rather limited horizons when it came to finding out about their subjects: extracting tax revenues and military recruits, while imposing some measure of political control, often in tandem with enforced religious conformity. Scott pointed out that the methods employed to attain these goals were frequently haphazard and arbitrary. But during the nineteenth century European governments adopted a more purposeful stance. The population was to be rendered more "legible" through policies designed to simplify and standardize the complexities of rural life. The point was to make the central state more powerful and efficient. Scott emphasized the introduction of consistent units for weights and measures – the most enduring of which was developed in revolutionary France: the metric system (meter/liter/kilogram). Similar state-sponsored efforts at standardization and uniformity were to be found in the enthusiasm with which nineteenth-century governments eliminated internal tariffs and privileged tax exemptions while instituting a legal code, a single currency, and "national" maps. For rural inhabitants the most tangible effects of this impulse were the campaigns to draw up cadastral surveys, the consolidation of scattered landholdings, and the elimination of communal property and collective use rights. The point is that Weber's analysis, based substantially on official documents, said much more about how "peasants" were increasingly subjected to the authorities' attention and interest, and much less about rural dwellers themselves. Scott's concept of "legibility" suggested that Weber's argument could be turned on its head: it was not that modernization eventually drove "peasants" to become "Frenchmen" during the last quarter of the nineteenth century. Rather, it was only in this period that the French state at last developed the mechanisms to document its rural citizens in a comprehensive and consistent manner.[25]

The timing of state intervention was similar in other parts of Europe, and there seems little doubt that enhancing "legibility" was regarded as a matter of profound political importance. The Stolypin "reforms" in Russia were among the most ambitious and self-serving. Profoundly shaken by a combination of military defeat, urban revolutions, and rural uprisings in 1905, the Russian government's responses included plans for a massive land redistribution in order to create for the first time "a class of small proprietors." The measure did not aim primarily at economic or social amelioration in the countryside. Stolypin justified his policy by observing that such people would be the "natural adversaries" of seditious politics, and would thus form "the basic cell of the state."[26]

Comparable pressures operated in Italy, where a national Direzione di Statistica (Directorate of Statistics) was created in the immediate aftermath of unification to undertake the country's first census. As Silvana Patriarca demonstrated, the gathering of official information in Italy was not merely a pragmatic exercise to provide Italy's new government with political and ideological legitimation. Nor was it a project which enabled the ruling elites simply to take stock of the country's resources, both human and material. Rather, insisted Patriarca, the process of collecting and publishing national statistics was a far more wide-ranging, constitutive process, whose influence was just as significant in preparing for unification during the decades before 1861 as it was in subsequently consolidating the new nation's sense of purpose. In these ways, the nineteenth century's obsession with national statistics contributed to the creation and diffusion – or as Anderson would prefer, the "imagining" – of national identity.[27]

Yet this was a daunting task. Nearly a decade after its creation the Italian Direzione di Statistica publicized its achievements to date. By 1869, according to Patriarca's summary, sixty reports had been compiled: twelve on commerce, eleven on population, nine on public and private schools, eight on industries, four on charities, three on weather and mineral waters, and another three on communes, provinces, and their finances, two on public health, and two more on savings banks and friendly societies, and one on elections. A further six volumes were devoted to reporting the meetings of the International Statistical Congresses (the latest of which had been held in Florence), and there was a summary volume of miscellaneous data. Not a single enquiry had been undertaken into agriculture. Even though the agricultural world continued to predominate in terms of both population and economic output, the rural environment was particularly "illegible" because of the persistence of local and regional particularities.

That illegibility reinforced officials' perceptions of the cultural differences between themselves and the inhabitants of rural communities.
Such attitudes often found expression in reports that commented on the "foreignness"
of peasants and their ways of life. In 1902
Pierre Buffault was a young forestry official at
the beginning of a long and active career. But
like many of his colleagues he felt frustrated by
the difficulties of trying to convince small
landowners that the law had curtailed their collective use rights (especially pasturing animals
and gathering firewood) in "public" forests.
Buffault did not hesitate to record his dismay:
to a regional conference he complained that
this was yet another instance of the instinctive
indolence and resistance to change that were
typical of peasants in this mountainous region;
comparable stubbornness might be found
only among Arabs. Although these insensitive
remarks could have come from the outpost of
any colonial empire, they actually appeared in
the heart of Europe: Buffault was referring to
the Béarn region of the Pyrenees.[28]

On the other hand, the persistent difficulties of gathering and processing information
meant that state authorities were never fully
informed – their policies for the control or con-
tainment of rural communities were invariably
flawed by a lack of detailed knowledge on key
issues. Nor did government agencies represent
a monolithic entity – they vied with each other
for budgetary allocations, staff and status, often
based on assessments of the priorities that
suited their own interests. Official ignorance
and bureaucratic in-fighting created opportunities for obstruction and maneuvering by peasants and other rural inhabitants. A host of
official files, prime among them the records of
criminal justice systems, carefully documented
various forms of popular opposition to the
demands and intrusions by the central state and
its agencies. These consequences of "cultural
conflict" have proved valuable to several scholars, particularly those like McPhee, Mooser,
and others who appreciated that criminal
justice records might offer insights not just into
the expectations and plans of powerful policymakers, but also the responses and resistance
of peasants and other non-elite groups. Yet the
documents generated by legal/judicial systems,

as Muir and Ruggiero put it, are invariably
"polluted by authority": we can read (or hear)
the "voices of the past," but not in an unmedi-
ated fashion – indeed, they were often translated, in many cases literally, in part due to the
prevalence of dialects, regional languages, and
illiteracy, but also because the records of police
and court proceedings have in all cases been
written in a form of legalese.[29]

Such sources nonetheless have an impressive
potential to tell us about aspects of rural life
that were documented in no other ways. Alain
Corbin's study of an "unknown" man's life
was one striking example – the reader learns
very little about Louis-François Pinagot
(1798–1876), the man about whom no
"private" records survived, and who was
selected by Corbin for precisely that reason.
But we are introduced to rich descriptions of
working and family life in nineteenth-century
Normandy (northwestern France), thanks in
large part to the wealth of local judicial and
notarial records. For the Ionian Islands, a
British protectorate from 1816 until being
absorbed into the Greek state in 1864, Thomas
Gallant investigated a formal colonial setting.
The extensive documentation generated by the
occupying power's efforts to govern and "civilize" the islanders allowed Gallant to explore
many of the ways in which both sides negotiated the strains imposed by their enforced
relationship. By employing anthropological
techniques, particularly to the analysis of police
and judicial records, Gallant was able to show
how colonial institutions (such as foundling
hospitals and even the courts themselves) were
incorporated by Greek women and men into
their daily lives in ways that were unexpected
and sometimes subversive.[30]

Resistance and accommodation went hand
in hand in the nineteenth century. But while
historians underscore the resilience of Europe's
rural inhabitants in the face of massive
upheavals, some observers of the time came to
view them with a degree of regret and even
nostalgia. Surely it was no coincidence that
the countryside's most significant bequests to
the twentieth and twenty-first centuries were
notions of regional identity that had a distinctly
rural flavor? Celia Applegate's survey of the
recent historiography of "regionalism" in

Europe showcased the powerful and enduring effects of that legacy.[31]

NOTES

1   Simpson (1995: 45–6, 74–8).
2   Mayer (1981). See also chapter 6, below.
3   Woodhouse (1991); Herbert (1976: 84–7, 137–40).
4   Blum (1978: 272).
5   Young quoted in Mingay (1975: 59).
6   See, for example, Bairoch (1973); Pounds (1985: esp. 187–247).
7   S. Clark (1999).
8   Mitchell (1992: 3–11, 141–58).
9   Milward and Saul (1977: 278–88, 326, 517).
10 McPhee (1992: 15–35).
11 Overton (1996a).
12 Young quoted in Allen and Ó Gráda (1988).
13 Thompson (1968); Zanden (1991).
14 Mathias and Davis (1996: 1–16); Petruscewicz (1996); Fonseca (2003).
15 Bull and Corner (1993).
16 McPhee (1999).
17 Mooser (1986: 52–80).
18 Ogilvie and Cerman (1996: 1–11).
19 Cerman, "Proto-Industrial Development in Austria," and Magnusson, "Proto-Industrialization in Sweden," in Ogilvie and Cerman (1996: 171–87, 208–26).
20 Bourke (1990: 161).
21 Sayer (1995).
22 Segalen (1983: 24, 28, 108, 128, 156, 160).
23 Weber (1977).
24 Harrison (1989: 180–7).
25 Scott (1998: esp. 22–52).
26 Stolypin quoted in Spulber (2003: 52).
27 Patriarca (1996: esp. 1–12, 122–30, chs. 6 and 7). Cf. Anderson (1991: 163–85).
28 Buffault quoted in Ogé (1993: 161–2).
29 Muir and Ruggiero (1994: ix).
30 Corbin (2001); Gallant (2002).
31 Applegate (1999).

GUIDE TO FURTHER READING

Case studies of "agricultural revolution" in Europe and the issues involved in assessing productivity gains appeared in Campbell and Overton, *Land, Labour and Livestock*. Anderson's *Explaining Long-Term Economic Change* summarized and evaluated a number of explanatory models. Several regional and national studies of historical geography have challenged Anglocentric views about the changing relationships among landholding patterns, farming methods, and rural manufacturing. Hoppe and Langton, *Peasantry to Capitalism*, who focused on Sweden, and Simpson, *Spanish Agriculture*, offered detailed examples.

National histories with a special interest in rural developments during the nineteenth century included Wintle, *An Economic and Social History of the Netherlands*, and McPhee, *A Social History of France*. The importance of access to land was underlined by Whited, *Forests and Peasant Politics in Modern France*, who showed how rural history can take a wider view of environmental management and the competing interests involved.

Relations between rural inhabitants and their landlords were surveyed by contributors to Gibson and Blinkhorn, *Landownership and Power in Modern Europe*, while elite representations of Russia's rural population were analyzed in Frierson, *Peasant Icons*. Clarkson's *Proto-Industrialization* assessed the early literature on this theme, and various perspectives subsequently made up a special issue of *Continuity and Change* 8 (1993). Changes in rural employment (both agricultural and industrial) during the nineteenth century had wide-ranging implications for gender relations, as Bourke's *Husbandry to Housewifery* demonstrated in the case of Ireland. The extent of emotional attachments among country people was given prominence by Thompson, "The Sale of Wives" in *Customs in Common*.

Lehning's *Peasant and French* provided a robust critique of Weber's modernization thesis. Schulte's *The Village in Court* dissected the internal tensions of rural communities as revealed in judicial records from Bavaria. Frank's *Crime, Cultural Conflict and Justice in Rural Russia* explored divergences between elite and popular attitudes to law and justice. An innovative study of popular beliefs, local identity, and the sounds of the French countryside by Corbin, *Village Bells*, drew extensively on the records of rural disputes.

CHAPTER FOUR

Industrial Revolution, Commerce, and Trade

ROBERT LEE

Introduction

Until recently it was common to view the process of European industrial development in the nineteenth century through British eyes: the process started in Britain with the "first industrial revolution" and its continental replication was "a purely and deliberately imitative process."[1] Such an approach increasingly appears to be conceptually narrow. It is based on a questionable interpretation of the industrialization process, whether in Britain or continental Europe, and fails to explore the possibility of different paths to economic growth, some of which may well have been no less effective than the British model and actually preferable in terms of long-term development, social cohesion, or other cultural criteria. This chapter will reassess the nature of the industrial revolution within the framework of existing theoretical explanations of nineteenth-century development and the diversity of European experience.

Any attempt to examine the extent and nature of industrial development in nineteenth-century Europe has to contend with significant data limitations. Despite considerable refinements in constructing national income series, data quality in the case of many European states, including Austria-Hungary, Denmark, and Holland, remains debatable or poor, while information on agricultural output and money wages is often problematical or restricted in its coverage. The pre-1914 Maddison national income estimates are less reliable for some European countries, such as Belgium, the Netherlands, Russia, and Switzerland, and very problematic in the case of Central and Eastern European states, in part because of boundary changes. New estimates of national income growth are also gender blind, ignoring the changing contribution of female labor to sectoral output.[2] The attempt to construct proxy variables based on such selective indicators as life expectancy, school attendance rates, and letters posted per capita provides an alternative measure of economic growth, particularly for the pre-statistical era. Although it is seldom an adequate substitute for a national income approach, it does help to place in context the economic changes of nineteenth-century Europe. Contrary to earlier assumptions, technological change measured by rising industrial productivity was not a necessary and sufficient cause of economic growth, which had been evident both in different parts of Europe and selective regions of the world well before the onset of the "first industrial revolution."[3]

Reappraising the "Industrial Revolution"

The industrial revolution lies at the heart of our understanding of the origins of modern economic development, whether in Europe as a whole or within an international context. But the British industrial revolution itself remains a problematic, if not a contested, concept. On the one hand, there is a well-established tradition that emphasizes the inherent discontinuity between 1760 and 1830 in a wide range of macroeconomic indicators, including national income, GDP per capita, capital formation, and productivity. It was also a period characterized by technological discontinuities as a result of increased technical innovation, profound changes in the organization of production and marketing, and an equally radical transformation of economic and social relations.[4] Few authors would argue that the structural changes associated with the industrial revolution were either all-embracing or pervasive. The emergence of a national market was constrained by the continued absence of uniform weights and measures until the mid-nineteenth century; there was a pronounced element of regional diversity in terms of the operation of capital and labor markets; and there was a considerable lag between the introduction of advanced manufacturing processes and their general consolidation in the 1830s and 1840s.[5] Nevertheless, the sustained pace of change, particularly in a number of regions and sectors, was impressive: by the early nineteenth century only about a third of the labor force was still engaged in agriculture, and urban growth in England alone accounted for approximately 70 percent of total increase in urban population in Europe as a whole. Irrespective of the precise causal factors behind early industrialization, including the operation of specific property rights, supportive institutional developments, or even the emergence of a free business press, the British economy underwent a series of structural changes between 1760 and 1830 which represented a perceptible break with the past.[6] To this extent, a radical change had occurred which had important implications for the development of continental Europe and the world as a whole.

By contrast, the concept of an industrial revolution has been increasingly challenged by recent research. It is now argued that the changes within the British economy up until the 1840s did not represent a "progressive, unitary phenomenon," but reflected longer-term development processes which had a very uneven and selective impact on economic performance and social structure. Indeed, prior to 1815, industrial growth was relatively slow.[7] Although there were clearly dynamic industries characterized by technological developments, such as cotton or iron, the pace of economic growth was diluted by the continued predominance of slow-growing sectors, and the relative weighting of "traditional" and "modern" sectors would have precluded any abrupt change in the pattern of economic growth. Even within "modernizing" sectors the secular trend was seldom uniform: the role of steam power as a major driving force for growth has been overstated; and the development of the cotton industry in Lancashire was not accompanied initially by the emergence of a competitive labor market or a significant reduction in information and search costs. Domestic work frequently remained the dominant form of production, as in the case of the hosiery and lace industries in the Midlands, and there was a marked continuity in the nature of women's work, as was the case in London before 1850.[8]

Reinterpreting Industrial Development in Nineteenth-Century Europe

The fact that the traditional view of the "first industrial revolution" is increasingly contested and no longer tenable has considerable implications for our understanding of economic growth in nineteenth-century Europe and the development of the modern world. First, it undermines the applicability of general theories of European development based on a single, British model predicated on the existence of a number of specific factors. According to various authors, from Marx to Rostow, the process of European industrialization was divided into specific stages, with the latter emphasizing the importance of a critical turning point of 30 years when fundamental advances in production techniques were achieved in conjunction with a significant rise in the savings ratio.[9] But the British case no longer provides evidence for the existence of a stage model associated with the onset of an industrial revolution. In reality, the experience of Europe in the nineteenth century reveals a variety of different paths to economic growth, some of which may well have been no less efficient than the British model and, perhaps, even preferable in terms of long-term development. Second, it places in question the extent to which the industrialization process in Britain can be viewed as a separate or exceptional phenomenon. A number of major variables, including increased population pressure with a concomitant upward trend in relative prices during the second half of the eighteenth century and greater pressure to rationalize agricultural production, operated across Europe in general. Continental Europe, like Britain at the beginning of the nineteenth century, was also characterized by uneven regional development, with industrial production in Germany, for example, particularly concentrated in Saxony, Silesia, the Ruhr, and Berlin, in contrast to the increasing emphasis on export oriented grain monoculture in the eastern provinces of Prussia. Even technical innovation was not restricted to Britain. In France, for example, Jacquard invented a silk loom, Réaumur popularized new methods of producing iron, and Berthollet invented chlorine bleaching. Despite continuing deficiencies in the communication and transport infrastructure, information dissemination throughout Europe was relatively rapid and factor mobility quite extensive. As a result, political elites, entrepreneurs, bankers, craftsmen, and primary sector producers were increasingly aware of the opportunities and challenges of modern economic development as part of a gradual leveling-up process.

Nevertheless, the general model developed by Gerschenkron, which postulates that growth rates in relatively backward European economies were characterized by a big spurt discontinuity, still attracts support. The more backward a country was, the more important were institutional factors such as banks and the state in determining both the speed and nature of industrial development, with a specific emphasis on producer rather than consumer industries and a greater pressure on consumption levels in order to facilitate capital formation. In certain cases, such as Austria-Hungary, the period between 1870 and 1914 witnessed unprecedented rapid growth, in line with Gerschenkron's paradigm, as Central Europe took advantage of its growth potential as a low income region, but the performance in the western half of the empire remained disappointing, primarily because of an outflow of capital to Hungary. Spain, another "relatively backward" state, demonstrated few advantages as a latecomer, with a progressive yearly decline in industrial output of 2 percent between 1860 and 1910, and the degree of backwardness in Southern Europe as a whole was arguably too large by 1870 to be overcome by the outbreak of World War I. However, despite its limitations, the concept of "relative backwardness" continues to offer a useful basis for analyzing the economic history of nineteenth-century Europe, particularly in terms of the ongoing debate over the trend towards relative convergence or peripheralization, and it will be used in this context as a basis for exploring a range of important issues.[10]

The Role of Banking in European Development

Previously it was assumed that nation-states needed to increase their savings ratio to achieve economic growth by raising the rate of productive investment from approximately 5 percent to over 10 percent of national income. The available data seldom confirm this hypothesis. The level of capital required to finance early industrialization was not excessive. Total investment in the cotton industry, for example, remained within reasonable bounds because of its rural base and different sectoral growth patterns. Moreover, pressure on capital costs could be minimized by leasing industrial premises and by reducing the amount of trade credit. Many parts of Europe undoubtedly suffered from poor credit facilities in the first half of the nineteenth century, with the possible exception of Belgium, where the foundation of the Société Generale de Belgique (1822) and the Banque de Belgique (1835) led to efforts to develop payments by check and overdraft facilities for businessmen and firms. But despite supply-side weaknesses, there is no clear evidence that economic growth was seriously hindered by capital shortages. In Germany, for example, there was a reduced demand for capital in the 1820s and 1830s, in part as a response to agricultural crises; the average interest rate in Prussia fell from 8 to 3 percent; and there were no liquidity problems even in the 1840s.[11] The diversification of successful merchant houses into private banking, direct transfers from the primary sector (in particular through industrial investment by members of the landed aristocracy, whether in Austria, Baden, or the duchies of Schleswig and Holstein), and the increasing willingness of traditional banking houses to handle commercial accounts represented useful sources of capital for industrial development.

By contrast, the significant growth in industrial output during the second half of the nineteenth century was accompanied by the development of a more sophisticated banking structure and increased institutional diversification. Most national banks effectively became lenders of last resort; 40 investment banks modeled on the Credit Mobilier were established throughout Europe between 1852 and 1880; and different banking structures were created to meet specific needs, whether for popular credit in Italy and France (from 1864 and 1878, respectively), for the primary sector, as in Germany (Raiffeisen) and Russia, or for small-scale businesses (Handwerkerbanken in Germany). The actual number of banks registered in individual countries increased significantly and even in Russia the total number of banking institutions rose from 455 in 1875 to 2,390 by 1914. Although Switzerland registered the highest growth rate in its financial institutions ratio, significant improvements were evident in other European states, including Belgium, Germany, the Netherlands, and Norway.[12]

Ultimately, there was a high degree of homogeneity in terms of banking type, but the timing and extent of institutional development, even within a specific region such as Scandinavia, often reflected the role of cultural and political factors. In Italy, by contrast, the pattern of development was determined by external factors with the establishment from the early 1890s of universal banks on the German model by German-led syndicates. However, the posited distinction between the UK and continental Europe, or between a market and bank oriented system, is difficult to sustain. Not only were the major commercial banks in the UK more heavily involved in providing overdraft credit to business enterprises than was previously thought, but also a number of continental countries failed to follow the German model in developing a mixed universal banking system. Despite their status as "relatively backward" economies, neither Greece nor Norway witnessed the creation of large-scale universal banks and there was only limited involvement by the banking sector in industrial share ownership. The benefits of universal banking in latecomer economies such as Germany and Italy have also been exaggerated. Despite the existence of interlocking directorates and long-term involvement with industrial firms, the system as a whole was not necessarily a catalyst for high rates of economic growth. There was a restricted focus on specific sectors of the economy, risk aversion to "new industries," and limited influence on the performance of large firms. Although universal banks helped to reduce transaction costs by overcoming the problem of asymmetric information, they only provided development assistance to the strong, although firms without banking attachments often performed equally well. In Germany, an increasing proportion of investment was financed by the banking sector from the late 1870s onwards, but smaller provincial banks had a wider customer base. To this extent, the European banking system was less differentiated in terms of its structure and function than had previously been assumed; the expansion of the banking sector seldom, if ever, preceded economic growth; and banks did not necessarily play a disproportionate role in the development of relatively backward economies.[13]

The Role of the State

In contrast to the British case, where economic growth (according to the traditional view) was largely a result of market forces, it is often argued that the state was actively involved in the industrialization process in continental Europe, whether in clearing away some of the obstacles to economic development, or in responding to the structural problems generated by relative backwardness. In France state policies helped to create the conditions for a market economy, particularly in grain; in Russia the adoption of a uniform currency cut transaction costs; in Bohemia the lifting of customs boundaries (1851–63) and the abolition of guilds (1859) were important factors in development; and even the general introduction of quarantine measures to control plague can be justifiably viewed as a public good. Where government power was absent, development-retarding domestic conditions were allowed to persist.[14] In a wider context, the state often provided the preconditions for successful industrialization by abolishing the feudal agrarian regime in a process that extended from the start of the enclosure movement in Sweden (with the Storskifte Act of 1749), the abolition of enforced residence (Stavsbaand) in Denmark in 1788, and the peasant emancipation edict in Russia of 1861, to the Romanian Agrarian Law of August 1864. Of equal importance was state involvement in facilitating technology transfer, dismantling guild controls, implementing financial and administrative reforms, supporting the creation of social overhead capital (particularly in the case of railway construction), and in providing an appropriate legal framework for capitalist production. Finally, state support for education was an important contribution to industrial development, with tangible benefits in terms of technical training, technology transfer, and the inculcation of appropriate attitudes within the working class as a whole. Despite some noticeable national differences, the nineteenth century witnessed a trend towards institutional convergence in terms of educational provision, a significant improvement in school attendance rates at both the primary and secondary levels, and a rise in general literacy rates, particularly among women.

But the posited contrast between the role of the state in Britain and more "backward" areas of continental Europe is difficult to sustain. On the one hand, the eighteenth century witnessed significant growth in the role and function of the "fiscal-military" state in Britain: at its peak it was the largest employer, purchaser, and borrower in the domestic economy. There was a progressive dismantling of corrupt practices

from the 1770s onwards, a process that was reinforced by parliamentary inquiries that placed sensitive information in the public domain, while the parliamentary system itself, despite franchise limitations, facilitated the emergence of interest groups which were able to secure policy innovations (for example, the repeal of the Bubble Act in 1825). Selective policies, as in the treatment of raw cotton imports, had benefits for the long-term development of the textile industry.[15]

On the other hand, the effectiveness of state intervention in many continental European countries has been increasingly questioned. State priorities in terms of economic policy were not always appropriate: some of the south German states, such as Baden and Bavaria, attempted to maintain small-scale handicraft production in a manner that militated against large-scale industrialization, while the Spanish Board of Trade granted privileges to individual manufacturers which restricted competition and trade. Economic policy frequently reflected fiscal considerations and concern over government debt: it was often determined by state bureaucrats, whether in Prussia or the Ottoman Empire, and influenced by dominant interest groups or members of the established elite.[16] Indeed, the role of the state in fostering economic development can only be understood within the framework of a comparative analysis of the changing nature of government and the articulation of political power. Despite the growing emphasis on the importance of the nation-state during the course of the nineteenth century, its development and structure were both diverse and complex. The British state differed from its European counterparts: there was a uniquely powerful single legislature, no regional assemblies after the Anglo-Scottish Act of Union, and corporate privileges were comparatively weak. In Italy, even after political unification in 1861, the legislative framework of individual states was still very diverse and marked by significant institutional heterogeneity. There were many competing factions within the Prussian state in the early nineteenth century, and the continued existence of numerous federal states with well-defined administrations after the creation of the Reich in 1871 meant that Germany was characterized by a persistent fragmentation of political power, which directly encouraged the emergence of interest groups and their articulation of economic demands.

To this extent, the role of the state in fostering economic development was constrained by political factors and a predisposition to protect vested interests. Indeed, it would be wrong to overestimate the effectiveness of state intervention, particularly in view of the unequal pace of state formation. The abolition of feudalism in France was "excessively complicated" and the Russian peasant emancipation edict was seriously flawed, while the outcome of liberal land reform in Spain was not always as intended. The ability of central government to control events at the local level or to modernize administrative structures was undermined by the continued strength of vested interests, with southern Italy, in particular, characterized by both administrative and political chaos; and the continued recruitment of higher civil servants from the landed aristocracy, whether in Prussia or other German states, inevitably encouraged a conservative approach to many contemporary issues. In many cases, institutional rigidities were only gradually eliminated and entrepreneurs in both France and Spain continued to suffer from a restrictive legal framework, in particular in relation to joint stock company formation, while chronic budget deficits continued to crowd-out investment.[17]

Even in relation to improvements in educational provision and the quality of human capital, the role of the state may well have been relatively limited. Although Germany was one of the first countries to develop an extensive program of public education, the elementary school curriculum was inadequate, secondary education only provided limited opportunities for social mobility, and trade schools remained fee paying. Agricultural schools were only established at a comparatively late date in both Denmark and France, despite the continued role of the primary sector, and open-market forces (including mass migration and international capital flows) were more important in determining Swedish economic growth than high literacy levels and school enrolment rates. In the mid-nineteenth century the population of England and France was less literate than Ireland, Scotland, or Sweden, which were less developed economically, and a clear correlation between state educational provision and "innovative drive" is difficult to establish on the basis of the existing evidence.[18]

Market Forces: The Role of Demand and Supply Factors

A number of historians have argued that demand factors were of critical importance in accounting for the onset of the "industrial revolution" in Britain and its development in continental Europe. Expenditure by the wealthy and increasingly by the "middling sort" created a trickle-down effect which sustained an increase in demand, particularly for consumer goods. In reality, the impact of the court or aristocracy on contemporary taste and style tended to decline during this period and there was no mass market for fashionable clothing even at the end of the nineteenth century. Nevertheless, the role of demand should not be dismissed out of hand, as the evidence for increased consumer demand, specifically in the British case, remains "compelling."[19] There was undoubtedly a growth in the number and quality of possessions, even in eighteenth-century Europe; there was an increase in per capita consumption of coffee, tea, and sugar (whether in the English provinces, the Kingdom of Hanover, or Sweden); and demand for consumer durables was sustained by a reduction in their relative cost and a rise in agricultural incomes. Long-term changes in European society, with a growing number of merchants, shopkeepers, and members of the professions with a high consumption propensity, reinforced this upward trend, while the establishment of department stores in major European cities in the latter decades of the nineteenth century was a reflection of the growth in middle-class incomes.

But an increase in national income as a result of industrialization did not necessarily lead to a greater income transfer to the poor: in fact, there is evidence of a further exacerbation in income inequality, whether in Sweden during the second half of the eighteenth century or

France between 1830 and 1866. Despite an increase in labor intensity (characterized by de Vries as an "industrious revolution") due to a reduction in the number of non-working days and the adoption of more labor-intensive forms of production, there was generally an inverse relationship between economic development and living standards. Although real wages remained consistently higher in Northwest Europe in comparison with the Southeast, there was no visible increase in French living standards before the 1830s. It was not until the latter decades of the nineteenth century, specifically from the 1870s onwards, that real wages began to rise in Denmark, the Netherlands, Germany, and Sweden, as the opening up of new grain markets enabled workers to improve their relative purchasing power, at least in Western European states with an increasing dependency on food imports.[20]

However, the industrial revolution together with improvements in agricultural output undoubtedly prevented a dramatic fall in consumption levels at a time of considerable population increase which, in turn, was an important demand factor that affected the industrialization process. The period between 1750 and 1900 witnessed an increase in Europe's population of almost 200 percent (from approximately 144 million to 423 million) and the highest rates of population growth were often registered in the first half of the nineteenth century, as was the case in the German territories (1816–20), Italy (1821–31), and Norway (1815–65). At the same time, this period was characterized by a significant rise in urbanization: Europe's urban population increased from 14.5 to 43.5 percent of the total between 1800 and 1910, with an acceleration in large city growth evident in the early decades of the nineteenth century in both Britain and Belgium.[21]

The relationship between population growth and economic development is complex, although both the nature and timing of demographic change in nineteenth-century Europe had, on balance, a positive impact. High rates of population increase in some European regions undoubtedly led to greater land fragmentation and diversification out of agricultural dependency, while stimulating the development of rural industries and the emergence of distinct proto-industrial regions, whether in Britain, Sweden, Switzerland, or other European states. A great deal of recent work has increasingly questioned the degree of discontinuity implicit in the concept of the agricultural revolution, but the gap in labor productivity between Britain and France had widened appreciably from ca. 1700 onwards and by the early nineteenth century productivity levels per head in English agriculture were already markedly superior to those of continental Europe. During the nineteenth century, the response of the primary sector to increased demand varied substantially: between 1840 and 1900 productivity rose throughout Europe, but the estimated increase of 30 percent and 45 percent in Russia and Austria, respectively, compared poorly with the performance of Switzerland (90 percent) and Germany (190 percent). Where land reform was weak and its benefits selective, as in France and Russia, or development was constrained by physical obstacles and unfavorable factors, as in the case of Spain, agricultural performance was disappointing, particularly at a regional level. By contrast, although proto-industry did not necessarily lead to factory-based industrial development, in certain cases it facilitated capital accumulation and in a wider context it contributed significantly to both regional specialization and labor mobility.[22]

What characterized the process of industrial development during the nineteenth century was its regional profile, whether in Britain (Lancashire and the Black Country), Belgium (the Sambre-Meuse region), Germany (Saxony, the Ruhr, and Silesia), or Spain (Catalonia, the Basque country, and Valencia), which, in turn, was often the result of a disproportionate growth of specific sectors of the economy, namely the textile industry (in particular, cotton), coalmining, the manufacture of pig and bar iron, and mechanical engineering. Although regional divergence was evident in pre-industrial Europe, this was often accentuated in the course of the nineteenth century, as the increasing concentration of industrial production in specific localities and the emergence of new industrial centers and "leading industrial regions" such as Roubaix-Tourcoing and the area between Basle and Glarus in Switzerland were accompanied by a greater emphasis on agricultural employment in other areas.[23] In contrast to the growth of producer goods industries in the Ruhr, the eastern provinces of Prussia became heavily dependent on extensive cereal production, while the southern states of Baden, Bavaria, and Württemberg became more agricultural relative to the national average. Regional variations remained predominant in Spain, while the persistence of strong regional divergence in Russian grain prices reflected the markedly disparate nature of industrial development.

The regional basis of early industrialization, whether in Britain, Belgium, or elsewhere in Europe, together with rising levels of urbanization, generated important demand effects within national economies, which, in turn, encouraged further specialization in sectoral production, which was often dependent on underlying factor endowment.[24] Internationally, the demand effects of industrialization were considerable in terms of core–periphery relations and the opportunities for some European countries to exploit the potential for export-led growth. During the nineteenth century, the structure of European trade was characterized by a relative stability in imports from more developed countries and a disproportionate increase in the share of colonial or Third World exports. At the same time, an increasing diversification in international trade, improved technical organization, and an extension of national transport systems with the development of railway networks contributed to significant growth in trade activity: between 1860 and 1890 the overall value of world trade rose annually by 4.8 percent.[25] In the case of Denmark, Norway, and Sweden, demand for agricultural exports (including dairy produce, oats, and timber), particularly from Britain, played an important role in encouraging economic growth, but the contribution of market-widening and supply side factors should not be neglected. By contrast, foreign trade dependency in the case of Portugal led to increased peripheralization and there were no visible benefits from an increased exploitation of Spanish mineral deposits by Britain and France following the 1869 tariff, although the export sector

as a whole was not responsible for Spain's relative backwardness.[26]

Tariffs or other protective measures adopted by individual states, according to international trade theory, only serve to undermine the operation of market forces. Within this context, the gradual dismantling of protectionism in Britain, culminating in the abolition of the Navigation Acts in 1849 and the budgets of 1853 and 1860, was an important factor in stimulating international trade and the operation of market forces. This trend had been accompanied by a tentative reduction in mercantilist measures in other European states (as in Prussia in 1818 and Russia in 1823), but it was not until the Cobden-Chevalier Treaty of 1860 between Britain and France that the era of free trade was effectively initiated. However, this was to prove a comparatively short interlude, as many continental states resorted again to tariff protection following the severe downturn of 1872. But tariff policy was invariably the result of interest group pressure and had a selective impact on the pattern of trade development and the growth of national industries, depending on its sectoral scope and level of protection: it also had distributional implications within national economies. Despite considerable support for the retention of tariffs to protect infant industries in continental countries faced with the initial technological superiority of British manufacturing industry, an absence of tariff protection could also stimulate trade in goods and facilitate technology transfer. This was the case, for example, in relation to the imports of British coke pig iron into the German Zollverein prior to 1843–4 which helped to modernize the domestic iron industry, although this process was only completed by the adoption of import substitution as a result of the higher levels of duty imposed in September 1844.[27]

It is difficult to compare tariff levels across European countries, but by the end of the nineteenth century there were significant differences. Britain continued to adhere to the principles of free trade, but most other European states relied increasingly on tariff protection, primarily as a means of protecting agrarian interest groups threatened by the fall in international grain prices. The average rate of protection imposed on Spanish imports amounted to 40 percent, despite increasing evidence that increased tariffs from the 1880s onwards only served to reinforce traditional agricultural practices and contributed to backwardness in the primary sector. The adoption of agricultural protection in Germany in 1879 was an important factor behind the growth in domestic agricultural production, but this was at the cost of urban consumers and delayed the process of structural modernization in the primary sector. The impact of tariff protection on the development of the chemical industry was marginal: although it helped to exclude British soda imports from the German market, this was accompanied by negative welfare effects from the 1880s onwards. By contrast, the level of tariff protection in some of the smaller European states, such as Belgium, Holland, and Switzerland, remained modest, and these were among the more buoyant European economies.[28]

Technological developments associated with the industrial revolution were also largely demand induced. France was arguably more advanced in terms of scientific research in the eighteenth century, but the major technological breakthroughs occurred initially in Britain and there was often a substantial gap between scientific invention and industrial application. Even outside the technological inventions associated with the "industrial revolution" in iron production, textile manufacture, and steam power, the role of demand could be considerable. Both in ceramics and small wares, technological change from the late eighteenth century onwards was a result of demand-driven product innovation which, in turn, encouraged process inventions. In general, there was rapid diffusion of new technology throughout Europe, although the transfer from Britain was seldom systematic. The diffusion process was facilitated by a variety of mechanisms: state-sponsored visits (funded, for example, by the Prussian and Swedish authorities); the recruitment of British industrialists and support for new enterprises (such as William Cockerill's ironworks at Seraing); the migratory culture of both entrepreneurs and artisans; and industrial espionage.[29] Europe, despite extensive state boundaries, was already highly integrated and

the mobility of entrepreneurs, craftsmen, ideas, and inventions should not be underestimated.

However, the successful application of new technology was often dependent on supply side factors, including the relative cost and availability of capital and labor, as well as environmental conditions. Whereas the high cost of steam engines in Germany even in the 1840s (whether imported from Britain or supplied by domestic manufacturers) delayed the widespread adoption of the new technology, the continued viability of handloom production in the French cotton industry at the end of the nineteenth century (particularly in the Rhone and Loire regions) was a result of the continued availability of low cost labor. Moreover, the significance of technological innovation for economic development should not be exaggerated: once the productivity gains of the modern sectors in the British economy (1780–1860) were subtracted from national productivity growth, the contribution of "other sectors" was negligible; in more backward European countries, such as tsarist Russia, the continued predominance of traditional methods of production in many areas of the economy further reduced the overall impact of technological change.[30]

The contribution of entrepreneurs to European development was also affected by supply side factors. The fact that France failed to maintain the high growth rates of the early nineteenth century has been attributed to the predominance of family concerns, excessive individualism, and the importance of the social role of the industrialist. By contrast, Germany's lead in developing the newer industries of the late nineteenth century (chemicals and electricity) was due, in part, to the adoption of effective sales and publicity techniques; a willingness to adapt administrative structures to meet new demands; an increasing emphasis on technical training; and an acceptance of the need for corporate cooperation, drawing heavily on state bureaucratic traditions, in order to minimize individual risk taking. In reality, the role of the entrepreneur was often circumscribed by a wide range of social and cultural factors which affected individual decision making. Confessional affiliation was an important factor in constructing business networks (as was the case with members of the Unitarian congregation in Liverpool and the Calvinist entrepreneurs of Alsace, where strict endogamy helped to strengthen social and work ties). The social security provided by the state to the Old Believers (*raskolniki*) in Russia enabled members of the dissident religious group to play an important entrepreneurial role, while ideological tolerance in eighteenth-century Cadiz helped to foster commercial activity by providing a mechanism for assimilating foreign merchants.[31] Property rights, together with the legal framework affecting joint stock company formation, also varied considerably. Whereas the retention of official controls prevented a series of incorporations in Sweden in the 1850s, legislative provisions in both Belgium and Britain were considerably more liberal. To this extent, the entrepreneurial function itself was influenced by non-economic variables, including cultural factors, institutional structures, and ideological constraints.

Finally, despite the absence of any simplistic correlation between increased investment in educational systems and the growth of national economies, part of the efficiency increase visible in a number of European economies between 1870 and 1914 (including Britain, France, and Germany) was almost certainly due to improvements in the quality of human capital. By the end of the eighteenth century there was a thriving book market in France and Sweden had attained a high literacy rate of 80 percent. Prussia was one of the first states to develop an extensive program of public education and by the end of the nineteenth century a number of European countries had achieved high primary school attendance rates. In Italy, by contrast, only 36 percent of all children between 5 and 14 years actually attended any school by 1900. There was a tendency towards institutional convergence in terms of secondary education, but the level of provision varied considerably, particularly if Germany is compared with Britain. Although the net contribution of increased educational investment was limited, both in the case of Prussia and the Netherlands, even the development of the cooperative movement in Denmark was dependent on increased literacy, and the closing of the traditional gender gap had a wider significance for changes in female labor force participation that were

already visible before 1914. On balance, poor countries (such as Norway and Sweden) with good schooling provision were better placed to exploit open market opportunities than some of the Southern European states, including Spain, where there was a persistent lack of concern for educational issues. However, defensive demarcations between different interest groups often delayed the reform of technical education: as a result, it seldom had a direct causal effect on industrial development.[32]

Conclusion

According to the traditional view, the "industrial revolution" witnessed the implementation of new technical knowledge and profound changes in the organization of production, in marketing, in the commercial infrastructure, and in the organization of the firm. Traditional forms of economic activity governed by hierarchically defined institutional arrangements and customary practices were replaced by economic transactions which reflected the operation of impersonal, competitive markets. Even in the case of Britain, as the "first industrial nation," such a view can no longer be sustained. Despite the significance of the changes associated with nineteenth-century industrialization, the transformation of Europe's economy was a long-run process. Well before the onset of industrialization the expansion of proto-industrial production in many areas of Europe had fostered important changes in the regional division of labor and a greater diversification in urban function, while larger units of centralized production (*Manufakturen*) had been established in various German states and other European countries. Economic development was inherently uneven throughout the nineteenth century: regional differences were aggravated by increased specialization, while traditional forms of production were retained well beyond this period, not only in "relatively backward" economies of Eastern Europe, but even in Britain. There is also evidence of convergence. British dominance in key sectors of production was gradually threatened by the industrialization of continental Europe, although German industrial productivity still lagged behind British levels even after 1900. All the

Scandinavian countries benefited from catch-up, in part as a result of export specialization, while Central Europe took relative advantage of its growth potential after 1870. By contrast, the relative gap between the more advanced economies and Southern Europe (including the Iberian peninsula and the Balkans) widened. Portugal, for example, was less developed by 1870 than previously thought and the initial degree of backwardness was too great to be overcome by the start of the twentieth century.[33]

Because of the historiographical focus on the British "industrial revolution," it is understandable that the analysis of European development has been based primarily on the European nation-state. However, given the initial and increasing divergence between different regions within individual states, national models must be viewed with increasing skepticism. In reality, there was no common model for European industrialization, just as there was no single factor behind economic success, although high agricultural productivity and increased urbanization were often important. Some of the major variables, such as population growth and concomitant trends in relative prices, operated across Europe in general, while factor mobility (both of capital and labor) was greater than previously assumed. There was no single path to modern economic growth and existing explanatory models – whether based on Britain's classical "industrial revolution" or Gerschenkron's paradigm of "relative backwardness" – are seldom convincing. If demand factors were important in stimulating development, the response at a national, regional, and local level varied considerably. Indeed, supply side factors, including the quality of entrepreneurship and human capital in general, may well have played a critical role. But these factors, in turn, were influenced by the political and social culture of nineteenth-century Europe, which ultimately had a perceptible impact on the process of economic change.

NOTES

1   Pollard (1981: vi).
2   Maddison (1995); Christensen et al. (1995); Buyst, Smits, Zanden and Luiten (1995); Koergård (1990: 283); Schulze (2000: 313); Zanden (1999); Griffiths and Meere (1983: 564); Good and Tongshu (1999: 106); Berg (1993).
3   Crafts (1995b); Jones (1988).
4   Hudson (1992); Sullivan (1989); O'Brien, Griffiths, and Hunt (1991); Mokyr (1993); Szostack (1989).
5   Hoppit (1990); Randall (1992); Beckett and Turner (1990); Hudson (1989).
6   Wrigley (1994); Slack (1990).
7   Wrigley (1988: ch. 3); Crafts (1995a); Harley (1993).
8   Pollard (1981: 106–10); Huberman (1996); Rose (1988).
9   Rostow (1960, 1963).
10 Gerschenkron (1966, 1968). For a reassessment of the applicability of Gerschenkron's general model, see Sylla and Toniolo (1991), Good and Tongshu (1999: 110), and Lains (2002).
11 Ziegler (1997); Cameron (1967: 129–50: "Belgium").
12 Cassis (1997: 158).
13 Cohen (1977); Collins (1998); Wixforth and Ziegler (1994); Pohle (1995); Tilly (1986).
14 Miller (1991); Senghaas (1985: 41).
15 Brewer (1994: 60); Harling (1996); Harris (1997).
16 Ribalta (1997); Brose (1993: 9); Özmurur and Pamuk (2002: 296).
17 Sutherland (2002: 2); Lee (2001); Riall (1993: 56); Aceña (1987); Molinas and Escosura (1989: 393).
18 Henriksen (1993); Baker (1996); O'Rourke and Williamson (1995).
19 De Vries (1993: 103); see also Crossick and Jaumain (1999: 1–45).
20 Lindert and Williamson (1983); Magnusson (2000: 140); Baten (2000/1); Hoffman et al. (2002: 348).
21 See chapter 5, "Demography, Urbanization, and Migration."
22 O'Brien (1996); Simpson (1995: 33).
23 Lawton and Lee (1989: 8); Pollard (1981: 101).
24 For a discussion of urbanization, see chapter 5.
25 O'Brien (1983); Fremdling and Knieps (1993).
26 Molinas and Escosura (1989: 395).
27 Fremdling (1991a); Pierenkemper and Tilly (2004: 54–5).

28 Molinas and Escosura (1989: 394); Krause and Puffert (2000).
29 Bruland (1991).
30 Temin (1997); Baker (1978); Wood and French (1989).
31 Fernández Pérez (2000); Lane (1987: 61); Hau (2000: 304–6).
32 Jarrick (1999); Lundgreen (1988/9); Clemens, Groote, and Albers (1996); Fox and Guagnini (1993: 5).
33 De Brabander (1981); Fremdling (1991b: 39); Lains (2002: 42).

GUIDE TO FURTHER READING

For an understanding of European industrialization in the nineteenth century, Sidney Pollard's *Peaceful Conquest* is still indispensable. Sylla and Toniolo's *Patterns of European Industrialization: The Nineteenth Century* provides a useful reassessment of Alexander Gerschenkron's concept of "relative backwardness" as a means of explaining the development process of different European states, while the collection of essays in Aldcroft and Ville's *European Economy 1750–1914* offers some helpful contributions on specific themes, including enterprise and management, transport and communications, and technical change. The nature of industrial development in many, but not all, European countries has been analyzed in detail in a manner that is accessible to English-language readers and some of the contributions are particularly helpful, such as Zamagni's *Economic History of Italy 1860–1990* and the succinct analysis of Germany by Pierenkemper and Tilly, *The German Economy During the Nineteenth Century*. However, it is always instructive to view the experience of Europe in the nineteenth century within a broader international framework, where the volume by Eric Jones, *Growth: Recurring Economic Change in World History*, is still well worth reading.

CHAPTER FIVE

Demography, Urbanization, and Migration

ROBERT LEE

Introduction

This chapter will analyze the process of European population growth within the framework of dominant explanatory models, in particular the theories of the demographic transition and the epidemiological transition. It will explore the extent to which the pattern and timing of national population growth in Europe followed different trajectories and examine the complex relationship between demographic change and economic development. The chapter will focus on a number of central themes: the determinants of fertility and mortality change; the impact of urbanization and migration on the demography of nineteenth-century Europe; and the extent to which population growth affected the nature of contemporary economic development.

The relative magnitude of population growth in Europe from the mid eighteenth century onwards is impressive: total population (including Russia) rose from approximately 144 million in 1750 to 274 million in 1850 and 423 million by 1900. This represented an annual growth rate for the two subperiods of 0.90 and 1.08 percent, respectively: by comparison, the posited average rise over each two-century period between 1000 and 1650 had been slightly over 20 percent. Furthermore, Europe's share of world population also increased from 19.2 percent in 1750 to 24.9 percent by 1900, despite high rates of emigra-

tion, particularly in the second half of the nineteenth century. At the same time, estimates of sectoral output and GDP per capita provide evidence of significant economic growth in many parts of Europe, even if the concept of an "industrial revolution" can no longer be sustained. What then was the connection, if any, between these two phenomena? What was the relationship between economic growth, involving extensive industrialization and increased urbanization, and corresponding population movements? Was there a causal link? Did the "industrial revolution" create its own labor force, or did population pressure, as an exogenous variable, stimulate modern economic development?

Demographic Transition Theory

For many years, the theory of the demographic transition, as developed by Thompsom (1929), Landry (1934), and Notestein (1945), provided a convincing framework for interpreting population change both in nineteenth-century Europe and elsewhere.[1] In essence, the theory postulated the existence of a three-stage model of population development which had a general applicability in the modern period. In the pre-transition period, European society was confronted with high mortality and high fertility rates, but this was followed by a period of

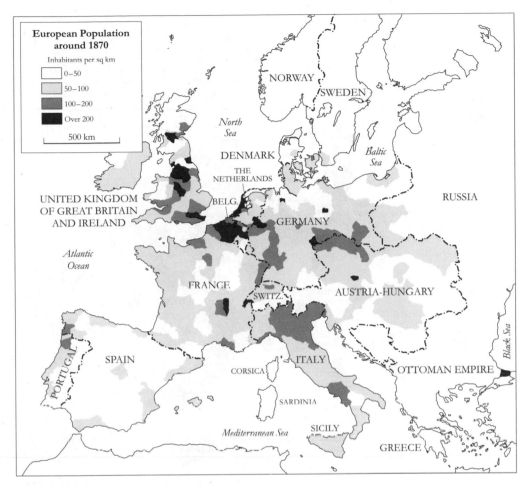

Map 4 European population around 1870

destabilization characterized by falling mortality levels, increased rates of population growth, and ultimately by declining fertility. The final, post-transition phase was dominated by low rates of mortality and fertility. The initial fall in mortality was seen as a prerequisite for the onset of the demographic transition: it was a result of "modernization," improved living standards, and a reduction in epidemic disease, primarily as a result of better hygiene, vaccination, improved diagnosis, and a more effective treatment of disease, as well as a reduced frequency of famines and deaths from violence. It was more difficult to account for the subse-

quent fall in fertility because it was less responsive to modernization, but a variety of explanations was put forward, including an increased use of contraception, rising individual aspirations, a greater emphasis on the health, education, and material welfare of individual children, and a negative response to a reduction in their relative utility.

Unfortunately, recent research has shown that only in a few European countries did the pattern of population growth reflect the assumptions of the demographic transition theory. Sweden was a classic case, with an initial fall in mortality followed by a wide plateau of

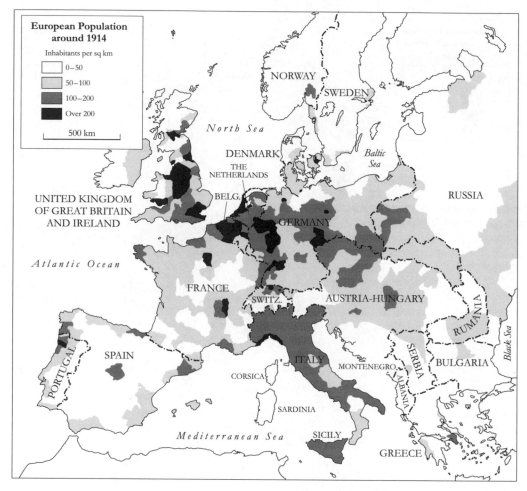

Map 5   European population around 1914

increased population growth as a result of a delayed fertility response which only became evident from the 1860s onwards. By contrast, France was characterized by a very early decline in fertility from the late eighteenth century onwards and a low rate of natural increase during the transition period: because fertility and mortality declined almost simultaneously, population growth tended towards equilibrium except for the period between 1815 and 1845.[2] Within Europe as a whole, three distinct demographic transition models can now be detected (a Northern Scandinavian, a Western, and a Southern variant), while the experience of individual states was very diverse. Whereas there was a significant level of pre-transition population growth in Russia, as a result of high fertility rates, mortality in Spain only began to fall at a comparatively late date; and Ireland was at the opposite end of the spectrum to France with a U-shaped profile. In general, proponents of the demographic transition model ignored the existence of substantial variations in pre-modern marital fertility and assumed incorrectly that a fall in mortality invariably preceded a decline in fertility. Moreover, as evidence from a series of local studies confirms, the decline in mortality was not necessarily a result of socioeconomic modernization. In Norway, for example, very high rates of population growth were registered in the late eighteenth and early nineteenth centuries, reaching an annual peak of 14.7 percent during the 1820s, despite the fact that the country remained to a large degree relatively underdeveloped. To this extent, demographic transition theory is merely "a description of a vague set of empirical correlations": it lacks a robust theoretical framework and fails to reflect the demographic experience of many European countries.[3]

The Determinants of Fertility Change

In line with demographic transition theory, the traditional view of marital fertility was that it remained remarkably uniform throughout the period from the sixteenth to the nineteenth century: there was little variation over time between different European countries; "natural" fertility was generally predominant; and there was no evidence of any significant recourse to family limitation until the 1880s and 1890s. Such an approach has been undermined by the work of the Cambridge Group, which provided a major reformulation of the original Malthusian model. This posited that the rate of growth of the labor force and of the population as a whole was a function of the real wage: if the supply of labor was perfectly elastic at a certain real wage corresponding to subsistence requirements, then the population would grow at whatever rate would keep the wage at this given level, with changes in fertility acting as the intervening variable. The original study by Wrigley and Schofield utilizing back projection emphasized the central role of marriage and nuptiality in determining the population development of England and Wales between 1680 and 1820 and the most recent analysis based on a family reconstitution of 26 parishes largely confirms their earlier findings. Age at marriage fell substantially and in a consistent manner from the 1720s onwards and by the

early nineteenth century, when nuptiality reached a peak, women were marrying on average 2.5 years earlier than their grandmothers. Although marital fertility rose steadily during this period, it was a relatively slow, long-term trend which resulted from a significant fall in the incidence of stillbirths and neonatal deaths (both of which reflected the nutritional status of the mother), and a rise in fertility rates above age 35.[4] The coincidence in the late eighteenth century between increased nuptiality and falling real wages was explained by the lagged generational response to changing employment conditions. By contrast, any improvement in overall mortality remained limited.

These views have not gone unchallenged. Concern has focused primarily on the reliability of a national aggregate approach and the unrepresentative nature of the parish sample, which excludes every major city and fails to reflect the overall population density of England and Wales. The "national" distribution of occupations is derived from a questionable source (namely from parish Poor Law overseers) and the classification scheme ignores the complexity of the domestic economy. The study suffers from a selection bias and migration censoring. It is also clear that the timing and propensity to marry was influenced significantly by local sex ratios, as well as by changes in employment opportunities, while the precise mechanisms affecting marriage propensity remain unclear, particularly in the context of substantial rural out-migration.[5]

Moreover, it is unlikely that increased fertility played such a critical role in determining population growth in other European countries. Although an increase in both legitimate and illegitimate fertility has been attributed to a rise in employment opportunities (for both men and women) in cottage industries and the service sector, a positive relationship between the growth in capitalist production (whether in agriculture or industry), marriage frequency, and age at marriage can only be established in a few regions of Central Europe, including Saxony, Thuringia, the East Elbian provinces of Prussia, Bohemia, and Moldavia. In other areas of Europe there was no replication of the pattern evident in England and Wales; the nineteenth century witnessed a reinforcement of traditional marriage patterns; and the reimposition of official marriage restrictions in some south German states, such as Bavaria and Württemberg, from the 1820s onwards may have reduced marriage frequency.[6] In general, nuptiality throughout most of Europe remained relatively stable, despite underlying changes in the structure of production, and the registered trends in the two key components of overall fertility (the proportions ever married and age at first marriage) were seldom significant. In Sweden, despite a rise in total population of 40 percent between 1810 and 1850, the marriage rate fell from 8.5 to 7.2 per 1,000 inhabitants between the 1790s and 1840s: there was a similar downward trend in both Austria and Prussia in the first half of the nineteenth century, although from higher starting points. The proportion of married females in Spain between 16 and 50 years of age only varied slightly between the censuses of 1797 and 1900, while in France the proportion married was almost static over a 200-year period.

The evidence from family reconstitution studies seldom points to a significant reduction in average age at first marriage. In a sample of German villages, there were only moderate changes in the age at marriage for women and the impact on fertility was accordingly "modest." Although the development of both proto-industrial and factory-based production sometimes provided an opportunity for earlier marriage, this was not invariably the case and in predominantly agricultural regions, such as Bavaria and the Black Forest in Germany, the average age of brides tended to increase during the first half of the century.[7] Moreover, marital fertility in Europe as a whole tended to remain relatively stable. There was a slight increase in rural eastern Flanders towards the end of the eighteenth century which was not maintained; a rise of approximately 15 percent in the index of underlying fertility (M) in three parishes in southeast Kent (1800/34–1865/80); and a gradual reduction in birth intervals in Törbel (Switzerland). But marital fertility in France was already in decline by the 1820s and the age-standardized index of marital fertility (Ig) for a number of German villages fails to reveal any clear trend, despite substantial variation.[8]

Only in the case of illegitimate fertility is there any evidence of a significant increase. In most pre-industrial societies bastards constituted only a very small proportion of total births, despite the operation of rigid settlement laws. By 1845–50 illegitimacy rates (per 100 live births) had risen in many parts of Europe to unprecedented levels, ranging from 4.8 in the Netherlands to 20.5 in Bavaria. In Sweden the proportion of children born out of wedlock rose from 2.4 to 6.0 percent between 1751–60 and 1851–60, while a moderate increase in illegitimacy in rural France was accompanied by high urban rates: between 1820 and 1829 Lyon had an illegitimacy rate of 14.3 and Rouen 24.1.[9] Various hypotheses have been put forward to explain this phenomenon: it was a result of a "sexual revolution" as the gradual permeation of market values encouraged illicit sexual encounters, or the disruptive effect of economic change on marriage expectations at a time when pre-nuptial pregnancy was still relatively common. Alternatively, the rise in illegitimacy may have been caused by changing courtship and marriage patterns or by a lifting of formal sanctions and social checks. It is important to note, however, that the highest illegitimacy rates were often found in marginal or relatively underdeveloped rural areas and the persistence of pronounced local and regional variations, whether in Germany or Sweden, highlights the importance of economic and cultural factors in determining the social significance of marriage.[10] The overall significance of rising illegitimacy rates for population growth, however, was limited: most births continued to take place within marriage (particularly in Italy, the Netherlands, and Spain) and high levels of infant mortality reduced the demographic impact of illegitimate births.

However, research on fertility in the pre-transition period has been of fundamental importance in providing a more effective context for understanding the later secular decline in marital fertility. Unlike many areas of Asia, where most women married at a comparatively early age, pre-industrial Europe had a unique marriage pattern with two distinctive characteristics: a high age at marriage and a significant proportion of people who never married at all. In fact, the original distinction made by Hajnal between a northwest and southeast marriage pattern is itself a simplification of what was in essence a highly adaptable system. At the beginning of the nineteenth century the proportion of women never marrying in rural communities varied considerably from 8 percent (Belgium) to 23 percent (Iceland); the mean age of women at first marriage often reflected a consistent class pattern; and marriage propensity at a regional level continued to be influenced by local inheritance practices and economic opportunities.[11] Moreover, fertility control within marriage was practiced not only by privileged groups, including ruling families, the nobility, and the bourgeoisie, but also by ethnic minorities (such as the German-speaking Jewish community in Prague and Calvinist families in the Ormansag region of Hungary), as well as by specific subgroups within rural society. There was considerable variation in the index of marital fertility in German village populations and clear regional differences in nuptiality in England and Wales, which reflected the dominance of specific industries and a relative imbalance of gender-specific employment opportunities.[12] To this extent, Europe was not characterized by "natural fertility": there were large differences in fertility and its various components well before the onset of industrialization; and individual communities were able to regulate nuptiality in response to economic conditions.[13]

The Secular Decline in Fertility

Controversy still surrounds any attempt to explain the fertility decline which affected most areas of Europe from the 1870s and 1880s onwards. With the exception of France, where the total fertility rate fell by 20 percent between 1800 and 1870, it was only in the late nineteenth century that Europe as a whole witnessed the onset of a gradual, but irreversible, decline in fertility.[14] Modernization was initially seen as an "absolute prerequisite" for determining the onset of this trend, in the mistaken belief that there were no earlier attempts to limit births within marriage because the concept of family limitation was "alien to the mentalities of the population in the pre-

transition age."[15] But other attempts to isolate specific causal factors, whether improved literacy (and higher educational attainment levels), secularization, a fall in infant mortality, or urbanization, have only limited explanatory value: there is no consistent relationship between education and fertility and marital fertility declined under a wide variety of infant mortality conditions.[16]

Most traditional explanations have stressed the existence of class-specific attitudes to family limitation and the general diffusion within the population of middle-class values. The fertility decline in Britain, for example, was a result of the "conscripted socialization" of the nonplanning elements of the population into a distinct bourgeois "future-time perspective," and a social diffusion process reinforced by relative income compression.[17] The changing economic utility of children, influenced by the introduction of compulsory primary education, reduced employment opportunities (at least in formal markets), and their more limited insurance function (given improvements in adult life expectancy), reinforced the contemporary emphasis on quality rather than quantity and the underlying rationale for family limitation. But the European fertility transition was a highly differentiated process, even if the extreme examples of an early onset (France) and a late decline (Albania and Ireland) are excluded. The fact that the fertility decline occurred virtually simultaneously in Britain and Hungary, despite marked differences in key social, economic, and cultural variables (including secondary sector development, living standards, urbanization, and the role of children), makes it difficult to establish a clear correlation between these phenomena, while recent work on late Victorian Britain has undermined the applicability of a class-specific trickle-down effect or the operation of a filtering down process within the social hierarchy.[18]

In general, it is assumed that fertility control was achieved primarily through stopping, reflecting increased confidence in the use of different birth control methods, including *coitus interruptus*, abstinence and available contraceptive devices. Information was probably disseminated by word of mouth, at least within the working class and, as married couples seldom had symmetrical interests, women were often the driving force in adopting family limitation, although the increasing willingness of men to exercise some self-restraint suggests a convergence of attitudes in relation to the perceived value of children.[19] More recently, however, evidence has been forthcoming of child spacing within the working class, particularly in late nineteenth-century British textile centers. If it is accepted that working-class couples were just as capable as their middle-class counterparts of maintaining supportive and mature relationships, then child spacing may well have represented a more sensible strategy of fertility control.[20]

The Determinants of Mortality Change

There can be little doubt that a decline in mortality during the nineteenth century was a significant factor in the rise in Europe's population. In the Netherlands the crude death rate (per 1,000) fell from 26.6 (1840–9) to 15.7 (1900–9); there was a marked degree of regional conformity in the downward trend of almost all mortality indicators in Sweden; while the fall in mortality "propelled Norway's population into one of the fastest growth rates in Europe." Even in the case of England and Wales, there is evidence to suggest that mortality, in particular infant mortality, was declining in the second half of the eighteenth century and changes in death rates between 1800 and 1829 were more significant for accelerated population growth than changes in birth rates. Death rates began to stabilize as mortality crises (whether induced by famine or pestilence) became less frequent, and the age of receding pandemics (as outlined in Omran's concept of the epidemiological transition) was followed by a decline in the incidence of infectious diseases, gradual (but perceptible) gains in life expectancy, and the eventual dominance after 1900 of degenerative or man-made diseases.[21]

The earlier work of Mckeown and others, drawing on evidence from England and Wales, as well as other European countries (including France, Hungary, and Sweden), appeared to offer a robust framework for understanding long-run mortality change: it analyzed the available cause of death data in order to infer the most likely causes behind a reduction in mortality, whether economic, environmental, or epidemiological. It certainly demolished the traditional view that improved medical practice and institutional provision played a critical role in achieving higher survival rates: any significant breakthrough in medical or scientific knowledge, with the exception of smallpox inoculation and vaccination, post-dated the long-term decline in infectious diseases; typhus disappeared from the British Isles many years before the identification of the body louse as a critical vector; and hospitals before the development of bacteriology were frequently gateways of death. In the case of England and Wales, sanitary reform was responsible for roughly 25 percent of the registered decline in mortality, whereas a rise in living standards, as reflected in the declining incidence of tuberculosis, accounted for approximately half the total reduction in mortality. The fall in tuberculosis mortality was already evident before 1851, but its downward trajectory was not the result of changing exposure levels, housing improvements, or sanitary reform, but was attributable to increased per capita food supply which became the key variable for explaining the registered fall in death rates. By implication, a similar mechanism operated in continental Europe: the decline in tuberculosis mortality in Sweden, as well as the reduced importance of infectious diseases in France, was also a result of increased agricultural output, while the late adoption of sanitary reform (such as the Hungarian Public Health Act of 1876) only had a limited impact on contemporary mortality trends.[22]

More recent research, however, has placed many of these findings in doubt. First, criticism has been directed at the use of a reductionist methodology and a simplistic reliance on contemporary cause of death data. Even though exposure to respiratory tuberculosis in childhood (from 0 to 9 years) is invariably sensitive to welfare differences, its aetiology is highly complex and other risk factors (largely ignored by Mckeown) have to be taken into consideration, including the incidence of other infectious diseases, overcrowding, poor housing conditions, and general psychological stress. Many diseases also have a depletion effect, increasing individual susceptibility to other infections.[23] Secondly, the interpretation is based solely on the use of aggregate statistics and ignores important compositional effects, specifically in relation to the changing extent of urbanization in individual European countries and the significance of the "urban penalty" as expressed in the mortality gradient between rural and urban communities. There were also diverse urban demographic regimes in nineteenth-century Europe with distinct mortality profiles: for example, port cities such as Bremen, Liverpool, and Malmö were prone to an increased risk of exposure to infectious diseases because of their extended transport links, while cholera was often spread along established shipping routes resulting in a disproportionate impact on ports and adjacent coastal areas.[24] In addition, increased urbanization, together with improved communications and higher rates of migration, may have affected the balance between the virulence of infectious diseases and the relative immunity of the human host, while the fall in scarlet fever mortality during the second half of the nineteenth century represented a spontaneous decline due to a variation in the virulence of the heomolytic streptococcus.[25]

It is also premature to reject the role of human agency in securing mortality improvements. Quarantine measures had first been introduced in a number of Italian city states (e.g., Florence) in the seventeenth century, followed by a slow diffusion of "best practice" to other parts of Europe: the imposition of *cordons sanitaires* by the Austrian authorities during the eighteenth century limited the spread of bubonic plague to Central Europe, while the emergence of relatively stable governments with a visible interest in population resources was accompanied by a decline in epidemic disease.[26] Although hospital provision remained highly uneven, its impact may not have been quite so negative: some hospitals had low in-patient mortality rates, primarily because of a selective admissions policy, while cross-infection was only a serious problem for patients undergoing surgery between the early nineteenth century and the gradual adoption of Lister's antiseptic principles in the 1870s.[27]

Moreover, a decline in the incidence of classic sanitation diseases such as typhoid and cholera, whether in Britain or Germany, played an important role in the overall fall in mortality, and their gradual elimination was due primarily to the implementation of public health measures in the second half of the nineteenth century. In Victorian Britain, for example, the estimated improvement in the urban disamenity index between the 1840s and 1905 was a result of "enormous improvements in sanitation" which reflected, in particular, the expansion of water supply systems in expanding urban areas. French urban mortality was directly affected by the development of water support systems, despite the late creation of *bureaux d'hygiène* in individual cities. To this extent, human agency, whether represented by the drainage of swamps, the removal of burial sites from inner-urban areas, or the implementation of sanitary legislation, may have been a factor in achieving more effective disease control.[28]

A primary reliance on increased food consumption and an improved diet as a means of explaining mortality trends in the nineteenth century is also problematic. In many parts of Europe, including eastern Prussia, the growth in agricultural output was achieved by the incorporation of more marginal land and a reliance on more labor-intensive systems of cultivation, with negative implications in terms of the work load of women, their net nutritional status, and the quality of infant care. In Sweden, increased agricultural output may only have allowed the population to grow without any tangible improvement in nutrition, while it failed to keep pace with increased urbanization in Britain. There was no perceptible increase in food intake in France until the 1830s and 1840s, and recent research has suggested that there must have been widespread malnutrition in many European countries prior to 1850 because of poor food production levels.[29] Moreover, food entitlements varied substantially across Europe, primarily as a function of economic status and social class, while evidence of increased primary sector production cannot be regarded as synonymous with improvements in per capita consumption. Differences in regional diets persisted in many European countries; food adulteration became an increasing problem in urban communities; and industrial development was often associated with an increased female dependency on male earnings, with an adverse impact on the distribution of household resources and women's living standards.[30] Finally, it is important to note that the pre-industrial life expectancy of elite groups within European society, including members of the English aristocracy and Scottish barristers, was no better than that of their less privileged contemporaries. If it is assumed that these social groups already had access to sufficient nutrition, then increased life expectancy during the eighteenth century and beyond is unlikely to have been the result of dietary improvements or higher levels of per capita food consumption.[31]

Evidence on living standards and height is also inconclusive. The longstanding debate between pessimists and optimists in assessing trends in the standard of living during the British "industrial revolution" remains unresolved, but despite a perceptible improvement in real wages, in particular after 1815, the food consumption levels of 1760 were not regained until around 1840. There was no visible increase in French living standards before the 1830s and it was only after the 1860s and 1870s, respectively, that real wages rose in the Netherlands and Germany, well after the registered decline in mortality rates.[32] By contrast, height data have been used to support the view that living standards improved in Britain until the early 1830s, although in other European states (e.g., Austria-Hungary) the late eighteenth century witnessed a decline in age-by-height profiles as a result of population pressure. Despite the claim that there was a positive relationship between height and real wages, there was no strict correlation in the case of the Netherlands during the first half of the nineteenth century. Periods of significant growth (as in the United Kingdom between the 1820s and 1840s) could be accompanied by a marked fall in average height, and height increases among Swedish army recruits from the 1850s onwards were unevenly distributed by district and social class. Evidence derived from data on height and nutrition may not necessarily be an accurate indicator of changing living standards: information on height is often

derived from military conscription records and subject to changes in minimum requirements and recruitment districts; the income elasticity for food diminishes with rising income; and urbanization may have been accompanied by a reduction in per capita food demand, a shift to higher value-added foodstuffs, or an increased reliance on starches. More importantly, the assumed link between height and mortality is dependent on a bivariate model with exaggerated claims in terms of its predictive power. In fact, although malnutrition tends to lower the efficiency of the average immune system, its impact is non-linear: temporary malnutrition, or a moderate reduction in nutritional status, does not cause a proportional loss of immune competence. Not all diseases (including measles and tuberculosis) are nutritionally sensitive and exposure risk is often a critical factor in determining infection. Indeed, even the increasing use of weight data to produce a more robust body mass index is unlikely to provide a completely reliable predictor of mortality risk and morbidity, as final height will inevitably reflect the nutritional costs of surviving a range of infant and childhood diseases (including smallpox) which were not in themselves nutritionally sensitive.[33]

Finally, any analysis of long-run mortality trends must take into consideration differential changes in age-specific mortality rates. Infant deaths, in particular, were a key determinant of overall mortality with important indirect effects on fertility. The initial fall in mortality, at least in England and Wales, France and Sweden, was most apparent among infants and children, whereas adult mortality only tended to decline from the mid-nineteenth century onwards. In England and Wales there was a significant fall in infant mortality during the eighteenth century, with London's Quaker community also registering a downward trend, although much of the decline occurred after 1800. At the national level, however, there was little evidence of any further improvement between 1840 and 1900: in the late nineteenth century infant deaths accounted for almost 20 percent of total mortality and mortality rates remained persistently high despite a deceleration in the pace of urbanization. In Sweden, the decline in infant mortality was a continuous process, with a 50 percent reduction in death rates during the nineteenth century, while an early fall in France between 1795 and 1825 was followed by a plateau and a persistent downward slope after 1880. By contrast, infant mortality rates remained relatively high in other parts of Europe (e.g., Austria, Germany, and Russia), even at the end of the nineteenth century, prompting speculation on the existence of a number of distinct regional models of infant mortality decline. Moreover, infant mortality in most European countries was characterized by significant regional variations. The highest infant mortality rates in Germany were recorded in the southern states of Bavaria and Württemberg, as well as in the eastern provinces of Prussia, whereas comparatively lower rates were registered in the northern and western regions; the Alpine districts of Austria had consistently lower mortality than the surrounding plains; and regional variations in infant mortality in England and Wales remained persistent throughout the late nineteenth and early twentieth centuries.[34]

A key determinant of infant mortality for most of the nineteenth century was the method of infant feeding. In general, there was an inverse correlation between breast feeding and infant mortality, particularly in the case of illegitimate children. Where breast feeding was not practiced or only adopted for a short period, infants were twice as likely to die prematurely, primarily because of the inappropriateness or poor quality of substitute foodstuffs in a context where the impact of dietary deficiencies was frequently aggravated by inadequate domestic hygiene. As a result, digestive diseases remained a major cause of infant death. However, it is difficult to explain local or national variations in infant feeding practices and the extent to which the failure to breast feed was a result of cultural or economic factors. On the one hand, it is generally assumed that breast feeding was the norm in England and Wales during the early nineteenth century, while an extensive reliance on substitute foodstuffs in Bavaria reflected customary practice reinforced by an implicit acceptance of postnatal family limitation (*himmeln lassen*, which reflected a belief that any infants who died shortly after birth would immediately

ascend to heaven). On the other hand, increased urbanization was accompanied by a significant decline in breast feeding: the growth of employment opportunities for married women may have enabled them to purchase extra nourishment for the family, but it also meant that they were increasingly unable to breast feed their children. At the same time, the adoption of labor-intensive production methods in the primary sector (as was the case in the eastern provinces of Prussia) affected both the extent and pattern of female work in a manner which restricted their ability to breast feed, while the persistence of gender-specific health conditions in many nineteenth-century households meant that women's poor nutritional status led to low birth weights and a reduced supply of breast milk.[35]

In general, income and social class were important factors in determining infant mortality levels, but not necessarily the timing or rate of the mortality decline.[36] More significantly, there was a direct correlation between infant mortality and urbanization. In general, towns and cities were associated with increased mortality risks for infants, whether in Britain or Germany. Increased population density in English industrial parishes in the early decades of the nineteenth century was accompanied by higher infant mortality rates, primarily because of a greater risk of exposure to disease pathogens and problems of waste disposal, while even in the late 1870s Berlin had an infant death rate of 400 per 1,000 live births. Moreover, the environmental risks of urban residence were not evenly spread across the infant population at risk: although the summer months increasingly posed the greatest threat for all infants (given the gradual decline in breast feeding in many European towns), socioeconomic status and residential location were often critical factors in determining their overall survival chances. Although the increasing availability of pathogen-free milk in urban areas from the 1890s onwards may have reinforced the downward trend in infant mortality, the strategies adopted by some local authorities to improve infant survival rates, including the provision of better quality milk and attempts to encourage a greater reliance on breast feeding, had little tangible effect. The poorer elements of urban society failed to benefit from milk supply programs, while courses on infant care seldom attracted the target groups whose infants were particularly at risk in the urban environment.[37]

However, the decline in infant and child mortality may well have affected survival chances later in life, given evidence which suggests that disease exposure during childhood (particularly in the first year of life) influences both physical development and later life mortality. Swedish age-specific mortality data suggest that a reduced disease load during infancy and childhood had a positive impact on adult cohort survival, while the provision of improved water-supply and sewerage systems in French towns such as Lyon had a positive cohort effect by reducing the exposure of children to water-borne diseases.[38] To this extent, the decline of infant and child mortality, whether as a result of urban sanitary reform, a reduced incidence of infectious diseases, or a change in disease virulence, may explain part of the long-run fall in European mortality and improvements in adult life expectancy in the second half of the nineteenth century.

Urbanization, Migration, and Demographic Change

For modern Europe as a whole, urbanization "lies at the very heart of demographic change."[39] Although there was a substantial urban network in Europe by the end of the eighteenth century, the rate of urban growth during the nineteenth century was unprecedented, with the emergence of new industrial towns, a rapid expansion in the population of major ports as a function of the growth in international trade, and the increasing predominance of large cities, including metropolitan centers. However, the timing, pace, and level of urbanization varied considerably. By 1851, 37.6 percent of England's population lived in towns of over 20,000 inhabitants: the comparative figure for Germany (1871) and Sweden (1891–1900) was 7.7 percent and 12.0 percent, respectively. There was an acceleration in large city growth in the early nineteenth century in both Britain and Belgium, primarily as a result of industrial development, but this

phenomenon was only visible in most other areas of Europe towards the end of the period.[40] Urban growth was largely (although not entirely) a result of extensive in-migration, and the persistence of substantial urban–rural differences in both fertility and mortality rates reinforced the significance of the urbanization process for the overall pattern of demographic change in Europe.

Although it is difficult to calculate the exact scale of urban migration, particularly before 1850, the labor force requirements of pre-industrial cities were met by extensive, age-specific in-migration. Many urban centers, including capital cities (Paris and London) and larger regional centers (Bordeaux and Marseille), had clearly defined migration hinterlands and individual towns had an attractive power for migrants beyond that created by population size alone. However, for a significant number of in-migrants, urban residence was by definition temporary. Guild controls and restrictions on the acquisition of citizenship, as well as Poor Law regulations, contributed to a high turnover of journeymen and servants, and urban communities were generally characterized by high mobility. It is estimated that there was a fourfold rise in the scale of urban in-migration from rural areas in the first half of the nineteenth century, followed by a further threefold increase between 1850 and 1890, as industrialization reinforced the role of migration in urban growth. The growth of Genoa and Glasgow was primarily a result of large-scale in-migration, while net in-migration accounted for 54 percent of the increase in Prussia's urban population between 1875 and 1905. The precise configuration of migration flows was often dependent on city type, but the rise in mass emigration after 1850 reflected the increasing attraction of overseas destinations, while population mobility within late-nineteenth century Europe was characterized by the growing importance of long-distance and inter-urban migration.[41]

Extensive rural–urban migration, if followed by eventual marriage and settlement, may have had a positive impact on overall fertility levels. In reality, this was seldom, if ever, the case. In Prussia, both marital fertility and the proportion married varied according to the socioeconomic structure and prevailing function of individual cities, but urban fertility prior to its secular decline was invariably lower than in rural areas: in other German states, such as Bavaria, there was a 26 percent difference. A similar pattern was evident in France, Holland, and Spain. Despite a favorable age structure, itself a result of age-specific in-migration, most European towns had lower fertility than the surrounding rural areas: in Dublin there was a shift to lower fertility from 1811 onwards and, in general, the onset of the fertility decline took place at an earlier date in urban communities. Urban expansion in the course of the nineteenth century was not accompanied by any noticeable increase in marriage or birth rates (except in rapidly expanding industrial towns), reproductive behavior reflected the early adoption of family limitation, and in-migrants were often at the forefront of fertility control. The available evidence confirms that they tended to marry at a later age than the indigenous population and completed family size was noticeably smaller.[42]

Most early modern towns were unhealthy, with the poor in particular suffering from below average life expectancy, but the urban mortality penalty was reinforced during the early stages of industrialization and was evident even in comparatively small urban communities. Rapid industrial development, whether in Eindhoven or Ghent, was associated with a deterioration in environmental conditions and rising mortality levels as the existing urban infrastructure was unable to respond to new pressures. In Germany there was a gradual increase in urban mortality until the early 1870s, while death rates in capital cities such as Copenhagen, London, and Stockholm were frequently very high. Because of their transport links, port cities suffered from increased exposure risks as shipping routes facilitated the spread of infectious diseases: Liverpool was notoriously unhealthy; the cholera outbreak in Hamburg in 1892 killed almost 10,000 people; and Toulon registered high mortality levels well into the twentieth century. Although cities were particularly hazardous for infants and young children, all age groups suffered from higher death rates across a wide spectrum of diseases in comparison with the rural population.[43]

It has also been argued that the impact of mortality on cities has been exaggerated: in most cases the permanent residents registered a natural increase, while any excess mortality was mainly the result of deaths among temporary migrants, many of whom were single. Although it is difficult to reconstruct the differential mortality of in-migrants and the native born, the available evidence supports such an interpretation, particularly for the early stages of industrial development: the temporary nature of migration, economic marginality, and crowded labor markets which discouraged settlement led to a deterioration in health conditions among in-migrants and higher mortality rates. Only towards the end of the nineteenth century, with a greater prospect of permanent migration to the city, was there any improvement in their life expectancy. But this was also a period when there was an increasing convergence in the mortality profiles of urban communities, whether in Germany or Sweden, perhaps because of a trend towards a more unified urban environment and the cumulative implementation of sanitary reform. In some European countries there is only a weak association between public health reform and urban mortality trends, but the provision of improved water-supply and sewerage systems often contributed to a decline in urban infant mortality (at a time when breast feeding was becoming less common) and the eventual elimination of the urban penalty.[44]

Population Growth and European Economic Development

The relationship between economic growth and demographic change is complex. Whereas rapid population growth within a Malthusian framework might lead to a fall in per capita income and the eventual operation of positive checks, low rates of growth could equally depress aggregate demand and restrict the supply of labor. Population growth is only one of many factors which influence economic development and its net effect is often dependent on the operation of specific demographic variables and the contemporary sociocultural and political context. On balance, the nature of demographic change in nineteenth-century Europe had a positive impact on economic growth. The rise in total population from the mid-eighteenth century onwards placed new demands on the agricultural systems of many states and acted as a stimulus for structural reform in the primary sector. It also contributed to the development of rural industries and the regional division of labor. Moreover, the decline in mortality, in particular in infant and child mortality, served to reduce the dependency ratio and led to an increase in the relative size of the productive age group. There is little evidence of shortages in labor supply during industrialization (except, perhaps, in the case of France) and the growth in the work force was accompanied by quality improvements in human capital as a result of rising literacy rates and better educational opportunities. Population growth can also contribute to increased labor force mobility and both urbanization and industrialization in the nineteenth century was dependent on higher rates of urban in-migration. At the same time, it is salutary to note that European population growth rates were seldom excessive. Indeed, were it not for the rise in overseas emigration (from 2.1 million to 11.2 million between the 1850s and the first decade of the twentieth century) and the general onset of the secular fertility decline from the 1870s onwards, the effect of population growth on individual European states may not have been as positive as it often was.

NOTES

1 Kirk (1996); Van de Kaa (1996: 389–432).
2 Chesnais (1986: 222–4).
3 Alter (1992: 19).
4 Wrigley and Schofield (1981); Wrigley et al. (1997); Wrigley (1998).
5 Levine (1998); Ruggles (1999).
6 Tilly, Scott, and Cohen (1976).
7 Knodel (1988: 124.)
8 Heywood (1995: 187); Reay (1994); Netting (1981); Van de Walle (1979).
9 Lee (1977a: 124); Norman and Rogers (1985: 46).
10 Norman and Rogers (1985: 52); Mantl (1997).
11 Hajnal (1965, 1982).
12 Livi-Bacci (1986); Vasary (1989); Lee (1977b: 45–8).
13 Weir (1984).
14 Coale and Watkins (1986: 29).
15 Simon Kuznets cited in Kirk (1996: 369).
16 Coale and Watkins (1986: 420–50).
17 Banks (1981).
18 Garrett (1990).
19 Seccombe (1992).
20 Seccombe (1990).
21 Lee (1979: 14); Mercer (1985); Omran (1971).
22 Mckeown (1976); Mckeown and Record (1962); Mckeown, Brown, and Record (1972).
23 Johansson (2004: 39–41).
24 Kearns (1988); Woods (2003); Szreter (1988); Lee (1998: 151–5).
25 Kunitz (1983).
26 Kunitz (1986: 280).
27 Brändström and Tedebrand (1988: 343–69); Cherry (1972).
28 Szreter (1994); Guha (1994); Riley (2001).
29 Lee (1990).
30 Horrell and Humphries (1992); Nicholas and Oxley (1993).
31 Hollingsworth (1977); Johansson (1991).
32 Feinstein (1981); Lindert and Williamson (1983).
33 Floud, Wachter, and Gregory (1990); Komlos (1995); Baten (2000/1); Voth and Leunig (1996); Riley (1994).
34 Landers (1987); Corsini and Viazzo (1993).
35 Kintner (1985); Dyhouse (1987).
36 Haines (1995).
37 Huck (1994); Williams (1992); Beaver (1973); Vögele and Woelk (2002).
38 Fridlizius (1989); Bengtsson and Lindström (2000).
39 Lawton and Lee (1989: 1).
40 Kearns, Lee, and Rogers (1989: 9–10).
41 Wrigley (1967); King (1997); Hochstadt (1983); de Vries (1984: table 10.1). The literature on European emigration is extensive. See, for example, Baines (1991); Norman and Runblom (1988); Hoerder and Moch (1996: 21–51).
42 Knodel (1974: 96–8); Pérez Moreda (1987: 22).

43 Kearns (2000).
44 Sharlin (1978); Lee (1999); Brändström and Tedebrand (2000).

GUIDE TO FURTHER READING

There are some excellent studies of the demographic development of individual European countries during the nineteenth century, but not all of them are available in English. For Britain, readers should consult the two books by Robert I. Woods, *The Population of Britain in the Nineteenth Century* and *The Demography of Victorian England and Wales*. The most recent synthesis of research on Germany is provided by Ehmer's *Bevölkerungsgeschichte und Historische Demographie 1800–2000*. Few authors have succeeded in producing a comparative analysis of European population history in the nineteenth century, but Michael Anderson's earlier contribution is still readable: *Population Change in North-Western Europe, 1750–1850*. By contrast, there are a number of useful books on individual themes which include material from a wide range of European states. The volume edited by Coale, Watkins and Cotts on *The Decline of Fertility in Europe* continues to raise a number of important issues, while Riley's *Rising Life Expectancy. A Global History* offers an interesting interpretation of the possible causes of the fall in mortality within a wider geographical framework. Two volumes edited by Richard Lawton and Robert Lee provide an insight into the demographic consequences of European urbanization: *Urban Population Development in Western Europe from the Late Eighteenth to the Early Twentieth Century* and *Population and Society in Western European Port-Cities, c.1650–1939*. Moch's *Moving Europeans: Migration in Western Europe since 1650* offers an excellent insight into the complex migration processes which were evident throughout Europe.

CHAPTER SIX

Lords and Peasants

CARL LEVY

This chapter focuses on the cultural, political, and social relations of the rural elite with the peasantry of Europe. It also looks at how the balance of social forces in the countryside affected European politics at the national level. During the long nineteenth century the freeing of millions of Europeans from the shackles of serfdom and rural servitude, and the decline of the power of their masters, indeed the beginning of the end of a thousand-year-old peasant civilization, is epic. It has spawned a rich interpretive and analytical historiography over the past forty years. Anthony Cardoza's meticulous account of the decline of the landed aristocracy of Piedmont in Italy from unification to the interwar period is enriched by comparisons with Calibrians and Sicilians as well as the Junkers of Prussia.[1] David Cannadine's account of the decline of the British aristocracy is enriched by examination of the English, Scottish, Welsh, and Irish roots of this formidably resilient class, as well as their continental cousins.[2]

After setting this chapter within the key interpretive framework – which has set the research agenda for historians of the lords and peasants of the long European nineteenth century – I proceed to look at three themes. The decline of serfdom and other associated forms of servitude in Europe took nearly one hundred years to be accomplished and followed in train with the mutation and evolution of a variety of forms of free labor and an accompanying variety of systems of land tenure. This is the first theme.

The second theme is the struggle for political hegemony in the countryside. This section will examine the extent to which the lords of Europe retained control of the new forms of mass politics (new secular ideologies and nationalism) that affected all parts of Europe as the century wore on. Forms of religion practiced by lords and peasants had varying effects on this struggle. The role of aristocrats and great landlords as leaders of local and national electoral politics or as patrons of peasant organizations in Western and Eastern Europe will be discussed. So too will the fraught relationship between the modernizing state bureaucracies of Western, Central, and Eastern Europe and the landed elite.

The third theme is the varieties of cultural hegemony manifested in the countryside by examining how nationalism employed rural themes to heighten its appeal. A good deal of historiography has been devoted to the way aristocrats set the tone for fashion, literature, and architecture, even after their economic power was in decline. The stately home/chateau/manor house, the sports of aristocrats, and their family names were talismanic markers for other classes – especially the urban bourgeoisie, the educated middle classes, and the rural notables. But the peasantry, too, had an influence: did the French state make peasants French (as Eugen Weber famously argued),[3] or was the story rather more of a two-way exchange between the French "metropole" and its neighboring "foreign" countryside? To what extent were the Balkans or vast swathes of the heartland of the Russian Empire "peasantized"? How was the "authenticity" of peasant culture used in these contests of competing hegemony?

The Persistence of the *Ancien Régime*?

In his account of the persistence of the premodern order in Europe, Arno Mayer sought to demonstrate that contrary to the assertions of modernization theorists and most Marxist historians, the premodern order held power and set the tone in Europe until 1914. Thus he argued that the peasant economy, the old fashioned small business, the nobility, and the church overshadowed the rising force of industrial capitalism and dominated the mass politics of the age.[4] Superficially, there is a powerful force to Mayer's argument. One need only recall the belligerent royal cousins King George, Kaiser Wilhelm, and Tsar Nicholas. Mayer overplayed his hand, however. He failed to see the major transfer of landed property in Britain (especially in Ireland) or Russia by 1914. And even if the carapace of the bureaucracy in Germany or Britain still seemed to reflect the values of pre or anti-industrial values learnt in public schools or universities, the individuals in the driving seat were far less aristocratic than those in the mid-nineteenth century and achieved their success and fame through merit or mass politics rather than aristocratic lineage.

Mayer's central theme is in fact a global extension of the *Sonderweg* thesis, which argued that the path from Prussia-Germany to Adolf Hitler lay through the manor houses of East Elbian Junkerdom. This neatly introduces the other major text that has shaped the historiography of lord and peasant in the long European nineteenth century. More or less concurrently with Mayer, David Blackbourn and Geoffrey Eley argued that the power of the Junker class in Wilhelmine Germany was greatly exaggerated.[5] Germany experienced a silent bourgeois revolution at the grassroots of civil society: through voluntary societies, a new civil law code, local politics, and industrial power the *ancien régime* was discreetly undermined. Though the thrust of their arguments was different, both Mayer and Blackbourn and Eley were skeptical of developmental models, which foresaw the neat decline of a feudal class and its replacement by a modern bourgeoisie. They forced historians of Britain and France to revisit their own first assumptions about the role of the landed elite in their respective countries. The modernity of industrial Britain or republican France was at best an ideal type. All countries followed their own roads to industrial society.

Thus, even in the first "modern" society, historians have noted the role of the aristocracy in forging capitalism, the parliamentary constitutional state (if not democracy), and the ruling class of the United Kingdom of Great Britain and Ireland. Martin Wiener's intervention (contemporaneous with Mayer and Blackbourn and Eley) argued that British capitalism declined because it was infused with aristocratic values.[6] This led to a twenty-year engagement with Wiener's thesis, which was criticized for its literary evidence and parochial reasoning. Why did the industrial might of Germany grow if Junkers or at least an anti-industrial culture played such a major role in Britain's chief competitor? Others concluded that British industrial capitalism had been pioneered by landed aristocrats between 1780 and 1830. Or, alternatively, that a gentlemanly form of financial and imperial trading capitalism attractive to the aristocracy was always more important than the brass and muck of the Midlands bourgeoisie, as argued by José Harris and Pat Thane.[7] More generally, it was argued that a European plutocracy arose out of the landed and capitalist elite by the late nineteenth century, so the argument about a feudalization of the bourgeoisie became meaningless. And indeed this fusion is foreshadowed by the incorporation of bourgeois merchants into the landed elite of France within a few generations of buying land and titles in the pre-revolutionary regime.

In a similar fashion historians of Napoleonic and post-Napoleonic Europe argue that the break-up of the great estates and church lands was not a straightforward triumph of the moneyed bourgeoisie over the feudal lords. A fused class of rural notables (from the nobility, middle class, and peasantry) dominated the politics of much of nineteenth-century France, Spain, and Italy. Even more radically, historians have come to realize that the notion of a uniform class of European lords or aristocrats is perhaps not so very helpful. There is a vast difference between the service nobility of tsarist Russia, the court nobility of *ancien régime* France, and the landed gentry of Prussia and England. Indeed, there is even a vast difference between the latter two. Whereas in England by the eighteenth century the landed gentry and the peers of the realm became a ruling class whose "clubs" were the House of Commons and the House of Lords, the landed gentry of Prussia (the Junkers) always behaved as a pressure group who used the state to advance their own interests rather than those of Prussia or (later) the German Empire, in much the same fashion as the Hungarian nobility "owned" the Hungarian nation through much of this period.

Thus we must be alert to the nuances and complexities of the historiography of lords and peasants in nineteenth-century Europe. Indeed, one other weakness of Mayer's argument is his figurative and literal rendering of the peasantry as mere cannon fodder – they were much more than that, and the historiography of their political and human agency will be discussed below. The remainder of this chapter will unpack these subtle differences.

Serfdom and Emancipation

The demise of formal serfdom took nearly one hundred years to accomplish, stretching from the initial emancipation decree of the House of Savoy in 1771 to the liberation of the Roma slaves of the Danubian Principalities of Moldavia and Wallachia in 1864. A total of 33 initial decrees of emancipation were issued. But the process only slowly liberated the peasantry of Central and Eastern Europe from the obligations, dues, and humiliations associated with servile status. The redemption payments owed by the Russian serfs and their descendants lasted until 1906 and it has been claimed that payments were collected during the 1920s in

Germany. The liberation from serfdom involved a series of freedoms gained over an extended period of time. True liberation meant personal freedom, equality before the law, personal and occupational mobility, and the abolition of the system of estates. If we take the first three of these as benchmarks, then the process took 21 years in Savoy, 43 years in Prussia, and 73 years in Denmark.[8] By using all four, David Moon extends the process of the ending of serfdom in the Russian Empire from 1762 (when Peter III abolished compulsory noble state service) to 1917 (when the society of orders was destroyed by the Russian Revolution).[9] In any case, the most humiliating aspects of servile status persisted for years after formal emancipation. More than fifty years after emancipation, noble landowners in Denmark still claimed their right to flog peasants, and courts in Russia in 1904 sentenced peasants to whippings, a form of punishment banned for other subjects.[10] The contentious seigniorial rights to hunting, fishing, and the fruits of the forest plagued relations between emancipated peasants and their former masters for the entire period surveyed here.

In the late eighteenth century, with the exception of Britain, the Low Countries, and parts of Scandinavia, farmers did not hold freehold, but servile tenures. This does not tell us that much, since obligations to a lord could amount to certain limited dues in kind or amounts of annual unpaid labor. Generally speaking, as one moved further east, servile status approximated that of outright slavery, although geographical determinism can be overdone. The case of Ottoman Europe is interesting.[11] The enslavement of the Roma was widespread in the Romanian possessions where the Ottomans ruled indirectly, and other peasants were treated almost equally badly there and in Bosnia (another autonomous zone), approximating conditions in the nearby Great Hungarian Plain or Galicia. However, Balkan Christian peasants elsewhere may have been freer than many of their European compatriots. The indigenous landowning aristocracy had been swept away by the Ottoman conquest, and legally nearly all the arable land was owned by the sultan. Ottoman soldiers were awarded estates, but these were not easily passed on to the next generation. Estate holders demanded produce from the peasants, but these peasants were not servile possessions of landlords. Thus we find here "a fundamentally different form of society from that found elsewhere in Europe,"[12] in which lay the roots of the peasant regimes of post-1918 Balkan Europe.

Russian serfdom deserves discussion in itself. It has been central to comparative analyses of forms of slavery elsewhere and that of European servility. Its legacy has haunted the histories of twentieth-century Russia and the Soviet Union. The very course of Russian history to our own times, it may be argued, has been traced by the unique impact it had on the development of Russian society before and after 1917. The relationship between the development of Russian capitalism and a nascent civil society before and after emancipation in 1861 has undergone much analysis. From the classic examples of Lenin and Chayanov to more recent efforts of historians such as Richard Pipes and Orlando Figes, the great debate about Russia's road to modernization has revolved around the role played by the freed peasantry in Russian capitalism before 1917,[13] and relates to the nature of Russian civil society and the absence of a robust middle class before the revolution. Within the Russian Empire, serfdom had always shared room with church, crown (appanage), and state: peasants paid dues to their superiors, but were not legally serfs. Serfdom was most predominant in the Moscovy heartland of the Russian Empire. In the borderlands and certainly in Siberia (Russia's "North America") it was less conspicuous. Also, military communities of free Cossacks were an alternative and a magnet. State and crown peasants, as well as the Cossacks, stoked the ideal of emancipation for the servile peasantry of the Russian heartland.

Was the position of the serfs of the Russian heartland therefore unique in Europe? In a comparative study of various forms of servitude in modern times, one can discern differences and similarities in Russian serfdom to the servitude experienced by the peasants of Eastern and Central Europe.[14] By the early nineteenth century, serfs in the Moscovy heartland of the Russian Empire remained as they had been, a source of rental income for their masters. The

development of commercial demesne farming (in a parallel fashion to the Prussian Junkers of East Elbia) in the central and southern borderlands created demand for the labor of the serfs for profit-making agriculture. Nevertheless, the majority of Russian serf owners still derived their profit from rents rather than the "surplus value" generated by their human property. On the other hand, the proportion of serfs to the population as a whole was lower than in Hungary or even compared to the newly acquired Baltic and Polish provinces (70 percent). Percentages of around 50 percent in the Russian heartland were similar to those in Brandenburg-Prussia and Austria-Bohemia. However, the prevalence of communally held land and the practice of repartition of the land between families of the *mir* were unique to the Russian heartland. Russian serfs paid their masters rent and labor, but these obligations and taxes owed to the state were negotiated through the elders of the communal unit. In the Baltic and Polish borderlands, peasants possessed family farmsteads through which their landlords exacted their servile dues.

In Russia the customary traditions of the *mir* created a counter-society which eventually destroyed the Tsarist Empire in 1917–18, while in the rest of Central and Eastern Europe, where civil society was more developed, law was used to defend customary and even "civil" rights. In Brandenburg-Prussia, for example, by the end of the eighteenth century, the introduction of *urbaren*, or labor contracts, allowed at least rich peasants to contest the amount of labor services they owed their lord. William Hagen has demonstrated a relished tradition of litigation by the peasantry to escape the overweening power of the Junkers.[15] Lucy Riall has also noted this mania for litigation by the inhabitants of the Brontë estate in post-feudal Sicily.[16]

What factors finally brought about the liberation of Europeans from servile status? This, too, has given rise to a great deal of debate among historians. Four factors can be delineated: (1) the sovereign (and his or her struggle with the nobility) and the state, (2) peasant revolts, (3) revolutionary ideology, and (4) the capitalist mode of production. An older mechanistic Marxist approach to the end of serfdom is not even advanced by Marxist historians today. Who in their most sophisticated incarnations will now argue that the educated lawyer classes and even the disenchanted nobility undermined serfdom, whose unintended consequences allowed for the free market in land and human labor to flourish in the wake of the French Revolution. In this respect the role of secular ideologies which undermined the God-given nature of the old order was important: an age-old hegemonic worldview was replaced by a dynamic belief in the rights of man and the mobilizing power of the nation-state. Others have pointed to the sovereign's self-interest. The liberation of the serfs would undermine the power of the nobility and open up new sources of support and taxation from the peasantry. However, the French Revolution, Napoleon's conquests, and even the revolutions of 1848 slowed the pace of reform and emancipation for fear that the entire old order would be swept aside. Indeed, only in France was emancipation initiated and carried out by a non-absolutist state. Napoleon's abolition of feudalism in his empire was permanent in Italy, but merely temporary in parts of the Habsburg lands, for example. And it can be argued that the Napoleonic empire was a curious mixture of the revolutionary anti-feudal ideals of 1789–93 and the reforming and calculating guile of the absolutist monarchies of the eighteenth century. Peasant revolts could be the final nail in the coffin (as they were in Galicia in 1848), but usually only determined the course of emancipation, as perhaps they did in Russia. Indeed, the peasants of Galicia and Croatia was granted their freedom from a grateful emperor for their opposition to the national revolts of their Polish and Hungarian overlords.

The final and decisive factor was international power politics. Defeat in war by Prussia in 1806 and Russia in 1856 was attributed to outmoded forms of technology and administration tied to the creaky old order. The interests of state power determined the fall of the old order itself. The rise of Russian serfdom in the seventeenth century was motivated by the Moscovite tsars' desire to bind the peasants to the lands of the noble *boyars*, to assure them a standing army to defend the vast borderlands from attacks from Swedes, Tartars, or Ottomans. A deal was made whereby the landed magnates served as officers in the army and as officials in the empire's bureaucracy, but once the tsar seized the lands of the church in 1762 and noble service was ended, the logic of the system was undermined. Victory over Napoleon merely hid a problem, which was brewing among the disgruntled intelligentsia who had been "liberated" in 1762. The Decembrists and other revolutionary groups of intelligentsia demanded a constitutional monarchy in which they were to have full participation in government, not merely serve as the lackeys of the tsar. And in order to compete on the world stage the empire needed a professional army that did not rely upon a servile population under the control of landed magnates. Thus the needs of reform were set even if arguments over compensation for lost serf income, the amounts of land awarded the freed serfs, and the need to create new state structures to control the countryside led to acrimonious debate between the tsarist court and the landed nobility.

Varieties of Land Tenure and Labor Service

Several types of land tenure can be identified in Europe after the old order faded away. Thus in the Netherlands, England, Wales, and parts of Scotland tenant farmers integrated into national markets, although this was certainly not the case in Ireland, where subsistence peasants increased their numbers until the terrible famines of the 1840s. Albeit in a summary of recent scholarship, Alun Howkins asserts the even England may have remnants of a peasantry in parts of the countryside.[17] In France the revolution created a much more substantial group of peasant proprietors. Peasant proprietors can also be found in parts of Italy and in Spain. They were also found in the borderlands of the Russian Empire, in Serbia and Bulgaria (as mentioned), and in Sweden. But in Spain (especially in Navarre and Catalonia), central Italy, southern France, western Germany, and parts of Scandinavia, complex varieties of sharecropping were dominant. Elsewhere to the south and east large landowners of aristocratic and middle-class provenance reduced tenants to landless laborers. Thus in Andalucía, Puglia, Bavaria, Austria, the Baltic borderlands, Hungary, or East Elbia new and older forms of control tied many to the land and the untrammeled authority of a great landlord. The Junker is often cited as the stereotype. Thus his power over his *Gut* was exercised through his control of local justice and administration through the *Landrat*. In this case, the Junkers became integrated into the world grain trade and took a direct interest in their business in the same way as the modernizing great landlords of the Po Valley in Italy from the middle of the nineteenth century. Land was also used as collateral for real estate speculation in the cities and absentee landlords used the bailiff to manage his enterprise as in the grain-growing areas of Sicily, Andalucía, Romania, and Ireland. Thus in the Sicilian or Romanian countryside, for example, the landlords' rent collector and enforcer, the *gabellotto* and the *arendaşi*, respectively, became an independent force to be reckoned with and the target of peasant fear and hatred. Spanish *desamortización* (disentailment) bore a resemblance to the process in Italy whereby feudal and church privileged property was transformed into private property. But in this case, as in Russia, the lords were compensated; in Spain, outstanding feudal dues were converted into Treasury obligations and thus the feudal elite was preserved to a certain extent by the liberal state. This old regime nobility was also reinforced, as in Italy, by the professional and banking middle classes, which bought disentailed lands. So the large estates in Spain retaining near-feudal lords rubbed shoulders with more modern farms and systems of tenure.[18]

Categorizations risk over-generalization. As Niall Ferguson has pointed out, land tenure and forms of labor in Europe "differed widely even within quite small regions: tenurial customs, after all, were legacies of the age before integrated markets."[19] In East Elbia, for example, it has been argued that the prevalence of the large Junker estate was something of a myth. "While there were some wealthy nobles in Silesia," Robert Gildea writes, "nobles in the core Prussian provinces of Brandenburg and Pomerania were often poor, and estates turned over rapidly because few were entailed."[20]

The Italian example brings out clearly the complexity of systems of land tenure and labor. Italian lands were ruled by a variety of political regimes and tied to peninsular and world markets in complex ways. The end of the old regime in the countryside resulted in at least three types of employment and land tenure. The south and Sardinia were noted for a mixture of latifundia and peasant farming. Central Italy and the northern Alpine areas were dominated by varieties of sharecropping, albeit the Agro Romano (the area around Rome) possessed estates owned or rented to tenants by the Roman "black aristocracy" (the aristocracy of the Papal States or even relatives of the pope).[21] And the Po Valley – although witnessing the development of large commercial farms and armies of landless laborers – also possessed complex varieties of leaseholds. To make matters more confusing, geographical pigeonholing is not always useful. Thus the rice farms of Piedmont's Vercellese had much in common with the large commercial farms of the Bolognese. The lemon groves outside of Palermo were extremely valuable operations dependent on tastes for marmalade in New York and London, but in a nearby part of the wheat-growing center of Sicily it was land as collateral for absentee landlords (not as a productive factor in a world commodity trade) that largely counted. And when we turn to labor control it is also difficult to generalize. So if Frank Snowden has pointed to the brutal and simple, and perhaps unique, American plantation-like labor control found on the great wheat-growing *latifondi* of Puglia's Tavoliere in the late nineteenth and early twentieth centuries, Marta Petruscewicz's study of the immense Baracco *latifondo* in Calabria in a slightly earlier era argues that in this diversified operation different tasks "commanded a specific labor relationship": "sheep raising gave rise to participatory arrangements, grain farming to day labor, and licorice manufacture to wage labor."[22]

Thus it would be foolish to generalize about tenure and labor. Nevertheless, if one had to point to unique areas they would be the large peasant proprietor classes in France, Sweden, and Bulgaria. Then there were the vast numbers of landless laborers in Andalucía, the Po Valley and parts of Apulia, and the Great Hungarian Plain. Standing alone (after 1861) were the communal rural communes of the Russian heartland (*obschina*) in which land was owned communally and families of the commune owned temporarily scattered strips of land (there were analogues in the Irish rundale, Scottish runrigg, and the Serbian *zadruga*).[23] In Russia, rising population put great pressure on communities and raised tensions between the landed gentry and the freed serfs. Russian modernizers were stymied for the most part. It is not true that vast numbers of freed peasants left for the cities once all restrictions were lifted. In fact, the results were somewhat paradoxical. The government encouraged independent land owning, especially Stolypin after 1906, but the results were very mixed. Elder control, the communal tradition, the lack of resources, and types of family structure prevalent in the heartland of Russia militated against the widespread emergence of the variety of land tenure systems we noted for Italy. In fact the temporary migration of peasants to cities and the supplementing of family incomes back home gave the communal village a new lease on life – "to the system of large and complex households at the very time when the growing rural population was forcing peasants off the land." Thus, as David Moon argues, "the reforms did not fundamentally alter Russian peasant society, but changed the relationship between peasant society and the ruling and landowning elites."[24]

The end of the servile order in the countryside did not mean that great landlords were not very noticeable owners of lands in Europe before 1914. There are certainly turning points in the nineteenth century: seizure of church lands and the end of feudalism during and after the Napoleonic era in Latin Europe and the emancipation of the serfs of Russia. The Great (Agricultural) Depression of the last decades, and land and tax reforms experienced in the United Kingdom (especially and dramatically in Ireland), undermined the position of the great landlords of Europe. But the *aristocratic* landed elite faded from 1880 to the Great War: the *deluge* occurred only after 1914. They exercised power in and through the countryside by

marriage into the plutocracy, through the commercialization of large estates, and their successful transformation in Eastern Europe into brewers, distillers, refiners of beetroots, and mine owners. In this way we can draw certain parallels to the economic fortunes of the Whiggish aristocracy of an earlier period of British history. Sharecropping also allowed for a form of "seigniorial share tenancy" in which the old nobility and the upstart notables of Spain, France, and Italy could meet the needs of modern markets, while at the same time exercise a near-feudal power of oversight over extended families of sharecroppers, as several studies of the Italian case and an interesting cross-national comparative study have demonstrated.[25]

Nevertheless the ownership of land by a restricted group of older and younger branches of the aristocracy or landed gentry did decline. In 1861 land ownership was most concentrated in Britain: 710 individuals owned one-quarter of the land of England and Wales and "nearly three-quarters of the British Isles was in the hands of less than five thousand people."[26] As David Spring points out, "no Continental landed elite owned so large a part of its nation's territory as did the English."[27] Perhaps the Spanish rank second, followed by the Prussians, with the French and Russians lagging far behind. In the lands of the Habsburg Empire one also encountered highly concentrated land ownership. Around 1900, 151 families of the Bohemian *Hochadel* (the high aristocracy) owned 1.5 million of the crownland's 5.2 million hectares and one-quarter of the land of Moravia was owned by just 73 noble families. In Hungary in the early 1900s, less than four thousand people owned 32 percent of the land: the vast estates of the princes Schwarzenberg, Lichtenstein, and Esterházy were quasi-empires.[28] But at least in England the landlords did not face a land-hungry peasantry, nor did they face the autocratic land-rich Russian state. "If," Spring concludes, "the undisputed possession of much land was a measure of power, the English landed elite was indeed powerful."[29]

The dramatic land reform in Ireland destroyed the territorial landed elite by 1914 and lessened its presence in Wales considerably, with Scottish magnates resisting the best. In England the effects of the agricultural depression, death duties, and income tax led to the greatest transfer of property since the dissolution of the monasteries in the sixteenth century. The situation was also dramatic in Russia. The landed elite had been in permanent decline since 1861. In 1914 there were still immense estates: 699 estates existed of more than 5,000 acres. However, this hides a change. In 1861 the nobles held 120,000 *desyatiny* (hectares) or half of the land in European Russia, but Norman Stone has calculated that by 1914 they owned less than a tenth of its arable land.[30] In Germany the aristocratic elite survived in greater numbers than was expected, but both the Russians and the Prussians were still poorer than their British counterparts. However one looks at the statistics, pre-industrial Europe was overwhelmed by wealth derived from mines, factories, or urban property. Middle-class millionaires far outnumbered the wealthy from the aristocracy. In this respect, Arno Mayer's argument about "the economic preeminence of pre-industrial forms of wealth is unconvincing."[31]

Social Control and Mass Politics: Lords and Peasants

The end of the servile order and the modernization of the European state during the long nineteenth century were the two overriding political issues facing the lord of the countryside. How would the lords confront the new balance of forces introduced by the end of servility? How would the lords confront a bureaucratic and centralizing state? These sets of issues force us to address a point that we have dealt with ambiguously throughout this chapter. Who exactly are the lords? Jerome Blum argued that the seigniors of the servile lands belonged to the nobility, "that they were members of an hereditary caste, composed of families who enjoyed rights and privileges denied to the other members of society." But if this is the case, then England did not have a nobility, since except for their right to sit in the House of Lords, they "did not form a legally defined order with specific prerogatives guaranteed by law and tradition in such matters as taxation,

ownership of land, monopolies, judicial authority . . ."[32] As Gildea puts it, "England had nobles, it did not have a nobility."[33] The British aristocracy was much smaller than its continental counterparts because only the eldest son inherited the title. Cannadine examines the landed elite of Britain and rather pragmatically announces that his book discusses "the titular aristocracy, the territorial baronetage and the landed gentry."[34] No other European land had a peerage similar to the House of Lords, except perhaps Hungary. The legal definition in Germany between high and low titled aristocracy had been significant. But the Junkers, usually untitled gentry, are more important to the themes of this chapter than the *Standesherren*, descendants of the nobility of the Holy Roman Empire, defunct in 1806. In France and Italy, revolution, constitutional reform, and/or unification meant that landed aristocracy no longer had legal representation in government and in this respect had less formal power than the Junkers or the British peers. Of course, a legalist approach can also mislead. In a strongly argued case, Anthony Cardoza demonstrates that in Italy at least the Piedmontese aristocracy may be different to other Italian aristocrats where the ruling house did not inherit the throne in Rome. He argues that close ties between the House of Savoy and the Piedmontese aristocracy placed them in a rather analogous situation to the Junkers, "providing local titled families with a host of advantages not shared by other aristocratic groups on the Italian peninsula." Thus the Piedmontese aristocracy retained cohesion based on "caste-like exclusivity, land ownership and military service."[35]

However, the centralization of the modern state exposed a rift between old and new elites throughout Europe. The older pre-Napoleonic elite yearned for a return to the order of ancient estates and provincial autonomy, but Restoration monarchies rather liked the centralized administration, police forces, and governmental reach that Napoleon had left them. In Italy, for example, the older nobility resented both the centralization of Napoleonic dominance and the centralization imposed on them by the Restoration monarchies. Thus the great barons of Sicily resented the hand of the Bourbons after their return to Naples. Later, in 1861, the Piedmontese "conquest" aroused similar reactions: there was much support for regionalization among the Tuscan nobility in the 1860s. But in Italy some southern barons supported violent mass movements of peasants and the displaced Bourbon clergy. The Carlist Wars in Spain had a regional dimension fueled by certain traditionalist grandees' resentment of Madrid centralization. In the Habsburg Empire the Croatian, Hungarian, and Polish nobility were suspicious of the modernizing bureaucrats of Vienna; after 1867 the Hungarian nobility's autonomy was recognized in the constitutional settlement which created the Austro-Hungarian Empire. In Germany the *Standesherren* in the south fought against the confirmation of the destruction of their rights and autonomies which the Restoration states kept after the defeat of Napoleon. In Prussia the Junkers eventually embraced the rhetoric of middle-class nationalism and bureaucratic reform in the first half of the nineteenth century, once they were assured that their manorial power was preserved and crucial seats in the military and the government of the king (and later the kaiser) were secured.

Methods of control changed in the countryside. In Russia, the land captain, a member of the local nobility, became the new link between Moscow and the peasantry. Local power was to be exercised also through the *zemstvo* established in 1864, but it only really started functioning after 1905 and came into its own during World War I. In France, Spain, and Italy the prefect played a similar role, but middle-class bureaucrats struck up relationships with the local notables. In Spain the largest landlords surrendered political power to *caciques*, and local bosses managed politics and mediation with the center, in much the same way as former *gabelloti* (now important landlords) did in Sicily.

Thus what drew together old and new, titled and untitled landed elites and the state and the monarchies was the necessity to replace the old order of servility with a new system of social control in the countryside – what Michel Foucault called a disciplined society. The aura of the old order, its cultural mores of deference and honor, were harnessed to newer forms of control.[36] In the French, British, German, Italian, and Spanish cases, the old and new blended. Law and order were guaranteed by national militarized police forces. But when they were too even-handed in labor and land disputes one could always rely on private militias. Deference earned by the older aristocracy could rub off on the new patricians of the countryside, or at least their peasants knew it was wise to continue to play the game of being deferential. Thus as Marta Petruscewicz notes in the case of Italy, the post-Napoleonic settlement reinforced older certainties in a new setting: "It was not the noble origin that defined social hierarchies and the dominant system of values – in fact, the Napoleonic period brought into landownership a vast urban patriciate and *galantuomini* – but simply the centrality of land."[37] And the dominant values of land and landed elites remained paramount in Italy until at least the early twentieth century. Patronage and clientelism may have had their roots in a feudal order of dues and customary rights, but in this case one asked the landlord to secure jobs for relatives in the post office or pensions for soldiers of the national state. And this power to bestow such gifts was tied to the bundle of votes the landlord grand electors or their boss agents "guaranteed" a government in the capital city. Ideology and hegemony were final factors identified by Blinkhorn and Gibson, to which we will turn in a moment. But it is worth recalling the contradiction behind this mixture of the old and new. As Adrian Lyttelton noted in the Italian case, nineteenth-century liberalism wished to see the abolition of old barriers to free trade in land and labor, but its landlord advocates in Italy and elsewhere "wanted to modernize the agrarian economy while preserving traditional patterns of social relations."[38] This faced its logical limits once the peasantry started to organize as a cohesive force to challenge these rules of the game.

Even in Europe's most modern but least bureaucratic society, Britain, which had seen servility fade away centuries ago, the local administration "was monopolized by aristocratic Lords Lieutenant and gentry Justices of the Peace."[39] And when local government was opened to a wider electorate, these "natural

leaders" for a very long time remained as fig-
ureheads even when politicians of more humble
backgrounds began to pull the strings. This
chapter only tangentially deals with the relationship between the middle class and aristocracy, but it is worth noting that on the
continent the bureaucracy became the recruiting ground for the educated middle classes and
did so slightly later in Britain after local government and civil service reforms. With the
exception of the diplomats and the officer
corps, throughout Europe by 1914 the middle
classes were prominent in the judiciary and
government departments. Nevertheless all
surveys demonstrate that whereas the numbers
of aristocrats declined in the parliaments of
most of Europe, they retained the whip-hand
in the cabinet of the German Empire until
1914. The Junkers were still the most significant power in the Prussian army through their
control of the patterns of socialization and
recruitment, but also by the presence of brilliant military intellectuals in their ranks. This
warrior class modernized itself even while it
promoted pseudo-feudal notions of honor with
rituals demanding satisfaction and dueling. Its
victories against Austria and France and its continued strength in the following decades in
most cases dampened the criticisms of the
middle classes, who in any case were more
frightened by the urban socialists. But in
Britain the terrain was different: the House of
Lords – which had the final say over the House
of Commons – surrendered its veto power with
far less resistance than the die-hards had fore-
cast. The most powerful landed class of mid-
century Europe had surrendered a great deal of
its economic and political power before 1914.

One of the defining issues that sheds light
on the different nature of the Junkers and the
British landed elite is the question of agricultural protection. In older standard accounts
of the German *Sonderweg*, "the marriage of
iron and rye" is seen as a significant step in
Germany's road to militarist hubris and disaster, whereas the repeal of the Corn Laws and
parliamentary reform ushered in an age of
peaceful evolution to parliamentary democracy
in Britain. While much of the teleological logic
has been undermined by recent and not so
recent work, this still throws up interesting

comparisons between these nations' landed
classes. Between 1874 and 1905 British Tory
governments ignored the agricultural lobby,
which was even less successful once the Liberals came to power. The landed classes and their
lobby groups were divided and ineffectual. The
Prussian case was very different. Although most
Junkers feared democracy and equality, they
had never been in the vanguard of liberty for
the nation. Most Junkers thought like a corporate group, not a self-assured reforming ruling
class such as the former Whig oligarchy.
The Junker's *frondeur* spirit "fed from the
thought that his family had antedated the
Hohenzollerns in Prussia and the reality that
the Junker squire was more or less a king on
his tiny estate realm."[40] The great difference
was that these little kings were modern enough
to help create the Bund der Landwirte (the
Agrarian League), an agrarian pressure group
that united Junker and peasant interests and
had no equivalent anywhere in Europe, let
alone in Britain.

In Russia, whereas the landed elite had lost
land and much money since 1861, its power in
the Duma did not really make up for the losses
in the countryside. Tsar Nicholas II, once revolutionary threats were suppressed, believed
himself an autocrat who considered constitutional and parliamentary constraints conditional encumbrances. Russia was also unique in
another way. Revolution and social protest
threatened the position of the landed elite in
1848 throughout Europe, in Italy in the 1860s
and 1890s, in Ireland, Scotland, Wales, and in
a lesser key in England in the 1870s and 1880s,
and in France and Romania in 1907. But it was
only in Russia in 1904–6 that the landed elite
and the state loss near-complete control of the
situation. In Britain and Germany an alliance of
the richer tenants and peasants and the elite fostered stability, whereas Russian reformers had
failed to create this situation before world war
broke out. Stolypin had sought to create an
alliance of "strong peasants" and noble landlords, but he was assassinated. The tsarist
system before emancipation had been founded
on personal and patrimonial ties between the
"Autocrat and his officials" and was "supposed
to be duplicated on the local level between
noble landowners and their serfs." But this

arrangement "was destroyed by the efforts at 'modernization' which logically entailed the disappearance of these very personalized bonds."[41]

The Politics of Peasants and Lords: Overview

Did peasants in Europe have their own politics during the long nineteenth century? The standard responses have been twofold. First, there is Eric Hobsbawm's contention that "insofar as the peasantry mobilized electorally, they did so under non-agricultural banners, even where it was clear that the fate of a particular political movement or party rested on the support of farmers or peasants."[42] Then there is Eugen Weber's contention that the politics of French peasants "remained in an archaic stage – local and personal – into at least the 1880s."[43] Let's start with the last assertion first. Historians of France have roundly criticized Weber's claim that peasants were pre-political until the last decades of the nineteenth century. Magraw notes the active participation of the peasantry in the revolutionary years of 1789–93, and their activism during the revolutions of 1830 and 1848. Magraw, Tilly, Margadant, and McPhee see the insurrections during 1851 in the wake of Louis Napoleon's *coup d'état* not as a series of parochial and confused acts, but motivated by lucid strategy.[44] In a similar fashion, Hobsbawm characterized the peasant anarchist insurrections of Andalucía as millenarian. Yet Temma Kaplan demonstrated that these were motivated by coherent trade union-like demands and fueled by self-educated peasants who communicated with artisans in the nearby towns of the Jerez sherry-growing district.[45] McPhee takes this argument one step further by claiming that the peasantry of the French Second Republic (1848–51) did not require the mediation of town-based artisans, lawyers, or teachers to shape their political worldview.[46] This conveniently takes us to Hobsbawm's first assertion that peasants followed other party banners, since it is assumed that a peasant party would have to be run and organized solely by peasants. This line of reasoning would not take us very far if we applied

it to workers' and socialist parties of the late nineteenth and early twentieth centuries, as Hobsbawm would be the first to realize. The lower middle class and the intelligentsia were significantly represented in these parties throughout Europe.

Nevertheless it is certainly true that peasants could be found in parties and movements led by former masters and lords. A useful way of conceptualizing their attachment is as an "agrarian fundamentalist" ideology, cooked up by the urban intelligentsia of Berlin, Munich, London, Paris, Bucharest, Florence, and Moscow. It argued that the rise of capitalist society and the decline of the old order undermined all that was good and healthy in the nation. The nation's soul rested in its organic attachment to the soil and the peasantry, and their rude but just lords were its guardians. Alien socialists and Jews or other outsiders undermined the healthy life of the nation by introducing notions of equality, secularism, and unmanly weakness. Financial capitalism was criticized and corporate or anti-industrial socialist remedies were sometimes invoked, although social imperialism was also usually endorsed. Agrarian fundamentalism might have its counterparts, parallels, or forerunners in the revivals of traditionalist religion (such as the Carlists in Spain or earlier the San Fedisti in Italy). It might also find more benign echoes in variations on what English Tories called "one nation" politics. Indeed, in the most industrialized nation in the world agrarianism – the yearning to solve the "Condition of England Problem" by returning to the farm – was even important in Chartism, as Malcolm Chase showed some years ago.[47] Echoes are also found in Russian Populism and more closely in the movement of middle-class Russian Slavophiles who opposed Russia's aping of the West. Perhaps the most famous cases of agrarian fundamentalism can be found in Imperial Germany, where both Bismarck and the Agrarian League constantly employed its motifs.

But peasants were autonomous rational agents. As already mentioned, peasant protest was not merely futile lashing out. The revolts of peasants in Sicily in the 1890s (Fasci Siciliani) and in France's Midi were part of broader movements. The Fasci were an alliance of the peasants, small town artisans, and the Sicilian intelligentsia and educated lower middle classes, resembling in many respects Chartism. The revolt of the Midi was for all intents and purposes collective bargaining through riot. The aims were negotiable.

Peasants and farm workers were not immune to unionization. Thus the landless laborers of Andalucía, the Po Valley and Apulia, and the Great Hungarian Plain formed unions inspired by anarchist and syndicalist ideologies. But they also fought for higher wages and the control of the labor force in their areas. Other peasants and farm workers in Italy formed unions inspired by socialism or Christian Democracy and were open to using the government in Rome to press their claims against intransigent landlords. The boycott copied from the Irish tenant farmers in their struggle against their landlords was imported into Italy. In all these cases, elemental demands of the propertyless for what the Spanish called the *reparto* – the division of the lands – was transmuted into modern trade union demands. In Italy, as Frank Snowden has shown, the trade union struggle of the female rice weeders (*mondine*) was joined by the campaign of dedicated doctors to wipe out the curse of malaria bred in the rice fields. Medical science, social conditions, and trade union rights were merged in this struggle.[48]

Trade union organization also spread to the sharecroppers of Catalonia, France, and Italy. Swedish peasants had experienced little servility. They had been represented in the *Riksdag* in their own estate, and in the parish community hall they honed debating skills and created their own rural public sphere. Their interests had been anti-landlord, but with the rise of a landless population and the industrialization of the countryside they sided with their former enemies. These skills were transmuted to the fledgling labor movement, which was nourished originally within this rural sphere. Scandinavia was also the scene of cooperatives (particularly in Denmark), so that by 1914 the majority of the rural population belonged to one of a myriad of organizations. Germany also saw a twenty-fold increase in cooperatives between 1883 and 1910, when they numbered 23,751. German cooperatives were mainly

credit unions. European Russia also witnessed a mushroom growth of such institutions by 1914 (with over 6 million member households). Italy, too, had a vigorous cooperative movement in the countryside, run by the Reds (socialists) or the Whites (Catholics) – from food and credit cooperatives to labor cooperatives, which engaged unemployed landless laborers in the Po Valley during the dead season.

Thus the agrarian population could be found in all manner of parties and movements: anarchist and socialist, Carlist, conservative, and Christian Democrat, populist and republican and radical. But where were the peasant parties? It is true that in a society such as France, which by the turn of the century could be plausibly defined as a peasant republic, they were not to be found. The peasantry served as the bulwark of the republic and supported a range of parties, from the radicals to a variety of republican parties, to the socialists. On the whole the weight of gravity ensured a moderate or even conservative republic, but they did not advance their own interests under the banner of a peasant party with its own peasant ideology. The countryside was experiencing a boom in these years, so the city was not a threat and France was a republic of small towns surrounded by the countryside of independent peasants. Schooling and the role of the church may have stirred passions, but the Dreyfus Affair did not seem to be that significant in the countryside. Rural antisemitism may have been noticeable in Alsace and traditionalist Catholicism in the West, but these areas had their specific historical legacies. For the most part the peasantry stabilized the republic and did not demand its own party.

Before 1914 peasant or agrarian parties were founded in Sweden and elsewhere in Scandinavia and played an important political role. But it was in Eastern Europe that a range of peasant parties truly made their mark. Thus: the Bulgarian National Agrarian Union (1899 and as a party in 1901), the Czech Agrarian Party (1899), the Russian Socialist Revolutionary Party (1901), the Serbian Peasant Unity Party (1903, became Serbian Peasant Party, 1919), the Croatian Peasant Party (1904), the Peasant Party of Greater Hungary (1906, became Hungarian Smallholder Party, 1909), and the Polish Peasant Party (1895).

These parties held that the virtues of peasant society could be preserved side by side with industrial capitalism. Thus the collective traditions of the *zadruga* and the *mir* were proposed as alternatives to urban individualism. Industrialization would follow the natural rhythm of national peasant traditions and not merely sweep away all before it. Parties such as those in Bohemia, Poland-Galicia, and Bulgaria were optimistic reform movements, where the expansion of the franchise would allow improvement through parliamentary and legal channels. In Russia the Socialist Revolutionaries proposed revolution. But in the future – after autocracy was overthrown – they envisaged the widespread usage of direct democracy, initiative, referendum, and recall. All of these parties envisaged some form of land reform, which ranged from socialization through the village community to the promotion of small-holdings, and thus reflected the land tenures of a given national case. They promoted productive peasant households, cooperative organizations, and the pooling of capital through rural organizations.

Some of these parties had a larger peasant membership than others. Chernov in the Socialist Revolutionary Party, Radić in the Croatian Peasant Party, and slightly later Stamboliski in Bulgaria were highly educated individuals. But before 1914 the Croat and Bulgarian parties were almost exclusively peasant in membership. The Czech, Romanian, and Polish parties became multi-class parties (indeed, the Czech Agrarian Party became the strongest Czech party in the parliament in Vienna in the last two elections before 1914). However, all of them had a strong nucleus of self-educated peasant leadership. Thus, the organizational base for the Polish and Bulgarian movements was found in their reading rooms, rural lecture circuits, and lending libraries. But they were also noted for their factionalism. One of the great issues was the national question, which diverted their "peasantist" focus. In Russia, although they were much larger than the Marxist parties, they were less agile. The Bolsheviks also recruited their most hard-bitten self-educated militants from ex-peasants in the cities, who expressed a bitter loathing for their bucolic origins.

Politics: Nationalism, Lords, and Peasants

Two types of nationalism have been identified in Europe during the long nineteenth century. In one case the nation is a historic identity which takes its shape from a well-established state with well-defined borders, such as England or France. In the other, the nation is recreated or "imagined" from a coterie of lands which share cultural and ethnic kinship, with the state form lending this imagining its coherence and cohesion. Thus the examples of Germany and Italy spring to mind.

Peasant culture played a signal role in the formation of the idea of a nation in the second category and bucolic themes were not absent from the reformulation of nationalism in the first. "Authentic" folk culture became the touchstone for the birth of modern nationalist movements in the lands that were still part of the multinational empires of Central and Eastern Europe (but decidedly not in Italy, where Mazzini and other nationalists were tone deaf to peasant culture or peasant economic needs). Thus, typically, German-speaking nobles and middle-class enthusiasts created the first dictionaries and grammars of the Estonians and Latvians. The Swedish upper classes "regularized" the Finnish language in its bucolic settings. Gypsy tunes, peasant art, and peasant folk tales became the main inspiration for a host of nationalist composers in Eastern Europe. Peasant arts and crafts became the rage for the growing middle classes of the urban centers of Eastern Europe and Russia. Ethnic nationalism linked with the peasant parties because they shared a form of populism grounded in the "authentic" national culture. Further afield we can see that in Ireland a Catholic nationalist populism grounded in tenant farmers' struggles against the Protestant territorial elite and seconded by the Irish middle classes of the towns had many parallels with Central and Eastern Europe.

Nevertheless, state-based nationalism was not absent. So in countries which "maintained a tradition of uninterrupted statehood (Poland and Hungary)" the "golden freedoms" of the swollen Polish *szlachta* or the Hungarian nobility were used to mobilize (with some hesitation) the non-noble segments of the population.[49] Jozef Piłsudski, a young noble of Lithuanian descent, founded the Polish Socialist Party in 1892, and invoked the insurrectionary traditions of pre-partition Poland (with yearnings for the earlier massive Polish-Lithuanian Commonwealth) and the heroic legacy of his noble ancestors. In the Czech case, however, where the ancient nobility had been smashed in 1620, the new nationalist movement had to invoke the issues of language, culture, economic development, and educational policy. Thus the famous battle with the German speaking population of Prague over the language to be used in high schools, and the use of the Czech language in official institutions, which offered career advancement to the sons and daughters of the Czech middle classes.

By 1914 nationalism had had an uneven effect on the European countryside. In the Balkan Wars that led up to the conflagration, one peasant living in a disputed part of Macedonia told an observer that his father had been Greek and no one mentioned the Bulgarians. But if the Serbs won he would not object, although now "it is better for us to be Bulgarians."[50] It is arguable if the bewildered Sicilian peasants forced to fight on the treacherous rocks and crevices separating them from the Croat and Slovene troops of the Habsburg imperial army felt much differently. The rout at Caporetto in 1917 seemed to many Italians as a failure of the national spirit. Indeed, the commanders of these peasant troops had little faith in their fellow countrymen. But the French peasantry consumed itself at Verdun with an appalling stolidity. French schooling and the French military had nationalized them, or at least they had internalized the national message under their own terms. In Russia the story was different. The emancipation of the serfs had deepened the divide between lords and peasants and opened a widening gap between the formerly sacred aura of tsardom and the peasant. Peasants may have risen up in previous centuries in support of a tsar pretender, but

now the entire notion of autocracy lost its allure. When the regime collapsed in 1917, the armed peasantry "were eager to go back to their villages, and beat their rifles into ploughshares, and their bayonets into pruning hooks."[51]

Conclusion

This chapter has reviewed the historical literature pertaining to three themes covering the decline and fall of servility, the struggle for hegemony in the countryside, and the role of cultural dominance as filtered through the emergence of nationalism. A red thread running through all of these themes has been the persistence of aristocratic and peasant cultures in a modernizing Europe. It seems clear that the aristocracy and the lords of the land retained an oversized presence in national life until 1914. But the question of how far they experienced a relative decline is still one of the major sites of controversy in historiography. Perhaps the relative importance of the peasantry and family farmers in Europe has still been under-researched. As we have seen, peasants and farmers were influential in politics before 1914, but their influence varied quite widely and across parties, depending upon which part of Europe one investigates.

NOTES

1 Cardoza (1997).
2 Cannadine (1990).
3 Weber (1977).
4 Mayer (1981: 12).
5 Blackbourn and Eley (1985).
6 Wiener (1981).
7 Harris and Thane (1984: 215–34).
8 Rösener (1994: 185).
9 Moon (2001: 1).
10 Blum (1978: 430).
11 Mazower (2001: 28–9).
12 Ibid, p. 29.
13 Pipes (1990); Figes (1997).
14 Bush (2000: 153–4).
15 Hagen (2002).
16 Riall (2003).
17 Howkins (1990: 117).

18 Schubert (1990: 58–60).
19 Ferguson (2000: 97).
20 Gildea (2003: 290).
21 Lupo (1990: 126).
22 Snowden (1986); Petruscewicz (1996: 13).
23 Stone (1999: 170).
24 Moon (1999: 343).
25 Jonsson (1992: 191–217).
26 Cannadine (1990: 55).
27 Spring (1977: 4).
28 Berend (2003: 159, 184–5).
29 Spring (1977: 4).
30 Stone (1999: 170).
31 Lieven (1992: 243).
32 Blum (1978: 11).
33 Gildea (2003: 170).
34 Cannadine (1990: xii).
35 Cardoza (1997: 10–11).
36 These are succinctly outlined in Gibson and
    Blinkhorn's (1991) survey of landownership
    and power in modern Europe.
37 Petruscewicz (2002: 97).
38 Lyttelton (1979: 131).
39 Lieven (1992: 10).
40 Ibid: 19.
41 Raeff (1983: 117).
42 Hobsbawm (1987: 90).
43 Weber (1977: 241).
44 For a good summary of these accounts of the
    French peasantry, see Moon (1996: 51–2).
45 Kaplan (1977).
46 McPhee (1992).
47 Chase (1988).
48 Snowden (2003).
49 Banac and Bushkovitch (1983: 11).
50 Mazower (1998: 94).
51 Moon (1996: 67).

GUIDE TO FURTHER READING

There is still nothing to replace the magisterial account of the end of servility by Blum, *The End of the Old Order in Rural Europe*. Another useful survey is Powelson's *The Story of Land*. There are several interesting comparative works by Kolchin (*Unfree Labor* and "After Serfdom") and Bush (*Servitude in Modern Times*) which tackle the issue of serfdom in its Russian variety and other forms in comparison to the plantation slavery of the New World. Russian serfdom is covered by Moon in *The Russian Peasantry 1600–1930* and

The Abolition of Serfdom in Russia, 1862–1907, who also gives a good account of the Russian peasantry.

There are several excellent overviews of the changing position of the lords in the European countryside during the long nineteenth century. Of especial note are the comparative works of Spring (*European Landed Elites in the Nineteenth Century*), Gibson and Blinkhorn (*Landownership and Power in Modern Europe*), and Lieven (*The Aristocracy in Europe, 1815–1914*). See also the case studies (Britain and Piedmont/Italy) by Cannadine (*The Decline and Fall of the British Aristocracy*, "The Making of the British Upper Classes") and Cardoza (*Aristocrats in Bourgeois Italy*). They demonstrate that the grander theories of Mayer's *Persistence of the Old Regime* and Blackbourn and Eley's *Peculiarities of German History* – although excellent for stimulating discussion and research – should be accepted only with reservations. A very good recent comparative overview can be found in Malatesta's "The Landed Aristocracy During the Nineteenth and Early Twentieth Centuries."

For two different critical accounts of the gentrification thesis, centering on Britain but with European comparisons, see Rubinstein's *Capitalism, Culture and Decline* and Thompson's *Gentrification and the Enterprise Culture*. However, also see Frevert's "Honour and Middle-Class Cultures," Kaelble's "French Bourgeoisie and German Bürgertum," and especially Mosse's "Nobility and Middle Classes in Nineteenth-Century Europe." A revised Marxist approach to the decline of feudalism is found in Mooers' *Making of Bourgeois Europe* and Pilbeam's *Middle Classes in Europe 1789–1914*, which is suspicious of the concept of the "notable."

A serviceable history of the European peasantry can be found in Rösener's *Peasantry in Europe*, but in truth we await several additional global syntheses, which is amazing considering that the peasantry comprised the vast majority of the European population well into the nineteenth century. Excellent national or local studies are Moon's *Russian Peasantry 1600–1930* and Kotsonis's *Making Peasants Backward*, which emphasizes how all social strata of tsarist Russia outside of the peasantry viewed them as childish barbaric "foreigners." Dennison and Carus, in "The Invention of the Russian Rural Commune," question the universality of the Russian rural commune. And Hagen's *Ordinary Prussians* is a very interesting account of East Elbian Germany. There are useful overviews of the European peasantry in the nineteenth and early twentieth centuries by Stone (*Europe Transformed*), Sperber (*Revolutionary Europe*), and Gildea (*Barricades and Borders*). Weber's *Peasants into Frenchmen* and Lehning's *Peasant and French* present two different sides to the political integration of the peasants into France. Of great interest is Moon's comparative essay "Peasants into Russian Citizens?," which compares the very different trajectories of the French and Russian peasants.

The Italian case in English is covered in several overviews and articles. Of particular interest are Lyttelton's "Landlords, Peasants and the Limits of Liberalism," Bull and Corner's *From Peasant to Entrepreneur*, Riall's "Elites in Search of Authority," and Snowden's "Mosquitoes, Quinine and the Socialism of Italian Women." A good comparative account of nationalism and the peasantry of Eastern Europe can be found in Berend's *History Derailed*. The concept of "agrarian fundamentalism" is discussed by Koning in *The Failure of Agrarian Capitalism*.

CHAPTER SEVEN

Bourgeois Society

PAMELA PILBEAM

Introduction: Defining the Bourgeoisie and Its Power

In nineteenth-century Europe "bourgeois" was used as an adjective to define social, cultural, and political attitudes and also to describe society as a whole. "Bourgeoisie," "middle class," or "middle classes" were nouns used to describe all groups in society between nobles and workers, peasants and the very poor, literally "the middling sort."[1] As a description of a section of society, "bourgeois" meant little beyond the assumption of tolerable material comfort, a "clean hands occupation" for the men and a comparatively leisured domestic existence for wives, daughters, children, and the elderly members of the family circle. Nor was "bourgeois" much of an indicator of exclusive attitudes and norms. "Bourgeois" was especially useless when used to claim that certain political opinions were unique to the middles classes. Despite this the term bourgeois was and is used in all these different ways, often without distinguishing between them. One of the aims of this chapter is to make you aware of the limitations of social descriptions that sound quite precise.

The word bourgeois began life in France; the comparable German word is *Bürger*. Those who write about the bourgeoisie often divide them into upper, middle, and lower, but this is no more than a pretence of precision. Bourgeois and middle class are habitually used, as in

this chapter, as interchangeable categories. German historians sometimes talk about the very rich as bourgeois and less wealthy groups as middle class or *Mittelstand*.[2] In origin both simply meant a prosperous town dweller who had bought certain civic privileges. By the early nineteenth century the bourgeoisie included members of the professions, state servants, and men with financial, commercial, or industrial interests. Many were landowners. Buying the estate of an impoverished noble was regarded as a sign of status, whether it was Lopakhin buying the cherry orchard in Chekhov's play of the same name or rich bankers in Germany acquiring Junker (noble) estates. The most wealthy would certainly have included themselves within the "upper class," but snobbish members of the nobility would have looked down on them, although if they were impecunious they would marry their children to rich bourgeois progeny to repair their depleted fortunes. While the number of noble families remained fairly stable in the nineteenth century, there was an astronomic growth in the bourgeoisie at all levels. Contemporary observers were most conscious of the expansion of the entrepreneurial element, but there was a dramatic growth in the professions and especially in state service, where there was a virtual explosion of lower middle-class clerical jobs.

It was the 1789 revolution which contributed most to the definition of the bourgeoisie as a social class and the notion that "bourgeois" involved specific political as well as social attitudes. In these years class was replacing traditional concepts that society was divided into estates or orders. In France the clergy were the first estate, nobles the second, and everyone else constituted the third estate. A person was born into an estate or order; over the centuries families had bought or acquired certain responsibilities to the state and varying privileges which defined them as a member of an estate. An estate did not correspond to different levels of wealth: there were poor nobles and very poor clergy. In the second half of the eighteenth century the idea that society consisted of organic layers of estates was giving way to the notion that a person was defined by how, and how successfully, he earned his living. In his influential pamphlet "What is the Third Estate?" published on the eve of the calling of the Estates-General (an assembly composed of representatives from all the estates) in France in 1789, the abbé Sieyès claimed the Third Estate was the real nation. For practical purposes Sieyès actually included only the wealthy bourgeoisie. Sieyès was using the terminology of estates, but talking in the newer language of class, where how much money a person had counted for more than traditional privilege.[3]

Key episodes in the French Revolution of 1789 contributed to the definition and increase in power of this middle-class elite, particularly the abolition of the privileges of clergy and nobility on the night of August 4, 1789 and the Declaration of the Rights of Man and Citizen later that month. Resistance to the dismantling of traditional privileges of birth helped to fuel a counter-revolution and with it, not only class definition, which pleased the bourgeoisie, but also class conflict, which alarmed them. The noisy and belligerent emigration of opponents of the revolution quickly transformed liberal definitions of bourgeois citizenship into intolerant exclusions based on rough-and-ready class-type distinctions. The revolution became anti-"aristo," even for a time, anti-bourgeois. Ultimately, however, it was the traditional professional, official, and landowning bourgeoisie which gained most from the revolution, both in land and political power as well as within the state bureaucracy.[4] The Revolutionary and Napoleonic Wars (1792–1814/15) ensured that similar social changes occurred in the huge amounts of Europe France conquered. As in France the bourgeoisie bought confiscated church land and acquired jobs in the state bureaucracy. The year 1789 thus enriched the middle classes and defined bourgeois as a political category.

At the end of the eighteenth century Adam Smith was one of the first commentators to note that the old society of orders, where concepts of duty had in theory predominated, was being replaced by the idea of class, where entrepreneurial wealth was increasingly prominent. It was assumed that the bourgeoisie were the main beneficiaries of economic change, which was defined as either the triumph of liberal economics or capitalist exploitation, depending on the politics of the observer. In the early nineteenth century people became obsessed by the idea that society was dominated by class divisions and conflicts and that these inevitably led to political upheaval.

Economic modernization served to increase both the size and political power of bourgeois groups. For generations people believed the analysis made by Karl Marx in the second half of the nineteenth century. He asserted that economic development would inevitably mean that the entrepreneurial sections of the bourgeoisie would take over political power. In Russia the extravagant lifestyle of the nobility and their decreasing willingness to engage in trade and industry led to the rapid decline of some families. Within a couple of generations, long before the emancipation of the 1860s, ambitious serfs began to take a leading role in economic change, gain their freedom, and establish themselves in the cotton industry, banking, and trade. Families such as the Morozovs, transformed from serf ribbon sellers into a commercial and industrial bourgeoisie, dominated the government of St. Petersburg and Moscow in the second half of the nineteenth century.[5] Elsewhere, the high profile of cotton and railway kings encouraged the view that a capitalist bourgeoisie was taking power. Publicists like Samuel Smiles eagerly created the idea that entrepreneurial growth liberated society from old bonds, offering new opportunities for the "self-made" man. In the mid-eighteenth century the brewer Whitbread bought big estates and a seat in parliament. In 1830–1 successively two bankers, Jacques Laffitte and Casimir Périer, were chief ministers in France. Marx assumed that their elevation showed that the 1830 revolution had replaced the nobility with a financial aristocracy. In fact the·entrepreneurial middle classes were rarely "selfmade" Cinderellas; most business and industrial enterprises were created by established families.[6] Nor were entrepreneurs as numerous or as dominant in political life as the short-lived elevation of Laffitte (1830–1) and Périer (1831–2) might indicate (Périer died in the 1832 cholera epidemic).

Social change accompanying economic innovation was far less rapid than some commentators feared. Marx's expectation that a bourgeois revolution would occur was not realized. The revolutionaries in France in the 1790s raged about "aristos." Heads of families, many of them noble, who emigrated during the revolution lost some land, but the proportion of noble-owned land fell by only 5 percent to 20 percent. Recent research has shown that the nobility was still the richest group in France well into the second half of the nineteenth century. The revolutionaries abolished nobility in the 1790s, but Napoleon created new titles, and in 1814 a hereditary chamber of peers shared legislative power with an elected chamber. From 1831 no new hereditary titles were created in France, but families continued to luxuriate in the social snobbery of the plethora which survived, and to invent new ones. Both before and after 1789 French nobles shared political and economic power with the wealthier elements in the bourgeoisie. In Prussia nobles retained control of the top jobs in the state and army throughout the century, alongside some newer bourgeois families whose fortunes had been made in banking, trade, and industry. In Russia although the wealthy industrial and banking bourgeois families ran St. Petersburg and Moscow, successive tsars continued to appoint nobles as provincial governors, senior bureaucrats, and army officers. In addition, much of the investment for railway construction and rapid industrial growth in Russia at the end of the nineteenth century came from French, British, and German banks and did not stimulate the development of a native middle class. Thus in 1914 the Russian middle class was tiny, fragmented, and in no position to claim a substantial role in government.

In Britain the power and wealth of the aristocracy actually increased in the nineteenth century. Between the "Glorious Revolution" of 1688 and the 1780s the number of aristocratic families had stayed constant at about 200, but their wealth had grown immeasurably. Some, like the Bedfords and Devonshires, were richer than some German princes. Land was the basis of their wealth. There were the considerable rewards of patronage and government office. The richest owned very prosperous mines. All built or "improved" large houses on their country estates. Investment in trade and in innovative transport developments completed a portfolio more varied than that of most other European aristocrats. The emergence of a money market at the end of the seventeenth century offered the large landowner alternative investments in property development and as directors of joint stock companies. Britain was supremely dominated by aristocratic rather than bourgeois entrepreneurial groups, to an extent unmatched elsewhere in Europe.[7]

The Bourgeoisie and the State

It was the landed and professional middle classes, already established in state service, whose numbers and influence increased most rapidly in the century. The real bourgeois revolution was not so much a consequence of industrialization, as of the increase in the power of the state and the consequent vast growth in the number of official appointments at all levels from menial to managerial. These were often acquired by the middle classes, although the most senior posts in Russia, Germany, and elsewhere habitually went to nobles.

The growing number of opportunities for the middle classes in state service was gained at a cost. In the eighteenth century those who ran the judiciary in France, Prussia, and elsewhere had a degree of autonomy and could hold rulers at arm's length. Centralization meant the ruler exerted his total dominance. The response of state officials and professional groups, particularly lawyers and doctors, was to assert their claims to be heard by inventing a new language of political representation and national sovereignty of which they were the main beneficiaries. Lawyers and doctors took a lead in French politics in the 1790s. Faced with defeat by successful French armies, other European rulers accelerated their efforts to centralize and modernize the apparatus of the state. Previously semi-autonomous professional bodies were brought under the control of the rulers.

The Bourgeoisie and the Professions

Obviously, the professions predated 1800, but it was during the nineteenth century that the various professions took steps to "professionalize" themselves. Each profession turned itself into an almost impenetrable caste and gave this section of the bourgeoisie more of a common identity than other sectors of the middle class. Professionals saw themselves as a service elite, with a particular sensitivity to social duty and honor. With population increase, urbanization, industrialization, and above all the growing role of the state, the size and character of existing professions altered and new jobs jostled for recognition as professions. The need for definition became acute as traditional fee-earning professionals were joined by salaried sectors, the first being the expanding army of bureaucrats. They led the way by defining a new professional ideal in which public esteem rather than independence was the prime feature.

Professional men began to demand specific educational prerequisites for acolytes and standardize training under their corporate control to develop a new sense of professional identity. A profession became an increasingly closed corporation, similar to a medieval guild or a semisecret society, limiting membership by various means to protect "standards," but also to defend the income of existing members and to ensure that access to the professions was restricted to a wealthy bourgeois elite. In France in the 1860s, 80 percent of law students were upper middle class. It was common for sons to follow fathers as lawyers or doctors.

The very act of defining their profession to try to assert their social exclusivity and auton-

omy, which was close to the heart of lawyers, doctors, engineers, and so on, allowed state power to increase. Educational and professional qualifications and the role of the professions came increasingly under the scrutiny of the state. Doctors, lawyers, engineers, and teachers began to demand educational prerequisites, the first of which was a certificate of secondary education. These were taught and examined in state-run institutions. In Prussia degree courses were officially validated and no one could practice as a lawyer without a state appointment. In the early nineteenth century changes in the Prussian legal system made it the norm that after ten to twelve years of expensive legal training, a man had to spend nearly as long again working unpaid within the courts before he could hope to secure an official post. Even then his prospects for promotion were less than those of a generation earlier. In France, although lawyers could practice without an official post, they complained that the rationalization, standardization, and centralization involved in creating a single legal system for France in the 1790s reduced the autonomy of their profession.

Vocal sections of the leading professions remained critics of the state in the years up to 1848, and not entirely for selfish reasons. In Prussia and other German states members of the judiciary were prominent in demands for written constitutions on the model of the French constitution of 1814. Such individuals took the lead in the 1848 revolution. But partly because they were alarmed at the scale of popular unrest their protest engendered, lawyers were subsequently mostly transformed into faithful and obedient servants of autocracy. Their reward was employment; job opportunities in the German bureaucracy increased and from the early 1880s the growth was astronomical as lawyers were allowed to practice privately.

Bourgeois doctors had key roles in movements for social reform and in the 1848 republic in France. Their politicization was ethical and altruistic. A generation of European doctors was appalled at the social effects of industrial and urban change. In England in 1830 Dr. Kay drew attention to the plight of women and children cotton operatives. In

France Drs. Villermé and Buret wrote influential commentaries, the first detailing conditions among workers, especially women and children, in all of the textile industries, the second comparing their circumstances in England and France. Villermé, although sympathetic to capitalism, drew up the first French legislation restricting child labor. Republican socialist doctors like Guépin in Nantes and Raspail in Paris set up free clinics to help the poor. Professional associations were formed. The professions reinforced their social elitism, but ironically they continued to be drawn into an expanding state bureaucracy, doctors vaccinating children against smallpox, taking part in state health insurance schemes, and so on.

Bourgeois Attitudes

Education

Education was crucial to the growth, definition, and development of middle-class groups. The huge expansion of education during the century was the product of middle-class initiative and was mainly for their benefit. Secondary and tertiary education was formalized by the introduction of state-administered secondary leaving certificates as well as certificates for specialized tertiary colleges. Revolutionary France led the way. Much-criticized church-run secondary establishments were replaced by *lycées* providing a secular, state-run education. In 1808 the baccalaureate, or secondary leaving examination, was introduced. The failings of existing universities were compensated for by the creation of high level colleges for aspiring state engineers, civil servants, and army officers. These included a series of *grandes écoles*, the *école polytechnique*, *écoles des mines*, *école des ponts et chaussées*, and others. Other states imitated the French example.

Such secondary and tertiary education was strictly limited to the elite by cost and content; high fees and obligatory Latin. There were some scholarships to the Napoleonic *lycées* in France, but they were available mainly to sons of officials and army officers. Secondary school-leaving certificates, such as the new baccalaureate in France and the *Abitur* in Germany, were rarely completed by pupils from poorer families. They became prerequisites for professional training and access to higher education.

Secondary education was enjoyed by a tiny bourgeois minority. In France roughly 60 percent of candidates, constituting 0.5 percent of the age cohort, successfully passed the baccalaureate. From 1812 secondary education in the German states consisted of annual examinations which had to be repeated if the student failed, culminating in the *Abitur*. In 1820, 1,000 boys passed the *Abitur*. By 1830 this number had doubled, but was to fall subsequently due to a panic that there was a glut of qualified men, who were likely to be disaffected. Only in 1860 did the figure rise again to 2,000. In Germany in 1870 only 0.8 percent of 19 year olds had the *Abitur*; in 1911, it was 1.2 percent. As in France and elsewhere, many pupils left without the *Abitur*, or attended other schools teaching the far less prestigious modern/scientific *Abitur*.

The secondary syllabus, whether in a French *lycée* or a *Gymnasium* in Germany, Italy, or Russia, was almost 50 percent Latin and Greek. In a Prussian *Gymnasium* typically 46 percent of the time was spent on Latin and Greek, 17.5 percent on maths, physics, and philosophy, and 4 percent was devoted to French. Until well into the second half of the nineteenth century only the full classical secondary schools were allowed to prepare pupils for the secondary leaving certificate. Middle-class families often preferred classical secondary education, which would have no direct career significance even when more modern scientific and technical alternatives emerged later in the century. There was a common assumption that unmitigated scientific learning bred socially discontented citizens, even revolutionaries. Classical learning conferred status. In some countries, Russia for instance, it gave automatic exemption from military service and a position in the Table of Ranks, the elite system developed by Peter the Great in the early eighteenth century that led, through state service, to noble rank. In Germany, too, classical education was regarded as a sign of status. In 1879 German civil engineers objected that graduates of non-classical secondary schools should qualify for their branch of state service, not because they made any use whatsoever of classical languages in their work, but because they claimed classical learning was character building and conferred status on their profession. The upper layers of the middle class tried to use education to define themselves and create an impermeable barrier to social advance from below.

Education was a tool manipulated by the middle classes for social control as much as for enlightenment. Primary schooling was developed to train the lower middle class and urban and rural workers to accept their station in life. Primary schooling was a dead end. There was no opportunity to transfer from a primary to a secondary school. Primary schooling provided basic learning in the preferred national language and taught obedience to the state. Technical schools provided the chance to "advance" to foreman status, and teacher training colleges allowed sons and daughters of the lower classes to train as primary school teachers. Education was strictly divided along gender as well as class lines. Until almost the end of the century girls were not educated beyond primary levels and in Roman Catholic states many girls' schools were run by nuns.

Women and the family

The family was honored as the basic unit of society by all nineteenth-century bourgeois observers. Only a tiny number of socialists and the occasional satirist doubted the significance of the institution. Monogamous, lifelong marriage was the norm. Families were essentially patriarchal. In France the authority of the father was enhanced by the new Civil Code, completed in 1804. A wife lost all control over the dowry she brought to a marriage; if she worked, her income was paid to her husband; she could not hold a bank account without her husband's consent; her husband could dictate where she lived. In 1814 the law permitting divorce, which had been voted in 1792, was abolished and not restored until 1884. The alternative, "bodily separation," was automatic if a wife committed adultery, but a wife could only secure such a declaration if her husband demanded that she cohabit with him and his mistress.

Throughout the nineteenth century an adult French woman had the status of a child.

In other countries a woman's status was no better, although there were some improvements in the legal and political rights of women in Britain towards the end of the century. In some respects France was less retrograde than others. The inheritance laws passed during the revolution gave equal distribution of property among all surviving offspring, regardless of sex. In reality wealthy bourgeois families, like the aristocracy, effectively practiced primogeniture. In other countries where primogeniture was the norm, only the male could inherit. In all states middle-class women only achieved a degree of independence when they were widowed. Then their autonomy would depend on how wealthy their husband had been. Even by the end of the century a sign of middle-class respectability was that women did not work for a living outside the home. Confining a daughter and a wife to a totally domestic sphere was proof of a family's prosperity. In the artisan economy, when workshops adjoined the home, wives had been accustomed to keep the books. As factories developed, wives were restricted to raising the children and managing the servants and the home.

Women were often idealized as the spiritual and moral force within the family. The Roman Catholic cult of the Virgin Mary served to intensify this notion, which was vital to the image of the Catholic church because, increasingly, it was only the women who attended services. As a consequence women took a prominent role in organizing charity, running laying-in societies and crèches. Through charitable and educational organizations run through the various churches bourgeois women in Protestant and Catholic societies found a public role outside the home.

Morality and sexuality

That women were held to be endowed with particular spiritual and moral qualities was based on the assumption that the sexual make-up of men and women was different. Well into the modern period scientists believed that procreation was entirely initiated by the male. It was argued that males produced both sperm and ova. The male implanted both into the uterus of the female, who was merely the receptacle in which the embryo was nurtured. Although scientists exposed the fallacy of this assumption, the corollary, that women were mere passive tools in sexual activity, persisted during the nineteenth century. The sex drive was held to be unique to the male, women merely endured sex with dutiful stoicism. Only the male possessed a passionate nature.

Sexual morality was thus a very different matter for the two sexes. A high and polygamous sex drive was held to be an essential feature of masculinity. It was quite normal for the male to be fully sexually active long before marriage with whatever range of partners was available, from family servants to prostitutes. On the other hand, unmarried women were supposed to be ignorant and uninterested in sex. After marriage some cultures expected the husband to seek and maintain a mistress or mistresses. A French wife would be likely to consider her husband inadequate if there was no mistress in the background. Whether or not extramarital attachments were an expected part of sexual morality, it was assumed that husbands would be discrete and publicly hold to monogamy. The wife, however, was expected to feel no urge to stray. Any criticism of this hypocritical standard caused uproar. The early socialist Fourier urged that a harmonious society would only emerge when women were liberated to acknowledge that they had the same urge for a variety of sexual partners as men. Building on his ideas, which Fourier expressed in so obscure a language that few read his books, the Saint-Simonians recommended trial marriage and multiple sexual partners. As a consequence, in 1832 their leaders, Prosper Enfantin and Michel Chevalier, were arraigned on a charge of subverting public morality and imprisoned.

This ambivalent code of sexual conduct was particularly bourgeois. Royal and aristocratic men were often flagrantly and colorfully immoral, while an even odder double standard was applied to the poor, who, it was believed, lacked respect for even formal codes of sexual morality. Prostitution was seen as an unavoidable consequence of the need of men for sexual experience and opportunity. Since bourgeois wives were assumed to be sexually frigid, sexual hygiene demanded a pool of available women to satisfy male needs. Poor women filled the void, but it was never totally clear whether prostitutes were supposed to act solely from financial need, or whether poorer women were thought to have sexual appetites because they were nearer to lower orders in the animal kingdom. What did become apparent during the century was that unsupervised prostitution led to an alarming increase in sexually transmitted diseases, particularly syphilis.

Culture and leisure

Culture was another area where the middle classes exercised an increasing influence on the whole of society. By the beginning of the century the age of the private patron of the arts was rapidly giving way to patronage by the state and municipalities. Art galleries, museums, theatres, concert halls, and libraries were built by governments, local authorities, and sometimes by private associations of wealthy citizens. The first public art gallery was opened in Vienna in 1781, and in Paris the Louvre opened in 1793. The National Gallery in London was launched in 1823 when the Austrians repaid their war loan. Soon municipal pride demanded that every substantial town had its own gallery/museum. The main consumers of such culture were bourgeois citizens and their families; the poor were excluded by price, or a variety of strategies. The British Museum, which opened in 1759, demanded a letter requesting a ticket of admission. Such establishments provided "rational recreation" approved by middle-class opinion.

Royal and noble private collectors of art were joined by the most wealthy bourgeois, who bought at annual salons or by direct commission. Industrialists and businessmen in northern England amassed impressive collections of art. A prosperous dry-salter in Manchester, William Hardman, owned paintings by Titian, Canaletto, Veronese, Ruisdael, Rembrandt, Wilson, Wright, and Fuesli. A family of Manchester cotton manufacturers, the Ashtons, owned a collection that included Constable, Turner, Collins, Holman Hunt, Egg, and Leighton.[8] Thomas Holloway, a manufacturer of patent medicines, not only collected Constable, Turner, Holman Hunt, and other fashionable artists, but also endowed a women's college that became part of the University of London and a sanatorium. Similar examples can be cited throughout Europe. In Moscow a small number of serfs who had bought their freedom and gone on to become millionaires also amassed art collections. The present outstanding collection of Impressionist art in the Tretyakov gallery is the result of such enterprise. Savva Morozov, whose family began as itinerant serf ribbon sellers, helped to found the Moscow Arts Theatre.[9]

The middle classes busied themselves running academies and literary societies such as the Literary and Philosophical Society (Manchester, 1781; Leeds, 1819). Mechanics' Institutes and Schools of Design were popular. They organized art exhibitions and concerts. In Manchester there were Gentlemen's Concerts, and a calico printer named Hermann Leo initiated Charles Hallé's long-lasting orchestral association with the city in 1848. In Leeds the musical association organized recitals in members' homes.[10]

Middle-class observers poured scorn on the preferred leisure activities of workers, music halls, prize fights, and public hangings. Middle-class pressure groups made the second and third of these illegal (1868) and music halls were subject to constant criticism because they combined food and entertainment with, worst of all, strong drink. Temperance and Sunday Observance societies were always busy to ensure that the working classes did not enjoy their very limited leisure. During the nineteenth century municipalities and private charities run by the middle classes began to "civilize" working people by creating public reading rooms and libraries and providing better housing, hospitals, and clinics for working people.

For those with money, leisure was a way of life, not just a matter of a few hours' rational recreation. Until the improvement of roads and especially the construction of railways that made even distant places easily accessible, the European bourgeoisie was inclined to ape the aristocracy and "do the season." The whole family would spend several months of the summer away from home. Spa towns such as Bath were attractive to wealthy families. Town centers were developed with luxury housing and public gardens in which the wealthy could "promenade" safely for hours, discussing marriages (and more informal liaisons) and maybe business arrangements. Elegant and commodious Assembly Rooms were built to house their entertainment. Here too there was space to show off glamorous and fashionable clothes, to see, and even more important, to be seen. Leisure activities, theatre companies, exhibitions, even waxworks adapted by touring from town to town to capture and serve this temporarily static captive market. Madame Tussaud, who brought her collection of wax royals and revolutionary deaths' heads from Paris in 1802, spent the next 33 years touring Britain and Ireland. Pickfords' removal company did well on such touring. Madame Tussaud acquired her own fleet of touring caravans built with the Tussaud's logo painted on the side in gold letters. As soon as there was a dip in profits in Brighton she would load up her growing collection of coronation displays and executed villains and move on to the next center of bourgeois recreation.

The railway revolutionized leisure and entertainment. It put Brighton a mere two hours from London. Although the cost was still substantial (in 1862 the price of a ticket was only one-third less than a coach ticket in 1820), far more people made the trip. On Easter Monday 1862, 132,000 people took the Brighton train. The "season" was dead. The middle classes went to Brighton for a day, indeed it became so crowded that the very rich abandoned the place. Theatre companies and others began to travel far less. The railway meant that customers rather than the entertainment did the traveling. At first most of this traveling was limited to the comfortably off, although special excursion trains allowed workers to go on day trips to the sea. In 1846 a mill in Swinton negotiated the first trip to Blackpool for its workers for 1 shilling per return trip. In general, however, cheap tickets came much later; third class carriages were introduced in the 1870s.

As travel became less a mark of prosperity, the rich began to travel further. Queen Victoria set the trend when she decamped from the Royal Pavilion in Brighton, but she set her sights modestly on the Isle of Wight. Others mimicked the aristocratic Grand Tour of earlier times by venturing abroad. Normandy became popular with the British, but the Mediterranean more chic. The tourist population of Nice rose from 575 in the winter of 1815 to 5,000 by 1861. There were fifty hotels in the city, twenty more than in 1847.[11]

The concept that leisure should be built into the working life of the less wealthy middle classes developed. Annual seaside holidays within Britain became the norm. Thomas Cook led the way. The first Cook excursions were to the Great Exhibition of 1851. As government legislation gradually limited the working day, leisure was no longer confined to the middle classes. In Britain a 10 hour working day became the law in 1847, in France in 1848. Some firms introduced half-day work for Saturdays. In 1871 in Britain came a Bank Holiday Act and paid holidays were gradually introduced. Leisure ceased to be the preserve of the bourgeoisie.

Consumption

With increasing prosperity bourgeois women became the spearhead of a consumer society. The center was the department store that provided for, or invented, all domestic needs. For the first time one store could provide clothes, shoes, hats, and underwear for the entire family, plus bedding, towels, furniture, jewelry, cosmetics, and even food. The first department stores opened in the 1860s. In Paris, capital of culture at the time, the most famous, the *Bon Marché*, was the first, opened by Aristide Boucicaut and his wife in 1869. It was to be Emile Zola's model for *Au Bonheur des dames* (1883) in which he tried "to create the poetry of modern activity."[12]

Department stores revolutionized mere shopping, creating a new culture of consumption. The main customers were bourgeois ladies, attracted by the safety, respectability, comfort, cleanliness, and elegance of the buildings, which were well lit and fitted. Stores stressed that ladies could visit their stores knowing that nothing would jar with their feminine sensibility and moral uprightness. The department store was a freely available public space, but the female cus-

tomers were reassured that it was a home-from-home that they could visit alone, unlike a theatre or concert hall, where it was assumed ladies would have a male escort.

The stores did far more than satisfy the needs of their customers. They also taught them what they ought to buy. In the later years of the century the catalogues of these "palaces of purchasing" shaped the standards of the middle-class home. They taught those who aspired to be more middle class the ground rules of the game. The stores and their catalogues cultivated a fantasy of culture, decorating the departments to turn them into an enchanting fairyland of design, color, and light. The shopper was invited to move from her own mundane domestic existence to a dream world of exciting drapery, mirrors, entrancing perfumes, and endlessly courteous staff.[13] Department stores presented themselves as the peak of modernity. Technical advances facilitated this process, whether it was plate-glass windows to replace earlier tiny panes of glass, or gas and later electric lighting. This was still luxury consumption for a small elite, but with the appealing illusion of democratic availability.

These "churches" to consumerism were staffed by male and female employees. Stores stressed that their sales staff were a "cut above" the average worker. Unlike the women seamstresses of earlier times who were often obliged to supplement their meager earnings with prostitution, department stores watched over the moral welfare of their employees. Their paternalism knew no bounds; the store presented the illusion that it was a philanthropic family rather than a commercial enterprise.[14] Wages were low, but all staff received free meals. In the *Bon Marché* an upper floor housed a large kitchen and four dining rooms exclusively for staff. These were carefully segregated by sex and status. The largest dining room, reserved for men, could serve meals to 800 people at one sitting. The women sales staff ate in one room, the women who were employed in the workshops in another. Department stores also provided accommodation for their employees on the upper floors. A total of 90 young men and women were housed in-store at the *Bon Marché* in 1878. The shop took care to segregate male and female living quarters strictly.

Care was also taken to civilize sales staff so that customers' sensibilities would not be harmed. There was a common room for the women residents which had a piano, a real sign of bourgeois respectability. The men had a games room with a billiard table. In 1872 the store offered employees free evening classes in English and German at the store. The best English students were sent to London for sixth months' tuition at the expense of the store. There were also lecturers in science, literature, and history to occupy the evening hours. In addition, the Boucicauts provided in-store free evening fencing and music lessons. There was a library with 400 volumes and evening concerts for staff, who were taught to mimic their bourgeois customers in all but income. Finally, in what came close to Fourier's ideal of a socialist community, there was a doctor on duty to provide free consultations for employees. Staff were encouraged to save money by a bonus of 6 percent interest on savings accounts at the store. In 1886, 3,200,000 francs had been banked by 927 employees.[15]

Associations – from political to social

The middle classes organized themselves into, and excluded the poor from, a vast range of associations, from cultural and sporting to political. Even in sporting fraternities there were attempts to exclude working people from participation. The most successful associations from which workers and also women were excluded were representative assemblies. The liberal bourgeoisie tried to manage their rulers and contain the potential subversive poor by asserting the principle of the sovereignty of the nation in elections. The French revolutionaries experimented unsuccessfully with representative institutions in the 1790s and acquired a dictatorial emperor at the head of their modernized state. After the Napoleonic Wars British radicals demanded reform of the House of Commons and the French argued over voting rights within a constitution modeled to some degree on that of Britain. Campaigns for suffrage reform were mainly (but not entirely) the initiative of middle-class reformers. In Britain the Chartist movement of the 1830s and

1840s, backed by some members of the lower middle classes, artisans, and better-off factory workers, pressed for a democratic electorate, as did societies like the mainly middle-class Friends of the People in France. The French enfranchised all adult males after the 1848 revolution and in 1867 all male householders got the vote in Britain. Elected assemblies at all levels, municipal to national, gradually became the norm in all countries. Until 1919 none rivaled the French by enfranchising all adult males. Few worried that the 50 percent of adults who happened to be female had no vote.

The extension of the right to vote tended to perpetuate traditional elites. In Britain the Reform Act of 1832 had no impact on the composition of parliament. In 1840, 80 percent of members still represented the landed interest and the proportion of bourgeois entrepreneurs (97 of a total of 658 MPs) was the same as at the end of the eighteenth century. Perhaps this was unsurprising, given the limited nature of the legislation. However, the same was true in France, even after the introduction of universal male suffrage in 1848. In 1861 the new united Italy adopted a 40 lira tax qualification for voters, which produced an electorate comparable to that of France before 1848. The Italian ruling elite was not only wealthy, it was also almost exclusively northern. Universal male suffrage had to wait until 1919. Frederick William IV of Prussia established a graded suffrage for the elected *Landtag* in 1849 which allowed the richest 18 percent of taxpayers to elect two-thirds of the new legislative assembly he created. The *Reichstag*, the representative assembly for the whole German empire created in 1871, was elected by all adult males, but the government was appointed by the emperor, not the majority in parliament. When elected local councils, *Zemstvos*, were set up in Russia in the 1860s and an imperial parliament or *Duma* after the 1905 revolution, an even narrower hierarchical voting system was inaugurated. Elected assemblies only began to find a role for themselves in Russia during World War I. Unsurprisingly, in an age of unpaid MPs, assemblies tended to be staffed by, as well as represent the interests of, wealthy bourgeois elites. In Germany a decreasing number of MPs were businessmen or industrialists. By 1914 the socialists were the largest single group in both the German *Reichstag* and the French assembly, and a growing, though a very divided, number in Italy. In the German *Reichstag* a majority of both socialist voters and assembly members were workers, a situation facilitated by a salary paid by the SPD to members of the assembly. Over half the German socialist MPs (122 out of 215) were journalists.[16] In France and Italy, where socialists were considered heirs of the revolutionary tradition, the proportion of lower middle-class socialist voters was much higher and the assembly members were predominantly middle class, often lawyers.

Throughout the century middle-class groups were concerned that radicals and socialists would exploit the very evident social and economic inequalities which increased as a result of modern industrialization. Marx preached inevitable proletarian revolution as the ultimate consequence of capitalist development. However, although the century was punctuated with revolutions in 1830, 1848, and in 1871 in Paris, tensions were defused by social insurance schemes, private and state-run, by the legalization of trades unions, by the provision of state-organized education, and by the unifying impact of compulsory military service. The development of parliamentary institutions created the illusion of consultation and democratic control and the promotion of nationalist and imperialistic sentiments stimulated the illusion of all social groups sharing common goals. The Socialist International's demand for international proletarian solidarity in 1914 went unheard. Yet, although society may not have become polarized quite in the way socialists (including Marx) had predicted, the gap between rich and poor widened. This was most visible at the top. In Britain in 1803 the top 2 percent owned 20 percent of the wealth of the country; by 1867 they owned 40 percent.

Wealth had always corresponded pretty closely to power. The elites of the nineteenth century institutionalized the equation, while pretending to eliminate privilege. Hierarchically structured education systems, professions, and assemblies of all sorts, plus improved policing, military control, and the monitoring and managing of public opinion, allowed a narrow section of society to dominate. One should take care, however, not to assume that this was a "bourgeois" century. As we have seen, at the very top, aristocratic families maintained their economic, social, and political control. Within the bourgeoisie the dominant professional middle classes were not part of a "class," but a series of powerful corporate interest groups. The extent of their privilege is masked when they are labeled a "class" and particularly when they are lumped together with the numerically much more numerous lower middle classes and white collar workers, who took up minor posts in the massive bureaucratic expansion of the second half of the century.

Politics

We have seen that Marx's argument that the financial, commercial, and industrial bourgeoisie constituted a consolidated ascendant class, destined to become politically dominant, was not applicable in the nineteenth century. Professional and bureaucratic elements tended to take the lead in elected bodies, voluntary associations, and in government. If there was no united middle class, to what extent did shared attitudes give the bourgeoisie common political ideas? Certain common political concepts can be identified, including a belief in human progress, in the existence of national identity, in the usefulness of education, in constitutional government, in the value of individual effort, in the significance of family structures, and in individual freedom. However, when these basics are tested, it is quickly apparent that all of them, particularly constitutional government and individual freedom, meant different things to different groups at different times. In addition, some of these political concepts would be shared with social groups both below and above the middle classes. Liberalism is often spoken of as the creed of the middle classes. In reality, as we have seen, although many members of the middle classes may have favored somewhat elitist, rather than democratic, political systems, the middle classes ranged among all political formations and attitudes, from right wing to socialists, from nationalist to internationalist, and from laissez faire to more protectionist economic ideas.

Conclusion: How Homogeneous was Bourgeois Society?

Although it is easy to use terms like "the bourgeoisie" or "middle class society," the aim of this chapter has been to encourage the reader to appreciate the diversity and huge range of occupations, income, and attitudes within the bourgeoisie. Middle-class groups came nearest to unity in ideas on education, on the family, the role of women, and on culture. They were furthest apart on politics. If bourgeois liberalism had been a reality instead of a myth and a convenient shorthand, the liberals would have united to secure liberal constitutional as well as economic objectives[17] in return for their concurrence with Bismarck's cynical manipulation of nationalist sentiments, the constitutional monarchy would have triumphed over fascism in Italy, and the Russian Revolution would have been avoided. Class did not correspond to political interest and identity.

NOTES

1 Pilbeam (1990: 1–22); Maza (2003); Harrison (1999).
2 Blackbourn and Evans (1991: 1–10).
3 Pilbeam (1996).
4 Cobban (1964). For a recent synthesis, see Sutherland (2003).
5 Rieber (1992).
6 Wahrman (1995).
7 Lieven (1992).
8 Wolff and Arscott (1990: 33).
9 Pilbeam (1990: 36).
10 Wolff and Arscott (1990: 33).
11 Haug (1982: 17).
12 Miller (1981).
13 Williams (1982).
14 Miller (1981: 225).
15 Ibid: 105–8.
16 Blackbourn (1992).
17 Prussian liberals secured substantial legislation promoting their notions of economic liberalism in return for their tolerance of Bismarck's nationalist policies in the 1860s. See Kitchen (1978).

GUIDE TO FURTHER READING

Pilbeam's "From Orders to Classes" provides a brief overview of European society. A more detailed survey of the middle classes can be read in her *Middle Classes in Europe*, which focuses on Germany, Italy, France, and Russia. Bush's *Social Orders and Social Classes in Europe since 1500* contains chapters on aspects of different countries, while Crossick and Haupt's *Shopkeepers and Master Artisans* offers a comparative analysis of sections of the lower middle class. The upper echelons of the bourgeoisie are examined in Howarth and Cerny's *Elites in France*, Higgs's *Nobles in Nineteenth-Century France*, and Lieven's *Aristocracy in Europe*. For greater detail on the middle classes in different countries it would be worth consulting Blackbourn and Evans' *German Bourgeoisie*, Kitchen's *Political Economy of Germany*, Evans's *Forging of the Modern State*, Raeff's *Understanding Imperial Russia*, Rieber's *Merchants and Entrepreneurs in Imperial Russia*, Shubert's *Social History of Modern Spain*, and Davis's *Italy in the Nineteenth Century*. Bourgeois culture may be approached through Miller's *Bon Marché*, Pilbeam's *Madame Tussaud*, Schwartz's *Spectacular Realities*, and Williams's *Dream Worlds*.

CHAPTER EIGHT

The Disappearance of the Traditional Artisan

JAMES R. FARR

The "Traditional" Artisan

Most historians agree that the "traditional artisan" disappeared during the nineteenth century.[1] Multiple forces – legal, political, demographic, and economic – converged during the era of industrialization, and one result was the destruction of the culture of the traditional European artisan and the consequent transformation of his identity. There is little doubt that Europe's cities in 1750 held hundreds of thousands of men (and some women) who more or less conform to the cultural profile of the "traditional artisan" and by 1900 very few did. But what was the "traditional artisan"? A danger of a general characterization is underrepresentation of heterogeneity and diversity within the ranks of the artisanry and overdetermination of similarities. And yet, amid all of this diversity, certain salient qualities stand out that most artisans shared, and these qualities in turn comprised the constituent parts of a more or less coherent European artisan culture that had endured for half a millennium before the nineteenth century and had been largely obliterated by the outbreak of World War I in 1914.

According to varieties of records where individuals were identified by occupational labels, artisans in the eighteenth century comprised varying percentages of the overall population of Europe's cities and a dwindling proportion of the inhabitants of the countryside. Whereas

perhaps 5 percent of Europe's rural population were artisans (and many of these doubled as farmers), the numbers in the cities ranged from nearly 80 percent of the male citizenry in Nördlingen in 1724, to about 40 percent in Madrid in 1757, to 25 percent in Dijon in 1750. These figures represent males, and although there were females who practiced handicrafts (notably seamstresses), the profile of the traditional artisan is a masculine one because, if little consensus can be gained from artisanal demographics, something most urban artisans had in common was the importance in their lives of organizations called guilds, and with only rare exceptions these were exclusively male in membership. As is well known, these institutions had regulatory powers governing economic activities, largely focused on containing competition through monopolies over the production and sale of specified commodities to preserve the livelihood of artisans and channel quality goods to the consuming public at a fair price.

The guild, however, was more than an economic institution. Indeed, the guild was a central cog in a theoretical system of order that emerged in the late Middle Ages and endured into the nineteenth century that historians call corporatism.[2] Corporatism, and the guild that was one of its fundamental institutions, was a constitutional system that did not simply organize work, but framed artisan lives by a representation of status and rank based upon the cherished principles of paternalism, hierarchy, and discipline of subordinates. Membership in guilds proclaimed a certain status for the guildsman, and thus access to this charmed circle (among guild artisans called mastership) was closely regulated. An entire way of life rested upon the corporate ideal.

Until recently, historians had argued that the guilds with their elaborate regulatory system had impeded economic activity and stifled economic growth. More recent research has proved this assumption mistaken, supporting instead a view of normal economic practice as a freewheeling affair where licit and illicit activity constantly revealed how inadequate the regulatory apparatus was to actual production, distribution, and consumption. Indeed, the "pre-industrial" craft economy holds many similarities with that of the nineteenth century; as we will see, the difference being often one of scale rather than kind.

The craft economy in pre-industrial Europe could be quite complex, with many sectors of it immersed in a diversified and far-flung market economy long before historians have customarily assumed.[3] Galloping diversity and specialization were characteristics that already marked the urban artisanry since the late seventeenth century, in some places even earlier, catalyzed by a "consumer revolution" that spiked demand, and would continue apace well past 1850. Because of this diversity and specialization in the division of labor, the most noteworthy feature of production in artisanal manufacturing was its decentralization. Artisans produced according to the logic of "constant returns to scale," an economic rationality whereby "growth of output required proportional growth of the inputs of labor and raw materials."[4] In a system guided by such logic, expansion was accomplished by increasing the quantities of labor and materials rather than by enlarging the physical plant because concentrated production was cumbersome, relatively expensive, and fraught with the problem of labor indiscipline (a product, in part, of the well-organized journeymen brotherhoods that affected labor markets). As long as manufacturing operated according to the logic of constant returns to scale, pressures to expand production exerted by increased demand, then,

would be accommodated by decentralization, not concentration. Only gradually over the course of the eighteenth and nineteenth centuries did manufacturers abandon this logic and the decentralized production it called for, embracing piecemeal economies of scale in some product lines where high volume, standardized and concentrated production would become the rule.

Most artisanal enterprises, even for much of the nineteenth century, did not organize according to scale, however, and responded to increasing demand by a proliferation of very small and increasingly specialized trades linked by elaborate and complex networks of subcontracting. The manufacture of the gun nicely illustrates such an interconnected system of production. Ostensibly made by the gunmaker, by the eighteenth century it in fact involved nine different craft processes as the lock, stock, and barrel passed through different "independent" shops on its way to final assembly in the gunmaker's shop.

Subcontracting was a rational application of the logic of constant returns to scale. The organization of labor followed this logic as well. It appears that from the Middle Ages right into the nineteenth century master artisans in many towns had kept a core of well-trained workers (usually journeymen but sometimes fellow masters jobbing themselves out) in permanent employment, and, when business was good, added workers (sometimes journeymen, but also non-guild semi-skilled wage workers) drawn from the mass of migrants that wandered from town to town seeking work, and laid them off when business slowed. A minority of artisans therefore formed a sedentary core surrounded by a periphery of transients in short-term employment.

In 1791 in Paris, for instance, the fifteen largest hat-making shops employed an average of over sixty workers each, with each employee assigned a particular task. Similarly, among the locksmiths of Marseille in 1782 about 4 percent of the masters employed almost 20 percent of the journeymen available in the labor market in shops with nine or more, but 80 percent of the masters there employed half of the journeymen in shops of three or fewer workers. Or take the joiners of Amiens in 1765–6, where the pattern of concentration and peripheralization is even more pronounced. There, 90 percent of the masters employed half of the available journeymen and put them to work in shops where they worked alongside three or fewer of their fellows, while only 3 percent of the masters hired nearly a quarter of the available journeymen, putting them to work in shops where they were joined by more than ten of their fellows.

For the majority of artisans – master, journeyman, or semi-skilled wageworker – economic insecurity was a constant fact of life. Margins were thin, and unemployment often came with the next sag in demand or bottleneck in distribution. The logic of constant returns to scale, subcontracting arrangements, and organizing labor relations in cores and peripheries did little to allay the fears that arose from such insecurity, but they did preserve the image of independence so staunchly defended by artisans, masters and journeymen alike. The tradition of independence among artisans had deep roots, and one's claim to respectability and therefore the all-important social status in a hierarchical society hinged upon maintaining it. Artisans would cherish these values well into the nineteenth century.

Independence was the badge of respectable social rank for artisans, and thus was at the core of their identity and culture. From the late Middle Ages well into the nineteenth century artisans were defined and defined themselves not primarily as producers as their occupational labels may suggest, but rather as members of an *état*, a rank or "degree," a *Stand*. Occupational label signaled less what an artisan did (it often did not) than his status, and status shaped identity (artisanal, or any other during the Old Regime). Status-based identity, moreover, was rooted in community, groups of people cohering around shared values and activities, formed through erecting and maintaining boundaries between an imagined "us" and "them." To keep the howling chaos of experience at bay, groups imagine boundaries of their communities in part by locating and defining activities in specified places – homes, workplaces, churches, taverns, alehouses, pubs, and so on – and delimiting who belongs within them. By including or excluding individuals from those places or from performing those activities, they

spell out the membership of the group, and so contribute to the ongoing process of shaping a culture. Moreover, the bonds of community and the desire of craftsmen to construct them often entailed great attention to ritual and ceremony.[5] As we will see, as sites changed and membership altered with the growing dominance of commercialized mass culture in the final decades of the nineteenth century, the intensely communal quality of traditional artisan culture was eroded.

It is worth recalling that social structure, far from being a static given, is the constantly renewed and revised product of human agency, however much that agency is framed by inherited circumstances. Simultaneously and inextricably artisans established and reestablished their place within the taxonomic structure of society through an apprehension of difference, distinction, and status. Old Regime taxonomy was a structured system of hierarchical differences which reached its high-water mark in the seventeenth century, and as society's elites increasingly distanced themselves from the craftsmen, artisans in turn became increasingly keen on defining the distance between themselves and their inferiors. At all social levels this process of dissociation was visualized by cultural markers, and artisanal status swung on the hinge of respectability based on independence. For the master craftsman, respectability could mean economic solvency and heading one's own reputable business and respectable household, while for a journeyman it surely meant being subject to no one's discipline, with no restrictions on one's freedom of movement.

However segmented the traditional artisanry had been, most artisans entered the nineteenth century with a corporate, communal sense of themselves, and exited it without one. In the interim, they had passed through a filter that dismantled the political, legal, and intellectual framework of corporatism, and, while suffering the unrestrained violence of the capitalistic market and eventually the emergence of a commercialized mass culture that engulfed them, left them to their own devices to shape a new meaning to their existence, and a new sense of who they were. The traditional conceptual tools for making sense of the world gradually ceased to be adequate to reduce it to meaning and to place oneself satisfyingly within it. The template against which status was measured and identity was constituted was irrevocably transformed, and the traditional artisan disappeared as a result.

The Splintering of the Artisanry in the Nineteenth Century

Over the course of the nineteenth century corporatism was gradually supplanted by a rival ideology: liberalism. Both articulated organizing principles which informed social, legal, political, and economic life. Where corporatism embraced the principles of collectivism, paternalism, hierarchy, and discipline in the social and political realm, and the economic principle of containing competition and channeling production and distribution toward what was perceived as the public good, liberalism subsumed everything within the principles of self-determined and autonomous individuals seeking self-interest in an unregulated or "free" economy based in what was thought to be "natural" market exchange (often called "liberty of commerce").[6]

Liberal legislation was often enacted piecemeal, and was sometimes repealed, but the trend over the nineteenth century was clear. As liberalism triumphed it proved corrosive to corporatism in general and to guilds in particular. For a guild member before the nineteenth century, rank had been represented by mastership and guild membership, conferring a distinction which helped secure a living, but also which conferred a social identity. The abolition of corporatism undermined that.

All corporate bodies, including guilds, were officially abolished in France by the Allarde Law enacted on March 17, 1791. Between 1808 and 1811 Prussian guilds lost their legal privileges through a series of laws, and even though guilds were not formally abolished, it was no longer necessary to belong to one to practice a trade. A citizen simply needed to pay a licensing fee. In Spain guilds met their demise in 1812, in Sweden in 1847, in Austria in 1859. The list could be extended. In 1869 the North German Confederation passed legislation for freedom of trade (a key component of liberalism and antithetical to corporatism), and that law was adopted by the German Reich in 1871.

The abolition of corporatism was not the only development that undermined traditional artisan culture. Population growth across Europe in the late eighteenth and nineteenth centuries triggered overcrowding and underemployment in most trades in most of Europe's cities, and the market for consumer goods that moved more regularly by developments in the transport system, expanded dramatically and became increasingly well integrated. This opened up local markets as never before and introduced greater competition, often on a national scale. "Liberty of commerce" brought the deregulation of prices, of craft entry, and of production levels, all of which structurally altered most trades in the towns of Europe well before mechanization and factory production became the norm.

In Prussia between 1800 and 1843, for instance, the handicrafts remained steady at about 15 percent of the total population, but because the numbers of Prussians surged by 50 percent, the ranks of the artisans swelled and led to severe overcrowding in trades.[7] To take another example, in France in 1815 population growth and underemployment in the country side drove migrants to cities where many tried to practice a craft. Unregulated entry into the trades, however, resulted in overcrowding here as well. By the1830s and 1840s the French working world was rumbling with discontent. One result was the emergence of the workers movement, treated elsewhere in this volume. Some decentralized custom work certainly gave way to concentrated factory production. But for those artisans who did not slide into the ranks of factory workers, what became of them? Many shifted to repair work, others to specialized retailing of factory-produced goods, marketing products locally that were imported from other areas via factors and national merchant operations. But a surprising number remained in small-scale production.

Determining the fate of the traditional artisan immediately comes up against a question of typology. Even contemporaries were unclear about what to label "artisans" in their censuses in the nineteenth century. In Great Britain in the 1860s the terms "working man" and "artisan" were still interchangeable and meant, according to Patrick Joyce, "the skilled, respectable working man."[8] Such a definition would have rung familiarly in the ears of artisans of a century earlier, but does little for historians trying to clarify a typology in the later nineteenth century. Nor do French censuses under the Third Republic do much to clarify the muddled typology. These records use a three-part division between employers, employees, and workers. Closer examination of the 1872 census reveals that 231,000 "manufacturers" registered as employers, a category that included 75,000 contractors, and 200,000 "employers" listed themselves in the vague subcategory of "workshop chiefs" (small producers with a workplace in their home). These figures show little clear distinction between an artisan as a family-based producer, a subcontractor, an entrepreneur, a semi-trader, or a substantial manufacturer. The situation in Belgium and Germany was no clearer. In the Belgian census of 1896, 20,000 men practicing a craft were listed as "workers," but a closer enquiry found that these men claimed to have no employer.[9] As late as 1907 in Germany the census had a category *Handwerker* or "handicraftsman" and placed it in the industrial sector, but whether these were small producers or skilled wage-workers was left imprecise. Evidently, Europeans at the time had no clear notion of where being an "employer" ended and an "employee" or "worker" began.

Still, behind the confusing typology that frustrates the historian's desire to count and classify, we can be sure that, like the working class, the number of small producers grew during the industrial revolution. Many craftsmen retained their own shops and worked the interstices of large-scale industry (like making and repairing the new machinery). The description of Britain as the workshop of the world, or Paris a city of workshops, was apt. In London in 1841 a census listed 840 separate craft occupations, reflecting the traditional response to increased demand which was the continual subdivision of the steps of production within "crafts" and the organization of production in a series of separate component tasks.

In London a decade later a census reveals that three-quarters of London's firms still employed fewer than five men, and 86 percent fewer than ten. In France as late as 1867 there were 67,000 mechanical looms in the textile industry, but still 200,000 hand looms, demonstrating that rural production and factory production coexisted, and even expanded.[10] In 1906 we still find that half of the French workforce was employed in firms hiring five or fewer workers. The 1907 German census listed 31 percent of the industrial workforce working in a firm of five or fewer employees.[11] This has led many historians to conclude that industrial production could follow a path other than, and alongside, that of factories or capital-intensive technology, through the proliferation of wide varieties of dispersed production, many of these small firms by century's end using the new electric and gas motors on a small scale.

Of course, large industrial production *did* come to dominate the economy – no historian disputes that – it just came to dominate more gradually, along multiple paths, and certainly later than has often been suggested. Indeed, throughout the nineteenth century the economy of Europe appears bifurcated, with small firms working alongside increasingly large ones. In 1896 in Germany, for example, 62 percent of establishments had fewer than ten wage earners, but 21 percent had two hundred or more. Much current research points toward the last quarter of the nineteenth century in some parts of Europe (Britain, Germany, the Low Countries, to a lesser extent, France), the early twentieth century in other parts (Southern Europe), when we see a quantum transformation in production, processing, and retailing enabled by regularization of demand smoothed by the dramatic changes in transport and communication, price elasticity, capital intensive and increasingly standardized production culminating in the assembly line, and, ultimately, the scientific management principles of "Taylorism" and "Fordism."

Amid such changes, small firms continued to exist, but they increasingly lost their independence. Often, they were subcontracted to larger firms and, in effect, paid wages for their work. The competition for such contracts was brutal, and their access to credit, raw materials, labor, and markets was increasingly dependent upon capitalist merchant operations or factors. So, even though the small-scale production sector of the economy continued to employ men and women, it did so in a way that severed these people from the traditional artisan culture rooted in independence. Amid such changes, the traditional artisan did not suddenly disappear, but the artisan did become something altogether different, gradually but ineluctably more integrated into production and distribution networks that were controlled by large capital. Intensive subdivision of tasks and subcontracting continued apace, but as independence became increasingly a chimera, the identity of the artisan was transformed.

Class and Culture

As the historiographical focus of industrialization brought small-scale production and specialized retailing into its view, historians began to explore how the former traditional artisanry became part of the new classes of the industrial era, that of the workers and that of what has been called the petite bourgeoisie. Much, of course, has been written of the former, but relatively little of the latter. Both, however, were products in part of a sundering and transformation of a culture through which the traditional artisan had gained his identity.

There existed clear connections between corporate craft traditions and early forms of socialism, and there were pronounced continuities between the "rites of labor" that defined the journeymen brotherhoods of the Old Regime and those of the era of industrialization.[12] William Sewell has found that even in 1848 skilled workers were still thinking in terms of distinction determined by membership in *états*, evidence of a reconfiguration of corporatism, and that "unskilled" workers were so designated not because of a glaring lack of technical aptitude, but because they had no corporate traditions.[13] This picture that portrays connections between worker collectivism and Old Regime corporate attitudes has been confirmed by scholars working on Italy, Spain, Britain, Germany, and elsewhere.

At the outbreak of the revolution of 1830 in France master craftsmen and skilled artisans launched several newspapers written by themselves to voice grievances and help organize a collective movement. Significantly, they described themselves as "the most numerous and most useful class of society . . . the class of workers." On the pages of *L'Artisan*, *Le Journal des ouvriers*, *Le Peuple*, and *L'Atelier* artisans envisioned a labor movement along class rather than occupational lines, decrying the deskilling caused by mechanization and calling for shorter working hours, protection of the small workshop from subcontracting and ruinous competition, and the establishment of producer cooperatives financially supported by the national government.[14] Many of these disgruntled artisans joined Etienne Cabet's communistic Icarian Movement in the 1840s. Its ranks were filled by handicraft artisans with little or no property, however, and predictably drew poorly from master artisans with larger property holdings. Thus, in the revolution of 1848, the terms "working class" and "proletariat" did not refer to factory or mine workers as they would later in the century, but rather loosely to handicraft workers, some waged and others small producers employing a handful of workers in their workshops, or, in times of economic downturn, none at all beyond family members.[15]

Germany witnessed a similar development. During the first half of the nineteenth century German artisans confronted economic conditions that destroyed the independence of many by denying them the means to acquire and maintain property (a key if now unofficial badge of mastership). By 1848, notably at the Frankfurt Assembly, many artisans sought to find means to preserve their burgher status while others felt a sense of solidarity with wageworkers and struggled to convince the government to secure and improve working conditions. The revolutionary leader Gottfried Kinkel summed up the situation thus: "Half the artisans belong to the bourgeoisie . . . the other half sends its children to the poorhouse and lives a mean and miserable life on its daily earnings."[16]

In England between the 1820s and 1850s, as in Germany and France, small producers with a stake in property straddled an emerging working class and a petite bourgeoisie, often and awkwardly sharing the values of each. They relinquished traditional artisan values of collectivity only slowly and piecemeal, witnessed by massive membership in the burgeoning "friendly societies" that existed – much as guild confraternities had – to provide mutual assistance to their members. Many artisans, both lesser masters and journeymen, joined the Chartist Movement or formed trade societies and labor exchanges to free the artisan from dependency on merchants and factors, seeking institutional protection from the liberal market economy. By the 1860s across Europe many artisans could be found in the increasingly organized labor movement, while others slid into the ranks of a petite bourgeoisie that included small producers and shopkeepers along with lesser government officials, school teachers, and clerks.[17] But such a dichotomous picture is a bit misleading, for there were many artisans who toiled in small workshops as employers who sympathized with some of the objectives of the labor movement, yet as employers might also embrace some of the values of the bourgeoisie.

Moreover, to speak of a petite bourgeoisie as a class would be misleading, for the men who filled its ranks showed no sense of class consciousness. They did, however, share some defining common characteristics, especially its proprietary artisans and shopkeepers. In Britain and Belgium, these men were committed to economic liberalism, but everywhere in Europe they identified more with the values of the larger bourgeoisie whose ranks they hoped (usually in vain) to join than with those of the emerging working class. The world of small enterprise (proprietary artisans and shopkeepers) was one where livelihood derived from both its labor *and* its capital (rendering it distinct from the working class and the bourgeoisie), with the family at the center of economic activity.[18] Above all, the petite bourgeois, like the traditional artisan, desperately sought to maintain a certain status marked by a strict concern for respectability rooted in the possession of property. They were desperately keen on separating themselves from the wage-earning and propertyless working class that lived around them and whom they increasingly viewed as dangerous.[19]

Respectability and the independence it was ideally rooted in were not easy to preserve, however, for lack of capital, and dependency for credit, materials, and access to markets on merchants, bankers, and factors, made the world of small enterprise precarious in the extreme. Bankruptcy was never far away and was far from uncommon, a fate that would shove many a petit bourgeois or their children into the propertyless and disrespected world of the wage workers. Mobility studies in France in fact show that there was more movement of the proprietary craftsman and shopkeeper into the working class than into the bourgeoisie.[20] To be "credit-worthy," then, was all-important, and this entailed running the firm according to the bourgeois values of individualism, thrift, sobriety, and respectability.

The stratum of the petite bourgeoisie felt its status to be perpetually threatened, sometimes reaching near panic, as in Germany in the late nineteenth century. This fear powered its politics, as in the *Mittelstand* movement in Germany or the right-leaning *Ligue syndicale du travail, de l'industrie et du commerce* in France, the latter organization reaching 140,000 members in the 1890s. The *Ligue* tried to use its influence for legislation to arrest the loss of customers, on the one hand, to department stores purveying ready-made goods and, on the other, to the growing working-class cooperatives.[21] More generally, though, the petite bourgeoisie responded to the threat to status by trying to place their sons and daughters in the world of white collar work that was rapidly expanding in the second half of the nineteenth century.

Free market economies and the abolition of corporatism did much to undermine the independence and sense of social status of the traditional artisan, prompting many to join the emergent working class and others to aspire to bourgeois status. In both cases, the traditional artisanry was redefined. There were other forces at work, however, that equally assaulted artisan culture and helped transform the identity of the traditional artisan. Between 1750 and 1900 Europe experienced a period of intensified attempts to reform and regulate popular, or "plebeian," culture. Often spearheaded by evangelicals, these reformers sought to make "the people" more godly. This meant their lives at work and at leisure must be more rational and more disciplined.[22]

These reformers emphasized labor discipline as a means to moral improvement, preaching that idleness leads to temptation. Thus, reformers leveled their attack on recreations of the "people," a category in Europe's cities that encompassed many artisans, both journeymen and masters. One eighteenth-century English reformer, Josiah Tucker, advocated a tax on popular recreations that he assumed would "prevent idleness [and] promote industry." The activities he wanted to tax provide the historian with a list of sites of popular leisure: "all places of public resort and diversion, such as public Rooms, Music-gardens, Play-houses . . . Horse racing . . . Ball courts, Billiard Tables . . . Skittle Alleys, Bowling Greens and Cock Pits."[23]

Not all reformers wanted to abolish popular recreations, however. During the 1830s and 1840s their goal was to "rationalize" them, by which they meant organized and disciplined activities. Popular recreations had been rooted in a parochial and collective identity, and were not easily absorbed in a society increasingly governed by an anonymous mass market, contractual relationships, and individualism, all played out in large congested cities. The reformers targeted organized sports as the best vehicle to reform the lower classes because these activities taught self-control and team work. Already in 1840 the English moral reformer William Howitt announced "a mighty revolution has taken place in the sports and pastimes of the common people."[24] Bear-baiting and cock-fighting gave way by late in the century to increasingly rule-bound organized sports like football or, in England, cricket. Even traditional sports like boxing were changed, more and more governed by rules. During the second half of the century, especially during the 1880s and after, such sports took hold among what now was increasingly referred to as "the masses," a group that included many artisans. Sports took place in new sites as urbanization engulfed the open fields where sporting activities were played before, and more and more the new ball fields were designed to accommodate spectators.

Organized sports were only a part of the emergence of mass culture which encompassed many artisans and served as yet another powerful force redefining the traditional artisanry. As Vanessa Schwartz points out, the rise of spectacle in late nineteenth-century cities like Paris "created a common culture and a sense of shared experiences through which people might begin to imagine themselves as participating in a metropolitan culture."[25] Along with the democratization of politics and increased standards of living, this culture became part of the foundations of mass society.

This new mass culture, of which artisans were such prominent participants, was the result of a combination of the drive for moral reform and structural changes in society and the economy. Higher wages, especially among the skilled artisans of the emergent working class, powered a rising demand in an increasingly commercialized consumer culture focused on leisure (which was increasingly severed from the world of work). This demand caused the proliferation of drinking establishments, music halls, horse race courses, mass spectator sports, circuses, and a mass popular press. Indeed, newspapers pitched directly to the lower classes publicized and popularized these activities.[26] Such consumerism was an important part of the transformation of urban culture that was occurring at this time, and the artisans that were such a prominent part of it found their culture transformed as well.

Drinking establishments everywhere in Europe during the nineteenth century doubled as meeting places for workers (and many artisans), reading rooms, and sites for sporting events. They increasingly became the powerhouse for the development of popular culture, where the traditional culture of the people (including artisans) was modified through commercialization. As urban construction increasingly encroached on space for leisure activities, drinking establishments were built or remodeled to accommodate swelling numbers. They typically had fewer seats, and had large, open spaces indoors. To gain an appreciation of the ubiquity of such establishments, consider, for example, that in 1861 in England and Wales there was a drinking establishment for every 186 inhabitants.[27]

Drinking establishments retained their popularity among artisans within the new mass culture in every city in Europe, but another institution also arose that was immensely popular and reflects by its clientele a further homogenization in which artisans were encompassed into a commercialized culture of the masses. This was the music hall. It developed out of the "singing saloons" of the midcentury, and by the 1880s had become immensely popular and counted among its regular paying customers many an artisan.

Many contemporaries in Europe's cities attest to the popularity of the activities and locales of mass culture among men often loosely described as "artisans." Most likely, these were the artisans that identified more with the emergent working class than those who strove to join the bourgeoisie. The artisans in the latter category engaged in different cultural activities, activities that nonetheless departed from the traditional culture of the artisanry and served no less to redefine the identities of these men. The artisans striving to join the bourgeoisie usually embraced the idea of self-improvement (in England notably in the evangelical movement of Primitive Methodism), and by mid-century, according to Henry Mayhew, many in England had joined the "workingmen's clubs" that had recently sprung up. These clubs, in his words, were comprised mostly of "lower middle class, well-to-do artisans and petty tradesmen."[28] At these clubs these men heard uplifting lectures and musical concerts, and participated in decorous games. These artisans were most likely proprietary employers, and in these clubs among others like them they could separate themselves from the undisciplined, idle, and wasteful activities that seemed to them to characterize the leisure time of their employees.

Often, these men's clubs had reading rooms, attesting to the widespread literacy of their members. Before the industrial era about two-thirds of Europe's master artisans could read and write, but relatively few journeymen and fewer wage workers could. Largely as a result of mass schooling, by the early twentieth century nearly all workers in England, Germany, and France were literate, with the greatest advances occurring during the last thirty years of the nineteenth century. Reading, consequently, became an increasingly important element in their lives.[29]

Education and literacy, for all their benefits, were active agents in the refashioning of traditional artisan culture, for they brought with them a different way of knowing about physical work. In England by the 1830s, for example, Mechanics' Institutes were being set up to teach "scientific" production techniques to working men. They were intended to be an educational medium through which occupational skills would be learned. Indeed, technical schools of this time cropped up all over Europe. By 1850 artisans were awash in a flood of printed guides to various trades, each manual specifically laying out the techniques and production practices of the given craft. Traditionally, and, during the nineteenth century, informally, apprenticeship was the way occupational knowledge was taught to skilled workers, with know-how and technique handed down from older workers to younger ones on the job in the workshop. Schools like the Mechanics' Institutes and printed occupational manuals challenged this educational process, and exposed in formal instruction and writing what had been the "secrets" or "mysteries" of the trade.[30]

The schools and guides were in part a response to the greater specialization and more specific techniques that were taking hold in the workshops of the nineteenth century as the capitalistic economy increasingly linked profit to efficiency. Artisans were mixed in their reaction to the Mechanics' Institutes and the published manuals. Some small manufacturers embraced them (many of them had in fact helped establish the technical schools), while other artisans resisted them. Those who resisted did so because they believed that the schools and guides threatened to obliterate a corpus of knowledge that they felt could not be codified. Traditionally, artisans had considered this body of knowledge – their mystery and art – to be a common property possessed by craftsmen that had been handed down from generation to generation. Fundamentally, this knowledge had restricted and controlled entry to the trade and gave master artisans power over the labor market (and discipline of their workforce, a key marker of status) as well as the production process. For journeymen, this knowledge separated them from the mass of unskilled wage workers who continually threatened their position. If this training function were replaced by schools and printed work manuals, then the gates to their trade would be thrown open. If this happened, artisans feared all craftsmen would suffer a further loss of status and power, yet another invasion of their cherished independence. In short, schools and technical manuals joined to further refashion the artisanry by altering the traditional template by which artisans had known who they were.

As the culture of the traditional artisanry was fragmented and transformed, many of the artisans that were small producers and retailers sought to embrace the social values of the middle class. Above all, this meant the family. Artisans of the emerging petite bourgeoisie aped middle-class values by increasingly spending their leisure time with their family, within the home, or in sites specific to middle-class activity, like public parks. At home the well-appointed parlor was where visitors would be received, which together with strolls through the park with the family, offered these men the opportunity to project their status through their possessions and the appearance of themselves and that of their wives and children. Indeed, strolls in the park amid the bourgeoisie were the prime time to wear one's "Sunday best" clothing and so demonstrate the financial means to own them. Such private and public display demonstrated financial means, which, in turn, announced economic independence and thus proclaimed respectability.

Conclusion

Over the course of the nineteenth century the culture of the traditional artisan that had taken shape during the early modern period was eroded and finally obliterated. Handicraft production continued alongside emergent industrialization, but political, legal, demographic, economic, and cultural changes transformed the world in which artisans had rooted their sense of who and what they were. Most artisans entered the nineteenth century with a corporate, communal sense of themselves, and exited it without one. Over the nineteenth century they saw corporatism and their guilds dismantled, while they suffered the unrestrained violence of the free market that liberalism embraced. Both liberalism and capitalism combined to undermine the traditional artisan's cherished sense of independence and put at risk his respectability. Many artisans joined the emergent working class, while others embraced the values of the bourgeoisie. During the second half of the nineteenth century the emergence of a commercialized mass culture further altered the template of artisanal identity, encompassing many artisans in a new popular culture, others in a literate one, that shaped a new meaning to their existence, and a new sense of who they were. By the early twentieth century, artisans as small commodity producers or as handicraftsmen working for wages could still be found, but the "traditional" artisan and the culture that he had defined and that had defined him had disappeared.

NOTES

1 Farr (2000: ch. 8); Crossick (1997: introduction).
2 Farr (2000: 20–32).
3 ibid: ch. 2.
4 De Vries (1976: 91).
5 Farr (2000: chs. 6, 7).
6 Ibid: 277.
7 Kitchen (1978: 21).
8 Joyce (1991: 58).
9 Hentenryk (1984).
10 Charle (1994: 83).
11 Kelly (1987: 13).
12 Truant (1994).
13 Sewell (1980).
14 McPhee (2004: 142).
15 Johnson (1974: 156–8).
16 Sagarra (1977: 326).
17 Behagg (1984); Miles (1999: 178).
18 Crossick and Haupt (1984: 9).
19 ibid: 79; Hentenryk (1984: 126).
20 Crossick and Haupt (1984: 106).
21 On the *Mittelstand*, see Volkov (1978); on France, see Charle (1994: 145).
22 Goldby and Purdue (1985: 10).

23   Quoted in Malcolmson (1973: 98).
24   Quoted in Malcolmson (1973: 170).
25   Schwartz (1998: 6).
26   Goldby and Purdue (1985: 12, 34).
27   Bailey (1978: 16, 88); Goldby and Purdue (1985: 118).
28   Quoted in Bailey (1978: 119).
29   Kelly (1987: 34); Vincent (1989: 1, 98).
30   Ibid: 108, 117.

GUIDE TO FURTHER READING

The most complete and current survey of what I have called in this essay the "traditional artisan" is my own *Artisans in Europe, 1300–1914*. For scholarship on nineteenth-century European artisans, no one has done more to develop the field than Geoffrey Crossick, both in his own work and in edited volumes. For the former, see his *Artisan Elite in Victorian Society*, and for the latter, see Crossick and Haupt's *Shopkeepers and Master Artisans in Nineteenth-Century Europe* and Crossick's *The Artisan and the European Town*. Other important studies of artisans in England are Behagg's *Politics and Production in the Early Nineteenth Century*, Prothero's *Artisans and Politics in Early Nineteenth-Century London*, and Schwartz's *London in the Age of Industrialization*.

On France, the essential work is Sewell's *Work and Revolution in France*. Christopher Johnson, in addition to the book cited in this essay, has written several important articles, notably "Economic Change and Artisan Discontent: The Tailors' History, 1800–1848."

On Germany, Jürgen Kocka connects the artisanry with the emergence of the working class in "Craft Traditions and the Labour Movement in 19th-Century Germany," while Volkov's *Rise of Popular Antimodernism in Germany* examines political sentiments.

Much less work in English has been done on nineteenth-century artisans in Spain and Italy, but useful information on Spanish artisans can be found in Martin's *The Agony of Modernization*.

CHAPTER NINE

The Social Condition of the Working Class

JUTTA SCHWARZKOPF

In the long nineteenth century, fundamental changes were wrought under the impact of industrialization. Although taking off at different points in time in each country, with Britain leading the van, by 1914 the effects of the new mode of production had made themselves felt in varying degrees of intensity, directly or indirectly, all over Europe. Industrialization has been most aptly defined by Eric Hobsbawm as "self-sustained economic growth by means of perpetual technological revolution and social transformation."[1] It is the latter aspect, the deep-reaching social changes attendant upon industrialization, that this chapter focuses upon, paying particular attention to the ways in which the lives of ordinary men and women were transformed as their traditional plebeian way of life came under pressure by the dynamics of evolving industrial capitalism.

For those people existing on their wages alone, it was the mechanization of production processes and their relocation into factories which changed their experience of work in fundamental ways. The separation of workplace and home was coupled with workers' subjection to factory discipline, exerted most forcefully by two kinds of mechanical device: the clock and the machine. The strict regimentation of time by the clock required a crucial shift in workers' orientation from completing the task in hand to spending a prescribed amount of time exerting themselves, a shift of mentality the deep-reaching implications of which

were analyzed by E. P. Thompson as one important facet of the alienation working people experienced on entering the factory.[2] Regularity of effort was most effectively imposed by machines running relentlessly at an even pace, which workers had to learn to keep up, regardless of fatigue and exhaustion. Such conditions were typical of textile mills, which came to be seen as the epitomes of the factory system. Only when operatives had fully adapted to machine work were they able to begin to derive at least some degree of satisfaction from skillfully manipulating the technical means of production.

Employers did not rely on machinery alone to produce a workforce displaying the kind of disciplined behavior that was a prerequisite of smooth production. An abundance of regulations, which listed in minute detail the musts and must-nots of factory work, was aimed at bringing about the desired degree of application. Contraventions were punished by fines or dismissal. Factory regulations were also clearly gendered in that male workers were frequently penalized for rowdiness, while female workers made themselves liable to fining by behaving in ways deemed unfeminine, such as displaying a spirit of contradiction.

In contrast to workshops, factories assembled a much larger number of workers, and the close contact, even collaboration, between master and men in the artisan trades gave way to marked social distance between factory owner and workforce, who were separated by vastly dissimilar lifestyles based on widely different levels of income. When employers did take an interest in the people in their pay that went beyond seeing them merely as hands operating machines to generate profit, this was often motivated by the wish to extend their control of workers' lives beyond the gates of the factory.

Mechanization proceeded unevenly, which made for marked variation in the degree of control workers were able to exert over the labor process. Mechanization and the operation of machines in purpose-built structures usually occurred first in textiles, with cotton leading the way. In iron and steel, by contrast, production had been concentrated in large units long before industrialization set in. Here, teams of workers wielded a considerable degree of control over the labor process. This was increasingly undermined as mill owners strove to make the flow of production continuous by imposing longer hours, shift work, and overtime. Pay incentives to increase output and the fining of scrap production proved powerful mechanisms of pitting worker against worker.

In engineering, most plants were something in between manufacture and factory, combining the odd steam-powered machine-tool and a great many workers, most of them with an artisan background. Although they used traditional tools such as files, hammers, and chisels, it was the collaboration of men from a variety of trades which distinguished these sites of production from traditional workshops. This organization of production persisted during the industry's period of rapid expansion. Not until the advent of specialized machine tools did relative shopfloor autonomy begin to be eroded as the designs to which they worked were less and less of operatives' own making.

Where the factory regime was harshest and mechanization made the greatest inroads into workers' control of the labor process, as in textile mills, employers initially faced great difficulties in recruiting labor. This is one important reason why, unlike heavy industry and engineering with their exclusively male labor forces, the early textile mills relied on the large-scale employment of women and children. Only in Bulgaria did women, who had predominated in the domestic manufacture of textiles, fail to make the transition to factory production. While children had little choice in the matter, having to do their parents' bidding, women took up factory employment not because they minded the harshness of the work regime less than men, but because their priorities differed from those of their menfolk. If the earnings yielded by a mill job helped ensure family survival, they would take it rather than clinging to the increasingly elusive independence of an unmechanized trade.

The early stages of industrialization saw marked fluctuation among the factory workforce. This has been seen variously as unsteadiness, signaling the lack of readiness to apply oneself to the task in hand, and to do so regularly, or as a form of protest, individual or collective, against conditions deemed intolerable. This behavior can also be viewed as a deliberate attempt to better oneself by switching to a job that yields higher pay or requires less effort. Regarded in this light, fluctuation would testify to confidence in one's ability to find alternative employment and to accommodate oneself reasonably quickly to unfamiliar conditions. The latter two interpretations emphasize workers' agency rather than depicting them as being acted upon by forces beyond their control. Fluctuation was typical of first-generation factory workers. Subsequent generations had their exposure to factory discipline eased by an upbringing in which their sights were set on mill work and which facilitated the acquisition of "factory skills," a term coined by Maxine Berg to denote workers' ability to reproduce a limited number of operations accurately and speedily.[3] Yet not even then was factory work a lifelong occupation, with workers usually leaving the mill when past their prime in terms of physical fitness and ability to keep up the degree of speed and concentration required in the tending of machines.

While any mechanization of production involves the transfer of human skills to machines, the extent of the deskilling that occurred in the course of industrialization has tended to be overrated. Both the deficiencies of the machinery, particularly in the early stages of its development, and the wide variations in the quality of the raw or intermediate product to be processed – of which cotton is only a particularly salient example – relied on workers' experience and their labor process-related faculties and abilities to yield satisfactory results. Yet "skill" is not simply an objective measure to be read off the requirements of a given labor process. Skill is also socially constructed, being determined as much by the degree of control a strong union is able to exert over the recruitment of labor, as Turner has pointed out,[4] as by gender.[5] Skill, on which rested the claim for a reasonable level of pay and relative job security, was moreover an important weapon in the struggle between capital and labor over control of the labor process, being constantly challenged and contested, defended and shored up. One important way of doing so was by giving skill a masculine connotation, tying it to the mechanical knowledge required for the operation of specific machines or to physical strength. Hence, by definition, women's work counted as only semi- or unskilled. Skill could have ethnic overtones, too, as a result of better paid jobs being made the preserve of indigenous workers, forcing members of ethnic minorities to take up whatever paid employment they could get, only to be accused of undercutting.

Productivity increase and mass production did not rely on mechanization alone. An extreme division of labor coupled with product standardization achieved the same, as instanced by the clothing trades of the European metropoles. Here, small masters and journeymen were transformed from artisans into homeworkers dependent for their supply of raw material and the marketing of their products on a putter out. In addition, the division of labor enabled the latter to employ large numbers of allegedly unskilled labor, mostly female, who were paid by the piece at very low rates. Wherever the local labor market was highly segregated by gender and industrial employment confined to men, their female kinfolk formed a pool of reserve labor ready to be tapped. The women brought to their employment abilities they had acquired in the course of their upbringing, such as sewing, which were seen as naturally inhering in women and therefore did not count as skill. Yet meager though they were, these women's earnings

were indispensable for the survival of families which could not subsist on a male wage alone. Such conditions seriously curtailed workers' bargaining power. A low degree of mechanization coupled with the employment of workers in their own homes, obviating the need for any workshops, greatly reduced overheads, thus minimizing the amount of capital required to set up in business. What's more, this mode of organizing production made for a high degree of flexibility, enabling sweaters, as such employers were graphically called, quickly to respond to any changes in the market. This was particularly marked in the clothing industry, which was subject to changes in fashion. Such flexibility rendered employment highly spasmodic and job security elusive.

Over the nineteenth century, and not least as a result of industrialization, the middle class expanded while tending to do increasingly well. The number of servants employed became a marker of a household's prosperity, turning service from a rural into a predominantly urban phenomenon. As the home became marked off as the core of the "domestic sphere," presided over by the middle-class housewife, whose aspirations to ladyhood required the delegation of menial labor to servants, domestic service became overwhelmingly female, remaining the largest sector of women's employment in industrializing and fully industrialized countries until the end of our period. Servants' conditions were determined by the prosperity of their employers. Those women toiling as "maids-of-all-work" in households unable to afford more than one general servant were exploited more harshly than those hired by wealthier families, who were able to take on domestic staff to carry out their assigned duties as part of a finely graded hierarchy. Unlike factory work, domestic service was unmeasured and working hours were potentially unlimited. The highly personal nature of the relations between mistress and servants not only marks a field in which women wielded power, but also reveals the kind of personal dependence that made domestic service an employment option shunned by women able to find other openings on the local labor market. As housework was increasingly planned and rationalized over the nineteenth century, servants became subject to closer control and were made to follow ever more precise instructions, which circumscribed what little autonomy at work they had had. Moreover, the difference in background and education led to growing segregation between employers and servants, as relations in middle-class families became increasingly intimate. Servants' quarters and servants' entrances were among the visible signs of this segregation.

Although working-class people had to contend with harsh conditions whatever their employment, the attention of contemporaries focused on the factory as the epitome of economic and social change. Working hours there were long, but limited, marking factory workers off from sweated labor, who had to drive themselves relentlessly to eke out a living. Yet hours in the factory were imposed, not by the self-discipline of workers, but by mill owners intent on maximizing profit. In the early stages of industrialization, hours were far from standardized, varying by region as well as between factories. As long as machinery was water powered, dry summers as well as spring floods caused mills to be closed and laid-off workers had to seek alternative sources of income for the duration. The working day, too, was porous, affording opportunities for turning factory time to one's own purposes. Thus women employed in the early textile mills were known to do their own sewing and knitting. As machinery was speeded up, having become less liable to breakdown, and water power was replaced by steam, the pressure on workers intensified. They experienced the mental strain produced by the need constantly to watch quickly moving machinery so as to be ready at all times to take the requisite action when something went wrong.

Large numbers of machines running at great speed made for a high level of noise on the shopfloor. Depending on the material processed, noxious, even toxic, substances polluted the atmosphere, which insufficient ventilation did little to cleanse. Lighting, before the advent of gas and, later, electricity, was inadequate, too. Apart from the noise, all this was equally if not more true of the conditions of homework, where the effects were even more pernicious given that they pervaded rooms used for producing goods as well as eating and sleeping. As a result of conditions on the shopfloor, many factory workers had both their hearing and their eyesight impaired, as well as suffering from a variety of respiratory and other occupational diseases. While these were the long-term effects of exposure to such conditions, the machines, which initially lacked any protective devices, posed severe risks to workers' limbs. Accidents, involving hair or fingers caught in the moving parts of the machinery, were commonplace, leaving victims maimed or dead. Only when observance of protective legislation was made subject to effective monitoring by factory inspectors did conditions on the shopfloor begin to improve.

Women workers, moreover, had to contend with all forms of sexual harassment. Depending on the industry, the organization of production enabled men in positions of authority to extort sexual favors from female workers in return for preferential treatment at work which enhanced their pay, for instance by giving them better material to work or assigning them a larger machine complement. Yet the congregation of large numbers of women in the workplace afforded some degree of protection, because they could rely on each other in their efforts to resist undesirable male behavior. Domestic servants, by contrast, were rendered more vulnerable by their isolation. Once found pregnant as a result of an encounter with one of the masters of the house, they were usually dismissed on the spot without any character reference, which was indispensable for finding a new position. This is why domestic servants formed a disproportionately large group among unmarried mothers and women found guilty of infanticide.

Wages, graded by level of skill and calculated by the hour or by the piece, leading workers to drive themselves to maximize income, displayed marked variation even within the same industry. Not until trade unions had become sufficiently powerful to force employers to engage in collective bargaining did wages become more standardized and eventually start to rise.

The transition to an industrial way of life was eased by the plebeian family, which itself came under pressure generated by the new mode of production. The family linked the spheres of home and work both in the ways its needs shaped the labor market participation of its members and the manner in which conditions of work and pay reacted upon household composition and power relations in the home. In a period of fundamental change and growing insecurity, only the family could be relied upon for support, both material and immaterial. Individuals lacking this source of relative security were distinctly disadvantaged. Although deprived of its productive function in the course of industrialization, the family continued to operate as a joint wage economy to which all members contributed their earnings acquired from a large variety of cash-generating activities. With the spread of the factory system, the payment of wages to individual workers rather than the family unit of production became universal, making apparent the precise size of each member's contribution to family income. This threatened to erode the material base of male dominance in the family, particularly when the earnings of wife and children exceeded those of the husband and father.

Child labor looked back upon a long tradition in both agriculture and domestic industry, because, in plebeian families, there had always been a need for all members to contribute to household income. Children were employed away from home mainly in those industries in which they had been engaged prior to mechanization. In the factories, they initially had to work the same long hours as adults and subject to the authority of the grown-up worker whom they assisted. Their very low pay reflected the market value of their labor power, which was controlled by both the limited range of employment options open to them and their need to earn money to help their families. It was the number and spacing of children which had a major impact on the poverty cycle all working-class families went through. Any newborn signaled the advent of an extra mouth to feed, thereby diminishing family income. Yet in the long run, children were assets rather than liabilities on account of their increasing ability to contribute to the family budget. While they might start off making the odd penny by running errands, as they grew older their earning capacity increased to the point at which

they were able to support aging and often ailing parents. When elementary education became compulsory and school-age children were effectively removed from the labor market, the financial burden this imposed on working-class parents by extending the period during which they had to support their offspring led them in the long run to adopt the course followed by some of their peers and reduce the number of their children.

Neither was women's paid work the result of industrialization. What was novel was the site on which it occurred. While previous forms of women's paid work had taken place within households, the employment of women in factories, semi-public sites that could only be reached by traversing public spaces, made for a degree of visibility which was heightened by contemporary middle-class notions of the private, domestic sphere as women's proper realm. Like that of children, women's paid work varied in form and extent over the course of the family's poverty cycle. Accustomed to seek out opportunities for earning from an early age, daughters' contributions to family income increased as they grew older. Once they began having children of their own, their family of procreation became even more dependent upon a second income apart from that of the male. Women, including mothers of young children, would continue to work away from home until the earnings of their children were sufficient to make up for loss of maternal income. Abandoning factory employment was not tantamount to complete withdrawal from the labor market. Women continued to support their families by taking up homework, by taking in lodgers or people's washing, by minding children or charring.

Rather than marking a breach with tradition, women's paid work in the period of industrialization displayed the continuity of traditional values and behavior under changing conditions. Accordingly, families sent their daughters to work in factories or other people's households as a way of profiting from expanding employment opportunities. Thus working-class women's paid work continued to be circumscribed by their families' needs and requirements. Manifold forms of female self-exploitation, that is their readiness to take up paid work regardless of the conditions offered, suggest that women gave priority to securing family survival, with scant regard to the personal price they had to pay.

In the period of industrialization, new employment opportunities opened up for women, who were sought after because they were expected to prove adaptable to novel conditions on account of both their different priorities from men and their long-time exclusion from an artisan work culture, the standards of which contrasted markedly with labor under factory conditions. In Britain, where they predominated in the early factory workforce, women and children may rightly be regarded as pioneering mill work. The assumption that it was women's cheapness as compared to men which rendered them attractive to employers is difficult to uphold. Any comparison of the waged work of both groups is virtually impossible due to the gendering of jobs and status and is further obscured by the large difference in wages within each gender group. Moreover, employers' readiness to accommodate women's need to keep shifting between work in the factory and work at home in accordance with the requirements of their families indicates that they were genuinely valued as workers.

As industrialization progressed, women's employment in industry contracted as the result of the collusive efforts of trade unions, employers, and the state. By effectively closing certain occupations to women, trade unions responded to the concern, widespread among their male membership, about safeguarding their economic power as the material base of male dominance in the family. In many instances, unionized workers colluded with employers intent on rendering women's work compatible with middle-class notions of femininity. The state, too, for reasons that will be examined below, enforced regulations that circumscribed women's employment opportunities. Their exclusion from a number of industries, particularly the more recently mechanized and flourishing ones, pushed them into badly paid forms of employment, such as homework, and a large number of precarious cash-generating activities, because contracting employment options did not reflect families' lessening need for a female income.

What little time working-class people had to dispose of freely – which was even more curtailed in the case of women on account of the double burden they had to shoulder – was not usually spent in homes characterized by overcrowding and the lack of even the most basic facilities. Instead, people socialized in streets and pubs. In the course of urbanization, large numbers of migrants from the countryside headed for towns ill-prepared to cope with the onslaught of people in search of both work and accommodation. With the provision of housing left to the operation of market forces, supply could never meet the volume of demand by people unable to afford more than the lowest of rents. Hence the internal overcrowding, the subdivision of tenements typical of working-class districts. In this way available housing stock was stretched to the utmost, while the extremely limited living space reflected the restrictions imposed by tight and precarious budgets. Where new housing within the financial reach of working-class tenants was built, it was densely packed, made of inferior materials, and lacked the most basic sanitary facilities as a way of economizing on the outlay of capital on which only minimal return could reasonably be expected. Such conditions made for little domestic comfort and rendered cleaning, which was a never-ending battle against grime, soot, and, often, vermin, even more arduous by the need to haul the necessary water over long distances and sometimes up several flights of stairs.

Overcrowding was partly also the result of ways devised by working-class families to cope with women's need to juggle employment away from home with childcare and housework. This need had arisen from the separation of home and work, while the gender division of labor in the family persisted. In Preston, a typical cotton factory town, for instance, many couples with young children chose not to establish households of their own, sharing with a set of parents instead. While making for very crowded conditions, "huddling," as this practice was called, spread the outlay on rent over a larger number of earners and ensured both the reliable supervision of children and the discharge of housework by a grandparent while the young mother continued to earn at her factory job. For the older generation, this arrangement alleviated the poverty the infirmity of old age usually entailed. The setting up of an independent household had to wait until children began to earn. In the absence of grandparents, lodgers, either kin or strangers, were taken in.[6] These findings by historical demographers clearly refute the long-held belief that mothers working away from home inevitably had to neglect their children.

Working-class neighborhoods were characterized by a high degree of social homogeneity, with workmates, neighbors, and kin often overlapping. The settlement patterns of new arrivals from the countryside, who tended to seek accommodation near relatives, demonstrate both the wish to maintain family ties in a period of mass mobility and the importance of kin in procuring housing and jobs as well as easing the transition to an urban way of life. These strategies, brought to light by historical demography, significantly reduced the dislocation and disorientation that industrialization entailed, casting serious doubt on the picture of general social disorder frequently painted of this period. The similarity of conditions under which people lived and worked bred a feeling of togetherness and solidarity, which showed in the manifold ways in which neighbors could be relied on for support in times of need. Women were central to weaving these neighborhood support networks, and a woman's ability to stay on good terms with her neighbors had a crucial impact on her family's comfort. Neighborhood support networks stepped in whenever families eking out a living at subsistence level failed to find the extra resources to help a member in need. Based as it was on reciprocity and solidarity, the help provided by neighbors was not blighted by the bitter feeling of degradation engendered by private charities giving assistance only after careful scrutiny of applicants' behavior. Yet the poor were in no position to be selective about the sources of support they turned to. Reliance on family as well as neighbors, on charity as well as begging and pawning, on petty theft as well as prostitution, made up what Olwen Hufton has called the "economy of makeshifts," by which alone many of the poor managed to survive.[7]

Working-class living conditions were manifestations of the marked degree of social inequality characteristic of industrializing societies. It affected virtually all aspects of working-class life, with large internal variation by level of skill. Skilled workers commanded better pay than the less skilled, and this began to decline later in their lives because their capacity to earn was less closely related to physical fitness; they enjoyed some measure of job security, and their higher degree of control over the labor process implied better treatment by employers. Given the gender and ethnic connotations of skill noted above, women and workers from ethnic minorities were systematically excluded from the relative privileges of skill. Access to education and housing differed between classes, too, but the impact of an individual's social status even extended to their chances of survival, affecting the incidence of sickness and mortality rates.

As industrialization progressed and further mechanization was used by employers to increase their control over the labor process, divisions on the basis of skill became blurred. This resulted as much from the erosion of the privileges attendant upon it as from an improvement in the position of the less skilled. Yet gender divisions were deepened, as noted above, while ethnic divisions persisted.

Despite the rise of real wages in all industrialized countries in the concluding decades of the nineteenth century, earnings remained precarious for all except a tiny layer of male workers at the top, and the vast majority continued to live near or only slightly above subsistence level. Working-class living standards were determined not only by the level of pay attained, but, at least as importantly, by the regularity of income. Only few could and did reasonably believe that relatively comfortable financial circumstances would last. This is the chief reason why extra income was spent on the satisfaction of immediate needs rather than laying the base for a different lifestyle, on paying for more and better-quality food, especially meat, and better clothing rather than on better-quality housing. Improved levels of nourishment increased physical stamina, enhancing one's capacity to earn. Furthermore, expenditure on food was immediately adjustable to varying levels of income, while the long-term commitment involved in signing a lease for better housing was not.

The period of industrialization was characterized by mass mobility, which was geographical rather than social in nature. Apart from urbanization, the marked swings of the economic cycle forced people to keep moving about in search of a livelihood. Although instances of working-class upward social mobility were highly exceptional, the mass mobility of incipient industrialization bore the potential of bettering oneself, for instance by exchanging the doomed existence of an agricultural laborer or cottager for a job in some urban-based industry.

Apart from the everyday strategies they devised to cope with the exigencies of the new economic and social order, working people also organized collectively to safeguard themselves against the insecurity that dependence on a precarious cash wage entailed. The vast array of associations aiming to afford members at least a modicum of protection from the risks of a waged-labor existence coalesced to form an outright culture of self-help. Many of these clubs evolved from an artisan culture, which had revolved around the guild and journeymen's associations based on sociability and reciprocity. Membership in any of these required the ability to pay a subscription, small though it may have been, on a regular basis. Despite their efforts, hardly any of these associations was sufficiently prosperous effectively to shield their members from the vagaries of life under capitalist conditions, and in times of crisis, such as the long-term unemployment of many, their funds were quickly depleted.

In the course of the nineteenth century, governments, too, began to take measures which, in the long run, reduced social inequality somewhat. One field of state activity was education. At the beginning of our period, literacy showed marked variation by class and gender, with female illiteracy rates exceeding male ones everywhere. As instanced by Britain, which boasted a well developed culture of autonomous working-class instruction, the absence of compulsory elementary schooling was not necessarily tantamount to the total lack of educational facilities. As more and more states introduced compulsory elementary education and expanded the supply of qualified teachers, national literacy rates increased accordingly, without, however, quite closing the gender gap. By the end of the nineteenth century, state-provided elementary education had been extended to the majority of the population in Northern, Western and Central Europe, with the remainder of the continent lagging behind.

Another area of state activity was housing. The explosive growth of towns had produced overcrowding with large numbers of people squeezing into any available – and, more importantly, affordable – accommodation, as noted above. It was growing concern about public health caused by epidemics such as typhus and cholera sweeping through the towns of industrializing Europe and the inability to prevent them from spreading beyond densely populated slums that sharpened the perceived need for state intervention. Initially, this was confined to regulations stipulating minimum standards to be observed in the building of working-class housing. In the second half of the nineteenth century, states in many parts of Europe became more actively involved. Their activity was premised upon the belief that the demand for housing was to be satisfied by the market and that it was the individual family which was primarily responsible for meeting its accommodation requirements. In whatever way the building of working-class housing was promoted, whether by encouraging building societies to be set up or builders to increase their activities by means of incentives in the shape of subsidies or tax exemptions, all of these measures were temporary, introduced and sustained only during periods of acute crisis, and therefore remained relatively ineffective.

True, those working-class families sufficiently well off to afford accommodation in one of the newly developed working-class suburbs did experience improved standards. They were in a position to benefit from the housing policies implemented by many European governments from the 1880s. These aimed to promote the self-contained family dwelling, which would offer sufficient space for a "decent" life, and upheld the ideal of property for those able to afford it. Policies were thus geared as much towards improving material conditions as morality, because middle-class observers had been particularly alarmed by the lack of gender segregation in the sleeping arrangements of working-class families, often crowding into only one room. Yet the policies adopted failed noticeably to solve the housing problems of the majority. On the contrary, government-initiated slum clearance programs, designed to demolish housing stock unfit for human habitation along with neighborhoods in which were concentrated people deemed of undesirable mores and dubious morality, exacerbated housing conditions for the poor, who saw their dwellings being knocked down with no affordable accommodation put in their place.

While housing policies stopped short of interfering in the workings of the market, legislation regulating the factory work of, first, children and, subsequently, women saw the state actively intervening in the economy. Only where industrialization was dominated by heavy industry boasting an exclusively male workforce, where women's factory work was negligible and that of children virtually nonexistent, as in Hungary, did the state fail to introduce protective legislation. The intervention it involved was particularly difficult to legitimize where the tenets of economic liberalism prevailed. This difficulty could be overcome by highlighting the essentially dependent condition of women and children. Unlike men, who were seen as free agents, able to negotiate the conditions of their employment themselves, women and children were construed as legitimate objects of state protection.

The shortening of hours for child labor and the laying down of a minimum age for taking up factory employment were demanded by paternalist philanthropists, who focused their criticism on the physically and morally degrading effects of factory work on working-class children deprived of the educational influence of parents or school. Parents' own concern for the wellbeing of their children revolved around the exercise of parental (particularly paternal) authority in supervising and training their offspring that passed to strangers when their children entered the mills. Yet the wish to preserve their authority and to spare them the ills of

factory work was tempered by their desperate need for their children's earnings.

The debate about female factory labor initially focused on the "working woman," portrayed as forced to neglect her domestic duties and particularly her children while employed away from home. Women themselves, provided they could afford it, wished to be relieved of at least part of their burden, while male workers, by demanding shorter hours or the banning of night work for women, hoped to rid themselves of unwelcome competition. As middle-class men, employers concurred with regulations according men and women what they perceived as the rightful place of either group in society, while in their capacity as capitalists, they were eventually won over to the state laying down the rules governing competition for all. Factory legislation was thus always informed by the wish to buttress the gender hierarchy at work and, by implication, in the family, but given the interdependence of workers in many production processes, men often benefited, too, from measures designed solely for the protection of women, such as shorter hours. Nevertheless, by being construed as a group in need of paternalist government protection, women were positioned differently from men in relation to the state. Significantly, Austrian legislation passed in the 1880s and limiting working hours to eleven included adult men as well. This deliberate curtailment of the liberty of industrialists formed part of an overall attempt by a socially conservative and highly authoritarian regime to revert to the social and economic relations characteristic of pre-industrial society.

Towards the end of the nineteenth century, the attention of many governments shifted to the "working mother," focusing on women's reproductive capacity. In a period of increasing economic and military competition between states, concern with the "quality of the race" mingled with anxiety about declining birth rates. Both threatened a loss of the manpower required to maintain national economic and military status. This period saw the passing of legislation affording women some protection during pregnancy and after childbirth, which only became effective when maternity leave was coupled with payments compensating at least in part for loss of earnings. Such legislation was partly also a response to demands by increasingly vociferous national women's movements, which wished the state to acknowledge women's specific contribution to the nation as an important step towards winning the vote. Yet protective legislation, which consisted essentially of factory laws in this period, left unchanged the conditions of the large number of workers in non-factory employment.

The concluding decades of the nineteenth century were also the period in which the question of where responsibility for individual welfare ultimately lay was being reconsidered in a number of European countries. From the start, the conditions engendered by industrialization had been debated extensively among contemporaries. These debates both fed upon and occasioned an abundance of evidence, ranging from the impressionistic travel account to the systematic investigation of specific aspects of the new industrial order. The participants in this debate were motivated by a number of concerns. Some felt deeply disturbed by what they perceived as the degradation in which the working class were forced to exist and genuinely wished to see misery abolished. Yet the quality of their desire was no guarantee for the effectiveness of the measures proposed. Others were deeply worried that the alienated masses might turn to revolution in order to improve their condition. A certain measure of material security for all was advocated as the best way to integrate these marginalized groups into society and thus to avert revolution. Such notions were clearly motivated by the wish to preserve the social and economic order.

The idea that at least some of the problems engendered by industrialization were beyond the scope of individual or collective self-help or charity and required state action for their abatement was entirely novel. It was predicated upon the growing recognition that neediness was not the result of personal deficiency, the unwillingness to work and to provide for periods of want, but caused by the workings of the economy and therefore beyond individual capacity to counter. A consensus took shape that the three traditional causes of working-class poverty – sickness, unemployment, and old age – could only be addressed effectively by the state. The

reaching of this consensus was speeded up by the challenge posed by labor movements whose growing support, expressed in terms of membership as well as votes cast by the emerging working-class electorates, turned them into a force to be reckoned with.[8]

The nascent social security systems that were devised at this historical juncture thus in no way followed inevitably from industrialization. Its negative impact on working-class living conditions needed to be perceived as a problem not of the individual, but of the community, a change of perception undoubtedly furthered by insistent working-class protest on a mass scale, for state action to be taken. This is borne out by differences in the timing of such measures and its lack of correspondence with the degree of industrialization attained. Thus Britain, the pioneer industrial nation with the most thoroughly proletarianized population in Europe, lagged several decades behind Germany, which was in the throes of accelerating industrialization in the 1880s when social security laws were passed. This points to conceptions of the state as accounting for such differences. Not only did Britain strictly adhere to the tenets of economic liberalism, requiring a fundamental change in outlook for state intervention to become possible, but thanks to the relatively strong constitutional position of its parliament, the political system also enjoyed greater legitimacy than was the case in the authoritarian monarchies of Germany and Austria. Yet these two countries looked back upon a long tradition of "reform from above." The social security policies implemented in the countries of Central, Northern, and Western Europe in the closing decades of the nineteenth century tended to follow this sequence: insurance covering accidents at work was introduced first, to be succeeded by provisions for old age, invalidity, and sickness. Unemployment was tackled only significantly later. This sequence possibly mirrors both the widening distance from principles of economic liberalism and the increasing sophistication required in administrating the coverage of each of these risks. While insurance against accidents at work could be seen as evolving from older conceptions of individual responsibility for damage caused, insuring against unemployment ran counter to previously prevalent notions of individual responsibility. Moreover, the principle of general coverage necessitated the setting up of completely novel state machinery. Only in the Netherlands were the risks of working-class life covered fairly comprehensively by handouts from the Protestant and Catholic churches, whose increasing influence in Dutch politics after 1850 confined the state to a subservient role in this field.

Whether building up their funds from tax or from the contributions made by workers, employers, and the state, social security policies differed fundamentally from all previous forms of assistance in that payment was claimed as a rights-based entitlement and came without any of the stigma that used to attach to recipients of relief. Yet up until 1914 the social security systems in place fell far short of effectively alleviating poverty. Initially, the payments made were woefully inadequate, proving unable to prevent the living standards of recipients from deteriorating rapidly. Many therefore had to supplement payments by relief. Furthermore, the system was far from comprehensive, covering only specific groups of workers. In Germany the system targeted industrial workers, deemed to be most dangerous in terms of the threat they posed to the political order. Moreover, any insurance system (which Germany had opted for) is premised upon the ability of those covered to pay regular contributions. By definition, such a system excludes particularly needy groups, such as agricultural or homeworkers, thereby deepening internal class divisions. By contrast, tax-financed provision, such as the old age pensions introduced in Britain in 1911, potentially turns the social security of all members of the community into a central aspect of citizenship, though initially payment was subject to testing the means and the moral probity of claimants.

Most importantly, the social security systems established were saturated with notions of proper family relationships. In Britain they were based upon the male breadwinner family, aiming to uphold a man's ability to support himself and his dependent wife and children. This complied with the view, prevalent in the labor movement, that the state's principal role was to insure male heads of families against loss of wages, and directly to provide for women

and children only in the absence of men. Women's receipt of benefits was thus crucially mediated by their relationships with men in their function as housewives and mothers.

In Germany, too, social insurance operated to reinforce women's dependence on men. Unless they had paid towards an old age pension of their own, widows were not provided for. Yet by allowing women to reclaim their own share of paid-up contributions on marriage, the system encouraged them to look to husbands for long-term support rather than seeing themselves as independent wage earners assuming responsibility for providing for their old age. Such failure to tackle the conditions that rendered especially precarious the livelihoods of single women, and particularly widows and those with dependants to support, ensured that poverty retained its predominantly female aspect.

In France, by contrast, the debate, which had a strong pronatalist bias, focused on state provision for children as a way of inverting the secular decline of the national birth rate. True, assistance was to be paid to the male-headed family, considered the norm. Yet by targeting children, French policymakers ultimately left negotiations over the gender division of labor to individual women and men.

This outline of the social condition of the working class in the long nineteenth century has had two aims. First, by highlighting those areas in which the contrast between a pre-industrial way of life and living conditions in an industrializing society were most marked, the account has directed attention to the adaptive feat accomplished by contemporaries. Secondly, as industrialization progressed, a trend towards improving the social condition of the working class as well as the agents effecting the alleviation of misery have been identified. Given the different timing in the onset of industrialization across Europe, in the years immediately prior to the outbreak of World War I, the social condition of the working class was marked by great diversity. At the economic level, this can be traced back to differences in the degree and extent of industrialization witnessed by a given country. Especially in the southeast of the continent, this interacted with the degree of national self-determination attained. Also at the political level, conceptions of the state, molding as well as molded by the form and strength of national labor movements, emerge as those factors shaping the social condition of the working class in relevant ways.

By 1914, the extremes with regard to degree and extent of industrialization were marked by Britain on the one hand, which boasted the largest and most thoroughly proletarianized population in Europe, and large parts of Southeast Europe – Romania, Bulgaria, Serbia, Montenegro – where the working class was a negligible quantity due to the near-complete absence of industrialization. Only Greece had seen some economic development. In Russia, the industrial workforce was insignificant numerically, while highly concentrated geographically. Up to 50 percent of workers kept shifting between tending their machines and tending the fields in their villages of origin, thus displaying all the signs of being half-peasant, half-proletarian. Alternating between factory and field was quite common in Italy, too, where the economic and social rift between north and south was widening as industrialization was confined to the former part of the country.

By 1914, apart from Britain, industrialization had progressed furthest in Germany and Belgium, as well as Austria and the Czech Lands in the Habsburg monarchy. The Scandinavian countries of Sweden and Norway, along with Denmark and Finland, had seen industrialization set in, as had the Netherlands, while France, from about the 1880s, had begun to transform into an industrial society in earnest. The comparatively late onset and halting progress of industrialization in Italy, Spain, and Portugal had produced pockets of varying degrees of industrialization – thoroughly so in the peripheral regions of Spain, less so in northern Italy – with their working-class populations surrounded by predominantly agrarian societies. The example of Hungary demonstrates how some measure of domestic autonomy, attained in 1867, acted as a spur to economic development. Conversely, it was precisely the necessity to curb the centrifugal forces of the emerging nationalist movements in order to preserve the political unity of the multi-ethnic Habsburg monarchy that acted as a brake on economic development in the eastern and southern parts of the empire.

Accordingly, the social condition of the working class varied across Europe with the progress of industrialization in each country. In Southern and Eastern Europe, there prevailed the misery of early industrialization, unchecked by any countervailing forces. In Western and Central Europe, where industrialization was most advanced and the state had moreover taken the first steps towards tackling some of the social effects produced by unfettered competition, improvements in working-class living conditions began to be discernible.

Yet it was really only in Northern Europe – in Norway, Sweden, and Denmark in particular, all of them relative latecomers in terms of industrialization – that social inequality was seriously eroded. The sociocultural leveling witnessed by these countries was partly the result of the expansion and improvement of state schooling, producing the highest literacy rates in Europe. Even more importantly, these countries boasted a vast array of autonomous plebeian organizations, which promoted both the wish and the ability to press for one's interests in a political environment that afforded increasing opportunities of doing so successfully as a corollary of growing democratization.

Despite the marked variations in the social condition of the working class across Europe before 1914, there do emerge a number of points that apply generally once industrialization has set in. Firstly, nowhere did the mechanization of production seize all branches of manufacturing industry simultaneously or evenly. With the exception of only a few countries, textiles was the first industry to mechanize, while also relying largely on women and children to staff newly erected mills. Secondly, everywhere the family played a central role in easing the transition to living under the conditions of industrial capitalism by providing an indispensable, albeit multiply perforated, safety net in a period marked by great uncertainty. Thirdly, industrialization occurred in societies that were deeply and variously gendered, and while the process of economic and social transformation was unfolding, the conceptions of masculinity and femininity and of their relation to each other changed too, though not in a uni-linear way across the board.

By the end of our period, in the industrialized parts of Europe, working-class people had fully accommodated to the conditions imposed by industrial capitalism as well as shaping them in the process, thereby developing a distinct working-class way of life. The social inequality which had been traceable in every aspect of their lives began to diminish as a result of social security systems set up by states, not least in response to working-class protest. By stressing the need to integrate a group which was socially marginalized and politically disaffected, the manner in which poverty began to be tackled only confirmed working-class people's self-perception of belonging to a social group apart, the members of which, despite any differences that might exist between them, had far more in common with each other than with any other social group. Much of this feeling of commonality was rooted in their experience of coping with the forces of change that industrialization had unleashed.

NOTES

1 Hobsbawm (1975b: 34–5).
2 Thompson (1993: ch. 6).
3 Berg (1986: 265).
4 Turner (1962: 193–4).
5 Phillips and Taylor (1980).
6 Anderson (1971).
7 Hufton (1984: 363).
8 See chapter 13, this volume.

GUIDE TO FURTHER READING

Lenard Berlanstein's *Industrial Revolution and Work in Nineteenth-Century Europe* assembles previously published articles that demonstrate the diverse directions in which the historiography of this period has developed. Bock and Thane's *Maternity and Gender Policies* examines the impact of national women's movements on the shaping of welfare measures by the state by focusing on the visions of gender which both of these processes embodied and helped to construct. Flora and Heidenheimer's *Development of Welfare States in Europe and America* presents the general conclusions reached from a number of comparative projects investigating the development of social security systems, which ultimately gave rise to the welfare state. Pooley's *Housing Strategies in Europe, 1880–1930* investigates housing policies in transnational perspective.

Scott and Tilly's *Women, Work and Family* is a classic treatment of the impact of industrialization on women's work, charting developments in terms of the transition from family economy to family wage economy. Simonton's *History of European Women's Work: 1700 to the Present* brings Scott and Tilly up to date and takes in more countries than just England and France. Stearns's *European Society in Upheaval* is one of the very few surveys of Europe in the age of industrialization, yet quite dated in seriously playing down working-class agency. Wikander, Kessler-Harris, and Lewis's *Protecting Women* investigates the gender biases inherent in protective legislation via national case studies.

PART III

Political Developments

CHAPTER TEN

Revolutions and Revolutionaries: Histories, Concepts, and Myths

SHARIF GEMIE

It is probably impossible to give a coherent definition of the meaning of the term "revolution" in the context of nineteenth-century history. In previous ages, the word's meaning had been clearer: a revolution meant a completed circular movement. In political or social terms, it meant returning a country or a society *back* to its original state: thus the "Glorious Revolution" of 1688 *returned* a Protestant monarch to the British throne. The key concept here was one of "righting wrongs," of ending corruption and abuses so that society could recover its original purity. During the course of the eighteenth century the word began to change its meaning, and philosophers and politicians began to use it in a new sense, as indicating a fundamental and innovative change, one that destroyed all traces of the previous state of things. It has often been used to indicate a contrast between step-by-step reforms, which merely introduce minor improvements, and wholesale, root and branch transformations. At first sight, the French Revolution of 1789 and the Russian Revolution of 1917 both certainly seem to merit the term.

The problem with the term, however, comes when its use proliferates. In our own time, every other domestic cleaning device or car attachment seems to be advertised as "revolutionary," to the point where the word has now become banal and devoid of any real meaning. Even in historical studies concerning the nineteenth century, the word is stretched across

events, issues, and political cultures. It appears in the most unexpected guises, as the basis of a new nation-state (in France), the transformation of an economy (the Industrial Revolution), the application of new experimental methods (the Scientific Revolution), or the creation of a new family form (the demographic revolution). To some extent, one can understand that many of these applications of the term are intended as metaphors. In recent decades, many historians have grown cautious about this careless use of the word, and – for example – most economic historians would prefer a term like "industrialization" to "Industrial Revolution," precisely because the word "revolution" suggests a single moment of dramatic transformation, while they consider that they are studying a centuries-long process of accumulated change. One way of making our task a little simpler is to cut out these metaphorical uses of the term "revolution": in this chapter we will be studying political revolutions and related social movements.

Even after making this exclusion, however, we still face some major issues. Nineteenth-century writers seem to have been obsessed by all sorts of revolutionaries. They appear as bloodthirsty, calculating, near-psychopaths in novels such as Fyodor Dostoyevsky's *The Devils* (1871) or Emile Zola's *Germinal* (1885); as violent, blundering idiots, almost laughable in their fanaticism, in Joseph Conrad's *Secret Agent* (1907); and as rather intriguing, mysterious activists in Henry James's *Princess Casamassima* (1886). Politically, revolutionaries can be internationalists, nationalists, socialists, liberals, syndicalists, anarchists, or republicans; they can be centralists or decentralists, feminists or misogynists, reactionaries or futurists, pacifists or terrorists, Christians or atheists. Turning to consider France in particular, it is worth remembering that by – for example – 1905, a politician invoking the immortal revolutionary principles of 1789 could well be a modest conservative patriot, intent on preserving the privileges of the propertied and the order of the state. Lastly, to compound this confusion, it remains perfectly logical to argue that the greatest revolutions may also be the most silent: consider, for example, the type of "civilizing process" outlined in the works of Norbert Elias, which describe a gradual disengagement from violent forms of human interaction that occurred without any barricades and manifestos.

The issues raised so far suggest one simple point: it would be foolish to attempt to provide some textbook-simple 15-word definition of the term. Not surprisingly, previous researchers have often made similar points in their works. When the great British philosopher Isaiah Berlin turned to study the Russian "Populist" revolutionaries of the nineteenth century, the first line of his essay read: "Russian populism is the name not of a single political party, nor a coherent body of doctrine."[1] Carl Levy has produced the most convincing and coherent analysis of Italian syndicalism. He bluntly notes at the start of his essay that "it is impossible to give the reader a one-sentence definition of Italian syndicalism."[2]

The years 1789 and 1917 stand, like bookends, at either end of the period under discussion: they frame its beginning and its end, and the images which flow from and to these two events provide the raw material for many of the most important political cultures of the "long" nineteenth century. The term – or rather the term's resonances and associations – captures in a neat and memorable form something particular about the political culture of this period, in which everything seemed destined to change, and during which even the most marginalized, exploited, and repressed peoples could still retain a sense of hope that their future would be better than their past. While it would be foolish to attempt to define the concept "European" in this short and already methodologically challenged chapter, one brief point can be made about this issue. Revolutions formed part of a common European experience in this period; they therefore contributed to a sharper sense of European identity.

Rather than attempting to provide a single, neat definition, let us consider a little further how nineteenth-century people themselves understood revolutions. We can begin such a debate by examining two great evocations of revolutions: Jules Michelet's *Histoire de la révolution française* (written between 1847 and 1868) and Leon Trotsky's *History of the Russian Revolution* (completed in 1930). Placing these two works together, we can note some interesting similarities and some intriguing differences. The first similarity is simply that of length: both are massive works, some eighteen hundred pages long in the case of Michelet, a mere twelve hundred pages for Trotsky's work. The reason for this size becomes clear as one begins to turn the pages. These are both works which attempt to capture the entire life of a nation during a profound moment of historical change. Both authors consider that their respective revolutions were a result of long-term development; both make some effort to set them within a wider historical context. Continuing with the similarities, one notes a sharp, even angry tone to these works. These studies are not mere repetitions of accepted commonplaces: they present arguments which are vital to national and political traditions, and which must be argued through, vigorously, even violently. In both cases, part of this polemic relates to the subject matter. Both Michelet and Trotsky claim that previous authors have merely scratched the surface, or have confused minor symptoms with profound matters. Their works will, they claim, out-argue previous studies because they have noted the role of – and here the studies lose something of their claimed clarity – the masses, the people, the nation, the working classes, the working class, or the proletariat.

These similarities are surprising when one considers the significant differences between the two authors. Jules Michelet (1798–1874) had an established social position: he was a professor of history at a prestigious Parisian college. His views brought him into trouble with the authorities, and he was dismissed from his post in 1849. Politically, he was a republican, but never a socialist or a Marxist. He was born after the great events which he evokes in his history. Leon Trotsky (1879–1940) was a member of the Bolshevik Party in 1917. He had been a revolutionary leader and a government minister in the first communist governments of post-1917 Russia. He was exiled, however, in 1928. He had participated in many of the events described in his work. Unlike Michelet, he explicitly informed his readers of his politics: a fervent and loyal follower of Lenin and, often, a creative Marxist thinker in his own right.

In both works, "revolution" is portrayed as something like a natural process, perhaps a tide, which can be temporarily slowed, but which cannot be stopped. But revolutions do not simply destroy: they are also a moment of the coming together of peoples, forming new communities. Michelet, in particular, insists on the role of the 1789 revolution in constructing French national identity. At times, such processes are invoked with a peculiar, passionate, quasi-sexual or familial language:

> The great nation . . . opened her arms to hug them. Everyone threw themselves on her, and all forgot themselves, no longer remembering from which province they were from . . . They had been isolated, lost children until then. Now they had found their mother: they were something more than what they had thought [they were], when they had believed themselves to be Bretons or Provençals . . . No children, learn this properly, you are sons of France.[3]

Curiously, one finds echoes of a similar argument in Trotsky's work, though in somewhat less extravagant form. For example, in 1917, Trotsky finds "a nation was beginning to form itself out of impersonal prehistoric raw material."[4] In Trotsky's work, however, the construction of a collective national identity runs in parallel with other forms of social construc-

tion, principally the formation and assertion of a strong working-class identity. As might be expected, Trotsky's work concentrates more on these social processes than does Michelet's.

Some of these works' most important differences are in their respective styles. Michelet's *Histoire* is often described as "lyrical," but this term is not quite accurate. Michelet certainly writes "from the heart" and – referring to the militants and activists of 1789 – even claims that "eventually, I was one of them, a familiar figure in this strange world."[5] Much of the force of his work comes from its powerful and effective descriptive passages. But there are few pages in which his prose style really soars into the imaginative intensity of a great novel. Instead, we often have the impression that this is something more like the retelling of a familiar folktale, in which we already know the story, and – like expectant children – we wait for our favorite episodes to come round. On occasion, Michelet surprises by retelling an element of the story in a new way. The dominant tone, however, is that he is telling us something that we already know: "The Revolution is in us, in our souls: outside, she has no other monument."[6] Unlike Trotsky, Michelet refuses to present his study as the result of a method of historical research. He even refuses to footnote his references, believing that such references will disturb the flow of the narrative. His *Histoire* is – he argues – simply *the* story of the revolution, retold with greater clarity and feeling than previous versions.

Trotsky's *History*, on the other hand, is presented in a more philosophically sophisticated manner. In his preface he raises methodological issues: how does one write a history of the illiterate masses? When comparing the two works, it is clear that Trotsky is far more confident than Michelet in finding the appropriate methods by which to analyze working-class and peasant life. He cites, for example, statistics concerning food supplies, strike rates, and industrialization. He informs us that although he was a witness to many key events, this is not a work of autobiography. When his presence is recorded in the narrative, it is in the third person. Marxism explicitly structures and guides this study, producing – for example – the survey of Russian economic history in the first chapter. Moreover, Trotsky's style is sharper and tougher than Michelet's. There is none of Michelet's rather flabby narration: instead, Trotsky reveals a genuinely encyclopedic knowledge of history, integrating references to previous revolutions, Proust's novels, events in contemporary Spain, and the nature of psychology into his narrative. Lastly, in Trotsky's work one gains a far stronger impression of the *organization* of a revolution. One constant throughout his study is his contempt for those who present a riot or a movement as merely "spontaneous." Trotsky might well reply that there was nothing more difficult to organize than spontaneity! For Michelet, revolution is something which happens, more or less of itself, when the time is ripe; for Trotsky, history always needs a push – and it has to be the right type of push, by the right militants, with the correct leadership.

Curiously, however, one's final impression of Michelet's and Trotsky's respective studies is of their similarities. Both seem caught in the same paradox. In the last pages of his work Michelet claims that "until now, all histories of the Revolutions have been essentially monarchic . . . This is the first republican history, it is the first to have smashed the idols and the gods. From its first to its last page, it has only one hero: the people."[7] For Trotsky, "the most indubitable feature of a revolution is the direct intervention of the masses in historic events."[8] But in both works, this "people," these "masses," remain curiously anonymous. They appear, briefly, in the big set-piece dramas; they provide the muscle for the confrontations and struggles; their loyalty or their slowness to rally is occasionally referred to and sometimes measured. But, in both works, they seem like a single bloc, a team, whose role is simply to carry out the task that history has set for them. Trotsky does devote a page or two to describe the people who joined the Bolshevik Party, but his words about them sound quite unbelievable:

> Bolshevism created the type of the authentic revolutionary, who subordinates to historic goals irreconcilable with contemporary society the conditions of his personal existence, his ideas, and his moral judgment. The necessary

distance from bourgeois ideology was maintained in the Party by a vigilant irreconcilability, whose inspirer was Lenin.[9]

For a moment we could believe that we had stepped back into the pages of Dostoyevsky and his nightmare figures of calculating psychopaths! Trotsky's words are more an evocation of a certain "ideal type" of party member, rather than a rounded description of actual militants.

Both works are also marked by a form of historiographical telescoping, through which the history of the revolution becomes the history of the leadership of the revolution and then, eventually, the history of the leader of the revolution. Michelet claims the People as his hero, Trotsky scorns studies of individual psychologies, but eventually both tell stories concerning tiny elites within vast mass movements. The result, in Trotsky's case, is particularly incongruous. One can almost hear the historiographical gears crunching when we read sentences such as the following: "Lenin was not an accidental element in the historic development, but a product of the whole past of Russian development. He was embedded in it with deepest roots."[10] Both authors have devised similar solutions to the same problem: while they set out to analyze the experience of an entire population, the historiographical conventions of their period meant that they would inevitably concentrate substantial elements of their studies on the actions and words of a revolutionary leadership. Both attempt to resolve this dilemma by claiming that there is some unique, almost magical quality to political life during the revolutions, which brought people, nation, political life, and leaders into a close harmony. They therefore claim that in these particular circumstances, a speech by a Robespierre or a Lenin could be taken to represent the entire population.

Returning to the question raised previously, how do these two works help us understand the nature of "revolution"? These two very different authors have written studies of revolution as national and/or social dramas, as traumatic births of identities or regimes, as turning points in historical evolution. In different ways they confirm the commonplace understanding of revolution as a wiping clean of the slate, and as a new beginning. Moreover, they both offer an insight into the nature of revolutionaries which contrasts with the sensationalistic images that pepper the nineteenth-century novels referred to at the beginning of this chapter. For Michelet, the revolutionaries of 1789 were big-hearted, brave, and creative men, somewhat akin to secular saints; for Trotsky, they seem closer to a team of fanatically well-organized office staff. Both works are rich in observation and metaphor, although one might well concede that Michelet's method, his claimed intuitive identification with the revolutionaries of 1789, has survived less well than Trotsky's creative use of Marxism. Curiously, however, both works seem marked by a similar flaw: they observe, study, and invoke a process, they mark its relative success or failure, but they are weak when it comes to explaining the motivation of the participants, shifting – in Michelet's case – to some cloudy sub-mysticism concerning the national soul, and – for Trotsky – to some particularly dubious suppositions about relationships between historical development and leading individuals' psychology or identity. And yet this moment of identification, when a largeish minority (in reality, despite our two authorities, *never* a majority) begins to assert itself as an autonomous political agent, must be the key moment in any revolutionary process. In its place, we get similar accounts of speeches in political bodies, or bold leaders' courageous decisions from both authors.

In other words, while both works certainly help us see what nineteenth-century people understood by the term "revolution," what they fail to explain is why the term had such resonance. Why did prominent novelists produce so many hostile caricatures of revolutionaries? And, more importantly still, why were so many nineteenth-century political movements inspired by the concept of revolution? To answer these questions, we need to move from studying the many revolutionary processes to considering what motivated the revolutionaries themselves.

When reading first-hand, autobiographical accounts of revolutionary moments, one is also struck by the passion with which a deep, heartfelt sense of community is evoked. A dramatic

example of this can be found in an unusual text by the Russian anarchist Michel Bakounine (1814–76). Following his participation in the revolutions of 1848 in France and Germany, he was captured by the authorities and eventually transferred to a Russian prison. There he wrote a confession of his activities, to be read by the tsar. The purpose of the document was to plead for clemency, but – in Bakunin's hands – the text served many other purposes. Here is his account of the revolutionary agitation during March 1848 in Paris.

> Sir, I cannot give you an exact record of that month in Paris, as it was a time in which my soul was drunk. Not only was it as if I was drunk, but we all were: some with a mad fear, others with a mad ecstasy or with insane hopes. I got up at 4 or 5 a.m., I went to bed at 2 a.m., and I was up for the rest of the day, going to all the assemblies, meetings, clubs, processions, marches, and demonstrations. To sum up, I took in the intoxication of the revolutionary environment with all my senses and all my pores. It was a party without beginning or end. I saw everyone and no one, for each separate individual was merged into this numberless and shifting crowd. I spoke to everybody, without being able to remember what I had said or what was said to me, as – with each new step – my attention was seized by events and new sights, by unexpected news . . .
>
> It seemed as if the entire universe had been overturned. What had been incredible was now normal, the impossible became possible, and the possible and normal seemed mad. In a word, people were in such a state that if someone had said "God has been chased out of Heaven and a Republic has been declared there!," everyone would have believed it and no one would have been surprised.[11]

Such images of revolutionary ferment feature in most first-hand accounts. There is some quality evoked here which is lacking in Michelet's and Trotsky's studies, something far deeper, far more exciting than the sight of a crowd listening intently to a revolutionary leader.

In a sense, Bakounine's memories of revolutionary intoxication could be compared to records of life under wartime: there is the same impression of coordination, of meaning, of people pulling together, working to their fullest to realize a common goal, and putting aside petty differences and quarrels. As in wartime, such emotions are heightened by the real sense of danger: by choosing to participate in a revolution, each individual is making a choice which puts his or her life in danger. Above all, these accounts evoke that deep, poignant emotion which we can only term "community," although it often seems to be something closer to a sense of love that transcends individuals and grips a whole crowd. There is, however, one important difference between such accounts of revolutionary experiences and accounts of wartime life. During wars, that new sense of community is at least partly structured by state authorities who – if they possess intelligent officials – mobilize propagandists and police forces in order to encourage a sense of communal self-sacrifice. The efforts of the revolutionary crowd in 1848 were – with apologies to Trotsky – far more spontaneous. They were not obeying instructions from above, but creating their own cultures and rituals.

In many cases, these dramatic accounts of intoxicated revolutionary community are given added poignancy by the subsequent fate of the revolutionaries. The classic example of this must be the Paris Commune of 1871. Here a crowd of relatively innocent, generally nonviolent municipal radicals, whose first demand was merely the right to elect their own city council, was confronted by the French army. French state authorities stigmatized these activists as degenerates, alcoholics, hooligans, and prostitutes, and instructed the army to show no mercy as it retook the city in May 1871. One myth which circulated widely was that of the *pétroleuse* or female petrol-bomb thrower. As the army shelled the city, fires started. In some cases, these may have been the work of radicals adopting a scorched earth policy; it is far more likely that most of the fires were the result of the army's own shells. Soldiers were told to search out suspect women. Such orders meant that any woman carrying anything capable of holding a liquid – such as a bucket or a pot – was in danger of being shot in cold blood. The final result of the army's actions was a bloodbath. A conservative,

minimum estimate for the number of Parisians shot by soldiers would be fifteen thousand; some serious historians have suggested that the total killed could be as high as fifty thousand.[12]

This dreadful massacre structured the manner in which the Commune was remembered. The Communards had no agreed political program: some looked back to images of the French Revolution of 1789, others followed the early anarchist thinker Pierre-Joseph Proudhon (1809–65) in searching for a decentralized, federalistic society, some were more influenced by the first trade unions, and a few by Marx's ideas. These currents crisscrossed and interacted with each other. Far more important than their improvised and often rather vague political pronouncements, however, was the simple drama of the episode. As political refugees fled from France into Spain, Belgium, Germany, and Britain, the message was spread. An established nation-state had turned its army against its own people. In place of political actors, martyrs were created. Significantly, this moment was also the first time that the name of Karl Marx (1818–83) became known to a wider public. His publications in the 1840s, 1850s, and 1860s were only read by a tiny audience of German radicals and exiles. In 1871 Marx was in exile in Britain: he was one of the few thinkers in that country who dared to defend the Commune. His pamphlet *The Civil War in France* was firstly an attempt to argue that there was a logic to the Communards' project. These rebels were not vandals and hooligans: their actions were symptoms of the manner in which class forces were evolving in nineteenth-century Europe. In fact, Marx had little personal sympathy for the revolt, and had advised radicals against taking action. But, following the horror of its repression, he could not stay quiet.

The memory of the Commune, the myths and images which it generated, provided an ultra-clear, devastatingly stark sense of political identity. Previously, there had been much political confusion: what was the difference between a nationalist with a social conscience and a socialist? An anti-clerical and an anarchist? A republican and a trade unionist? After 1871 there was a clear sense of "us and them," not constructed by any coherent elaboration of political programs or philosophical values, but by identification for or against the Communards and therefore, by implication, for or against "thc" rcvolution. In many ways, this legacy held back the political development of socialism, for it muddied the differences between socialism, social-nationalism, and radical republicanism.[13]

Obviously, not all nineteenth-century revolutionaries participated in the Commune. But it probably is not much of an exaggeration to say that all of them were *virtual* participants. The episode of the Commune provides a lucid illustration of two of the most important aspects of the nineteenth-century cult of revolution: the sense of community, and the ever-present danger of participation. And these points allow us to go some way to responding to the dilemma noted at the start of this chapter. While it is difficult to present a *political* definition of what constituted either a revolution or a revolutionary, there was some real sense of a shared experience and perhaps of shared values that contributed to a sense of revolutionary community. Similar arguments have been developed by other researchers examining congruent fields. Isaiah Berlin found some cognate quality when he studied the Russian revolutionary groups. There was no one organization which dominated their political culture; they were "loose congeries of small independent groups of conspirators or their sympathizers." They did possess, however, "sufficient moral and political solidarity to entitle them to be called a single movement."[14] Carl Levy presents the following observation about the manner in which Italian syndicalism functioned: it was "a field of force for an unstable ensemble of different social classes and individuals who shared a deep alienation from liberal Italy."[15] These cultural or moral qualities that the revolutionaries shared are probably more important than their formal political commitments.

These observations lead us somewhat further. Our two great guides – Michelet and Trotsky – produced studies of revolutionary processes in which the momentum of revolution seems almost to have a life of its own, whether due to the generation of a national mystique or to the development of socioeco-nomic forces. Both historians are weak in explaining exactly why particular individuals chose to participate in such processes. Our brief survey of 1848 and the Paris Commune of 1871 reveals, however, something else. Revolutions are lived as moments of passionate participation. Moreover, revolutionary organizations, at their best, generate and preserve something of that same ideal. In order to understand more fully the revolutionary cultures of the nineteenth century, we need to study further this sense of revolutionary community.

Why did people become revolutionaries? The decision to join a revolutionary organization was a dangerous one: at worst, it could mean arrest, prison, and even death. At best, in the relatively liberal countries of Western Europe, it could still mean social ostracism, the end to hopes for promotion, and dismissal from work. Indeed, it was the well-founded fear of persecution which led socialists, trade unionists, and anarchists to establish organizations, for without some permanent structures to offer militants jobs and wages, they would be left defenseless. At first sight, joining one of these groups seems a senseless act of self-denial.

The answer to this question lies, once again, in the nature of revolutionary community. In the quotation by Bakounine given above, relating to 1848, revolutionary community appears as a unique, hallucinogenic moment of individual transcendence. It should be remembered, however, that revolutionary community could take far more prosaic forms. Pamela B. Radcliff has written one of the best-researched studies of how an early twentieth-century revolutionary organization actually functioned. Her work is set in Gijón, a small port town in northern Spain, and concerns the Spanish anarcho-syndicalist organization, the Confederación Nacional de Trabajo (CNT – The National Confederation of Labor), which was created in 1911 and may have had over a million members in 1936, making it arguably the largest trade union federation in Spain. Radcliff draws together records of the CNT's activity during the periods when a degree of state toleration allowed it to operate semi-legally. It provided a wide range of services to its members. As might be expected, it organized strikes or boycotts of exploitative employers. But, beyond this, it also ran a job placement agency, advising members of employment opportunities across Spain. It provided medical services for those who were ill, and arranged funerals when members died. CNT members could learn to read and write in CNT evening classes; they could attend technical training courses arranged by the CNT; they could borrow books from CNT libraries; they could participate in CNT theatre groups; they could listen to dramas, or folk and classical music concerts performed by CNT groups. At weekends and on holidays they could attend demonstrations and processions organized by the CNT, which usually ended with picnics and dancing. More than these practical services, the CNT offered something perhaps still more important: an ethic, a critical perspective on working-class life. While most male members of the CNT had grown up within the confines of an established working-class leisure culture, structured around football, drinking, and gambling, the CNT attempted to introduce new concerns, such as education, and made some efforts to ensure that CNT activities were open to women as much as to men.[16] Radcliff's conclusion is important: "At this point, the labor movement had become the indispensable source of economic and social solidarity and mutual aid."[17]

The CNT was not a unique organization. Bizarrely, although the Marxist-inspired political culture of the German SPD (Social-Democratic Party) was quite different from the CNT's anarcho-syndicalism, the range of services it offered to its members and – above all – its ethic of self-improvement and education were clearly similar to those offered by the CNT.[18] In other words, for many working-class people, joining a revolutionary organization was not some act of heroic self-sacrifice, but a simple, practical necessity. These revolutionary groups offered resources and services which were not available elsewhere.

Examining the practical work undertaken by groups such as the CNT and the SPD certainly challenges the conventional stereotype of the revolutionary as social outcast, whether in the form of Dostoyevsky's psychopaths, Michelet's secular saints, or Trotsky's fanatical bureaucrats. But, it might be objected, the CNT's and

SPD's "social services" were not *really* revolutionary. After all, had not Karl Kautsky (1854–1938), the SPD's principal political theorist, called for a fundamental shift in socialist political strategy, from "overthrow" to "attrition"?[19] And, while anarcho-syndicalism has a terrifying reputation for revolutionary intransigence, does not Radcliff note the CNT's "flexible moderation"? While the founding documents of anarcho-syndicalism insisted that revolutionary trade unions were to refuse all contact with political parties, in practice the Gijón CNT often adopted a policy of quiet cooperation with selected parties on particular issues. Radcliff talks of the "fluid boundary that changed according to circumstances" lying between the CNT and Spanish republican groups.[20]

Clearly, these are important questions which draw us back to the issue of defining "revolution" and "revolutionary." Are the actions undertaken by the CNT and the SPD examples of the decay of a revolutionary spirit? Or, on the contrary, should we learn from them, and accept a more prosaic, less sensationalistic concept of "revolutionary"? We will return to this issue in the conclusion.

To some extent, in considering these issues of definition, we are also raising the question of the differences between a relatively liberal Western Europe and an authoritarian Eastern Europe. While socialists and syndicalists could found organizations that hovered between legality, semi-legality, and illegality in the West, no such opportunities existed in the East. Western revolutionaries learnt very quickly that, above all, Russia was different. Bakounine noted: "The basic force in Russia is fear, and fear destroys all life, all intelligence, any noble movement of the soul."[21] Alexander Herzen (1812–70), his contemporary and fellow revolutionary, described Russia as "this kingdom of darkness, lawlessness, silent death, mysterious disappearances, gagged and tortured prisoners."[22]

Under these circumstances, joining a revolutionary organization was a considerably more serious matter in Russia than in Western Europe, and the penalties potentially far greater. There was no margin of legality: mass organizations like the CNT or the SPD simply could not exist. One striking example of this difference is the absence of political demonstrations in Russia: the first such public protest occurred in St. Petersburg in 1861, and was promptly repressed by the police.[23] And yet, for all these significant differences, one also notes important similarities.

Of necessity, nineteenth-century Russian revolutionary organizations were far smaller than their sister organizations in the West. Becoming a revolutionary meant adopting a second identity, and accepting a life of secrecy and danger. It was often preceded by a severe moral or psychological crisis. Vera Figner became a leading member of the People's Will, a terrorist group. In her autobiography, she outlines the process which led her to join: in the months before, "I began to deny everything" she writes.[24] Venturi, in his masterly study of Russian revolutionary groups, notes how often individual activists asserted a "complete scepticism which is so necessary so as to be able to begin everything again."[25]

Most strikingly of all, many members of Russian revolutionary groups were young people from relatively privileged families. They joined a movement which made "complete dedication and self-sacrifice" its basis.[26] Why had they made this sacrifice? When we raise this question about the workers of Gijón, the answer seems to lie in the practical benefits that could be drawn from CNT membership. No similar observation can be made for these civil servants' daughters and priests' sons, these children from the petty nobility and the merchants.

Herzen provides us with the beginnings of an answer. Arguably, Russian official culture and in particular Russian family forms were growing stricter, more rigid, and more hierarchical during the nineteenth century. These future revolutionaries grew up in cold, formal households, in which their parents were distant and uncaring figures. The one element of emotional relief for them was provided by the servants. To Herzen, servants seemed like big children, and thus their "mutual attachment" was created. The sight of the cruel punishments which servants suffered was extremely upsetting: Herzen notes that in his family, while the corporal punishment of servants was *almost* unknown, it was common to dismiss unruly or disobedient servants by sending them off for conscription. The result, for Herzen, was "a rooted hatred for slavery and oppression in all their manifestations."[27]

The new generations of young revolutionaries from relatively privileged families were marked by both an acute sense of personal guilt for the comforts they had enjoyed, and an intense love for the suffering and exploited Russian masses, in particular for the peasantry. Such emotions came to a climax in the 1873–4 movement "to go to the people." In the summer of 1874 thousands of young students and connected activists from Russia's urban centers attempted to shed their old identities. They learnt manual trades or studied how to be teachers, they swapped their smart clothes for those of the artisans and peasants. They were motivated by a "passionate longing for liberation which took as its banner the repudiation of learning in order to find a true, healthy and simple life."[28] They then headed out to the villages, to work among the peasants and to preach a new gospel of social liberation. The peasants were amazed, puzzled, and often suspicious. The police authorities were quick to act: some four thousand were arrested, and 770 were eventually tried.[29] From the failure of this movement, and the severity of the authorities' repression, came the turn of many Russian revolutionaries to conspiratorial methods and terrorist tactics.

What motivated these young people to express their humanitarian feelings in these desperate, dangerous forms? We can provide some answer to this question by noting, in particular, the prominent participation of young women. One study finds that in the 1860s some 3 percent of Russian revolutionaries were women, some 12 percent in the 1870s. There were two major mass show trials of revolutionaries in 1877; 16 of the 50 accused in the first were female, 38 of 193 in the second.[30] Obviously, women were far from a majority of these groups, but such comments miss the point. The predominant cultural and social forces of Russian society worked to keep women ignorant and politically passive: they were accorded no official political representation whatsoever. By 1897, literacy rates among Russian women were still only 13.1 percent.[31]

It is therefore quite extraordinary to find this evidence for significant female political activism in revolutionary circles. (It should also be noted that while some male revolutionaries positively welcomed female participation, many were skeptical, if not hostile.) In turn, these women's presence teaches us something about the wider nature of the revolutionary organizations. Barbara Engel notes: "Russian society provided almost no options for a woman who thought critically about her family role and rejected the values that would have enabled her to endure it."[32] Similar comments could be made about the majority of young revolutionaries. The dominant structures of education, work, and culture created lives without any meaning. In this particular sense, one can make a comparison between a member of a tiny Russian revolutionary cell and a CNT or SPD member. In all these cases, the revolutionary organizations and cultures were providing them with something that the broader social structures were unable to provide: social services for Spanish or German workers; meaning and morality for disaffected Russian youth.

For one particular strand of nineteenth-century revolutionary political culture, these revolutionary communities were of crucial political importance. For most groups, they were seen as instruments to achieve a particular political goal: revolution. For the anarchist groups, revolutionary communities were not simply instruments to achieve a goal, but actual models of how a future just society might be run. To cite an old joke, anarcho-syndicalist groups did not simply want a bigger slice of the cake, they wanted to run the whole bakery. From this came the characteristic anarchist concentration on the *morality* of the organization: it must avoid authoritarian forms, it had to be open, and – if possible – consensual. Marxist groups, on the contrary, tended to think of parties as temporary instruments that would "wither away" after the Revolution.[33]

Let us return, however, to the question asked at the beginning of this chapter. Is there any quality which unites these philosophers and terrorists, workers and nobles' children, bureaucrats and saints, psychopaths and pacifists? What do the words "revolutionary" and "revolution" mean?

The key characteristic of all these groups is their relationship to the dominant means of communication and culture. The German political philosopher Jürgen Habermas has identified the emergence of a "public sphere" in the seventeenth and eighteenth centuries. To simplify his rich and intricate arguments, one could state that prior to this period, culture and politics were structured around two poles: the public life of royal courts and early states; and the private life of the workplace and the family.[34] A third pole, the "public sphere," was created when private individuals began to act *as if* they were public officials: when they began to publish commentaries on events and to discuss ethical issues of state policy. Authorities were confused by the emergence of this new cultural force. Some (e.g., the Russian monarchy in the nineteenth century) were frankly hostile, and used censorship and police action to limit its presence. Others (e.g., the French monarchy in the 1780s) conceived of the public sphere as, potentially, a useful supplement to state action, and therefore gave its emergence a qualified welcome. The French Revolution of 1789 can be interpreted as the first example of the assertion of the political capacity of the public sphere. Nineteenth-century governments were therefore more guarded in their attitudes, and attempted to direct the public sphere by schooling, censorship, and state promotion of particular cultural forms. However, the nature of the public sphere as a free zone of debate was also being hollowed out from within: commercial pressures pushed authors to present their arguments and their texts in market-friendly forms.

Our revolutionaries emerge as rebels against these constricted forms of the public sphere. Their common first step is to demand, in Cornelius Castoriadis's words, the right to present "an explicit questioning" of power structures.[35] In other words, they refuse to accept that anything should be seen as holy, as sacrosanct, as beyond criticism, whether for religious, state, or commercial reasons. Their revolutionary communities function as critical, alternative public spheres. They refuse censorship, of course, but more importantly they refuse what might be termed "mis-education" by which populations are trained into an unthinking obedience. This second point explains the "social service" aspect of many mass revolutionary groups. For an articulate critical force to emerge, all aspects of lifestyles must be considered: work as well as education; sexuality as well as food.

These were explosive ideas. They attracted some of the best minds in nineteenth-century Europe, from Leo Tolstoy to Oscar Wilde, from Camille Pissarro to Karl Marx. But, in the late nineteenth century, a new challenge to them emerged. Right-wing forces had previously relied on the traditional deference to the priest and the squire to provide mass support for conservative groups. In the increasingly critical cultural atmosphere, deference was dying. A "new right" emerged, which consciously imitated the revolutionaries: it adopted an anti-establishment tone, complained about censorship, and spoke about the economic hardships suffered by honest patriots. On occasion, it even confronted police forces and state authorities. This "new right," however, was never committed to the libertarian ideals of the public sphere. Its long-term goal, always, was to end debate and popular cultural empowerment.[36]

This interpretation of the multifaceted revolutionary tradition of the nineteenth century also explains some of the difficulties faced by our two historians, Michelet and Trotsky. Both, in different ways, were interested in state building. Michelet, a history professor, wanted to assist in the recreation of the Republic in France. Trotsky was an ex-minister, with (in 1930) some hope of one day returning to government. But the revolutionary tradition, with its critical ideas and community ethic, was by its very nature an anti-state, anti-government tradition. Noting and celebrating the revolutionary communities created after 1789 and 1917 would have run counter to Michelet's and Trotsky's purposes: in place of secular saints or bureaucratic fanatics, our two historians would have been forced to note the real enthusiasms of naive, fallible human beings.

ACKNOWLEDGMENTS

I would like to thank Patricia Clark, Tadzio Mueller, and Fiona Reid for their helpful comments on earlier draft versions of this chapter.

NOTES

1 Berlin (1978: 210).
2 Levy (2000: 212, 223).
3 Michelet (1979, vol. 1: 324).
4 Trotsky (1977: 284).
5 Michelet (1979, vol. 1: 45).
6 Ibid: 31.
7 Ibid: vol. 2: 897.
8 Trotsky (1977: 17).
9 Ibid: 1016.
10 Ibid: 344.
11 Bakounine (1974: 80–1).
12 For an introduction to the Paris Commune, see Gemie (1999a: ch. 9). For a fuller account, see the older but still very useful work by Edwards (1971). On the campaign against the Commune, see Gullickson (1996).
13 On the memory of the Commune, see the useful essay by Rebérioux (1997).
14 Berlin (1978: 210).
15 Levy (2000: 212, 223).
16 However, as Radcliff notes, women's participation in anarcho-syndicalist organizations was often problematic. On this point, see also Berg (1996) and Gemie (1996).
17 Radcliff (1996: 233). On the Spanish anarchists' educational and cultural activism, see Litvak (1981).
18 On the pre-1914 SPD, see Evans (1990).
19 Kautsky (1983: "The Mass Strike").
20 Radcliff (1996: 178, 170).
21 Bakounine (1974: 112). See also Naarden (1992) for a useful, if flawed, discussion of how Western European socialists attempted to integrate Russian conditions into their theories and strategies.
22 Herzen (1956: 9).
23 Venturi (2001: 227).
24 Engel and Rosenthal (1975: 13).
25 Venturi (2001: 136).
26 Ibid: 586.
27 Herzen (1983: 45–55).
28 Venturi (2001: 503).
29 Ibid: 505–6.
30 Hillyar and McDermid (2000: 24–6).
31 Ibid: 105.
32 Engel (1983: 17).
33 These points are discussed in greater detail in Gemie (1994). See also the thought-provoking argument of Mueller (2003).
34 Habermas (1992).

35 Castoriadis (1990: 126–63).
36 On this "new right," see the interesting
    analysis by Blackbourn (1986: 152–84), and
    the case study by Hunt (1975).

GUIDE TO FURTHER READING

No single work can be recommended as a complete guide to the totality of nineteenth-century revolutions and revolutionary movements. Habermas's *Structural Transformation of the Public Sphere* is a dense, provocative consideration of the nature of nineteenth-century politics; while Castoriadis's *Le Monde morcélé* is a collection of acerbic essays by a master polemicist on the nature of modern political culture.

There have been many remarkable, innovative, and thought-provoking works written on aspects of this chapter's subject. For obvious reasons, Russian revolutionary movements have attracted the attention of many historians. Venturi's *Roots of Revolution* remains a classic work: at once encyclopedic in its scope, vivid and detailed in its style, and remarkably successful in making these distant figures and ideas come alive. Berlin's *Russian Thinkers* is somewhat narrower in scope, but rich in argument and observation. Hillyar and McDermid's *Revolutionary Women in Russia* is a more recent work that provides a clear introduction and a provocative perspective on women in revolutionary groups – a topic which is also explored in Engel's *Mothers and Daughters*. Herzen's cool, well-written autobiographical texts and political writings have been unjustifiably forgotten: his *From the Other Shore* and *Childhood, Youth and Exile* provide invaluable insights into the revolutionary mentality. And, as argued in this chapter, Trotsky's *Russian Revolution* is a classic example of Marxist historiography. Engel and Rosenthal's *Five Sisters* is a useful selection of autobiographical texts.

At various moments in the nineteenth century France almost seemed to be acting as a political laboratory for new movements. My *French Revo-lutions, 1815–1914* provides a concise introduction to them, and also includes excerpts from primary documents and suggestions for further reading. Edwards's *Paris Commune* is a classic work, rich in observations and analysis; Gullickson's *Unruly Women of Paris* stresses the importance of gender in 1871. Rebérioux's "Le Mur des fédérés" is an intelligent and well-written consideration on the memory of the Commune. Furet's *Interpreting the French Revolution* presents an acerbic and provocative analysis of the historiography of the French Revolution.

Arguably, the world's first mass socialist movement developed in nineteenth-century Germany. Evans's *Proletarians and Politics* is a well-written analysis of the development of the SPD, and Kautsky's *Selected Political Writings* is a useful collection of texts by its principal theorist. Germany was also the site for a significant pseudo-revolutionary "new right": its political culture is analyzed in Blackbourn's "Politics of Demagogy" and Hunt's " 'Egalitarianism' of the Right."

Anarchism developed as a mass movement in nineteenth-century Spain. Radcliff's *From Mobilization to Civil War* is an innovative and well-researched analysis of its presence and practices in a single Spanish town, while Litvak's *Musa Libertaria* considers the anarchists' cultural politics. Townson's *Republicanismo* is a fascinating collection of essays on the very varied Spanish republican traditions.

Long-neglected by scholars, anarchism is finally beginning to gain some of the attention it deserves. Marshall's *Demanding the Impossible* is a lively and encyclopedic review of the anarchist tradition. My "Counter-Community" and "Anarchism and Feminism" consider two important aspects of anarchist political culture. Levy's "Currents of Italian Syndicalism" is a compact, detailed essay on an important anarchist movement. Berg's " 'Free Love' in Imperial Germany" notes some of the contradictions in anarchist political culture, while Mueller's "Empowering Anarchy" discusses the relationship between anarchist and postmodern thought.

CHAPTER ELEVEN

The Rise of the Modern Leviathan: State Functions and State Features

Jörn Leonhard

Changing Semantics and Critical Discourses: Defining the State in a Period of Transformation and Crisis

From the end of the eighteenth century and against the background of both the French Revolution and the beginning of the industrial revolutions, the concept of the state underwent a fundamental change in Europe. Whereas classical authors of political theory such as Plato, Aristotle, or Hobbes concentrated on distinguishing the state from other types of human association like family, local community, or church, the late eighteenth and early nineteenth century witnessed a hitherto unknown distinction between state and society. Society, in this context, referred to the complex interactions between individuals who tried to satisfy their distinctive needs and interests, if necessary against the existing state authority. The idea of a homogeneous unity between state and society excluding conflict came under increasing pressure, and not only in political theory. During the French Revolution the politically self-conscious and socially influential part of the *tiers état* of French society proved to be capable of acting against the traditional state structures of the *ancien régime*. It was in the context of the French Revolution and its perception in Germany that Hegel for the first time warned against a confusion of state and "civil society." For him, the state in its fullest sense and in its developed form (Hegel thought about the Prussian example of his own days) represented the manifestation of a moral concept prior to the meaning of society.[1]

The changing meaning of the state during the long nineteenth century, covering the period between 1776/89 and 1914, was accompanied by numerous contemporary and often controversial discourses about the character of state and society. Later in the century and contrary to Hegel's assumption, Marx argued that the state could only be the result of particular class constellations and thus formed part of a superstructure determined by socioeconomic processes. However, when confronted with the developments in France between 1848 and 1852, Marx had to admit that if no class was strong enough to monopolize power, a state executive under a charismatic leader like Napoleon III could at least temporarily instrumentalize the state for its own purposes.[2] In contrast to Marxist interpretations, a more functional approach was developed by Max Weber towards the end of the nineteenth century. He referred to the state as a particular apparatus of rule, characterized by a monopoly to use force in a legitimate way.[3] Finally, in the twentieth century, the "totalitarian" state seemed to remove the historically important distinctions between state and society. As the quite different examples of Fascist Italy, Nazi Germany, and Stalinist Russia proved, a totalitarian state in distinct historical contexts and with distinct consequences seemed to reabsorb society and subordinate it to the will of a single party or a charismatic leader. The enormously destructive potential of these regimes in the twentieth century derived its force not least from the state and its developed instruments and infrastructures.

Against this background, this chapter concentrates on where the modern state, with its multiple functions and instruments, came from, which were the decisive structural processes behind the rise of the modern Leviathan in nineteenth-century Europe, and how particular functions and features developed in different historical contexts.

States and Modernization: State Traditions and Structural Changes since the Eighteenth Century

It is impossible to understand the development of the state in the nineteenth century without taking into account the earlier origins before 1800. Two types of early modern states are important in this context. First, there were absolutist monarchies, which had, with varying degrees of success, developed fiscal structures to raise taxes and standing armies as stabilizing factors both internally and externally. These traditions and institutions not only characterized France, Prussia, the Habsburg Empire, and Russia, but also Sweden, Denmark, Spain, and Portugal, as well as a number of states on the Italian peninsula and in the Holy Roman Empire. Second, there were states in which there had developed a complex compromise between the prince's and the estates' power. Britain, after the failure of absolutist experiments in the seventeenth century, represented this category, but a similar constellation also existed in Poland, Hungary, and in the Holy Roman Empire as a whole, with its tradition of elective emperors. Many of these territorial states of the early modern period did not survive the restructuring of Europe's political map between the 1790s and 1815. Indeed, this highly complex process of state building led to an enormous reduction in the number of territorial states. The number decreased from about

500 units around 1500 to about 20 states around 1900. This process, much intensified between 1794 and 1815, was influenced by two new attractive state models: constitutional monarchy and nation-state. The success of both models in nearly all European states between 1789 and 1914 went hand in hand with the expansion of state functions and the development of adequate bureaucracies.[4]

The early roots of these transformations and the bureaucratic apparatus of modern states point back to the second half of the eighteenth century. Under the influence of Enlightenment philosophy and its European variants, the ideal of a well-ordered state machinery, based upon rational, economic, and uniform administration and justice, began to develop. Especially in the period of enlightened absolutism under Frederick the Great in Prussia and Joseph II in Austria, this ideal of a reform-oriented state, which no longer served the monarch but an abstract ideal of the common good, became a dominating feature. At the same time, these reform-minded monarchs began to provide their bureaucracies with special privileges in order to make them loyal instruments, independent from aristocratic clientelism, and to prevent corruption.

More importantly, European societies since the late eighteenth century were confronted with new and structural challenges which necessitated new institutions and infrastructures. The most fundamental of these challenges was clearly the demographic revolution: Europe's population grew from approximately 130 million in 1750, to 266 million in 1850, and 400 million in 1900. This enormous increase, indeed a demographic explosion in the long term, meant that migration began to affect an ever greater part of the population. It has been estimated that up to 85 percent of the population were directly or indirectly affected by migration within Europe. Some 70 percent migrated from the countryside to new and rapidly expanding cities. Since much of the migration was caused by a lack of traditional employment, migration also went hand in hand with social conflict, crime, and an increase in the use of collective violence. Therefore, the state apparatus not only had to secure the raising of taxes, the recruitment of military conscripts, and the safeguarding of public order. Especially towards the end of the century, mass migration led to ever greater social problems in crowded cities, so that the concentration of so many migrants necessitated an interventionist state bureaucracy, able to deal with social problems and public health.[5]

This underlines that a particular constellation was responsible for the rise, development, and expansion of the modern state in Europe: on the one hand, a fundamental social and economic transformation of society, caused by demographic transformation and industrial modernization; on the other hand, bureaucratic traditions of the eighteenth century, originating from the enlightened ideal of a well-ordered state and its function to reform and educate society on the basis of progressive ideals. This tension between an active role of state bureaucracies and their response to structural changes, the ambivalent position between their fear of revolution and their will to plan the future, became one of the most striking characteristics of the modern state in the nineteenth century.[6]

Men and Money: European Wars as Causes and Catalysts of State Expansion

In a long-term process that intensified from the late eighteenth century onwards, European states influenced and penetrated more and more aspects of everyday life. The wars of this period, and the military conflicts against revolutionary France since 1792 in particular, served as one of the most important catalysts in this process, because they led to the mobilization of money and men through the means of mass conscription and raising taxes. The ability to raise taxes and standing armies had already been a dominant feature of continental monarchies before 1789 (and neither should the rise of the military-fiscal state in Britain during the eighteenth century be underestimated), but the dimension of the European wars between 1792 and 1815 went far beyond this traditional paradigm of monarchical state building of the European *ancien régimes*.[7] If the combination of conscription and taxation

in wars served as a fundamental catalyst for the expansion and intensification of state functions, the focus on the European war periods between 1792 and 1815, 1854 and 1871, and before 1914 becomes obvious. Going beyond the direct consequences of war and defeat, state functions changed because wars provided criteria to judge the state's ability to perform successfully in periods of national crisis and collective challenge. Hence war experiences indirectly stimulated other state activities, for example regulating the public, directing education and providing welfare structures, thus replacing the old corporatist structures of the *ancien régime* with its numerous guilds, corporations, estates, and orders which had fulfilled many of these functions before the beginning of the century.

Wars and defeats also forced the import of new administrative structures and led (especially between 1792 and 1815) to the creation of new states which had to integrate numerous new territories and populations. Thus the French Revolution and the subsequent Napoleonic empire meant a fundamental watershed, not only for France, but also for large parts of continental Europe as they came under direct French rule or under French influence. The ideal of a centralized and uniform state administration was first meant to communicate and implement the will of the revolutionary regimes in Paris and later of the emperor in all parts of France. Countries occupied by the French, especially Italy, Spain, and Belgium, experienced this new ideal of strong administrative centralism. With the end of the Holy Roman Empire, the reshaping of Germany's political map after 1800, and the disappearance of numerous tiny principalities, the emergence of new post-revolutionary states such as Prussia, Bavaria, Baden, or Württemberg led to a new wave of state intervention and dynamic activity. Bureaucratic reforms "from above" were intended to make political and financial survival of the states possible.

Taking a *longue-durée* perspective, military competition and confrontation between states generated the fundamental prerequisites for modern state structures on the European continent, such as the princely court, the standing army, and the fiscal institutions which allowed the effective raising of taxes. While the states monopolized the use of violence, the military-fiscal state absorbed ever more resources. Between 1500 and 1800 the European population doubled, whereas the number of soldiers increased tenfold.[8] Between 1800 and 1945 this process was further intensified and accelerated because of technical innovations and the introduction of mass conscription in the aftermath of the French Revolution and the Napoleonic Wars.[9]

Military defeats, throughout European history, also led to substantial political, administrative, and legal reforms. It was defeat which illustrated the necessity for these reforms in order to make the state strong enough to meet the challenges ahead. Thus the era of Prussian reforms, which witnessed an extraordinary but only temporary freedom of action for bureaucratic state reformers, dated from Prussia's military defeat against Napoleon in 1806. Similarly, the defeats of 1918 and 1945 meant turning points in the history of state bureaucracy and administration in Germany. For the Habsburg Empire, the defeats in 1748 against Prussia, in 1859 against Italy and France, and especially in 1866 against Prussia necessitated far-reaching reform initiatives. Russia's internal problems became obvious in the defeats in the Crimean War of 1854 and contributed to the bureaucratic reforms of the 1860s focusing on the abolition of serfdom and limited self-government on the basis of local and regional Zemstvos. Of equal importance was the military collapse in the naval war against Japan in 1904/5, which forced the tsar to make substantial concessions and led to the transformation of autocratic power into a constitutional monarchy with an elected Duma.

But however obvious state expansion in the nineteenth century was, its overall financial dimension remained relatively limited. After the end of the wars in 1815, war spending and mass conscription as new means of state activity came to an end, thus also avoiding two major causes of popular unrest. As a result, state expenditure declined. For example, in Britain it declined throughout the century, and even in France with its developed state infrastructure and its tradition of centralism and state activism, it remained at a modest level compared with later developments in the twentieth century. Despite the military campaigns between 1854 and 1871 and the arms race before 1914, state spending in Europe by 1913 was only 10 percent of gross national income, compared with up to 50 percent in the post-1945 period, indicating the enormous impact of the two world wars and the development of welfare structures on a hitherto unknown scale.[10]

Professionalization and Centralization: The Emergence of a Functional State Elite

"The chains of muzzled humanity are made from office-paper."[11] Thus commented at the beginning of the twentieth century the German-Austrian writer Franz Kafka on the enormous significance of the modern state and its bureaucracy. He pointed to the fact that there seemed to lie a sophisticated and well ordered system of repression through anonymous bureaucracies behind the rather boring routine of administration. Kafka also anticipated that totalitarian dictatorships would not only incorporate modern centralized administrations in order to implement their orders, but would in fact be heavily dependent on them: totalitarian command structures in many ways represented a bureaucratic ideal, an emotionless implementation of orders, irrespective of their ideological background, but often in the name of an abstract ideal of effectiveness and necessity.

The professionalization of legal education and the importance of trained lawyers in administrations became crucial for the development of functional state elites. Already in the early modern period the perception of Roman Law at continental universities had led to the emergence of a particular legal tradition which facilitated legal codification projects in the later eighteenth and nineteenth centuries. The idea of a state founded on the rule of law became a cornerstone of legitimizing modern states and their expansion. However, not all of continental Europe was affected by this tradition in the same way. Whereas Northern and Central

Europe, but also the Iberian peninsula, France and Italy, were directly influenced by the tradition of Roman Law, Eastern Europe, Poland, Hungary, and Russia were not (or only partly) affected by it. This also explained why in the nineteenth century the implementation of the principle of the rule of law proved much more difficult in these parts of Europe.

A further factor was the emergence of a self-confident administrative nobility, a nobility not by birth but by function. Since the fifteenth century, lawyers at the high courts in France, Spain, and Italy and in the larger states of the Holy Roman Empire had achieved equality with the other aristocratic members of administrative institutions. This led to the long-term development of a new educated elite, often with non-noble social backgrounds, but with experience of special training in law, characterized by a strong *esprit de corps*, an identity distinct from other groups of society. In France, but not only there, a *noblesse de robe* emerged which was privileged by the monarch and which regarded itself as the most loyal backbone of the French state.[12]

This new functional elite which the state needed to perform its administrative duties also developed abstract concepts of common good and *raison d'état*, transcending merely individual or group interests. Many of these state civil servants even survived the formal end of the *ancien régime* after 1789 and became very influential in the post-revolutionary reform period (and not only in France, as the examples of Prussia after 1806 under the influence of the leading reform minister Hardenberg, of Baden under minister Reitzenstein, and Bavaria under Montgelas after 1803, demonstrate). In these cases leading officials were no longer primarily loyal to the person of the monarch, but to a more abstract notion of the state and the common good as represented by the state. This "revolution in the good sense of the word," in the famous words of Hardenberg in his Riga Memorandum, were meant to safeguard the public good as defined by bureaucratic reformers who had been educated in the spirit of enlightened principles of the later eighteenth century. In some cases, notably in Italy and in some of the German states, this also explains why so many officials became crucial

for the development of early liberalism, which developed as bureaucratic liberalism seeking a consensus between state and society.[13]

State Models and Variants of State Activities in the Nineteenth Century: Four European Cases

Within a general European trend there existed enormous differences between distinct state traditions and transformations. From a comparative perspective, four cases illustrate the diversity of responses to the challenges of socioeconomic transformation and political change during the nineteenth century.[14] Especially in the case of France, this illustrates how important the export of a bureaucratic model of the state could become for other European countries in the crucial period of the French Revolution and the subsequent Napoleonic empire.

France, with the emergence of the revolutionary state, the Napoleonic model, and its export to other continental European states, marked a watershed in the history of the modern state.[15] Three particular elements of the revolutionary and imperial era were exported to countries which were directly occupied by the French or indirectly influenced by developments in France: the new legal codification of the Civil Code which represented essentially bourgeois values, new legal institutions and procedures (especially jury courts), and a modernized and highly centralized administration. Revolutionary France had replaced the administrative chaos of the *ancien régime*, characterized by the contradicting functions of various offices, with a clear organization of new ministries: interior, justice, treasury, foreign policy, and defense. These ministries recruited their personnel from the *ancien régime's* old administration and from those who had politically benefited from the revolution. The result was a new bureaucratic elite, fusing old and new elements. Even more important was the development of special administrations (e.g., for ship building and mining), which recruited their personnel from newly created state institutions.

In these *écoles* (e.g., the *École polytechnique* or the *École normale supérieure* in Paris) a technocratic state elite with a strong identity was generated.

The post-revolutionary bureaucracy represented a highly centralized ideal of administration. It destroyed attempts, especially during the earlier part of the revolution, to achieve at least a certain degree of administrative devolution by allowing local self-government. Thus, even large French cities became subordinate units of the capital's ministries. Only from the later 1870s onwards were municipal councils given the right to elect their mayors. France's administrative structure, as generated by the revolutionary and Napoleonic era, was based on three elements: the local and municipal level, the regional level in the form of *départements*, and the national level in the form of central ministries in Paris. This administrative model was imitated in many other parts of Europe in order to integrate new territories and to implement a centralized government, as for instance in Bavaria and Baden (which, because of the enormous territorial changes between 1803 and 1806, had become much larger middle-states), but also in the new Kingdom of Italy after 1859.[16] The administrative chiefs of the French *départements*, the prefects, were directly appointed by the emperor. They were not only responsible for the implementation of orders from Paris and the organization of elections, but also for the appointment of local mayors and municipal councils. The emperor himself appointed all mayors of larger cities. This state centralization completed and perfected a long-term process which had already started in the *ancien régime*, when French monarchs of the eighteenth century had begun to use the new institution of royal intendants to contain the influence of feudal and corporative powers on a regional and local level. This process was accelerated after 1792 by revolutionary commissioners who had been sent from Paris to all French regions in order to ensure the proper implementation of revolutionary policies. Compared with the authoritarian and repressive nature of this bureaucratic state centralization, the legal system represented, at least to a certain degree, essentially liberal values: property rights, unlimited exchange of goods,

and legal equality. Despite a reform of the judiciary under Napoleon, the revolutionary ideal of a separate and independent third power besides legislative and executive remained theory. All political turning points of French history in the nineteenth century – 1814/15, 1830, 1848, 1851, 1870/1 – led to political purges of the judicial institutions. In terms of a social history of the French state, it is remarkable to see that despite the aim to fuse noble and bourgeois elements into a new loyal elite of *notables*, the social profile of the Napoleonic bureaucracy was essentially bourgeois: 85 percent had started their career after the revolution, and 70 percent had a middle-class background. Privileged by the imperial regime, they owed their careers no longer to being born into an already privileged estate, but to their talent and their education.[17]

A second type of state can be described as dynastic military, represented in different ways and with contrasting consequences by Prussia and the Habsburg Empire. Both Austria and Prussia had initiated far-reaching reform projects in the eighteenth century. These had been motivated by enlightened principles under Frederick the Great and Joseph II, and the aim to make the state more effective in mobilizing its resources. Raising taxes and strengthening military power remained the two main motives behind these reforms. Confronted with the victories of the revolutionary and Napoleonic armies, these apparently successful models of enlightened absolutism were questioned and forced to embark on a new era of reforms. Indeed, following the Prussian defeat against Napoleon, a generation of Prussian bureaucratic reformers had a temporarily extraordinary freedom of political action. This resulted in attempts to transform the corporatist society into a non-feudal, liberal market society, characterized by legal equality and socioeconomic modernization. The abolition of serfdom in 1807 was an important step in this direction, but the former landlords succeeded in maintaining many reserved rights, which in Prussia survived until the end of World War I.

Whereas the Prussian imitation of the French administrative model based upon central ministries as well as the separation of the judiciary from the administration proved to be successful, the Prussian road to a state founded on the rule of law and a constitutional basis proved to be much longer and much more difficult. Only in 1849 was a constitution granted by the Prussian king, and it included a restrictive three-class franchise which was only abolished in October 1918. Since the 1820s Prussian state bureaucrats had lost much of their reform reputation and many liberals, despite the state's role in fostering economic reforms, regarded the bureaucratic state more and more not as a potential ally but as part of the problem of political paralysis.[18] In contrast to France, Prussia's administrative structure did not follow a consistently centralist model. The *Landräte* as the chief administrative officers of the regional districts were not recruited from a centrally trained elite in Berlin, but from the class of the regional estate owners. They represented both the Prussian monarchy and the interest of the landowning class. Even in 1910 no less than 58 percent of the Prussian *Landräte* were of noble origin – a remarkable difference compared with the dominating bourgeois social profile of the French prefects.[19] Furthermore, and again different from France, Prussia allowed her cities to develop much more autonomous self-government, as the early municipal reforms of Freiherr vom Stein after 1806 underlined.

Compared with Prussia, the Austrian bureaucratic state reforms had a much more limited impact, due to the end of enlightened reform absolutism after Joseph II and the restorative tendencies under Metternich after 1815. If reforms were carried out, they clearly followed a pattern of military and autocratic implementation, such as after 1848/9 in Hungary, where still-existing feudal institutions were abolished. However, overall, the bureaucracy after 1815 lost all reform initiative and became an institution more and more identified with the preservation of the status quo, a development furthered by political and religious censorship and the reemergence of aristocratic patronage. The administration of the multiethnic Habsburg Empire was centralized, but highly complex because of various intermediate institutions. With the exception of Hungary – where, after the compromise of 1867, civil servants were recruited from the Magyars – the empire was governed by a German elite.

Britain remained on a special path in the development of modern state structures, very much characterized by the long-term reform of self-government. Here the failure of continental absolutism in 1688/9 led to a unique constellation. In stark contrast to continental experiences, the development of a bureaucracy as the monarchy's central administrative institution was stopped, allowing the landed gentry to maintain fundamental administrative functions. This type of aristocratic self-government became a most persistent factor in the development of British bureaucracy even in the nineteenth century. Local self-government, as represented by the landed nobility, dominated the counties, where for example justices of peace were recruited from the landed nobility until the late 1880s. Local self-government meant that the power of central administrative institutions in London remained rather limited and developed relatively late, for instance regarding Poor Law regulations and their implementation.[20]

Only as a consequence of early industrialization did this begin to change in the 1830s, when, responding to the social problems in larger cities, the Poor Law Amendment Act of 1834 provided for state inspectors responsible for maintaining centrally defined standards. The 1830s also witnessed far-reaching reforms of municipal self-government, which was now based upon elected municipal councils, leading to a rise of municipal services and communal bureaucracies in the second half of the century. Compared with this strong tradition of local self-government, the development of central institutions primarily followed a pattern of fiscal and military functions. In contrast to continental cases, the central ministries only developed a larger infrastructure from the 1830s onwards, especially in the case of the Home Office, which was responsible for recruiting inspectors for the Poor Law regulations, for schools, and health policies. They also cooperated closely with local governments. But compared with the continental experiences of France, Prussia, and Austria, the British central state bureaucracy remained a relatively small and loose organization of various old and new institutions in London. Only in 1870 was a system of central examinations introduced for those applying for posts as higher civil servants. In contrast to the continental dominance of lawyers among the bureaucratic elite, most officials in Whitehall had experienced an education in Oxbridge, underlining the amateur ideal of generally educated gentlemen. However, the much more progressive characteristics of modern bureaucracies in the British case developed in the colonial administration, the Indian Civil Service and the Colonial Office, which became much more of a centralized and highly elitist organization, characterized by special training.[21]

Finally, the history of the state in Russia marks a fourth European type, a case of imitating modernization. In contrast to the cases described above, Russia did not experience any constitutionalization before 1905, underlining the contemporary reputation of an autocratic regime with corrupt bureaucracies. However, this interpretation overlooks the fact that the Russian bureaucracy was the product of imitation of Western examples. Peter I and Catherine II had studied and copied models of absolutist and enlightened state administration of their Western neighbors – the reforms of 1775–82 which introduced *gouvernements* and districts followed West European examples – whereas the legacy of revolutionary and imperial France did not have a lasting influence. Until 1861 the Russian state had delegated all legal and police functions to local landowners. Local self-administration was based upon the village community, which was collectively responsible for the payment of taxes and the distribution of land.

This constellation limited the central state's ability to penetrate the countryside, and indeed the administration on the levels of *gouvernements* and districts remained largely ineffective and weak. Attempts to achieve a more effective noble self-government were only partly successful, as the limited impact of local *Zemstvos* institutions illustrated in the later 1860s. It took more than three decades until these new bodies could stimulate any improvement of public services such as road construction, public health, and schooling. This particular structure was very much due to the fact that

St. Petersburg – with its central administrative institutions, and its political and cultural attractions – increasingly absorbed the talented and ambitious from the regional provinces and deprived local and regional self-government of a reform-oriented and self-confident elite. In combination with a fragile financial basis, caused by the lack of industrial development and by the agrarian sector's low productivity, the tsarist bureaucracy's attempts to stimulate the country's modernization remained extremely limited. It proved unable to imitate successfully the state-building process of Russia's Western neighbors in a period of socioeconomic change and political tension. It was World War I that served as a catalyst for bureaucratic modernization in Russia, which continued after 1917, when Bolshevik Socialism marked the start of a new era of state intervention on a hitherto unknown scale.[22]

New Functions, New Conflicts: Communication and Infrastructure, Education and Social Welfare, and the Emergence of the Interventionist State before 1914

Three basic processes accompanied the development of modern state bureaucracies in Europe from the mid-eighteenth century onwards. Towards the end of the nineteenth century, especially after 1880, these processes combined and led to a new constellation in which the early roots of the modern interventionist state became obvious, though with remarkable differences in distinct European contexts: first, the dynamic demographic development and its consequences, especially mass migration within Europe; secondly, the industrial transformation of societies which absorbed the human surplus. Both processes led to social transformations and also social unrest, but they affected European regions to different degrees. Whereas the northwestern part of Europe – starting in England, then expanding to North and Central Europe, including the northern zones of the Mediterranean (northern Italy, northern Spain/Catalonia) – became industrialized, the south and east remained very much excluded from these processes and maintained a primarily agrarian structure. Industrialization meant an enormous potential for increasing and intensifying state power through raising taxes, and indeed one can observe that states and societies in the northwest of Europe since the 1870s experienced the most rapid and far-reaching expansion of modern administrations.[23] In many European contexts, and especially in the case of socioeconomic latecomers, state governments and their bureaucracies acted as agencies to stimulate modernization through a "revolution from above," by state regulation of the agrarian and manufacturing sectors, through legal and educational stimuli, and through state investments in industrial developments, especially in railway building.

Thirdly, the nineteenth century witnessed a revolution of communication with far-reaching consequences. This process accompanied the increasing mobility and expanding exchange of information among ever greater parts of society. It was based on technical innovations – the railways, telegraphs, and telephone – which reduced distances in time and space and led to a hitherto unknown intensity of exchange of information: letters, books, newspapers, and journals contributed to the dynamic circulation of information and to the development of a better informed public. The bureaucratic state of the nineteenth century was in many ways one of the motors behind this process: by the invention of modern statistics, by regulating time and orthography, by encouraging, stimulating, and enforcing literacy, by directing and administering railway building, post, and telegraph.[24] Administrative communication used the new media, thus serving as a catalyst for technical improvements and their implementation. This also meant that the new bureaucracies needed well educated and trained personnel; school and university education therefore became a vital precondition for effectively functioning states machineries.

Thus, new functions of the state developed when the industrial revolution intensified in continental societies. Railwaymen, postmen, policemen, and teachers, an army of state civil servants, became everyday symbols of the various state functions. Railway building in the 1840s became a key component of investment, and in many cases (e.g., in the German states and France) it was state governments which led the way. State investments in post and telegraph stimulated mass communication. Primary and secondary education and the maintaining of public order were regarded as primary state functions. As a consequence of these processes, the number of state civil servants exploded, especially after 1850. Between 1870 and 1900 the numbers rose from 210,000 to 405,000 in Germany, from 99,000 to 395,000 in Britain, and from 224,000 to 304,000 in France, indicating the relatively modest level from which Britain started, compared with the already large state apparatus on the continent, but underlining the dynamic growth in the last third of the century, which became a European feature of the period.[25]

Two key state activities in the late nineteenth century deserve special attention, because they demonstrate not only the state's expansion, but also the potential limits and conflicts connected with this process. Education was no longer regarded as a private matter. It had to serve the state's interests and thus, in the eyes of contemporaries, legitimized the state's primary role in directing schools and universities – more directly in the French Third Republic than in the British monarchy. It became a prime target of state governments in Northern Europe between 1880 and World War I, and the funding of primary schools, trained teachers, and free education was reflected in state budgets, which also underlined the enormous differences between the north and south of Europe. In 1901 Germany spent no less than 12 percent of its state budgets on public education, England 10 percent, and France 8 percent, but Spain only 1.5 percent. The most important motive behind intensified education politics was national integration, which was of special importance not only for the French Third Republic after 1871 and the new nation-states of Italy and Germany, but also for the multiethnic empires of Russia and Austria. A common language seemed to be a more successful instrument of achieving unity than just a dynasty.[26]

But the state's activity in education also led to new conflicts, as the bitter antagonisms between state governments and the Catholic church in countries with large Catholic populations demonstrated. In France, the republican governments expelled teaching congregations from the primary school sector in 1886, provoking the growth of private Catholic schools which did not receive any state funds but attracted many pupils. In Germany the *Kulturkampf* between the government and the Catholic church was not only about the church's educational influence, but also represented a bitter conflict over loyalty to the new nation-state of 1871. In the eyes of German liberals, Catholicism stood for a "Romish" and hence universalistic set of ideas which was deemed unpatriotic, and they also pointed to the antagonistic ideologies between apparently enlightened liberal tendencies on the one hand and reactionary Catholic on the other. Here the conflict between state and church only concealed deeper-rooted conflicts over identity patterns in a period of nation-state building. In Italy the anti-clerical left unsuccessfully tried to abolish the catechism in state schools. In Spain the new state school reform of 1902 which introduced state-paid teachers and supervision by local and regional boards, provoked strong resistance from the Catholic church and Catholic politicians and associations. In all these cases the expansion of state activity met fierce resistance and underlined the complex and often limited nature of this process.[27]

In the context of rapid industrialization and urbanization, which affected more and more continental societies in the second half of the nineteenth century, European states were confronted with dynamic social change that questioned the traditional instruments of social welfare offered by churches, mutual aid corporations, and other charities. The social question of the day made it obvious that state repression was not an adequate response to the legitimate demands of industrial workers.[28] The case was particular in Germany, where universal manhood suffrage became part of the constitutional basis of the new nation-state of 1871. Here, Bismarck, who had believed in the natural conservatism of the workers, was confronted with the growing organizational and

political strength of German socialism as the representative of the German proletariat. Bismarck's response was a dual strategy of repression on the one hand (based on anti-socialist legislation which also provided a common ground for his cooperation with the Catholic centre) and worker-friendly social legislation on the other. It followed the model of "reforms from above," initiated – as in the days of the Prussian reforms after 1806 – by state governments and bureaucrats in order to avoid a further gap between state and society. Paradoxically, state socialism set the pace for innovative and modern social legislation and the origins of the modern welfare state in Germany, but the motives behind it were at the same time dominated by political conservatism. In order to achieve conservative ends, Bismarck was prepared to apply progressive means – without success in the long term, because neither anti-socialist legislation nor social state legislation could prevent the rise of the SPD, which by 1913 became the strongest political party in *Reichstag* elections.

Although the dimensions of the social insurance schemes of the 1880s (consisting of compensation for industrial accidents, sickness benefits, and old age and disability pensions) should not be overestimated – the full pension, for example, was only received at the age of 70, after 48 years of contributions, and could not be passed on to a widow or children – it signified the change from a traditionally reactive position of the state and a laissez-faire strategy to a proactive and potentially intervening welfare state. This not only had a deep impact on the meaning of the paternalist state and expectations of state activity in a period of dynamic social change in Germany, but also stimulated other European countries.

In the case of Britain, the influence of industrialists and their focus on freedom of contract and the ideal of self-help limited the development of an interventionist social state legislation for a long time. In contrast to Germany, there was no strong tradition of state-led and proactive reforms from above. Furthermore, the development of an independent labor party was a relatively late development, hence the government was under less political pressure to respond to a powerful representative of the

④ Russia - copied Western bureaucracy
 • less centralized → cannot modernize
* Does he not see constitutionalization as imp.?
Indust. → Taxes → State Expansion
• Communication (new tech) implemented by bureaucracies
• Education comes under the state → Nat'l Integration
 → Conflict w/ Church

• Dynamic social change → questions traditional
instruments of social welfare
 • Bismarck applies progressive means to achieve
 conservative ends
 • Laissez-faire → Welfare
 • British tradition of self-help slows social
 reforms

Ch. 11: Rise of the Modern Leviathan
         State Functions & State Features

early 19th c. - New distinction btw State & Society
→ French Revolution

- Rise of bureaucracies out of Enlightenm
sense of order & to deal w/ demograph
rev.

- War ⇒ Expansion of states through
mobilization of money & men (conscription
& taxes)

    · Defeat ⇒ Reform

- Difficult to implement rule of law in
states not influenced by Roman Law

✳ 4 cases reflect DIVERSITY of response
to socioeconomic transformation & political chan

① Rev. France, Napoleonic Model ⇒ exported
    · Centralization through départements
    · Legal System, Bourgeois, Liberal

② Dynastic Military - Prussia & Austria

③ Britain = aristocratic self-government
- Dev. of Bureaucracy in mid 19th c.

industrial workers. Some progress was made under the Liberal government of 1892–5, but Joseph Chamberlain's demands for poverty and unemployment legislation did not lead to large-scale schemes. Despite the Conservative government's cautious steps, the Workmen's Compensation Act of 1897 indicated a clear shift towards an interventionist and proactive state policy.[29]

In France, a government of moderate republicans and radicals initiated social legislation in the late 1890s, when the socialist Millerand took over the ministry of commerce. The Factory Act of 1900 reduced working hours for men and women in workshops. In Catholic countries such as Italy, both the state and the church focused on the social issue. Pope Leo XIII's encyclical *Rerum Novarum* was meant to encourage Catholic associations in order to weaken socialism.

Looking at the architectural incarnations of European states – its heritage in the numerous town halls and court buildings all across Europe's capitals, imitating and at the same time often overshadowing dynastic palaces as if it symbolized the state's emancipation from traditional types of rule – it seems obvious to regard the rise of the modern state in nineteenth-century Europe as an unbroken and somehow inevitable process.[30] But a closer look at the limits and resistance – as illustrated by the antagonisms between state and church as well as between state and working classes – may warn us about such a simplistic perspective. The history of the modern Leviathan is also the history of the many bitter conflicts which its rise provoked.

NOTES

1 Entrèves (1967); Mager (1968); Oppenheimer (1975); Poggi (1978); Dyson (1980).
2 Marx (1852); Cowling and Martin (2002).
3 Weber, "Politics as a Vocation" (1919) in Gerth and Mills (1948); see also Beetham (1985).
4 Tilly (1975: 21); Raphael (2000: 17).
5 Raphael (2000: 13); Schulze (1995: 150–2).

6 Barker (1944); Genet (1990); Reinhard (1999).
7 I. A. A. Thompson (1976); Hochedlinger (2003); Gantet (2003: 119–21); Brewer (1989).
8 Parker (1988: 24); Raphael (2000: 20).
9 Moran and Waldron (2003).
10 Tombs (2000: 16).
11 Quoted in Raphael (2000: 10).
12 Ibid: 21–2.
13 Rosenberg (1958); Mueller (1984).
14 Raphael (2000: 41–75).
15 Ponteil (1966); Church (1981); Rosanvallon (1990).
16 Fried (1963); Davis (1988).
17 Charle (1980: 20–32); Raphael (2000: 49).
18 Gillis (1971); Lüdtke (1979).
19 Witt (1985).
20 Chester (1981); Pellew (1982); Waller (1983); Emsley (1983); Corrigan and Sayer (1985); Eastwood (1994).
21 Young (1961); Cell (1970); Kaminsky (1986).
22 Starr (1972); Pinter (1980); Lincoln (1990).
23 Raphael (2000: 13–14).
24 Perrot and Woolf (1984).
25 Tombs (2000: 17).
26 Gildea (1987: 351).
27 Ibid: 353.
28 Ibid: 356–60.
29 Mommsen and Mock (1981).
30 Lane (1983).

GUIDE TO FURTHER READING

There is still a relative lack of systematically comparative works on the emergence of the modern state. The best overviews are still Barker's *Development of Public Services in Western Europe*, Dyson's *State Tradition in Western Europe*, and Tilly's *Formation of Nation States in Western Europe*, which concentrates on the relation between nation and state building in comparative perspective. See also Schulze's *States, Nations, and Nationalism* for a more recent and stimulating overview. Mommsen and Mock's *Emergence of the Welfare State* provides an innovative view on Germany and Britain, thus challenging some notions about apparent pioneers and latecomers. The crucial role of wars for state-building processes has been analyzed for the British case by John Brewer's excellent and groundbreaking case study *The Sinews of Power*, which should now be read in combination with Moran and Waldron's *People in Arms*.

Useful works on the different European cases which, if read together, allow comparative perspectives include Chester's *English Administrative System* and Palmer's *Police and Protest in England*

and Ireland for Britain in the long nineteenth century; Church's *Revolution and Red Tape* and Payne's *The Police State of Louis Napoleon Bonaparte* on France. For Italy, see Davis's *Conflict and Control*. On Prussia, see Mueller's *Bureaucracy, Education, and Monopoly* and especially Lüdtke's *Police and State in Prussia*.

CHAPTER TWELVE

The Democratic Experience

JOHN GARRARD

This chapter will focus on the experience of the political elites presiding over whatever liberalization and democratization there was, and of the adult population participating in the politics that resulted. I will examine not just enfranchisement and elections, but also experience within the civil associations now often seen as underpinning viable liberal democracy. I shall concentrate on experiences in Britain, France, Germany, Scandinavia, Italy, and Russia. However, first we should explore the political and social contexts wherein, at vastly contrasting rates, this experience began.

Contexts

Widely varying political regimes found themselves in situations where none was immune from having to react, flexibly or inflexibly, conservatively or liberally, to ever-growing pressures for the popularization of their political systems. These ranged from France's temporarily revolutionary and democratic regime in 1789 through constitutional, parliamentary, albeit deeply oligarchic, systems like Britain's and Norway's, where monarchical power, though still often highly significant, had been limited for some time, to the varyingly absolutist and heavily monarch-centered regimes across most of Europe. Democratization theorists would see initial regimes as important: authoritarian, still more totalitarian, regimes, and the cultures they tend to produce, are gen-erally less friendly to democratic development than more liberal ones.

All these regimes initially attempted to suppress or harass "dangerous" political tendencies, but none was capable of (or wanted to) control to the point achieved by twentieth-century totalitarianism – where not just actions but also thoughts, even whole popular mindsets, were up for grabs. Russia aside, all had concepts of consultation and representation, if only through the constrained and irregular medieval estates system; none possessed police or other resources sufficient to attempt such domination. Absolutism could seriously inhibit civil society, but, across Europe, once socioeconomic change began generating mass political articulation, control was necessarily limited. Thus it is easier to envisage liberal democracy emerging from absolutist regimes than their totalitarian successors, because the former were far less able to prevent the emergence of underpinning democratic cultures. This was somewhat true even of so ambitiously absolutist a regime as tsarist Russia's – though here control achieved levels where significant parts of emerging political civil society were themselves authoritarian in both self-administration and aspiration.

Yet we should also note that those regimes showing even temporary signs of liberal or constitutional development before 1789 were among those most likely eventually to emerge as successful democratic states. These include regimes in Britain, the Netherlands, Norway (loosely controlled by Denmark until 1814, thereafter equally loosely by Sweden), and Sweden, which became a limited monarchy from 1723, reacquired absolutism after Gustav III's coup in 1772, then returned permanently to constitutional monarchy after Gustav IV's 1809 abdication. There were, however, also determinedly absolutist regimes like Denmark's up to 1848 that emerged as perfectly success-ful democracies. Some autocratic regimes, like Germany, could have so emerged had it not been for the interwar economic catastrophes.

Capitalization and its companions – indus-trialization, urbanization, and expanding com-munications – were creating situations and social groups challenging the political bases of all regimes. Existing ruling elites had to react to these challenges. Absolutist monarchs occa-sionally remembered to consult the estates, but invariably dismissed them and, by 1800, they had sometimes forgotten them altogether. Pre-revolutionary France had three: nobility, clergy, and commons. So did Sweden: nobles, clergy, and burghers – adding peasants in 1723. Austrian emperors, contemplating their vast dominions, thought there might be five: nobles, clergy, burghers, knights, and peasants. In all these cases estates were hardly represen-tative of the people and the same is true for many eighteenth-century parliaments. Though historians now view the eighteenth-century House of Commons and its electorate as more representative of Britain's social structure than their predecessors,[1] its franchise, still more its constituency boundaries, were increasingly at odds with accelerating social change and pop-ulation movement.

Social change created conditions favorable to mass politicization. It was no accident that the 1848 revolutions centered upon towns. Migration uprooted rural people, often causing even those remaining to feel more conditional about their attachments. For both migrants and non-migrants, social and political defer-ence was likely to be eroded at least in the short term. Industrialization and urbanization greatly increased social complexity, doubly so because their initial impact, while often dramatic, also varied greatly across any given country. People were gathered into situations – large work-

places, towns, neighborhoods (particularly once these began stabilizing as in Britain in the 1870s) – likely to facilitate exchange of experi-ence. They developed common if varied senses of identity, and enhanced their means of defending and advancing their perceived interests. Urban dwellers, at least those even marginally above subsistence, organized for common purposes, whether social, sociable, economic, or political. Given that subscriptions were paid to those organizations, some form of internal democracy was thought of as the best means of holding accountable those who administered them. The growing communica-tions revolution invariably centered on towns and made organization easier. The emerging civil society flourished in the new urban centers.

Because it was associated with individualism, capitalism has frequently been seen as naturally friendly to liberal democracy, to a point where the latter is perceived as almost inevitably flowing from the former.[2] In fact, capitalism's more specific effects were rather ambiguous. Its impact upon artisans illustrates this: it enriched some while deeply immiserating others in less advantageous market positions. But capital-ism's periodic ability to produce rising real incomes for those being politically included was highly beneficial. In Britain, substantial working-class male inclusion in 1867 and 1884 was followed by an extended period of rising real wages, as was women's inclusion, along with remaining men, in 1918 and 1928.[3] The same is true of nineteenth-century Scandinavian and German politics.

However, agriculture still dominated most European economies for most of the century. As socioeconomic change was rapidly eroding rural deference, there was no necessary incom-patibility between agriculture and democracy. However, the rural situations were certainly less encouraging to democratic political culture than their urban counterparts.

Finally, the French Revolution gave a major boost to the European democratic experience. It changed France's regime and political culture fairly permanently and in decisively democratic directions. It also conditioned political experi-ence and expectations among wide segments of many European societies: inspiring some, terrifying others. It boosted opinion politics over those impelled by deference and bribery. Whatever its leaders intended, the revolution and its aftermath put popular sovereignty, alongside liberalism and nationalism, upon European political agendas, outside perhaps Russia.

Elite Experience

Elites were crucial to nineteenth-century democratic success or failure. In democratization's "first phase,"[4] they were likely to exert the greatest influence. Legislative and governmental initiatives depended on them. Elites were socially, culturally, economically, and politically dominant across Europe. France aside, they came predominantly from aristocratic or gentlemanly hereditary landowners who dominated governments, held exclusive sway in most upper legislative houses, and heavily influenced lower-house personnel. They oversaw the transformation towards mass politics, substantially influencing the terms and conditions under which larger segments of the population were included in the political system. At the absolutist and economically least-developed end of Europe, Russia's government in 1914, even its recently created Duma, was noble-dominated. At the other end, in Britain, much the most industrialized and urbanized European country, the landed classes dominated national governmental, parliamentary, and administrative elites until at least the 1880s. Along with wealthy business families with whom they were merging to produce "a generalized upper class,"[5] they remained centrally important until at least 1914. Even the Liberal cabinet that curtailed the Lords' veto over Commons legislation and produced a land tax was substantially suffused with landed personnel.

With the intermittent exception of French elites, none exactly welcomed mass politics. They disliked the idea of sharing power with those they regarded as their social inferiors. Most, mindful of the French Revolution and its ensuing aristocratic carnage, initially reacted to popular pressures with fear and hostility, and some (as in Russia and Austria) continued thus until 1914. Even French elites generally shared their European counterparts' fears about "the dangerous classes,"[6] these determining their

perceptions of the 1848 revolutions and 1871 Commune. Outside France, even among elites consenting to expand formal political inclusion, none initially saw their actions as ushering in democracy. Rather, as in Britain, they were including those rendering themselves "politically fit" – by demonstrating they possessed rationality, appropriate and politically undisruptive values, and "a stake" in the existing system. Only a minority within any European elite included women within this charmed circle. Most eventually made varying degrees of peace with popular politics while determinedly trying to ensure its introduction occurred in ways compatible with their own continued power and privilege. This was why most regimes chose to *stage* the process of political inclusion, long-retaining property and education as a significant basis of enfranchisement. It was also why liberalization, outside Britain, proceeded equally cautiously: many countries – notably but not exclusively Germany, Austria-Hungary, and Russia – remaining significantly absolutist until the end.

Thus these perceptions considerably affected how all elites reacted to pressures for political inclusion. All, even the most despotic, were eventually forced into some compromise with those below. All were impelled into more significant negotiation with dominant economic forces beyond their mostly landed ranks. However, two patterns of reaction are broadly distinguishable, roughly coinciding with countries east and west of the Rhine. First, there were elites who, after varying periods of resistance, made their peace with popular forces – in staged and managed ways, permitting degrees of popular participation by enfranchising groups as they were deemed "politically fit," and explicitly allowing degrees of influence upon the political process. Most had reached manhood suffrage by 1914, thereby admitting "a right" to vote; all except Finland (1906) included women only in or after 1918. France, with the least traditional elite, democratized most rapidly. Having briefly flirted with manhood suffrage during the 1789 revolution, and then returned to something much more propertied under Napoleon and the Bourbon and Orleanist monarchies, it reembraced formal male democracy in 1848 – retaining it thereafter, Napoleonic and even Third Republican manipulations notwithstanding. With the 1875 constitution, governments became clearly responsible to parliament. Having briefly liberalized in 1789, 1830, and 1848, French politicians commenced more permanent, though hesitant, liberalization from 1863.

Other countries conducted the process in more stately fashion, leaving copious counterbalances in place. Britain, for example, having long-since established regular elections and constitutional monarchy, substantially expanded urban middle-class voters and representation in 1832. It then conducted substantial cohorts of urban and rural workingmen into the system in 1867 and 1884. It permitted female household heads the municipal vote in 1869, and finally established universal suffrage in 1918 and 1928. Sweden, having finally discarded absolutism in 1809, began a similarly staged democratization of the resulting constitution. It did not abolish the ancient estates representational system until 1865, but then it established regular elections in roughly equal constituencies whereby 20 percent of adult males could vote for the upper house and 40 percent (though with plural voting) for the lower. Qualified manhood suffrage and PR emerged in 1909, and universal suffrage in 1918. As in other Scandinavian countries, movement towards parliamentary (rather than monarchical) sovereignty was even slower, with ministerial legislative responsibility not clearly established till 1905. Denmark, having abandoned absolutism by popular pressure only in 1849, began a multi-stage democratization process from a situation where one in seven of the adult male population could vote for the lower house in 1849, to universal suffrage and proportional representation (PR) in 1915, though some women could vote nationally as early as 1866.

The Italian states experienced brief but well-remembered flirtations with parliamentarism and universal manhood suffrage under Napoleon in 1796 and during the twilight of hereditary rulers in 1848–9. However, Piedmont aside (developing a constitutional monarchy from 1848), they remained resolutely, even ferociously, absolutist until Italy began to be an independent entity after Austrian defeats by France in 1859. There then started slow progress towards universal manhood suffrage via successive erosions of heavily propertied franchises for Italy's national and myriad local governments in 1880, 1882, 1887, and 1912. The destination, reinforced by PR, was finally reached in 1918–19. Again, the establishment of parliamentary government and erosion of kingly discretion was even slower, though the former had been fairly clearly established by 1900.

Similar patterns of staged political inclusion, conducted mostly by traditional elites, and laced with slowly declining monarchical intrusion and autonomy, are observable in Norway, Finland (notwithstanding loose Russian control), Belgium, and Holland. However, Italy's example takes us over the hazy borderline into the second group, mostly but not exclusively east of the Rhine. Here traditional elites, after varying periods of resistance, and to varying degrees, also made peace with popular forces by liberalizing and popularizing their regimes. However, unlike most West European elites they did so within political frameworks intended to remain basically autocratic, even while sometimes permitting some popular influence. Germany's example demonstrates how the desire to retain authoritarian political regimes mixed with powerful liberalizing forces to produce "a hybrid."[7] There were intermittent signs of constitutional development among German states in 1814–15 and again in 1830. Though both were suppressed or discontinued, rulers universally yielded to the 1848 revolutionaries, granting constitutions leaning heavily in liberal, even democratic, directions. Though rapidly subjected to further and sometimes brutal suppression, these mostly survived, becoming bases for further grudging liberal-democratic development after Germany's forcible unification by Prussia in 1871. Most states formally guaranteed liberal political freedoms; most possessed legislatures regularly elected, directly or indirectly and sometimes having formidable powers. By 1914, some states, particularly south German ones, had manhood suffrage and governments at the edge of legislative responsibility.

At the national level, Bismarck had introduced manhood suffrage for the North

German Federation in 1866 and retained it for the federal *Reichstag* elections in 1871, reinforced less intentionally by secret voting. This lower house held sway over the budget, and had significant powers at least of delay. The persecution of Catholics was abandoned in the 1870s and the 1878 Anti-Socialist Law lapsed in 1890. More generally, in spite of periodic repression and harassment, federal and state governments by 1900 had arrived at grudging tolerance of the existence and activities of most political movements, including working-class and socialist ones. By viewing these as interest groups, most regimes felt able to grant them significant concessions. Unsurprisingly, this was most evident with agriculture and heavy industry. However, substantial gestures were also made towards the increasingly complex rural and urban *Mittelstand*, Catholics, even the socialist-oriented working class. Though state and federal governments and heads of state retained very substantial autonomy, this was not different in kind from those still retained by Italian, Danish, or Dutch rulers, located in the first, more democratically hopeful group of countries.

However, despotic continuities also need emphasis. The 1830 and 1848 revolutions were firmly, even brutally, repressed, and the surviving constitutions often reduced, certainly in the medium term, to elegant formalities. Many (particularly north German) states resolutely restricted or otherwise qualified their franchises to the very end. Most notorious was Prussia's unchanged three class franchise of 1849, which though granting votes to most adult males, divided them into three equal groups, with the propertied upper two together electing twice as many as the third, even though this comprised three-quarters of the population. Bismarck granted manhood suffrage in the confident aristocratic belief that the lower orders (being largely rural or small-town) were safely deferential, could neutralize dangers represented by troublesome liberals, and be manipulated into nationalism.[8]

Governments actively and passively attempted political control. As far as possible, given a burgeoning press, news was carefully managed. State-level elections were vigorously manipulated. Bureaucracies, assisted by gerry-mandered boundaries, were expected to manage them, and their efforts often created amenable parliaments. *Reichstag* elections were not manipulated, but constituencies, roughly distributed according to population in 1871, were never changed. They became increasingly maldistributed in favor of rural areas in face of ever-accelerating demographic change.

The *Reichstag*'s influence, like its state counterparts, was substantially counterbalanced by often-appointed and invariably landed upper houses. This merely formalized the German landed/military caste's general power, not different from, but far exceeding, landed influence in first-group polities. If regimes permitted and conciliated representations from below, it was because groups allowed themselves to fit into traditional and still highly autocratic pictures of subjects "petitioning" their rulers. This points to the central fact that neither federal nor state governments were drawn from or effectively accountable to legislatures, however democratically elected. They were appointed by and responsible to royal rulers, who thought themselves ultimately accountable only to God. Finally, even if governments grudgingly tolerated political movements, this did not stop their police watching and harassing the rather wide spectrum considered dangerous. Given the passing of the ultimately restrictive 1908 Law of Associations, the reversion to more inflexible chancellors after Bülow's 1909 resignation, it is hard to know where tolerance was headed by 1914. While the distinction between, say, Italy (which also passed an anti-socialist law in 1894) and Germany appears hazy, other second-group regimes appear more emphatically and enduringly despotic. This is true of Austro-Hungary for which there is no room here. Even more is it true of Russia, which remained a largely unreconstructed despotism until at least 1905.

The Russian tsar and his ministers were subject to no constitution, untroubled by any legislature (representative or otherwise), and darkly suspected all popular movements. The only points where rulers were obliged to hear their subjects were via the supplicatory channels of petitioning. With no constitution, there was not even formalized recognition of liberal freedoms; political parties indeed were banned before 1905. Though Alexander II established a local governmental network in 1862, the franchise was heavily property weighted, and the *Zemstvos* were perceived and long-treated as administrative arms of government, without political significance – though they increasingly became something more. When the Duma was finally conceded in an effort to sidestep the 1905 revolution, it had limited legislative powers, and was popularly elected on a class basis. This heavily advantaged property, disadvantaged its opposite, and separated voters from their ultimate deputies by stages of selection that multiplied the further down the social scale the voters were located. The Duma was juxtaposed against a state council, "elected" by clergy, *Zemstvos*, nobility, academy of sciences, and trade and industrial organizations. When the first Duma proved disappointingly unaccommodating, it was dissolved. When subsequent elections failed to produce something more pliable, a virtual *coup d'etat* produced a third Duma elected on a franchise even more restrictive and advantageous to landowners. Meanwhile, toleration even of clearly constitutionalist political civil society (the Kadets and Octobrists, for example) was barely grudging and remained heavily laced with police surveillance and harassment.

However, as with Germany, historians have recently been less pessimistic about tsarist Russia's political direction by 1914. Though limited, Duma powers to enact and refuse legislation were considerable. Historians have not just emphasized the relative vibrancy of civil society and the *Zemstvos*, but also the third Duma's limited susceptibility to government pressure.[9] Government ministers, particularly Stolypin – Russia's last effective prime minister – are seen by some as learning to conciliate at least some non-landowning interests, play them off against each other, and build alliances for the 1910 social reforms.[10] Though political education was occurring very late, probably too late given social change and pressures developing from below, elites were certainly less inflexible than their predecessors were fifty to a hundred years previously – even if their royal master remained as intractable as ever, and even though, after Stolypin's assassination, the system took another lurch towards reaction.

One reason why most European elites could make some sort of peace with manhood suffrage, if not democracy, was that even the most liberal ones actively manipulated the results. They did this through electoral manipulation, exploiting paternalism and deference, social control, manipulating political agendas, and constraining, shaping, and incorporating civil society. All elites felt themselves at the beginning of a process whose consequences were uncertain, possibly dangerous, and required careful management. Britain's elite, significant because it probably presided over the most liberal, if not the most democratic, polity west of the Rhine, can stand testimony for all. This is so even though the efforts were often ultimately more subtle and self-confident than elsewhere.[11]

As noted, Britain's franchise was periodically expanded to take account of socioeconomic change, but also of spreading "political fitness" and thus safety. Parliamentary seats and constituency boundaries were redistributed to allow enhanced representation for the country's rapidly expanding urban and industrial areas. Yet also operative were calculations of political advantage for parties in power. Furthermore, until 1885, population was never explicitly admitted as a criterion for seat distribution. New towns were selected as constituencies in 1832 and 1867 because they were "communities" with their own visible local elites, commanding deference and respect – in other words because their burgeoning populations were safely under reasonable control from above. In 1885, numbers became the primary basis for drawing boundaries and distributing seats; notions of "community were substantially abandoned. Yet even here, county constituencies were shaped to conserve the parliamentary presence of gentlemanly rural leaders. Paternalism was part of the British calculus. Just as they had long before 1832, nineteenth-century local elites, now including manufacturers, made extensive and often successful attempts to pull the strings of dependency among their voting tenants and employees.[12] Supplementing this until at least 1872 was extensive bribery.

There were also linked attempts at political education, social control, and influence over the political agenda. After 1867 local political parties, controlled as they generally were by local socioeconomic elites, mounted vigorous programs to educate and inform new voters, with talks ranging from "The British Constitution" through historic figures like Cromwell to current affairs.[13] Newspapers were purchased and working-class members urged to read them. There were also persuasive talks about self-help, thrift, and sobriety – the bibulality of Tory clubs notwithstanding. Members were also given opportunities to "mingle" with their betters, thereby improving themselves. Here parties were supplementing much longer-term efforts to civilize the lower orders from charities and other middle- and upper-class-led civil organizations.

The national state added a range of punitive measures to achieve the same result: the New Poor Law was intended to spread habits of self-help by rendering itself baleful in the eyes of those unwisely seeking state assistance. The pauper's lot, whether on indoor or outdoor relief, was rendered visibly shameful. Although the law was originally passed in 1834 and thus social rather than political in intent, its vigorous revival for twenty years after 1871 was more clearly linked to lowering expectations of the state among the newly enfranchised.

British political elites also used the press extensively to promote their own values and ideas. Earlier and more enthusiastically than any other European elite, Britain's elites tolerated, embraced, and incorporated civil society. With formal censorship long-since abandoned, the never-very-effective "taxes on knowledge" began formally eroding in 1837, disappearing altogether in the early 1850s. After attempted repression around the Napoleonic Wars, governments removed the Anti-Combination Laws in 1824–5, and in rival party bids for working-class support, confirmed and safeguarded the right to strike in 1871 and 1875. Having early decided friendly societies were both safe and actively functional in a laissez-faire society, governments set about supervising, regularizing, safeguarding, and encouraging them, starting in 1793 and completing in 1875. Retail cooperatives were similarly encouraged, indeed granted privileged trading status which was never revoked, shopkeeping outrage notwith-

standing. Although working-class radical activity occupied a legal limbo for some decades, governments eased active repression and surveillance after 1832, abandoning it altogether after the mid-1840s.

Finally, with the political agenda partly controlled, national and local political elites, socially elevated though they were, proved remarkably adept at competitively appeasing emerging groups within and even on the margins of the expanding electorate. Politicians like Peel, Palmerston, Disraeli, and most spectacularly Gladstone, along with multiple local counterparts, skillfully tapped into the values and aspirations not just of the urban middle class, but also respectable workingmen. Some of this was rhetorical (important nevertheless), some ceremonial and about giving respectable status within national and local communities; some – like safeguards for friendly societies, cooperatives, and trade unions – altogether more concrete.[14]

In this controlling, manipulative, appeasing, and incorporating behavior, British politicians were part of much broader European patterns, as evident among relatively liberal as more authoritarian regimes. The only difference was that British elites learnt to do it earlier, more subtly, and with less prohibition and repression. French governments, even republican ones, employed their network of prefects and mayors to influence elections just as enthusiastically as their counterparts in the German states. Approaches to trade unions by regimes west of the Rhine were enduringly suspicious, barely less so than those to the east. Sweden fully legalized them only in 1864, granting rights to strike only in 1882; France conditionally and partially in 1884.

Mass Experience

Given the varied ways political elites reacted to prospects of democracy, the varied things they did about it, and the varied socioeconomic contexts across Europe, it follows that the political experience of the adult masses also varied. That experience was shaped both by influences and political contexts set by those above, and pressures created from below. Given this, how many were drawn into politics, how did they perceive their participation, and what affected their perceptions?

Formally speaking, the answer to the first question seems simple. The size and composition of European electorates, even once they started existing, varied according to country, and mostly expanded dramatically over time. The resulting experience was almost exclusively male, but (Russia excepted) embraced most male adults by 1900, still more (including Russia with qualifications) by 1914. However, even then, in most countries it mattered who the voter was. The votes of people from lower social classes were frequently qualified by sometimes multiple votes available for those further up. In some cases, they were qualified also by the latter's more direct and heavily weighted access to the business of actually electing legislators, as distinct from merely choosing those who did – through their "Class" in Prussia or Austria-Hungary or their Curia in post-1905 Russia.

However, nineteenth-century political participation was rarely confined to those legally included. This is so in several senses. First, given restricted or non-existent franchises and rapid socioeconomic change, the more politicized of those politically excluded were likely to demand entry in rapidly increasing numbers, and indeed press for other reforms even before admission. Britain's vast Chartist Movement, with its often massive meetings, demonstrations, and reform petitions (that in 1842 being signed by an only somewhat imaginative 3.5 million), is a spectacular example, as are connected pressures for other sorts of reform from the Anti-Poor Law and Factory Hours movements. Similar agitations could be found at various points in many European countries with liberalizing regimes. Women's suffrage campaigns developed widely around 1900, and in Britain and elsewhere were long-preceded by pressure for widely varying moral causes from movements wherein women, particularly middle-class ones, were substantially, even dominantly, represented.

Other pressures for change from political outsiders are harder to classify in "modern" ways. Rural riots about food prices or taxes, which were dying away in Britain early in the century but persisted much longer elsewhere, were often set within basically deferential frameworks and aimed at causing local landed rulers to perform paternalistic duties of protection. Even where less "respectful" of authority, such disturbances were normally conservatively directed – making government aware of what would not be tolerated, but under the banner "long live the pope" or "keep the old laws."[15] The same is true of the habit of petitioning royal rulers for redress, which persisted in Russia throughout the century. None of these popular interventions focused on demands for long-term political participation as of right, though these could emerge. On the other hand, the many thousands of mainly urban people participating in the century's frequent attempts at revolution were far more likely to produce demands for liberty and enfranchisement, even manhood suffrage, alongside those for national liberation.

Secondly, outsiders also participated in more routine electoral ways. In Britain at least, elections provided access to non-electors as well as electors. This had long been so. Eighteenth-century elections, when contested, even in constituencies with microscopic electorates, engulfed entire communities[16] – rich and poor, women and men. Some of this was about pleasurable ritual, some about getting very drunk. However, some provided access for much more radical action. Such intervention was even legitimized by one meaning of "virtual representation" and justification for open voting – electors *represented* non-electors, and could be legitimately pressurized by "exclusive dealing," even modest terrorization. This continued until 1867, and was one reason why urban parliamentary candidates found it advisable to hold meetings of, and make promises to, non-electors. In one sense, this steadily faded out as the franchise extended, disappearing well short of even manhood suffrage. In another sense, and for women, it expanded. In their tens of thousands, they were one of the most crucial elements staffing the mass parties as they emerged in Britain and elsewhere from the 1870s, particularly with the emergence of bodies like the Women's Liberal Federation and the Primrose League.[17] They provided vehicles for transmitting, even formulating, women's political demands.

Pressures from beyond the political pale could be equally evident in local government. In Britain, Sweden, and some German cities, legitimized participation was more widely available in local than in parliamentary elections.[18] Local electorates were often broader than parliamentary ones. Parish meetings, at least in Britain and Sweden, could be almost totally open, providing access for entire adult communities, doubly so because legitimate participation was hard to police. This was why parish meetings in Britain, particularly before 1850, became vehicles for radical anger over issues like church rates, poor relief, even franchise reform.

Given all this, it is unsurprising that, once people were enfranchised, they often participated in great numbers and exultant enthusiasm. In Britain between 1867 and 1914, urban turnouts of 85 percent were routine – in by-elections as well as general ones, in municipal as in parliamentary contests. This was partly produced by an electoral registration system advantaging the politically committed. However, high turnouts also rapidly characterized French elections after manhood suffrage in 1848, as they did within a decade or so of its appearance in Germany in 1871 – reaching 84 percent in 1907 and 1912. Partly, such apparent enthusiasm was born of novelty, quite often celebration of long fought-for citizenship. Elections were also wonderful entertainment. In drab cities and dull small towns, the tumultuous "hustings," colorful processions, and massively attended meetings, with their formidable speaking contests and constant repartee between candidate and audience, together presented the best show in town.

However, what did all this mean for those participating, legitimately or on the fringes? Were people expressing genuinely held political opinions, or acceptance of their place in the hierarchy, or gratitude for alcoholic and other largesse made available during or between elections? Deference and bribery were certainly important in fueling political behavior, particularly until around the early 1880s. In Britain, these had long been central to elections – in rural counties with their substantial but dependent electorates; in small towns with their small, often malleable and easily corruptible

ones. These habits were even evident among the scattering of large "open boroughs" before 1832. Such traditions continued in spite of the enlarged electorate after 1832, supplying central reasons why the landed elite dominated parliament for so many decades.[19] Indeed, factory paternalism and party-subsidized inebriation were key features of politics in many industrial towns into the 1880s.[20] Shock about the drink-sodden 1868 election persuaded Liberal politicians – always more puritanically inclined than the Tories – to pass the 1872 Ballot Act.

Such behavior was equally evident in France, and a key reason why elections became so vastly expensive with manhood suffrage in 1848. Peasants were often naturally deferential to landlords, many obedient to pressure from local prefects and priests, and everyone liked wine, particularly when provided by someone else. These were important reasons why Louis Napoleon was elected president in 1849, and won elections and plebiscites under the empire from 1851.[21] German electorates could show considerable obedience, particularly when faced by fearsomely paternalistic landlords or industrial employers.

However, the reality was more complex. Borderlines between deferential, corrupt, and opinion-based political behavior were hazy. In Britain, before and after 1832, deference was often conditional upon performance of paternalistic duties in terms of civic improvement, charitable donation, or other largesse. Voters could withhold their respect from patrons perceived to fall short. Bribery, officially condemned but still frequent, and defined as rewards given *during* rather than between elections, indicated still more instrumental relationships between voters and candidates. Furthermore, while some constituencies (particularly cathedral towns!) were anybody's, voting for whoever corrupted most generously, electors in others expected "customary" payments for what they planned to do anyway based on previously formulated opinion. Thus bribery could coincide with high levels of partisan voting.[22] Meanwhile, French peasants, obediently voting Bonapartist during the Second Empire, have been portrayed as implicitly, sometimes explicitly, bargaining with local prefects over the distribution of governmental largesse.[23]

Overall, opinion voting was advancing in all European countries where elections were held, even if somewhat intermittently. However, there were limits to the "democratic-ness" of this emerging culture. Voters often celebrated rights to citizenship. This did not necessarily mean they wished them extended to others. British middle-class males seeking franchise access in 1830–1 did not generally want it extended to their working-class radical allies – one reason for the latter's subsequent sense of betrayal. Respectable workingmen, gaining access in 1867, had just as many reservations about admitting "the residuum," even more about women, as did the aristocratic politicians who let them in. Such reservations also beset most Central European middle-class liberals during the 1848 revolutions, and were central to the Frankfurt parliament's inability to broaden its base by appealing to more radical and less socially elevated forces. Later, they underpinned center and right-wing party attitudes in the German states, and their willingness to cooperate to hamper the SPD by introducing more restricted franchises.

Nevertheless, opinion voting was increasing. Why was this; why was it more evident in some locations than others? It was partly produced by franchise expansion itself: electorates became too large to bribe comfortably. Furthermore, while industrialization and urbanization permitted the emergence of industrial paternalism in the medium term, their longer-term tendency was to undermine deference – as cities got larger and industrial employers more impersonal. Opinion voting was also produced by rises in issues dividing people, particularly those based around religion and class. Among these, franchise agitation itself could produce surges of opinion voting – as in Britain in 1830–1 when most borough patrons temporarily lost control of their electoral property.[24] Franchise expansion enhanced the trend, particularly once electorates reached sizes where mass parties emerged to compete for attention. Another consequence was that states became more interventionist, and parties began making competitive offers of government aid. For some voters anyway, private bribery could pass seamlessly into governmental largesse. These general trends were evident not just in clearly liberalizing countries, but also in more enduringly authoritarian ones. German elections after 1871 were marked by increasingly vibrant debate about major issues. Similar trends were evident during the French Second Empire's last decade. In both locations, authoritarian governments were steadily losing control – hence the rapid electoral rise of French republicanism and German socialism.

Elections themselves were educative, given the vast size of many election meetings, their extensive coverage in the immensely serious nineteenth-century press, and the inexhaustible oratory of elite politicians. Perhaps this is most evident in the least democratically hopeful place. Russia, the decidedly exclusive *Zemstvos* aside, lacked experience of popular consultation until the 1905 revolution. Indeed, the multiplication of electoral layers leading up to the selection of the Duma was designed to neutralize, or at least muffle, the popular will, particularly for peasants and workers who had the greatest number of tiers between themselves and the deputies ultimately selected. Yet the effect was rather different. Ascending from village assembly level and through succeeding layers, one seems to witness peasants and their representatives learning to articulate their interests, and bargain over them with other interests like those of larger landowners, and with emerging political parties over the content and meaning of their programs.[25] Peasant political culture had far to go in this respect, particularly since many saw the process less in terms of regularized and rightful popular consultation than in that of the traditional and occasional business of petitioning the tsar for redress.[26] Nevertheless, further cultural progress did not seem inconceivable by 1914.

The European-wide move towards opinion politics was also strengthened by the associational life rapidly filling the space between state and family. Some was overtly political – like political parties and pressure groups. Some was primarily economic – employers and professional organizations, trade unions, cooperatives, friendly societies. Some was social like charities; and some purely sociable like workingmen's clubs. Nevertheless, many associations were creating points of resistance and articulation against pressures from above, whether from the state or from employing or other elites. Potentially, they were also agencies of "political training" of multiple sorts. How widely available was such civil-associational experience? Membership provides crude though useful indicators. In 1800 it was sparse among peasants and rural and urban workers (friendly societies often excepted), but in 1900 it was far more widespread among all but the most marginal ones, Russia excepted. Membership was higher in Western than in Eastern Europe. It was highest in Britain. But by 1870 the *Mittelstand* and lower middle classes were better organized in France or Germany than they ever would be in Britain. This aside, civil organization was far more evident in Britain than France or Italy, though café society provided alternative, if less formal, venues for discussion of common concerns for all social groups in these latter countries. More generally, and for reasons already explored, organization was far more evident in large urban and industrial areas almost everywhere than in small towns or rural areas. This last dimension remains evident even though rural groups became increasingly organized in the late nineteenth century – witness the vibrant emergence of national and land-reform organizations in Ireland, rural trade unionism in Britain, and vibrant peasants' organizations in France, Italy, Germany, and Scandinavia.

As this suggests, organizational participation also varied by class and more importantly by segments within classes. Among middle-class people, interests were well articulated in the burgeoning ranks of professionals everywhere – both pre-industrial ones like doctors and lawyers, and the new science-based professions like the various sorts of engineers, each of which had often produced societies for exclusively exchanging and reinforcing scarce expertise by the 1860s. Among individualistic entrepreneurs, organization was more patchy – though business groups, both specialized (associations of cotton masters, ironmasters, etc.) and general (chambers of commerce, federations of industry), became increasingly formidable by the 1880s in most countries. This partly connected with the general emergence of

limited companies and cartels. However, for urban middle-class men and women everywhere, charitable activity was so widespread by mid-century (as was religious observance) that it became part of their class identity. So too was participation in moral reform organizations like temperance and prison reform. For similar reasons all middle-class ranks were party-politically active, particularly as mass parties began emerging from the 1860s.

Significantly, there was no automatic fall-off in associational activity upon passing into the working class – though there were clear demarcations within that class. Skilled male workers, industrial or pre-industrial, tended to high levels of associational activity. With democratic work patterns and relative economic security, they were generally the initial and most enduring sources of friendly society/mutual aid, cooperative, and union activity. It then tended to spread downwards into the ranks of the secure semi-skilled and then in late-century the unskilled. In all respects, associations emerged first and most vibrantly in Britain. British friendly societies, always the most numerous of any working-class organization across most of Europe, had around 650,000–750,000 members by 1801, roughly 4,000,000 by 1872, and at least 5,600,000 by 1904 – thus covering most working-class families in some way. Trade unions also emerged early, expanding steadily after legalization in 1824. TUC affiliated unions numbered 500,000 by 1880, 1,2000,000 by 1900 (with 822,000 in unaffiliated unions), and 2,682,357 (plus 1,462,643 unaffiliated) by 1914, covering 25 percent of manual workers. With later levels of industrialization and more hostile governments, working-class organizations emerged later in continental Europe, but were widely evident by late-century, accelerating in prewar years. By 1914, for example, France had 1,026,000 trade unionists (10 percent coverage); by 1913, Germany had around 3,000,000 and 15 percent coverage.[27] Party political activity was also an increasing fact of working-class life almost everywhere except Russia. The mass parties, spreading across Europe from the 1870s, drew heavily upon manual workers. This is true both of older elite-led parties like Britain's Liberals and Conservatives; even more of the newer and largely continental socialist parties. Most spectacular was Germany's SPD, with around 1,000,000 members by 1914, but others were also growing fast.

One frequent underpinning for much political and other civil-associational activity was organized religion. The nineteenth century saw the emergence of religious defense organizations of all kinds concerned with defending themselves in their frequently ambivalent relationships with the secular state. Churches also inspired vast ranges of charitable and political activity.

Russia, because of its ambitiously absolutist elite, and far lower levels of urbanization and industrialization, provided the least hospitable context for the emergence of a strong civil society. Trade union membership was far smaller than the other countries reviewed here, though Russia's population was far larger. Parties started emerging around 1900, even more after 1905, but memberships were modest even by 1914. Yet due to partially relaxing controls after 1905, the advent of real elections and accelerating social change, civil society was advancing even here. The *Zemstvos* had long since ceased simply being agencies of central government and were acquiring new roles – for example, as aid coordinators during the famine resulting from the Russo-Japanese War, and representatives of their areas. By 1905 they had their own national consultative organization: the General Zemstvos Organization. In the classic way of civil society, *Zemstvos* also unwittingly trained political leaders, providing both Kadets and Octobrists with much of their leadership at all levels. Associational life was developing rapidly in larger cities – 600 were recorded in Moscow's directories by 1912.

What did all this activity entail; why and how far should we see it as democratically positive? First, associations were important because they were generated from below. Though nineteenth-century despotisms had far less impact on people's lives and minds than their totalitarian successors, their rulers still aspired to considerable levels of control. It was thus important that people should have or create spheres autonomous of the state if liberal democracy was eventually to take hold. Working-class people in particular needed bases

from which to resist the intrusive and suspicious attentions of their early political elites, still more the dependence and deference levied by landowners and employers. Secondly, much associational activity concerned the articulation of interest and opinion of all kinds. In 1870s Britain, most imaginable contemporary interests were being significantly articulated for purposes of self-help, negotiation with other interests, or with central or local government. Articulation of interest was emerging along gendered lines: middle-class women had begun building on their crucial charitable roles to produce the first suffragist organizations; some would shortly reach across the class divide to campaign against prostitutes' legal disabilities. This later became the basis for broadening feminist activity – mass suffrage organizations, and more tentative middle-class-led activity to unionize female manual workers and empower women cooperators.

The burgeoning presence of nineteenth-century newspapers strengthened civil society everywhere. They were expanding rapidly in numbers (even modest-sized British cities boasted two or more dailies by the 1870s, alongside several local weeklies). From around mid-century, their circulations accelerated. Multiple reading, particularly among workingmen, meant that they reached an ever wider readership. Local, provincial, and eventually national papers were unnerving cornucopias of serious information – providing readers with opportunities to discover and understand their world as never before. This was available not just generally but also to more intimate interests. Newspapers carried voluminous reportage about all kinds of civil associations, providing vast extended platforms for those who ran them. Interests and identities could therefore be articulated and rendered available to very wide audiences, enabling people scattered across a country, or even between countries, to see their experiences and struggles as similar to those elsewhere. This was doubly true as papers became ever more specialized – as working-class radicals, unions, cooperatives, religious groups, professionals of all kinds, national minorities, feminists, and many others began producing their own often-multiple organs of information and propaganda. Newspapers thus became crucial means of eroding social and political deference and the essentially local worlds and hierarchies upon which it so often depended.

Thirdly, civil society helped build more democratic political cultures via attitudes and expectations created and reinforced by the internal processes of associational life. For many people, intermittent participation in the bits of their polities that were becoming more democratic was being replicated and anticipated by frequent, sometimes intense participation in the governance of economic, social, or political organizations. Information about how civil associations ran themselves is scarce. Historians have been far more interested in how organizations presented themselves to the world than in their internal processes. Some were clearly more internally democratic than others. All civil organizations had mechanisms of accountability, especially the annual general meeting open to all members, where reports were read, committees elected or reelected, and issues raised, debated, and decided. This was central to associational culture and it became the preferred, because most effective, procedure even in authoritarian countries. However, members of middle-class organizations often appeared content with oligarchic modes of governance: the sparsely attended AGM with reports delivered to an unexcited few, after which committees were once more reelected and expected to operate for a further twelve months without greatly troubling the membership. Most charities, for example, operated in this way.

Among respectable workingmen, who benefited most from political incorporation across nineteenth-century Europe, civil-democratic commitments seem to have been more vibrant. In Britain, friendly society lodge meetings appear to have been generally well attended – perhaps unsurprisingly given their alcoholic conviviality and the intimate and personal nature of their decisions about benefit distribution. Skilled unions showed similarly strong attachments. Though branches reconciled themselves to some centralization, they resisted amalgamation because it eroded local control. Unions remained strongly attached to direct democracy long after friendly observers like the

Webbs thought was good for the flexibility their leaders needed in negotiation with employers.[28]

Not all civil association was democratically functional. The Catholic church, with its authoritarian self-governance and suspicion of most radicalism, was always problematic in liberalizing societies, though its papal-centered international orientation created ambivalent relationships with all secular regimes, even authoritarian ones. While skilled and semi-skilled working-class associations were vibrantly democratic, organizations embracing the unskilled were far less so. Unskilled jobs produced neither pride nor attachment, and economic desperation precluded interest in consultation processes. Thus unskilled unions were always less democratic than their skilled counterparts; and large insurance companies, pitilessly exploiting the need for respectable burial, were wholly undemocratic.

Matters were more problematic in authoritarian regimes. The latter were suspicious of civil associations, and prone to harass and even suppress political organizations, particularly radical ones. Internal democracy rendered the latter vulnerable to such attentions. Consequently, groups tended to emerge and survive that were authoritarian both in aspiration and self-governance. Austrian governance in Italy until 1859 produced multitudes of secret societies, and the tradition survived, producing enduring problems for the slowly liberalizing post-independence regime. Russia, much the most enduringly ambitious despotism, eventually permitted democratic organizations to emerge, but not before more authoritarian strands had begun capturing the imaginations of many peasants and workers, most notably the Social Revolutionaries and the Bolshevik-producing Social Democrats.

Overall, levels of democratization before 1914 substantially influenced the path of European societies after 1918. Those countries emerging as stable liberal democracies after 1918 were those where elites had shown themselves to be flexible, where political cultures were more democratic, and where associational life was rich and varied. Meanwhile, those with the least flexible elites, and least developed or democratically dysfunctional associational life in 1914, were the ones whose subsequent liberal democratic experience was either non-existent or terminally problematic.

NOTES

1 O'Gorman (1990).
2 See, for example, Fukuyama (1992).
3 Garrard, Tolz, and White (1999: 37); Scott (1988: 460); Blackbourn (2003: ch. 7).
4 Rustow (1970).
5 Guttsman (1963); for a Europe-wide view, see Meyer (1981).
6 Tombs (1996: 14).
7 Blackbourn (2003: 304ff.).
8 Steinbach (1992: 134ff.).
9 Levin (1966, 1973).
10 Conroy (1998), esp. ch. 5.
11 For a fuller account of the argument, see Garrard (2002: ch. 3).
12 Joyce (1980).
13 Garrard (1988).
14 Biagini (1992); Kirk (1985).
15 Clark (1996: 71).
16 O'Gorman (1992); Rogers (1989).
17 Pugh (1985: ch. 5).
18 Scott (1988: 187ff.); Garrard (1983); Applegate (1992).
19 Gash (1969).
20 Joyce (1980).
21 Tombs (1996: 103).
22 Phillips (1992).
23 Tombs (1996: 108ff.).
24 Phillips (1992).
25 This seems the implication from the evidence in Emmons (1983).
26 Ibid: 242ff.
27 Garrard (2002: 172–3); Mommsen and Husung (1985: 67–73).
28 Webb and Webb (1897).

GUIDE TO FURTHER READING

The most analytic general works are Tombs's *France 1814–1914*, Clark's *Modern Italy 1871–1995*, Blackbourn's *History of Germany 1780–1918*, Nordstrom's *Scandinavia since 1500*, and Scott's *Sweden: The Nation's History*. All contain substantial information and insight about European political elites, their changing relationship with their variously politicizing publics, the legal process of political inclusion, and the varied strength and character of civil society. My own *Democratization in Britain* discusses the role of political elites in democratizing British politics, the development of British political culture, and the role of civil society in this development. As far as I know, no other source explores democratization in the same conscious way – for Britain or any other European country. However, though originally written in 1966, Moore's *Social Origins of Dictatorship and Democracy* remains a stimulating place from which to start thinking more broadly about these themes, and provides conscious inspiration for Tilly's *Contention and Democracy in Europe, 1650–2000*.

The best comparative source specifically on European elites is Mayer's *The Persistence of the Old Regime*, even if one finds it harder to accept his more general thesis about the relationship between the resilient European aristocracies and, first, the allegedly subordinate bourgeoisie, and secondly the outbreak of World War I. There are also relevant books on particular national elites and their political and other relationships with diverse groups in society: for example, Thompson's *English Landed Society in the Nineteenth Century*, Guttsman's *British Political Elite*, and on Germany, Struve's *Elites Against Democracy*. Struve's view of the authoritarian perceptions of German traditional elites, and of the despotic character of the system over which they presided, was shared by other historians of nineteenth-century German politics in the 1960s and 1970s, most notably Dahrendorf, in *Society and Politics in Germany*. This contrasts with the less pessimistic and less "top-down" analyses offered by more recent historians like David Blackbourn. It contrasts even more with recent interpretations of the political sensitivities and skills of contemporaneous British local and national elites – for example Biagini's *Liberty, Retrenchment and Reform*, Kirk's *Growth of Working-Class Reformism in Mid-Victorian England*, and Garrard's *Leadership and Power in Northern Industrial Towns 1830–1880*. Recent historians of Russian politics have also been more prepared than their predecessors to recognize political instincts emerging among its elites – for example, the contributors to Conroy's *Emerging Democracy in Late-Imperial Russia*.

For European elections and the varied underpinnings of electoral behavior, there is useful analysis on Britain in O'Gorman's *Voters, Patrons and Parties*, Phillips' *The Great Reform Bill in the Borough*, Gash's *Politics in the Age of Peel*, Nossiter's *Influence, Opinion and Political Idioms in Reformed England*, and Hanham's *Elections and Party Management*. On Germany, there is useful material in Jones and Retallack's *Elections, Mass Politics and Social Change in Modern Germany*, Sperber's *The Kaiser's Voters*, and Suval's *Electoral Politics in Wilhelmine Germany*. I am less aware of comparable material on other European countries, though Emmons's *Formation of Political Parties and the First National Elections in Russia* contains much useful examination about post-1905 elections to the Russian Duma, and stimulates consideration of the very rapid political learning process by parties, electors, and groups about what electoral politics entailed and how interests could be articulated. The most useful source of election statistics across Europe is Mackie and Rose's *International Almanac of Electoral History*.

In this chapter, civil association in all its forms is seen as a major force underpinning political culture. The most directly available source on this aspect in Britain is my own *Democratization*. This draws on the multitude of studies of protest groups, trade unions, and other interest and pressure groups undertaken by British social historians. Analysis of this aspect of politics elsewhere in nineteenth-century Europe can be found in several of the works already cited. Other examples include Evans's *Society and Politics in Wilhelmine Germany*, Blackbourn's *Class, Religion and Local Politics in Wilhelmine Germany*, McPhee's *Politics of Rural Life*, and Smith's *Tariff Reform in France 1860–1900*. Comparative studies include Mommsen and Husung's *Development of Trade Unionism in Great Britain and Germany* and Breuilly's *Labour and Liberalism in Nineteenth-Century Europe*.

CHAPTER THIRTEEN

Labor Movements

STEFAN BERGER

Introduction

The birth of the modern labor movement is dated to the nineteenth century. Social conflict and even social movements predate the nineteenth century – one only needs to think of the English Levelers of the seventeenth century. Ideas of a more just society and the struggles to achieve it are nothing peculiarly modern or even nineteenth century. But it was the growing size and density of the industrial working class and the proletarianization of artisans which gave rise to the classical organizational forms of the labor movements: trade unions and political parties. Small property owners, artisans, and skilled workers were strongly represented in the first labor organizations of the nineteenth century, as it was among them that notions of a "moral economy" and a just social order were particularly prominent.[1] Demands for greater social justice resurfaced strongly amid the revolutionary ferment created by the French Revolution of 1789 across Europe. Throughout the entire nineteenth century the French Revolution remained an important reference point for the socialist labor movement in Europe. Its slogan *liberté, egalité, fraternité* was adopted, and the revolution influenced diverse revolutionary theories of leading representatives of labor. Even when reformist socialists moved away from ideas of insurrection and violence and embarked on the parliamentary road to social-

ism, the ideals of 1789 remained an important programmatic marker.

Apart from the political demands for greater participation, a major change in the economic system was occurring over a long period of time which meant that, by the nineteenth century, most social processes were market driven and the commodification of all social relationships had proceeded with unprecedented speed. The new relations of production produced similar types of industrial workers with similar lifestyles across Europe. The Genoa-Milan-Turin triangle in northern Italy, the Ruhr in Germany, St. Petersburg in Russia, south Wales in Britain, and the Pas de Calais region in France – they all saw the emergence of the factory worker as proletarian existences. These existences were characterized, above all, by insecurity. Insecurity bred social conflict. And the labor movement was the most important institutional attempt to regulate such social conflict. These industrial regions of Europe were in many respects islands of change within predominantly rural and agricultural societies. In most of Europe the numbers of industrial workers grew slowly. In France, for example, over 60 percent of the population was still rural in 1914. Russia was perhaps the most peculiar juxtaposition between vast stretches of agricultural country and pockets of industrialization, especially in Moscow and St. Petersburg, in which an urban working class employed in huge factories grew rapidly. Industrialization affected different countries in diverse ways. Germany, for example, was transformed from an archetypal backwater of industrial Europe around the middle of the nineteenth century to the leading industrial nation on the continent by 1914. It replaced the industrial pioneer, Britain, which, during the first half of the nineteenth century, had been very much the exception: up until the end of the nineteenth century few other European societies could rival Britain, as far as the size of the working class in new large conurbations was concerned. Uneven economic development characterized industrialization in Europe, and thus the birth of modern societies, not any longer organized around the idea of estates, but around the new notion of class, was also a regional phenomenon.

The new working classes were perceived primarily as a problem by most social commentators of the nineteenth century. Social reformers demanded greater protection for workers, especially children and women. From the 1830s onwards the languages of "class" entered diverse European societies, and the emerging labor movements would build on and develop these languages of class, especially where they had a socialist orientation. But the nineteenth-century labor movement can by no means be equated with socialism. Hence, the first part of this chapter will talk about the different ideological factions which made up the nascent European labor movement. The second part will then introduce some of the major organizational forms of the labor movement, while the third part will look at some of the characteristic features of nineteenth-century labor movements: their dedication to workers' education, their avant-gardism, and their gendering of the term "labor." Finally, we will analyze the degree of integration of labor movements into existing European state structures and ask how important the labor movement's internationalist orientation was.

Different Ideological Avenues

In the first half of the nineteenth century, liberals were the champions of a range of progressive causes, including social and political reform. Many workers and artisans therefore looked to liberalism, which seemed to offer a combination of radicalism and respectability. Working-class liberalism did not assume any necessary conflict between workers and employers. By contrast, both had a mutual interest in the economic success of their company, and both should work in harmony and social partnership to achieve this aim. However, employers also had to accept workers' representatives, improve working conditions, and pay workers a "fair wage." The belief in inter-class cooperation was widespread among early radicals: Giuseppe Mazzini in Italy, John Stuart Mill in Britain, and Georg Forster in Germany were democrats who believed in integrating the working class into a wider movement for political and social reform. The problem, though, was that the majority of liberals were unwilling to follow them. They identified property and education as the twin preconditions for citizenship, and as workers possessed neither, most liberals were in favor of excluding them and their organizations from the polity. Hence it was only among left liberals and democrats that notions of an alliance of workers' organizations with liberalism remained strong. The strongest working-class liberalism could be found in Britain between the 1850s and the 1880s. The Gladstonian Liberal Party forged an enduring alliance with the trade union movement and set itself up as defender of the people's interests against a corrupt aristocracy. A respectable party of progress and limited step-by-step reform was attractive for the labor movement, although even in Britain there was considerable tension between the willingness of liberals to consider reforms in the political sphere and their staunch defense of the inequalities produced by the existing economic order.

This is exactly why socialist labor movements advocated independent working-class education (i.e., a break with liberalism). Early socialist thinkers included Claude Henri de Saint-Simon, François-Charles Fourier, and Robert Owen, whose major writings were published in the 1800s and 1810s. They denounced competition, egotism, and individualism and instead championed ideas of cooperation, associationalism, and collectivism. They aimed for a more rational organization of society, which they saw as based on notions of autonomous and small communities.[2] In the mid-nineteenth century Karl Marx and Frederick Engels devoted themselves to the task of unmasking the "utopian" character of these early socialisms and replacing them with a more "scientific" socialist theory. They famously postulated that the entire history of humankind was the history of class struggles. Class conflict between workers and the owners of the means of production, the capitalists, was inevitable, as was the ultimate overthrow of capitalism and the coming of socialism. Socialism was understood very much as the public ownership of the means of production. A change in the economic system would be the key to changes in the political system and the way in which societies were organized. According to Marx and Engels and their followers, the key agents of change were the workers and their organizations. The labor movement carried out the class struggle in the economic and political sphere. One of the assumptions of Marx was that industrialization would make the workers the vast majority of the population. However, in many areas of Europe the labor movement was faced with the fact that industrial workers were a distinct minority.

Towards the end of the nineteenth century socialist revisionists such as Eduard Bernstein based their fundamental critique of orthodox Marxism on their empirical findings that the industrial working class might never form a majority of the population. The logical conclusion that reformist socialists drew from this was that the working-class parties either needed allies or they ideally would reorient themselves and move beyond their one-sided orientation towards the electoral mobilization of industrial workers. They had to move from class-based parties to people's parties which would be capable of attracting the vote of non-working-class sections of society. Ethical socialists tended to support this move strongly. They had always been doubtful about the class struggle as the main motor of social change. Instead, they anchored their demands for greater social justice in ethics, arguing that capitalism was essentially an amoral economic system based on the exploitation of people. It was not the laws of history but the laws of morality that demanded its transformation. Elections and parliaments were perceived as the main instruments of social reform. Socialists in the nineteenth century, however, remained torn between a desire to transform capitalism by way of revolution and a willingness to work for step-by-step social reform through political channels, notably parliaments.

It was this political orientation of Marxists and ethical socialists which was criticized by anarcho-syndicalists. They regarded politics generally as a detraction from the real struggle, which had to be fought at the workplace. The aim was public ownership of the means of production as with the Marxists, but anarcho-syndicalists were much clearer than Marxists about who would take control of the factories and of society following the socialist transformation. The workers themselves would organize their everyday lives and societies. Marx had always stayed clear of being too precise about what would follow the revolution, and other socialists, such as Ferdinand Lassalle in Germany, had been strongly statist in their blueprints for a future socialist society. Anarcho-syndicalists, by contrast, distrusted the state. Anarchist movements in Italy made many converts among middle-class and artisan radicals. Elsewhere, they could recruit strongly among autonomist and anti-clerical groups (e.g., in Romagna or Catalonia). They also successfully mobilized agricultural workers in Andalucía and textile workers in Catalonia. Their social base was thus remarkably diverse, but territorially they tended to be most successful in Southern and Eastern Europe. France, Italy, Spain, the Balkans, and Russia saw the emergence of particularly strong anarcho-syndicalist movements. They could be insurrectionist, such as in Bologna in 1874 and Benevento in 1877, or they could be terrorist, such as in Eastern Europe, where they could only organize in clandestine illegal ways. In Western Europe, notably in France and Spain, they could also build strong trade union movements which had a considerable influence on the industrial relations systems in their respective countries.

Socialist labor movements were not only ideologically diverse and internally divided. They also faced powerful rivals, not only from working-class liberalism, but also from working-class Catholicism. Distinctive Catholic workers' organizations emerged in Germany, Italy, France, Belgium, and other European states. They tried to implement the social teachings of the Catholic church, as entailed in the encyclical *Rerum Novarum* of 1891. Based on a fundamental critique of modernity, it envisioned the renewal of a corporate state in which different sections of society would all occupy their due place, each with different functions and roles and all together forming one harmonious whole. Catholic parties and Catholic trade unions were often strongly antagonistic towards socialist organizations, which were perceived as godless and materialist.

As this short overview demonstrates, the nineteenth-century labor movement was ideologically diverse. It consisted of several labor movement milieus which often remained tightly segregated from each other. Organizationally, as we shall see below, this state of affairs weakened the labor movement considerably.

Working-Class Organizations

Some of the earliest organizations for working people were friendly societies or mutual aid societies. As they tended to concentrate their activities on insurance and entertainment and often eschewed direct political concerns, they were, in some parts of Europe, the only legal form of workers' organization. On the other hand, in many countries they also provided the germ for a nascent trade unionism and its concern about working conditions and deskilling. In the 1820s, London alone had about 200 friendly societies. By 1914, 7 million workers in England and Wales were members of friendly societies.

Another important pillar of the labor movement was the cooperative movement. It organized millions of workers as producers in producers' cooperatives to ensure the abolition of "idle profit" and the just sharing of the rewards among those who had earned them. And it organized millions of workers as consumers in consumers' cooperatives which aimed to circumvent the profits made by trading and middlemen. Early consumer protests had often included notions of the "just price" and were connected to riots over rising prices of basic foodstuffs, such as bread or beer. Cooperatives sought to organize consumers so as to ensure the "just price" and avoid rioting. They also played an important role for millions of working-class families as saving and credit institutions. Producers' cooperatives were often formed by agricultural laborers. So, for example, in the Po Valley in northern Italy groups of laborers tendered collectively for work. Many of these cooperatives became fertile breeding grounds for socialism. Cooperation always entailed an alternative view of how society should best be organized. However, cooperatives had a great variety of political orientations. Thus, in Britain, many remained liberal in orientation and were skeptical about socialism and the nascent Labour Party. In Germany, by contrast, the Social Democratic Party soon dominated the cooperative movement, and cooperatives became part and parcel of the wide ancillary network of organizations established by German social democracy.[3]

Producer cooperatives were all about fair wages and the abolition of the profit of land or factory owners. Another part of the labor movement, the trade union movement, was also set up to defend workers against exploitation by those who owned the means of production. Before the emergence of trade unions there existed what Eric Hobsbawm once famously called "collective bargaining by riot": machine breaking and other violent and spontaneous forms of protest. Luddism in Britain, which reached its high point between 1811 and 1816, is a good example. Once again it was Britain, as the industrial pioneer of the nineteenth century, which saw the earliest formation of associations of workers in trade unions. Following the repeal of the Combination Acts in 1824, trade unions emerged and expanded rapidly. The Grand National Consolidated Trades Union was the first attempt to build a national trade union organization, but it collapsed in 1834. In the 1840s and 1850s craft unions organized skilled workers across various industrial sectors in Britain. They were geographically widely spread, financially sound, and well organized. Craft unions protected sectional interests (i.e., the status and pay of skilled workers in a particular trade). Craft unionism remained the dominant form of unionism in Britain throughout the nineteenth century. More skilled workers were in a much better position than the less skilled to form trade unions, as they tended to work fewer hours, had better working conditions, and were better paid. Early efforts to organize the unskilled in 1829 and 1834 came to nothing. It was only with the so-called new unionism from the 1880s onwards that concerted efforts were made in Britain to organize unskilled sections of the working class.

Craft unions also flourished elsewhere in Europe, and certain groups of workers, notably printers, served as European pioneers of craft unionism. But during the second half of the nineteenth century industrial unionism became more prominent. In Germany in particular, rapid industrialization in the second half of the nineteenth century saw the emergence of trade unions which no longer organized workers along skill lines. They sought to organize all workers in a particular industry. Industrial unionism had the advantage of producing fewer and bigger, more powerful organizations which could speak with one voice when it came to representing workers' interests *vis-à-vis* employers. In much of Southern Europe neither craft nor industrial unions organized along national lines became the center of trade union activities. In France, trade unionism emerged out of the journeymen's *compagnonnages* and out of mutual aid societies which functioned as *de facto* trade union organizations defending the interests of artisans, masters, and journeymen alike, against attempts by the merchant class to replace them with less skilled and lower-paid workers. In the republic after 1871 municipalities often set up so-called labor exchanges, *Bourses du Travail*, which coordinated union activities locally. In the absence of a strong and united union movement, these local offices played an influential role in defending workers' interests. The Italian chambers of labor, the first of which was established in Milan in 1890, were modeled on the French *Bourses*. As in France, they became a vital coordinating center for local trade unions, which provided leadership in industrial conflicts. They also were not averse to organizing

the unskilled and representing the unemployed. Again, the flowering of the chambers of labor can be linked to the weakness of national trade union federations, which emerged relatively late in Italy. The first national federation, the Confederazione Generale del Lavoro, was only founded in 1906 – specifically to counter the advances of the anarcho-syndicalists in the Italian labor movement.

In some areas of Europe, in particular Spain and Italy, syndicalists proved particularly adept at organizing agricultural workers. The Ruthenian Radical Party, founded in eastern Galicia in 1890, very successfully mobilized Ruthenian peasants in the Habsburg Empire in the name of socialism. Considerable agricultural unrest also broke out sporadically in Russia throughout the nineteenth century, and in the 1880s and 1890s it accompanied the first significant strike movements by industrial workers. Some Russian socialists, such as Alexander Herzen, idealized Russian peasant communes, arguing that they were built on collectivist principles which already made socialism part of their everyday lifeworld. But overall, trade unions and the socialist labor movement more generally were not too successful in mobilizing agricultural workers and organizing them on a more permanent basis. The German social democrats in fact were unable to attract significant support in rural areas, despite the fact that small peasants and landless laborers frequently suffered from the dominance of large landowners. Apart from the paternalistic structures of landed society, the SPD's rigid commitment to socialization and its inability to come up with an attractive program for small farmers contributed to the rejection of socialism by all segments of rural society.

Throughout Europe political divisions weakened the unity of the trade union movement. In mid-century Britain many craft union leaders were liberals who formed strong alliances with the Liberal Party. Socialist ideas infiltrated the trade union movement with the new unionism and generally became stronger after 1900. In Germany socialist unions had powerful rivals in Catholic and ethnic trade unions, such as the Polish miners' union in the Ruhr. Syndicalist unions in Italy and Spain often opposed social democratic unions.

Regional differences could further weaken trade union movements, especially where they were bound up with ideological differences. Thus, for example, conflict between Catalan moderates and Andalucían militants weakened the Workers' Federation of the Spanish Region, founded in 1881.

Disunity was all the more deplorable as trade unions in many countries faced an uphill struggle against hostile state administrations and employers. Britain was the only European country where a system of collective bargaining was functioning reasonably well before 1914. Trade unions were not generally perceived as a threat to the existing social and economic order. Rather, they were widely accepted as interest organizations of the working classes which were in fact beneficial to the economic life of the nation, as they helped to ensure workers' discipline at the workplace. Elsewhere in Europe trade unions were not so well received. In nineteenth-century Germany the majority of employers refused to accept trade unions as bargaining partners, and the state did not produce a legal framework which would have recognized trade unions as legitimate interest organizations of the workers. In France trade unions were legalized only in 1884 in an attempt to promote "responsible trade unionism" along British lines. However, even then many employers would have nothing to do with unions. Employer paternalism was a major obstacle to the formation of strong independent trade union movements. Through company housing, department stores, schools, hospitals, and pensions, employers tightly controlled their labor force and interfered with many aspects of their everyday lives. Trade unionists were threatened with dismissal and exclusion from all the benefits that "industrial feudalism" brought. The Krupp factories in Germany or the Peugeot works in France are good examples of such paternalist practices. The state also often responded negatively and violently to trade union activities. During the 1906 miners' strike in France the government sent 95,000 soldiers into the mining villages to keep order and to arrest several leading labor leaders. Churchill, as home secretary, sent the army to Tonypandy in south Wales in 1910 to keep unionism at bay.[4] In Sardinia the army killed miners during a strike at Buggerru, thereby provoking the 1904 general strike. The heavy hand of the state contributed to a radicalization of the trade unions.

Generally, strikes became more widespread and bigger affairs in the last third of the nineteenth century. As early as the eighteenth century, strikes were quite common events in the British textile and clothing industries. But these were localized and small affairs compared with the massive strike wave which rolled through Europe in the decade preceding World War I. Levels of unionization had risen considerably. Nowhere was the trade union movement stronger than in Britain, where levels of unionization reached 25 percent of the entire workforce in 1913 and membership of trade unions stood around 4 million in 1914. It was a highly fragmented movement with hundreds of often small trade unions representing rather small sections of workers. On the other hand, some bigger unions increasingly came to dominate the movement before 1914 and millions of workers were covered by agreements between unions and employers. Elsewhere, unionization levels were also on the rise: just before World War I they stood at 20 percent in Denmark, 15–16 percent in Belgium and Germany, and 10–11 percent in Italy, France, and Norway.[5] Conciliation procedures were well established in Britain, but they were also developed in a range of other European countries. The British Conciliation Act of 1896 was followed by the September agreement in Denmark in 1899 and similar agreements in Sweden, France, and Italy before 1914. Factory commissions in Italy often served as channels of communication between employers and workers' organizations. They aimed at reducing the number of wildcat strikes and moving towards more stable and negotiated systems of industrial relations.

Despite considerable moves towards a more "responsible" trade unionism, strikes were becoming more frequent. They were often triggered by the harsh working conditions, high accident rates, low wages, and heavy-handed management strategies, which included the promotion of company unionism, the employment of blacklegs, lockouts, and the use of *agents provocateurs*. Strikes expressed pride, exasperation, and anger. They often had devastating effects on entire industrial communities, especially if they ended, as they mostly did, with the defeat of the trade unions. But workers could also experience strikes as means of empowerment, which raised the specter of wider emancipation. Within the socialist labor movement strikes were regarded by some (most notably Rosa Luxemburg and various anarcho-syndicalist theorists) as an important revolutionary tool which raised the political consciousness of workers. But ideas of the general strike as the most potent weapon of the revolutionary working class met with considerable resistance – not the least from "responsible" trade union leaders who were averse to risking the misery of trade union members and the potential destruction of the organization itself for consciousness-raising objectives. They often were equally skeptical of plans of international socialists to use the mass strike as a weapon to counter the threat of war in Europe. For many trade unionists, including many socialist trade unionists, strikes were the ultimate weapon to defend the economic interests of the workers and should not be used lightly for political reasons. This opened up a division between the trade unions and the working-class parties.

Political organizations of the workers, mostly in the form of political parties, are the final organizational pillar which made up the edifice of labor movements in Europe. Mass political parties belong to an age of mass politics, which can be dated to the last third of the nineteenth century. At the beginning of the nineteenth century political groupings of workers often took the form of clandestine and secretive cells. Auguste Blanqui became the apostle of this conspiratorial tradition, which flourished under conditions of illegality. He believed fervently in the value of secret revolutionary brotherhoods which would prepare the revolution and sweep them to power. The often tiny and elitist circles of dedicated revolutionaries thought of themselves as the most advanced troops of the proletariat, chosen to lead the workers into the promised land of socialism.

Where workers could organize more freely, political mass movements also emerged which were only loosely based on central organizations and tended to focus on specific issues. One of the most important mass movements with a considerable working-class input was Chartism, which reached the high point of its activities between 1837 and 1842. It could organize hundreds of thousands of people through mass meetings and petitions which all demanded an extension of the franchise as the center point for wider demands for political and social reform. Chartism's demands were formulated in the national charter, and the National Charter Association had 300 branches in 1841, but their make-up and orientation were incredibly diverse. Britain's relatively liberal political system and the strong alliance between liberalism and working-class representatives allowed such a mass movement to flourish. In the German lands, where political conditions were less favorable and liberals less inclined to integrate workers into the polity, we find a much earlier break between "bourgeois" and "proletarian" democracy leading to the formation of independent working-class political parties. The process started in Germany with the formation of the General German Workers' Union, founded in 1863. It was the precursor of the German Social Democratic Party (SPD), which became the biggest socialist party in the world before 1914 and was emulated as a model party across Scandinavia, the Low Countries, Italy, and Eastern Europe. What many European socialists admired about the SPD was its success in recruiting a mass membership – over a million individual members on the eve of World War I. It was a strongly neighborhood-based party which built a whole range of ancillary organizations and aimed to care for its members from cradle to grave. From socialist kindergartens to socialist burial associations, the social democrats offered everything from youth organizations, women's organizations, sports clubs, choirs, trade unions, and libraries. Its financial prowess allowed it to finance a network of over 150 socialist newspapers and journals and to employ a range of full-time organizers and party officials, which in turn were crucial in mobilizing and integrating wider groups of workers into the party and its milieu. The SPD was essentially a working-class party and was most successful in urban industrial areas. It was also essentially a Protestant party, with most Catholic workers remaining loyal to the Catholic Center Party. And it recruited much better among skilled than among unskilled workers.

Other socialist parties in Europe, founded in Spain in 1879, in Austria and Switzerland in 1888, in Sweden in 1889, in Italy in 1892, and in Britain in 1900, found much to admire and emulate in the SPD. However, as they developed within different national frameworks, they all had their own distinct characteristics. Thus, for example, the British Labour Party did not know any individual membership at all before 1914, and the Italian socialist party can hardly be described as a working-class party, as it contained a considerable middle-class, university trained element. It had some of its strongest electoral support not among industrial workers, but among the farmworkers of the Po Valley. A number of socialist parties, for example in Finland, Norway, Sweden, Bulgaria, and the Ukraine, were successful in winning substantial rural support. Yet, overall, there was still a considerable correlation between the strength of working-class parties and urban areas which were at the same time areas of heavy industry and/or mining. But everywhere in Europe working-class parties fought for an extension of the franchise, as this was obviously the most important means of obtaining a greater share of the vote and thereby more influence in national parliaments. In France universal male suffrage was granted in 1848. In Britain most urban male workers were enfranchised by the reform of 1867. For German national elections a universal male suffrage was first implemented in the North German Confederation in 1867 and then taken over in the constitution of the German Empire in 1871. However, in regional and local elections far more restrictive franchise systems applied, with the three-class franchise in Prussia being the most notorious among discriminatory systems. The SPD spent considerable energy in trying to reform the Prussian franchise before 1914, but it was ultimately unsuccessful. However slow and imperfect the enfranchisement of the masses was in nineteenth-century Europe, it allowed working-class parties to mobilize substantial support for the aims of the labor movement at the ballot box.

The more successful the parties were in acquiring representation in national parliaments, the more sections of the socialist parties moved away from the revolutionary perspective and endorsed ideas of piecemeal step-by-step reform. This brought further political fragmentation – with many socialist parties divided between reformists and adherents of revolutionary forms of Marxism. Revolutions in nineteenth-century Europe such as the 1830 revolution in France or the 1905 revolution in Russia generally had a strong politicizing effect and raised political and social expectations among workers. On the whole, however, the adherents of revolution lost ground to the reformists before 1914. The revisionism debate originated in the German SPD and centered on Eduard Bernstein's critique of orthodox Marxism, which was refuted repeatedly at party congresses. This, however, could neither prevent the spread of reformism in the prewar SPD, nor hold up the European-wide repercussions of this debate in other socialist parties across Europe. The isolation and self-isolation of socialist parties did not help their electoral orientation. In much of Eastern Europe socialist working-class parties could only exist under conditions of illegality. In much of Central Europe police repression remained a distinct possibility. Even where the parties tried to win allies among other parties, they often found it difficult to overcome their political isolation. Hence socialist parties were not parties of government anywhere in Europe before 1914.

They could, however, take pride in impressive electoral results. The Finnish socialists, with just 85,000 members, managed to obtain a staggering 43.1 percent of the vote in the national elections of 1913. The Swedish socialists achieved 36.5 percent in the 1914 general elections and the best result of the SPD came in 1912, when it reached 34.8 percent. Social democratic parties were strongest in Scandinavia and Central Europe. The second biggest membership of any socialist party in Europe behind the SPD could be found in the Czech lands, where 243,000 people had joined the Czech socialist party. But nowhere did they win an outright majority. They also made significant gains at the local and municipal level. Ideas of municipal socialism were first developed before 1914. In fact, Sesto Fiorentino in Florence was a municipality controlled by the socialists before 1914, and it distinguished itself by building a range of municipal facilities in the areas of health, education, and public transport.[6] But on the whole it needed the extension of the local franchise, which by and large only happened after World War I, to make municipal socialism a more viable option.

In Germany at least, party unity was maintained before 1914. In other countries, most notoriously France, the political labor movement was far more hopelessly fragmented into different feuding sects. Under pressure from the Second International various groupings finally came together to form the Section Française de l'Internationale Ouvrière (SFIO) in 1905. It had the same tensions between Marxists and reformists that characterized so many parties of the Second International. Unlike the SPD it did not draw most of its support from the industrial working class, but recruited heavily from the petite bourgeoisie and the peasantry. A strong anarcho-syndicalist movement in France further weakened the SFIO. The same was true for working-class parties in Spain and Italy. Overall, labor movements across Europe came to rest on a dense network of organizations, including political parties, trade unions, cooperatives, friendly societies, and a wide array of ancillary organizations. We need to ask next what, apart from its ideological fragmentation, gave the labor movement its distinct character.

Autodidactism, Avant-Gardism, and the Gendering of Labor

I would like to emphasize three characteristic features of European labor movements which I take to be among the most important. The first feature has to do with the self-understanding of the labor movement as an educational movement. Wherever it had the opportunity to do so, the labor movement built up institutions of working-class education. It did not trust the state, which was frequently seen as hostile, repressive, and an enemy of working-class emancipation. Workers could only be educated and converted to the aims of the labor movement through independent working-class education. *Gewerkschaftshäuser* in Germany, labor halls in Britain, *casa del popolo* in Italy, and whatever they were called elsewhere in Europe, formed the backbone of the educational efforts of the labor movement, which ranged from basic literacy courses to lectures on literature, economics, history, and philosophy. The labor movement also put great emphasis on training its own officials. Many leaders of the labor movement were working-class autodidacts, who had taught themselves the basics of European culture: great European literary figures, composers, and architects were very much regarded by labor leaders as their heritage. They wanted workers to appreciate "high art," an understanding of which, they argued, would make them better human beings. The aim of improving the worker always remained a central one for European labor movements. This notion of the labor movement as an agent for the betterment of the workers brought with it a high degree of tension between an often more highbrow labor movement culture and a more "base" working-class culture. Socialists famously despised the drinking, gambling, and whoring habits of the lumpenproletariat. They equally disliked the modern forms of popular leisure entertainment, such as the music halls or early cinemas and spectator sports, which they tended to denounce as forms of escapism. Labor movement education and culture thus was in many respects set apart from the world of ordinary workers. They formed the basis of largely inward-looking communities of solidarity which defined themselves in opposition to what they regarded as "bourgeois culture" and often set out to create a proletarian counter-culture. But *de facto* labor movement culture sat uneasily between working-class and bourgeois cultural forms.

The emphasis on improving not only the workers' material situation, but also on bettering the workers morally and intellectually, leads us straight into our second defining characteristic of European labor movements: their avant-gardism. Labor movements were often dominated by the better-off, more skilled workers and artisans who had a higher income, more job security, and greater educational opportunities. They defined themselves as belonging to an elite of "respectable" workers which was a world apart from the rougher elements of the proletariat. Where they had adopted the socialist creed, they saw it as their task to educate their fellow workers and guide them towards the promised land of socialism. Many of the charismatic leaders of nineteenth-century labor movements (e.g., August Bebel and Carl Legien in Germany, Ramsay MacDonald and Arthur Henderson in Britain, Georgi Plekahnov in Russia, Arturo Labriola in Italy, Pablo Iglesias in Spain, and Jean Jaures in France) saw themselves as members of an avant-garde who would have to lead the workers along the path to socialism. Even where these leaders had come from the working class and had been autodidacts, they had little inclination to listen to ordinary workers and their concerns. Rather, they already knew the answers and where workers failed to agree with them, it was a matter of lacking political consciousness. This avant-gardist self-understanding of the labor movement was one of the most woeful consequences of the Blanquist conspiratorial tradition, and it formed the basis of the Leninist understanding of the Communist Party as the ultimate fountain of all wisdom and the irreproachable guide on the road to socialism.

A third distinguishing feature of European labor movements was its maleness, which could at times deteriorate into "proletarian anti-feminism."[7] Thus, for example, men went on strike across Europe to exclude women from paid employment in the factories. Many male trade unionists were concerned about women undercutting male wages, but even where this was not the case, they tended to oppose female employment. Thus, the French printers' union decided in 1913 to expel a member for getting his wife a job, despite the fact that she was paid union rates. Many trade unions had specific clauses not allowing women to become members. Even where they could join, they rarely occupied positions of authority and leadership within the trade union movement. Labor leaders were all too willing to buy into the

bourgeois ideal of the woman as the "angel in the house." Women had their duties around homemaking and childrearing. Theirs was the domestic sphere, not the worlds of work and politics. As women were very rarely voters before 1914 (among European countries, only Finland in 1906 and Norway in 1913 introduced the franchise for women), working-class parties could easily ignore their concerns and problems. Chartism's proposals for a more democratic constitution in Britain expressly excluded votes for women. The Parti Ouvrièr Français shied away from actively increasing its support among female textile workers in the north for fear that it might lead to a backlash from male workers who, after all, were the only ones who could vote in elections.[8]

Social events organized by the labor movement not infrequently excluded women or typecast them in the role of homemaking and motherhood. They baked the cakes and served the tea, they brought the children to family outings, but they were absent from the smoke filled back rooms of pubs, where political meetings were held. It was extremely difficult for women to negotiate their feminism with their socialism:[9] everywhere feminists were accused by male socialists of sowing the seeds of disunity among the working class. Women's emancipation, they insisted, would have to wait until after the revolution and the transformation of capitalism. The emancipation of the working class took precedence over the emancipation of women.

It would, however, give an entirely false impression were we to describe the labor movement simply as yet another means of repression of women. By contrast, the women of Europe had few more genuine champions of women's rights than could be found among sections of the socialist labor movement. Early socialists such as Fourier and Owen were outspokenly in favor of full equality for women and attacked the bourgeois family as the single most oppressive institution standing in the way of such equality. August Bebel's *Woman under Socialism* (first published in 1878) became one of the founding texts of European socialism. It went through countless editions and was translated into at least fifteen European languages before 1914. It amounted to an ardent and spirited defense of women's rights and included demands for equal wages for equal work (on average, women earned about 40 percent less than comparable male workers), marriage reform, property rights for women, access to the professions and better education, as well as sexual reform. Political parties and cooperative movements built up women's sections which did get involved in politics and debated questions of political reform closest to many women's concerns, such as family, health, and education. The SPD's women's organizations could boast 200,000 members on the eve of World War I and the Women's Cooperative Guild sought to represent in particular the interests of housewives administering the often tight family budget. Working women, such as the female textile workers in Germany, devised a variety of strategies to negotiate the parallel and complex demands of work, leisure, and family commitments.[10] There is very little hard evidence to suggest that female workers were either less likely to strike or to join trade unions than their male colleagues. In France, for example, women workers made up 10 percent of the entire unionized workforce, which was far below the percentage of women workers among the employed population as a whole, which was closer to one third. But this was no doubt partly to do with the fact that women workers were not welcome by male-dominated unions and that it made little sense for women, many of whom regarded paid employment as a transitory phenomenon in their lives, to join a union.

Labor Movements Between National Integration and Internationalism

If labor movements were predominantly for working-class men, their members strove hard to be recognized as full citizens with equal rights and duties in the nation-states. Yet their integration proved to be problematic almost everywhere. Even the British state, arguably one of the most liberal of its kind in nineteenth-century Europe, became rather heavy-handed at times when it felt threatened by so-called radicals. Between the 1790s and the 1810s it

deported and imprisoned them, using the 1794 Acts against subversion. The Peterloo massacre of 1819 and the Metropolitan Police Act of 1829 demonstrated that the state was wary of political forces construed as a danger to the system. However, overall, wide sections of the labor movement retained their confidence in the existing legal and political system and did not explicitly set out to overcome existing state structures. Lib-Labism and progressivism, at its high point between 1850 and the 1870s, remained the most influential political orientation of the British labor movement at the end of the long nineteenth century. This looked different, where more authoritarian and repressive regimes produced more radical labor movements.

Following the Bonapartist coup in France in 1851, the political labor movement was severely repressed. This strengthened the arguments of those anarcho-syndicalists who thought of politics as an irrelevance and called on its followers to concentrate on the struggles in the workplace. Even in the Third Republic after 1871 those reformists most keen to exploit the possibilities for social and political reform found it difficult to capture the working-class imagination. Responding to strikes and anarchist terrorism, the Italian state put into effect stringent emergency laws in the 1890s. In Spain powerful alliances of local landowners, church, and state established between the 1830s and the 1850s held the labor movement at bay. Local notables, *caciques*, controlled politics and the social order by means of patronage and corruption. Following two attempts on the life of the German emperor in 1878, the Anti-Socialist Laws banned the SPD from campaigning and laid the foundations for the ruthless harassment of known Social Democrats. The long memory of persecution in the 1880s prevented any full integration of the SPD into the German nation-state long after the Laws had lapsed in 1890.

Yet even in Germany one finds the social democrats attempting to forge alliances with other political forces to bring about social and political reform, especially in the more liberal southwestern German states in the 1890s and 1910s. The emergence of the welfare state under Bismarck also furthered the identification of socialists with the nation. The birth of the welfare state was meant as an antidote to socialism, but socialists across Europe often acquired a stake in the development and running of welfare systems. In Scandinavia and the Netherlands, working-class parties allied themselves to left liberals to bring about franchise reform. The repercussions of the Millerand affair in France highlighted the ambiguous position of labor movements between integration and isolation. Alexandre Millerand, a well-known socialist, had joined the republican government of René Waldeck-Rousseau as minister of commerce in 1899. He helped implement important social reforms, but his appointment sparked debates across the socialist movement in Europe as to whether socialists should participate in bourgeois governments. The influential SPD in its majority remained steadfastly opposed to such collaboration, and was, in turn, attacked by reformist socialists across Europe for its attentism and verbose but ineffectual radicalism.

By the end of the nineteenth century more powerful and highly organized labor movements were far more integrated into their respective nation-states than was the case at the beginning of the century. The identification with the nation was particularly strong in socialist movements in large multinational empires and states. Polish, Czech, Hungarian, Finnish, and Irish socialists were invariably also nationalists. One interesting exception is the Belgian socialist movement, where Flemish and Walloon activists operated across the language divide. Their common struggle to extend the franchise made them largely immune to the "national question" which increasingly divided Belgian society before 1914. By and large, socialists who thought about the "national question" in nineteenth-century Europe came to accept the idea that each people was entitled to its nation. Austro-Marxists such as Karl Renner and Otto Bauer emphasized the division between state and nation so as to allow for national autonomy within multinational empires. If the state was not used to reinforce the national identity of any one group, then it could stay clear of the potentially disruptive forces of nationalism. Lenin and the Bolsheviks in Russia largely accepted that the different

nationalities making up the Russian Empire would go their own way after the socialist revolution. Many socialists, following Marx, tended to underestimate the power of national identity over people's imagination in an age of mass politics. "The working men have no country," Marx had famously stated in the *Communist Manifesto*. Rosa Luxemburg was one of the few Marxists who opposed the principle of national self-determination. Anarcho-syndicalists also had no truck with the language of the nation. But the vast majority organized in labor movements across Europe did feel strong ties to their respective nations and states.

The borders of nationalism were at times crossed. This is particularly obvious when examining the attitudes of labor movements to foreign immigrants. The Irish in England, the Poles in Germany, the Italians in Switzerland, the Belgians in France – they were invariably met with xenophobia and exclusion. Trade unions often were not interested in organizing them and instead cast them as strike breakers and wage cutters. Labor activists set themselves up as patriots who were ready to defend the fatherland against foreign aggression. Labor movements right across Europe were convinced that their particular national culture represented the highest stage of civilization, and as Europeans they were equally adamant that their culture was superior to those of the "natives" in European colonies. Socialists undoubtedly were among the strongest critics of imperialism, but at the same time many were affected by colonialist discourse, which was commonplace in Europe before 1914. Socialists often shared vague notions of the racial superiority of the "white man" and believed in the responsibility of Europeans to civilize the rest of the world. The Boer War badly divided the British labor movement, and the war in Libya did the same for the Italian labor movement. Especially in southern Italy, many socialists saw colonialism as an alternative to mass migration. In shipyard towns or where armaments industries were significant, colonialism guaranteed jobs.

If labor movements partook in nationalism and racism to a considerable extent, they were also among the most internationalist-minded movements in the nineteenth century.

Socialists and trade unionists set up the First International in London in September 1864. Following divisions between the followers of the Russian anarchist Mikail Bakunin and Karl Marx, the International declined and was finally dissolved in 1876. But the thought of the workers' struggle being an international one remained powerful, as a Second International was founded in Paris in July 1889. Its member parties held regular international congresses which discussed a wide range of issues, including working conditions, social policy, unemployment, the general strike, migration, franchise reform, relations with bourgeois parties, militarism, colonialism, and the threat of war. The anarchists were excluded from the International at its London congress in 1896. A separate Socialist Youth International was founded in Stuttgart in 1907, and the trade union movement also organized international information bureaus, trade secretariats, and federations which were meant as forums for discussion and means to disseminate information. But they also coordinated their activities, helped fellow unionists during lockouts and strikes, and supported members who traveled between different countries. Worker mobility in late nineteenth-century Europe was remarkably high, and among labor movements the idea was widespread that workers (by and large white and European workers) had something in common and needed to organize internationally to defend their interests. By 1914, 32 international trade secretariats did this kind of work across Europe. After 1886, pan-Scandinavian trade union congresses were attended by socialist unions from Sweden, Denmark, Norway, and Finland. An international secretariat of national trade union federations, founded in Dublin in 1903, had affiliated member organizations in 19 European countries in 1913. Yet, when war broke out in 1914, the national orientation of labor movements proved stronger than their internationalism almost everywhere in Europe.

Conclusion

Labor movements traveled a long way in the long nineteenth century. They emerged with industrialization and the growing commodification of all social relationships, and helped to construct diverse languages of class which gave meaning to their own activities and the social world around them. They built a variety of organizations and came to rest on the three pillars of the cooperative movement, the trade unions, and the working-class political parties. Ideologically divided into Christian, liberal, socialist, and anarcho-syndicalist wings, the labor movement was at heart an educational movement which aimed to educate workers to become better human beings. It was a vanguardist movement whose activists thought of themselves as spearheading a wider working-class movement for emancipation, and it was a male movement whose ideas about social order were strongly gendered. Its international aspirations were difficult to square with the increasing nationalization of European labor movements, which acted primarily within the framework of states and nations that dominated Europe. Affected by increasing racism and nationalism, they were at the same time the most ardent champions of the political, economic, and social rights of working people. They organized perhaps most successfully around issues of electoral reform as they set out to extend the franchise. Their call to remove the causes of social misery helped bring about welfare states. Overall, they extended the notion of human rights from individual to collective rights, and thus proved important pathfinders to some of the solutions to social problems which would be implemented in the twentieth century.

NOTES

1   Thompson (1971).
2   On the early French socialists, see Pilbeam (2000); on Owen, see Harrison (1969).
3   Prinz (1996).
4   D. Smith (1980).
5   Eley (2002: 70).
6   Bell (1986).
7   Thönessen (1973).
8   Hilden (1986).
9   Hannam and Hunt (2000).
10 Canning (1996a).

GUIDE TO FURTHER READING

Voss and Linden's *Class and Other Identities* provides succinct historiographical surveys on important themes in European labor history. Geary's *Labour and Socialist Movements in Europe Before 1914* provides a reliable country by country introduction to nineteenth-century labor movements in Britain, France, Germany, Russia, Italy, and Spain, with some comparative perspectives provided by the editor's introduction. Geary's *European Labour Protest* focuses on a comparative analysis of levels of radicalism in the European labor movement after 1848. Although older, Stearns and Mitchell's *Workers and Protest*

1880–1914 remains a very readable and comparative analysis of a wide range of largely Western European labor movements in the final decades of the long nineteenth century. Breuilly's *Labour and Liberalism* consists of a series of comparative studies on nineteenth-century German and British labor movements. Linden and Thorpe's *Revolutionary Syndicalism* introduces a variety of European anarcho-syndicalist movements in Europe. Biernacki's *Fabrication of Labor: Germany and Britain, 1640–1914* explores the ways in which different meanings of the term "labor" determined the shape and outlook of national labor movements. Schwarzmantel's *Socialism and the Idea of the Nation* analyzes the relationship between socialism and nationalism.

CHAPTER FOURTEEN

National Movements

STEFAN BERGER

Introduction

The nineteenth century was the classical century of nationalism and of the aspiring nation-state. What follows will seek to shed some light on those social forces behind this most powerful ideology, which, in the primeval loyalties it engenders, can only be compared with religion and with violence. After reviewing some of the major theories and typologies of national movements, the remainder of this chapter will explore the ideas and tropes used by the national movements and investigate their promises of participation and inclusion, as well as their threats of persecution and exclusion. We will analyze the importance of states for the success or failure of national movements and ask how the diverse national stories in Europe were constructed and perpetually reconstructed throughout the nineteenth century. The emergence of mass nationalist movements across Europe was accompanied on the one hand by a significant reduction in the number of European states prior to 1914 and, on the other, by the expansion of Europe into the far corners of the world. Colonialism and imperialism had a major impact on national movements and will have to be discussed in some detail. Up until 1914 the landscape of Europe was still dominated by major multinational empires, such as Russia, Austria-Hungary, and the Ottoman Empire, and multinational states such as Spain and Britain.

We will have to explore the diverse ways in which these multinational entities reacted to the challenges of national movements within their borders.

Typologies and Theories of National Movements

In 1955 Hans Kohn published an influential book on nationalism in which he claimed that nationalism changed its meaning and significance when it traveled from Western to Eastern Europe in the course of the nineteenth century.[1] He perceived the Western idea of the nation as predominantly voluntarist, culturally inclusive, and founded on liberal political principle. Eastern Europe, by contrast, was haunted by ethnic nationalisms, culturally exclusive, and politically authoritarian. In the political context of the Cold War the liberal parliamentary British nation, the revolutionary American nation, and the republican French nation became the shining examples of Western nationalism, whereas the Russian autocracy was regarded as the best example of the East European type of nationalism. Kohn's dichotomous setup of the terms of the debate has remained hugely influential. A whole string of theorists of nationalism built on and expanded on Kohn's ideas, but hardly anyone ignored the basic distinction he made.

Theodor Schieder divided European national movements into three types, distinguishing between those movements which went back to a revolutionary foundational moment, those which emphasized culture and came to fruition through unification, and those which resulted from often violent secessions from multinational empires.[2] Like Kohn's two types, Schieder's three types had a strong territorial dimension. Western European national movements could look back to revolutionary founding moments (e.g., the French nation to the Great Revolution of 1789, and the British nation to the Glorious Revolution of 1688). Central European national movements, by contrast, emphasized their roots in a common language and culture and strove to unite areas which had previously been disunited. Schieder here picked up on the famous distinction made by Friedrich Meinecke between cultural nations and political nations, implying that some nations were bound together by subjective contractual obligations, whereas others were bound by more objective ties of a common language, culture, and heritage.[3] Italy and Germany were prime examples of cultural unification nationalism. Ironically, successful unification nationalisms could highlight the divisions more than the unity. Take, for example, Italy, where Italianness ultimately could not be built on Catholicism because the pope was hostile to the Italian national movement, and despite the fact that a strongly patriotic and Catholic neo-Guelph movement was very successful in the 1840s. The fractured nature of Italian society, the strong linguistic diversity and regionalist attachments, as well as massive social conflict and the poor education system – all of these factors made the Italian nation a rather volatile and crisis-prone project. Finally, according to Schieder, a variety of national movements in Eastern and Southeastern Europe often resorted to violence and terrorism to achieve their goals of emancipating their respective nations from the grip of multinational empires.

One of the most influential theorists building on Schieder's typology is John Breuilly, who brought to the debate a strong sense of power. Power relationships and in particular the powers invested in the modern state were of crucial importance for the development of national movements across Europe.[4] Breuilly asked primarily what nationalism was used for and by whom. This functionalist approach to the history of national movements yielded important results, as it highlighted the crucial significance of states and those elites who ran states in promoting diverse nationalisms. At first sight, Breuilly's interest in structures and functions seems at odds with the recent boom in studies using linguistic approaches (such as discourse analysis) to shed light on the ideas and the symbolic repertoire of national movements. Their foundational text is Benedict Anderson's *Imagined Communities*.[5] The constructed nature of nationalism and the importance of modern national movements for "inventing" national stories has also been the subject of a pathbreaking edited collection by Eric Hobsbawm and Terence Ranger.[6] This emphasis on invention and construction was taken one step further by Homi Bhaba's insistence that nations were basically narratives which had no foundation in "real" history. Nations were narratively constructed by those promoting nationalism.[7] Ideas of inventing, constructing, and narrating the nation had a huge impact on a whole generation of nationalism scholars who sought to provide empirical evidence for the constructivist camp and against the dwindling minority of those scholars who still maintained that nations were natural and had deep roots in the past. If the search for invented traditions has at times lost sight of the uses that such inventions were being put to, there is, as Breuilly himself has pointed out, nothing to prevent historians from connecting their research on symbols and ideas with the question of power relationships.[8]

The wilder shores of constructivism have also been worrying Anthony Smith, one of the foremost scholars on nationalism and national identities over the past decades. He has been skeptical about those scholars who talk about the nation as a mere invention, and has, instead, insisted on the importance of having something on which to build constructions of the nation. In other words, according to Smith, some nations found it easier to construct national pasts than others because they had more building blocks. Somewhat controversially, he has argued that nations have ethnic cores: they are built most successfully on notions of a common ethnicity. He has steered clear of biological essentialism, instead arguing that ethnicity relied on history, culture, language, and traditions.[9] Especially long and continuous periods of independent statehood helped enormously in the nineteenth-century construction of national narratives. Linking the aspiring or existing nation of the contemporary world to a long and continuous history framed in the notion of a proud national past was one of the most effective tools of national movements across Europe.

The Search for Origins and the Modernity of National Movements

Establishing a historical pedigree was of utmost importance to national movements. They regularly celebrated foundational moments from which they could construct such continuous national narratives. So, for example, the Swiss celebrated 600 years of Swiss national history in 1891, remembering the confederation of the Swiss cantons in 1291. Nineteenth-century national stories traced the national idea to the dawn of time itself. Many of the ideas and tropes "discovered" by nineteenth-century nationalists went back a very long time. In England, for example, a national movement formed around the idea of parliament in the sixteenth century: 1688 then marked the moment when the national movement fused monarchical and parliamentary principles. Notions of parliamentary liberty were also closely bound up with Protestantism. The strong identification of the nation with Protestantism developed in the sixteenth century. Henry VIII used national sentiment and arguments to break the autonomy of the church. The German princes in conjunction with Luther did the same during the German Reformation. In the Holy Roman Empire notions of Germanness were present among the circles of sixteenth-century humanist scholars and at the court of Maximilian I. Strong links between humanism and the national idea were also noticeable in Italy (the cradle of European

humanism) and other parts of Europe. An early modern Dutch national movement rose to prominence in the context of the Dutch revolt against Spain in the sixteenth century. Here again, religion was to the fore, with Dutch Calvinism pitched against Spanish Catholicism.[10]

It was, however, only in the long nineteenth century that the concept of the nation was broadened to incorporate potentially all members of an "imagined" nation-state community. Previous references to the nation tended to be restricted to a small and select number of people, usually feudal and clerical elites. Between 1750 and 1850 the nation acquired a qualitatively new meaning under the impact of the breakthrough to modernity.[11] Although some scholars have argued that there were early modern and even medieval forms of nationalism, most historians continue to see nationalism as a thoroughly modern phenomenon.[12] Those espousing nationalist ideas were modern men intent on overcoming what they perceived as the straitjackets of the old feudal regimes.[13] Industrialization and urbanization changed social structures fundamentally in that they brought a commodification of all social relationships. In their wake a new group of people – businessmen, but also a new class of state civil servants, free-flowing intellectuals serving an ever-increasing book market, and state-employed university and school teachers – sought to frame a new role for themselves. This new middling group of people did not really fit the traditional estates-based social order. They were, in Elie Kedourie's famous phase, "marginal men," who took up nationalism as it promised them orientation and new perspectives.[14] More specifically, it allowed them a greater say in the affairs of the state. The "marginal men" were staking out their claim to become more central. They discovered the national idea as a powerful vehicle to foster their own interests in society and they often became the main carriers of national movements in Europe.

In a pathbreaking study on the social origins of national movements, Miroslav Hroch has argued convincingly that European national movements went through three stages of development: in the first stage, nationalism is espoused by small groups of intellectuals debating how to fill the category of the nation with meaningful content. In the second stage, a more organized movement takes shape which propagates the idea of the nation among wider groups in society. The third stage is characterized by mass mobilization around the idea of the nation.[15] What is characteristic for the early nineteenth century is that highly educated middle-class elites formed a powerful alliance with the youth of Europe to challenge the existing social, economic, and political order. The national movements were in many respects the first major European youth movement. But in certain instances (e.g., early Risorgimento Italy) nobles also played an important part in mobilizing national sentiment.

If industrialization was clearly important to the rise of national movements, there was no automatic mechanism between the strength of national movements and the degree of industrialization. By the middle of the nineteenth century Italy, for example, had only pockets of modern industrial development, but a vibrant national movement. In contrast, Britain was already a pioneer of industrial capitalism in the eighteenth century, but organized mass nationalist movements only developed towards the end of the nineteenth century. In Germany Friedrich List's disappointment about the limited success of attempts to construct the nation through political acts made him a champion of the idea of a Customs Union, which was ultimately set up in 1834. Economic union was envisioned as the key stepping stone to national unity. Since then important traditions of thought from within the German national movement have imagined the nation primarily in economic terms.[16] A national school of economics rose to prominence and sought to link nation building to the creation of a powerful national economy. "Made in Germany" became the most influential slogan (ironically, coined by an Englishman), encapsulating national pride in German economic achievements.

Political and social developments also played a major role in shaping the way in which national movements constituted themselves in the nineteenth century. Here the deep impact of the American and French revolutions needs to be mentioned. The revolutionaries in the USA and France stipulated that the third estate (i.e., ordinary people) were the backbone of the nation and that they, as citizens, should have an equal say in the affairs of the nation. Thus, for example, Abbé Sieyès famously defined the French nation as a community of people sharing the same legal framework and being equally represented in the national assembly. The political will of the nation was supposed to find expression in political institutions which guaranteed universal human rights. Commitment to the nation was an act of political will, a "plebiscite de tous les jours," in the famous phrase of Ernest Renan.[17] Liberal and democratic nationalists across Europe supported the American War of Independence and greeted the revolutions as the beginning of the long-awaited age of freedom. The ideas emanating from the double revolution in America and France were a huge export success, with democrats being far more enthusiastic than liberals, on balance. Even in autocratic Russia the revolutions inspired attempts to introduce political definitions of the nation, such as the attempt of the so-called Decembrists to introduce constitutional rule to Russia in 1825.

However, the vast majority of liberals were soon disillusioned by the way in which the French revolutionaries drowned that freedom in blood. In their eyes the nation could no longer be justified with reference to the language of universal rights. Instead, they turned to national languages and cultures to validate claims for greater inclusion and participation. Johann Gottfried Herder and Johann Gottlieb Fichte – key German theorists of the nation in the late eighteenth and early nineteenth centuries who were to develop a truly European significance – relied heavily on "objective" factors such as culture, literature, history, geography, climate, customs, and religion to construct the unique national characters of diverse peoples. Almost every nation or aspiring nation had its Herders and Fichtes in the nineteenth century. With most of them, the people (*Volk*) remained the basis and backbone of the nation, but its meaning now became nationally specific.

The very term "people" signaled diverse connotations in different European languages. The Russian *narod* often carried strong ethnic and religious overtones, whereas the German *Volk* focused on cultural and historical roots and the French *peuple* as well as the English *people* remained most strongly connected to sometimes quite different political meanings of the word. References to culture and history remained shot through with participatory political demands. It became almost a common assumption among national movements that national communities had to share a particular culture and a common language and that they had to be of a certain size to be viable.

Yet many European nation-states had to come to terms with ethnic minorities and minority languages. Nineteenth-century national movements, often encouraged by national states, tended to attempt to introduce linguistic uniformity. Following the French Revolution of 1789, regional languages blossomed, but soon the French state put restrictions into place and after 1792 only publications in high French were officially encouraged. And in the 1870s and 1880s the state led a "civilizing mission" in the French provinces aimed at driving out regional languages and establishing a uniform linguistic and educational standard. German nationalists found it equally difficult to endorse ideas of multilingualism. In the Frankfurt parliament of 1848/9 the majority of the national movement vowed to protect the rights of linguistic minorities, but in imperial Germany the balance soon shifted towards an emphasis on nationalizing the linguistic minorities inside the Reich. Unlike the eighteenth-century reforms of Joseph II in Austria and Frederick II in Prussia, which also aimed at creating a more unified linguistic community, nineteenth-century efforts were not primarily motivated by concerns for the more rational organization of the state. Language did become a major issue in Belgium in the middle of the nineteenth century, when pressing social problems in Flanders led to protests against the inaction of the Francophone Belgian state. The Flemish leaders came to resent the hold of the French language over Flanders and mobilized popular resistance to such linguistic imperialism after the extension of the franchise in 1893. Identifying Flanders with the Dutch language and strengthening notions of linguistic separation created major and lasting problems for a united Belgian identity.

Ironically, linguistic uniformity could also be a major problem in cases where it was perceived as a stumbling block to nation formation. The Norwegian national movement, for example, struggled to come to terms with the fact that Norwegian was almost indistinguishable from Danish. There were huge debates on whether the Danish used in Norway should be Norwegianized or whether the Norwegians should even invent an entirely different national language. But more often than not linguistic diversity was more of a problem than linguistic unity. Switzerland was in fact one of the few examples which went against the grain of assumptions of linguistic uniformity. Its nation building incorporated multilingualism and spanned different cultural traditions, although the antagonism between Catholic and Protestant cantons remained an important feature of Swiss national identity. Nevertheless, the Swiss successfully organized around a set of institutions and a range of assumptions surrounding their particular geography. Thus, for example, the idea of the mountain nation, isolated from the outside world, was of major importance to the Swiss national movement.[18] Size, language, and culture all mattered when it came to nation building, but as the Swiss case demonstrates, history, politics, and geography could be equally successful in constructing a sense of nationhood. Frederick Engels' famous distinction between "historic" and "unhistoric" nations was based on the search for criteria to distinguish between those nations who had a claim to statehood and those who had not. Engels' crucial reference to history again points to the ultimate importance of anchoring national identity in the past. Hence modern nationalist movements were so keen to discover kindred spirits in centuries long gone and proclaim an essential continuity of the nation from the earliest times possible.

The Importance of Cultural Capital and Symbolic Repertoires

National movements across Europe constructed national narratives which were meant to underline the credibility of their claims. Symbols of the nation played an important part in rallying the people to the national cause. National flags were designed and national anthems composed. Where these national symbols either were absent or weak or where they were hotly contested, such as in nineteenth-century Spain or Germany, national movements struggled to produce secure and stable national identities. Where these symbols were strong, such as in France or Britain, we observe the opposite trend. Giving symbolic expression to the nation often involved forms of mythical remembrance. Myths of origins such as the idea of an *Ur-Volk* (a preexisting people which preceded nation and state) were invariably popular. Most foundational myths related back to either antiquity (especially Greece and Italy) or the Middle Ages. National movements defined their nations according to whether they had been successor states to Rome or opponents of the Roman Empire. National myths also surrounded the histories of particular ruling houses, key national heroes, texts, and battles. Those intent on constructing a national story were keen to identify a particular moment or event from which, they argued, nation formation had reached a point of no return. Those points of no return were often connected to stories of conquest and war.

European history between the late eighteenth and early twentieth centuries was, after all, characterized by the violent redrawing of European borders, which reduced drastically the number of European states. Hundreds of formerly independent and semi-independent entities were removed from the European map. The Napoleonic Wars and the subsequent Vienna settlement of 1815 contributed to stirrings of national movements across Europe. Subsequently, many representatives of national movements looked back to this period as the birthplace of their respective modern national movements. They regarded it as a time of national awakening. In established nation-states such as Britain the Napoleonic period reinforced nationalism. In Spain the national movement constructed the Spanish resistance to Napoleon as the major obstacle to the French emperor's success. The "Spanish thorn," in Napoleon's own words, had led to

his defeat and Spain could be proud of that legacy. Major defeats of Sweden and Denmark by Napoleon meant that the national movement began to stir in Norway. In the stateless nations of Central and East Central Europe the Napoleonic Wars brought expressions of national sentiments which did not yet reach a mass audience. But national movements in alliance with state power eventually brought about the unification of Germany and Italy between 1859 and 1871 – again, through military conflict and war. States in which the national narratives drew heavily on war and conquest tended to become highly militarized societies, such as Germany before 1914, France after 1871, and Britain during the Boer War.

The themes of war and conquest were often connected to notions of a golden age. The Netherlands in the 1600s, Spain in the fifteenth and sixteenth centuries, Italy during the Renaissance – national movements in the nineteenth century looked back on these periods with pride, as they signaled either the nation's great power status, or a particular economic, cultural, or political significance. Thus, the Dutch national movement held up the Netherlands' proud legacy of tolerance and diversity: Amsterdam was celebrated as the print capital of Europe during the seventeenth century. Books that were banned elsewhere could be freely printed there. The strong connection between liberalism and the national movement found expression in celebrations of constitutional traditions throughout Europe. In Spain, for example, liberal nationalists denounced the period of the Inquisition as a dark age which destroyed great cultural potential. Instead, they looked towards the first constitutional convention held in Cádiz between 1810 and 1813 as a promising antecedent of the kind of nation-state on which they wanted to build.

Wars, golden ages, and even constitutional reforms produced heroes. National heroes tended to be "great men," such as monarchs, generals, politicians, businessmen, explorers, and scientists.[19] Thousands of national monuments dedicated to such "great men" still litter the landscape of European nations today. In the late nineteenth century hundreds of Bismarck and Wilhelm II memorials were erected in imperial Germany, overwhelmingly paid for by civic associations at no extra expense to the German taxpayer. National monuments became the focal points for national festivities organized by national movements across Europe.

Those who constructed the nation were predominantly male. National clubs and associations at times did not even allow women to become members. Women were, of course, also routinely excluded from citizenship and from army service. All perceived enemies of the nation were continuously feminized in nationalist discourse. In a patriarchal society their ultimate inferiority was demonstrated by showing them to be the female "other." At the same time, however, the nation was widely imagined as "family."[20] In the family, women clearly had an important role to play: hence national movements did allow women to participate in national festivals and to fulfill the "typically female" functions connected with housekeeping and childrearing. The nineteenth-century bourgeois women's movement argued persistently that women fulfilled vital services to the nation. They bore the future generation of soldiers and reared them in a national sense. They also nursed those soldiers in times of war and fulfilled a wide range of charitable and social roles in society. Nationalist women's associations often belonged to the biggest national associations. On the political right, they championed a racialized and ethnic discourse of the nation, whereas more left-leaning women's associations tended to appropriate the language of human rights and citizenship.

The national movement aimed for a mass audience. Hence, communication was crucial for its success. The massive improvement in the transport system – especially the forward march of the railways, but also the roads, canals, telegraph, and post office – ensured that news traveled more easily across distances and that people moved more freely as well. National newspapers came into wider circulation, and national festivals could draw mass audiences. The Wartburg festival in Germany was attended by no more than a few hundred students in 1817. The Hambach festival in 1832 drew tens of thousands of supporters of the German national movement. Sports events increasingly became national competitions. The Olympic Games, first organized in Athens in 1896, was a kind of substitute war between nations carried out in a stadium.

As the national movement acquired a mass following, "banal nationalism" became more and more important.[21] The nation was becoming part and parcel of everyday routines and procedures through games for children with a national theme, china depicting national heroes, landscapes, monuments, naming ceremonies for ships, exhibitions and sports events drawing mass crowds, and collectors' cards or postcards with national motifs. Travel and mass tourism increasingly became important means of propagating national identity.[22]

National Movements and States

Where the state preceded modern mass nationalism, it also often encouraged national movements to develop the full repertoire of national symbols and narratives. It actively promoted nationalism to further its own political ends. Hence nationalism as an ideology often flourished where it was adopted and promulgated by states. Germany would be a classic example. National movements existed and clamored for national unity long before unification of the country in 1871, but any genuine nationalization of the masses arguably only occurred under the impact of the state-driven nationalism in the German Empire. It relied on monarchical and ethnocultural constructions of the nation and downplayed civic and political traditions. Furthermore, different ideas of the state had a major impact on the shape and content of diverse national movements. Thus, the idea of the state as a neutral arbiter between different social forces in society encouraged statism in Germany. Liberal nationalists tended to abhor the thought of conflict between state and civil society. By contrast, the state was meant to banish partisan conflict and restrain the egotisms of civil society. Characteristically, the German term for "citizen" – *Staatsbürger* – included a more passive, subject-like element which was absent from the English term and also from the French *citoyen*.[23] Civil society was imagined as working in harmony with and alongside the state. The potential interest fragmentation and pluralism of civil society frightened many German liberals, who saw in the state the only guarantor of a harmonious, classless, and leveled middle-class society.

Early modern "composite states,"[24] in which regions had traditionally enjoyed a great deal of autonomy (e.g., the Holy Roman Empire, the Swiss confederation, Italy and Spain), developed strong traditions of a federal nationalism. A prominent urban core was often at the heart of constructing broader regional identities and mediating those with local and national identities.[25] Especially where these regions were economically successful they tended to develop a strong identity of their own. Powerful alliances between urban elites and an agrarian hinterland produced regionalist sentiments which could be predominantly cultural (such as in France or Britain) or political-legal (such as in Germany and Switzerland). In some nations (e.g., Germany and Switzerland) the definition of citizenship was left to federal (i.e., subnational) territorial units – the cantons in Switzerland and the individual German states making up the German Empire after 1871.

Where a state was firmly committed to free trade, as in Britain and the Low Countries, strong financial interest groups often kept protectionist forces in check. Where this was not the case, as in Imperial Germany, the latter often exercised a stronger influence on national movements and strengthened an inward-looking and at times xenophobic nationalism. Where a state had a long and/or proud constitutional tradition, such as in Britain, Sweden, Belgium, and Norway, the constitution could become the key focus for national movements that would stress the importance of voluntarist and political definitions of the nation. Both the 1809 Swedish constitution, which ended absolutism and formulated a new relationship between crown and parliament, and the 1814 Norwegian constitution became near-sacred bases of identity constructions in these two Scandinavian countries.

To reach greater numbers of people a good educational system provided by the state proved crucial. The early nationalization of the peasants in Denmark would have been unthinkable without the school system. And the much-admired Prussian educational system proved to be an important vehicle for spreading the national movement's message. National movements and nation-states could make Germans, French, British, and Italian citizens, not the least because of their influence over the education system, their command over the army, and their alliance with the churches. Another important means to bolster a national ideology was monarchism. In the eighteenth and early nineteenth centuries nationalism had been an ideology largely opposed to monarchs and their feudal and authoritarian regimes. As discussed above, the national movement had an affinity with the liberal and democratic movements rather than with monarchism. But in the second half of the nineteenth century monarchism moved into the limelight as the single most important bulwark of the conservative forces against any further liberalization or democratization of the state. Conservatives everywhere in Europe had initially occupied strongly anti-national positions, as the nation seemed to threaten their feudal power base, but in the course of the nineteenth century they adapted to the new ideas. Ideologues such as Friedrich Julius Stahl and Wilhelm Heinrich Riehl were among the most powerful propagators of a national idea which focused on Christianity, folk culture, ethnicity, and language, and effectively depoliticized the national idea.

However, the nation also assumed a religious quality for its followers, who spoke about a "chosen people" in search of their "holy land." The nation replaced religion as the highest human value which had general application. National movements could call on their followers to die on the "altar of the fatherland" just as Jesus had died on the cross. Many symbols, metaphors, and myths were transferred from the religious context to the imagined worlds of the nation, referred to as "sacred territory." Members of the nation could think of themselves as laboring under a special covenant with God.

Everywhere in Europe state-driven nationalisms were challenged and contested by national movements in opposition to the state. In Germany, for example, left liberals and socialists opposed the state-driven monarchical and ethnocultural definitions of the nation and instead highlighted their commitment to a more pluralistic, a more civic, and a more political nation-state of the future. National movements often failed to live up to their promises of egalitarianism. Theoretically, every member of the nation was of equal value to them. In reality, however, liberal national movements practiced a range of exclusionary mechanisms directed against the lower social classes which were perceived as lacking the preconditions for political activity, namely education and property. A famous example is the German National Association, which set its membership dues so high as to prevent workers and poorer artisans from joining. Liberal nationalists were frequently opposed to any extension of the suffrage. Hence it is little surprise that socialist movements across Europe, speaking on behalf of the working classes, put forward rival, more democratic and open forms of nationalism.

Another group which often came up with alternative narratives of national belonging were Catholics. In some nations, such as Spain, Ireland, and Poland, Catholicism was firmly integrated into the official and dominant nationalist narratives. But in countries with Protestant majorities, their situation was more difficult. They often rejected the total claims of the nation-state for undivided loyalty, and sought to bring together their commitment to a transnational church with their loyalties to the nation. As a consequence, many national movements, especially in states with strong Catholic minorities, declared the Catholic church an unpatriotic and hostile force.[26] Jesuits and members of monastic orders were, for example, excluded from the otherwise extremely liberal 1814 Norwegian constitution. During the 1860s the *Kulturkampf* in Germany laid the foundations for making confessional affiliation the biggest single factor in dividing German national identity prior to 1914.[27] Anti-Catholicism, just like anti-socialism, was a common feature across European states, albeit to very different degrees.

Overall, mutually incompatible types of nationalism were put forward by different sections of society. In an age of mass politics during the second half of the nineteenth century, the nation-state could not be built from the top down. The state sought to ally itself to strong popular and civic movements which it influenced in particular directions. The state aimed at controlling public opinion, as it could no longer ignore it. Movements which threatened the official nationalism propagated by the state were often turned into "internal enemies" of the nation.

But the most important "internal enemy" of a whole host of European nation-states was "the Jew." Anti-Judaism had, of course, a long tradition in European religious thought. Christianity regarded Jews as the people responsible for killing Christ, and pogroms against Jews had been a feature of most European societies from the Middle Ages onwards. But in the last third of the nineteenth century anti-Judaism was overlaid with modern antisemitism, which did not hark back to religious arguments but foregrounded race in its rejection of the Jews. The strong reception of Social Darwinist ideas by national movements across Europe was responsible not only for the ethnicization of citizenship laws but also for the development of *völkisch* nationalisms. Notions of separate and hierarchically organized races spread after 1870, and national movements began to demand the purification of their particular race as a precondition for maintaining racial superiority. Even in Scandinavia the ethnicization of the national idea led to the strong endorsement of ideas of ethnic distinctiveness of Scandinavians deriving from common ancestors: the Norsemen of the old Icelandic sagas. A "literary medievalism" began to search for the common origins of the Scandinavian people, but it equally asked who could construct the purest lineage, or where the Norse people actually remained most "unpolluted" from "foreign" influences.

Strongly developed civil societies often were the precondition for powerful national movements, but civil societies were not necessarily tolerant and benign.[28] National movements often constructed national communities of solidarity against perceived internal and external enemies. External enemies were often direct neighbors with whom one shared histories of often violent conflict and between whom borders could sometimes be hotly contested. Many territories in Europe were being claimed by several national movements as belonging to their respective nation-states. Hence border regions often took on a particular significance for national movements: here, national identities had to be defended especially vigorously. But people in border regions were also often perceived as unreliable allies. Linguistic and cultural identities in border regions were not clearcut.[29] Nationalization policies of the central state often produced strong national conflicts, for example between Germans and Danes in the province of Schleswig, and between Germans and Poles in the province of Posen. The Franco-German conflict over the Rhine is another famous example, but equally, the Italian national movement was opposed to the Austrian seizure of Lombardo-Venetia. Borderland identities could set themselves against the nationalization ambitions of central states and emphasize their in-betweenness and hybridity; whether they were successful or not depended on a variety of different factors.

Overall, nations were inclined to define themselves strongly against national "others." Russian national movements defined Russianness against "the West," while, inversely, various nations in Europe had written Russia out of European history altogether, declaring it as Asian "other." Germanness was frequently contrasted with Slav identity, but it was also directed against the "hereditary enemy" France and against "perfidious Albion." Polish nationalists saw themselves surrounded by German, Austrian, and Russian enemies of the nation who had, twice in history, completely ended Polish stateness. The Dutch and Belgian national movements presented their national stories as ones of an emerging and ultimately victorious liberty against "foreign" attempts to oppress them. They were proud of their countries' free press, constitutionalism, and extensive rights of asylum.

If states were crucial in fostering and supporting national movements, many of these movements in nineteenth-century Europe did not have a state to sponsor them. Here they emerged out of a burgeoning civil society based in urban centers in which members of the new middling classes – in particular, intellectuals and state bureaucrats – were prominent. In some European countries, however (and here one thinks in particular of the Scandinavian

countries, but also some in Southeastern Europe), rural peasant communities played a vital role. In Norway the 1814 constitution explicitly incorporated peasants into the nation, recognizing their vital political role. Associations of peasant societies were also important backbones of the national movement throughout Denmark. Even where peasants played no major role in the national movement, reference to peasants as representing the true "national spirit" was commonplace, for example among Slavophiles in Russia or the early national movement in Serbia. Peasants were regarded as uncorrupted by "foreign" influences and expressing "authentic" national cultures – regardless of the fact that the vast majority of peasants in East Central or Southeastern Europe would not have any strong consciousness of belonging to a particular nation. The celebration of indigenous peasant or folk cultures was a characteristic of romantic national movements which sought to counter the claims of the liberal national movements, which often referred to universal Western models, most frequently Britain and France. The liberal nationalists often adhered to a discourse of "backwardness" which saw the comprehensive modernization of their societies (industrialization, development of civil society, and a more liberal political framework) as the precondition for developing a strong national consciousness. Whereas they aimed to make peasants into citizens of the nation,[30] romantic national movements declared that peasants already were the true standard bearers of the nation. Yet, in some cases (e.g., Poland), the aristocracy rather than the urban middle classes or the peasants played the most important part in constituting vibrant national movements (in the Polish case in particular the lower and middling aristocracy – *szlachta* – members of which had suffered economically and were virtually without political influence or representation).

Overall, very different social actors were active in diverse national movements across Europe. Stateless nations needed to construct national continuities. They searched for predecessors and anchored their national ambitions in the past. This was obviously easier where some kind of national state had existed previously. Thus, in Germany, the national movements could link the nation either to the Prussian state or to the Holy Roman Empire (the latter was, however, fraught with difficulties given the very weak state traditions of this empire). Under the impact of Romantic nationalism, notions of a hegemonic medieval Reich were used extensively throughout the nineteenth century to legitimate German territorial demands in the present. They also produced considerable tensions with neighboring national movements and nation-states. In Lithuania the national movement could look back to the Kingdoms of Lithuania as a predecessor of a Lithuanian state. The other Baltic states, Latvia and Estonia, by contrast, had no such traditions to build on and hence could only fall back on the notion of the people as the essence of their national identity.[31]

Medievalism combined with political Romanticism was a characteristic of many nineteenth-century national movements. In the Hungarian, Spanish, and Polish national movements, for example, the memory of a grand medieval past was prominently connected with claims that their nation had a particular role in protecting European civilization from outside forces, such as the Muslims in the Spanish Reconquista or the Tartars, Mongols, and Ottomans in the Polish and Hungarian national discourses. Political Romanticism favored organicist definitions of the nation: it imagined the nation as a body which developed over time, had a period of youth, followed by a period of maturity and decline, from where it needed some kind of rebirth. As parts of the body had no option of choosing whether they wanted to belong or not, so citizens had no choice: they were naturally a part of the nation which preceded them. Body metaphors emphasized harmony over interest fragmentation. Different parts of the body functioned as one. They supplemented each other and did not work against each other, except where the body had fallen prey to some kind of illness or disease.

Political romantics were champions of medievalism and idealized the peasantry and their allegedly authentic rural lifestyles, but the romantics themselves were often city dwellers. In the new urban centers dense networks of civic associations practiced a new kind of sociability among their (mostly male) members. Historical societies, musical societies, gymnasts, citizens' guards, and student fraternities were among some of the more prominent associations, which mobilized those social strata which saw in the national principle a powerful means to demand a greater say in the affairs of the state. Networks of communication and the emergence of a public sphere more generally were crucial for the emergence and development of national movements in Europe. In their voluntary associations they already practiced the kind of participatory democratic processes that they wished to introduce at state level. Everyone was supposed to be equal within the boundaries of the association, just as everyone was imagined equal within the boundaries of the future nation-state. Frequently, the model was that of a leveled middle-class society which wanted to protect itself against repression from above and revolution from below. This was particularly evident in the European revolutions of 1848–9. Everywhere demands for a more genuine liberalization and constitutionalization of politics combined with demands for the creation of nation-states. The so-called "spring of nations" had a strong liberal-democratic flavor, with national movements committed to a generous male suffrage, the rule of law, and constitutional government. But the issues of republicanism and democracy split the movements badly across Europe, with monarchist national imaginations opposed to republican ones and liberal constructions of the nation juxtaposed to democratic ones.

In Britain, as Linda Colley has emphasized, nation building went alongside empire building and war experiences.[32] In the eighteenth and nineteenth centuries, Britishness became the means to accommodate the Scottish and Welsh challenges to English dominance over the nation-state, and also the vehicle with which to make all the nations of the United Kingdom identify with its colonial empire. It reinforced notions of an "island nation" separate from and different to continental Europe. But everywhere in Europe a fascination with colonial conquest reinforced notions of cultural and racial superiority. The latter justified the ruthless exploitation of the colonies and the brutal treatment of the colonial subjects, perhaps most notoriously in the Belgian colony of the Congo. It could also underwrite notions of the civilizing mission of the Europeans, most often clothed in images of a "white man's burden" (Rudyard Kipling). But nation builders everywhere (e.g., Max Weber in Germany, Joseph Chamberlain in Britain, Jules Ferry in France) argued strongly, albeit in different national contexts, that building large colonial empires was the precondition for the success and the survival of the nation-state.

Issues of empire wrote themselves into the national narratives in a variety of different ways. The loss of empire, as in Spain's case, produced a fundamental sense of failure and unease with the nation-state. In Spain, it encouraged a discourse of decadence which decried Spanish backwardness and inferiority. It was no coincidence that 1898, when the USA pushed Spain out of its last remaining colony, Cuba, was also the foundational moment for the Catalan and Basque national movements. It was only after 1898 that the elite nationalism of the Catalans and the Basques made inroads into the masses. Ultimately, the Catalan national movement proved to be a more powerful challenge to the Spanish state, as linguistic differences had been retained more thoroughly in Catalonia. One of the economically most advanced regions of Spain, the professional and economic middle classes argued strongly that the Spanish state had failed Catalonia and that the country could rule itself more effectively than could a distant government in Madrid. Their voices were being increasingly heard by the Catalan people.

National Movements in Multinational Empires and States

National movements were particularly opposed to multinational empires, which still dominated much of Central and Eastern Europe throughout the nineteenth century: they often relied on dynastic loyalties to supersede sentiments of national belonging. The Romanovs in the Russian Empire, the Habsburgs in the Austrian Empire, and the sultans in the Ottoman Empire all mistrusted nationalism as an ideology, as they clearly recognized its explosive and

destructive potential for their multinational empires. They sought to counter it by introducing federal and decentralized forms of government which would grant varying degrees of cultural autonomy to their constituent nations. In 1848 the Habsburg emperor acknowledged that all nationalities within the empire were of equal status, and in 1867 he started a process of devolving power to the historic kingdoms and crownlands. The widest-ranging proposals for transforming the empire into a multinational federal state came from the Austrian Socialist Party. Its theoreticians, such as Karl Renner and Otto Bauer, understood nationalities as cultural communities which needed to be given institutional recognition within a federalist framework. However, right from the start, one of the major problems with the far more limited Habsburg settlements was that they did not treat the different national movements the same. Most privileges were given to Hungary, and the Croatian, Polish, and Czech national movements remained dissatisfied with the more limited rights they had been granted.

Ultimately, the idea to use federalism to take the sting out of national movements failed, because varying degrees of self-government were used to develop powerful state-driven nationalization processes threatening the very survival of the empire. Thus the Magyar political elite constructed a national narrative focused on history and territory. It emphasized the traditions of the old Magyar nobility and the importance of the historic Hungary, referred to as the "lands of the Holy Crown of St. Stephen." In 1860 the celebrations on St. Stephen's Day turned into a public condemnation of the Habsburgs, who were accused of repressing the Hungarian nation. In fact, the Hungarians themselves became oppressors. Other languages than Hungarian were actively suppressed, as the Magyar elites set about to Magyarize the large national minorities inside Hungary. Schools and universities espoused a Hungarian nationalism which had no regard for the Habsburg dynasty. In 1896 the Hungarians celebrated one thousand years of the first Magyar tribes arriving on Hungarian soil.[33]

In the Austro-Hungarian Empire the national movements of its constituent nations were far more advanced than in either the

Ottoman or the Russian empires. The Ottoman Empire functioned reasonably well because it combined central bureaucratic and military control with the granting of considerable autonomy to local notables, who could exercise control over economic and political decision making. It granted political privileges to the Greek Orthodox church, thereby making it difficult for national movements to exploit religious divisions. The Bulgarian national movement drew support from local resistance to the dominance of the Greek patriarchate in Constantinople, but in Romania the Greek Orthodox church was, for a long time, perfectly happy with the privileges granted to it by the Ottomans. Here it was a group of Romanian notables who were unhappy with the influence of the church and attempted to mobilize the peasants in the name of the nation. National movements in the Ottoman Empire arose out of local conflicts between different factions of notables/clergy striving for power and resenting the influence of other factions. They began to prosper in the late nineteenth century because the Ottoman center was weak and increasingly unable to sustain its complex alliances with local notables. Thus, for example, the Serbian national movement was rooted in the failure of the Ottomans to protect the local population from the arbitrary violence of the Ottoman soldiers, the Janissaries. Other European powers, sensing the weakness of the empire, exerted additional pressure to gain a foothold in the Balkans. Such external pressure was particularly vital for the consolidation of the Greek national movement. Ottoman attempts to deal with the crisis by centralizing control, introducing Turkish as the official language of the empire, and secularizing government only met with greater resistance among the different nationalities.

Among the great empires of Eastern Europe, arguably Russia had the least problems with strong national movements before 1914, if one excludes the strong Polish national movement on its western-most border clamoring for national independence in various forms and guises almost throughout the nineteenth century. In fact it was the alleged repression of the Polish nation by Russian autocracy which incurred the wrath of liberal nationalists across

Europe. Together with the European-wide sympathies for the Greek national struggle, the Polish case is a good example of the cosmopolitanism of early national movements. Members of the many Greek and Polish associations across Europe during the 1820s and 1830s were united in their belief in national self-determination everywhere in Europe. However, in the majority of the territories making up the Russian Empire, an overwhelmingly agricultural and illiterate population had little sense of national belonging of one sort or another. The Russian census of 1897 did not even ask about nationality, as the statisticians in Moscow feared that the peasants would be confused by such a question. Instead, they chose to ask about language and confession. The results revealed just how multinational the empire was. Only 43 percent of the population spoke the single official language of the empire, Russian. Many more were members of the Russian Orthodox church, but even religion was a problematic pillar in an empire which included large non-Christian minorities. Hence the Romanov empire could only propagate the idea of the imperial state as the basis of a Russian identity. An ethnocultural Russian national movement, which surfaced for the first time in the context of the 1905 revolution, threatened to destroy rather than save the Russian Empire. And yet the diverse nationalist groups were supported in monarchist circles and the Orthodox church. The tsar himself had considerable sympathies, blissfully unaware that nationalism ultimately undermined the very existence of his empire. Luckily for him the non-Russian territories lacked substantive national movements which could have reacted strongly to the nascent Russian nationalism at the beginning of the twentieth century.

National movements not only threatened empires in Central and Eastern Europe. They also began to surface in multinational West European states such as Britain and Spain. In Britain, Scottish and Welsh national movements stopped short of demanding their own nation-states. The Cymru Ffydd movement in Wales and the Scottish national movement were happy to find cultural and (in the Scottish case) institutional outlets for the expression of their differences, and on the whole endorsed the union as beneficial to all its constituent members. This was, of course, not the case for the Catholic majority in Ireland, which persistently demanded independence from Britain. Here, the movement of Young Irelanders constructed a cult of Celticism and the Gaelic language meant to reinforce resistance to what were deemed "foreign" Saxon influences. The British state reacted by putting forward (ultimately unsuccessfully) various schemes for Home Rule, which were fiercely contested among the different political factions in Britain. In Spain, Catalan and Basque national movements also challenged the dominance of the Castilian parts of Spain.

Conclusion

In 1914, when, in Lloyd George's famous phrase, the lights went out in Europe, national movements, in alliance with state power, had become one the most potent forces shaping domestic and foreign policies. They had been successful in creating narratives about nations which served as powerful focal points for the identities of a growing number of people across Europe. Nationalism as an ideology had become a mighty tool for nation-states and for those in search of a nation-state. They were busy undermining multinational empires and challenging, with varying degrees of success, multinational states across Europe. National movements and their ideas were responsible for producing the kind of climate which enabled World War I to happen. As such, they were arguably one of the most malign forces in the history of Europe, yet, depressingly, it was only after World War I that national movements and nationalisms in Europe radicalized themselves further and came fully into their own. It took the major upheavals of total war and genocide on a hitherto unprecedented scale to discredit nationalism and force a gradual rethinking of the dominant national narratives after 1945.

ACKNOWLEDGMENTS

I am grateful to Jörn Leonhard for his close reading of this chapter and for many good suggestions to improve it. The remaining infelicities are, of course, entirely my own.

NOTES

1 Kohn (1955).
2 Schieder (1992).
3 Meinecke (1970).
4 Breuilly (1993).
5 Anderson (1991).
6 Hobsbawm and Ranger (1983).
7 Bhaba (1991).
8 Breuilly (2002).
9 Smith (1986); see also his excellent introduction to the various debates in nationalism and national identity studies (Smith 2000).
10 Gorski (2000).
11 On the idea of an epochal breakthrough to modernity in the century between 1750 and 1850, see Koselleck (2002: 154–69).
12 For the debates between the "perennialists" and the "modernists," see Smith (2000).
13 Gellner (1983).
14 Kedourie (1960).
15 Hroch (1985).
16 James (1990).
17 Renan (1994).
18 Zimmer (2003a).
19 On the importance of national heroes to national history writing, see Eriksonas (2004).
20 Hagemann (1997).
21 Billig (1995).
22 Koshar (2000).
23 Keane (1988).
24 Elliott (1992).
25 Umbach (2002).
26 Clark and Kaiser (2003).
27 Smith (1995).
28 Trentmann (2000).
29 Donnan and Wilson (1999).
30 See the classic study for France: Weber (1977).
31 Wendland (2003: 205–38).
32 Colley (1992).
33 Freifeld (2000).

GUIDE TO FURTHER READING

An excellent starting point is the eminently comparative and wide-ranging survey by Eric

Hobsbawm, *Nations and Nationalism since 1780*. Very useful introductions to the theme are also provided by Hewittson and Baycroft in *Nationalism in Europe, 1789–1914*, Lawrence's *Nationalism in Europe, 1780–1850*, and Zimmer's *Nationalism in Europe, 1890–1940*. Slightly older but still extremely readable is Pearson's *European Nationalism 1789–1920* and Alter's *Nationalism*. Greenfeld's interesting but controversial study entitled *Nationalism: Five Roads to Modernity* compares nation-building experiences in North America, England, France, Russia, and Germany. It contrasts an "individualist-civic nationalism" in England and the US with more collectivist and xenophobic traditions in continental Europe. For country-by-country studies which focus on the characters of national movements in the modern period, see the series *Inventing the Nation*, published under the general editorship of Keith Robbins with Edward Arnold. For a good survey of the close relationship between gender and nationalism, see Blom, Hagemann, and Hall's *Gendered Nations*.

CHAPTER FIFTEEN

The "Woman Question"

KATHLEEN CANNING

The nineteenth-century "woman question" encompasses an array of theories and debates about the physiological nature, political capacity, moral character, and social location of women in European societies. The "woman question" was framed at the levels of law, philosophy, and policies of state, by discourses on morality, science, and social reform, and in political arenas ranging from salons to parliaments, religious revivals to suffrage campaigns. While each national polity and culture engendered its own "woman question," some debates and social movements crossed the borders of states and nations, lending a transnational or international character to the "woman question" and the women's movement by the last third of the century. The question of women's place in society and politics arose most acutely in times of turmoil and transformation – from the French Revolution and the Napoleonic Wars, through the revolutions of 1848–9, to the dislocations of industrial change, and the intensifying race for empire towards the century's end. Yet the "woman question" was also deliberated and debated at the level of everyday life, as women contested the limitations placed on their education, property rights, and status in marriage and family, and claimed new rights and duties as citizens in cities and communities, nations and republics. Moreover, the "woman question" was articulated in the arenas of both high and low politics and attempts to resolve it crisscrossed

disparate political and cultural milieus and transcended boundaries of class, ethnicity, region, and religion. At some point in the history of the nineteenth century, each nation and each social group addressed a "woman question" and sought resolutions according to its own capacities and ideologies.

As defined here, the "woman question" was almost always also a "gender question," that is a more fundamental query into the relational character of both sexes, the alignment of sexual and social order. At times "the woman question" signaled other crises – about the moral or biological integrity of families, illegitimacy or depopulation, or the perils of industrial growth – with women figuring as the most visible, vulnerable, or volatile presence within these constellations. While the "woman question" constituted a discursive complex, an ideological web, it is important to note that it also produced a social movement – the organized women's movement that formed across Europe during the last third of the nineteenth century. If the "woman question" swirled through different discursive arenas, encompassing an array of possible social issues and standpoints during the early nineteenth century, the congealing of national and international feminist movements around women's rights sharpened the lines between advocates and opponents. Finally, the nineteenth-century "woman question" did not mark the first time European societies explored the ideals of femininity and masculinity, marriage, family, virtue, and morality. In fact, the *querelles des femmes* that raged during the period between the late Renaissance and the early Enlightenment sometimes produced a thousand pamphlets in a single year for the literate urban populace.

Yet the nineteenth-century "woman question" did mark a departure from previous disputes in many respects. The momentous transformations confronting Europeans in this age – from the physical alterations of countryside and cityscapes, the melding of workers and burghers into new social classes, the founding of nation-states and expansions of empires, the new cultures and sciences of knowledge, the creeds of liberalism, nationalism, socialism, and feminism – dissolved previous social and cultural grids, including hierarchies of gender. The relentless and rapid pace of change meant that relations between family and state, women and men, were never peripheral to these transformations, but were instead in continuous need of the kind of reordering that constituted modernity. The "woman question" emerged as contemporaries sought to come to terms with these changes, engaged in and dispensed with projects of reordering society, politics, and culture, and confronted the contradictions inherent in the new ideologies of republican democracy, liberalism, and socialism. In doing so they availed themselves of the modern means of disseminating and galvanizing public opinion in increasingly literate societies – from newspapers and journals to statistics and scientific enquiries. Even if the nineteenth-century "woman question" was cast amid contention and crisis, it was rearticulated at various turning points throughout the nineteenth century and remained a crucial fault line in European societies during and after World War I.

The Inception of the Modern "Woman Question"

Although it became an identifiable discourse only during the mid-nineteenth century, the "woman question" originated in the philosophical and political upheavals of the late eighteenth century – the French Revolution and the subsequent embrace of Enlightenment ideol-

ogy that swept across the European continent in its wake. The congealing of civil society itself provided a new arena for the entry of women into politics and indeed the stakes of such "disputes about women" increased with their first claims upon the polity. The opening act of the nineteenth-century "woman question" began when the women of Paris took the stage as social actors, participating in the public acts that eroded the authority of the Bourbon monarchy and articulating their own visions of the republican rule that should replace it. Only a few female seamstresses and tradeswomen raised their voices in the collections of grievances (*cahiers de doléance*) collected on the eve of the revolution. Yet thousands of women led the march to Versailles in October 1789 that began with demands for distribution of bread and ended with the capture of the king and royal family and their return to their constituents in Paris. As the mainstays of the feudal monarchy were turned on their head and the National Assembly began deliberating the rights of "man and citizen," women filled the assembly halls to hear the debates and sought to join or institute revolutionary clubs. Not long after the Assembly drafted the Declaration of the Rights of Man and Citizen, revolutionaries themselves probed the limits of these rights. Noting that neither gender nor race should determine the capacity for citizenship, rather the ownership of property and the ability to be governed by reason, the Marquis de Condorcet issued his appeal for the "admission of women to citizenship."[1] As contests over the terms of citizenship intensified, women revolutionaries entered the debates to speak on their own behalf. The constitution of 1791 abolished some of the privileges men enjoyed in the realms of property ownership and inheritance and redefined civil majority in equal terms for men and women. Spokeswomen from the women's clubs assailed its shortcomings, emphasizing the differential place of women in the sections pertaining to marriage and family and asserting women's "natural right" to bear arms on behalf of the nation. Olympe de Gouges published the Declaration of the Rights of Woman in 1791, proposing a comprehensive blueprint for women's active citizenship rather than the passive status accorded by the constitution. Attaching sexual to political equality in her call to do away with husbands' patriarchal power within families, de Gouges contended that the "tyranny of men over women was the true wellspring of all forms of inequality."[2]

In the revolution's first phase the women of Paris became subjects on a highly visible stage of European politics, one that monarchs and aristocracies across Europe observed anxiously. Assembling in public political spaces to represent their own interests, they engaged in acts of "self-creation," performing, as Joan Scott notes, "the public/political role usually performed by men."[3] Women won certain concessions from the National Assembly in the realms of family law, gaining equal status to men in marriage and divorce in 1792, for example. In the eyes of its opponents, the revolution appeared to have inaugurated the emancipation of women – civil, political, and sexual – which they viewed as a violation of the fundamental political and domestic orders. Although still deprived of the right to vote, female members of the Parisian sans-culottes established the radical Society of Revolutionary Republic Women, symbolically refiguring citizenship by donning the tricolor cockade and adopting the language of virtue in their public speeches. The actions of French women inspired those in other countries: in Belgium, for example, women took an active role in the revolt against Austrian rulers in 1789.[4]

The dreams of equal citizenship were drastically curtailed when the Jacobins unleashed a wave of repression, closing popular revolutionary clubs, first and foremost those of women. Legislators moved to realign family and state, masculine and feminine roles, when they restricted the participation of women in politics, stripping them of their right to speak in public or to dress in revolutionary clothing. Highlighting women's tasks as mothers of citizens and educators of men, the ideology of republican motherhood reinscribed the gendered divisions between public and private posited by Enlightenment philosopher Jean-Jacques Rousseau. The expulsion of activist women from the public sphere contrasted sharply with the ascription of citizenship rights to men of the "common classes," based not least on their service in the revolutionary armies

that carried the ideals of French republicanism across Europe. If the vision of women's citizenship, which Olympe de Gouges outlined in some detail in 1793, was expunged from public life by the turn of the nineteenth century, the fundamental issues it raised would inform and shape the "woman question" across Europe for decades to come. The revolutionary and then Napoleonic Wars meant that the legacy of the revolution spread far beyond France. In Britain, Mary Wollstonecraft, who had first supported the "rights of man" in the early days of the French Revolution, issued her far more radical tract, *A Vindication of the Rights of Woman*, in 1792. Positing that women could not renounce their capacities as "rational and sexual subjects" in order to become citizens, Wollstonecraft accepted inherent differences between the sexes.[5] Crafting her own notion of republican motherhood as a vital contribution to civic life, she noted that its fulfillment required women's equal participation in both economy and politics. Wollstonecraft thus challenged male tyranny in quite different terms than de Gouges, seeking to redefine rather than to eradicate sexual difference. Yet, for Wollstonecraft, the emancipation of women was inextricably linked to "the social and political liberation of 'the people as a whole'."[6] Responding from the vantage point of Hohenzollern Prussia to the distinctions between active (male) and passive (female) citizens in the French constitution of 1792, intellectual and reformer Theodore Gottlieb von Hippel noted that women who had hoisted the flag of revolution had a "divine calling" to involvement in the affairs of state and warned that the failure to instill "the opposite sex" with the rights of citizenship would inevitably lead to "sexual strife."[7] Revolutionaries in the Dutch Republic also raised the banner of liberty, equality, and fraternity in the Batavian Revolution of 1795. Dutch activist Etta Palm D'Aelders, a prominent advocate of women's rights during the French Revolution who was expelled from France for her political activities in 1795, participated in the Batavian Revolution at home later. Applying the lessons of the French Revolution in the Dutch Republic, she issued a programmatic call for women to organize exclusively female political clubs and argued on behalf of their participation in the "governance of the nation."

As the revolution marched across the European continent, the images of women claiming citizenship in their own name became one of its key legacies for the nineteenth century. The contradictory precepts of the revolution framed both aspects of the "woman question": liberty and equality as universal "rights of man" on the one hand, its refusal of active citizenship to women on the other. Even if the term "feminism" did not emerge until nearly a century later, sexual difference was established, as Joan Scott has argued, "not only as a natural fact, but also as an ontological basis for social and political differentiation."[8]

The "Character of the Sexes" from Restoration to Revolution

The effects of the French Revolution continued to ripple across Europe during the era of the Napoleonic Wars. Amid the cycles of war, reform, and counter-revolution profound anxiety continued to fester about the specter of women's emancipation. The end of the revolution was only assured, many believed, when the hierarchies between the sexes were definitively restored. Yet instead of restoring an old gender system, the Napoleonic code and the awakening of national sentiment across the European continent actually fostered a new gender order for the nineteenth century. Although the Napoleonic Code had the "progressive" effect of abolishing feudalism and the guild system, lifting trade restrictions, and establishing constitutions in many principalities across Europe, it also aimed to decide any open questions about the equality or emancipation of women. If the revolution had permitted women to "violate" public spaces, the Napoleonic Code prescribed the return of women to the private realms of marriage, maternity, and domesticity. As Napoleonic troops engaged in battle across the continent, women joined nationalist or patriotic associations, crafting their own versions of female patriotism and emphasizing mothers' contributions to the unity and virtue of the nation. Patriotic women in Prussia, for example, were encouraged both to reject foreign or French influences in public and domestic life, and to mobilize material and emotional resources to support "national warriors."[9]

The restoration that followed Napoleon's defeat, embodied in the Congress System under Klemens von Metternich, aimed to expunge all traces of revolution from the European landscape, restricting civil liberties and associational life, and reinforcing the authority of monarchy, aristocracy, and church. The revival of rhetorics of tradition was meant to strengthen family structures and patriarchal household authority as bulwarks against continued calls for individual rights and the lingering menace of women's emancipation. New rationales were sought for restricting public political domains to men while assigning women to the spheres of domesticity and motherhood. The attempts to define the "character of the sexes" spanned the discursive arenas of political philosophy, pedagogy, science, and medicine, as each undertook its own mapping of physiological qualities onto mental or political capacities. Understanding the sexes in terms of oppositional characteristics – active–passive, bold–modest, reason–intuition – helped to fix the posited boundary between public and private. Men were thus "by nature predestined for public life" and social production, whereas women were suited "for a domestic role" and "private reproduction."[10] Science and medicine, early anthropology and later in the century, psychology and psychiatry, conveyed the sense that the polarity of the sexes was part of the "natural order of things" and could scarcely be altered by changes in the political or economic status of women. These debates that both determined and disseminated the "character of the sexes" rearticulated sexual difference so as to stabilize those societies that still harbored the memory of revolution and the "rights of man," and that had just begun to face the rippling effects of industrial and urban growth.

Although monarchs across Europe sought to hold both these forces at bay, the political and geographic terms of the settlement of 1815 were continually challenged, for example by nationalist uprisings in Spain, Naples, Greece, and Russia in the first third of the century, or through the persistent reformist activity that percolated below the level of formal politics. Debates about women's status and women's rights, sometimes couched in the languages of religious or moral reform, continued to flourish in the arenas of the informal public sphere: salons and social clubs, charity societies or educational associations. Across Central Europe the "Deutsch-Katholiken" (a branch of Catholicism known as German-Catholics, as opposed to Roman Catholics) mobilized women and men against the authoritarianism of the Catholic church, counting between 100,000 and 150,000 adherents at their high point of the 1840s.[11] Women, many of whom joined this movement independently of husbands or fathers, constituted a vital force in these and other revivalist or oppositional religious movements. Eschewing the "'unholy dualism' between the sexes," many of these movements granted women equal rights to speak and hold office within their institutions and addressed women's subordination within marriage and family.[12] So the German Catholics, for example, argued in favor of a "rational religiosity," highlighting women's particular capacity for rational thought. Affirming that gender distinguished the character of the sexes, dissident religious movements nonetheless advocated women's equality and women's emancipation.

The goals of moral reform and political participation were linked as well in the British anti-slavery or abolitionist associations of the 1820s and 1830s. Men predominated in the political and parliamentary struggles over slavery, but over seventy organizations of middle-class and upper-class women carried the day-to-day campaign against slavery in the decade before its abolition in 1834. Boycotting slave-grown sugar, circulating petitions, and raising funds, female activists drew parallels between the conditions of slaves and their own subjection, both familial and political. This presumption of similarity elided differences of race and class, and the political economy of slavery itself, a stance which bourgeois women's associations would repeat in the context of colonialism later in the century. Yet this assertion of solidarity also led the Birmingham Abolition Society to solicit

and publish the remarkable autobiography of Bermudan former slave Mary Prince in the late 1820s, thus making tangible to the British reading public a new and unfamiliar instance of female self-definition and self-representation.[13] Expanding this agitation to the persistence of slavery in the United States, the British anti-slavery movement became international in scope after 1833.

In the interstices of political repression, middle and upper-class women defined a "woman question" that reflected the concerns of their social milieu, namely access to higher education and professional training for unmarried women, legal reform of property rights, marital and divorce laws, and opportunities for meaningful engagement in philanthropy and charity work among the poor. Distinguishing their views of women's rights from the perceived excesses of the revolutionary era and fostering a creed of class and gender-specific respectability, embedded in family, marriage, and church traditions, bourgeois women of the Restoration era recognized sexual difference while insisting on improvements in women's status. In nations still fighting for unity or independence during this era – Italy, Poland, Finland, the Ukraine – middle-class women asserted their own claims to national belonging as educators of future citizens who were uniquely capable of instilling in their children knowledge of national language and culture and loyalty to the fatherland.

On the boundary between respectable and transgressive were those women whose salons formed a space of critical intellectual exchange, where censorship and the curtailed civil liberties of Restoration society could be circumvented. Salons were also a site of wide-ranging imagination about both past and future, not least about the potential for egalitarian marriages based in love rather than economic interests. Female salonnières like Madame de Staël in Paris or Rahel von Varnhagen in Berlin, delved into the meanings of sexual passion, romance, and tragedy, while upholding the values of freedom, equality, and civility. Inhabiting the purported boundary between private and public sociability, female intellectuals who hosted or participated in the subculture of the salons often spurned the expectations of respectable society: Dorothea Mendelsohn, daughter of Jewish Enlightenment reformer Moses Mendelsohn, left an unhappy marriage to join her lover, philosopher Friedrich Schlegel, while Caroline Michaelis Schelling pursued personal happiness rather than convention, marrying three times in the space of 15 years. The Berlin Jewess Rahel Levin, a free thinker whose love for a Prussian officer violated religious and social norms alike, withdrew into the intellectual freedom of her salon, marrying at the age of 43 a man 14 years her junior. As much as these unusual women flouted dominant customs of respectable love and marriage, the culture of Romanticism, prevalent in salon culture of the early nineteenth century, subordinated women in ways more subtle than jurisprudence or scientific tracts. Romanticism reified the polarity of the sexes, ascribing to men a place in the world of politics and economics, while women figured mainly as muses who inspired men's creativity or upward mobility. Male Romantics, for their part, proffered an optimistic view that passionate love could overcome the polarity of the sexes, fusing male and female, man and woman in a symbiotic rather than oppositional relationship.

While female intellectuals of the educated middle classes questioned and sometimes subverted bourgeois conventions of marriage and childrearing, more radically inclined women, including some working women, aligned themselves with the utopian movements that formed around Robert Owen, Charles Fourier, and St. Simon during the 1820s and 1830s. In Britain the Owenites envisioned much more than a reform of bourgeois marriage, calling for the collectivization of households and the transformation of the very fundamentals of "sexual culture" that subordinated women to the "tyrannical supremacy" of husbands and fathers. Owenism's combination of democratic and sexual radicalism revived and recast previous visions of women's rights, such as those of Mary Wollstonecraft. The "Appeal of One Half of the Human Race, Women, Against the Pretensions of the Other Half, Men, to Retain them in Political and Thence in Civil and Domestic Slavery," drafted by William Thompson and Anna Wheeler in 1825, echoed Wollstonecraft in its insistence that women's

political interests could never be "contained" in those of their fathers and husbands. Their appeal, as Barbara Taylor has noted, provided the "rudiments of a socialist feminist" worldview in its wider-ranging critique of the competitive individualism of bourgeois society that gave rise to the inequality between the sexes. Notions of sexual equality and difference were at the heart of the project of British radical utopianism that began to take on "a political life of its own" in the 1820s.[14]

In France the Fourierist movement of the 1830s also castigated the institution of marriage for its "oppression and debasement" of women, outlining a more fundamental restructuring of the economy to ensure the right to work for all. The status of women, Charles Fourier proposed, was a crucial measure of the progress and prosperity of "all humankind."[15] Flora Tristan, initially a follower of Fourier and advocate of utopianism, struck out on her own during the 1830s, writing and speaking across France on the conjoined issues of women's plight and workers' need for self-protection through unions. St. Simonism was the first of these utopian socialist movements to elevate the "woman question" to a central, rather than secondary, concern. Blending mystical religion with Romantic idealism and emotionalism, the followers of Claude Henri Comte de Saint Simon organized formally only after his death in 1825, rejecting Enlightenment rationalism and shunning the legacy of revolutionary violence and terror. While their early emphasis was spiritual, mystical, and visionary rather than political, the July Revolution of 1830 in France brought issues of class injustice, exploitation, and disenfranchisement of workers to the fore, galvanizing popular support for the St. Simonians. Considering the issues of male and female workers, St. Simonians sought to remedy social conditions through the founding of cooperative workshops and collective housing for both tailors and seamstresses in Paris and Lyons. The visible presence of women in the St. Simonian movement led to the arrest of male leaders in 1831 for the "corruption of public morals," leaving a space for women to found their own separate club and to begin publishing a women's newspaper, *The Free Woman*, which restricted its authorship to women and aimed to free "female thought" from male intervention. From the demands of St. Simonian women for reforms of working, housing, or health conditions emerged a new "woman question," one reflecting issues specific to women workers and identifying the need for a total liberation of women from economic, emotional, domestic, and sexual subjugation.

With the utopian projects of the 1820s and 1830s, debates about the status and rights of women had begun to divide along the lines of social class. Each time citizens challenged states, seeking to change the terms of governance and representation – as in the July Revolution of 1830 – women's social subordination and political disenfranchisement became a topic of debate. In Britain the passage of the Reform Bill of 1832 galvanized the first mobilizations of women for suffrage rights. Extending the suffrage to a broader swath of the male British population (based on property qualification), the Bill brought into sharper relief the disenfranchisement along class, gender, and ethnic lines, that is, of propertied women and Irish Catholic men. The differential politics of the British franchise worked to solidify the nation, as Catherine Hall has argued, by tightening the bounds of both gender and race at a time when Britain faced both slave revolts in Jamaica and intensifying demands from the Irish for Catholic emancipation.[16] The Chartist Movement of the later 1830s set its sights initially on universal manhood suffrage and an end to all property qualifications, but later compromised on the issue of women's suffrage, fearing loss of male support. Although not counted in the ranks of citizens, female sympathizers of Chartism claimed a role in politics by founding their own political unions and temperance associations. As ever larger numbers of men claimed a place as citizens in nation and civil society, women took up the language of citizenship both in their continued pursuit of suffrage and their efforts to end women's subjection in marriage and family.

The 1830s represents a turning point of sorts in the sense that the ferment over the "woman question" that began with the French Revolution became a regular feature of public life in nineteenth-century Europe and could no longer be quelled through wars, revolutions, or reform initiatives. At times an undercurrent amid turbulent change, in other moments in the foreground of debates about social and political change, the "woman question" traveled across national boundaries, part and parcel of the conflicts over constitutionalism, republicanism, and individual rights that spilled over into the German states and Italy, reaching to Scandinavia and Russia by mid-century.

Mid-Century Revolutions: Redefining the "Woman Question"

The revolutions of 1848–9 represented the culmination of conflicts that had simmered throughout the 1840s. The constitutional question, encompassing both limits on the power of monarchies and expansion of the rights of political representation for the middle and "popular classes," had been definitive in British and French politics, and in some of the states and principalities Napoleon had occupied. In Italy and most of German-speaking Europe the national question was the key pursuit of mid-century, with the goal of welding a nation out of disparate principalities and provinces. Although the social consequences of industrial transformation had already garnered reformers' attention in the most economically advanced regions of Europe during previous decades, only during the decade of the "hungry 1840s" did a broader social question emerge as a coalescence of the short-term crisis of poor harvests and widespread hunger with the longer-term and chronic impoverishment of journeymen and other workers displaced from their trades with the advance of factory production. The confluence of the national, constitutional, and social questions is what distinguishes these revolutions, as a European-wide phenomenon, from their predecessors. While the social question sparked popular protests in the streets of Milan, Paris, Berlin, Frankfurt, Prague, and Vienna, the national and constitutional questions preoccupied the parliaments that sprung up during the revolutions. Not only were women participants in these revolutions, but also the scope of the "woman question" both expanded and became more differentiated across these arenas – constitutional, national, and social – in the course of these conflicts. In Italy, where the desire for a unified nation and political reform had been cultivated by secret societies and salons since the Napoleonic Wars, the wave of poor harvests and economic hardship spurred the first wave of protests in 1847: women donned the Italian tricolor and took part in attacks on royal representatives and symbols such as members of the civilian guard or revolutionary armies. While the desire for constitutional rule was widespread, the issue of Italian sovereignty and national unification was primary. As in other instances of patriotic national movements, activist women configured themselves as citizens by sewing, cooking, and nursing for the national cause. Many enthusiastically embraced Guiseppe Mazzini's vision of nation and of "citizen-mothers," remaining active in this cause until the fulfillment of Italian unification in 1861.[17]

The revolution that broke out in Paris in February 1848 was primarily constitutional in nature, but the popular protests and street fighting during the June Days aimed at deeper social change, including the reorganization of labor in national workshops and wider-reaching rights of citizenship for workers. Under the leadership of former St. Simonians Jeanne Deroin and Pauline Roland, women formed clubs and began publishing newspapers in February 1848 to advocate not only women's rights, but also their emancipation. The liberal reforms enacted by the provisional government during the spring of 1848 included universal suffrage for "all Frenchmen," neither bestowing citizenship rights on women nor explicitly disavowing those rights. When outraged female activists demanded that the government take a position, the Assembly voted 899 to 1 against women's suffrage, and also dismissed a petition from the women's clubs to restore the right to divorce. Female activists elaborated the vision of citizenship first articulated by Olympe de Gouges in 1791, now linking claims to suffrage rights with the right to work. Radicalized by the Assembly's failure to undertake more expansive economic and social reforms, the

streets of Paris erupted in June, as armed workers battled the National Guard, leaving some ten thousand dead and some twelve thousand arrested or in voluntary exile, including the most radical female leaders. The post-revolutionary restoration of social and political order once again rested on the capacity of the state to expel women from the public by disbanding women's clubs and political journals. One outcome of the 1848 revolution in France was the elaboration and delineation of citizenship rights, encompassing not only property but also labor, not only rights, but also duties. These expanded terms of citizenship provided the framework for the "woman question" of the second half of the century, in which women's labor and women's duties to the nation would figure more prominently than the discourse of rights.

When revolution broke out in Berlin, Vienna, and Frankfurt in the spring of 1848, the women who joined clubs, initiated gazettes, and founded patriotic societies could not draw upon historical memories of women's protest or past evocations of female citizens in the republican polity, as French women had. Instead, the educated women who joined the men of their class in envisioning both a new nation and a constitutional form of government came to identify with these causes and to develop deep concerns about the social question through their activities in charity work, educational associations, or religious movements like the German-Catholics during the *Vormärz* period (before March 1848). The "woman question" that arose in the course of the revolutions in German-speaking Europe was, therefore, focused more on the prerequisites than the actual participatory practices of citizenship. Adopting a language of liberation and rhetorics of freedom, women activists argued that women should have access to higher education and professional training. Luise Otto, who published the *Frauenzeitung* (Women's Times) from 1849 through 1852, asserted women's rights to use all of their "powers freely to develop that which is purely human" and promoted an image of women as "responsible and self-determining citizens of the state." At the same time, however, Otto and other middle-class women encased the prospect of women's citizenship in notions of "true womanhood," of women's nature and social needs as mothers and wives. They upheld demands for women's rights for meaningful participation in society and politics, while emphatically rejecting notions of women's "emancipation" or eradication of "inalterable sexual characteristics" or sexual difference. The middle-class women's movement of 1848–9 endorsed visions of liberal democracy, even founding a Democratic Women's Association in 1849.[18] Yet democracy did not necessarily mean equal political rights for women or men of the lower classes. Rather, the middle-class women who confronted the social question embraced a broader vision of class-defined social reform as they set out to remedy the working and living conditions of those poor women workers who had filled the streets of Berlin and Frankfurt in the spring of 1848, demanding bread and economic independence. In Prague the 1848 revolution also drew attention to women's place in politics not because women demanded emancipation, but because they raised their voices as "citizens of the state."[19]

By 1849 the project of forging a nation had submerged the democratic longings expressed in the popular revolts of spring 1848. The networks of women's associations, clubs, and journals founded during the revolutionary period turned their attention to the issues of girls' education, professions for single women, and charity work among the poor. In the conservative aftermath of the revolution, the "woman question," which now centered on women's capacity to contribute to social, political, and national life, expanded its focus towards the ever more urgent "social question." In fact, one solution to the "woman question" – mobilizing middle-class women's skills to improve health, living standards, and hygiene among families of the poor – became intricately connected to remedying the social question. The fundamental belief that the sexes had distinct characteristics, capacities, and needs formed the foundation for the ideology of "social motherhood" and the conceptualization of citizenship in terms of women's duties rather than rights. Despite its emphasis on women's unique capacities, this vision of women's citizenship based on difference rather than equality was nonethe-

less threatening to the authorities of Prussia and other German states. The wave of conservative legislation in the early 1850s included new laws depriving women of the right to edit or publish newspapers or magazines.

Not only states where revolutions raised the flag of citizenship, but also autocratic Russia generated its own "woman question" in the circles of university students and intellectuals during the mid-nineteenth century. While law and custom deemed that women's relations with the state and broader society be mediated by men, the momentum for economic and political reform intensified in the wake of the failed constitutional revolt of the Decembrists in 1825. Tsar Nicholas I, who ruled from 1825 to 1855, sought to crush all civic activism and social critique through censorship and the establishment of a new political police force. Students and intellectuals, inspired by utopian socialists, German Romantics, and the wave of revolutions that swept across Europe in 1848–9, began to question both the power of the tsarist state and of male patriarchs within families. Led by a few ambitious women of the aristocracy and gentry whose main concerns were access to higher education for women, female reformers drew parallels between the "poor, limited education of women" and the conditions of the Russian peasantry during the 1850s and 1860s, striving to rouse them to revolt against their backward conditions.

The issue of women only began to constitute a broader social question in Russia after its defeat in the Crimean War in 1856, as many reform-minded intellectuals critically contended with Russian "backwardness" and the urgent need for reform. Originating in debates about women's education, the Russian "woman question" amplified in the next decade into a "full-scale anthropological discussion of women's peculiar genius and destiny." The opening salvo in this debate stemmed from the male poet and radical publicist M. L. Mikhailov, who critiqued both Michelet and Proudhon's theories regarding women's nature, marriage, and maternity. The "woman question" acquired economic dimensions with the emancipation of the serfs in 1861, as the family economy of aristocracy and gentry, thus far based on serfdom, began to modernize and the issue of women's employment was raised for the first time. Nikolai Chernyshevskii's novel *What is to be Done?* (inspired by the writings of George Sand) probed the choices facing a young woman as she came to terms with a loveless marriage and the search for a meaningful life. In the extremist climate of tsarist repression, many women of the intelligentsia began to identify with liberalism. For some, the embrace of individual rights meant a declaration of independence from families and customs, so like the "new women" of the 1920s they cut their hair, smoked in public, and dressed in unconventional clothing. Others pursued a more dramatic escape from political and familial subjection by joining the nihilist movement or the radical underground and preparing for "social revolution."[20]

The "Woman Question" as Social Question

By the second half of the nineteenth century the "woman question" had distinct meanings and resonances in different social and cultural milieus. While the development of "sexual science" emphasized that which women held in common – their physiology and corresponding capacities and proclivities of mind – the "woman question" in the realm of political debate was increasingly differentiated by class. Crucial aspects of the "woman question" for women of the bourgeoisie or educated middle classes were property rights, laws pertaining to marriage, divorce, and childrearing, and improvement of girls' schooling and educational opportunities. Prescribing the proper duties and boundaries of women in the middle-class household *vis-à-vis* husbands, children, and servants, the ideology of domesticity not only hinged middle-class respectability to the notion of separate spheres, but also imparted to women a specifically feminine power within the realm of home and hearth. Constructed across disparate discursive arenas ranging from moral and religious handbooks, to women's novels, household manuals, advice columns, and scientific and medical tracts, the ideology of domesticity shaped and informed the middle-class feminist movements that would work to oppose and transform it later in the century.[21]

Although domesticity as an ideal relied upon a sharp distinction from the world of work, feminist historians have analyzed the intensive female labor involved in acquiring, displaying, and maintaining the artifacts and symbols of respectability, as well as their indispensable economic contributions to households and family economies, from scrimping, saving, and sewing to the investment of dowries and the fostering of business relations.[22] The middle-class "woman question" first revolved around the capacities, limits, and needs of women within an idealized domestic sphere. Yet the causes of women's education, employment, or reform of property or divorce law quickly became intensely public matters, not least because of persistent campaigning by single and independent women, who by necessity or circumstance were forced to break open the confines of bourgeois domesticity. Independent women like Florence Nightingale, whose desire to contribute to the nation by caring for British soldiers during the Crimean War was matched by her drive to improve medical care and professionalize nursing, inspired other unmarried women to become involved in philanthropy or other care-giving professions.[23] Still other independent women subverted marriage and family within female subcultures of intimacy and same-sex love.[24] Sometimes betrothed or married women themselves defied the strictures of bourgeois domesticity by refusing arranged marriages, filing for divorce, or contesting the rights of husbands over property, the custody of children, or over their own bodies.

Although many of the struggles that defined the sides and positions *vis-à-vis* the "woman question" remained private or took place within households, others were sites of public and intensely political contest. The Married Women's Property Acts (1856, 1870, 1882) were repeatedly deliberated in the British parliament, but also mobilized considerable public opinion on both sides, coinciding partially with debates about female suffrage. In Britain at least, the confluence of these two issues was formative of the feminist movement. One definitive text that forged the links between the distinct spheres of women's rights was John Stuart Mill's "On Liberty" of 1859, which forms one of the crucibles of nineteenth-century liberalism. From his standpoint as an MP in parliament Mill, whose intimate relationship with Harriet Taylor formed one crucial influence on his thinking, worked to realize both equal political rights, above all suffrage for women, which was voted down for a second time with the passage of the Second Reform Bill in 1867, and property reform. His essay "The Subjection of Women" (first published in 1869) traversed the European continent, introducing the idea of women's emancipation in Italy, Austria, and Russia. "Was there ever any domination," Mill asked, "which did not appear natural to those who possessed it?"[25] Against the notion of the polarity of the sexes, now validated by scientific theories such as Darwin's emphasis on the importance of sexual selection, as well as scientific practices such as skull measuring, Mill contended that "woman's 'nature' could never be properly determined until all the legal and cultural constraints on women's full development, as human beings, were removed."[26] The dissemination, reception, and refutation of Mill's tract rendered the "woman question" a major philosophical and political issue of the age, one deserving of scholarly and political attention. Translated into every major European language, often by female activists and intellectuals who shared his views, Mill's essay exposed the contradictions of liberal and republican universalism and galvanized opposition to both liberalism and women's emancipation.

The "woman question" acquired other social dimensions with the beginning of the assertively public crusade of middle class women against the legal regulation (and hence sanctioning) of prostitution through the Contagious Diseases Act during the 1860s. Under the leadership of Josephine Butler, the abolitionist movement aimed not only to expose the underside of bourgeois marriage and respectability – the sexual double standard – but also asserted a complex stance of moral custody over vulnerable prostitutes whom state regulation now subjected to mandatory registrations, bodily inspections, medical treatment, and eventual incarceration in the case of refusal. In fact, the Napoleonic Code was first to prescribe in law the police registration and medical inspection of prostitutes. Similar regulatory laws were enacted in Sardinia and individual German states in the 1850s and took effect on a national level in Italy with unification in 1860 and in Germany in 1871. Prostitution galvanized middle-class women's activism on the continent as well, prompting both the founding of Protestant and Catholic "moral associations" as well as more liberally inclined abolitionist clubs during the 1860s. Abolitionism compelled the organization of women on an international basis in the mid-1870s when Josephine Butler initiated the foundation of the "British and Continental Federation against the State Regulation of Vice."

If prostitution became a "social question" of sorts for the middle-class women's movement, the working-class "woman question" was sparked by the expansion of female factory work as the pace of industrial development intensified during the last third of the century. Female industrial workers represented a minority among employed women, usually comprising about a third of the female workforce, yet they became a powerful symbol of the dangers many perceived in the transition from agrarian to industrial society and the changes it wrought across countryside and cityscapes. During the first half of the century in Britain, from mid-century on in France, Belgium, and the Netherlands, and during the last quarter of the century in German-speaking Europe and Italy, women became independent wage earners as factories displaced craft guilds and family workshops, in some instances turning masculine crafts into female trades. From the moment the first factories opened their gates, presumptions about female docility and dexterity underwrote the desire for women workers, as did the perception of women as "secondary earners" whose wages often comprised barely half of those paid to men. With each new technological innovation, machines and the tasks required to serve them were coded masculine or feminine. Yet, as Joy Parr has shown, this process was enormously varied across regions and towns, industrial branches, and individual mills, so a job that was "clearly and exclusively women's work in one factory, town or region" could have been "just as exclusively men's work in another factory, town or region."[27] The "sex labeling" of factory machines and tasks is merely the most obvious example of the powerful ways in which ideologies about gender shaped shopfloor hierarchies and relations. The sexual division of labor discussed elsewhere in this volume represented a coalescence of ideologies and interests – those of employers, male "breadwinners," the workers' first unions, and later the policies of states – each of which sought to define and limit the boundaries of women's work outside of the home. Male craftsmen's fears of "feminization," of "men turned into maidens," imparted to the process of "proletarianization" a gendered language of protest, which would echo in the slogans and campaigns of workers' organizations during their formative years, inflecting the vocabularies of class and citizenship.

If the "social question" of mid-century turned around the issue of pauperism – that is, the fear that early industrialization had permanently impoverished a sector of both urban and rural craftsmen – in the course of the next decades the working-class family was identified as the locus of social instability. At the heart of the impending crisis of the family was the problem of women who worked outside of the home. By the last third of the nineteenth century the social question of female factory labor constituted a discursive site at which the more fundamental relationship between public and private, production and reproduction, factory and family, men and women, was defined and contested. The extent to which women's work threatened to undermine the polarity of the sexes is revealed in the chagrined assessments of Germany's most eminent social scientists: Ferdinand Tönnies, sociologist and member of the Association for Social Policy, assigned female factory labor a leading part in his analysis of the dissolution of the *Gemeinschaft* (community) and the formation of the modern *Gesellschaft* (society). Entry into the "struggle to earn a living" not only rendered a woman "a contracting party and possessor of money" with the capacity to "develop her rational will." As a result of this struggle, Tönnies claimed, "the woman becomes enlightened, cold-hearted, and conscious. Nothing is more foreign and terrible to her original inborn nature, in spite of all later modifications."[28] His eminent colleague, Lujo Brentano, elaborated

his "ethical" objections to female unions or clubs, noting that if women organized unions or went on strike to defend their interests, this would occur at the price of a "hardened character," undermining women's "moralizing influence on male workers." Ultimately, the organization of women's unions or strikes would mean "poisoning family and society at their very source."[29]

The stream of enquiries, statistical and scholarly studies, and political and religious debates about the dangers of female factory labor situated working women at the heart of the social as the arena of contest and collaboration between state and civil society over the reproduction of labor.[30] Discourses about the question of women's labor coalesced, linking the views of social reformers, liberal and clerical, with those of state bureaucrats and employers whose growing demand for labor rendered this question more acute as the end of the century neared. The worries about married women's employment outside the home that saturated social reform debates of the 1880s and 1890s, especially in Germany and France, involved not only the moral and sanitary quality of life in workers' quarters and concern that female "wage-cutters" had undermined the respectable "male breadwinner wage." During the last quarter of the century, they also revolved around the added dimension of declining birth rates and infant mortality: more specifically, the fears that married women's labor outside of the home would leave an indelible mark on national birth rates and the quality of population in an age of imperial competition and expansion.[31] These concerns led reformers to campaign for a legal ban on married women's factory employment in Germany during the late 1880s, which proved economically unfeasible for employers and working families themselves.

States nonetheless sought to respond and mediate the sense of acute crisis by enacting protective labor laws across Europe from the 1870s. The Factory and Workshops Act of 1874 and 1878 in England restricted women's work to 54 hours per week, while in Germany the first protective labor laws for women and youths went into effect in 1878 and were expanded in 1891. By the early 1890s most fully employed women in Germany, France, and England worked 10–11 hours per day, were prohibited from working at night, had acquired three to four weeks of maternity leave after birth, and were banned from sectors of production deemed most dangerous to their reproductive health. The attempts of these states to solve the social question of female factory labor laid the foundation for the protective aspects of later welfare states, and for the bifurcation of social citizenship into male and female streams: protective labor measures thus aimed to meet the perceived needs of women, families, and children by contrast with benefits such as social insurance, granted to men as the outcome of their mobilizations for social and political rights. Thus this "woman question" was not solved by banishing married women from the workplace; rather, state social policy mediated and regulated the relationship between sexual and social order through its first interventions in the realm of protective labor legislation.

Another face of the working-class "woman question" was that of a less visible female figure, that of the dissolute working-class wife, whose domestic and childrearing capacities fell short in the project of national regeneration, failing to bind the working-class man to family and home, leaving him vulnerable not only to the vagaries of the labor market, where he now had to compete with women for jobs, but also to socialism, anarchism, strikes, and other social protests. In other instances, debates and reform initiatives concentrated on the single mill girls, like the young Irish women who flooded into the silk and cotton mills of the Lower Rhine in the 1870s and 1880s. Living in company dormitories or boarding houses without supervision, the arrival of mill girls in towns across the textile belt of the Rhineland prompted fears among local elites about foreignness, licentiousness, leisure, and luxury – all bound up with the fact that young women were now living away from home, cut off from communities and clerical influence, earning and spending an independent wage. The dire consequences for family and social economies included the erosion of both domesticity and morality – young women would no longer learn to care for households or wait for marriage – so pregnancies out of wedlock, and unkempt and unhygienic households were the likely outcome. An array of moral, hygienic, and health-related initiatives sprang up in response to perceptions of these dangers – from cooking and sewing classes for young, single women, to health initiatives for maternal and infant welfare, such as home visits by public health doctors or nurses, or dispensation of hygienic household hints by middle-class women's reform groups. Armed with a wide array of new scientific knowledges about contagion and disease, heredity and social vice, reformers undertook an unprecedented scientification of the social, in which working-class women became the chief objects of middle-class women's projects of enlightenment and intervention.

The coincidence of fears of depopulation with measures aimed to restrict or ameliorate the living and working conditions of lower-class families took place not by chance as the competition for empire entered a new phase from the mid-1880s. In fact it is fruitful to consider the ways in which the social, as a field of intervention and imagination, now stretched from the workers' dwellings of Manchester, Paris, or Berlin to the colonial realm. The fears of declining birth rates or feeble populations clearly threatened to weaken empires at the height of European expansion and the solution for these fears was to be found not only in the subordination and settlement of new colonies, but also in the remedial undertakings of middle-class reformers in the cities of the metropoles. Indeed, the success of this undertaking relied upon an intriguing reciprocity of the middle-class and working-class "woman questions." The face of the late nineteenth-century women's movement was namely the new "maternalist" feminist who embraced an ideology of social motherhood, mobilizing the unique qualities of womanhood on behalf of nation and empire. Their visions of citizenship prioritized duty over rights, moral reform and social intervention over suffrage. In fostering social activity on behalf of health, hygiene, and housing improvements at home, maternalists in France and Germany delineated themselves along class lines from the working-class or indigent women whom they sought to reform, while British middle-class feminists took a similar stance, inflected by both class and race, towards improving the lot of women in India.[32] In Germany many of the same maternalist feminists who fought most stridently to expand maternity leave or reduce work hours for female factory workers identified equally vigorously with colonialism and were eager to claim a place for themselves in imagining and establishing colonial rule, even in governing the realm of sexual relations between white men and "native" women. By the end of the century, then, maternalist social reform projects were deeply entwined with empire, both in their participation in colonial associations and settlements, and in their efforts to prevent "race deterioration" at home.[33]

Maternalist feminism, often termed the "feminism of difference," took organized form in Germany by the 1890s, where the majority of bourgeois women's groups favored the notion of "spiritual motherhood" over suffrage. In France a proliferation of Catholic women's associations rallied to defend church and family from the incursions of republic and socialism. In Britain by the 1890s feminists of different hues, embracing equality rather than difference and spurred on by reforms they had won in the realms of education, property rights, and marital law, overcame their disputes in order to form a united suffrage movement under the leadership of Millicent Garrett Fawcett, which would be challenged after the turn of the century by the militant suffrage group founded by the Pankhursts. By the last decade of the nineteenth century working-class women, whose protests and claims of citizenship had alarmed the European public during the June Days of 1848 and again during the Paris Commune, formed their own organizations and began mobilizing for more sustained struggle. In England the matchgirls of London waged a determined and controversial strike in 1888 that galvanized British public opinion and attested to the importance of working women's organizations. Female textile workers initiated a powerful suffrage movement of their own during the late 1890s, linking the right to vote to working conditions and unionization and thus echoing the demands of the French revolutionary women in 1848. In Germany

socialist women, forced by the laws of association to found separate organizations, not only demanded the right to vote, join unions, and strike, but also challenged the "proletarian anti-feminism" that underwrote the politics of class in the powerful German socialist movement. August Bebel's *Woman under Socialism* (first published in 1879) offered the first systematic socialist analysis of the "woman question," tracing the origins of women's oppression to the system of private property and analyzing women's dual subjection as workers and as women.[34] Bebel's text went through several editions by 1900 and helped to galvanize the formation of a powerful socialist women's movement in Germany, led during the 1880s and 1890s by Clara Zetkin, who vigorously eschewed most cooperation with the bourgeois women's movement.

Women's movements in those European nations still seeking unification or independence (e.g., Poland and Czechoslovakia) usually subordinated questions of women's rights to the project of nation building. They were generally led by women of the educated middle classes who seldom appealed to working-class women. The women's movement in the Czech lands, for example, prioritized women's contribution to the struggle against Austrian rule and Germanization rather than seeking to contest male domination in Czech public life. Polish women entered the public sphere in the era after the 1863 uprising against Russia as mothers rather than as claimants of individual rights, but by the late 1880s they began to embrace many of the same campaigns pursued by British, French, or German women on behalf of higher education, professional employment, and equal rights in civil and political realms.[35]

The "woman question" culminated in the founding of organized women's movements in nearly every European country, from Scandinavia to the Mediterranean, from Spain to Russia, during the last two decades of the nineteenth century, representing a wide range of responses and interpretations of this question. Not all of them embraced the program of feminism which became part of public parlance in the late 1880s and many, in fact, mobilized explicitly to defend against the prospect of women's emancipation. Those women (and some men) who did take up the term "feminist" aimed to liberate women "from social subordination and male dominance" and to fulfill their "rights of self-determination." Others, such as the organizations of Catholic women in France, defined themselves as anti-republican and anti-feminist advocates of church, family, and traditional gender hierarchies in public and familial realms. Even in those European movements where feminism thrived, it had many faces. In Germany, for example, only those radical advocates of both suffrage rights and sexual equality took up the language of feminism, while socialist women and the mainstream middle-class women's groups distanced themselves from feminism, embracing (respectively) social revolution and spiritual motherhood instead. As the examples of the Czech and Polish women's movements suggest, feminism was sometimes compatible with movements for national unification and in other cases appeared as a diversion or disruption of the national cause. For women in some parts of Eastern Europe and Russia, the vocabulary of feminism arrived as an import from the West that lacked resonance where liberalism had yet to flourish. Finally, by the end of the century, the "woman question" had engendered international movements – from the anti-vice or abolitionist organizations that were founded across Europe in the 1870s and 1880s, to the suffrage and pacifist coalitions that emerged in its last decade. Across Europe a gulf arose between those who on the one side increasingly defined the "woman question" and the women's movement in international terms, and on the other side those who approached the "woman question" as definitive of the quest for national unity, integrity, or vigor. This chapter has thus emphasized the importance of contextualizing the "woman question" and the movements it produced with respect to nation, class, ethnicity, and empire.

Regardless of their stance on feminism, women became a vocal and persistent presence in the public sphere of the late nineteenth century, founding their own newspapers and joining public debates and demonstrations on a wide range of social and political issues. Still lacking political rights in most countries until the second decade of the twentieth century, women mobilized for equality in marriage and property law, against vice, and for the expansion of empire and the protection of women workers. Casting themselves as citizens in terms of either equality or difference, and assertively wielding the expertise they had gained in previous decades, the proliferation of new women's organizations, bourgeois and socialist, religious and secular, pushed open the boundaries of the public sphere during the last decades of the century, securing a place for themselves from which they could no longer be easily banished by the turn of a pen or a law. The fact that the "woman question" produced a broad palette of responses, from the discursive to the institutional, attests to its significance as a framing question of the nineteenth century, one that was formative of ideologies and politics, social movements and subjectivities.

NOTES

1 Landes (1988: 11–17).
2 Sledziewski (1993).
3 Scott (1996: 3 37).
4 Polasky (1993).
5 Taylor (2003).
6 Taylor (1983: 6).
7 Bock (2001: 99–101).
8 Scott (1996: 4).
9 Hagemann (2004).
10 Hausen (1981).
11 Herzog (1996: 13).
12 Frevert (1989: 7–75).
13 Midgely (1995); Prince (1993).
14 Taylor (1983: 1–18, 2–25).
15 Fraisse and Perrot (1993: 5–55).
16 Hall (2000).
17 Howard (1980); Offen (2000: 121).
18 Frevert (1989: 7–80); Gerhard (2001: 5–65).
19 Maleová (2004).
20 Stites (1978); Engel (1983: 8–102).
21 On the ideology of domesticity, see Poovey (1988).
22 Most notable here is the classic by Davidoff and Hall (1987).
23 Vicinus (1988).

24   Vicinus (2004).
25   Quoted in Smith (1989: 251). See also Rendall (1984: 28–91).
26   Offen (2000: 13–43); Bock (2001: 12–27).
27   Parr (1988); see also Freifeld (1986); Rose (1992).
28   Tönnies (1974: 186, 191). For further elaboration of this point, see Canning (1996b).
29   Quoted in Else Conrad, "Der Verein für Sozialpolitik und seine Wirksamkeit auf dem Gebiet der gewerblichen Arbeiterfrage" (dissertation, University of Zurich, 1906), pp. 86, 88.
30   On France, see Scott (1986); Cole (2000).
31   Offen (1984).
32   Burton (1994); Mayhall (2002).
33   Davin (1978); Wildenthal (2001).
34   Bebel (1971).
35   On the women's movement, see generally the contributions in Paletschek and Pietrow-Ennker (2004).

GUIDE TO FURTHER READING

On the origins of the "woman question" in the Enlightenment and French Revolution, readers might begin with the much-debated book by Joan Landes, *Women and the Public Sphere in the Age of the French Revolution*, as well as Scott's *Only Paradoxes to Offer*. Indispensable in the history of the middle-class "woman question" is Davidoff and Hall's *Family Fortunes*; Lewis's *Labour and Love*, and for Russia, Engel's *Mothers and Daughters*. A starting point for the history of women workers is Valenze's *First Industrial Woman* and the comparative collection of essays *Gender and Class in Modern Europe*, edited by Frader and Rose. For a contrast between the middle-class liberal and working-class socialist "woman question" the definitive texts by John Stuart Mill, *On the Subjection of Women*, and August Bebel, *Woman under Socialism*, which were read across Europe, form an essential foundation. For further study on the ways in which the "woman question" informed nationalism and nation-state formation, see the comparative essays in Blom, Hagemann, and Hall's *Gendered Nations*.

More general histories of women and gender in European history include Smith's *Changing Lives*, Fraisse and Perrot's *Emerging Feminism from Revolution to World War* (volume 4 of *A History of Women*), Bock's *Women in European History*, and Abrams' *The Making of Modern Woman*. More specifically on the history of feminism and women's movements, see Rendall's *Origins of Modern Feminism*, Offen's *European Feminisms*, Stites' *Women's Liberation Movement in Russia*, and the excellent comparative history of women's movements edited by Paletschek and Pietrow-Ennker, *Women's Emancipation Movements in the Nineteenth Century*. For methodological considerations of women's history and gender history, see Poovey's *Uneven Developments* and Scott's *Gender and the Politics of History*.

PART IV

Intellectual Developments
and Religion

CHAPTER SIXTEEN

Political Ideologies: Liberalism, Conservatism, and Socialism

EDMUND NEILL

Introduction

At first sight, the task of delineating the major political ideologies of liberalism, conservatism, and socialism, as they existed in theory and practice in Europe from 1789 to 1914, might seem a relatively straightforward one, on the basis that they can all be identified as essentially creations of the early nineteenth century. According to such an argument, while all three have a more or less reasonable claim to being at least as old as the seventeenth century, nev-ertheless it was only in the nineteenth century that liberalism, conservatism, and socialism truly came into being as fully-fledged ideologies, as responses to Enlightenment thinking in general and to the French Revolution in particular. Thus, according to this position, liberalism's commitment to greater individual liberty, both in the political and economic spheres, can be traced to the Enlightenment's skepticism of political and religious authority, and its contention that men (at least in the Western world) are equally endowed with fundamental reasoning abilities. This meant that rather than relying on traditional institutions and religious beliefs as guides for how to behave, humans could instead have confidence in their own capacity for working out how best to act, both because this would enable them to achieve greater material prosperity, and because it would mean they can more fully realize the abilities inherent in their character. By contrast,

conservatism in its full-blooded form is claimed to have arisen precisely to combat such tendencies – in other words to uphold the author-ity of the *ancien régime* in general, and that of the church in particular. Finally, socialism is said to have developed due to the Enlightenment's commitment to the potential improvement of humanity, and more specifically by the convic-tion of radical groups in the French Revolution that this necessarily implies trying to ensure a greater degree of socioeconomic equality between classes, rather than just the achieving of greater political liberty for individuals.

However, although such a picture is far from entirely false, the reality of the situation proves to be considerably more complex, and for two reasons in particular. Firstly, although political thinkers of every stripe were certainly strongly affected by the Enlightenment, and particularly by the experience of the French Revolution, their ideological reactions were not nearly as neatly distinguishable as this picture implies, not least because Enlightenment thought itself cannot be reduced to a simple set of mutually consistent propositions – on the contrary, the intellectual inheritance it bequeathed was highly variegated, and open to a wide range of interpretations. Rather than defining them-selves as being either "for" or "against" the Enlightenment, political thinkers all tended to emphasize the preeminence of certain *aspects* of the Enlightenment heritage, so that some thinkers emphasized the importance of "progress," others of "autonomy," and others again of "equality," to name but three significant examples, moreover doing so in importantly different ways. This had the result not merely of causing there to be considerable overlap *between* liberalism, conservatism, and socialism, but also of causing considerable divergence *within* particular ideologies.

Secondly, identifying streams of thought in the earlier nineteenth century as either "liberal," "conservative," or "socialist" is, in any case, a somewhat arbitrary exercise, since these terms are in fact – to a greater or lesser extent – retrospective impositions on the thought of such thinkers. Thus, although there is a good case for using the term "liberal" as a classificatory term to identify a particular stream of thought at this time, since it is possible to use it to pin down a certain kind of thinker, this is far less clear in the case of conservatism and socialism. In short, therefore, all three ideologies tended to evolve over the course of the nineteenth century, with all three altering their presuppositions somewhat, and conservatism and socialism becoming more coherent. We will therefore examine liberalism, conservatism, and socialism as they existed at the beginning of the nineteenth century, comparing and contrasting their premises with those of Enlightenment political thought, before proceeding to observe how all three ideologies altered during the course of the nineteenth century.

Liberalism, Conservatism, and Socialism in the Earlier Nineteenth Century

If we turn, then, to examining the nature of what was arguably the dominant political ideology in the early nineteenth century, namely liberalism, we find that although it took a number of quite different forms, all of these were broadly based upon the Enlightenment aim of securing greater freedom for individuals, but reinterpreted in a new context. More specifically, they all had five fundamental normative goals in common which were designed to achieve this end, which were largely drawn from Enlightenment thought. They tended to

be political individualists who were committed to the principle that greater political liberty was desirable, because they argued that mankind in general had a broadly equal potential to reason, rather than this being an ability that is confined to the higher orders of society. Secondly, they tended to stress the beneficial effects that mankind could accomplish with the free use of this reason, often linking this contention to a confidence that societies would develop and progress if this were the case. Thirdly, this claim about progress was commonly linked in the first half of the nineteenth century to the contention that only government by a nation-state could guarantee prosperity and freedom, thus providing liberals with a specific normative goal in the sphere of government. Fourthly, liberals tended to stress the importance of individuals having economic freedom, as opposed to laboring under "artificial" constraints of government regulation and monopolies, on the basis that this would aid the prosperity of society as a whole, while, fifthly, they also respected property rights and property laws, since these were necessary, apart from anything else, to maintain basic order and security within a given state.

If, however, all early nineteenth century liberals broadly had these major aims in common, they nevertheless differed quite sharply among themselves as to which of these normative ends was ultimately to be regarded as most fundamental, and in consequence what precisely they advocated in practice. To some extent, these differences can be put down to differing national political traditions. However, in general, they can best be explained by putting them down to fundamental ideological differences, particularly as to what actually constituted individual freedom, and the circumstances that best guaranteed it, rather than to idiosyncratic historical differences, or indeed to more fundamental philosophical disagreements. Essentially, liberal thinkers put forward three competing views as to what constituted and guaranteed individual liberty in the early nineteenth century, and we will briefly examine each in turn.

First, then, some liberals in the early nineteenth century took it as all but self-evident that the most important way to safeguard individual liberty was to limit interference from others, but especially from the state, so that individuals had the maximum liberty possible in both political and economic spheres. As such, these liberals tended to define liberty on a purely individual basis, without reference either to others in society or state institutions. However, even within this group, liberals did so for two importantly different reasons. Thus, on the one hand, some liberals, and most influentially Jeremy Bentham, particularly in his *Constitutional Code*, argued in favor of increased personal liberty for utilitarian reasons. At first sight this might seem surprising, since Bentham's insistence that all moral judgments and legislation be grounded on the principle that they create "the greatest happiness for the greatest number" seemed to allow a very high degree of state intervention – and indeed did so to the extent that it sanctioned the clearing away of corrupt institutions, and a vigorous attack on vested interests in society. However, it likewise followed from Bentham's principle that the value of personal freedom from all kinds of intervention was also very important, since one of the most important ways in which an individual's happiness could be furthered was to allow him or her the freedom to pursue their own life plans.[1] This was reinforced by Bentham's conviction (following Hume) that since, in any case, there were no particular principles by which states could judge directly what would make individuals within society happy, it therefore followed that the best a state could do for individuals was to provide them with the security to make their plans in peace. Hence Bentham's strong commitment to upholding the value of personal liberty.

By contrast, other liberals, including most clearly Wilhelm von Humboldt, but also to some extent J. S. Mill, particularly in his later works, were equally emphatic that increased personal liberty was vitally important, but were so not on a utilitarian basis, but rather on the grounds that it was essential for individuals to be able to develop their personalities – both morally and aesthetically – to the maximum extent possible. In fact, Humboldt's liberalism, most pungently expressed in his work *The Limits of State Action* (1792), was, if anything, even more vehement than Bentham in arguing for freedom from the state, since Humboldt largely ruled out even government action to protect individuals against one another as being illicit, since he seemed to believe that a society, if left alone, would naturally be harmonious.[2] Indeed, Humboldt's liberalism verged on being anti-political and utopian, since it appeared to assume that individuals would naturally develop into being cultured and sophisticated members of society, provided there was no interference, ignoring almost altogether, at least in the early *Limits*, the question of how much education they needed, and the degree to which they had to participate politically. Instead, it was left to Mill in his later essays, *On Liberty* (1859) and *Considerations on Representative Government* (1861), to specify both a minimum level of education that the state should guarantee (if not provide), and a set of institutions designed to ensure that individuals "developed themselves" not only aesthetically, but also politically.

Secondly, by contrast, other early nineteenth-century liberals were far less convinced that simply guaranteeing individual freedom from state intervention alone was sufficient to guarantee true liberty, since they were not as strongly individualist as Bentham or Humboldt, but instead maintained that the way a given society was constituted, sociologically, was a critically important factor in determining how free individuals were. Rather than simply seeking to find ways of restraining the ability of the state to interfere in the lives of individual citizens, in other words, which had led Bentham and Mill among others to become increasingly strong advocates of democracy and franchise reform, these other liberals, who included Benjamin Constant and Alexis de Tocqueville, maintained that new societal circumstances required a different form of government altogether. For, such thinkers maintained, what the individualists had ignored was that the threat to liberty faced in the early nineteenth century was not primarily a political problem, but was rather caused by the rise of a more commercial society, and the resultant destruction of traditional local political and economic institutions. This, they argued, had led citizens to demand equal rights before the law, since there was no longer any other body to which they could appeal for justice, hence inevitably causing the state's power to grow.[3] This meant that attempting to control the state by democratic means was to treat the symptoms rather than the cause of the problem. Moreover, such thinkers argued, liberty could not simply be equated with freedom from coercion by the state, but also consisted in the performing of virtuous customs, customs that had been largely destroyed by the advent of modernity. At first sight, such an argument might seem rather conservative. But although both Constant and Tocqueville expressed some regret for the waning of the premodern age, ultimately both regarded modern society as an improvement on the old – as Constant argued explicitly in his famous essay comparing *Ancient and Modern Liberty* (1819). For as is made most clear in Tocqueville's great work, *Democracy in America* (1835/1840), they believed that modern solutions to the problem of the rise of the state were possible, but only on the basis of adopting some form of federalism to disperse its power and to inculcate new virtuous social *mores*, rather than by directly seeking to restrain it through democracy.

Finally, other early nineteenth-century liberals, by contrast, notably G. W. F. Hegel and various British Whigs, argued that although it was important for individuals to have certain rights against government intervention, it was nevertheless only in the context of the nation-state that they could gain true liberty. To some extent they resembled Constant and Tocqueville, in that they rejected the contention that liberty could be gained just by ensuring that individuals had freedom from constraint to pursue their own life-plans. However, where Hegel and the British Whigs differed importantly from these French thinkers was by arguing far less ambivalently that the nation-state itself represented an improvement on previous governmental arrangements, and was, moreover, an important motor of progress, rather than laying as much emphasis on the degree to which its power should be restrained. They of course also differed significantly between themselves on various issues; particularly as to what precisely "progress" consisted of. Thus although the Whigs were inclined to agree that "the commercial interest" should be brought within the pale of the constitution, so

that everyone with a certain amount of property should be awarded with a vote, they also tended to adhere to the idea that the ultimate foundation for their arguments was an "ancient constitution" that was unique to Britain, which meant that there was inevitably a conservative side to their thought;[4] moreover, although they were certainly in favor of "progress" in general, their conception of this was essentially an open-ended one. By contrast, Hegel famously sought, particularly in *The Philosophy of Right* (1809), to delineate a state that would definitively reconcile individual freedom with the objective needs of the state without nearly such a strong reference to the past, taking as his premise the idea that humans could only be truly free in the context of a morally virtuous community that enabled them to develop themselves fully, a process that inevitably, according to Hegel, pointed to the valuing of a particular character-type.[5] So Hegel's view of liberalism, though sensitive to past developments, was far more firmly linked to the idea of future development than that of the Whigs. But this should not obscure the significant similarities in their views: both put forward a form of liberalism that linked individual and state far more directly than either of the other early nineteenth-century versions.

Essentially, therefore, despite its many varieties, in general early nineteenth-century liberalism was a relatively coherent ideological position, which was based, fundamentally, upon the aim of increasing individual freedom. By contrast, insofar as it existed as a coherent intellectual position, early nineteenth-century conservatism was a far looser body of thinking, which consisted of a diverse set of reactions to a number of different targets, including, variously, the Enlightenment assumptions that all men had more or less equal powers of reasoning, skepticism about religious belief, and liberal demands for greater political and economic freedom from the state. Crucially, however, virtually no conservative regarded it as feasible to reject the whole of the Enlightenment heritage *tout court*, either intellectually or in practice, so that few of them sought either to resurrect the *ancien régime* in its entirety or to argue that all aspects of Enlightenment thought were mistaken. At most, what they sought to do was to raise doubts about some more optimistic Enlightenment thinkers' belief that reason could be fruitfully applied universally to political and social problems, drawing significant inspiration from the rise in historist thought in the late eighteenth and early nineteenth century. We can see this by examining two prominent thinkers who each represented a different strain of conservative thinking, namely Edmund Burke and Joseph de Maistre.

Thus, firstly, Burke's brand of conservatism, particularly as put forward in his *Reflections on the War in France* (1790), did not advocate an entirely reactionary outlook, repudiating neither modernity nor the post-Reformation religious settlement, but instead sought to delineate what truly provided stability and permanence in modern commercial society. Where Burke differed from the liberal Whig position, in other words, was not that he objected (as, for example, Rousseau had done) to the effects of modern commerce on society, or to the increasingly free movement between aristocracy and middle classes in Britain, but rather that he believed that such Whigs were mistaken about the relationship between commerce and traditional social customs. Instead of maintaining, as Scottish Enlightenment thinkers and their liberal successors had done, that social stability and civilized manners were dependent upon increased commercial freedom, Burke contended that in fact it was the continuing heritage of chivalric manners that provided the conditions for social stability and hence for vibrant commercial interaction.[6] This heritage had actually been fatally undermined in France, Burke argued, by an over-rigid distinction between the aristocracy and the commercial classes, and made worse by a mounting public debt. This had ultimately led to the extremes of the French Revolution, where the "monied interest" had sought to despoil church lands to regain the money sunk in this national debt, in the process destroying the *ancien régime* altogether. However, even in England, where there was no such rigid split between the aristocracy and commercial classes, Burke argued, especially in his *Letters on a Regicide Peace* (1796–7), the "energy" of certain new government officials presented a potential challenge to the settled political and commercial order. For through advocating a policy of bureaucratic national aggrandizement, such officials were also increasingly coming to pursue a policy of confiscation, with similar threats to the social order – in other words to the very order of modernity that liberals themselves upheld.[7] So while Burke differed from early nineteenth-century liberals in the way that he thought that the modern order should be upheld, he was nevertheless in many ways seeking to uphold a similar vision of society to that of liberal Whigs.

Secondly, if we consider the work of Joseph de Maistre, who approximated most closely to the model of a reactionary conservative, even here we find that his position was not completely untouched by the ideas of the Enlightenment. It is certainly true that Maistre's brand of conservatism was considerably more reactionary than that of Burke, since Maistre would have been quite happy to uphold the political and social system of the *ancien régime* in France, had not the French Revolution intervened so catastrophically. Thus, in such works as the *Study on Sovereignty* and the *Essay on the Generative Principle of Political Constitutions*, Maistre, unlike Burke, upheld the importance of monarchy on an explicitly divine-right basis, arguing that an individual's obligation to state and nation rested fundamentally on a religious basis, on an emotional bond, rather than because it was the best way of securing freedom, however defined.[8] Moreover Maistre, unlike the representatives of other forms of early nineteenth-century conservatism, was much readier to attack certain fundamental tenets of Enlightenment thought, exhibiting an extraordinarily strong admiration for primitive over civilized mankind that rivaled Rousseau in its enthusiasm. However, despite all the authoritarian and reactionary elements of his thought, Maistre was nevertheless far from immune from Enlightenment influence. Despite a tendency to scorn the Enlightenment attempts at describing mankind in terms of universal laws, Maistre himself sought to make intelligible the development of mankind in universal terms, substituting a providential grand narrative for a fundamental faith in a universal human nature. Moreover, crucially, despite his dislike of republics and representative institutions, even in his most virulent writings Maistre did not advocate overturning the new political arrangements in France, arguing instead that coming to terms with the new institutions was the lesser evil. Even in the work of the foremost reactionary conservative ideologue of the early nineteenth century, in short, the impact of the liberal Enlightenment was not entirely absent.

If, as we have seen, both early nineteenth-century liberalism and conservatism can be successfully analyzed as reactions to the Enlightenment and the French Revolution, early nineteenth-century socialists tended to take their cue instead from the significant changes in social organization that occurred due to the impact of the "industrial revolution." For while older patterns of production continued to exist alongside new ones, so that the laboring classes continued to include both artisans and agricultural workers, nevertheless the dual shift to using new technology and new methods of industrial production increasingly led to the creation of a genuine industrial proletariat. Perhaps inevitably, such far-reaching changes caused considerable anxiety and resentment among significant sections of the working classes, as traditional patterns of work, and hence of community life in general, were undermined, and early socialist thinkers sought above all to address these. To do this, such diverse thinkers as Claude-Henri de Saint-Simon, Robert Owen, and Charles Fourier all tried to put forward a normative vision of society that reestablished a harmonious relationship between workers within society, a task they tended to attempt by delineating a completely new set of social relationships. Because of this, they were often labeled "utopian" socialists, despite their often close study of contemporary social trends, and their attempts to examine societies more scientifically than they had ever been before. They concurred with one another that forming socially harmonious associations of workers would be desirable because this would enable workers to regain a sense of community analogous to medieval guilds, and to increase their wages through the reduction or elimination of private competition. Although often grouped together, however, especially by subsequent Marxist thinkers –

who criticized them for being insufficiently radical – the "utopian socialists" were nevertheless importantly divided among themselves as to how to achieve the "harmony" in society that they sought. Thus they disagreed both as to the nature of these associations, and on how they should be formed. We will therefore briefly examine the differences between them.

If we consider Saint-Simon's position as put forward in such works as *Industry* (1817) and *The Industrial System* (1821), it is clear that, for him, the key to organizing society successfully was to ensure that the whole of it became one harmonious association, a task he believed could be best accomplished by promoting the interests of the "intellectuals" – namely a society's scientists and artists – and of the "industrial class." To do this, he argued, spiritual power should be handed to the intellectuals within society, who were far better qualified to offer moral guidance than the church. Meanwhile, he maintained, the temporal power should be passed to the outstanding representatives of those working in industry, who were themselves far more naturally virtuous than the traditional aristocratic class, since, through being productive, they were thereby necessarily oriented towards the common good. Such changes, according to Saint-Simon, would represent a crucial first step towards a complete overhaul of the way in which society was governed; a process that Saint-Simon believed would culminate in a completely new conception of the state. For rather than being concerned with the traditional *political* concerns of maintaining order and security, the state in the future, according to Saint-Simon, would be mainly concerned with *administrative* tasks, and in particular with ensuring the productivity of industry. As such, the state would potentially enjoy extensive authoritarian powers over individuals, and particularly over private property. However, such would be the harmonious nature of society, Saint-Simon maintained, in view of its greater social cohesion and increased morality, that in fact very little state intervention would be necessary in practice.[9] For Saint-Simon, in short, to regain harmonious social relationships, one needed to alter the whole state system, although ultimately its new orientation towards social good was based as much on moral renewal as it was on economic reorganization.

By contrast, Fourier, in such works as the *Theory of Universal Unity* (1822) and the unpublished *New Amorous World*, and Owen, in his well-known work *A New View of Society* (1812–13), took a somewhat different view of how harmony was to be achieved in the future. In particular, the two diverged from Saint-Simon by being far more wary of the idea that society could be reformed all at once, arguing instead that in order to be virtuous and harmonious, associations, initially at least, would have to be organized on a much smaller scale. Superficially, this was simply because neither thinker was as convinced as Saint-Simon that a centralized state could be run on a purely altruistic basis. So while Fourier and Owen agreed with him that simply insisting upon the importance of greater individual rights against the state in the manner of liberal thinkers would not be sufficient to ensure that workers' lives improved without more fundamental changes in social organization, they were nevertheless suspicious of Saint-Simon's bureaucratic solution. More fundamentally, however, their disagreement with him rested on their more equivocal attitude to the impact of industrialization, since they did not believe that this necessarily led to a more morally cohesive society. So even if one gave power to the most "enlightened" members of society, in other words, as Saint-Simon advocated, there was no guarantee that greater happiness would follow. Hence the advocacy of both Owen and Fourier of smaller-scale communities, in which it was easier to control the factors affecting social cohesion.

It should be stressed, however, that they did so for different reasons. Thus, Owen largely advocated the setting-up of small-scale communities due to his materialist determinism, arguing that since human agents were entirely at the mercy of the circumstances that affected them, this was the mode of organization that would ensure the greatest happiness for the greatest number.[10] By contrast, Fourier maintained (in a manner akin to Rousseau) modern society and modern philosophy had imposed illicit restraints upon mankind such that its true nature had been prevented from expressing itself,[11] a predicament that could only be remedied by creating small-scale communities called "phalansteries," in which men and women would be truly able to express their love for one another. But this should not undermine entirely the similarity in the advocacy by Owen and Fourier of small, harmonious communities, or, indeed, more loosely, of important parallels between their thought and Saint-Simon's. Broadly speaking, all of them sought to create genuinely harmonious human associations; but they differed importantly as to how best to go about it.

Later Nineteenth-Century Political Thought: Liberalism, Conservatism, and Socialism Transformed

In the second half of the nineteenth century the nature of liberal, conservative, and socialist political thought shifted appreciably. This was due to various developments that took place both intellectually and in practice during the course of the nineteenth century, and to two in particular. Firstly, political thinkers increasingly tended to base their arguments not simply on an ahistorical *a priori* definition of the self, but instead upon more sociological and evolutionary analyses of human communities. This was a development that was partly stimulated by actual changes associated with the formation of a genuinely industrialized society, but also by the increasing popularity of historist and social evolutionary theories in the nineteenth century, a popularity importantly (but by no means exclusively) stimulated by Social Darwinism. And it had far-reaching effects. The effect on liberals was generally to induce them to connect the value of personal freedom more firmly with the normative goal of self-development, although the reality of an increasingly industrialized society confirmed other theorists in their belief that a more sociological solution to the problem of how to secure freedom was required, or even that putting forward the goal of self-development was a mistake, since individuals had irreducibly competing ideals. Meanwhile, if in general the effect of taking a more sociological and historical starting point to political thinking was to confirm socialist confidence in the possibility of a genuinely altruistic future society, it also increasingly provided ammunition for conservatives who sought to stress the importance of traditional social relationships within nation-states. In the second place, on a more concrete level, the combination of the establishing of nation-states, and the franchise generally being widened, was significant. For not only did it tend to induce liberals to move on to stressing the importance of obtaining socioeconomic freedom for individuals, rather than of merely gaining political liberty, it also increased the confidence of socialists to aim to reform the whole of society. Furthermore, it also had the effect of inclining conservatives to move into the areas that liberals had vacated ideologically, the latter increasingly stressing the importance of free trade, personal liberty, and nationalism. We will firstly examine the various new forms that liberalism took in the second half of the nineteenth century, before considering those of conservatism and socialism.

Broadly speaking, then, liberalism in the later nineteenth century was to take two main paths. The first was exemplified by the movement in Britain known as "New Liberalism," whose most distinguished intellectual representatives were the theorists L. T. Hobhouse and J. A. Hobson. Such thinkers were still recognizably liberals, since they continued to stress a number of core liberal tenets, including the value of personal liberty and the importance of extending the franchise and of international free trade. Moreover, following the Hegelian tradition of liberalism, they continued to believe that the nation-state had a vital function to play in securing personal freedom for individuals, rather than seeing the state as an end in itself, as conservative nationalists were inclined to do, or maintaining that it was really a vehicle for class oppression, as more radical kinds of socialists were increasingly maintaining. But they also differed quite significantly from what had been some of the dominant tenets of liberalism. Thus, in particular, in such works as *Liberalism* (1911) and *Social Evolution and Political Theory* (1911), Hobhouse departed from earlier liberals' suspicion of state intervention by advocating that the state should provide a far greater level of public ser-

vices, including state-maintained libraries and museums, and support for hospitals and public transport. Moreover, he claimed, in contrast to the mid-century advocates of a stricter system of free trade, the state needed to intervene in the economy in order to ensure individuals' right to work, since otherwise they could not be said to be truly free.[12] And these deviations from the earlier liberalism were justified economically, particularly in Hobson's works, by the argument that wholesale state intervention was necessary to maintain free competition, since otherwise it would be distorted by an inevitable tendency towards private monopoly and therefore inequality of opportunity.[13]

In contrast to these relatively optimistic reactions to the changed circumstances of the later nineteenth century, other liberal thinkers in this period, such as the sociologists Max Weber and Emile Durkheim, and British pluralists such as J. N. Figgis and F. W. Maitland, reacted with considerably more pessimism to these developments. Such thinkers were all still recognizably "liberal" in political orientation, since they tended to support granting more freedom to individuals within society, being inclined to support the principles of an increased franchise, secular governance by the state, and the rule of law, and were generally supportive of the idea that social changes necessitated giving the state a larger role in providing welfare for the poor. However, unlike the New Liberal thinkers, such theorists were far less convinced that the social and political problems created by the industrialization of society could largely be solved by state intervention, although they were divided among themselves about how best to solve them. Thus for Weber, the fundamental problem to be addressed in the late nineteenth century was not simply that the state needed to intervene more in the economy to ensure that individuals were free in practice as well as in theory, but was also more fundamental. Rather, it was that some of the very forces intrinsic to modernity that allowed individuals more freedom were also at the same time the most potentially destructive. Thus, in such works as *The Protestant Ethic and the Spirit of Capitalism* (1905) and *Politics as a Vocation* (1919), Weber argued that although an efficiently organized industrialized society granted individuals more free choice, this came at the cost of them having "irreducibly competing ideals," and indeed of a certain "disenchantment" with the world, since there were fewer traditional norms to bind them together. For since such efficiency inevitably caused individuals, whether in politics or elsewhere, to think purely in terms of instrumental "ends," and of how best to achieve them, the result was that traditional bonds between individuals were necessarily undermined. This meant agents increasingly came to be related to one another bureaucratically, since this was the most efficient way of achieving instrumental ends, inevitably limiting their capacity for spontaneous free action.

According to Weber, therefore, any idea that one could reorient individuals towards a rational and harmonious common good, based upon an agreed character-type, as the New Liberals had maintained, was impossible; rather, one had to fight for the very continued existence of spontaneous free choice against bureaucracy. To do this, given that both mass democracy and bureaucratic political parties were inevitable, he believed, the only partial solutions that were possible, he argued in *Parliament and Government in Germany* (1918), were to strengthen parliament as a buffer against bureaucratic officialdom, and to try to ensure that charismatic leaders inserted some spontaneity into the political system.[14] And while Durkheim and the British pluralist thinkers were considerably less pessimistic, since both eschewed such a harsh critique of modernity, they nevertheless also both differed sharply from the New Liberals as seeing a "common good" as impossible. Instead, for both, real freedom consisted of the experience that one had in more voluntary social groups, so that it was through trade unions, churches, and communal life (for the British pluralists) and through corporations (for Durkheim), rather than being something one gained directly from the state.[15] And since the growth of the modern state seemed to be increasingly curtailing such freedoms, they, like Weber, viewed the future with some trepidation.

Broadly speaking then, later nineteenth-century liberals, in common with their earlier counterparts, continued to maintain that the most important function of the state was to secure political and economic freedom for individuals, although they differed from earlier liberal thinkers as to how best to achieve this. Equally, while conservative thinkers continued to argue for the importance of their core commitments to (landed) property, the church, and nationalism, and more generally of traditional values over rationalist arguments, they too had to adjust their strategy to take account of the changed circumstances of the later nineteenth century. Partly, this represented a challenge for conservatives, since they had to find new ways of making them attractive to a new working-class audience, in view of the general trend towards an increased franchise. But it also (perhaps surprisingly) represented an *opportunity* for them, since they were increasingly able to present their position as a contrast not only to an increasingly vibrant socialism, but also to liberalism. Because liberalism (as we saw above) became increasingly preoccupied with the task of securing universal equality of opportunity by advocating a certain measure of state intervention, conservatives were thus able to present themselves as upholding the traditional liberal values of freedom from the state, defense of commerce, and (usually) laissez-faire – having largely already taken over the mantle of nationalism from liberalism after the failure of the 1848 revolutions.

We can see this if we examine the arguments of the British social theorist Herbert Spencer, who earlier in the nineteenth century had been regarded as a staunch supporter of liberalism, given his railing against aristocratic privilege, and his insistence on the importance of a minimal central state. However, while Spencer's views on politics had remained reasonably constant, by the end of the century, when he wrote the angry polemic *The Man Versus the State* in 1884, his strident denunciation of state intervention and upholding of individual liberty, coupled with his increasing worries about extending the franchise, left him in many ways closer to moderate conservatives.[16] For while the structure of his argument remained too rationalist for later nineteenth-century Burkeans such as Lord Hugh Cecil, there is no denying the similarity between Spencer's work and the latter's *Liberty and*

Authority (1910), despite some differences over franchise reform and imperialism.[17] Moreover, Spencer's "conversion" was hardly unique: other moderate liberals such as Henry Sidgwick also began to be identified as "conservative" in the later nineteenth century – to some extent for similar reasons.

However, it would be misleading to argue that this was the only form that late nineteenth-century conservatism took, since there were also two more full-blooded versions. Firstly, some conservatives actually reacted so pessimistically to the new circumstances of the later nineteenth century that they sought not only to reject socialism and the newer forms of liberalism, but also in fact to reject modernity as a whole. This tendency had been latent in some earlier nineteenth-century conservatives' arguments, and in Maistre in particular, but tended to become more explicit as the century proceeded, as industrialization and economic and political liberalization altered the political landscape. Thus, to give but one British example of this, while Burke at the end of the eighteenth century still sought – in true Whig fashion – to reconcile commerce, culture, and religion, by the middle of the nineteenth the Romantic William Cobbett was criticizing modern life in general from the Reformation onwards, since he believed the latter event was responsible for the crime of capitalist ownership. It also found notable expression in the work of Thomas Carlyle, who, in such works as *Heroes and Hero-worship* (1840) and the *Latter-Day Pamphlets* (1850), argued romantically against industrialization and representative government, seeking instead to uphold the virtues of religion and of heroic despotism. But it was in Friedrich Nietzsche's work above all that this tendency found its fullest and most radical expression. For in such works as *The Genealogy of Morality* (1887) and *Beyond Good and Evil* (1886) Nietzsche sought to criticize not merely modern social and political arrangements, but also Western tradition itself for its adherence to ascetic Christian norms of charity and forgiveness, arguing that such norms had inevitably weakened mankind's ability to express its potentially heroic nature. For by illicitly making individuals feel "responsible" for injuries to those weaker than themselves,

Nietzsche argued, the predominantly Christian Western tradition had led to a catastrophic misidentification of "good" conduct, preventing men from acting in a genuine and uninhibited manner.[18]

Secondly, rather than rejecting modern social developments as a whole, other conservatives increasingly emphasized the necessity of a stronger, more interventionist state to deal with the new situation. Rather than advocating this to ensure the true freedom of individuals, however, as liberals had done, conservatives did so because they believed it was crucial for states to be modernized so as to be able to compete effectively for colonies, influence, and foreign trade. This was a theme that was even to be found in more liberal theorists, such as Weber, who (influenced in fact by Nietzsche) believed that struggle between states was inevitable. However, it found most clearcut representations in the work of the nationalist Heinrich von Treitschke, and, influenced by Social Darwinism, in Benjamin Kidd's highly popular work *Social Evolution* (1894). For both of these thinkers, as for earlier conservatives, it was a fundamental mistake to take the individual as the ultimate standard for political thought rather than the nation or nation-state; where they differed was insisting that changes in social and historical circumstances now dictated a much more active and potentially *dirigiste* form of state organization.

Finally, if conservatism grew considerably more vibrant in the later nineteenth century, this was, if anything, even more true of socialism. Partly, this was because of the increasingly obvious social inequalities which were caused by rapid industrialization, and because the working classes were beginning to be enfranchised, hence having more of an influence on practical policy. All this tended to encourage socialist theorists to devise methods of reforming the whole of society, rather than simply advocating setting up utopian or small-scale communities, so that they increasingly tended to advocate state intervention to secure greater equality for new, industrialized working classes. However, socialism's increased buoyancy was also importantly stimulated by the work of one particularly radical and influential thinker, namely Karl Marx. Marx's work proved influential, not simply because he claimed to be able to predict future events, or because, more prosaically, he and his close associate Friedrich Engels were such vigorous polemicists and proselytizers. Rather, Marx's brand of socialism achieved its preeminence because it seemed able to explain the relationship between theory and practice, synthesizing the insights of Hegelian dialectic in explaining historical development with a firm grasp of the empirical realities of industrial capitalism – as put forward notably in Engels' *The Condition of the Working Class in England* (1844). According to Marx, it was no use attempting to set up utopian political communities to insulate the working classes against capitalism, or even to use the state to alleviate its grosser inequalities. Rather, he argued, the social and political inequalities of the capitalist period which prevented the working classes from achieving their full potential could only be overcome by establishing a completely new economic system, since ultimately both social and political relationships were determined by the question of who owned the means of production.[19] Hence the necessity for revolution to emancipate the proletariat, according to Marx, since only in this way could they gain control of these means of production, since the capitalists would never voluntarily surrender them.

However, Marx's explanation as to how precisely the revolution would be brought about varied considerably, since sometimes, especially in his earlier work, he argued that the proletariat would acquire the necessary revolutionary consciousness because they would increasingly be able to appreciate the way the capitalist system really worked, as it approached the point of terminal breakdown. Thus, in such works as *The Communist Manifesto* (1848), drawing on his earlier philosophical works *The German Ideology* (1847) and the *Economic and Philosophical Manuscripts* (1844), Marx argued that the "revolutionary consciousness" of the proletariat would be crucial for the successful securing of revolution. By contrast, later in the nineteenth century, after Marx had witnessed a number of failed attempts at actual revolution, he tended to argue – most notably in his famous work *Capital* (1867) – that revolution would inevitably occur due to the inherent contradic-

tions of the capitalist system. This solved the problem, but left followers of Marx with the continuing problem of explaining why revolution had not yet occurred. This led both Eduard Bernstein and V. I. Lenin to suggest that capitalism was able to stabilize itself more thoroughly than Marx had envisaged, though the latter argued that the imperialism responsible for this was but a stage before inevitable revolution,[20] while the former famously argued in *Evolutionary Socialism* (1898) that capitalism was itself moving in a socialist direction.[21] Despite the influential nature of Marx's *oeuvre* the predictive nature of his work led to divergences between his adherents after his death in 1883.

In any case, despite the highly influential nature of Marx's work, not all socialists in the latter part of the nineteenth century followed his analyses, even allowing for the emendations that Marxists found to be necessary after Marx's death. Broadly speaking, there were two main alternative responses to the changed circumstances of the later nineteenth century among socialist thinkers. Firstly, some, such as the Fabian socialists in Britain, including Sidney and Beatrice Webb among others, argued that, rather than necessarily being an agent of ruling-class dominance, as Marx had maintained, the state could be used far more positively to help secure greater socioeconomic equality for the working classes. To do this, the Fabians argued, an extended franchise was vital, since otherwise the electorate would be unable to secure the election of suitable governments, but almost more important was that the state should be run with administrative efficiency, and with the appropriate expert knowledge. So although the Fabians were to some extent democratic, in that they believed everyone should have the vote, they were also elitist in the sense of believing that only a relatively *dirigiste* state could come to rational solutions as to how to run the country effectively, and to allot resources properly.[22]

Secondly, in stark contrast, other socialist thinkers such as Alexander Herzen, Peter Kropotkin, and Georges Sorel put forward a vision of socialism that was based on the tenet that mankind was naturally cooperative, arguing, unlike the Fabians, that the role of the state in securing this cooperation was transitional at best. To some extent, therefore, these thinkers, who have generally been labeled "anarchist" socialists, can be viewed as following the tradition established by the earlier utopians, since they stressed the conceptual importance of social cooperation over both the elimination of class differences, and socioeconomic equality – albeit that these aims tended also to be important to them. However, there were also three important differences. Firstly, the anarchists tended to have less of an anti-technological aspect to their thought on balance, so that for example Kropotkin believed that modern technology would aid the establishment of a new integration within society,[23] and Herzen sought to find a way of retaining specifically Russian cooperative institutions while nevertheless advocating modernization of the economy. So although anarchist socialists tended to stress the importance of practical work rather than abstract learning, and were also generally critical of the positivist tendencies in nineteenth-century thought, they nevertheless had even less sympathy than the earlier thinkers with premodern social organization. Secondly, rather than advocating the setting up of communities within the existing state, as the utopian socialists had done, the anarchists tended to argue, like Marx, that this was pointless, since the extent of the social changes caused by industrialization meant that only transforming society as a whole would have an impact. Thirdly, partly as a result of this ambition to change society as a whole, the anarchists tended to be at least sympathetic to the view that violence would be necessary to effect such far-reaching changes. Thus Herzen advocated a revolution to remove oppressive and illiberal states, while Sorel, in his *Reflections on Violence* (1908), seemed positively to revel in the necessity of violence to create a new society. So while the anarchist socialists retained some of the aims of their utopian forebears, their thought was necessarily colored by the very different circumstances of the later nineteenth century.

Conclusion

In conclusion, while liberals, conservatives, and socialists retained certain core ideological com-

mitments throughout the nineteenth century, not only did all three groups evolve significantly throughout this period, they also continued to differ considerably among themselves. Thus although liberals retained their commitment to ensuring that individuals gained the maximum amount of political and economic liberty possible, they not only had to react to the changed circumstances of the later nineteenth century, but also did so in a number of different ways to ensure liberal goals. Conversely, while conservatives continued to define their position in opposition to normative liberal and socialist aims, not only did the changes in these goals dictate changes in conservatism, but also continued differences as to how to react. And although socialists continued to advocate greater social harmony and socioeconomic equality, not only did they have to adjust to the realities of a genuinely industrialized society in the later nineteenth century, they also continued to differ as to how to achieve their ends. In short, the enormous political and economic changes of the nineteenth century caused the three main political ideologies to become richer and more varied, rather than easier to define. But this was the price they paid for their increased intellectual vibrancy.

NOTES

1   Bentham (1983: 196).
2   Humboldt (1969: 108).
3   Tocqueville (1861).
4   Millar (1818: 131–4).
5   Hegel (1952: 160–1).
6   Burke (1826: vol. 5, 155).
7   Ibid: vol. 8, 240–1.
8   Maistre (1965: 99).
9   Saint-Simon (1975: 210, 229).
10 Owen (1927: 260).
11 Fourier (1971: 215).
12 Hobhouse (1911: 163).
13 Hobson (1974: 4).
14 Weber (1994: 222).
15 Durkheim (1957: 28).
16 Spencer (1909: 87).
17 Cecil (1910: 64–5).
18 Nietzsche (1994: 29).
19 Marx (1977: 289).
20 Lenin (1982).

21 Bernstein (1961: 147–51).
22 Webb and Webb (1897: vol. 1, 32).
23 Kropotkin (1899: 271).

GUIDE TO FURTHER READING

Freeden's *Ideologies and Political Theory* provides a stimulating overview of political ideologies from mid-century onwards, while individual ideologies are served by Ruggiero's *History of European Liberalism*, Lichtheim's *A Short History of Socialism*, Lindemann's *A History of European Socialism*, and Eccleshall and O'Sullivan's *The Nature of the Right*. For early nineteenth-century liberal thinkers, see Rosen's *Jeremy Bentham and Representative Democracy*, Ryan's *Philosophy of John Stuart Mill*, Vogel's "Liberty is Beautiful," Holmes's *Benjamin Constant and the Making of Modern Liberalism*, Welch's *De Tocqueville*, Burrow's *A Liberal Descent*, and Avineri's *Hegel's Theory of the Modern State*; for conservatives, see O'Gorman's *Edmund Burke* and Lebrun's *Throne and Altar*; for socialists, see Taylor's *Political Ideas of the Utopian Socialists*, Pollard and Salt's *Robert Owen*, and Ionescu's *Political Thought of Saint-Simon*. For later nineteenth-century liberal thinkers, see Freeden's *The New Liberalism*, Beetham's *Max Weber and the Theory of Modern Politics*, Lukes's *Emile Durkheim*, and Nicholls' *Pluralist State*; for conservatives, see Taylor's *Men Versus the State*, Strong's *Friedrich Nietzsche*, and Burrow's *Crisis of Reason*; for socialists, see Avineri's *Social and Political Thought of Karl Marx*, Carver's *Marx and Engels*, McLellan's *Marxism After Marx*, McBriar's *Fabian Socialism and English Politics*, Walicki's *History of Russian Thought*, and Jennings' *Georges Sorel*.

CHAPTER SEVENTEEN

Social Darwinism and Race

MIKE HAWKINS

Introduction

Social Darwinism and race: two bodies of ideas that have provoked heated scholarly debates for decades. As to the first, scholars disagree over its meaning, its relationship to the theories of Charles Darwin, the ideological usage to which it was put, and its historical significance. The concept of race is likewise subject to disputes over its precise meaning, over whether it is a modern phenomenon or one that has deep historical roots – perhaps even in human nature itself – and over the extent to which doctrines of race have permeated European culture during the past two centuries.

My concerns are, first, to examine the nature of Social Darwinism, to outline its salient features and its relationship to Darwin's own theories. Then I will discuss the application of Darwinism to the realm of race and look at some examples of European thinkers who made this connection an important focus of their theories. Throughout this chapter I will be stressing the complexity of Social Darwinism and the diversity of its ideological usage in nineteenth-century European thought.

One point that needs to be made at the outset is that Darwinism has been greatly enhanced as a theory of evolution by twentieth-century advances in population genetics and molecular biology. However, our concern in this chapter is with the Darwinism that existed in the nineteenth century, in many respects a looser and more eclectic theoretical system, often comprising elements that would nowadays be construed as inconsistent with Darwinism, for example the notion that physical changes incurred by an organism as it adapted to its environment could be transmitted to its offspring (the doctrine of the inheritance of acquired characters, associated with the French evolutionary naturalist Jean-Baptiste Lamarck, 1744–1829).

Darwinism and Social Darwinism

In 1859 the British naturalist Charles Darwin (1809–82) announced the existence of a "general law, leading to the advancement of all organic beings, namely, multiply, vary, let the strongest live and the weakest die."[1] This pioneering work developed an idea originally formulated by the economist Thomas Malthus (1766–1834). Malthus had argued that the rate of population growth always exceeded the increase in the food supply unless plague, natural disasters, warfare, and sexual restraint curtailed the former.[2] Darwin transplanted this thesis to the natural world, asserting that population growth placed pressure on the resources necessary for life, leading to a "struggle for existence" among organisms. This struggle occurred at three levels. First, organisms had to contend with their environment (e.g., climatic conditions); secondly, they were competing with other organisms for resources; and thirdly, they were competing with members of their own species, the most intensive form of the struggle, since conspecifics ate the same food and occupied the same ecological space.[3]

Darwin reasoned that any variations in an organism, however small, that gave it an advantage in this struggle (i.e., that enhanced its chances of survival and reproductive capacity) would, through the forces of heredity, gradually spread through the population. Nature thus "selected" certain biological traits, analogous to the way animal breeders and horticulturists who wished to produce strains with specific characteristics bred only from specimens exhibiting the traits in question. But Darwin went further, arguing that the cumulative effects of natural selection, working over long periods of time, could lead to the emergence of new species and account for the elimination of others, as evidenced by the fossil record.

If new species had emerged by the transformation of existing species rather than by divine creation, then humans must have developed from some animal predecessor. Darwin avoided speculation along these lines in the *Origin* in the futile hope of averting controversy, but other theorists in Europe and the USA were quick to take this course. Indeed, some went beyond this to claim that not only had the physical attributes of humans evolved through natural selection, but so too had many features of their mental and social lives, including morality, religion, marriage, and warfare.

It is this final step which constitutes *Social* Darwinism. It is quite possible to accept a Darwinian account of human origins while arguing that human culture represents an entirely different level of reality which cannot be adequately accounted for by biological processes. Social Darwinists, however, believe that these processes can and should be extended to the explanation of human behavior, psychology, and social institutions. Moreover, Darwin himself was fully of this view, as is clearly evident in his *Descent of Man*. By the time this book was published in 1871, others had already applied evolutionary theory to these areas, and

indeed Darwin drew upon some of these applications. However, it is apparent from his notebooks that he had entertained this ambition for many years before the publication of the *Origin*.[4]

What Social Darwinism represents, therefore, is a worldview governed by the belief that "everything in nature is the result of fixed laws."[5] Evolution through natural selection is one such law, made possible by the struggle for existence acting upon minute but useful biological variations and the action of heredity in spreading these variations. Finally, these laws of nature are also applicable to the mental and social aspects of human existence: human history, like natural history, was wrought by the forces of evolution.

To a modern audience attuned to the political conflicts of the twentieth century, the vocabulary of Social Darwinism will probably resonate with ideological implications. The focus upon competition and the "survival of the fittest" – an expression originally coined by the British philosopher Herbert Spencer (1820–1903) and subsequently adopted by Darwin – would be in accord with liberal individualism and the endorsement of the competitive dynamics of capitalism. Certainly, Spencer adhered to this position, and there is compelling evidence that Darwin, as well as his champion, the naturalist T. H. Huxley (1825–95), did so too.[6] Similarly, the idea of struggle and the success of some species and the elimination of others could furnish a rationale for warfare between nations or races as a natural condition of humanity. Such rationales certainly existed, as will become evident later in this chapter. But to equate Social Darwinism exclusively with these kinds of perspectives is vastly to oversimplify its ideological history, because it was also deployed for quite the opposite political positions.

For example, the editorial preface to an English translation of a book by the Italian socialist Enrico Ferri (1856–1929) insisted that Darwinism was not simply compatible with socialism but constituted its "scientific foundation."[7] A German thinker, Ludwig Büchner (1824–99), argued that the struggle for existence was itself subject to evolution, and among humans this took the form of replacing violent conflict with a competition among the products of the mind. Hence:

> Whilst the struggle between peoples was formerly a contest of weapons, strength of body, courage and ferocity, it now consists in an emulation in good and useful arts, in discoveries, contrivances and sciences. The time is past in which one people subjugated another or exterminated it to take its place; it is not by destruction but by peaceful competition that one can attain a superiority over the other.[8]

The Social Darwinist worldview, in effect, did not entail any specific ideological position and was mobilized by opposing camps: patriarchy and feminism, capitalism and socialism, militarism and pacifism, materialism and spiritualism. This flexibility derived from a number of areas of ambiguity within the original Darwinian formulation, which facilitated different interpretations of the same phenomena.

First, many Darwinists were happy to endorse the theory of the inheritance of acquired characters. If the environment was able to influence physical characteristics, this could be used to authenticate programs of reform aimed at improving social conditions in order to promote biological progress. However, other Darwinists, notably the German biologist August Weismann (1834–1914), insisted that the source of variations was innate and externally induced traits acquired during an organism's lifetime could not be inherited. This position could be used to dismiss environmental reform as irrelevant in favor of a policy of selective breeding. Neither biological position entailed either ideological position, but it is not difficult to see how different theories of the source of organic variations could be used to underpin divergent political strategies.

Second, Darwinism contained an ambiguity over the unit of selection. Darwin favored the individual organism as the unit upon which natural selection acted, although occasionally he saw evolution acting upon groups – the herd, clan, or variety. When transposed to humans, this could result in either a focus upon individuals or groups conceived as tribes, nations, races, or even classes as the elements

engaged in struggle. Many theorists, however, regarded both levels as either acting simultaneously, or else themselves subject to an evolutionary process in which one mode gradually became predominant. In France, Clémence Royer (1830–1902) – who published her translation of Darwin's *Origin* in 1862 – insisted that selection was ubiquitous, operating at all levels of existence, from species down to groups (including the family) and individuals. Hence: "The struggle between individuals produces the selection of individuals. The struggle between varieties decides their future. The struggle between species has as its consequence the triumph of some, the disappearance or emigration of others."[9]

A different picture was presented by Benjamin Kidd (1858–1916), a self-educated clerk turned highly successful popularizer of evolutionary theory. Kidd, like Royer, depicted selection as an all-pervasive, inexorable, and primarily progressive process. However, for Kidd, this struggle initially took place among humans in the form of warfare between primitive bands and then increasingly organized societies. In modern times this competition still occurred (albeit not necessarily in the form of warfare) but was complemented by peaceful competition within societies of an ever-increasing intensity. This rivalry was among individuals and had become "the leading and dominant feature of our civilisation. It makes itself felt now throughout the whole fabric of society."[10] It was the relentless nature of this struggle among individuals for resources, position, and esteem which, for Kidd, had contributed to the progress of civilization and the dominant position of the West.

For Kidd, individual selection was a more advanced form of the struggle. In contrast, for the French theorist Vacher de Lapouge (1854–1936), the reverse was the case. Among early humans the struggle was among individuals, but evolved into group competition. "In man, the struggle for existence changed character with the intervention of solidarity. The struggle of each against all continues, but gives way to the struggle of groups in which individuals found themselves unified against the common enemy."[11] According to Lapouge, this struggle was now among races, and so savage and unremitting was it that, unlike Royer and Kidd, he regarded Darwinism as totally incompatible with any belief in progress.[12]

The differences over the direction of evolutionary change relate to a third area of ambiguity. Many theorists – including Darwin[13] – believed that evolution produced progress, while aware that change could also be regressive in character. This latter possibility became the explicit focus of some Darwinists who warned that degeneration (i.e., a reduction in the adaptive capacity of organisms) was as likely an evolutionary outcome as progress.[14] Indeed, some became obsessed with the idea of an accelerating human degeneration brought about by the suspension of the forces of selection due to the emergence of social institutions and practices which encouraged the survival of the "unfit" (e.g., improvements in medicine and charitable concern for the welfare of the indigent and afflicted). As we shall see below, this focus on degeneration was an important component of a number of theories of race.

Finally, Social Darwinists interpreted the struggle for existence in a number of ways. Warfare, industrial competition for markets and resources, natural disasters and epidemics, hereditary illnesses, inter-personal rivalry and competition, the battle of ideas – all were invoked as instances of selective pressures. Social Darwinists varied in their choice of these pressures, and some arranged them in an evolutionary sequence, though differing over the ordering of these pressures. But it was this ambiguity as to which *human* interactions were analogous to the forces of *natural* selection that provided Social Darwinism with its ideological range and flexibility. Thus, depending on whether one saw warfare as endemic to the human condition or as a primitive mode of selection, which was discarded as evolution advanced, it was possible to be a Social Darwinist and either a militarist or a pacifist.

Social Darwinism, however, was not so loose and bland that it lacked coherence and rhetorical bite. On the contrary, all Social Darwinists believed that humans were governed by the same laws that regulated the rest of nature, linked humans to an animal ancestry, and perceived them, both culturally and physically, as the products of an evolutionary past in which the forces of natural selection and heredity had played important roles. This was a distinctive worldview (i.e., an integrated perception of nature, human nature, and time).

Although fiercely contested from a variety of quarters, Social Darwinism rapidly grew in popularity during the last four decades of the nineteenth century. Paradoxically, evolution through natural selection waned in importance among biologists until it was integrated with population genetics in the 1920s and 1930s in what has been termed "the Modern Synthesis."[15] But the social application of Darwinism occupied an important place in sociopolitical thought throughout this period. There are perhaps two reasons for this. The first is that in a period of rapid change affecting all areas of existence, accompanied by a decline in traditional moral and epistemological certainties, Social Darwinism offered a view of the world that was comprehensible to any reasonably educated person and could be accommodated to a large number of ideological positions. Secondly, it laid claim to scientific status, which helped legitimate its assertions about human nature, social reality, and history. In the world of the late nineteenth and early twentieth centuries, one of bewildering complexity and threatening change, Social Darwinism provided a rather straightforward means of organizing and interpreting the data of experience. Indeed, it accorded existential centrality to change while showing that the latter was not random but patterned in accordance with the laws of evolution. How were these ideas applied to the issue of race?

Social Darwinism and Race

The term "race" was in vogue when Darwinism appeared, although it had a number of senses. "To start with it was used to identify a lineage, a set of individuals of common descent who, because of out-marriage, could be of varied appearance. When race was used in the sense of type, this was to identify a set defined by their phenotype or appearance."[16] During the nineteenth century there was a marked tendency to equate race with an ethnic group which could be distinguished by certain hereditary physical and psychological traits.

Darwinism showed that such traits were subject to change over time, but the implications of this were not developed until the following century, and many Darwinists considered races to denote fixed types, even separate species. Nevertheless, race remained an imprecise concept and was often conflated with nation or applied to ethnic aggregates (e.g., the "European race").

Well before Darwinism, a number of theorists had classified races according to skin color, hair type, and cranial features. The efforts almost always ranked races according to some criterion of inferiority/superiority, often accompanied by warnings about the dangers of interracial breeding. In some extreme examples of this genre, the Western world was depicted as suffering from a profound degeneration due to the triumph of inferior races and miscegenation. This was the theme of the Frenchman Arthur de Gobineau (1816–82) in his *Essay on the Inequality of the Human Races* (1853–5) and by a Briton who became a naturalized German, Houston Stewart Chamberlain (1855–1927) in *The Foundations of the Nineteenth Century* (1899).

Neither of these writers was a Social Darwinist, but they popularized the notion that races were distinct, biologically grounded types, could be ranked along a scale of superiority/inferiority, and that those at the bottom of this hierarchy posed a threat to those at the top. In an imperialistic Europe these ideas would have fallen on fertile soil. The majority of Europeans believed in their superiority to the native inhabitants of the Americas, Africa, Asia, and Australasia, and a good many regarded these differences as biologically (rather than culturally) generated. These notions were widespread, received the support of science, and would not be seriously undermined until the period between the two world wars in the next century. "Prior to that time, social differentiation based upon real or assumed racial distinctions was thought to be part of the natural order."[17] While most people would not have endorsed the apocalyptic pessimism of de Gobineau and Chamberlain, they would have been receptive to claims about the dangers of racial crossing or the potential for racial conflict.

In such circumstances it was inevitable that, from its inception, Social Darwinism would be applied to the question of race. Royer had made a point of emphasizing racial inequality in the preface to her translation of the *Origin*. She argued that "human races are not distinct species, but they are clear-cut and highly unequal varieties; and it is necessary to think twice before claiming political and civic equality in a people composed of a minority of Indo-Germans and a majority of Mongolians or Negroes." Superior races were destined to replace lower races, and should not mix their blood with the latter, as this would lower the level of the entire species.[18] In Germany, Friedrich Rolle, a paleontologist and geologist, classified races by color, with the black races beneath the brown, yellow, and white races. Races were subject to natural selection because they were engaged in a struggle for existence, especially for territory.[19]

Similar arguments appeared in the widely read popularizations of Darwinism by Rolle's countryman, the zoologist Ernst Haeckel (1834–1919). Haeckel divided humans into 12 species and 36 subspecies (using criteria such as hair type, skin color, and speech) and arranged them in a hierarchy depending on their proximity to the ape. These species were the equivalent of zoological species, and white Europeans – the "Mediterranean species" – were the most highly evolved of all. Haeckel contended that the differences between civilized races and the lowest "savages" were such that the latter should be classified with the animals He also believed that the differences could not be overcome by attempting to civilize savages, as this would only accelerate their extinction, to which they were doomed in the struggle for existence with superior races.[20]

In England, Alfred Russel Wallace (1823–1913), the co-discoverer of natural selection, proposed in 1864 a Darwinian explanation for the existence of races. He hypothesized that humans were originally homogeneous and subject to the action of natural selection which, over time, produced racial differentiation. However, with the emergence of mind and social organization, selection ceased to act on the physical constitution of humans and worked on their intellectual and moral capacities. This explained why the physical traits of different races had remained fixed for thousands of years, while their mental traits had continued to evolve. Wallace concluded that "it must inevitably follow that the higher – the more intellectual and moral – must replace the lower and more degraded races." However, the continued operation of natural selection on the higher races would lead to increasing perfection to the point where "the world is again inhabited by a single homogeneous race, no individual of which will be inferior to the noblest expressions of existing humanity."[21]

Darwin, in his *Descent*, proposed a different explanation for racial differences: sexual selection. Animals competed for mates, either by conflict among the males (as in deer) or by the male seeking to attract females. This was the reason for the plumage of the peacock, which seemingly would increase its exposure to predation. By attracting more females, however, the gaudiest peacocks were able to enhance their reproductive success. In this way, sexual selection would account for male–female differences and the development of distinctive traits designed to acquire or attract mates.[22] Darwin applied this thesis to humans, arguing that natural selection could not account for the physical characteristics of races since these were rarely useful in the struggle for existence and so would escape the action of natural selection. However, mate selection based upon different conceptions of beauty could account for such characteristics. Thus "the differences between the races of man, as in colour, hairiness, form of features, etc, are of a kind which might have been expected to come under the influence of sexual selection."[23] Natural selection, though, would continue to operate on the intellectual and moral faculties, while the high rate of population increase would exacerbate the struggle between the higher and lower races. Darwin speculated that in "some future period, not very distant as measured by centuries, the civilised races of the world will almost certainly exterminate, and replace, the savage races throughout the world. At the same time the anthropomorphous apes . . . will no doubt be exterminated."[24]

These early examples of Darwinian thinking about race illustrate the assumptions of Cau-casian superiority, that racial differences include a moral dimension which allowed races to be ranked in a hierarchy of ascending excellence, and certainty over the continuing struggle among races in which the "savage" races would be extirpated. For all of the theorists, race denoted not only physical but also psychological and behavioral traits. The fact that a generally liberal outlook among these thinkers accompanied these attitudes on race is indicative of their pervasiveness across the ideological and political spectrum. Wallace was a socialist, and, interestingly, abandoned Social Darwinism a few years after the presentation of his paper on race, renouncing his claim that natural selection could account for human intellectual and spiritual attributes.[25]

None of these thinkers made race the primary focus of their theories. Rather, race was one area to which they sought to apply Darwinian evolutionary theory, although it is significant that these foundational figures in the development of both Darwinism and Social Darwinism should have considered the topic sufficiently important to do so. There were, however, Social Darwinists who made race, or more particularly, interracial conflict, the central theme of their writing, and it is to such that we now turn.

Social Darwinist Theories of Racial Conflict

In 1883 the Polish professor of public law at the University of Graz in Austria published a book on racial struggle: *Der Rassenkampf*. Ludwig Gumplowicz (1838–1909) went on to make the idea of group conflict the basis of a sociological theory which drew heavily on Darwinism. This took the form of applying the theory of the struggle for existence to social evolution. The antagonism and competition endemic to the interaction between nations were explicable by general laws that could be extended from states to "all groups and social circles."[26]

Gumplowicz argued that the first human group was the primitive horde: "a group of men who are still dependent upon the simplest animal impulses."[27] These impulses were those of obtaining food and sex, which produced violent conflicts between hordes over women and resources. With the conquest of a numerically superior horde by one less numerous but of greater mental ability there appeared the state, "the organised control of the minority over the majority."[28] Material interests drove states into violent competition with one another, while within each state the various classes formed by the division of labor were likewise driven by self-interest and were also competing, albeit non-violently. He described this conflict as a "race-war, for such is its inexorable animosity that each group that is able, tends to become exclusive like a caste, to form a consanguineous circle. In short it becomes a race."[29]

This was how races came into existence; humanity "is composed of an endless variety of species" the characteristics of which were transmitted by inheritance. None of the extant races were pure due to inter-breeding, but such pure races probably existed in the past.[30] Each social group is thus a unit opposed – either actually or potentially – to all other social groups. The motive which drives each group is self-interest, and it is insatiable because no group remains content with what it has. The satisfaction of material interests necessitates the exploitation of human labor, which is not impeded by humane considerations. The exploited group belongs to another race or social class. Yet it is through these twin mechanisms of self-interest and the exploitation of foreigners that evolution through the struggle for existence occurs. "Moreover, this evolution cannot cease. For nature has provided that man's needs shall not stand still. Higher and 'nobler' wants are constantly awakened. At the very point where natural ethnic divisions would disappear, artificial 'social' distinctions arise to perpetuate the antagonism of human groups."[31]

Despite his assertion that "Man's psychological character, his mental evolution and so also his mental activity is conditioned by the stage of his political and social evolution,"[32] Gumplowicz apparently did not regard evolution as a process in which human nature and hence motivations were liable to radical alteration over time. This is because he saw no difference between the psychic dispositions and behavior of primitive hordes and modern states and races. Both were governed by "the blind laws of nature" to the extent that no ethical constraints on the action of either could be effective, only "the fear of the stronger," and nothing would prevent either from seeking its own interests if the opportunity arises.[33]

When Gumplowicz did refer to evolution resulting in social progress, this seems to take the form of increasing social complexity and size through conquest and absorption and internal differentiation through the coerced division of labor. This inexorable conflict enhanced civilization since it produced the conditions for prosperity and leisure, which in turn facilitated culture. However, he did not interpret this as a continuous process, but rather a cyclical one, in which large social groups were eventually sundered by internal conflict or defeated by enemies. This sort of catastrophic outcome was certainly possible for Europe, for though it was not menaced by barbaric tribes, the instincts of the latter "lie latent in the populace of European states."[34]

The sociology of Gumplowicz thus made the struggle for existence among humans the primary source of change, and although his use of race was broad and often conflated with class and caste, he helped popularize the idea of a *Rassenkampf*, a ubiquitous war among races. This notion was central to my next example, the French theorist mentioned earlier, Vacher de Lapouge.

Lapouge was convinced that Darwinism enabled one to "grasp the laws of the life and death of nations" by applying the principles of struggle and selection to humans. Man did not occupy a privileged position in nature, but was merely a primate.[35] The key to understanding him was "race," human types differentiated by hereditary physiological and psychological characteristics.[36] The individual could not escape this racial heritage: "He cannot change the traits of his visage, any more than he can efface from his soul the tendencies which make him think and act as his ancestors acted and thought."[37] Races were thus "zoological" phenomena, species in the making, and racial traits were innate and could not be altered by education. This meant that there could never be racial unification, as this was "contrary to elementary biological laws."[38]

Lapouge championed a new discipline of "anthropo-sociology" on these foundations. This was mainly concerned with two racial groups – *Homo Europeaus*, or Aryan, and *Homo Alpinis*. The former was tall, blond-haired, and long-skulled (dolichocephalous), the latter small, dark, and short-skulled (brachycephalous). The Aryans were intelligent, innovative, creative, and energetic; natural leaders in warfare, business, the arts, and science; promoters of progress. *Alpinis*, on the other hand, was servile, mediocre, and lazy, capable only of performing menial, unskilled tasks.

Although naturally superior, the Aryans had been in serious decline for several centuries, whereas *Alpinis* was multiplying. This was because natural selection had been replaced during this period by "social selection," which had the perverse effect of encouraging the proliferation of inferior specimens who were better adapted to modern social conditions. For example, whereas warfare in the past had eliminated weak and sickly individuals, modern warfare subjected strong and fit young men to mass slaughter, leaving criminals and the physically and mentally impaired to propagate the race. The reduction in the numbers of the warlike Aryan left Europe in a precarious position in the imminent racial wars that Lapouge foresaw.[39]

Moral selection also promoted inferior at the expense of superior social elements. Charity fostered the survival and reproduction of those who would not work, while humanitarianism allowed criminals to flourish and transmit their deviant traits to their offspring, rather than eliminating them by extensive use of the death penalty.[40] Particularly pernicious was "political selection." According to Lapouge, the French Revolution had been "above all the transmission of power from one race to another."[41] It signaled the arrival of democracy, an environment conducive to the Aryans in countries where they were still numerous (e.g., Britain and the USA), but a disaster in France where they had already been drastically reduced. Here it had produced an impotent albeit oppressive bureaucratic

regime compatible with the sheep-like mentality of the brachycephals, who made excellent citizens because they were tolerant of abuse.[42]

As a consequence of social selection, much of Europe was in serious racial decline and would succumb to Russia. Sometimes Lapouge saw degeneration as ultimately destroying Britain and the USA, who could not protect themselves from it;[43] on other occasions he thought it was conceivable that the USA, in alliance with England, would triumph.[44] But disaster might be avoided if countries adopted policies aimed at halting racial degeneration. Lapouge speculated about the creation of a racially superior caste through the artificial insemination of women by a small number of perfect men, and over the beneficial consequences of allowing degenerates to destroy themselves by making free alcohol available to them. But he considered it unlikely that public opinion would tolerate the use of these (for him) quite feasible selectionist techniques.[45]

Lapouge did not find a receptive audience among his fellow countrymen, which is hardly surprising given his views on the acute racial degeneracy of the French. But his publications are important because they vividly illustrate certain trends in Social Darwinist theories of race that were clearly marked by the end of the nineteenth century. First, there is the insistence on race as a biological type, with racial traits established through the forces of selection, transmitted by heredity and virtually ineradicable. Second, there is an emphasis on the inexorable nature of the struggle for existence, particularly among the different races. Third, there is a ranking of races in accordance with some criterion of intellectual and moral worth, with white Europeans occupying the summit of this hierarchy. Fourth, there is an obsession with racial deterioration that threatens the supremacy of Europeans, sometimes through interbreeding with "inferior" races, but also through social institutions and practices which suspend or pervert the action of natural selection. Fifth, there is a belief that this degeneration can be arrested, if not reversed, by the appropriate eugenic policies. This connection between race, Social Darwinism, and eugenics will be explored below.

Eugenics and Social Darwinism

In 1883 Darwin's cousin, Francis Galton (1822–1911), proposed "eugenics" (from the Greek for "well-born") as a means of improving the racial quality of a population. This could be achieved by a twofold process: negative eugenics was aimed at preventing the breeding of putatively inferior elements in the population, while positive eugenics encouraged the breeding of the "higher" elements. This was necessitated by the fact that natural selection no longer appeared to be operating, with the result that the "unfit" rather than the fit were surviving and proliferating.

These concerns are plainly apparent among the early Social Darwinists. Royer had attacked misguided charity and welfare policies for protecting "the weak, the infirm, the incurable, the wicked, . . . all those who are ill-favoured by nature" because they allowed defectives to spread their hereditary taints throughout the population.[46] Haeckel had also attacked institutions and policies which produced an "artificial selection" that protected criminals and the incurably sick, or else, as with military service, exposed the young and the fit to untimely death.[47]

One of the starkest portrayals of the consequences of contradicting natural selection was made by a Scot, William Greg. He argued that while natural selection still took place *between* races and nations, this was no longer the case *within* nations. Here the effect of civilization "is to counteract and suspend the operation of that righteous and salutary law of 'natural selection'" which ensures that the fittest individuals survive and procreate.[48] This occurred because "we have kept alive those who, in a more natural and less advanced state, would have died." Greg's target here was "the ineffective and incapable, the weak in body or mind" who in uncivilized tribes are unable to care for themselves and hence die.[49] But he also attacked people who had acquired wealth by inheritance rather than merit despite being incapable of sustaining themselves through their own efforts, and who married "to produce enervated and unintelligent offspring."[50]

Greg concluded it was possible to conceive of a polity in which paupers were forbidden to procreate, and people who intended to have children should have to pass a competitive examination "so that paternity should be the right and function exclusively by the elite of the nation."[51] However, no modern nation would endure the despotic regulation necessary for the restoration of natural selection, and in any case, "a result so acquired might not be worth the cost of acquisition." Greg thought it just possible that the spread of enlightenment and moral responsibility among the masses might be effective, and on this race between enlightenment and physical deterioration "the destinies of humanity depend."[52]

These arguments appear in the *Descent* where Darwin, citing Greg, underlined the deleterious consequences of charitable and medical care for the sick, the maimed, and the poor in civilized societies, which prevent their elimination and enable them to reproduce. No animal breeder would allow his worst specimens to breed, but this is precisely what happens in the case of man. He counseled celibacy for the impoverished, but also warned that if the natural rate of increase was diminished too much, natural selection would no longer take place and humanity would stagnate.[53]

Well before Galton's advocacy of eugenics, then, Social Darwinists had expressed concern that social progress appeared to be undermining the process of natural selection and the survival of the fittest. By the end of the century this concern had blossomed into proposals for government-led schemes to arrest the process of decline in the mental and physical quality of the population. In Britain the philosopher F. H. Bradley (1846–1924) argued Darwinism entailed a revision of our ethical codes, with their stress on individual rights, and called for a "moral surgery" in which criminals, but also the insane and sufferers from hereditary diseases, should be eliminated for the good of the community. Punishment had to be separated from questions of guilt and justice, and should rather be regarded as a Darwinian imperative in order to maintain selection and prevent the spawning of the diseased and the morally vicious.[54]

Bradley's proposals were particularly harsh, but the advocates of eugenics shared the view that the survival of the national or racial community in the struggle for existence took moral precedence over any consideration of individual rights. The British physiologist John Berry Haycraft believed that the "clamorous appeals for personal rights" were ceding place to a sense of obligation to others, particularly future generations, and this could entail individuals making sacrifices in the interests of racial reconstruction.[55] Whereas previously diseases such as whooping cough, scarlet fever, leprosy, and tuberculosis were selective in their impact, carrying off the weakest individuals, advances in medicine and improved social conditions now prevented this selection from occurring. But if selective processes were removed without being replaced, the result would be racial decay. Haycraft proposed that criminals and people who refused to work should be prevented from marrying and procreating, while "incapables" (i.e., the sick and insane) should be segregated, though well treated.[56] But while Haycraft was appalled at the prospect of the "swamping" of the capables by the incapables, he was against birth control. "The world will fall to the share of those who produce most offspring. Let us be sure that in our own nation it shall not be the offspring of the deteriorated."[57]

Conclusion

By the end of the nineteenth century both the rationale for eugenics and different schemes for its implementation had been worked out by a number of theorists. However, the movement did not really gain momentum until the first decades of the next century, when eugenics societies were established across Europe and in the USA. There are many reasons for this rather sudden upturn in interest in eugenics, but one important factor was a fall in the birth rate in European societies. This fueled fears of national or racial decline, particularly since among manual laborers and the underclass the birth rate remained high. This, coupled with mounting concern over the statistics of criminality, suicide, mental and physical illness, alcoholism, and prostitution, provided a context in which racial decadence appeared clearly evident.

The development of eugenics, and its adoption in countries such as the USA, Sweden and, most horrendously, in Nazi Germany, is beyond the scope of this chapter. What is relevant here is the manner in which a Darwinian view of human physical, psychological, and social evolution was used to support the call for eugenics. If the world was an arena of conflicting races or nations and yet civilization was counteracting or suspending the action of natural selection within nations, then the resulting deterioration in the quality of the population could have serious consequences. These themes were articulated in Nazi ideology, which made the struggle among races for resources and living space the key to understanding history. The concomitant of this was the elimination or exploitation of "inferior" ethnic groups like the Jews and Roma, and the eugenic cleansing of the master race itself to avoid inner deterioration by the tainted genes of criminals, homosexuals, the mentally and physically sick, and opponents of the Third Reich.

Although historically there has been a close link between Social Darwinism and eugenics, it must be stressed that there is no *inevitable* connection between them. Some Social Darwinists were vigorous opponents of eugenics. T. H. Huxley, for example, poured scorn on the claims by eugenicists to be able to determine fitness in a population, and on the despotic and ruthless "pigeon-fancier's polity" which their policies would require.[58] On the other hand, some of the staunchest proponents of eugenics were anti-Darwinian, such as the playwright G. B. Shaw.[59]

What, then, of the connection between eugenics and race? Undoubtedly, many eugenicists were convinced of the reality of racial differences, of the inequality of races, of the inevitability of interracial competition, and therefore of the need to maintain the vitality and integrity of one's own race in order to be able to survive in this context. But the unfit could often be construed as comprising the urban underclass, paupers, criminals, alcoholics, and those afflicted with hereditary illness, as well as "inferior" races. Although eugenics appealed to all shades of the political spectrum, many of the stigmatizations in play here derive from class prejudices, and indeed the vocabularies employed in class and in racial descriptions overlapped considerably.[60] Both terms tended to be used as simultaneously descriptive and evaluative, assigning moral significations to whatever physical and mental attributes were used as criteria.

The consequences of this configuration of race, class, and eugenics could be harsh for certain groups, not just in Nazi Germany, but also in the USA, where eugenic policies were implemented in some states until the 1970s.[61] In Britain eugenics failed to exert a major impact on state legislation, but its ramifications were felt nonetheless.[62] Thus it has been argued that an analysis of the death sentence for military offenses during World War I shows that it was passed and carried out disproportionately against those perceived to be racially inferior (e.g., Irish, Indian, and African soldiers) and individuals who, on mental and moral grounds, were deemed to be worthless as soldiers and as men.[63]

During the last four decades of the nineteenth century, then, Social Darwinist theories of race were formulated that would play a significant role in the history of the following century. It is important to reinforce the theme of this chapter, however, that this was not the only ideological role of Social Darwinism, although the appropriation of the latter by race theorists was always probable until the scientific validity of race was vitiated during the twentieth century by the demonstration that there was greater biological variation *within* than *between* ethnic groups. That there is no inevitability about the connection is shown by the fact that Social Darwinism is currently powerful in the disciplines of sociobiology and evolutionary psychology, but rarely are these disciplines concerned with racial differences.

NOTES

1   Darwin (1968: 263).
2   Malthus (1992: 28–9).
3   Darwin (1968: 117, 126).
4   Desmond and Moore (1991).
5   Darwin and Huxley (1983: 51).
6   Weikart (1998); Desmond (1998).
7   Ferri (1905: v).
8   Büchner (1872: 156).
9   Royer (1870: 520, 14).
10 Kidd (1895: 39–40, 53).
11 Lapouge (1899: 374).
12 Lapouge (1896: 451).
13 Darwin (1968: 459).
14 For example, Lankester (1880).
15 Huxley (1894); Bowler (1983).
16 Banton (1987: 95–6).
17 Barkan (1992: xi).
18 Royer (1866: lxi).
19 Rolle (1866: 116, 140).
20 Haeckel (1876: vol. 2, 307–9, 325, 363–5).
21 Wallace (1979: 53, 54).
22 Darwin (1906: ch. 8).
23 Ibid: 308.
24 Ibid: 241–2.
25 Desmond and Moore (1991: 569–70); Clements (1983).
26 Gumplowicz (1898: 188).
27 Gumplowicz (1963: 193).
28 Ibid: 200.
29 Ibid: 227.
30 Ibid: 161, 171–8.
31 Ibid: 206.
32 Ibid: 301.
33 Ibid: 229.
34 Ibid: 309.
35 Lapouge (1896: 1, 11).
36 Ibid: 5–6.
37 Lapouge (1899: 351).
38 Ibid: 369.
39 Lapouge (1896: 224); Lapouge (1899: 501).
40 Lapouge (1896: 119, 321–4).
41 Ibid: 251.
42 Lapouge (1899: 232–3).
43 Lapouge (1896: 444–5).
44 Lapouge (1899: 499–502).
45 Lapouge (1896: 472–7, 486).
46 Royer (1866: lvi).
47 Haeckel (1876: vol. 1, 170–4).
48 Greg (1868: 356).
49 Ibid: 358.
50 Ibid: 360.
51 Ibid: 361.
52 Ibid: 362.
53 Darwin (1906: 205–6, 944–6).
54 Bradley (1894).
55 Haycraft (1895: 156, 161–2).
56 Ibid: 98–102, 108–9.
57 Ibid: 153.
58 Huxley (1894: 22–3).

59 Shaw (1931).
60 Lorimer (1978).
61 Crook (2002: 363–81).
62 Thomson (1998).
63 Oram (1998).

GUIDE TO FURTHER READING

Social Darwinist theories are comprehensively reviewed in M. Hawkins, *Social Darwinism in European and American Thought, 1860–1945*. For a briefer, European focus, see Corsi and Weindling's "Darwinism in Germany, France and Italy." For an exploration of the implications of Darwinism for conceptions of human nature (including recent versions of Darwinism), see Richards, *Human Nature after Darwin*. There is a detailed account of Darwinian theories of psychology and morality in Richards, *Darwin and the Emergence of Evolutionary Theories of Mind and Behavior*. There are analyses of the wider manifestations of Darwinism in Beer's *Darwin's Plots* and Chamberlin and Gilman's *Degeneration*. Hannaford's *Race* surveys the career of the notion of race in Western history. For a study of the relationship between Darwinism and conflict which highlights the complexity of this relationship, see Crook's *Darwinism, War and History*. For a review of recent literature on the connections between Social Darwinism, race, and eugenics, see Crook's "American Eugenics and the Nazis."

CHAPTER EIGHTEEN

The Age of Catholic Revival

ODED HEILBRONNER

There is good reason to describe nineteenth-century Europe as the "Age of Catholic Revival" rather than the "Age of Revolution," the "Age of Capital," or the "Age of Imperialism."[1] It was a period marked by several powerful religious revivals, an increased popularity of religious literature, and deep religious controversies in both Catholic and Protestant camps. Against the background of the sustained attacks on the Catholic church between 1789 and 1815, one can only wonder how European Catholicism emerged in post-1815 Europe as more populist, much more ultramontane, and generally better equipped to survive in a more rational, industrial, liberal, and secular Europe.[2]

No wonder that more and more historians speak of nineteenth-century Europe as a "second confessional era." The reference here is of course to the "first confessional era" of the Counter-Reformation in the sixteenth and seventeenth centuries.[3] In both eras one can discern close relations between state building and the fixing of confessional identities. Nineteenth-century European Catholicism adapted well to a new religious and political situation by aggressively revamping its institutions. At the same time, European Catholicism of the nineteenth century (as in the early modern period) was also marked by the persistence of popular religious enthusiasms which were still influencing individual and group identity.

At the center of this chapter stand the relationships between popular religion, the politics of Catholic church institutions, various Catholic social groups, and the surrounding Protestant societies. These relationships shaped the Catholic milieu, or, in my words, the Catholic ghetto. At the same time, one cannot speak about the ghetto and its walls without describing the world outside, namely the institutions of the European nation-states, chiefly the civil-liberal institutions, some of them Protestant.

This chapter aims to demonstrate how religious and political settlements, which originated in the Counter-Reformation period and disintegrated in the period of the French Revolution and Napoleonic period, were revised during the first half of the nineteenth century. From the mid-nineteenth century onwards new political settlements heightened confessional sensitivities, especially in the religion of the Catholic people and the Catholic institutions. One of the main results of these developments was the creation of a Catholic ghetto. However, by the eve of World War I, one could discern rising dissatisfaction among many Catholic groups, especially among the middle class and workers who were trying to "get out" of the Catholic ghetto. In this chapter, then, the story of European Catholics is one of heroic recovery from the trauma of the French Revolution and a justifiable struggle against the new repressive, industrial nation-state.

Preconditions: The Confessional Age and the Age of Revolutions

During the late sixteenth century and as a result of the Catholic Reformation some fundamental changes were taking place in Western and Central Europe. Three modern church systems were founded on specific confessions of faith, thus generating specific confessional cultures, political cultures, and mentalities. These were the Lutheran system, the Calvinist system, and the Catholic system. The Catholic confessionalization (as well as the other two confessions) not only affected religion and theologies, but also signified fundamental change with deep effects on European politics and culture.[4] If medieval Christianity was magical and pagan, post-Reformation Catholicism was characterized by modernity. It was keen to combat popular superstitions, train new clergy, and evangelize in the non-European world. Furthermore, the church's administration was reformed and Catholicism undertook new initiatives to stop the dissolution of traditional primary ties (family, kinship) and the push toward individuality. It also constructively engaged with a state welfare system, reform of school and pedagogic systems, and the adaptation of new economic values and political cultures.

Comprehensive church reform was analogous to the process of state building by European absolute rulers.[5] One should remember that the Age of Reason was also an Age of Faith. Catholic missions and orders flourished all over Europe and outside of the continent. Popular festivals and superstitions were widespread among the lower classes. The mingling of magic with the religion of simple people was just as evident as it had been hundreds of years earlier. The cult of saints, certain forms of faith healing, and the superstitious goals of pilgrimage were popular in many Catholic regions of Europe. Many of the these phenomena were initiated against the will of official Catholicism.[6]

The Enlightenment is often associated with deliberate efforts to undermine religious belief and organizations: it was a time of "disenchantment of the world" and an age which was characterized by the "rise of modern paganism." The way of seeing the world as full of magical or spiritual powers and forces collapsed. God was confined to working through natural causes and obeyed natural laws accessible to human study.[7] Although one should distinguish between the Enlightenment in Catholic Europe (where Catholic enlightened thinkers and scholars were speaking of reform within the Catholic church and called upon the church to play a more useful role in society) and Protestant Europe (where the Enlightenment was anti-Christian and still more anti-Catholic), both looked with horror at the popular Catholic revival.[8]

Popular (Catholic) religion and the Enlightenment reflected deep changes within European societies of the eighteenth century. Demographic changes, changing economies, urbanization, and increased literacy are some important phenomena within the European infrastructure. They meant that religious conformity and the complete fit between Catholicism and society became impossible to maintain. They also meant that the church had to adapt itself to these changes, a step which the Catholic church initially refused to accept.

Against the background of these changes one can understand the revolutionary upheaval of the late eighteenth century. The French Revolution symbolized the birth of the modern age, which was characterized also by the birth of secularization, both rooted in the Enlightenment discourse. There can be no doubt that Enlightenment (anti-Catholic) ideas which flourished in France influenced the religious policies of the French revolutionaries, for France played an important role in Catholic Europe. It was not only the country with the largest Catholic population, it was also the country in which the monastic orders had their largest number of houses, and the country where theological influence was particularly strong. The Catholic church in France was an official institution linked to the Old Regime, with many political, juridical, and financial privileges.

From this perspective one can understand the strength of popular anti-clericalism and anti-Catholicism in the 1790s. In November 1789 the National Assembly nationalized church property. In July 1790 the Assembly made clerics civil servants, a step which made the Catholic church in France completely dependent on the state. In November 1791 the Assembly voted the Ecclesiastical Law that required each priest to swear loyalty to the constitution and the state. The law split the Catholic church in France and initiated widespread resistance which lasted well into the twentieth century.[9]

The anti-church laws in France reflected widespread anti-clerical sentiments all over Europe as the French revolutionary armies advanced eastward. Priests, monks, and orders were persecuted in France as well as in Central and Southern Europe. Churches were closed, vandalized, or converted into secular institutions.[10] Although towards the last year of the 1790s Catholic worship in France once again became legal and one can discern Catholic religious revivals in some French regions, it was not financed by the state and was dependent mainly on local lay initiative to reopen churches and reestablish sacred life. The main consequence of the revolutionary period was that "French people were no longer automatically Catholic, simply by the fact of being French."[11]

During the Napoleonic period Catholicism was recognized as the religion of the majority of Frenchmen, but other religions such as Protestantism and Judaism were legally equal. The Concordat that was signed by Napoleon and the Catholic church in 1801 signaled the inability of the church to return to its pre-1789 leading position. The Napoleonic state appointed bishops and priests. The priests were to swear an oath of loyalty to the state and prayers for the state were said in all churches. In countries where Napoleonic regimes were established that same anti-Catholic policy took place. The church surrendered property. Churches and monasteries were closed. Priests and bishops were persecuted and many Catholic states in Central Europe were secularized. The traditional political culture on the eastern bank of the Rhine – before 1791 one of the main strongholds of Catholic Europe – disappeared in the face of secularization, which put an end to dozens of Catholic mini-states, independent bishoprics, duchies, and principalities. The Catholic infrastructure there (as well

as in Spain, Italy, and many parts of Austria) was completely destroyed. It took the church many years to recover from the Napoleonic trauma.[12]

The new order in Europe that emerged from the Napoleonic Wars marked the most serious challenge to the Catholic church since the days of the Wars of Religion. As Owen Chadwick argued: "Napoleon overthrew the settlement inherited from the wars of religion and left a new Europe in which Protestants were politically far stronger than Catholics."[13]

One of the main results of the French Revolution and wars was that the church had to compete with other religions and political ideologies. The most important of these in the first half of the nineteenth century was liberalism. Between 1815 and 1860 the main components of liberalism, such as nationalism, secularization, free trade, urbanization, materialism, scientific progress, and Protestantism, were in deep conflict with the church. Although rural Europe maintained high levels of compliance with Catholic doctrines, the cities of Europe, most of them strongholds of liberalism, expressed mainly indifference to church rituals and festivals. From the 1820s onwards many middle-class and bourgeois liberals, together with growing numbers of workers, saw the church as an enemy. As heirs of eighteenth-century rationalism, many liberals found themselves at odds with Catholicism. The Catholic church in the Restoration period and before the revolutions of 1848 (as well as after, as I will show later) opposed certain basic liberal beliefs such as religious tolerance, a free-trade economy, a free press, a non-religious educational system, and private ownership. No wonder that the Catholic church found its allies among the Restoration governments in continental Europe who – with important regional variations – saw liberalism as their enemy.

The church saw socialism and radicalism in pre-1848 Europe as even greater enemies than liberalism. The church perceived them as godless, and looked at their cosmopolitan ideas as a secular religion whose main interest was to destroy the old world, including Christianity. The workers hated the pre-1848 church because of its alliance with the most aristocratic and conservative powers in Europe. Mutual hostility fed much of the outbreaks of violence between the two forces in the 1848 revolutions.

The main efforts of the Catholic church in the first decades after the Napoleonic Wars were directed towards its adjustment to the political settlement of the Congress of Vienna. In most West and Central European countries (except Portugal and Austria) the ecclesiastical structure had been destroyed and it was necessary to build new dioceses and new ecclesiastical institutions, according to the new political boundaries. In France, the basic structure of the church was already in line with the new conditions. In western and southern Germany the revolutionary wars and Napoleon's secularization policy had resulted in a profound shock for Catholic institutions, and for the church there were also important territorial changes to which it had to adjust.[14]

In Central Europe, where Catholic and Protestant regions and towns had intermingled for more than two centuries, article 16 of the constitution of the German Confederation from 1815 gave religious minorities the status and rights of a minority.[15] However, the reality looked different. The strongest state of the German Confederation, Prussia, was a Protestant state with a strong minority of 30 percent Catholics living in the Rhineland and Westphalia and in some eastern regions such as Silesia. Here the state claimed wide-ranging supervisory and controlling power over the Catholic church. Conflicts became unavoidable as soon as the interests of the Prussian-Protestant state and the Catholic church contradicted each other. The arrest of the archbishop of Cologne at the beginning of the Cologne riots in 1837 because of his position over the question of marriages between parents of different denominations – as well as the huge turnout at the pilgrimage to the Holy Coat in Trier in 1844 (which turned into an anti-Prussian demonstration) – revealed the problems of state–religious minority relations under the new territorial boundaries after the Napoleonic Wars.[16] If, especially in Protestant states, Catholicism became a beleaguered religion in nineteenth-century Europe, this tended to reawaken popular Catholicism and strengthen the hand of Rome.

The European Culture Wars and the Reaction of the Catholic Church

The nineteenth-century Catholic ghetto[17] was characterized by a great body of shared religious organizations, experiences, rituals, and relationships which gave to the believers a strongly felt common identity and separated them from their Protestant, Jewish, or Liberal neighbors who did not participate in these organizations and did not share in any of these experiences. The Catholic church used those sentiments in its struggle against the European nation-states and European modernity more generally. Apart from the events of the Reformation, the French Revolution, and its impact on the Central European regions, it was the *Kulturkampf*, the struggle of several European states (and especially their liberal elites) against the Catholic church, which led to the emergence of a Catholic ghetto. This struggle, which began in southern Germany in the 1850s, was to reach its culmination in the German state of Prussia in the 1870s and continue in one form or another throughout Western and Central Europe.

There is no doubt that the focus of the European *Kulturkampf* lay in the Catholic regions in the German state of Prussia, but the experience of the Catholics there was replicated in many other Western and Central European regions. The *Kulturkampf* began on a local level as a reaction to the general suffrage instituted by Bismarck. The growing power of the priests, who were now more easily able, by means of elections, to enlist the support of the Catholic masses and thus to increase the power of the church, was perceived as a threat.[18] And finally, on the Catholic side, the *Kulturkampf* was exploited in order to institute a democratization of the church, to augment the power of the priests, to introduce changes in the traditional Catholic elites, and to replace the old class of leaders with a younger leadership, more bourgeois in its background. The struggle helped the new generation of priests to gain positions of leadership in the *Zentrum* and in the ecclesiastical hierarchy, which, from the 1870s onwards, needed increasingly to consider the priests' opinions. The struggle faced the hesitant and those who declined to enter the Catholic ghetto (which began to take shape at the end of the 1860s) with a difficult decision. It was not just a question of loyalty to ultramontane principles. The attacks by the Prussian government on the church and its representatives necessitated the adoption of a clear position. One had to take a stand either "inside or outside the walls," knowing that "outside the walls" would inevitably mean collaboration with the Prussian bureaucracy.

The Catholic educational system was at the center of the conflict. The Prussian educational laws of March 1872 lessened the church's control over Catholic schools.[19] Additional laws were passed in 1873 and the years that followed. These were accompanied by discrimination, isolation, sentencing, and sometimes violent action. In general, it can be said that on the bureaucratic level there was a definite anti-Catholic bias, and the whole administrative system was pressed into the struggle.

The actual implementation of the laws was sometimes a problem. In most cases, the laws were not carried out in their entirety. They were promulgated but not implemented. However, the blow represented by the Kulturkampf was also felt in other areas and regions throughout Central Europe. Many priests were arrested and imprisoned. Their congregations were disbanded. Five of the eleven bishops in Prussia were arrested and imprisoned for short periods and their positions were left unfilled, and Catholic newspapers and associations were placed under police supervision. Most of the Catholic public in the Catholic regions of Prussia supported the church's position, as was shown by a massive enrollment in the ultramontane associations. The attacks on it strengthened their mutual ties. The Catholic lower strata, who were more vulnerable to manipulation, saw the attacks on them not only as a blow against their faith, but also as an attempt by the Protestant (and part of the Catholic) bourgeoisie to perpetuate their inferiority. In some regions the Kulturkampf took on the character of class struggle, where there was a clear division between Protestant factory owners and Catholic workers (some of whom were Polish). Even the priests in rural areas commiserated with their congregations for the economic exploitation that they suffered from the Protestant bourgeoisie or from Catholics with high economic positions in the village or the local town.[20]

The German and the European Kulturkampf, together with economic, political, and demographic processes of tremendous social significance (industrialization, the rise of the nation-state, the change in the status of women, the increasing birth rate, etc.), helped to give some European Catholics a mentality of self-imprisonment within a geographical, social, economic, and political fortress. At the same time they also led to an intense internal debate in Catholic society, and especially its bourgeois sections, on how to break out from behind those walls.

Hence, most studies on European and English Catholicism present a liberal-secular chronicle of a struggle between the principles of separateness and union. The desire to leave the confines of the church fortress is juxtaposed with the right to remain within them. The claims of a backward ghetto mentality stand next to the wish to belong to a modern liberal society which prided itself on its progress and modernity. This struggle took place simultaneously in countries with a Catholic majority (France, Austria, Spain, Italy) and in countries with a Protestant majority (Germany, Holland, Britain).

However, as the case of Catholic Spain in the second half of the nineteenth century demonstrates, this struggle could be interpreted not only in terms of a struggle between "good" (secular, liberal, reformist, modern principals) and "bad" (backward, tradition, anti-modern principals), but also as a struggle between New or Reform Catholicism which advocated new, militant Catholicism and called for a confessional-modern society based on a new understanding of the principles of Christianity, and anti-Catholicism (some say anti-clericalism) which advocated republican and liberal ideas based on the moderate and gradual separation of church and state and the gradual secularization of society.[21]

The Catholic ghetto provides the starting point for those scholars of European Catholicism who began producing critical studies of

European Catholicism during the last few decades. These scholars have studied several bishoprics in Germany and France, describing the patterns of cultural, social, economic, and political behavior that prevailed among the Catholics in these mainly agrarian regions as the model of the Catholic ghetto.[22] As in other European countries such as Austria, Spain, Ireland, Belgium, the Netherlands, and Switzerland, such Catholic ghettos were patterns that bore the definitive imprint of institutions such as the Catholic church, a Catholic political party, the Catholic school system, Catholic workers' unions, and Catholic voluntary associations.[23] They were "clerical citadels" as they were called by Julio de la Cueva, who studied the town of Santader in northern Spain, whose inhabitants lived their lives according to instructions issued from the pulpits and at the same time encountered "secular armies willing to put them to siege and eventually, to occupy them."[24]

Many scholars argue that the Catholic ghetto was a result of – and contributed to – popular piety among large sections of society. This popular piety was chiefly a result of personal and institutional actions, initiated most importantly by (1) social and religious associations; (2) acts of pilgrimage and missions to spread the faith, as well as the manipulative use of apparitions and popular beliefs; (3) the priesthood; (4) Catholic women; (5) hostility between Catholics and Protestants, which persisted until the first decade of the twentieth century; (6) the Catholic press; and (7) political Catholicism. Conversely, scholars also suggest that it was popular piety which laid the foundation for the Catholic ghetto, a piety which was spasmodic before the second half of the nineteenth century and represented after 1848 a sort of challenge to local Catholic authority and institutions.[25] The growing intensity of the cult of the Virgin Mary reflects what Ralph Gibson described as a process in which popular Catholicism "appealed to the heart rather than the head."[26] Most scholars agree today that the main engines in this emotional process were the local priest and Catholic women.

The parish priest was the most influential notable in the Catholic ghetto. In remote and underdeveloped villages, where most European Catholics lived until the turn of the nineteenth century, the priest was responsible for building the ghetto walls by controlling the religious life of the congregation and by restraining their desire to "leave the tower." Most scholars agree that it was impossible to build a Catholic ghetto without such clerical activity, where the guards of the ghetto were the priests and their superintendent was the bishop.[27]

Catholic women were the "human ammunition" of the Catholic church and its organizations and the "heroines" of Catholic piety. Research in this matter is still in its infancy, but it is clear that women were the popular force which moved the wheels of ultramontanism. Although they were of marginal importance for political Catholicism (as they did not have the right to vote), they constituted the majority in the various organizations and societies, especially the ecclesiastical ones. They were present more often than the men in confessional ceremonies: in church on Sundays, at the Easter communion, at the priest's sermons, on pilgrimages, at Catholic feasts and festivals, and, most important of all (from the priest's and the church's point of view), they were in attendance with the local midwife. As I will describe later, at the beginning of the twentieth century, the church lost an increasing number of adherents, but these were mainly men. The women stayed behind and "defended the walls of the ghetto."

Scholars have shown that a feminization of religion took place in the nineteenth century. Bonnie Smith, Caroline Ford, I. Götz von Olenhusen, and Hugh McLeod have seen it as chiefly a Catholic phenomenon, as have David Blackbourn and many others who have considered the matter.[28] In most studies women are represented as bearing the chief burden of the Catholic-ultramontane movement, which was paradoxically a male-dominated phenomenon.

Moreover, many bourgeois Catholic women, especially towards the end of the nineteenth century, sought greater equality in the relations between the sexes. One way to improve their status was by using their influence to increase their families' piety. Being responsible for running a bourgeois family, they were able to introduce religious elements into family life and thus increase the religious orientation of such a family. Davidoff and Hall made a similar claim in their classic study of evangelical women in the English bourgeoisie.[29] At the same time, women in families where the husband and wife had different religions were not able to decide the religion of all their children, but only that of the daughters. The fathers decided the religion of the sons.[30]

Of course, one should consider the possibility of the church's manipulation of Catholic women in the first decade of the nineteenth century in order to bring them into its fold and repair the losses to secularism. Was the feminization of religion a manipulative tool wielded by the Catholic church in order to prevent the flight of women from its ranks? Certainly, it would appear that the use of the "stigmata" by the Catholic church was directed chiefly towards women.[31] David Blackbourn describes the feminization of the Marpingen phenomenon and also notes the idealization of the child. But he stresses that the use of apparitions did not depend solely on the church. It could not have succeeded if the women had not been ready or even eager to accept a religious sign of this nature. The various apparitions created a new feminine identity which many women wanted. In addition women were also prominent participants in various rituals such as the Sacred Heart of Jesus, where Jesus himself, while showing his Sacred Heart to Jesuit Father Bernardo of Hoyos, promised him in 1733: "I will reign in Spain." It was an opportunity for women to express their personalities, and where piety was concerned, to demonstrate their superiority to men. In sum, since women were the main target of the Catholic church and its most enthusiastic supporters, the feminization of religion could only have occurred in places where ultramontanism flourished. In places like southern Germany or northern France where ultramontanism was weak, the phenomenon could not exist. Only in Catholic ghettos such as the Catholic communities in the German Rhineland, eastern France, or in Lower Austria could the feminization of religion and feminine piety flourish.[32]

Heterogeneous Movements Within and Outside the Catholic Ghetto

The diversity of the Catholic ghetto, its lack of ultramontane homogeneity, and its diverse attitudes to civil-liberal society led some German scholars to argue in favor of several *different* ghettos (they use the term "milieus").[33] They distinguish between "micromilieus" – local (usually village) societies with their specific habits, traditions, and institutions (family, neighborhood, friends); "mesomilieus" – larger areas (in Germany: the Catholic regions of Upper-Lower Bavaria, the Protestant districts of Upper Franconia), where a specific religious identity reflected local religious habits and institutions (e.g., Catholic workers' voluntary associations); and, finally, the "macromilieu" – the milieu of the whole of German Catholic society. All three ghettos are more or less closely related to the church.

Such diversity was a unique phenomenon within the Central European Catholic ghetto and it led some scholars to write about the European Catholic ghetto in contrast to the conditions of the Catholics in Britain. Accordingly, one can speak about the "relatively" open Catholic ghetto in Britain, where contact between Catholics and Protestants was much more widespread than was the case with the closed Catholic societies on the continent, where only minimal contacts existed between the two confessions.[34] On the other hand, in Britain "Catholics tended to become isolated in ghettos cut off from the dominant (liberal-Anglican) culture," whereas on the continent none of the major cultural-ideological groupings was dominant.[35]

The Catholic ghetto was culturally extremely varied (by "culture" I mean the totality of values, beliefs, modes of thought, and lifestyles common to a group of people living in a given area). The culture of the region is of crucial importance here, whether it is the culture of the German Pfalz, of Lower Austria, or eastern France, of Lancashire or northwestern France, or the German-speaking regions of Switzerland. Obviously, different regions will display diverging behavioral patterns in accordance with their cultural variables. Thus, different forms of Catholic ghetto existed in Liverpool, Brittany, the German Upper Pfalz, the regions of Fribourg (north Switzerland), and the Tyrol.[36]

The Swiss historian Urs Altermatt describes the components of the Catholic Swiss ghetto and stresses its strongly felt common identity.[37] He is doing it by asking first how it came about that so many Catholics in Switzerland were born in a Catholic hospital, went to Catholic schools, read Catholic newspapers, voted for a Catholic party, were insured against accident and illness with a Catholic welfare organization, and were buried as Catholics. His answers relate to the components of the Catholic's shared experiences in north-Switzerland, although, of course, many of these elements were also found elsewhere in Europe.

The ghetto was most developed in the Netherlands, where "Dutch Catholics became one of the most highly organized sections of the church."[38] Primary schools, a political party, a trade union, and newspapers were founded after the 1850s and formed part of the Catholic subculture, which was protected by a coalition between anti-revolutionary Calvinists and ultramontanists.[39] By the turn of the century a similar set of organizations existed in France, Belgium, and Austria. On the other hand, when one considers such important institutions as the Catholic Party and school system, then France lacked a political party and, after the turn of the century, a Catholic school system, and both the Belgian and Austrian Catholic school systems were limited to certain regions and did not constitute a general phenomenon. In Germany, there was no separate system of Catholic elementary schools at all after the 1870s.[40]

Regional and political peculiarities were important in other cases too. A unique element in Switzerland was that the Catholic ghetto was concentrated in German-speaking areas and not in French ones. In Austria, ultramontanist norms were established by exploiting an ecclesiastical autonomy authorized by earlier liberal regimes. A conservative coalition of German clerics and non-German ethnic groups, among whom Catholic feeling was strong, was created during the 1870s. Within the German-speaking ethnic group, Catholic politics and social organizations developed rapidly, particularly in the countryside, and were dominated by the clergy and local aristocracy.[41]

In particular the character of the Catholic semi-ghetto in England differed from the continental experience. By the mid-nineteenth century, anti-Catholicism was a prominent feature of British political culture. While defending themselves against outside attacks, Roman Catholics had to distinguish themselves from their hostile surroundings. Through a concentration on specifically Catholic devotional forms of piety, the almost ghetto-like character of late Victorian and early twentieth-century English Catholicism came into being. Popular public acts of devotion like benediction and the public rosary were common among English Catholics. They also had a social and political function: these rituals helped to draw a large number of working-class Catholics (in Liverpool, for example) and poor Irish immigrants into the ghetto. The sanctity of poverty as a means of unifying the church across class lines became a distinguishing mark of English Catholicism.[42]

Roman Catholics in the United Kingdom distinguished themselves from their brethren on the continent by another phenomenon: Irish Catholicism. In Ireland Catholic religion provided the fundamental basis for the identity, not of a class, region, or community, but of a nation. The economically subordinate position of Irish Catholics (who made up about 80 percent of the population) provided the most important common reference point for Catholics. The earliest nationwide movements such as the campaigns for Catholic emancipation in the 1820s and for the repeal of the Union in the 1840s depended heavily on the work of the clergy as local agents. New church buildings were another site where Catholicism and nationalism merged and they were another powerful symbol of the pride of the Catholic population.[43]

One could also speak of the social diversity among European Catholics. Not all Catholics lived within the walls of the Catholic ghetto. Middle-class Catholics in Belgium, the Rhenish bourgeoisie, the northern French bourgeoisie, and the rural bourgeoisie in southwest

Germany represent Catholic groups who lived beyond the ghetto walls.[44] A unique Catholic bourgeois and urban culture was characterized by its cultural habits, particularly in the sphere of learning: reading, writing, library activities, and disputes with the priests over cultural hegemony. The secularization process was the chief basis of their culture, which stood in sharp contrast to the ultramontane milieus which came into being in the cities of Central and Northern Europe in the middle of the nineteenth century. In this Catholic-bourgeois milieu, ultramontane religion became a problematic issue for many members of the bourgeoisie.[45]

The German scholar Thomas Mergel describes a crucial element of the Catholic Rheinish bourgeois culture: it had one leg in the liberal-secular bourgeois world and the other in the Roman Catholic church. This position forced many Catholics during the years of the *Kulturkampf* to choose one of three different worldviews (pro-liberal and radically anti-ultramontane, pro-liberal within the walls of the ultramontane ghetto, or liberal bourgeois) but without entirely abandoning Catholicism. According to Mergel, most bourgeois Catholics in Cologne chose the second worldview, and one can assume that during the years of the *Kulturkampf* the same process took place in other Catholic cities in Europe.[46]

The study of the European Catholic bourgeoisie by means of cultural analysis has increased our understanding of the reasons why class or religion played so important a role in all forms of daily life. Local notables (doctors, high school teachers, judges, etc.) and their families determined the local norms of behavior, values, beliefs, and modes of thought and could even wield an influence over local electoral patterns. Obviously, this stratum was always engaged in a struggle with other groups for local cultural hegemony (and hence for economic or political hegemony). It was often a struggle between the local Catholic bourgeoisie on the one hand and the traditional conservative Catholics or ultramontanes on the other. This was a typical situation in Catholic urban centers mainly after the 1850s.[47]

The Catholic bourgeoisie also found itself engaged in fierce struggles with its Protestant counterparts in mixed communities in Central Europe and the Netherlands.[48] At the local level, in everyday routine, popular Catholic culture deepened the gap between Catholics and Protestants. In southern and western Germany for example, anti-Protestant Catholic cultural sentiments centered on local cultural phenomena such as saints, customs, religious books, almanacs, and penny pamphlets. "For this Catholic audience," argued the American scholar Helmut W. Smith, "the words in bold print evoked a whole series of social, cultural and political associations: all of them negative, all of them directed against Protestants." So, in mixed communities in Central and Northern Europe, the Catholic ghetto and the Catholics who lived on the fringe of it or beyond its walls were dominated mainly by Catholic popular culture, where saints, superstitions, and anti-Protestant hatred played a major role. It was a way of life which stood "in contrast to the Protestant high culture which had become largely synonymous with German national culture."[49]

The Plight of the Catholic Ghetto before World War I

The European *Kulturkampf* served to strengthen the walls of the Catholic ghetto. The political-organizational structure of European Catholicism was built up in the 1870s.[50] The popes, in a number of ordinances issued in Rome from the 1860s to the 1890s, provided the spiritual "cover" for isolationist tendencies. Catholic parties gave political protection. Priests and women provided spiritual protection and moral drive, while the drawing-power necessary to prevent many Catholics from leaving the ghetto was provided by acts of pilgrimage, saints and angels, superstitions, and the newspapers of the Catholic Associations.

Nevertheless, internal changes to European Catholicism at the turn of the century led to a deep crisis. The social composition of the support for political Catholicism in Central Europe altered. The core of its electoral strength was provided by workers and members of the lower middle class. In its leadership, there were fewer and fewer priests and officials of the church and more and more middle-class members wishing to find their place in the modern bourgeois world. Workers, farmers/artisans, and members of the bourgeoisie were the three traditional pillars of political Catholicism. Their interests were increasingly difficult to bring together under one party.[51] In response to these challenges, Catholic parties sought to shed their clerical image and to represent themselves as Catholic, modern "people's parties." The necessity of maneuvering between the demands of the workers, the bourgeoisie, and the farmers somewhat diminished their strength, because there was always a group that was unsatisfied, whose interests were opposed to those of other groups which sought protection in political Catholicism.[52]

There were also other important processes which worked against the church's interests. The process of secularization, which was a major cultural phenomenon in all the European societies of the period, contributed to a weakening of the cultural infrastructure of Catholic communities and of course the church. Social problems, which were of tremendous importance in Western and Central Europe because of the swift transformation from an agrarian society to an industrial one, began to affect the Catholic ghetto as well. The case of the Catholic workers is an illuminating one. Although the Catholic faith with its symbols and institutions was for many workers a place of refuge from the daily vexations of industrial life, the drift of Catholic workers into the ranks of the social democrats and socialist groups was a problem for the church and its organizations. It was not only the attraction of the modern world "outside the walls" which caused the workers to leave the fold. The inadequacy of the ghetto in solving the social problems which arose at the time of industrialization also contributed to this desertion. Masses of Catholic workers, however, sought protection in Catholic associations, many of which combined social activities with charity. Many of them were village people who had moved to the towns as part of the process of internal immigration which took place in Europe in the course of the industrial developments of the second half of the nineteenth century. They became workers in factories, and the fact that they were rural

Catholics raised on ultramontanism, together with their disadvantaged position, drew them to the church, often via its charitable organizations.[53]

The churches (and not only the Catholic church) sought to expand their activities in the cities in view of the mass immigration from the countryside, which increased in intensity towards the end of the century. The Ruhr region in Germany, Lancashire in England, and northern France are good examples of areas where a strong bond was formed between workers and the Catholic church. There were obstacles, however, to the church's capacity to absorb them. The first was its limited material resources, especially after the *Kulturkampf*. The church did not succeed in every city in finding enough priests and in materially supporting the network of voluntary Catholic organizations with whom the workers sought protection. Another obstacle was of an ideological nature. The associations' anti-socialism turned a potential ally into an enemy. Furthermore, many workers were all too conscious of the fact that the leadership of political Catholicism often rested with bourgeois representatives who were primarily concerned with satisfying the interests of the middle and the lower middle classes.

A further difficulty for the church was the increase in hostile acts and discrimination towards Catholics even after various European states had officially abandoned the *Kulturkampf*. There were political, sexual, and class/economic conflicts – both open and hidden – but the most prominent of all was the Protestant–Catholic conflict or (in Catholic states such as France and some southern German states) Ultramontane–Liberal Catholic conflict.[54] This was the longest of the major conflicts in Europe, at least in areas where the two groups lived next to each other. The hostility between the two religions was especially intense and sometimes violent on the local level. This hostility helped to convince many Catholics in rural areas that life outside the walls was extremely dangerous, but, at the same time, the enmity made many wonder whether the ultramontane policies of the village priest and the church authorities were wise. These policies, after all, meant years of uncompromising struggle, and perpetual confrontation, and, worse still, they perpetuated the Catholic position of inferiority.

These problems should not be seen as something separate from the crisis in European societies on the eve of World War I. The cultural pessimism of the *fin de siècle*, so much a consequence of the ambivalence of modernism, formed part of the crisis of the Catholic church and the Catholic societies. The fear of modernism and the apprehension that its achievements might prove to be a fearful double-edged sword also found expression among the European Catholics. What should the direction of the future be: continued isolation in a ghetto or a change of values? An attachment to religious anachronism perpetuating deprivation and backwardness, or "leaping out beyond the walls"? Many Catholics all over Europe were struggling with these questions in one form or another.[55]

NOTES

1 Eric Hobsbawm famously described nineteenth-century Europe as an "Age of Revolution, Capital and Empire." At the same time he totally ignored the role of the churches and especially the Catholic church. See Hobsbawm (1962, 1975a, 1987).

2 Hubert Jedin as the editor of the authorized series *History of the Church* has dedicated three volumes to the nineteenth century, while only two deal with the period between the Reformation and the French Revolution. He justifies his decision by indicating the speed and the extent of the churches' growth. See Jedin (1981: vol. 7, ix). See also volumes 8 and 9 in the same series.

3 Blaschke (2000); Kretschmann and Pahl (2003); Harrington and Smith (1997).

4 Reinhard and Schilling (1995).

5 Reinhard (1989).

6 Chadwick (1981: ch. 1).

7 Thomas (1983: 640, 659).

8 Brockliss (2002).

9 Tackett (1986).

10 Bell (1995).

11 Gibson (1989: 55); see also Desan (1990).

12 Row (2004); Schieder (1987).

13 Chadwick (1981: 536).

14 Jedin (1981: vol. 7, 111–15).

15 Hubner (1954: 80).

16 Schieder (1974).

17 Heilbronner (2000); McLeod (1986).

18 Anderson (1986, 1993).

19 Lamberti (1989).

20 Sperber (1983); Heilbronner (1996).

21 Lannon (1987).

22 Ford (1993); Blackbourn (1991).

23 Jedin (1981: vol. 9, 190–217).

24 Cueva (2004).

25 Schieder (1974); Sperber (1984); Nipperdey (1988).

26 Gibson (1989: 265).

27 Singer (1983); Blaschke (1996); M. L. Anderson (1995).

28 Smith (1981: ch. 5); Ford (1990); Olenhusen (1995); McLeod (1988); Blackbourn (1993).

29 Davidoff and Hall (1987).

30 Mergel (1995).

31 Weiss (1995).

32 Gatz (1990).

33 Blaschke and Kuhlemann (1996).

34 Jedin (1981: vol. 9, 135–44); Obelkevich (1990); Supple (1993).

35 Coleman (1978: 64).

36 Lewis (1978); Wahl (1980); Ford (1990); McMillan (2003); Belchem (2000).

37 Altermatt (1972: 21; 1989).

38 McLeod (1997: 137); Margry and Velde (2004).

39 Wintle (1987).

40 Jedin (1981: vol. 9, 107–18); Lamberti (1989: 40–87).

41 Lewis (1978); Reif (1991).

42 Quinn (1993).

43 McLeod (1997: 20–1); Parry (2004).

44 Tollener (1990); Mergel (1994); Smith (1981); Heilbronner (1996).

45 Schloegl (1995).

46 Mergel (1994: 144).

47 Steinhoff (2002).

48 Anderson (2001).

49 Smith (1994, 1995).

50 Evans (1999); Becker (1984).

51 Evans (1984); Strikwerda (1995).

52 Loth (1991).

53 Sun (1999).

54 Hazaresingh (2004).

55 O'Meara (1991); Graf (2000).

GUIDE TO FURTHER READING

Jedin's *History of the Church* (Vols. 7–9) is still the best major work of scholarship on the Catholic (and Protestant) church in nineteenth-century Europe. McLeod and Scribner's *Christianity and Society in the Modern World* is a major series of book-length historical studies which explore the relationship between Christianity and its social context since the sixteenth century. Whyte's *Catholics in Western Democracies* is one of the best studies on the differences between Catholic societies in continental Europe and the Anglo-Saxon world, although it was published more than twenty years ago. Rémond's *Religion and Society in Modern Europe* studies religious practice and social attitudes across Europe since the French Revolution. Evans's *The Cross and the Ballot* discusses political Catholicism in Europe and stresses mainly the similarities in the activity of Catholic parties in several states. McLeod's *European Religion in the Age of Great Cities* deals mainly with the problems that the Catholic and Protestant churches faced with the growth in the size and number of cities and in the proportion of the population living in urban areas. A new edition of McLeod's *Religion and the People of Western Europe* discusses studies on European Catholicism published since the first edition in 1976. Frank Tallett and Nicholas Atkin have edited and written several studies on the conditions of the Catholics around Europe since the eighteenth century. *Catholicism in Britain and France since 1789* and *Religion, Society and Politics in France since 1789* are very useful collections of essays, as is *Priests, Prelates and People*, where Tallett and Atkin record lines of struggle between church institutions and the people and governments of modern Europe. Clark and Kaiser's *Culture Wars* is a collection of essays on the conflicts between the Catholic church and European (mainly liberal) states in the second half of the nineteenth century.

CHAPTER NINETEEN

Protestantism

ANTHONY J. STEINHOFF

Even before he set out for Lambarene in 1913, Albert Schweitzer had established himself as a major figure within late nineteenth-century Protestantism. Born in 1875, he followed in his father's footsteps and became an ordained minister of the local Lutheran church in 1900. For almost thirteen years he served as vicar in Strasbourg while also teaching at its prestigious university and establishing a reputation as a leading liberal New Testament theologian. A Bach scholar and organist of European renown, Schweitzer also promoted the cause of religious music in his native Alsace, performing with church music societies and giving concerts to subsidize the restoration of historic organs. Then in 1905 he felt the call to serve in Africa, although as a physician rather than as a minister, which prompted him to commence formal medical training. Eight years passed, however, before the theologically conservative Parisian Mission Society finally agreed to accept his services. Only then did Schweitzer begin the work for which he later received international attention.

Undoubtedly, Schweitzer was an extraordinary individual. Nevertheless, his biography speaks to several developments that defined the history of European Protestantism between 1815 and 1914. It was an age of Protestant revival in Europe, which split many churches into evangelical, orthodox, and liberal wings. It compelled hundreds of Protestants to spread the gospel – and notions of European civiliza-

tion – to the corners of the globe. The study of Protestant theology in this period, especially the New Testament, was dominated by German academics. The renewed sense of religious identity also had important consequences for European political and social life. It provoked tensions in church–state relations. It fostered powerful ideas about national belonging. It also generated social conflict, which increasingly found an outlet in politics. Finally, in his ministry and scholarship, Schweitzer – like Protestant clergy and laity throughout the century – struggled with the social and cultural challenges ensuing from religion's encounter with modernity.

This chapter examines the history of European Protestantism during the long nineteenth century from three main angles. It looks first at the changing face of Protestant faith and practice. It then investigates the relationship between Protestantism and politics, both in the sense of church–state relations and the links between Protestantism and nineteenth-century political culture. Finally, it explores the relationship between Protestantism and sociocultural change. As we will see, the landscape of European Protestantism during this period remained highly fractured along national and regional lines. Many of the trends shaping local Protestant life and practice were, however, European in nature. Furthermore, Protestantism remained highly relevant to European social, political, and cultural life after 1815, so much so that we may even label this era a Protestant century.

The Evolution of Protestant Life

Europe's religious landscape changed dramatically between 1800 and 1914. Secularization theory, however, no longer seems a helpful way of making sense of these developments, especially within European Protestantism. Churchmen's jeremiads about falling levels of church attendance in the final third of the century overlooked the reality that the churches were in much better shape in 1900 than in 1800. A European-wide renewal of religious sentiment during the first half of the century contributed substantially to this improvement. It also reflected advances in education, transportation, and communication, which permitted a more thorough degree of Christianization than in centuries past. As the century progressed Protestantism continued to evolve both theologically and organizationally. This led to greater diversity in the public face of Protestantism, while also providing new ways for individuals to fashion their own identities as Protestants.

In 1815 Protestantism remained largely a Northern and Northwest European phenomenon. The Anglican church was established in England, Wales, and Ireland, and large numbers of Protestants also stood outside these churches in nonconformist and dissenting communities. Calvinism held sway in the Netherlands, several of the Swiss cantons, parts of the Prussian Rhineland, and in Scotland, where it was called Presbyterianism. In Scandinavia and much of the German Confederation (Prussia, Hanover, Saxony, Württemberg), the official church was Lutheran. Protestants also formed a significant minority in France (predominantly Calvinist, but Lutheran in eastern France) and as a result of the territorial reorganization of the German lands between 1799 and 1815, in Catholic states like Baden and Bavaria.

As the nineteenth century began, Protestantism's future seemed bleak. Eighteenth-century rationalism had bred skepticism and indifference among the faithful. Rationalist ministers downplayed the importance of the mysterious and the divine. Jesus Christ, for example, was no longer the Son of God, but only an especially moral man. Since services were often little more than arid lectures on morals and ethics, many men and women stayed away from church and chapel. Institutional morale was also low. The Church of England, for example, was plagued with high rates of pluralism and absenteeism; extremes of clerical poverty and wealth went unchallenged. Lastly, from 1789 to 1814, thousands of Protestants on the continent lost access to church or minister.

By the time that the Congress of Vienna convened, however, a religious revival was already underway. This was the Awakening, a movement with roots in German Pietism and British Evangelicalism. Pietists and Evangelicals held that religion was not a matter of the head, but of the heart. Ministers like the Württemberg pastor Ludwig Hofacker (1798–1828) emphasized the need for individuals to develop a personal relationship with Christ, model their lives on Christ's, and undergo conversion. British Evangelicals such as Charles Simeon (1759–1836) encouraged people to read the Bible and spread the good news. Sin and repentance, wonder and grace – these were the themes awakened ministers and lay preachers emphasized. This romantic emphasis on religion as experience and feeling – a deliberate rejection of Enlightenment intellectualism – also characterized the thinking of Friedrich Schleiermacher (1763–1834), whose *Religion: Speeches to Its Cultural Despisers* (1799) and *The Christian Faith* (1821–2) helped revitalize Protestant theological study on the continent.

British Evangelicals played a notable role in spreading this new religious outlook to the continent. They established foreign missions, disseminated religious literature, and founded Bible and missionary societies. An exemplary key here was the Scotsman Robert Haldane. His protégés nourished contacts in Denmark that in 1815 resulted in the creation of the Danish Bible Society. That same year, Haldane traveled to Geneva and Montauban, where his lectures attracted influential men such as Henri Malan and Jean Merle d'Aubingné to the *réveil*.

From Geneva the awakening spread through-out Switzerland and, with Frédéric Monod's aid, into France. Swiss developments also had great influence on the Dutch revivals of the 1810s and 1820s. In comparison to British evangelicalism, Pietism's geographic reach was more limited. Nevertheless, it encouraged an upsurge of religious sentiment throughout the German Confederation. It also influenced revivals in the German-speaking cantons of Switzerland (especially Basel), in Alsace, and in the Scandinavian and Baltic lands.

What is most impressive about the early nineteenth-century Awakening was the enthu-siasm and fervor it unleashed. In areas touched by the revival, the size of congregations swelled. Increased levels of church giving per-mitted the construction of new buildings and the hiring of additional clergy, which profited both rural and urban regions. The Awakening also manifested itself in the establishment of a plethora of charitable and religious societies, many with only loose ties to the state churches. Bible societies from London to Geneva pro-moted the dissemination of accurate, affordable editions of scripture. Missionary societies based in London, Paris, and Basel spawned a network of affiliates that, together, spread the gospel message across the globe. And after 1850, the Inner Mission became a focal point of Pietist efforts in Germany and Scandinavia to combat the social and moral ills of industrial society.

Not everyone was pleased by the Awaken-ing. Initially, Protestant church leaders felt threatened by these spiritual impulses and tried to rein them in. Prussian churchmen clamored for the suppression of Pietist conventicles on noble estates. In 1817 Genevan officials even forbade their ministers from speaking on topics favored by awakened preachers (e.g., Christ's divinity or predestination). There were two causes for the churches' concerns. First, the Awakening directly challenged the validity of rationalist theology, which still dominated most continental church establishments in the first decades of the century. Second, by deempha-sizing the importance of church, sacrament, and formal theological learning, the Awaken-ing's proponents called into question the insti-tutional church's very *raison d'être*. Thus, even as rationalism fell victim to the romantic *Zeit-geist*, official discomfort with the awakening persisted.

By 1830 a second, confessional wave of religious revival was also gathering steam. The confessional Protestants – Calvinist, Lutheran, and Anglican – shared their awakened brethren's desire for spiritual renewal. But their romantic sensitivity ultimately led them back to the confessional era, the sixteenth and seven-teenth centuries, in search of guidance for defining Protestant community and piety. They reasserted the fundamental importance of the church community against the low-church ten-dencies in Evangelicalism and Pietism. Confes-sional Protestants reemphasized the authority of formal statements of faith such as the Augs-burg Confession and the Thirty-Nine Articles. The confessional revival also devoted significant attention to church liturgy, resurrecting the agendas and rituals of the past to foster a warmer climate of worship in the future. Neo-Calvinists, thus, sung from the psalter instead of the hymnal, whereas Lutheran ministers sung prayers in responsorial style with their congregations.

Theology also played a central role in the confessional revivals. Many ministers arrived at their orthodox positions after prolonged study and then took up the pen to defend them. In Germany, many of the most influential cham-pions of the confessional Lutheran cause were professors, notably Ernst Wilhelm Hengstberg (1802–69) of Berlin, who also edited the influ-ential *Evangelische Kirchenzeitung*, and Adolf von Harless (1806–78) at Erlangen. Similarly, the publishing and preaching of Oxford dons such as John Keble (1792–1866), Edward Pusey (1800–82), and John Henry Newman (1801–90) so dominated the Anglican revival that it became most widely known as the Oxford Movement.

The confessional revival had considerable appeal in a Europe that, in the 1830s and 1840s, was still quite traditional. But it also attracted a considerable degree of criticism. Although the Oxford Movement revitalized Anglicanism, its leaders were often accused of trying to lead the church back to Rome. This charge seemed especially accurate after both Newman and William George Ward embraced Roman Catholicism in 1845. Prussia harassed the "old Lutherans" who rejected the united church's liturgy and authority throughout the 1820s and 1830s, moderating its position only when Friedrich Wilhelm IV became king in 1841. Beginning in 1850, orthodox Lutherans in France also badgered church and state to restore the authority of the Augsburg Confession, protesting loudly whenever a "rationalist" or "unionist" Lutheran was appointed to the theological faculty at Strasbourg or to a position of church leadership. Confessional Calvinism was especially unsettling. Confessional concerns helped precipitate the Scottish Disruption of 1842, which produced the Free Church of Scotland. Efforts by the confessional majority to impose doctrinal uniformity at the national synod of 1872 so divided the French Reformed Church that by 1879 the single church existed in name only. In Holland, too, Abraham Kuyper's promotion of neo-Calvinist interests culminated in schism, the *Doleantie* of 1886.

Protestant religious revivals not only resuscitated the sense of religious community, they also diversified it. They presented contrasting and often rival visions of community, pastoral activity, and Protestant identity. In some cases, as in Britain, many of these options found formal expression outside of the establishment. But everywhere competition among evangelicals, confessionals, and liberals continued forth within the state churches. Thus after 1850 most state churches had conservative, orthodox (or confessional), and liberal wings, which continued to compete with each other to define the church and shape its policies. This competition had both positive and negative consequences. In some instances, "spiritual choice" promoted piety and religious commitment, since individuals did not have to content themselves with an outmoded or otherwise unappealing "product." However, the often heated conflicts among religious factions tarnished the churches' public image and caused some people to leave them altogether.

By 1850 Protestant clergy in many parts of Europe had registered the first signs of the phenomenon of *Entkirchlichung* or "unchurching." For a wide variety of reasons, including the lack of churches and ministers, new ideas of masculinity, and a sense of political or personal conflict with the church and its ministers, increasing numbers of Protestants attended services only infrequently, when at all. Down to the end of the century, *Entkirchlichung* tended to affect cities more than rural areas, working-class and educated upper middle-class men more than women, and industrial countries (Germany and Britain) more than less developed states (Norway, Sweden, Denmark).

Yet we should not equate "unchurching" with secularization. First, recent research has shown that the correlation between industrialization, urbanization, and *Entkirchlichung* is weak. In England, for example, a palpable drop in church attendance commenced only in the 1870s, suggesting that religious communities had held their own during the height of urban and industrial growth. Similarly, studies of German Protestantism have demonstrated that in some regions the countryside and not the city had the lowest rates of churchgoing. Second, at the family level, religion was still important. Wives and children continued to attend services even when husbands and fathers did not. Third, although churchgoing declined, rates of receiving religious rites of passage – baptism, marriage, Christian burial – remained strong across Europe. In Germany, church burials became even more common by century's end.[1] Individuals thus still retained important ties to formal religious communities. Fourth and finally, as the nineteenth century advanced, attending services was no longer the only way that one "got religion." One could belong to a religious association or read a religious newspaper. Sunday schools and mandatory religious education programs also exposed youth to Protestant practices and beliefs even if their parents rarely made it to services.

During the second half of the nineteenth century a significant shift in the very tone of Protestant teaching occurred. This also affected how individuals experienced Protestantism. A major figure in this transformation was the German theologian Albert Ritschl (1822–89). Long associated with the University of Göttingen, Ritschl argued that Christ was one's only source for knowing God and that, through Christ, God appears as a God of love. Moreover, Ritschl contended that Christians were called to contribute to the realization of God's kingdom through moral action in the present life. Such ideas had important practical consequences. They encouraged a warmer sense of church community. They prompted ministers to preach more about God's love and grace than about sin and damnation. Above all, Ritschl and his students laid the groundwork for a new theology of social action, which bore fruit in increased Protestant engagement with contemporary social concerns after 1850. This refashioning of Protestantism as "compassionate Christianity" was not limited to Germany. British evangelicals, too, increasingly downplayed the importance of the theme of eternal punishment, arguing that incarnation and not atonement was the centerpiece of Christian doctrine.

Liberal Protestantism also enjoyed a new lease on life in the decades after 1850. Despite the challenges of the Awakening, confessional revivals, and general conservative drift, the rationalist spirit had not expired. Prominent churchmen and laity still championed the cause of free religious enquiry and rejected the idea of binding dogmatic authority. In particular, liberals asserted that the understanding of faith and the organization of religious community had to evolve if religion and church were to remain relevant. Not all liberals drew the same conclusions from these principles. In some quarters we find a return to positions that could have been expressed during the Enlightenment. In 1860 a group of British liberals (the "Broad Church School") published the collection *Essays and Reviews*, which questioned the veracity of miracles, criticized the science of the Bible, and rejected the idea of inspired scripture. In France, liberals like Edmond Scherer and Timothée Colani (co-founder of the *Revue de Strasbourg*) presented Christianity principally as an ethical, instead of a divine, force. By contrast, men like Daniel Schenkel, founder of the German *Protestantenverein* (an organization that defended liberal religious interests), held firmly to belief in God and Christ but downplayed the importance of dogma. Still other liberals hoped to make the church more inclusive, by reaching out to the faithfuls' hearts as well as their minds. Herein lay the explanation for the renewed appreciation for liturgy and religious music in places like Alsace after 1870.

These trends in nineteenth-century Protestantism had one further consequence that deserves attention. Europe's Protestants created organizations to pursue a variety of religious and charitable goals that transcended national borders. They also established European confederations of regional and national societies. These developments had their roots in the Awakening, notably the establishment of Bible and missionary societies in much of Northern Europe during the first half of the century. By the 1840s organizations with an explicitly international character also materialized. The first was the Evangelical Alliance, founded by evangelical Protestants across Europe in 1846. National young men's associations reorganized themselves in 1856 into the World's Alliance of Young Men's Christian Associations (YMCA). Liberals, too, gathered at international conferences such as the World Congress for Free Christianity and Religious Progress. Finally, at the turn of the century, efforts to coordinate foreign missionary work resulted in the convening of the World Missionary Conference at Edinburgh in 1910, followed shortly thereafter by the launching of the *International Review of Missions* in 1912.

Protestantism and European Politics

The contention that the nineteenth century was a secular age has rested not only on a sense of declining religiosity, but also on the perception that religion – and Protestantism in particular – had lost its political and social significance. Here too recent research has exposed shortcomings in the secularization paradigm. Although a certain secularization of the state and politics occurred after 1815, religion continued to shape meaningfully the evolution of European political life. Religion remained a political matter, first, because it was a state controlled monopoly. States maintained established Protestant churches. They decided what other religious groups could enjoy a legal existence. Second, religious groups entered the political arena to pursue their goals and defend their interests. This activity helped keep religious questions in the public eye while also helping transform and modernize European politics. Lastly, Protestantism influenced the articulation of nationalist ideologies after 1850, an event of enormous consequence both at home and abroad.

Without question, demographic and social developments across Western and Northern Europe reduced organized religion's political importance between 1815 and 1914. To this extent, we can talk about a secularization of the state and politics. The spread of religious pluralism prompted states to endorse religious toleration and adopt a neutral stance towards members of recognized religious communities, thereby diminishing the privileges of established churches. National and local governments also came to define many functions previously performed primarily by churches, including education, public welfare, and the registration of vital statistics, as state responsibilities. Politicians on the left even sought to eliminate all state support for organized religion, although they achieved this only in France with the 1905 Law of Separation.

Although the churches' political influence waned after 1815, Europe's states remained heavily engaged in religious affairs, above all in Protestant countries. For the most part, Protestant churches were either part of the state itself or closely tied to it. In England, Prussia, and Sweden the head of state was simultaneously head of the established Protestant church. In 1817 King Friedrich Wilhelm III of Prussia even used his authority to unite the Lutheran and Reformed churches in the old Prussian provinces. State authorities set church law and established regulations governing church administration. Parliament fulfilled this function in Sweden and England, as did Hamburg's and Bremen's city councils. In Prussia and German states with Catholic ruling houses, special ministerial authorities assumed these prerogatives. A similar arrangement existed in France, where the bureau for "non-Catholic" affairs within the interior ministry watched over the two recognized Protestant churches. Well into the final decades of the century, clergymen also doubled as local administrators. They supervised public instruction and sat on local charity boards. In addition, states devoted significant portions of their annual budgets to maintaining the churches, paying the salaries of church officials and subsidizing the costs of church building and pastoral training.

For much of the century European governments also carefully controlled the right to worship publicly, largely by limiting the right to associate. Until mid-century, continental governments generally outlawed religious assembly outside of the established churches. Conventicles were legally outlawed in Scandinavia. The French Civil Code permitted informal religious meetings with the consent of local police authorities, which was rarely granted. Only in Britain were circumstances different. There Protestants had won the right of religious dissent with the 1689 Law of Toleration. But even these Protestants faced a wide array of civil disabilities during much of the nineteenth century. In short, religious toleration and parity existed only for the recognized and established churches' members.

With the loosening of restrictions on the right to associate beginning in the late 1840s, a more general sense of religious toleration become commonplace in Western Europe. It led to the creation of free churches in Switzerland, France, and Britain. The freer climate also promoted the growth of religious sects after 1848. From England came the Methodists, the Irvingians, and the Salvation Army. Swedenborgianism hailed from Sweden and the Nazarene movement from Hungary. American Baptist, Seventh Day Adventist, and Christian Science missionaries all attracted converts throughout Europe. Nevertheless, legally speaking, all of these religious groups remained but public associations, subject to varying degrees of police supervision and oversight. They enjoyed none of the financial, legal, or symbolic privileges associated with the recognized and established churches. Only in France and in Switzerland were all Protestant communities eventually placed on a roughly equal legal footing, thanks to the French Law of Separation and the disestablishment of the Swiss Reformed churches between 1907 and 1909.

The state's involvement in ecclesiastical affairs was not the only reason for religion's ongoing political importance after 1815. Churches and religious groups also increasingly used the political process for their own purposes. In part this was necessary because the state now monopolized the legal use of force. The conflicts between and within religious groups arising from the century's religious revivals were now channeled through the courts and, eventually, party politics. Thus, the state arbitrated between competing denominational interests. In Scotland, thus, disputes over the rights of proprietors to appoint Presbyterian ministers during the 1830s and 1840s routinely ended up in civil courts. Nevertheless, high levels of dissatisfaction with the state's resolution of these and similar cases still led 474 ministers to leave the established church in 1843, the so-called Disruption. State authorities in France and throughout the Rhine Valley also had to settle disagreements between Catholics and Protestants over issues ranging from the religious education of children from mixed marriages to the use of religious buildings and church bells.

Religious groups also mobilized politically to advocate their own interests, which had far-reaching consequences for European politics. Protestants played a central role in the extension of religious toleration and the emergence of a "neutral" state, as the British example demonstrates clearly. In 1828, dissenters and nonconformists finally managed to rescind the Test and Corporation acts, which had kept them out of municipal office and parliament. This then led to the political emancipation of Catholics in 1829 and Jews in 1858. Bitter disputes between nonconformists and Anglicans over marriage procedures resulted in parliament's 1836 decision not only to recognize marriages in licensed nonconformist places of worship, but also to authorize fully civil marriage. In Switzerland, Germany, and especially in France, Protestants also promoted a more secular state to protect civil society, as they viewed it, from ultramontane Roman Catholicism's anti-liberal and anti-modern aims. These attitudes contributed directly to the outbreak of the Swiss *Sonderbund* war of the 1840s as well as the German *Kulturkampf* of the 1860s and 1870s. Similarly, from 1814 to 1879 French Protestants routinely supported republican and anti-clerical positions in order to protect their very right to exist. And with the definitive establishment of the Third Republic

in 1879, Protestant politicians like Henri Buisson and William-Henry Waddington sought to secure religious liberty by promoting a thoroughly laicized French state.

For the most part, Protestants pursued these political goals through established means. British nonconformists, for example, overwhelmingly supported the Whig (and later Liberal) Party, sharing a common desire to weaken the Anglican establishment, which steadfastly opposed political reform. In Germany and in Switzerland it was precisely this perception that the main political parties represented Protestant interests that compelled Catholics to create their own political organizations after 1860. Only in Holland, however, did an explicitly Protestant political party emerge, the fruit of Abraham Kuyper's neo-Calvinist campaign against the liberal coalition in the Dutch government and Reformed church. Protestants also formed associations with clear political agendas after 1860. The most prominent examples were German: the *Protestantenverein* and the *Evangelischer Bund* (Protestant Alliance), which Willibald Beyschlag founded in 1886 to unite German Protestants and ward off Catholicism's growing political influence.[2]

Changes in the institutional organization of Protestantism also promoted Western European democratization. Over the course of the century, the organs of church government (themselves public institutions) became more representative and inclusive. In some instances, as in the revival of the Anglican Convocation in 1854, the goal was to broaden clerical participation in setting church policy. The dominant trend, however, was increased lay influence over church affairs, by establishing and revitalizing synods (especially in Germany and Scandinavia), regular church conferences (as in the Anglican diocesan conferences), and parish assemblies. Admittedly, the number of people who held positions in these bodies was limited. But they were selected by elections that were often conducted under fairly liberal franchises. For example, the French Decree-Law of 1852 allowed all Protestant men over the age of 30 to vote and hold an ecclesiastical office. After 1850 local organs of church government also enjoyed greater measures of self-government. Parish councils acquired greater autonomy in the administration of property and endowments. They also attained a voice in the choice of ministers, that is, state officials. In fact, by the end of our period, formal appointment of ministers by parishes was widespread in Switzerland and France. It existed *de facto* in much of Germany, the Netherlands, and Norway.

Recent research has called attention to one final area in which Protestantism exercised a significant influence on European politics after 1815: nationalism and national identity. Protestant countries increasingly framed the definition of national community in religious terms. In Denmark, the theologian Nicolai Grundtvig explicitly joined the cause of national with religious revival. The "fathers" of modern German nationalism – Herder, Schleiermacher, Arndt, and Jahn – were overwhelmingly Protestants with theological training. They portrayed the creation of a German nation as part of a divine plan. They also equated the essence of "Germanness" with Protestantism, noting that Luther had created the modern German language and freed Germany from the chains of papism. German nationalists framed the wars of national unification in confessional terms – Protestant Germany (Prussia) versus Catholic Austria and France – and construed Prussia's victories as signs of divine favor. Throughout the imperial period this self-perception as a Protestant state was constantly reinforced, not only through negative actions such as Bismarck's attack on the Catholic church (the *Kulturkampf*), but also through the use of Protestant churches for important state ceremonies and Emperor William II's prominent involvement in the Prussian United church's affairs.

Protestantism played a similar role in the definition of British national identity. At the beginning of the nineteenth century this association received its clearest expression in the Anglican and, in Scotland, Presbyterian establishments. Although nonconformists and dissenters successfully challenged the privileges attendant to these arrangements after 1828, they too viewed Britain as a fundamentally Protestant nation. Anglican and dissenter alike viewed Britain's political freedom, material prosperity, and cultural accomplishments as the fruits of her Protestant faith. Like its German counterpart, British nationalist rhetoric depended on a negative portrayal of Catholics and Catholicism. British discourse, however, focused more on Catholicism's moral and religious weaknesses than its potential political strength. By the end of the century even this language became less pronounced, because British Catholics enjoyed a considerable degree of toleration and equality. Moreover, Britain's main continental rival, France, no longer identified itself as a Catholic nation.

Interestingly, this emphasis on the religious dimension of national identity emerged most forcefully only in European states with considerable non-Protestant minorities (i.e., Britain, Germany, and Switzerland), where it played a central role in domestic political life. This is one of the main elements in the German historian Olaf Blaschke's depiction of the nineteenth century as a "second confessional age."[3] Where the state's religious identity was less at issue, as in Scandinavia, the Protestant dimension of national identity received much less attention. The situation in the Netherlands was more unusual. Although the Dutch were predominantly Calvinist, the growing influence of the liberal party after 1848 resulted in the deemphasizing of the state's confessional character. Orthodox Calvinists campaigned to reverse this trend after 1870, but they never succeeded in making the idea of an explicitly Calvinist Dutch identity the dominant component of Dutch nationalist discourse.

The self-identification of Britain and Germany as Protestant nations had consequences far beyond the realm of domestic politics. It motivated and legitimated imperialist activity across the globe, especially in the decades after 1870. The British had long regarded their empire as a gift from God for the purpose of propagating Christianity. Many of the great British colonial explorers, including David Livingstone, General George Gordon, and T. E. Lawrence, were devout Protestants. They saw themselves not as mere adventurers, but as missionaries spreading the gospel and humanity among the heathen. Moreover, Britain's gains in the late-century wave of colonial expansion seemed to confirm her status as a chosen nation, a fact increasingly celebrated by politicians, Anglican churchmen, and the public at large. Protestantism, colonialism, and national pride were also closely linked in imperial Germany. One of the most vocal imperialists in the Bismarckian era was Friedrich Fabri, a Protestant minister, church politician, and longtime director of Germany's largest Protestant mission, the Rhenish Missionary Society of Barmen. A co-founder of the German Colonial Association, Fabri advocated using Protestant missions to advance German national and colonial interests abroad. But even nominally non-confessional interest groups like the Colonial Association and its successor, the Pan-German League, justified Germany's colonial aspirations by invoking the confessionalized language of German nationalism.

Indeed, the nineteenth century was not only the great age of the Protestant mission but also the era of Protestantism's worldwide expansion. The missionary societies based in London, Paris, and Basel became truly international institutions, recruiting personnel and receiving financial support from across Europe and, eventually, even overseas. But all of Protestant Europe participated actively in the spread of the faith. In 1842 the Norwegian Missionary Society sent its first missionary to the Zulus in Natal; later on it established outposts in Madagascar and in China. The Danish Missionary Society, founded in 1821, was active in Greenland. It also cooperated with the Basel Mission on Africa's Gold Coast and with the Leipzig Mission in southern India. The Paris Missionary Society sent individuals like Albert Schweitzer not only into the depths of Africa, but also into China and Southeast Asia. Between 1815 and 1914, 15 separate Dutch organizations arose to plant the faith in the East Indies.

Protestant missions did more than spread the good news and civilization to Asia and Africa. They provided spiritual care for thousands of European Protestants engaged in international trade, diplomacy, and colonial administration in Bombay, Constantinople, and Shanghai. Organizations like the Evangelical Lutheran Mission of Leipzig and the British Church Missionary Society also tended to the needs of the millions of Protestants who emigrated from Europe after 1815. They sent clergymen and hymnals to Lutherans of German and Scandinavian origin in the United States and Canada. They helped Anglicans who arrived in Canada, Australia, New Zealand, and South Africa finance church construction and train future ministers. Indeed, because of these developments, by 1914 European Protestantism acquired a presence in the world of which it could only have dreamed in 1815.

Society and Culture

In the *Communist Manifesto* Karl Marx and Friedrich Engels described the nineteenth century as a bourgeois age. Capitalism became the dominant form of economic production. Middle-class attitudes determined the basic character of political, social, and cultural life. "Law, morality, religion," they argued, "are to [the proletarian] so many bourgeois prejudices, behind which lurk in ambush just as many bourgeois interests."[4] Peculiar as it may seem at first glance, this quotation is a useful starting place for reconsidering Protestantism's social and cultural impact in nineteenth-century Europe. In spirit, if not always in practice, Protestantism was the religion most directly linked to this middle class. It shaped bourgeois ideas about gender and gender roles. It influenced bourgeois attitudes towards the working classes and, critically, middle-class appreciation of industrialization's and urbanization's social consequences. Even the century's renewed interest in science and the search for truth had a distinctly Protestant foundation. Nevertheless, the association of Protestantism with the middle class remained problematic. Although middle-class men and women maintained that religion was important for social order, they themselves were responsible for some of the century's strongest challenges to Protestantism's social and cultural hegemony.

One of the most significant areas where Protestantism exercised a strong influence on middle-class attitudes was gender. The bourgeois ideal of masculinity, which emphasized self-control, rationality, industry, and thrift, grew directly out of the Protestant conviction that Christians were individually responsible for the salvation of their own souls. The Evangelical and Pietist revivals reinforced this association by emphasizing the importance of personal conversion for salvation. Protestant ideals also informed the trend towards a strict division between the home and the workplace, as Max Weber argued in *The Protestant Ethic and the Spirit of Capitalism*. This rationalization of business, in turn, gave new meaning to the age-old notion of "separate spheres." Thus, Alfred Lord Tennyson writes in 1847:

Man for the field and women for the hearth:
Man for the sword and for the needle she:
Man with the head and women with the heart:
Man to command and woman to obey;
All else confusion.
(The Princess: A Medley, 5.437–41)

The renewal of religious fervor in the nineteenth century further promoted the construction of these spheres by giving it biblical sanction. Evangelicals noted that God created Eve to aid Adam, to be his helpmate. Conservative groups recalled that St. Paul not only counseled women to obey their husbands but also decreed that women should be silent in the church, which they also interpreted as a prohibition against women exercising public authority.

Bourgeois notions of gender identity also shaped men and women's responses to organized religion. The central dilemma here was the emotional, sentimental, and intuitive dimension of nineteenth-century religiosity. Middle-class Protestant men increasingly had problems reconciling this understanding of religion with the rational and individualistic aspects of bourgeois masculinity. Studying theology provided one way to do this. Serving as a "soldier for Christ" in a foreign mission or in the armed forces was another. But the prevailing tendency, especially in Germany, was for Protestant men to stay home, while their wives and children attended services. Indeed, after 1815, active piety became closely associated with femininity and the cult of domesticity. This reflected, in part, the popular assumption that women were naturally predisposed to religion. But this "feminization of religion" also ensued from the division of labor implied by the ideal of separate spheres. Men encouraged piety in women because the latter were responsible for the moral upbringing of children. Likewise, women became increasingly active in the panoply of Protestant religious, social, and charitable associations because they saw them as the logical extension of their maternal responsibilities. Paradoxically, though, as deaconesses, charity workers, and Sunday school teachers, Protestant women also found a way to escape the confines of domesticity and engage themselves in the public sphere.

By its very connection to the self-image of the middle class, Protestantism was implicated in the development of class identities in nineteenth-century Europe. Nonetheless, the connection between Protestantism and social class remains complex. First, only a small fraction of Europe's Protestants were bourgeois, thus the very designation of Protestantism as a "bourgeois" religion is problematic. Second, working-class dissatisfaction with Protestantism stemmed to a large degree from the perception (and reality) that the official churches and their ministers served the interests of the political and social elites. But the very nature of official religion in urban parishes also pushed workers away. The scheduling of services, the moral and religious outlook of sermons, notions of "proper church attire," and pew rents all posed significant cultural and social impediments to working-class involvement in organized religion.[5] Recent research suggests, however, that if German workers were quicker to leave the church than their English counterparts, sizable numbers of working-class men and women in both countries still considered themselves active Protestants, often as members of sectarian communities.[6] Third, the increased recruitment of ministers from lower-class backgrounds across Europe estranged members of the educated, liberal bourgeoisie from the churches. Once again, the gap was as much cultural as it was social. These clergymen, it was felt, were incapable of discussing religion and spirituality in ways that appealed to the educated mind. Such sentiment provided further incentive for urban middle-class men and, to a lesser degree, women to seek their religious bread in places outside of the parish church.

Although the bourgeoisie's ties to organized religion ebbed as the century progressed, its social vision remained deeply indebted to Protestant values. Institutionally, Europe's Protestant churches were as slow as their Catholic counterparts to respond to the declining economic and social situation of a substantial portion of their flock. Herbert Spencer, for example, contrasted the "Church-of-England priests who think their duty consists in performing ceremonies, ... offering prayers, and uttering such injunctions as do not offend the influential numbers of their flocks" with individual ministers like his uncle, Thomas Spencer, "who held that it [was] within his function to expose political injustices and insist on equitable laws."[7] The Prussian Superior Church Council (*Oberkirchenrat*) expressly warned its ministers against getting involved in politics, even to promote social justice. In a 1879 circular, it repeated that the Christian way to improve society was not through political action, but rather through the "still, self-denying work of love towards the lost and the suffering."[8]

The *Oberkirchenrat*'s views were emblematic of Protestant thinking on the "social question," especially during the first two-thirds of the century. Protestant elites inside and outside the official churches regarded the problems of industrial and urban society as fundamentally moral in nature. Poverty was a consequence of personal failing, a sign of sin, which individuals could remove through work and self-betterment. Of course, more fortunate Christians were obligated to help the poor and suffering through loving acts of charity. Nevertheless, the primary responsibility for change lay with the individual sinner. Moreover, because the world was the product of a divine plan, it would be impious for humans to contemplate transforming society or interfering with the God-given economic laws that structured it.

This moral framing of the social question provided a powerful argument against state intervention in the workplace and state-sponsored social reform. This pleased laissez-faire industrialists and political conservatives, who wished to limit the size of the state and its budget. It also appealed to religious conserva-

tives, such as the preeminent Scots Presbyterian Thomas Chalmers, who insisted on the priority of private efforts. Indeed, the middle classes relied to a considerable degree on the churches and on voluntary associations with roots in the Protestant milieu to respond to the challenges posed by industrialization and urbanization. This also meant that private social initiatives tended to promote religion and middle-class views of social respectability in equal measure. For instance, Hinrich Wichern's *Raues Haus* in Hamburg aided wayward and orphaned youth. But it also worked to transform these boys and girls into useful members of church and society by giving them religious instruction and vocational training. Organizations like the City Mission, first established in Glasgow by David Nasmith in the 1820s, similarly sought to evangelize while attending to the urban poor's material needs.

A sense of Christian duty also compelled many Protestants to advocate a wide range of social reforms after 1815, which led them too into the political arena. British Protestants actively campaigned for prison reform and the abolition of slavery (achieved in 1834). Drawing on a paternalistic conception of the state, some Protestant leaders even promoted state regulation of the workplace. Members of the evangelical Clapham group thus supported the 1818 Factory Act. Later, the earl of Shaftesbury proved an outstanding champion of parliamentary legislation that improved working conditions for men, women, and children. In Germany, Otto von Bismarck's social legislation of the 1880s arose largely out of a desire to undercut socialism's appeal by adopting part of its program. But it also represented a conviction that a Christian state had a responsibility to assist the poor.

The rising challenge of socialism and organized labor, in fact, encouraged the ruling elites to advance not only a Christian view of the state, but also of society. In Victorian Britain and Wilhelmine Germany, Protestant groups campaigned tirelessly and with considerable success to impose middle-class standards of moral behavior on the rest of society. They mobilized for temperance and the limitation of work on Sundays. They fought against indecent literature and legal prostitution. However,

Protestant efforts to form a specifically Christian response to socialism had mixed results. The British Christian Socialist movement lasted barely a decade. Similarly, the German Christian Socialist Labor Party, founded by Prussian court preacher Adolf Stöcker in 1878, quickly foundered due to lack of support from either workers or church leaders.

Stöcker achieved greater success with the Protestant Social Congress, which first met in 1890. He hoped that this gathering of socially minded Christians would draw up a program of political action against the social democrats, a vision in keeping with the *Oberkirchenrat*'s recent decision to encourage Prussian ministers to involve themselves in the affairs of the working class. Instead, the Congress adopted a more neutral mission: to study current social conditions and recommend reforms in keeping with the gospel's moral and religious demands. In this form, the Congress became a prominent and influential forum for discussing contemporary social questions in Germany, attracting the participation of leading academics and social theorists such as Friedrich Naumann, Martin Rade, Ernst Troeltsch, and Max Weber.

These remarks about social policy serve as a useful reminder of Protestantism's continual contributions to the evolution of European intellectual and cultural life after 1815. The literature on European secularization has tended to emphasize the growing distance between faith and science. But theirs was as much a reciprocal as it was an antagonistic relationship.[9] Modern science worked from the Protestant belief in an individual Christian's right, even duty, to engage in intellectual enquiry and judgment. The notion that truth existed and that humans could discern at least a part of it, which provided such a powerful stimulus to scientific investigation, also had deep roots in Protestant tradition. Quite ironically, Protestantism helped produce knowledge that raised serious doubts about Christian theology and the very existence of God, ranging from new geological hypotheses about the earth's origins to biological evolution and germ theory. Men of science like Charles Darwin and Rudolf Virchow came to share Søren Kierkegaard's radical view that, ultimately, there was no intellectual proof of God. But instead of accepting the Danish theologian's conclusion that one accept God on faith alone, an increasing number of European scientists and intellectuals repudiated Christianity altogether, swelling the ranks of religion's "cultural despisers."

Nevertheless, nineteenth-century European Protestantism remained a devoted champion of learning and the open exchange of ideas. Protestants led the campaigns to improve public schooling for the youth of Western Europe. In Britain, groups like the National Society for the Education of the Poor and the National School Association sought to broaden the network of primary schools, while also breaking the Church of England's educational monopoly. In France, François Guizot drafted the landmark 1833 law on public education, which obligated communes to maintain primary and secondary schools. Prominent French Calvinists such as Samuel Vincent and Athanase Coquerel led the mid-century movement to establish a national system of public and compulsory education. Europe's Protestant communities also preserved close ties to the universities, for this was where most ministers received their formal training. To get around the Oxbridge monopoly on college degrees, British nonconformists established their own university at London in 1836; a move that Dutch neo-Calvinists duplicated by founding the Free University of Amsterdam in 1879. The close connections between Protestantism and European cultural modernity received their most infamous acknowledgment in Pope Pius IX's 1864 *Syllabus of Errors*. A major consequence of the encyclical's condemnations, however, was to increase the anti-Catholic bias in European higher education. Protestant faculty members felt that Catholics were incapable of conducting objective research and refused to hire them. When governments did try to appoint Catholic professors, this aroused great controversy, as evidenced by the nomination of Martin Spahn to a professorship at the University of Strasbourg in 1901.

In contrast to the Catholic church's conviction that modern learning could not benefit Christianity, rational and liberal Protestants in particular endeavored to employ new scholarly methods to develop a more contemporary and intellectually rigorous understanding of faith and community. The centerpiece of this endeavor was historical biblical criticism, which attracted attention far beyond its intellectual home in the German university. Theologians like Paul Anton de Lagarde (1827–91) of Göttingen and Lobegott Constantin von Tischendorf (1815–74) of Leipzig used modern linguistic methods to create more accurate versions of the Old and New Testaments. Much more provocative were David Friedrich Strauss and Ferdinand Christian Bauer, the founders of the so-called Tübingen school, whose Hegelian-inspired studies of the gospels and the Pauline epistles raised profound questions about both scripture's status as inspired text and the very origins of Christianity. These writings aroused a great deal of anger and protest. The University of Geneva even found itself forced to rescind its offer of a chair in theology to Strauss in 1839. Ultimately, however, conservative and liberal theologians responded to Bauer's and Strauss's challenges by pursuing their own scholarly enquiries, which by 1914 revolutionized prevailing wisdom on Jesus' ministry and the nature of Christian community. And it is on the basis of such findings that liberal Protestants, including German *Kulturprotestanten* like Martin Rade and Albert Schweitzer, as well as Broad Church Anglicans like Charles Kingsley and Benjamin Jowett, aimed to create a living church for modern times.[10]

The political, social, and cultural events that transformed Europe after 1815 had lasting consequences for organized religion. Considerable numbers of men and women reduced their attachments to organized religion; many severed them altogether. Christian churches no longer functioned as privileged centers of sociability. They lost influence over the course of European politics. Finally, science and socialism competed successfully with organized Christianity's truth claims, thereby diminishing its attractiveness as an all-embracing *Weltanschauung*. Nevertheless, as scholars have shown renewed interest in the nineteenth century's religious dimension, secularization theory seems to raise more questions than it answers. It fails to account for the enormous vitality of nineteenth-century European Protestantism:

the revivals of the first half of the century, the wave of church building, the renewed interest in liturgy, hymnody, and theology, and the impressive extension of European Protestantism throughout the globe. Moreover, secularization theory overlooks the strength of Protestant influences on modern nationalism and the rise of state sponsored social policy. On June 8, 1900 Friedrich Naumann told his Strasbourg audience during a lecture on Christianity during the nineteenth century: "Protestantism has become a [world] religion. As an overall historical force, and not [merely] as a church, it stands more dazzling at the end of the century than one could ever have expected."[11] Indeed, if ever there was a "Protestant century," it was the nineteenth.

NOTES

1   Reeken (1999: 331–4).
2   Smith (1995).
3   Blaschke (2000).
4   Marx and Engels (1975: 494–5).
5   Hempton (1994).
6   Brown (2001: 149–56); McLeod (1996: 5–28).
7   Vidler (1974: 90).
8   Besier (1994: 107).
9   Chadwick (1975).
10   Hübinger (1994).
11   Naumann (1900: 93).

GUIDE TO FURTHER READING

There is no recent detailed survey of nineteenth-century European Protestantism. However, two older works remain excellent starting points: Latourette's *Christianity in a Revolutionary Age* and Vidler's *Church in an Age of Revolution*. More recently, the initial chapters of McLeod's *Religion and the People of Western Europe* provide a useful overview of general trends. Brown's *Death of Christian Britain* is now essential reading for British developments, to be supplemented with Parsons' *Religion in Victorian Britain*, Wolffe's *God and Greater Britain*, and Brown's *Religion and Society in Scotland since 1707*.

There are few quality studies of continental Protestantism in English. Hope's *German and Scandinavian Protestantism 1700–1918* gives useful insight into ecclesiastical and theological developments in these countries, but is highly idiosyncratic and difficult to read. Wintle's *Pillars of Piety* provides a nice sketch of trends in the Netherlands. For those with reading knowledge of French or German, the following titles will be of interest: Encrevé, *Les Protestants en France de 1800 à nos jours*; Besier, *Religion Nation Kultur*; Nowak, *Geschichte des Christentums in Deutsch-land*; Pfister, *Kirchengeschichte der Schweitz*; and Lindhart, *Kirchengeschichte Skandinaviens*.

McLeod's *Secularization in Western Europe 1848–1914* brings the arguments over secularization theory up to date. Smith's *German Nationalism and Religious Conflict* and Van der Veer and Lehmann's *Nation and Religion* both usefully probe the relationship between religion and national identity.

CHAPTER TWENTY

Orthodoxy

SHANE P. O'ROURKE

The Orthodox world at the beginning of the nineteenth century was largely divided between two great empires: the Ottoman and the Russian. The history of that world is intimately linked with the history of these two empires. However, the Ottoman and Russian empires were not the only determinants of Orthodox history. The legacy of a third, long-defunct empire weighed heavily on the Orthodox world. The Byzantine Empire had been synonymous with Orthodoxy for over 1,000 years since the conversion of Constantine. Its imprint on the faith could not be erased even half a millennium after the destruction of the empire by Sultan Mehmet the Conqueror. Orthodoxy was steeped in the traditions and memories of the Byzantine Empire, but it was not alone in this. Even the secular powers were tied to the memory of Byzantium. In their different ways, the Ottoman sultans and the Russian tsars saw themselves as the successors to the Byzantine emperors and to the universal empire of Byzantium. The tale of the Orthodox world in the nineteenth century could be seen as the tale of three empires. Without an understanding of the different inheritances bequeathed by these empires, the history of Orthodoxy in the nineteenth century would be impossible to comprehend. But the context of the nineteenth century was worlds removed from that of the fourth or fifteenth centuries. New political ideologies, rapid economic and social change, and shifts in the international balance of power drastically altered the world in which Orthodoxy was situated.

The trajectories of the two halves of the Orthodox world diverged sharply in the nineteenth century. In the Ottoman Empire the history of Orthodoxy was dominated by the break up of the empire in Europe into national units. As part of this process, national churches appeared which repudiated the jurisdiction of the Patriarch of Constantinople and strove to establish autocephalous or autonomous churches. This created a bitter and damaging split within the church. Simultaneously, the new national churches had to negotiate relations with new national elites whose understanding of the correct form of church–state relations drew on the ideas of the Reformation and the French Revolution. Neither source had much in common with Orthodox tradition.

In Russia, on the other hand, the Orthodox church and religion enjoyed a preeminent position which was accompanied by almost complete subservience to the imperial state. In the nineteenth century both sides found the relationship less than ideal, but attempts to reform it proved frustratingly difficult. And in addition to dealing with the age-old problem of its relationship to the secular power, the church was forced to confront a series of new challenges. Among educated society and large sections of the ruling elite it was despised for its subservience and its lack of relevance to the modern world. Nor could the church take refuge in the piety of the peasantry, who were the overwhelming majority of the population in the nineteenth century. Everyone acknowledged the peasant's belief in the supernatural, but many educated observers argued that there was little that was specifically Orthodox or even Christian about these beliefs. No less disturbing was the tendency for peasants who were committed to the Christian faith to find their home in one of the numerous dissenting sects which continued to thrive despite official disapproval and persecution. The church was caught between an obdurate and unyielding state and a faithful who, many suspected, held to a very different version of Orthodoxy than that prescribed by the church.

The Byzantine Tradition

The traditions of the Orthodox church differed in significant ways from those of the Western churches. The conversion of Constantine to Christianity and his choice of Constantinople as the new imperial capital placed the secular and ecclesiastical powers in the closest possible proximity. The intense reverence for Constantine (equal to the apostles in the Orthodox tradition) transferred to the office of emperor in general. The church accepted the right of the emperors to interfere in the life of the church because his authority as emperor straddled both the secular and religious realms by right. The emperor was recognized as the head of the church as well as the state. This relationship was formalized in the doctrine of symphony in which church and state existed in mutual respect and interdependence. Of course, the emperor also possessed a monopoly of all the earthly instruments of power, which made it extremely difficult for the church to resist the will of the emperor. The great struggles of the medieval popes for supremacy over the secular powers in the West and later the Reformation had no counterpart in the Byzantine tradition. Later on, the Russian tsars, believing themselves the successors of the Byzantine emperors, would distort the doctrine of symphony to treat the church in a way that no Byzantine emperor would have contemplated.

The structure of the Orthodox church diverged from the universalism of the church of Rome and the national churches of the post-Reformation era. The Christian church, which in the early Byzantine era was still united, was divided into patriarchies based on the ancient sees of Rome, Jerusalem, Antioch, Alexandria, and Constantinople. Later on Serbia, Bulgaria, and Russia all achieved patriarchal status. Authority within the church was dispersed through the consiliar system. Each patriarchy was independent or autocephalous and none could make a decision binding on the others unless it was through a universal church council. Beneath the autocephalous churches were autonomous ones who were under the jurisdiction of one of the patriarchs but possessed a large measure of internal freedom. The Russian church was in this position until it achieved patriarchal status in 1488. The new national churches of the nineteenth century would have to come to terms with new secular authorities whose ideas on the proper relationship between church and state came from traditions wholly alien to the Byzantine world. Similarly, the issues of autocephaly and autonomy would be bitterly contested between the new national churches and the Patriarchate of Constantinople.

The Orthodox World Under the Ottoman Empire

When the armies of Sultan Mehmet the Conqueror breached the walls of Constantinople on May 29, 1453 and burst into the imperial city, slaying the last Emperor Constantine XII, the Orthodox world suffered an unparalleled catastrophe. The emperors and the empire vanished into history, but the church continued, although now wholly dependent on the goodwill of a Moslem ruler. By the standards of the contemporary Christian world, Mehmet was extraordinarily generous to the church. In the Islamic tradition as people of the book, like the Jews, Christians were recognized as a legitimate community entitled to practice their faith, albeit with certain restrictions. The Ottoman Empire classified people according to religion rather than ethnicity, race, or language. Accordingly, all the Orthodox within the empire were grouped into one nation or *millet*. The Patriarch of Constantinople became the head of the Christian *millet* responsible before the sultan for the behavior of his flock. Each *millet* regulated its internal life and enjoyed the protection of the sultan as long as taxes were paid and there was no disloyalty to the empire. Paradoxically, in some ways the Patriarch of Constantinople found his power considerably enhanced from Byzantine times. The formerly independent patriarchies of Bulgaria and Serbia were eventually absorbed back into the Patriarchate of Constantinople, since under the Ottoman dispensation they were Orthodox Christians and part of the Orthodox *millet*. A large degree of secular authority was passed to the church – something it had never possessed under the Byzantine Empire. Although nothing could compensate for the catastrophe of the fall of the Byzantine Empire, many in the Orthodox world recognized the possibilities of continued existence within the Ottoman Empire, regarding that as infinitely preferable to liberation at the hands of the West, for which the price would have been unification of the Roman and Orthodox worlds on Roman terms.

From the fifteenth to the nineteenth centuries the settlement of Mehmet the Conqueror provided the basic framework for church–state relations. His successors by and large respected the institutional position of the church within the empire even if they felt free to interfere in matters of personnel or organization. The Patriarch of Constantinople became a political player in the Ottoman system and had to play by the rules of that game, especially bribery and intrigue. Gaining the office of patriarch, and still more keeping it, necessitated the payment of considerable bribes to Ottoman officials. Understandably, these officials had a direct financial interest in the rapid turnover of the patriarchal office. Inevitably, an aura of corruption began to surround the patriarch, particularly as the faithful were forced to pick up the bill for the bribes through church taxes.

The domination of the church by the wealthy Greek families living alongside the patriarch in the Phanar district of Constantinople only deepened the sense of corruption. These Phanariot families alone had the wealth to pay the requisite bribes to Ottoman officials which gave them control over all the major offices in the church, both ecclesiastical and lay. The domination of these families extended into the Slavic areas of the empire. They ensured that hierarchies of the Slavic churches were filled with their appointees, who were always Greek. Since the appointments had been secured with liberal bribes the first task of the new bishop was to recoup his losses. Heavy taxes on the Slavic peasantry did little to enhance the prestige of the church or hierarchy, particularly as they were levied by Greek prelates.

Almost to the end of the eighteenth century the Orthodox community survived and sometimes thrived under Ottoman rule. Both the patriarch and faithful within the empire accepted Ottoman rule because it was not without benefits and the power of the empire doomed any challenge to the status quo and brought harsh retribution within its wake. Whatever difficulties the Orthodox faced in their day-to-day relations as a second-class community in a Moslem empire, the lack of any alternative had forced them to make the best that they possibly could out of the situation. The patriarch and his community had found for themselves a niche within the empire that, if not ideal, was at least familiar and reasonably predictable. The French Revolution and changes in the international balance of power brought the long period of mutual acceptance and harmony to an end.

The Disintegration of the Orthodox Oecumene

Throughout the eighteenth century the loss of energy and purpose within the Ottoman Empire accelerated. Corruption became more pervasive and consequently the condition of the Christian peasantry in the Balkans (the main tax base of the empire) deteriorated rapidly. Heavy, arbitrary taxation accompanied by copious amounts of violence undermined the stability and security that had been one of the great achievements of the Ottoman Empire in the Balkans. At the same time, the intellectual ferment and the destabilization of the international system set off by the French Revolution and Napoleonic Wars gave hope to the small groups of nationalists who dreamed of freeing their countries from the Ottoman yoke. A ailing empire, new ideologies, and a rapidly changing international balance of power foreshadowed turbulent times for the Orthodox church.

Nationalist revolutions broke out at regular intervals in the empire's European dominions from the start of the century onwards. Beginning with Serbia in 1806 and followed in Greece, Romania, and Bulgaria, the whole course of the nineteenth century was dominated by the struggle for independence. For the Orthodox church in the Balkans the nationalist revolutions were a volatile mixture of danger, opportunity, and ambiguity. For all that the empire had accepted Christians as a *millet* with rights as well as obligations, they were never allowed to forget that they had second-class status. The chance to be free of this burden and their Moslem rulers was a tempting proposition, particularly as the benefits brought by Ottoman rule receded into the past. Bitter experience, however, had taught the church that the empire was a formidable opponent who always took savage reprisals against rebellious territories regardless of individual guilt or innocence. Even in the event that revolt was successful, it would mean a great leap into the unknown for the church and its faithful. What relationship could it construct with these men from the cities or diaspora communities who proclaimed themselves leaders of the struggle for independence and who spoke about nations and constitutions? Independence would also threaten the disintegration of the Orthodox oecumene under the leadership of the Patriarch of Constantinople. Whatever grievances the Balkan churches had against the Greek domination of the church, hardly any wanted the break up of the oecumene. Yet how could relationships be maintained with a patriarch seated at the very heart of the empire against which the rebellions were directed?

If the churches in the Balkans found themselves in a dilemma over the nationalist revolutions, the position of the patriarch and church in Constantinople was precarious in the extreme. As head of the Orthodox *millet*, he was responsible before the sultan for the behavior and loyalty of his community. He would be called to account for the rebellions against the empire. The patriarch had always been vulnerable to intrigue and well placed bribes among Ottoman officials, but the nationalist rebellions exposed him to much more acute danger. The paranoia and hatred that gripped the court as it struggled to suppress the rebellions found an easy target for revenge in the person of the patriarch. However loudly the patriarch protested his loyalty to the empire and anathematized the rebels, the conviction that he was in league with them and the foreign Christian powers who supported them was widely shared among the sultan and his court. Even if the patriarch's protestations of loyalty were not futile, they inevitably caused great offense among his flock in the Balkans, who felt betrayed by his words and deeds. The nationalist revolutions were beginning to rip apart the whole Orthodox oecumene so laboriously maintained since Ottoman conquest.

The nationalist revolutions were initially the work of urban intellectuals inspired by the example of the French Revolution and by the Romantic nationalism of the early nineteenth century. Their problem was that most of the population of the nation in whose name they claimed to act remained blissfully ignorant of their Greek, Serbian, or Bulgarian identities. The identity of the population of the Balkans which was overwhelmingly rural was expressed in religious terms. Any notion of "native land" was restricted to the village or district and certainly did not extend to the abstract notion of the "nation" as expounded by the revolutionaries. If the revolutionaries were to have any chance of success, they had to find some way of mobilizing the rural population against their Ottoman masters. Only the church possessed the institutional means and the idiom to accomplish this.

Although the first rebellion against Ottoman power began in 1806 in Serbia, it was the Greek Revolution which began in 1821 that initiated the profound crisis that would grip the Orthodox world for the rest of the nineteenth century. The war for independence was launched by a group of Greek émigrés based on Russian territory. After some early successes, the Ottomans quickly crushed the movement. Much more serious was the revolt that broke out in the Peloponnese at the same time. Unlike the émigré-inspired insurgency, the one in the Peloponnese was a mass one. And it was the church that was the critical institution. It was the only institution that reached into every village, however remote. The priest was a figure of authority and respect within the village and one of its natural leaders. Once the hierarchy had decided to support the revolt, the whole of the church in the Peloponnese swung behind it. Critically, the revolt was cast in terms of freedom from the infidel oppressor and his hated tax gatherers, which spoke directly to peasant interests and understanding. Having made its decision, the rebellion had to succeed as far as the church was concerned. It could expect little mercy from the Ottomans in the event that it failed. Years of bitter struggle followed in which church property and buildings were destroyed and many priests killed. Once again the Ottomans showed themselves formidable opponents and would have crushed the insurgency but for the intervention of the Great Powers, who destroyed the Turkish fleet at Navarino Bay. At the end of the war, a new state had emerged. Its people were impoverished, its economy in ruins, and its church severely weakened. At its head was a new elite filled with grandiose ambitions to build a nation and unite all those Greeks still outside its borders.

If the war was costly for the church in Greece, it brought unmitigated woe to the church in Constantinople. In the recent past patriarchs had roundly condemned nationalist movements against the empire as a sin against the lawfully and divinely constituted authority of the sultan. While the agitation remained little more than isolated incidents, the Ottomans were satisfied with the declarations of loyalty made by the patriarchs. The Greek revolt, however, ripped a gaping hole in the empire; worse, its example threatened to unravel the entire empire in the Balkans. Patriarch Gregorious V had little sympathy for the revolt, but before he had a chance to publicly condemn it, he was arrested. On April 22, 1821 the patriarch, two metropolitans, and twelve bishops were hanged at the gates of his palace. It was an act of brutality that appalled Europe and damaged the Ottoman cause even among the conservative powers who had little sympathy for the revolt.

The execution of the patriarch and bishops was only the beginning of the church's woes. Gregory's low standing among the Greeks for his opposition to the rebellion was offset by his martyr's end. His successor, however, immediately condemned the revolt and anathematized the rebels. Relations between the church in Greece and Constantinople irreparably broke down, creating a *de facto* schism. The extreme precariousness of the patriarch's position in Constantinople made it impossible for him to recognize the independence of the Greek church in the early 1820s. Yet it was not only fear of the Turks that restrained him. The patriarch was loath to abandon his authority over the Greek church, since it would represent a major diminution of his authority and prestige, to say nothing of the loss of revenues. This pattern was repeated as more of the European parts of the Ottoman Empire won their independence. In Bulgaria the great mobilizing issue of the national movement had been the domination of the Bulgarian church by the Phanariots. When the Bulgarian church proclaimed itself autocephalous (with the sultan's approval) the Patriarch of Constantinople anathematized all those involved and proclaimed the Bulgarian church schismatic. Relations were not restored until 1945.

The New National Churches

Separated by force and circumstances from the Patriarchate of Constantinople and the sultan, the Orthodox churches found themselves in unfamiliar territory. Deprived of their religious and secular heads in short order, past experience and tradition offered little guidance for the future. The rupture of relations with Constantinople provide a *de facto* solution to the problem of religious authority. The new churches all repudiated the authority of Constantinople and proclaimed themselves independent. *De facto* solutions on their own were not sufficient. None of the new churches had the power to consecrate bishops without the approval of Constantinople. In the short term, this did not matter very much, but as the disputes rumbled on decade after decade it would become an acute issue. In the end all the churches restored relations with Constantinople, bringing an end to the very acrimonious and divisive schisms within the church.

If matters were necessarily fraught between the national churches and the patriarch, at least the churches could expect a better understanding with the new national regimes. The churches had been vital to the success of the nationalist revolts and were the single most potent source of national identity. This combined with their nationwide institutional network seemingly placed them in a very strong position with the emerging states. Yet, in all of the states, the churches found themselves very much the junior, subordinate partner. The new national elites looked not to the Byzantine Empire for their model of church–state relations but to post-Reformation national churches of Western Europe or more radically the Civil Constitution of the Clergy produced during the French Revolution. Sections of the new elites had a thinly disguised hostility to the church, believing it to be part of the problem of backwardness that they were so desperate to overcome. All of them believed that the undoubted power and influence of the church over the people should be harnessed and directed by the state.

The rules governing church–state relations – whether the Constitution of the Clergy in Greece in 1832, or the Romanian and Bulgarian equivalents – were largely dictated by the state and imposed on the churches. All of them gave extensive power to the new states to interfere in the running of the church. Clergy became state employees and the appointment of bishops was subject to state approval. Boards were installed to run the church with the decisive voice always belonging to the state. Monasteries were regarded as a luxury that the new states could ill afford. Many were closed or amalgamated and their lands confiscated. Very rapidly the churches found themselves stripped of all autonomy *vis-à-vis* the new states. This was not a reversion to Byzantine tradition in which both church and state had shared the same conception of a harmonious polity sharing spheres of influence, but a one sided domination of the ecclesiastical sphere by the secular. The Ottoman sultan and even the Patriarch of Constantinople had shown themselves far more respectful of church autonomy that the new states.

The single Orthodox oecumene that had been created by the Ottoman conquest disintegrated during the wars of national liberation in the Balkans. By the end of the nineteenth century the oecumene had divided into new national churches, inward looking and forgetful of the wider Orthodox community. The Patriarchate of Constantinople had shrunk to the remaining Greek population of the Ottoman Empire and would fall to numerical insignificance as a result of the disastrous Greek–Turkish war of 1922, when most of the Greek population left. With the break up of the Ottoman Empire in the Balkans it was probably inevitable that the Orthodox oecumene would also fall apart. Yet the extraordinary bitterness of the process was not inevitable. Even allowing for the acute difficulties and dangers surrounding the patriarchal church, it could have shown more flexibility and generosity. The habits of domination formed over the preceding four centuries were too deeply rooted to allow for a graceful surrender of power. The Bulgarian case in particular threw into sharp relief the stubbornness and rigidity of the patriarchal response, which could not be blamed on the Turks. The loss of universalism and its replacement with national churches removed one more restraint on the barbarism unleashed by the nationalist genie in the nineteenth century, which found its fullest expression in the twentieth.

The Orthodox Church in Russia

The entwining of religious and political authority in Muscovy was even more tightly accomplished than in Byzantium. The Russians had received their Christianity from the Byzantine Empire in 988 when Prince Vladimir of Kiev converted. The conversion of Kievan Rus to Orthodoxy was one of the greatest achievements of the empire and an event of unparalleled importance in Russian history. The particular qualities of Byzantine Christianity would reverberate in Russia for centuries after the empire itself had disappeared.

The Kievan Rus received from the Byzantines an extremely sophisticated form of Christianity which had centuries of learned disputation, philosophical discussion, and practical experience. It had been produced by a state that saw itself as the heir to the whole classical tradition and was the most highly developed polity in Europe, if not the world. Consequently, there was a widely held belief that the form of Christianity which had been brought to the Rus was perfect. The Russian translation of Orthodoxy, *pravoslavie*, literally means "right praising," which gives a sense of the importance the Russians attached to the exact form of Christianity which they inherited from Byzantium. The duty laid on the Rus was to preserve their faith in its pristine form and wait for the Second Coming. Any attempt to reform or change the faith in the meantime could only be diabolically inspired. This was to have grave consequences for Christianity in Russia later on.

The second great legacy bequeathed to Russia from the Byzantines was the conception of state power, particularly the interweaving of secular and religious authority. The standing of the emperor within the church provided a model for the Russian grand princes. Of course, while an emperor still existed in Constantinople, no Russian grand prince could claim an equal authority with the Byzantine emperor. But once the empire had fallen, the Muscovite grand prince began to see himself as the heir to the Byzantine emperors and their authority. Ivan III married Zoe Paleologue, the niece of the last Byzantine emperor, and so established a dynastic link with the last Byzantine dynasty. Tentatively at first, but with increasing confidence, the Muscovite grand princes adopted the title of tsar. Ivan the Terrible was crowned tsar in 1547, the first Russian prince to officially lay claim to the mantle of the emperor. Ivan's coronation completed the transformation of the Russian ruler from one Christian prince among many to the successor of Constantine.

But the Russian conception of the doctrine of symphony was far more rough hewn than the Byzantine. Instead of symphony between church and state, there was an unambiguous subordination of the former to the latter. In Byzantium, despite the emperor's position as head of the church and his possession of earthly powers, in most cases he recognized a distinction between what was God's and what was Caesar's. No such inhibitions existed in Muscovy. The tsar was head of the church in the same way he was head of the state: an unlimited, autocratic ruler responsible only to God for his actions. For the church as an institution it was extremely difficult to conceive of opposing the tsar, let alone actually doing so. The church felt besieged on all sides, with only the tsar standing between it and extinction at the hands of the heretical Catholics to the west or the infidel Moslems to the south and east. The habit of abject submission to the will of the tsar continued century after century down to the 1917 revolution. Individuals and communities would oppose very violently what they considered to be violations of the faith and traditions, but the church as an institution never did.

These two elements of the Byzantine legacy, the belief in the perfection of the Orthodox faith and the unlimited authority of the tsar, collided thunderously in the mid-seventeenth century. Patriarch Nikon reformed the liturgy and some of the ritual of church services to bring the Russian church back into line with the practice of the rest of the Orthodox world. These reforms struck at the heart of many believers' understanding of their faith. If it was perfect why did it need to be reformed? The answer was clear. The reforms were a sign that the time of the Antichrist was at hand. The Orthodox state of Muscovy had now gone the same way as Rome and Byzantium.

The church split between those who accepted the reforms and those who refused. The latter became known as Old Believers, or less charitably as schismatics. Many communities chose to immolate themselves in fiery holocausts rather than succumb to the temptation of accepting the reforms and thereby damming themselves. Others sought safety in flight in the endless frontier regions. The schism did incalculable harm to the church in the short and the long term, dividing the Russian church to the present day. Although the state's enthusiasm for persecution had waned by the nineteenth century, it still viewed Old Believers with suspicion and distrust. This distrust was fully reciprocated by Old Believers, who continued to regard church and state as heretical even if in not quite such apocalyptical terms as earlier.

The church had little time to absorb the shocks administered to it by Patriarch Nikon before it was subjected to a ruthless reorganization by Peter the Great. Peter's determination to mobilize all the human and institutional resources of Muscovy in his efforts to turn it into a great power embraced the church as much as any secular institution. Peter, for all his dislike of Muscovite ritual and his scandalous parodies of it, was committed to Orthodoxy and the church. He saw no contradiction in this and the unrelenting subordination of the church to his aims. When the position of patriarch fell vacant Peter did not appoint another one, thereby depriving the church of a leader and figurehead. Instead, a council, dominated by bureaucrats, replaced the patriarch. Many monasteries were closed and monks whom Peter regarded as surplus were drafted into the army. The church meekly accepted this wholesale attack on its institutional autonomy. Weakened by the schism and psychologically incapable of offering resistance to the wishes of the tsar, the church found itself reduced to a department of state run by bureaucrats. Catherine the Great deprived the church of any financial independence when she secularized church lands, turning the clergy into civil servants – and very poor ones at that.

The fortunes of the church at the start of the nineteenth century were at a low ebb with little prospect of improvement in sight. The clergy had become a closed caste deeply divided within itself and cut off from the rest of Russian society. The parish clergy (or White clergy as they were known) were married and each generation of sons followed in their fathers' footprints. The monastic clergy (or Black clergy) were unmarried and were the only clergy eligible to become hierarchs. Between the two sections of the clergy there was little understanding and much animosity. The nineteenth century, particularly the second half, would demand from the church exceptional flexibility and creative thinking. It was very poorly equipped to do either.

The first half of the nineteenth century brought no respite to the church from the state's consuming desire to make its control even more pervasive. While little was done in this regard during the reign of Alexander I, his brother Nicholas I was determined to regularize and systematize the effective but rather quirky control over the church exercised by the state. Nicholas had an obsessive passion for order, regulation, and discipline. The few remaining areas of autonomy left to the church hierarchy over personnel and the management of their dioceses were removed. The bishops who sat on the Holy Synod were even more marginalized by the lay members, especially the procurator, who in line with prevailing philosophy of Nikolaevan Russia exercised autocratic power over his constituency. Nicholas's aim – as with all his reforms – was to perfect the administrative apparatus in order to impose his vision of a disciplined, obedient, and submissive society.

Unfortunately for Nicholas, his reforms far from rejuvenating or equipping the church to carry out its mission, further stifled and restricted the church's activity. The centralization of decision making in Nicholas's Russia did not lead to the more efficient dispatch of business, but to ever greater backlogs even in the most mundane matters. Nicholas's mania for control certainly prevented any unwanted initiative or unauthorized actions by the church, but it produced not a disciplined, well run administrative organization but only institutional paralysis which grew decade after decade.

The church's problems evident at the beginning of the century multiplied through Nicholas's reign. The financial crisis gripping the church was as effective in paralyzing activity as Nicholas's system of control. The isolation of the church from all sections of society continued. Even Nicholas recognized that his system was failing and the church needed reform. Secret commissions were established to investigate the problem and propose possible solutions. Yet like all the commissions established by Nicholas to suggest solutions to the chronic problems of the empire, they came up against Nicholas's obsessive desire to centralize all decision making in his own person. Independence, creativity, and spontaneity differed little from anarchy in Nicholas's mind. Not surprisingly, nothing changed while Nicholas lived. Defeat in the Crimean War and the accession of a new tsar, Alexander II, provide the impetus for the reform of the whole of Russian society, including the church.

Although the church was not the highest priority of the government, it was important. Alexander and his small group of active reformers hoped to enlist the church in its efforts to raise the moral, educational, and patriotic level of the people, especially the peasantry. Instead of an exclusive concentration on ritual and ceremony, the government hoped that the clergy would adopt a more pastoral role, actively intervening in the lives of parishioners to help in the process of transforming them from serfs into citizens. The government wanted the clergy to raise the moral level of the peasants and make them aware of their new obligations and duties. Such aims proved very difficult to achieve in practice. The clergy and the peasantry for different reasons did not share the government's vision of the new order. Nor did the government have any money to fund any reforms. The treasury was bankrupt and as far as the government was concerned the church had to find the money itself. Of course, having stripped the church of most of its assets in the eighteenth century, the church likewise was in no position to fund any reform effort. Lack of money and radically different visions of what the role of the church should be by the government on the one hand and the clergy and faithful on the other did not leave much room for optimism.

After years of negotiating, commissions, and discussions with little direct result, the government suddenly announced a series of reforms. The hereditary nature of the clergy was abolished, allowing for free entry and exit from the caste. Provision was made for the involvement of parishioners in the running of the local church. In the end, however, the state drew back from releasing the church from its control. No autonomy was conceded to the church at the highest level. The tradition of seeing the church as an arm of the bureaucracy was too deeply rooted within the governing elite to allow them to surrender control over the church. Yet as long as the government insisted on treating the church in this manner, the church had little hope of fulfilling the role the government assigned to it in the new order.

The nineteenth-century clergy were ill-equipped to become the new, dynamic pastors envisioned by the government. The crippling problems of the clergy, particularly the parish clergy, remained the same under Alexander as they had under Nicholas: poverty, isolation, thwarted expectations. Not surprisingly, the White clergy (nearly all of whom were married with families) resented their limited opportunities. No less resented was their deeply unenviable position among their parishioners. Unlike the Catholic or Protestant clergy in the West, the priest had little respect from the faithful. Educated Russians often despised the lowly parish priest, who they regarded as peddling superstition and magic to a gullible peasantry. Peasants valued the office of the priest highly, particularly the performance of the rituals of baptism, marriage, and the last rites. This respect did not automatically transfer to the person holding the office, who had to work very hard to be accepted by his parishioners.

The desperate financial position of the parish priest compounded his humiliation. The priest's basic means of subsistence was a plot of land which he was forced to farm himself. Manual labor in the fields was the mark of a serf and did little for a priest's prestige. The incompetence of the priest as a farmer was proverbial, further undermining respect for him. The priest's income from farming was supplemented by charging his parishioners for carrying out the function of his office, particularly baptisms, marriages, and funerals. Haggling with peasants over the price of the great rites of passage demeaned the priest even more. Peasants deeply resented what they saw as the grasping, mercenary nature of the priest. They had ample opportunity to take revenge on him. After the harvest, for example, it was traditional for the priest to make the rounds of the village in order to receive from every household a sack of grain. The price for this was the insistence of each household that the priest drink a stiff shot of vodka with the family. After 20 or 30 houses, the condition of the priest can be imagined.

The morale of the parish clergy was not surprisingly very low. Many of those who arrived to take up their office full of enthusiasm for their calling were sooner or later ground down by their dismal circumstances. It was widely noted that far from raising the moral level of the peasantry the priest soon sank to the level of his parishioners. Peasants did not take kindly to having their way of life reformed and could make life very uncomfortable for a zealous priest who sought to impose a version of orthodoxy other than the peasants' own. Nor could the priest look to his superiors for a sympathetic hearing. The bishops ruled their clergy with iron discipline. Most of the parish clergy felt that the bishops had little understanding of their plight and even less interest. Priests who complained were liable to be labeled trouble-makers and could be removed from their parishes and sent to some of the remoter reaches of the empire.

Family life brought its own problems peculiar to the clergy. The priest was burdened with having a peasant's income but much higher expectations. Education in the seminary for his sons was necessary, but expensive. As the nineteenth century wore on, it was increasingly necessary to provide an education for his daughter if he wanted to attract a suitable husband for her. The wellbeing and happiness of his daughter was not the only consideration at stake. In the absence of any welfare system, the only barrier between the priest and destitution in his old age was the parish church. He passed his office on to his son-in-law on condition that he would support the aged priest and his family. The main criteria for the selection of a parish priest thus became a willingness to support the previous incumbent in his old age. Once free entry and exit were allowed from the clerical estate, there was an immediate exodus of young men seeking secular careers, creating a shortage of priests and throwing into jeopardy the precarious welfare system of the older generation. More than a few priests' sons found a new career in the revolutionary movement.

Of course, not all priests or even a majority turned into alcoholics. There were any number of men who struggled against their conditions and overcame them to provide the peasantry with deeply respected and beloved pastors. Probably the attachment of the peasantry to the clergy and the church has been underestimated despite all the problems that existed between

them. The fierce, desperate courage with which peasants defended their priests and churches against overwhelming odds during collectivization in the 1930s suggests that the estrangement of the priests from their parishioners was less than many had supposed.

By a long distance the peasantry was the largest group of orthodox believers in the nineteenth century, as they had been in previous centuries. Before the middle of the nineteenth century very little was known about popular beliefs. As long as peasants were not openly schismatic, both church and state tended to leave the peasantry alone. When popular religion became a subject of academic enquiry it appeared to show 900 years of Christianity had made remarkably little impact on peasant beliefs or practices. Beneath the thinnest Christian veneer lurked a teeming universe of pagan gods, spirits, goblins, witches, and wizards. It seemed that the Christian God and saints had been effortlessly absorbed into the preexisting belief system, leaving it essentially intact. Peasant religion was widely, and negatively, characterized as *dvoeverie*, literally "dual faith," signifying the mixture of Christian and pagan elements. Researchers were shocked to find peasants who were ignorant of the most basic tenets of the Christian faith, who could not recite even the Our Father, let alone possessed any understanding of doctrine or the Bible. Most researchers concluded that the peasantry saw Orthodoxy as a form of magic which was a necessary and useful tool in fighting off the numerous malevolent spirits that assaulted the peasantry throughout their lives. This ruthlessly pragmatic attitude to religion was devoid of any real spirituality.

It is hard to ignore the weight of evidence accumulated to support this representation of the peasantry. Yet, equally, it should not be taken at face value. Measuring the internal level of anyone's faith is extremely difficult and even more so for people separated from the observer by a cultural chasm. Most peasants left no account of their beliefs and those who did record them were not peasants. The hostility many of the intelligentsia had to the church not surprisingly found its way into their observations, which confirmed their own views of the degenerate and corrupt nature of the church.

This does not mean that what was recorded was wrong, but only that caution is necessary in its interpretation. Popular religion in Russia does not seem very different from popular religion elsewhere in Europe. *Dvoeverie*, with its implication of an intact pagan belief system, is misleading. Syncretism of popular beliefs and Christianity would be a fairer term. For there is plenty evidence of deep spiritual commitment by peasants as in any other group. They seemed to respond to good priests and were not indifferent to his qualities. Orthodoxy remained the religion of the majority of the Russian people and its roots among them were very deep.

One religious force undiminished in its appeal in the nineteenth century was sectarianism. The name implies a unity and coherence that did not in fact exist. Old Belief was continually fragmenting and generating new sects. Yet its overall appeal continued to grow in the nineteenth century despite continued hostility from church and state. Old Believers ranged from the vastly wealthy Moscow merchants, to the followers of the self-flagellists, to the self-castrators. In between lay communities of old believers keeping a low profile, but tenaciously holding their beliefs and their hostility to the official church. The variety of sects and the commitment of their supporters to them in spite of constant official disapproval and intermittent persecution is also testimony to the continued appeal of Orthodoxy, even if not in the form prescribed by the church.

Conclusion

The Orthodox oecumene in the nineteenth century was facing a new world where the certainties of the previous centuries no longer applied. The old dispensation in either the Ottoman or tsarist empires might not have been comfortable or ideal, but it was at least familiar and reasonably predictable. That familiarity and predictability was shattered in the nineteenth century in both parts of the Orthodox oecumene. The Balkan states began their long and ultimately successful struggle for independence from the Ottoman Empire. New national churches emerged out of the wreckage of the empire and the loss of authority of the patriarchal church in Constantinople. In Russia

the church struggled half heartedly to break loose from the suffocating embrace of the state, yet feared to rely on its own inner strength. The state toyed with various ideas to make the church more responsive to the needs of a modern state, but refused to allow the church the independence it needed. The acute problems of the church and its believers remained unresolved and undiminished. In the twentieth century, the Orthodox church would face problems of a much greater magnitude as it contended with much more powerful and overtly hostile states. Yet despite its manifest problems in the Balkans and Russia, the Orthodox church had survived as an independent branch of Christianity, surviving not just the three empires, but also the far more unpleasant regimes of the twentieth century.

GUIDE TO FURTHER READING

Knowledge of the world of Orthodoxy in the nineteenth century (and most other centuries for that matter) in the West is remarkable chiefly for its absence. Seventy years of communism in Russia and forty in Eastern Europe did little to advance understanding. Political instability and impoverishment since the end of communist rule have not helped either. The best place to begin is undoubtedly Obolensky's *The Byzantine Commonwealth*. The story is carried on admirably in Runciman's *History of the Great Church*. There is nothing comparable for the later period. Information on the church and religion is mostly to be found in the various surveys listed in the bibliography. A useful exception is Frazee's *The Orthodox Church and Independent Greece*. The situation does not seem likely to improve in the near future.

In Russia things are better. A new generation of scholars is adding greatly to our knowledge. A good introduction to the history of Orthodoxy in Russia is to be found in Pipes's *Russia Under the Old Regime*. An older if still useful account is Miliukov's *Outlines of Russian Culture*. By far the most important work on the church in the nineteenth century is Freeze's *Parish Clergy in Nineteenth Century Russia*. Belliustin's *Description of the Parish Clergy in Rural Russia* is a moving account of the difficulties of the life of the parish priest written by a dissident priest. Kizenko's biography of *Father John of Kronstadt* shows the reservoir of popular support the Orthodox church was still capable of mobilizing at the end of the nineteenth century. Ryan's *Bathhouse at Midnight* is an encyclopedic work on popular beliefs from the eleventh to the twentieth centuries. Shevzov's *Russian Orthodoxy on the Eve of Revolution* is arguably the most important book on Russian Orthodoxy for twenty years.

CHAPTER TWENTY-ONE

The Jews: A European Minority

DAVID RECHTER

The conceit of the "long nineteenth century" sits well with the trajectory of European Jewish history. It was the French Revolution that first emancipated the Jews, opening up for them the possibilities of participating in the brave new world of modern Europe, and it was World War I that brought down the multinational empires in which the great majority of Jews lived, changing at a stroke the structures that had shaped Jewish society. The Jews were an archetypal European minority – everywhere a minority and nowhere a majority – and diversity is at the heart of their story. It will become clear, however, that there is no single story, no master narrative that can comfortably incorporate the bewildering variety that is a defining characteristic of the Jewish experience in nineteenth-century Europe. There is no European Jewry, but rather many European Jewries.

Even if we take diversity and difference as a given, we can nonetheless find threads that connect the experience of the Jews across political and cultural borders. It is necessary to steer a course between, on the one hand, the wilds of a postmodernist fragmentation that denies the very existence of what I have just called the "Jewish experience" and, on the other, an older ethnocentric historiographical dispensation that viewed Jewish history as a unitary field and accordingly minimized the very substantial differences between Jewish societies in various parts of Europe. Despite the myriad ways in which Jews conceived of themselves and

were conceptualized by others, there were still some identifiable common experiences – for example, the push towards integration into the surrounding society and the encounter with antisemitism – that helped to define and shape European Jews and their history.

Jewish history is embedded in a number of contexts. The history of the Jews of Lwów/L'viv/Lemberg, for example, is partly Galician, partly Habsburg Austrian, partly Polish, partly Ukrainian, partly Soviet, while always Jewish and always local. For Eastern and Central Europe, such an example is entirely typical. But even for Western European Jews, the local, regional, national, and international levels must always be borne in mind. The Dreyfus Affair was undoubtedly of the greatest importance for French Jews and for France, yet it takes on a different complexion – and assumes a broader significance – when set beside the emergence in the preceding two decades of political and racial antisemitism in Germany and Austria, and the massive outbreak of anti-Jewish pogroms in the Tsarist Empire in 1881/82. There is certainly a pan-European component to the history of the Jewish minority, but these broader resonances grow out of local circumstances.

In capsule form, a standard rendering of the course of European Jewish history in the post-Enlightenment period revolves around the twin poles of emancipation and assimilation, and proceeds along a loosely delineated East/West axis that divides the premodern from the modern, the unemancipated from the emancipated, the unassimilated from the assimilated. The demands and opportunities of modernity fractured a stable and coherent European Jewish community into a kaleidoscope of national, religious, cultural, and social identities. Modernity and identity – elusive ideas at the best of times – are the conceptual keys to this longstanding and still influential paradigm of modern European Jewish history. It remains a useful guide to the broadest parameters of the story, highlighting the remarkable transformation of Jewish society that accompanied the achievement – and the aspiration to achieve – emancipation, along with its hoped-for byproduct, acculturation or integration (now regarded as more flexible and appropriate terms than assimilation in conveying the manifold ways in which Jews adapted to the societies around them). Emancipation plus acculturation equals modernity: here was an equation that represented the surest road out of the ghetto to a normal existence. The holy trinity – a most un-Jewish notion, to be sure – of emancipation, acculturation, and modernity retains a privileged position in the historiography of modern European Jewry, but has been substantially modified in recent decades in a number of important respects.

Diversity and difference are increasingly emphasized. Emancipation, for example, is rarely seen nowadays as a uniform process working its way across Central and Western Europe. Instead, we find close attention paid to the specifics of each case: revolutionary France with its quick and bold emancipatory declaration; the protracted struggle of German Jewry for civic equality; the strange non-event of British Jewish emancipation. The very idea of emancipation has been subject to scrutiny, its content and meaning one thing in the Russian Empire and something radically different in Habsburg Trieste or Victorian London. So, too, emancipation's concomitant, Jewish modernity, has been thoroughly examined. Modernity, like most broad historical terms, is elusive of definition, but most historians are willing to at least temporarily set aside their doubts and proceed on the assumption that they are able to recognize it when they see it.

Modernization often functions as a catch-all phrase, a useful shorthand to convey the transformative effects on European societies (and their Jews) of forces such as the Enlightenment, capitalism, and the rise of centralized authority and the nation-state. Industrialization, urbanization, secularization, increasing religious tolerance, social and economic mobility – all were part of the package of modernity and all were of tremendous importance for the status and role of Jews in Europe. The many and various ways in which European Jews became modern are now a staple of historical discourse in this subject. This was far from a trouble-free ascent into the promised land of the modern; rather, it was an obstacle-strewn journey that saw both great success and great failure.

Emancipation and modernity are by no means a spent force in historiographical terms, but there has been a degree of decoupling and decentering of these ideas, a consequence of the exponential increase of research in recent decades into new geographic and conceptual areas. Emancipation no longer necessarily equals modernity, nor is modernity a guarantee of emancipation. For example, Sephardi Jews, descendants of the expulsions and migrations from the Iberian peninsula that began in the late fifteenth century, constituted an acculturated and cultivated minority between the sixteenth and eighteenth centuries in Amsterdam, Italy, southwest France, and London. Often seen as forerunners of Jewish modernity, in that they engaged eagerly with the cultural, intellectual, and social influences and values of the surrounding society, they were "unemancipated" in the classic sense of the term, as despite their sometimes extensive privileges they did not enjoy legal equality of civic rights and obligations. If these Sephardi Jews were modern and acculturated but not emancipated, rural Ashkenazi Jews in France furnish a counter-example.[1] Fully emancipated, they nonetheless were slow to board the modernization train, preferring traditional Jewish mores to acculturation into French society for much of the nineteenth century. For Russian Jewry, emancipation on the Western European model was a non-starter. The Tsarist Empire, home to by far the largest number of Jews in the world (some five and a half million by

1910), allowed selected categories of "useful" Jews a measure of integration into its corporatist social system of estates. Although full civic emancipation was never on the agenda, this policy led to a degree of both modernization and integration for an elite of Russian Jewry that numbered in the tens of thousands. Finally, for Anglo-Jewry, a highly acculturated and comfortable non-Anglican religious minority until the late nineteenth century (i.e., prior to the large immigration to Britain of Eastern European Jews), the issue of emancipation only rarely became a pressing collective concern. Here again, modernity and acculturation were not umbilically linked to emancipation as a legal category. In all these examples, it is clear that the once dominant conception of emancipation as a purely legal act, of emancipated as a civic status – equality – is no longer either descriptively or analytically adequate. It has been overlaid – not replaced, as the formal side of emancipation remains important – with the idea of emancipation processes, of social and cultural emancipation, and with more differentiated approaches to Jewish status and identity that take into account the diverse frameworks in which Jews lived. In this way, the straightforward equation of emancipation and acculturation with modernity has given way to a more complex portrait, but its component parts still comprise – in some combination – the essential theoretical building blocks of most work on the history of modern European Jewry.

This broadening of conceptual and geographical horizons serves to complicate further, without erasing, the aforementioned East/West divide. Emancipation and modernity were traditionally the preserve of Western European Jewry, which enjoyed the privileges of liberty and equality (if not necessarily fraternity), while Eastern European Jewry most decidedly lacked these. In turn, this was a clear reflection of the identification of Eastern Europe as a relatively backward and underdeveloped region, the mirror image of the modern West. To be sure, East and West are rather crude descriptive tools, but from the perspective of European Jewish history they manage to transcend the merely geographic. The East/West divide is not merely a historiographic construct; it is also a product of the post-Enlightenment Jewish situation. By the nineteenth century, Western European Jewry was a relatively small religious-ethnic minority that had rapidly acculturated and modernized, whereas Eastern European Jewry was far more numerous, remained devoted to its own religion and culture, and largely eschewed assimilation or acculturation. Jewish Eastern Europe is commonly cast as a foil lacking the modern "attributes" of the West, a large, self-contained and socially stratified group that maintained a studied distance from the surrounding society, which in turn kept the Jews at arm's length. By contrast, Jews in Western Europe formed a more homogeneous, middle-class group that aspired to be an integral part of the wider society (a wish not always reciprocated). Naturally, the boundaries between East and West were not always clear, particularly since the stream of Jewish migration from East to West was constant from the middle of the nineteenth century and assumed massive dimensions from the 1880s. The continuous "East meets West" that resulted led to the development of enduring intra-Jewish instability and tension.

Underlying these conflicts were fault lines in Jewish society that were a function of divergent conceptions of Jewish identity, of self-definition and definition by others. European Jewry was at one and the same time a collective unto itself and a part of many other collectives. Like most minority groups, Jews spent considerable time and energy trying to establish where and how they might fit in the broader scheme of things. As Amos Funkenstein has remarked, "Few cultures are as preoccupied with their own identity and distinction as the Jewish,"[2] and historians of European Jewry have for many years placed identity, both individual and collective, at the heart of their work. What did it mean to be Jewish in modern Europe? Were the Jews merely a religious group, "Germans of the Mosaic Faith," in a standard phrase of the time? Or were they this and more? A "community of fate," perhaps, as another popular Western and Central European definition of the mid-late nineteenth century put it? An ethnic group? A people? A fully-fledged secular nation? European society asked similar questions from a different perspective. How should the Jews, as Jews, be accommodated into a nation-state? How much should be demanded of them in terms of adaptation to the majority culture? From the Enlightenment to the Holocaust, these were recurring dilemmas for Jews across Europe. For much of the nineteenth century this cluster of issues was commonly referred to as the Jewish Question, which, in reductionist and inelegant form, may be stated as: "What should be the place of the Jews in modern Europe?" It is in the shape of the Jewish Question – and its shadow, antisemitism – that those with an interest in the history of modern Europe most often encounter the Jews. As Jews rapidly emerged from their literal and metaphorical ghettos, they became a lightning rod for opposition to the ill-understood and much-feared forces of modernization, forces perceived by many as a threat to their traditions and way of life.

At the end of the eighteenth century there were slightly more than 2 million Jews living in Europe, making up approximately 90 percent of the world's Jewish population. More than half of Europe's Jews were in territory acquired by the Russian Empire in the partitions of Poland in 1772, 1793, and 1795. Right throughout the period under discussion, and in particular from the 1880s until World War I, Jewish population growth was more rapid than the general rate of increase, with Eastern Europe the site of the fastest growth. At the beginning of the nineteenth century Jews comprised perhaps 1.5 percent of the European population, rising to around 2 percent – 8.5 to 9 million – by the century's end. Jews, then, were a relatively small, non-Christian – or in the Ottoman-controlled Balkans, non-Muslim – minority that had lived in Europe for almost two millennia as a distinct group in a hierarchical society that distributed rights and duties among the population in unequal fashion. The definition of Jews was not problematic, nor was it especially difficult to explain their functions and status. One of the defining characteristics of Jewish society prior to the nineteenth century is its semi-autonomous nature, its partial self-government in administrative, legal, financial and, of course, religious affairs. Broadly speaking, Jews lived out their lives in

the Jewish community. Generally perceived as different and alien, their segregation was both self-imposed and enforced from without. They dressed differently, ate different foods, prayed to a different God, spoke a different language (Yiddish in Central and Eastern Europe, Ladino in the Balkans), and often lived in separate neighborhoods within towns and villages.

If one of the hallmarks of the nineteenth century for Western and Central European Jews was increasing integration into surrounding society, it is clear that this entailed a radical realignment of loyalties and identities. The French Revolution, as the moment of first Jewish emancipation, was a pivotal point in this process. The novel idea of Jewish equality did not of course come out of nowhere. Its foundations were provided by Enlightenment thinkers, who, as convinced social engineers, believed that an improved and enlightened society had no place for backwards and obscurantist groups. Even the Jews, therefore, were included in their vision of a better world based on secular and rational values. The beginnings of religious toleration, too, had a part to play, opening up the possibilities of a separation of church and state, an idea with obvious beneficial implications for Jews. During the French National Assembly debate on Jewish citizenship in late December 1789, Count Stanislaus de Clermont-Tonnerre supported equal rights for the Jews in France in the following terms: "The Jews should be denied everything as a nation, but granted everything as individuals . . . It is intolerable that the Jews should become a separate political formation or class in the country. Every one of them must individually become a citizen; if they do not want this . . . we shall then be compelled to expel them. The existence of a nation within a nation is unacceptable to our country."[3]

Clermont-Tonnerre succinctly articulated the quid pro quo demanded of the Jews by emancipation: in order to be admitted into the French fold, they would need to renounce any semblance of collective autonomy beyond the religious. At the same time that the French revolutionaries offered to include the Jews in the new society in the making, they stipulated that this inclusion was conditional on the Jews effecting a fundamental change not only in the way they viewed themselves but also in their relationship to society at large. These were the terms of the emancipation bargain that became the informal contractual basis for the admission of Jews into European society generally. The prize was inestimable, being the opportunity to join society, to be not just in France, but of France. This signaled a transition from the old world of exclusion – from a society in which political, socioeconomic, and cultural life was underpinned by religion – to a new world of inclusion, where Jews were equal members of society who happened to practice a different religion – and where religion was to be a private matter rather than the state's business. The cost, though, was also evident. Jews were required to divest themselves of much of the collective identity that defined them and were to merge into the body politic. Since, as already noted, they had for the most part lived their lives within the confines of their own community, this posed a direct challenge to the very core of traditional Jewish society. Unsurprisingly, Jewish ambivalence about the terms of this proffered deal was not inconsiderable. Doubts notwithstanding, the desire to integrate and acculturate proved well-nigh unstoppable. Emancipation was a revolutionary force with a ripple effect that spread across the continent.

For the 40,000 Jews in France in the late eighteenth century, emancipation took place in two stages. First, and with relatively little argument, the highly acculturated Sephardi Jews of southwestern France were emancipated in early 1790. The poorer, more traditional, and more numerous Ashkenazi Jews, concentrated in Alsace-Lorraine, were emancipated in September 1791 after spirited debate. Opponents felt that the Jews were a debased and corrupt people unprepared for equality, a refrain that was to be heard many times across Europe during the course of the nineteenth century. The French revolutionary armies brought emancipation in short order to Jews in the Low Countries, some southern German states, and parts of the Italian peninsula, although many of the emancipatory decrees were rescinded following Napoleon's downfall. It was in the German states that the most intense debate took place about whether Jews were worthy of equal rights. In contrast to the brief flurry

of discussion that preceded emancipation in France, German society engaged in protracted agonizing that was finally resolved only with the establishment of a unified Germany in 1871. Even armed with formal equality, the approximately 500,000 German Jews faced persistent obstruction and resistance to their integration in key sectors of society such as the army, the judiciary, and universities, to say nothing of continuing popular resentment which would soon issue forth in a resurgent antisemitic movement.

Germany was long regarded as the case study *par excellence* of the difficulties involved in the processes of emancipation and acculturation, but the once-common view that the fraught history of German Jewry can serve as a model for the course of Jewish history elsewhere in Europe has fallen by the historiographical wayside. The hundred years of German hand-wringing about Jewish emancipation saw the emergence into the public arena of the Jewish Question, which appeared and reappeared in different guises at different times. Emancipation's slow and halting progress in Germany impelled Jews – by the middle of the nineteenth century, mostly middle class and educated – to develop distinctive answers to the persistent and intrusive Jewish Question in the form of movements for renewal, their part of the emancipation bargain. As we shall see, these movements – the Haskalah (Jewish Enlightenment), Reform and *Wissenschaft des Judentums* (the Science of Judaism) – proved to be of great significance for nineteenth-century European Jewry in general. By way of contrast, with regard to the emancipation of Anglo-Jewry – numbering 30,000–35,000 by the middle of the nineteenth century – there were fewer and less severe disabilities to remove than almost anywhere on the continent. Subject to the same restrictions that applied to nonconformists or Catholics (i.e., those who were not members of the established church), there were no legal statutes in Britain spelling out what was permitted and what forbidden for Jews, nor did the state play an interventionist role in Jewish communal organization, which was entirely voluntary. Emancipation was granted in piecemeal fashion, with the various disabilities often dropped *de facto*, as demanded by circumstance rather than by legislative action. In a country where the Jewish Question at no time attained the degree of noxious intensity often found on the continent, most Anglo-Jews felt no great pressure either to renounce their traditional beliefs or to invent new ways of being Jewish.

These same key issues of Jewish emancipation, acculturation, and modernization also figure *mutatis mutandis* in the Balkans, carried into the area in the course of the nineteenth century on a potent tide of Westernization. By the end of the century, there were some 100,000–125,000 Jews (overwhelmingly Sephardi) in this region: the small communities of fewer than 5,000 in Zagreb and Sarajevo, just over 5,000 in Belgrade, under 10,000 in Greece, and 30,000 in Bulgaria were overshadowed by the 80,000 Jews in Salonika, a thriving port city with a large Jewish working class. Living in the main under Ottoman rule, but faced at the same time with the new realities of Balkan nationalism, Jews shared a common – but not uniform – language, religion, and culture. While the nineteenth and early twentieth centuries saw major shifts in the area's political frontiers, the four centuries of Ottoman rule decisively contributed to the creation and maintenance of a separate ethnic-religious identity and Jews remained a distinct minority in both state and popular perception.

This image of the Jews as an identifiable pan-European minority should not lead us to picture them as living in a hermetically sealed bubble, isolated from their environment. It should be clear by now that this was far from the case. Jews were indeed a recognizable minority, but this was not incompatible with active engagement with society at large. These are not to be viewed as mutually exclusive categories, but rather as points along a continuum. The perpetual interplay between minority group and "host" society is apparent in the above-mentioned movements for Jewish renewal. On the one hand, these movements grew out of the internal dynamics of Jewish society; on the other, they were part of the Jewish effort to fulfill their side of the emancipation bargain by remaking themselves into modern Europeans. They were part of the Jewish answer to the Jewish Question.

The first of these movements was the Haskalah, the Jewish Enlightenment, which developed in the final decades of the eighteenth century in Prussia, primarily in Berlin but with a strong presence also in Breslau (Wrocław) and Königsberg (Kaliningrad). Proponents of the Haskalah (known as Maskilim, or Enlighteners) demanded fundamental changes to Jewish society, reflecting their acceptance of the widespread Enlightenment view of the Jews as deformed and degenerate. No corner of Jewish life escaped their critique: religion, culture, social and economic behavior, and politics all needed regeneration and reform before Jews could be expected to make a worthwhile contribution to, or even properly belong to, general society. They promoted aspects of Jewish life that they presumed would be seen in a positive light by that society, such as the purity of biblical Hebrew, the stability of Jewish family life, the Jewish agricultural past, and Judaism's rich philosophical legacy. Inveterate modernizers, the Maskilim focused a good deal of attention on what they saw as the pernicious influence of traditional Jewish education, a hidebound system defective in both religious and secular instruction. Many of the first generation of Maskilim were products of this system and wished to dismantle it wholesale, substituting biblical study and Hebrew for the prevailing focus on Talmud (the authoritative corpus of Jewish tradition) and encouraging the study of natural sciences. To this end, they created a network of modern Jewish schools, first in the German states and subsequently as far afield as Kishinev, Odessa, and Riga. Transforming the system of education was linked to an overhaul of the Jewish socioeconomic structure: Jews were too poor and too concentrated in petty commerce and trade (i.e., they were not working the land); they were, in short, unproductive. In order to effect these changes, the Maskilim turned to the state. This was in and of itself an unusual step, since Jews had normally regarded external authority as something of a necessary evil. For the Maskilim, though, the state was a potential ally in the drive for reform and modernization, an approach that implied not only that the barriers between Jews and others should break down but also that the values of non-Jewish society were worthy of emulation. Drawing their religious and cultural values from the surrounding society, the Maskilim saw antiquated Jewish customs and religious beliefs as obstacles to integration. Invoking the views of the German Enlightenment about organized religion, they aimed to limit rabbinical authority and stressed the importance of reason, virtue, and morality, of natural law rather than revealed truth. Similarly, most took a dim view of Yiddish as a bastardized jargon that perpetuated Jewish isolation. While there were radical elements that looked to conversion as a solution, most Enlighteners sought to modify Judaism, hoping to shape it into a suitable faith for civilized people in a modern society.

By the 1820s the momentum of the Haskalah's modernizing impulse in the German lands and other parts of Western Europe had pushed the movement beyond its Enlightenment parameters, leading to new forms and expressions of Jewish renewal. From Prussia, the movement spread eastwards, through Habsburg Galicia into Russian Poland through the 1820s and 1830s and thence to Russia proper, where it was firmly established by the 1840s. Again, the role of the state was crucial in shoring up an institutional basis for the fledgling movement, which had its most important centers in Vilnius and Odessa. In the East, just as in the West, the Maskilim desired acculturation to the bourgeoisie, but in Eastern Europe this was neither as large nor as influential a target group as its Western European counterpart. The growth of a Russian-Jewish intelligentsia and merchant class, intimately bound up with the era of the Great Reforms of Tsar Alexander II, both reflected and carried forward the Russian Haskalah. Like its predecessor in the West, ideological coherence was not its strong suit. Divisions ran along generational and intellectual lines, revealed in contrasting attitudes, for example, to the role of Hebrew and Yiddish in Jewish culture (Russian was an agreed-upon common denominator), to levels and forms of religious observance, and to the appropriate relationship with the Russian authorities. Unlike some of their Western precursors, the Russian Maskilim hoped to make Jews acceptable to their neighbors without necessarily abandoning all distinguishing religious,

social, or cultural traits. Given that they were operating in an entirely different environment governed by different rules, this was no more than a concession to reality. The Maskilim were akin to a small boat of modernization and Westernization adrift in a vast sea of Jewish poverty and tradition. The difference in context also helps to account for the different course of the Russian movement. Whereas reformers and modernizers in Central and Western Europe no longer described themselves as Maskilim by the middle of the nineteenth century, in Russia the term remained in use much longer. Among the movement's signal achievements in Eastern Europe was that it laid the foundations for the emergence and development of modern Hebrew and Yiddish culture, both of which were indispensable to the growth of Jewish nationalist movements in the latter decades of the nineteenth century. By modernizing and popularizing existing cultural traditions, Hebrew and Yiddish *belles-lettres*, poetry, and journalism prospered. In the same vein, Jewish intellectuals, publicists, artists, writers, and activists of all kinds managed to create a Jewish public sphere across Europe catering to, and sustained by, a Jewish population conversant in the various vernaculars and/or Hebrew and Yiddish.

Never a mass movement, the Haskalah was nonetheless a powerful force in both East and West, propelled by the insistent drive towards modernization and integration. These were the very same aspirations underlying the development of the Reform movement and the Science of Judaism, both of which can in this sense be viewed as indirect outgrowths of the Haskalah. Religious reformers, coalescing as a movement in the German states by the 1820s, wanted to present Judaism in terms acceptable to the non-Jewish world, as an enlightened religion stripped of its antiquated external trappings. Religion should be relegated to the private sphere, where it would constitute but one component of an individual's life, a marked departure from the traditional Jewish view which saw religion and tradition as forming the essential framework and structure of daily existence. Reformers introduced a raft of changes in religious ritual, dispensing with elements they deemed inappropriate while at the same time suggesting improvements and innovations. Praying for a return to Zion was discouraged, as this might imply dual loyalties; religious services should be fewer and shorter; the use of Hebrew was minimalized; German-language sermons and organ music were introduced; women were to be included in religious life rather than marginalized. In place of the noisy and chaotic services typical in traditional synagogues, which they deprecated as "Oriental," the reformers wanted decorum and dignity. The direction of these reforms is clear: they moved towards establishing a Jewish church, aiming to reduce or eliminate ethnic, national, or tribal features of Jewish identity. Moreover, they wished to replace Jewish law (Halakhah) as the supreme authority in Jewish life, seeing it as yet another barrier to Jewish integration.

By the 1840s, reformed synagogues existed across Central and Western Europe and a generation of secular-educated reformist rabbis began to elaborate a theology to accommodate their adherents' determination to combine religious observance with civic integration. Sharp disagreements between radical and moderate wings of the movement soon led to the formation of competing versions of modern Judaism. One such version was Positive-Historical Judaism, whose foremost expositor was Zacharias Frankel. A Prague-born, Budapest-educated rabbi, Frankel worked in Teplice (Teplitz) Bohemia and in Dresden before being appointed head of the Jewish Theological Seminary in Breslau, a major rabbinical teaching college. He agreed with the reformers that Halakhah should no longer be the sole basis for Judaism and Jewish life, but offered a more moderate alternative to what in his view were the radical excesses of Reform. Frankel did not dispute that Jewish Law was rooted in divine revelation. Revelation, though, was not a single event; rather, it was a process transformed in and by the course of Jewish history. In contrast to the success of Reform and Positive-Historical Judaism in Western and Central Europe, and also in the United States, neither managed to establish a foothold in Eastern Europe. Partly this was due to the nature of Jewish society there: incomparably larger, more traditional, much poorer. But it was also a result, more broadly, of the fact that

these ideologies grew out of the challenges posed by the possibility of integration and emancipation, and by the existence of a liberal, or at least partially liberal, society – all of which were lacking in Eastern Europe.

The complex of ideas about emancipation and integration that set the Haskalah in motion also gave rise to the Science of Judaism, ideologically and institutionally part of the milieu of Reform and Positive-Historical Judaism. The *Wissenschaft des Judentums* movement first crystallized in the 1820s in Berlin, where a group of young university-trained Jewish scholars turned their attention to "the scientific study of Jewish religion, history, and philosophy," which in their eyes was under the sway of "ignorant, prejudiced rabbis . . . innocent . . . of any knowledge beyond their own narrow field."[4] It was incumbent upon the Jews to develop a critical historical consciousness, one of the markers of an authentically modern sensibility. But examining the past with the tools of modern historical methodology necessitated a sharp break with the traditional Jewish approach, which looked to the historical record to ascertain signs of God's work and strengthen belief in his authority. At work in the hearts and minds of these scholars was a liberal faith in positivism; they were optimistic that if they could only bring to light the "true and scientific" version of the Jewish past, the power of rationality and facts would persuade opponents of Jewish emancipation that their anti-Jewish prejudices were misguided. By the end of the nineteenth century the idea of the "scientific" or scholarly study of Jews and Judaism was well established in Europe and beyond, and its intellectual horizons had expanded exponentially to incorporate a vast array of subjects and disciplines. Although relegated to the institutional and intellectual margins of state academic infrastructures, this movement represents the precursor to modern Jewish studies in universities across the world today.

In response to these religious, cultural, and intellectual adaptations and modernizations, traditional Jews too were compelled to define and articulate their own attitudes, leading to the development of what came to be known as Orthodoxy, an umbrella term covering a wide religious spectrum. At one end of this spectrum was "Neo-Orthodoxy," a German product of the second half of the nineteenth century. Its leading thinker, Samson Raphael Hirsch, believed that Judaism could, and should, be responsive to the needs of the modern world and that observance of Jewish Law was fully compatible with participation in outside society. Secular education was permitted; Jews could adopt contemporary dress and the local language; minor modifications in religious practice were permitted, but the traditional liturgy was sacrosanct and Hebrew remained the exclusive language of prayer. Jews must maintain their distinctiveness, yet – within carefully circumscribed limits – should also acculturate to secular society. A more unyielding variant flourished in Hungary, where Reform – called Neolog in its Hungarian guise – also exerted considerable influence. Here we see the growth in the 1860s of a new strand, Ultra-Orthodoxy, resolutely opposed to all innovation and urging strictest adherence to Jewish Law. In pursuit of religious purity, Ultra-Orthodoxy in fact substantially recast tradition to suit its own conservative purposes. In other words, this is yet another example of the "invention of tradition."[5] Perhaps this was all the more necessary given Hungarian Jewry's unrivaled reputation for assimilation and acculturation. Hungarian Jews, numbering some 80,000 in the last decade of the eighteenth century, 340,000 by the middle of the nineteenth century, and 910,000 in 1910, uninhibitedly embraced the Magyar cause and during the second half of the nineteenth century came to occupy a key position in the country's economic and cultural life. Social integration, though, lagged somewhat behind external indices of success. By way of contrast, and as another example of the indelible imprint of the majority society upon the minority, a rather different form of Orthodoxy prevailed in Britain. Mainstream Anglo-Jewish Orthodoxy was on the whole indifferent to the niceties and formalities of religious observance, exhibiting little of the religious and ideological intensity common on the continent, a consequence perhaps of the fact that the British state and British society made fewer formal and informal demands of Jews. Pressure to conform and acculturate was by no means absent, but it was

less insistent and pervasive than in most European states.

The forces of tradition were most strongly entrenched in Eastern Europe, where reformist tendencies made only limited headway. In this area, the religious establishment was challenged from a different direction, by the revivalist movement of Hasidism. Hasidism developed in the second half of the eighteenth century in Podolia and Volhynia, southeastern lands of the Polish-Lithuanian Commonwealth which were incorporated into Russian Ukraine following the Polish Partitions of the 1770s and 1790s. (The term Hasid – pl. Hasidim – referred originally to a pious man.) It quickly became a mass populist movement, spreading rapidly across southern Poland, Lithuania, and Ukraine, into Habsburg Galicia and Bukovina, Hungary and Romania. Hasidic worship was notorious for its unbridled enthusiasm and joy, its singing and dancing; sobriety and rationality were not, the Hasidim believed, the best path to a close relationship with God. Their detractors accused them of laxity in their observance of ritual law, of contempt for traditional study of Talmud and Hebrew scriptures, and of an unhealthy proclivity for the Jewish mystical tradition, the Kabbalah. While Hasidism was a product first and foremost of the conditions and problems of Jewish society, and in particular the upheavals attendant on the collapse of the Polish-Lithuanian Commonwealth, it drew too on nonconformist Christian ideas in the same areas. A cult of charismatic leadership was a feature of the movement, with each community organized around a Tsadik (righteous or holy one), who held court in regal style. The Tsadik was considered a direct link to the divine, a healer and miracle-worker whose every action, thought, and word was invested with divine importance by his followers. The messianic tendencies inherent in this drew unrelenting opposition from Jewish community authorities who saw Hasidism and its powerful leaders as a threat to the status quo.

The anti-Hasidic forces, spearheaded by the Mitnagdim (literally, the "opposers"), pursued their campaign on two fronts. They were quite prepared to cooperate with the state authorities in harassing the Hasidim, regularly denouncing Hasidic leaders to the government as seditious, with the result that on occasion some were thrown into prison. Within the Jewish fold, they resorted in more than one instance to the blunt instrument of excommunication: "They must leave our communities with their wives and children . . . it is forbidden to do business with them, and to intermarry with them, or to assist at their burial."[6] Maskilim, predictably enough, were also fiercely opposed and, like the Orthodox, saw fit to bring the government into this internal conflict. For those preaching Enlightenment, the Hasidic movement represented a threat to all they held sacred – it was anti-modern, anti-rational, anti-integration. The contempt, naturally, was mutual. Even in the face of this determined resistance, by about 1830 Hasidism had grown from a small and harried sect into a commanding force in many areas of Eastern Europe (it was weakest in Lithuania, where it encountered its strongest opposition). Over time, it became an integral part of the religious establishment and successive waves of westward migration from the middle of the nineteenth century established it also in many parts of Western Europe and the United States.

Looking back from the vantage point of late in the nineteenth century, we can discern that the point of departure for the splintering of Jewish society along ideological, cultural, socioeconomic, and religious lines was the Haskalah, with its relentless push for integration and, by extension, modernization and emancipation. A point of departure, however, is not identical with a prime cause. Cultural and intellectual or ideological phenomena cannot be regarded as the sole determinants of change on this scale. Just as important, and in fact impossible to disentangle from the realm of the abstract, were the engines of nineteenth-century European modernization already referred to – foremost among them, capitalism and industrialization. These, always working in tandem with ideas, transformed European Jewry. There were by this time many and varied ways of being Jewish; Jewish identity, in its public and private modes, was a subject of debate, a moving target rather than a fixed point of reference. Much of this debate, as has already been made clear, first took place in the German states, where the Jewish Question was

at its most intense and most prolonged. But given that they were a minority dispersed throughout numerous states and regions, it is only natural that the incessant discussion about the Jews and their place in society was a pan-European phenomenon.

The Jewish Question, of course, was by no means a neutral concept, a subject for dispassionate and disinterested consideration. Quite the contrary. It was a sensitive and explosive matter, the destructive potential of which became clear in the 1870s and 1880s with the emergence of modern antisemitism in the wake of Jewish emancipation and integration in Central Europe. The antecedents of modern antisemitism are to be found in the long traditions of both Christian and post-Christian hatred of the Jews. Theological rejection of the Jews as Christ-killers led the church to segregate, repress, and expel Jews, while modern secular ideologies such as the Enlightenment and socialism dismissed them as outmoded relics of a bygone age. Modern antisemitism – the term was coined to provide a scientific facade for Jew-hatred – was political and racial, rejecting Jews not on religious or metaphysical grounds, but for concrete, practical reasons: the Jews were said unduly to dominate social, political, and economic life, and even the state itself. It took shape as a movement in Germany and Habsburg Austria (particularly its capital, Vienna), drawing on German romantic nationalism that presumed the *Volk* (people) to be the fundamental building block of civilization and culture; economic and cultural resentments engendered by the Great Depression of the 1870s and 1880s in many areas of Central Europe; and pseudo-scientific racial ideologies that divided humanity into lesser and more worthy races, with the Jews alien and Asiatic, and the Aryans the carriers of all that was best in Greek and Roman civilizations. In short, it was an ideological mélange with little coherence. It has been aptly described as a "cultural code"; to be identified as an antisemite was a convenient shorthand for a whole host of related attitudes: if you were an antisemite, you were also anti-modern, anti-democracy, anti-liberal, anti-capitalist, anti-Enlightenment, anti-French Revolution.[7] This was an ideological package deal, with antisemitism right at the core, which goes some way to explaining its potency as a political and social force.

Crossing geopolitical borders with ease, this package deal also had a right-wing, nationalist and clerical French version, an anti-Revolutionary, Catholic strain of anti-Jewish thought. Its most famous episode, the Dreyfus Affair, incorporated all these elements. Captain Alfred Dreyfus, a Jew from Alsace, was falsely convicted in 1894 of selling military secrets to the Germans. Imprisoned on Devil's Island in the Atlantic Ocean, Dreyfus found himself at the vortex of a scandal that for over a decade engulfed key institutions of French society, pitching secular republicanism against clericalism and advocates of a restored monarchy. That Dreyfus was Jewish played no small part in the affair and that antisemitism and the Jews were at the center of such a bitter and protracted conflict once more points to the way in which the Jewish Question was able to ignite larger issues that went to the heart of modern European society. Its power in this sense was to be only too evident during World War II, although this should not be taken to imply that nineteenth-century racial and political antisemitism inexorably led to the Holocaust. That particular teleology ought to be avoided; by the same token, a relationship of some sort must be acknowledged.

Antisemitism was a force to be reckoned with also in Eastern Europe and Russia, where popular antipathy focused on the Jews as an alien religious element and anti-Jewish animus assumed less overtly "scientific" and racial forms. Here, mob violence and pogroms were a constant threat, while antisemitism was used sometimes as an instrument of government policy, a characteristic that distinguished Eastern European from Western European antisemitism in the period prior to World War I. A good example of this semi-official antisemitism is the Protocols of the Elders of Zion, a document manufactured by the Russian secret police in the 1890s. Based on a French pamphlet that attributed ambitions for world domination to Napoleon III, the Protocols purported to be an account of a secret meeting of a shadowy group called the Elders of Zion, supposedly the leaders of world Jewry intent on enslaving the globe. In time, the Protocols became a favored prooftext for antisemitic conspiracy theorists. Similarly prominent in the antisemitic imagination was the late-nineteenth century revival of the medieval Blood Libel, or ritual murder charge, which brought into play almost all of the above motifs, combining modern and traditional modes of discourse with popular hostility, political maneuverings, and state involvement in the form of complex legal processes. Ritual murder trials were held in Hungary, Bohemia, Germany, Poland, and Russia, calling into question the very assumptions upon which Jewish emancipation and acculturation rested: that the Jews were not alien, that they were capable of being good citizens and civilized Europeans. Clearly, drinking blood from corpses murdered expressly for that purpose is barbaric rather than civilized.

It could be argued that it was not just antisemitism that was different in Eastern Europe. Jews were different there, too: greater in number and less integrated than in Central and Western Europe. In the Tsarist Empire, the Jewish population increased – more rapidly than the general population – from the approximately three-quarters of a million acquired in the Polish Partitions of the late eighteenth century (prior to this the tsars had permitted almost no Jews in their lands) to 2.5 million by the middle of the nineteenth century, and then to some 5.5 million by 1910 (of a total population of 130 million). Jews were a predominantly urban group, concentrated in petty commerce and in trades and crafts, with a small stratum of wealthy industrialists and financiers. The overwhelming majority was poor; hundreds of thousands were classified as *Luftmenschen*, people living on air, with no visible means of support. The Russian government imposed a vast web of restrictions on Jewish life, hampering the growth of economic, religious, cultural, and political institutions and leading to the poverty, overcrowding, and pervasive misery that gave the Jewish Question in Russia its urgency. The Jews did not suffer alone, of course. Life in Russia was comfortable for only a select few and the tsarist autocracy dealt with the Jews as it dealt with many other issues – policy and its implementation was inconsistent and ad hoc. Moreover, the Jewish

Question, while undoubtedly a constant thorn in the tsarist side, was far from their most pressing concern. Their approach to the Jews lurched back and forth between the desire to exclude them and the desire to integrate them partially. Nicholas I (ruled 1825–55), for example, conscripted young Jews for longer than the requisite 25 years in order to convert them, and he opened schools to Jews for similar reasons. Yet he continued Catherine the Great's (1762–96) policy of confining most of the Jewish population to residence in the Pale of Settlement, an area stretching from the Baltic Sea to the Black Sea, incorporating Ukraine and Belorussia and the northwest regions of the empire. By the end of the nineteenth century, nearly 12 percent of the Pale's population was Jewish, but in urban areas the percentage was far higher, as Jews made up a large minority and often a majority in many small towns and cities. Following Nicholas, Alexander II (1855–81) relaxed some of these restrictions, opening higher education to Jews, permitting selected categories to live outside the Pale (university graduates, army veterans, certain merchants, medical professionals), and reducing the burden of military service.

The combined impact of the grinding poverty, autocratic oppression, and volatile antisemitism that characterized the final decades of tsarist rule were met with two broad Jewish responses: flight and fight. Large-scale emigration was under way already during the 1870s, but the terrifying assault on the Jews launched in the spring of 1881 helped catalyze what eventually became one of the largest sustained mass migrations in history. During the course of 1881–2, hundreds of Jewish communities were attacked in a series of pogroms that began in southern Russia and spread quickly across the Pale. Jews were devastated by the violence of the attacks and disappointed by the lack of support and defense provided by the authorities and by their erstwhile allies in the liberal and revolutionary camps. A second, more destructive, wave of pogroms took place between 1903 and 1905, leaving around a thousand Jews dead and 7–8,000 wounded. Between 1881 and 1914, almost one-third of all Eastern European Jews migrated westward. In addition to those leaving Russia, substantial

numbers left Romania, home to 250,000 Jews at the end of the nineteenth century, and Habsburg Galicia, a formerly Polish province with some 900,000 Jews at this point. Tens of thousands went to Germany, France, Austria; 150,000 to England; while many looked even further afield – to Canada (about 100,000), Argentina (115,000), and South Africa (40,000). More than 80 percent, though, opted for the United States, which attracted approximately 2 million Eastern European Jews between 1881 and 1924, when immigration restrictions were introduced.

Mobility, it should be noted, is a thread running throughout Jewish history, not unsurprisingly for a group that lacked its own territory for so long. From the late thirteenth century until the late sixteenth century, Jews were expelled at various times from most parts of Central and Western Europe, settling in the Polish-Lithuanian Commonwealth and the Ottoman-controlled Balkans. In the late seventeenth century, Jewish migration changed direction, this time returning west. The great migration that began in the 1880s was part of a more general population mobility, but Jews moved at between three to four times the rate of general migration and, in Eastern Europe, they were six to seven times more likely to migrate than non-Jews. Jews constituted 5 percent of the Russian population, but made up 50 percent of Russian emigrants. (They made up 60 percent of emigrants from Galicia and 90 percent of emigrants from Romania.) Besides leaving in greater numbers, there were more women and children among Jewish migrants than among other groups. Most tellingly, more Jews left permanently than was true of other migrants; for the great majority of Jewish emigrants, this was a one-way ticket.

For those who chose to remain, or were left behind, politics offered the promise of a better world in Europe rather than abroad. Jewish responses to the Jewish Question and antisemitism were the motor for the development of Jewish political ideologies and movements. As was often the case in European Jewish history, this new politics took its cues and models from the available material in the general environment. Thus, as liberalism, nationalism, and socialism took form, so too did parallel Jewish versions of these ideologies. Here, too, an East/West division has some utility. In Eastern Europe, Jewish political culture took predominantly autonomous forms. A bewildering plethora of organizations and parties sprang into existence, devoted to secular nationalism, left-wing radicalism, or a combination of the two, aspiring to independent and sovereign action for the benefit of the Jewish people, who were defined as a nation like any other. Implicit in this approach was that Jews should tread a separate political and cultural path, either in the form of autonomy in Europe or in an independent homeland in Palestine (or elsewhere). In the Jewish context this was revolutionary, since it assumed that nothing less than a complete transformation of the Jewish condition could solve the Jewish Question. In response to this political mobilization, the large and influential Orthodox population of Eastern Europe created its own political structures, more conservative and highly resistant to secularist nationalism and socialism. The very process of increasing politicization among the mostly quietist and loyalist Jewish traditionalists, however, resulted in some blurring of these ideological boundaries, apparent, for example, in the growth of religious nationalism.

In Western Europe, Jewish liberalism was ascendant. Jewish liberals, organized in philanthropic, religious, social, and cultural groups, defined themselves as a religious – or sometimes ethnic – community, and their political goals were limited accordingly. They agitated for the emancipation of their less fortunate Eastern European "co-religionists," as they preferred to call them. Of particular importance were the various defense organizations established to protect Jews from antisemitism and foster Jewish pride. Bodies such as the Central Association of Germans of the Jewish Faith or the Austrian Israelite Union functioned as ethnic political pressure groups, but stopped deliberately short of defining the Jews as a separate people, something accepted without demur by both nationalists and the Orthodox in Eastern Europe.

The most successful and long lived of all Jewish political movements was Zionism, which spanned East and West. Launched as an international political movement in Central and Western Europe, its heartland of support and its earliest ideologues and activists were in Eastern Europe. Deriving its momentum from European nationalism and antisemitism, it was a protean force that aimed to achieve Jewish sovereignty in Ottoman-controlled Palestine. Zionism was part of a broader spectrum of Jewish nationalist thought that sought political solutions to the Jewish Question in nationalist variants of Marxism and liberalism; in forms of cultural nationalism and integral (right-wing) nationalism; in diaspora nationalism, which believed that territory was not a sine qua non of nationalism; and in territorial alternatives to Palestine. That the Jews were a distinct group was a given for all shades of Jewish political thought. Beyond this, though, little consensus was achievable regarding just what kind of group they were and how they ought to organize politically. This was the politics of a minority, driven by a sense of existential crisis about its security and identity, terminally divisive and fragmented, and with only limited access to the levers of state power. In all these ways, Jewish politics was an expression and a reflection of the Jewish encounter with the modern world.

The success or failure of modern Jewish politics is a vexed question; the same holds true for the broader enterprise of which this politics formed a part: Jewish emancipation. During the long nineteenth century, the vagaries of emancipation – its achievement, its travails, its absence – marked much of the experience of European Jewry. In comparison with what followed, however, this was an extended period of relative stability. World War I and its aftermath saw a revival of vicious antisemitism that challenged Jewish integration in Western and Central Europe, while the upheavals that ensued with the collapse of the Habsburg, Russian, and Ottoman empires, and of Wilhelmine Germany, notably intensified Jewish self-perception as a vulnerable, stateless minority. The war was particularly devastating for the Jews of Eastern Europe, where it shook the foundations of Jewish life, uprooting, impoverishing, maiming, and killing on a mass scale. The immediate postwar years were not much better: tens of thousands of Jews were killed in pogroms, while hundreds of thousands were wounded and made homeless. Much worse, of course, was soon to come.

Viewed against this background, it is little wonder that the nineteenth century has often been seen in a rather positive light by Jewish historiography. The magnitude and breadth of the transformations of European Jewish life between the French Revolution and World War I left no aspect of Jewish society untouched, altering almost beyond recognition the foundations and structures of the Jewish condition and of Jewish identity. Almost, but not quite. While it is true that the dimensions and contours of the collection of issues that comprised the Jewish Question had undergone far-reaching changes, many of the basic assumptions involved were nonetheless still operative. The Jewish Question remained an open wound for many Europeans. In this sense at least, the Jews ended the century as they had begun it, an identifiable and discomfiting minority dispersed across Europe.

NOTES

1 The Jewish world's primary ethnic division is between Sephardi Jews (*Sefarad* from the Hebrew for Spain) and the Ashkenazi Jews of Central and Eastern Europe, *Ashkenaz* being the old Hebrew term for Germany.
2 Funkenstein (1993: 1).
3 Mendes-Flohr and Reinharz (1995: 115).
4 So commented Eduard Gans, one of the first of these scholars, cited in Mendes-Flohr and Reinharz (1995: 218).

5 Silber (1992).
6 *Encyclopedia Judaica* (Jerusalem, 1972), vol. 7, cl. 1396.
7 Volkov (1978a).

GUIDE TO FURTHER READING

Gartner's *History of the Jews in Modern Times* is an informative and accessible survey. Seltzer's *Jewish People, Jewish Thought* offers a thoughtful account of the modern period. Good introductions to the diversity of Jewish experience can be found in Birnbaum and Katznelson, *Paths of Emancipation*, Frankel and Zipperstein, *Assimilation and Community*, and Katz, *Toward Modernity*. Almog's *Nationalism and Antisemitism in Modern Europe 1815–1945* and Katz's *From Prejudice to Destruction* capably chart the history of antisemitism.

On German Jewry, Meyer's *German-Jewish History in Modern Times* provides a broad synthesis. Fine studies of Czech and British Jews are Kieval, *Languages of Community* and Endelman, *The Jews of Britain 1656–2000*. Also useful are Benbassa and Rodrigue's *Jews of the Balkans* and Hyman's *Jews of Modern France*. On the Russian Empire, Baron's *Russian Jew under Tsars and Soviets* remains a standard, although slightly dated, text. More stimulating, but narrower in scope, are Nathans, *Beyond the Pale* and Stanislawski, *Tsar Nicholas I and the Jews*. Friesel's *Atlas of Modern Jewish History* is a helpful guide, while an excellent collection of primary documents can be found in Mendes-Flohr and Reinharz, *The Jew in the Modern World*.

PART V

Cultural Developments

Chapter Twenty-Two

European Culture in the Nineteenth Century

James A. Winders

The influential English critic Raymond Williams demonstrated in a number of literary and historical investigations that terms like "culture," "literature," and "art" began to take on their familiar exclusive, highly specific connotations roughly around 1800, a turning point also noted by social historians as a time for sharpening distinctions between public and private realms, each coded differently in terms of gender. For the purposes of this chapter, the operative definition of "culture" will be the more generally inclusive one more familiar to anthropologists. Thus, culture, for us, will refer as readily to popular entertainment as to lofty literary and artistic achievements.

Romanticism

The Romantic sensibility in the arts and in European culture generally was a complicated outgrowth of the late eighteenth century and the waning Enlightenment. It would cast a long shadow over the following century, and may even be said to continue in the lower-case form in contemporary culture. Traditionally, intellectual historians represented Romanticism as a sharp break with Enlightenment culture, but more recent scholarship has reminded us that an emphasis on sentiment, emotion, and even spirituality had been emergent within the late stages of the Enlightenment. Thus the story of Romanticism's relationship with the cultural *Zeitgeist* that preceded it can be shown

to be complicated and multi-dimensional. Jean-Jacques Rousseau (1712–78), the Enlightenment *philosophe* whose novels and essays inaugurated the shift in emphasis from reason to emotion, was perhaps the most significant transitional figure at the threshold of the Romantic era, and his profound influence on Immanuel Kant (1724–1804) led directly to the German Romantic writers.

The enormously influential Johann Wolfgang von Goethe (1749–1832) and his fellow poet Johann Christoph Friedrich von Schiller (1759–1805), the key figures of the late eighteenth-century literary movement known as *Sturm und Drang* ("Storm and Stress"), presided over the flowering of German Romanticism, as did the philosophers Johann Gottfried von Herder (1744–1806) and Friedrich Wilhelm Joseph von Schelling (1775–1854). Herder, in a break with the Enlightenment emphasis on universal human attributes, upheld the importance of unique ethnic characteristics that defined the nation as *Volk*. Schelling's *Naturphilosophie* ("Nature Philosophy") extolled the inspiring, sustaining role of the natural world for artistic creation.

William Blake (1757–1827), whose iconoclastic spirituality informed his visionary poetry and who thundered against the encroaching horrors of English industrialism in the prophetic tones of an Old Testament patriarch, prefigured the emphasis on nature and the individual creative genius that marked the efforts of first-generation English Romantic poets William Wordsworth (1770–1850) and Samuel Taylor Coleridge (1772–1834), the latter of whom was equally influenced by such German figures as Schelling. The generation that followed them included such towering poets as Percy Bysshe Shelley (1792–1822), John Keats (1795–1821), and George Gordon, Lord Byron (1788–1824), as well as the novelist Mary Wollstonecraft Shelley (1797–1851). Their counterparts in Germany, much the generation that followed Goethe and Schiller, included Friedrich Hölderlin (1779–1843) and Friedrich von Hardenberg, a.k.a. Novalis (1772–1801).

The critics and essayists August Wilhelm Schlegel and Friedrich Schlegel played the role of theorists/advocates for German Romanticism, and Coleridge championed their ideas in England, as did Germaine de Staël (1766–1817) in France. Her influence continued after her death, one result being that Romanticism took hold in France well after it had set the dominant tone in Germany and England. This applies as well to other Romance language areas such as Italy and Spain.

The major themes and motifs of the Romantic outlook may be explored through attention to individual artists, but the characteristics ascribed to many of these artists make for some striking contradictions. This is especially apparent when focusing on elite versus popular aspects of Romanticism. As for emotion, clearly the Romantic credo was that the creative artist should communicate directly to a reader, viewer, or listener the power of the emotional state that brought the work into being. However, the purpose of this exercise could have very different consequences for a popular response or political impact. Some writers, such as Adam Mickiéwicz (1798–1855) of Poland or the Italian Giuseppe Mazzini (1805–72), were nationalist leaders who intended their writings to rally their people. But more often the Romantic artist was someone who, however much inspiration he may have taken from "the people," embodied the figure of the necessarily isolated, often suffering genius who allows us a glimpse of the turbulent emotional life that makes possible his art. The poems of Wordsworth and Coleridge, despite their stated intention to model their poetic discourse on the natural language of the common folk, are good examples.

Political contradictions abound in Romanticism. Emerging during the heady years of the French Revolution and the Napoleonic Wars, Romantic artists ran the gamut from anti-clerical skeptics to those calling for a return to the Catholic faith and an embrace of medieval values. Napoleon Bonaparte, championed by some artists as progressive, was denounced by others as a tyrant. Ludwig van Beethoven abandoned one view for the other, tearing off the dedication page to Napoleon of his "Eroica" symphony (No. 3). Percy Shelley exhorted the slumbering masses to rise up and claim the earth as their own, while the brilliant and no less iconoclastic French writer François René de Chateaubriand (1768–1848) espoused reactionary monarchist views to match his return to orthodox Roman Catholicism.

Responses to industrialization likewise were strewn all about the political landscape. English Romantic poets appeared to object to the factories on aesthetic grounds, and such sensibilities found their counterpart in the nostalgic landscape paintings of John Constable (1776–1837), if not the proto-impressionist canvases of J. M. W. Turner (1775–1851). For some troubled by the changes to be found in a modernizing world, the appeal of the medieval settings of the wildly popular novels of Sir Walter Scott (1771–1832) was an escapist answer. Yet Romanticism sometimes informed the denunciations of socialists like Charles Fourier or indeed the writings of the young Karl Marx, who adored Scott's novels. If, for some, a reputedly nobler past beckoned, for others it was the promise of an emancipatory future. And some painters created visual denunciations of injustice, such as Francisco José de Goya (1746–1828) – whose *The Shootings of the Third of May 1808* commemorated atrocities committed by Napoleon's troops in Spain – and the French artists Théodore Géricault (1791–1824) and Eugène Delacroix (1798–1863).

Nature, to be sure, was held to be the antidote to all that was questionable in civilization, and Rousseau's teaching that contact with nature instructed one in virtue persisted through the later development of Romanticism. Nature also might serve as the setting for fantastic imagery and inspiration, something conveyed powerfully by the oneiric canvases of the German painter Caspar David Friedrich (1774–1840). The influence of Schelling's *Naturphilosophie*, wherein nature was viewed as an organic whole, even inspired research in chemistry and physics. It also informed the scientific researches of that polymath Goethe, who worked at a theory of optics that would reject what he viewed as the cold mechanism of the Newtonian model. Expressed in a variety of ways in Romantic art, the reverence for nature and the growing sense of ways in which modern development posed a threat to it may well be one of the movement's most lasting influences, extending down to the ecology movement of recent decades.

A perhaps even more lasting legacy of the Romantic movement was its great emphasis on youth. Viewed from the perspective of other world civilizations, the Western preoccupation with youth culture seems unusual, but historians who have looked into the question of generations and their consciousness of themselves as such have seen the Romantic era as the one in which this tendency, coupled with the inclination to see youthfulness as a virtue, first emerged. Scanning the above paragraphs and noting the life spans recorded for many of the principal Romantic artists, one will be struck by the many examples of those who lived exceptionally brief lives, even by the standards of an era with relatively low life expectancy (Keats, Shelley, Novalis, Byron, Géricault). The interpretation increasingly brought to bear on this grim phenomenon was that it was preferable to die young than to settle into mediocrity and decrepitude.

Music, the art that clung longest to Romanticism, embraced this and its myriad other themes. In fact, one could argue that Romanticism dominated all of nineteenth-century European music. If music is the art most able to produce emotional responses, the Romantic music did so in several deliberate ways. As with literature or painting, the goal was to recreate for the listener the profound emotional state that had inspired the composer. Dramatic themes, orchestral crescendos, or thundering piano chords were the aural equivalent of the stormy bold colors on a Romantic canvas. Romantic music emphasized performance at times more heavily than composition, and the cult of the virtuoso held sway throughout the nineteenth century. The violinist Nicolo Paganini (1782–1840) and the pianist Franz Liszt (1811–86) were accorded legendary status by their adoring audiences.

Ludwig van Beethoven (1770–1827) was very much a transitional figure in the history of European music, bridging the classical styles of the eighteenth century and Romanticism. His imposing nine symphonies variously invoke the beauty of nature, creative genius, and the joyousness of universal fraternal feeling, and his piano sonatas remain at the heart of that instrument's repertoire. The piano had undergone a technical transformation around the turn of the century, and Romantic composers devoted elaborate attention to the instrument's new capabilities. Frédéric Chopin (1810–49), the Polish-born composer and pianist who immigrated to France, produced some of the most beloved music for the piano with his *Études*, and embraced his native folk culture with his *Polonaises* and *Mazurkas*.

Nature in its specific settings often inspired Romantic composers, such as Felix Mendelssohn (1809–47), the German composer who was the personal favorite of Queen Victoria. His *Hebrides Overture* (1842) commemorated his journey to Scotland, which like many other Germans he admired and imagined as a land of ancient poetic inspiration for the Nordic races. Along with the *Tragic Overture* (1880) by Johannes Brahms (1833–97), Mendelssohn's is one of the best examples of the concert overture, a staple of Romanticism. Other composers explored inner psychological worlds and the dream state, both of which figure prominently in *Symphonie Fantastique* (1830) by Hector Berlioz (1803–69), one of the greatest but also one of the most misunderstood of all French composers. His most famous composition epitomizes the symphonic poem or "tone poem," an innovation of Romantic music that demonstrated the link between music and other arts.

Romantic music was closely allied with lyric poetry which, along with the fashionable interest in folk songs and ballads that marked the early nineteenth century, led to a great proliferation of songs – often for solo voice with piano accompaniment – in Romantic composition. The short-lived Franz Schubert (1797–1828) composed more than 600 such works, called *Lieder* ("songs"). The importance of vocal music certainly accelerated the growth and widespread influence of opera in the nineteenth century, which continued to be dominated by such Italian composers as Gioacchino Rossini (1792–1868), Vincenzo Bellini (1801–35), and Gaetano Donizetti (1797–1848). Romantic themes persisted in the operas of Giuseppe Verdi (1813–1901), the single most influential of all operatic composers. Late in the century, the operas of Giacomo Puccini (1858–1924) represent a turning away from Romantic toward more Realistic or topical subject matter. French grand opera reached spectacular levels in the early nineteenth century in the works in French of Giacomo Meyerbeer (1791–1864), who was nevertheless a German composer. By later in the century, *opera comique* and grand opera fused into French lyric opera.

For sheer energy and grandiose ambition, no composer could match the example of Richard Wagner (1813–83), who sought to synthesize theatre, music, and poetry into an all-enveloping *Gesamtkunstwerk*, or comprehensive work of art. His goal was nothing less than the revitalization of a national culture, which he perceived in terms of authentic *völkisch* identity. Wagner's greatest accomplishment was the multi-opera *Ring Cycle*, heavily indebted to Teutonic legend and lore. With his charismatic wife Cosima, Wagner settled in Bayreuth, Germany, where he staged his ambitious performances and where they presided over an ongoing salon of admiring younger artists. After the composer's death, Cosima significantly magnified the *völkisch* and antisemitic implications of much that could be found in Wagner's works.

Romantic – or perhaps Neo-romantic music – flourished until very late in the nineteenth century, especially in Vienna, where Richard Strauss (1864–1949) energetically continued the tradition of the "tone poem." Yet the most profound (albeit troubled) musical genius of

this milieu was Gustav Mahler (1860–1911), whose music met with incomprehension when first introduced. Mahler's music is dark, brooding, and dauntingly ambitious, especially his choral symphonic works. The somber overtones of his work match the tragic circumstances of his personal life, not to mention the indignities he suffered as a Jew in the antisemitic Hapsburg Empire. Mahler continued the Romantic *lieder* tradition, with his complex *Lied von der Erde* (1908) and the heartbreaking *Kindertotenlieder* (1901–4).

The Popular Press, Novels, and the Reading Public

Like their Enlightenment predecessors, Romantic authors addressed themselves to an attentive public, one gaining in literacy throughout the century. The early nineteenth century had seen the establishment of modern publishing practices, so that copyrights and royalties, concepts alien to writers of the previous century, were now part of the world writers could assume. As books gradually became more affordable thanks to lower printing costs and changes in their marketing, the prospect of impressive sales drove many authors to pursue writing as a means to a comfortable life. Honoré de Balzac (1799–1850) and Charles Dickens (1812–70) provide celebrated examples of writers who became prolific our of economic necessity as well as to satisfy the demands of an ardent readership.

Today, as we stand in awe before shelves filled with the volumes produced by such energetic authors, we lose sight of the fact that they and most other successful writers of prose fiction first found their readers in the installments they published in popular newspapers and magazines. The growth of the popular press remains one of the most striking cultural phenomena of the late eighteenth and early nineteenth centuries. It was an era of sweeping changes in the business of journalism, including in the way press publications circulated. And even though the contemporary German philosopher Jürgen Habermas has extolled the lively exchange of ideas to be found in eighteenth-century European coffee houses, where newspapers typically were available, if anything the vitality and impact of newspapers were even greater in the early decades of the nineteenth century.

Newspapers usually were available only in the form of individual subscriptions, something beyond the means of most readers. During most of the first half of the century readers availed themselves of public reading rooms – called *cabinets de lecture* in France – in order to peruse the latest newspapers. Here one would pay a modest amount to sit by the hour and peruse the papers. Readers in Paris flocked to read *La Presse* and *Le Siècle*, two dailies that first appeared in 1836. This was at the height of the July Monarchy, a time of frustrated political reforms, financial scandal, and legislative corruption. The latter was a major target of the great caricaturist and painter Honoré Daumier (1808–79), many of whose most politically charged cartoons appeared in *La Charivari*, a paper founded in 1835 that would become a major influence on the great British publication *Punch*.

The demand for newspapers increased apace with the rise of literacy and the growth of urbanization. Censorship remained an impediment in many countries, particularly in monarchies. Relatively speaking, British newspapers were much less threatened with censorship. But as the century unfolded, successful newspapers came to be established in major cities across the continent, including *Le Figaro* in Paris (1854), *Die Frankfurter Allgemeine Zeitung* in Prussia (1856), and the *Corriere della Sera* in Italy (1876). One of the most significant debuts with a far-reaching impact on the market both for journalism and popular fiction was that of *Le Petit Journal* in 1863. It was the first daily paper to be distributed throughout France, featuring material that would entertain rural readers as well as urbanites. The paper regularly published *romans-feuilletons*, or serially appearing novels, and this sounded the death-knell of *colportage*, or the itinerant book peddling trade that had long provided readers not living near bookstores or lending libraries with inexpensive books and periodicals.

Magazines likewise boosted their sales by serializing fiction. They also appealed to a wide readership through their prolific use of illustrations, eventually photographic reproductions.

The Illustrated London News, founded in 1842, was the prototype, inspiring imitators in other countries, for example the French *L'illustration*, the German *Die Woche*, and the American *Harper's Weekly*. Many successful literary careers were founded in large part on popular literary reviews, and Great Britain offered the greatest variety of these. Edinburgh alone boasted the *Edinburgh Review* (founded in 1802), the *Quarterly Review* (1809), and *Blackwood's Edinburgh Magazine* (1817). Prominent English novelists were associated with such London magazines as *Bentley's Miscellany* (founded in 1837) and *Cornhill Magazine* (1860). The former employed Charles Dickens as its first editor, the role William Makepeace Thackeray (1811–63) played for the latter publication. Significant literary magazines on the continent included *Revue des Deux Mondes* (1829), where some of the first works by the beloved novelist Victor Hugo (1802–85) appeared, the German weekly *Die Literarisches Wochenblatt* (1820), and *Nuova Antologia* (1866) and *La Cultura* (1881) in Italy.

The successful practice of serialization did much to make the novel the century's dominant literary genre. Certainly this was true of Balzac, whose 91 novels and novellas, many of them collected under his vast series *La Comédie Humaine*, often appeared first as *romans-feuilletons*. The rising consumer society increased demand, and novels written for the popular market circulated widely in inexpensively produced editions by publishers like Routledge in England and Reclam in Germany.

After the major new daily newspapers established themselves in the 1830s in France, readers of the day responded to the *romans-feuilletons* they featured as if they were "muckraking" journalistic pieces. This was true especially of the wildly successful novelist Eugène Sue (1804–57), whose *Les Mystères de Paris* (1842–3) and other novels appeared first in *Le Journal des Débats*. Sue's sentimental fiction portrayed the misery of the urban poor. The very popular novelist Aurore Dupin (1804–76), a.k.a. George Sand, known even more for her scandalous life than for her fiction, wrote novels that encouraged sympathy for peasants as well as urban workers and the poor, in a style that began to move from Romanticism to literary Realism.

Adventure stories formed another important part of popular fiction. Such novels as *Les Trois mousquetaires* (1844, *The Three Musketeers*) by Alexandre Dumas *père* (1802–70) first saw print in serial form, and their popularity prefigured that of the futuristic works of Jules Verne (1820–95) much later in the century. The gallantry of bygone ages had enormous appeal for popular readers, and the novels of Walter Scott continued to sell briskly throughout Europe. As the American mystique as a land of adventure and danger grew, novels set in that frontier enjoyed great popularity, an important example being the works of James Fenimore Cooper (1789–1851).

In England, novels by women authors dominated the literary landscape early in the century. Jane Austen (1776–1817) perfected the art of novels as comedies of manners that exposed the foibles and pretensions of women and men caught up in the rituals of courtship. Her fiction, largely unknown during her lifetime, preceded the era of the popular literary press described above. This was true as well of the brilliant Brontë sisters, Charlotte (1816–55), Emily (1818–48), and Anne (1820–49). Emily Brontë's *Wuthering Heights* (1847 – published the same year as Charlotte's *Jane Eyre*) in many ways established the model for what came to be called the "Gothic Romance," still a dominant force in popular fiction. Elizabeth Gaskell (1810–65), who enjoyed commercial success through the exposure her fiction gained in such publications as *Blackwood's Edinburgh Magazine*, did much to promote the posthumous reputation of Charlotte Brontë, whom she had befriended. Gaskell's greatest popular success came through *Household Journal*, to which Charles Dickens had asked her to contribute.

Recent scholars with an interest in gendered aspects of cultural history have observed that novels that appealed to women readers served, through their heavy emphasis on the emotional interiority of domestic life, to enshrine the Victorian "angel of the house" as the model for female virtue, within a social framework that assigned women to the private sphere while according men the privilege of its public counterpart. Novels seem to have been particularly well suited to an era that took as given the steady progress of increasingly complex national and urban development, accompanied by a decline in the centrality of rural existence. The genre, with its long, episodic organization of events and characters, appeared to mirror the drama of linear historical development through which Europeans felt themselves to be living.

Even though the majority of the population continued to inhabit the countryside, the nineteenth century was a time of increasing urbanization. In such major European cities as Paris, London, and Berlin a middle-class public with increasingly comfortable economic means and more plentiful leisure time arose and experienced their cities as stages on which the major modern actors – government, commerce, and culture – played starring roles. Paris during the July Monarchy (1830–48) saw the origins of what would become modern consumer culture, in the covered arcades of central Paris that, with their glass roofs and fashionable boutiques, anticipated the more upscale shopping malls of today. People could stroll and admire the goods on display, savoring the sense of abundance and modern accomplishment that would be epitomized by London's Crystal Palace Exhibition of 1851.

Realism and Naturalism in the Arts

However confident and self-congratulatory the attitudes of the comfortable classes of the nineteenth century may have been, the artists of the mid-to-late portion of that century often saw their role as one of exposing the many limitations and shortcomings of a world ravaged by industrialization and the degradation that urban existence brought to the unfortunate. The comprehensive vision of such novelists as Balzac, in his effort to encompass the entirety of Restoration Paris, exposed the social defects and outrages of that world, even if the author, himself a monarchist, might not have intended that emphasis. Other novelists, such as Hugo and Dickens, certainly intended such criticism, and in Dickens's case his novels led directly to parliamentary hearings about the abuses factory workers and miners suffered. Realism in novels could also focus on rural existence, as in the immensely popular novels of George Eliot, a.k.a. Mary Anne Evans (1819–80) and Thomas Hardy (1840–1928). Like their urban counterparts Dickens and Thackeray, their novels populated an entire fictional world.

Realist painting likewise highlighted the negative aspects of social existence, subjecting them to artistic dissection. Oil paints helped in this regard, as early and mid-century painters anticipated the kind of technical advantage that would come with photography. Paris, dubbed the "capital of the nineteenth century" by critic Walter Benjamin, was certainly the center for innovations in painting for Realism and the schools that superseded it. An acknowledged master of the oil medium was Jean Auguste Dominique Ingres (1780–1867), best known for his fantastic scenes of the Turkish bath. However, the theme of social class is more immediately apparent in such portraits of his as *Monsieur Bertin* (1832), where the sitter looms toward the implied viewer in his full bourgeois *gravitas*.

The caricaturist Honoré Daumier brought an aroused social consciousness to his depictions of working-class characters, such as his washerwoman (*La Blanchisseuse*, 1863), portrayed as she trudges home, leading her young daughter by the hand, bearing her load of wash. Here, Realism begins to shade over into its successor Naturalism, where more squalid examples of social existence would be spotlighted. This is similar to the approach of the great Realist painter Gustave Courbet (1819–77), well known for his radical political activism at the time of the Paris Commune (1871). Courbet in particular was remarkable for the casual matter-of-factness of his subject matter, nowhere more apparent than in his great canvas *Un Enterrement à Ornans* (1849–50, *Burial at Ornans*). Elsewhere in Europe, Realism in painting often meant a less obviously social or political message, more oriented toward exploration of light, color, and shadow. The implied subject matter could be much more ambiguous, as in the paintings, recently the subject of rediscovery and reevaluation, of Christoffer Wilhelm Eckersburg (1783–1853), the Danish artist whose portrayal – typically of female models – calls to mind the light-intoxicated canvases of Johannes Vermeer.

Naturalism, especially evident in literature, marked a step beyond Realism to represent less the social totality than its most unsavory aspects. Again, a French novelist is one of the most representative figures, and this is Émile Zola (1840–1902), whose novels, such as *Nana* (1880) and *Germinal* (1885), were meant to serve as a call to action and reform. Zola was most famous for his intervention on behalf of Alfred Dreyfus (1859–1935), the French military officer wrongly court-martialed for treason. An equally compelling example of a Naturalist writer was the hugely influential Norwegian playwright Henrik Ibsen (1828–1906). He laid bare the hypocrisy and unhappiness of middle-class families, particularly, in such plays as *A Doll's House* (1879) and *Hedda Gabler* (1891), with regard to women trapped in stifling marriages.

The modern novel continued to evolve out of Realist and Naturalist influences, responding as well to the aesthetic challenges of avant-garde movements in the arts. From the perspective of recent literary criticism, the single most significant nineteenth-century novelist for the development of literary modernism was Gustave Flaubert (1821–80), whose fiction contains elements of Romanticism, Realism, Naturalism, and much besides. He first attracted notoriety when five installments of his novel *Madame Bovary* (1857), published serially in the *Revue de Paris*, were condemned for indecency, resulting in a public trial at which the author and his publisher were defendants. The year 1857 was the height of Napoleon III's Second Empire, a time noted, among other things, for highly pious, if hypocritical, expressions of public morality, much of it inspired by the strong prejudices of the Empress Eugénie. Flaubert's novel, in which a bored country doctor's wife indulges in adulterous affairs, ran afoul of such sensibilities. Although Flaubert was acquitted of the charges he faced, the book failed to achieve the commercial success such publicity might have guaranteed. Readers found Flaubert's style complicated and baffling. Claiming in his correspondence that he had wished to produce a book "about nothing," the author adopted what he referred to as his "free, indirect style." At times, Flaubert seems to inhabit his protagonist, at other times he takes on the omniscient narrator's voice, but quite often the narrative point of view strikes the reader as disembodied, diffuse, and multi-directional. For some recent critics, this unprecedented style marks the work as "postmodern" *avant la lettre*, so to speak.

Symbolist Poetry, Impressionism, and the Avant-Garde

A long succession of artistic "isms" began to emerge after the mid-nineteenth century in ways that would define the essence of the modern arts. Paris was very much the center of this process. Symbolism was the movement in the arts, associated especially with French poetry, that encouraged the idea that the artist must create private symbols capable of giving the reader, viewer, etc. a powerful transformative experience made possible by the process Symbolists called this *synaesthesia*, defined as the ability of one kind of aesthetic experience to invoke an equivalent one in another artistic realm. For example, a literary work might call to mind a painting, or the latter might suggest a passage of music. French Symbolist poetry broke away somewhat from the Romantic tradition, and even more deliberately rejected the lofty "art for the sake of art" credo of the so-called Parnassian school.

The founding figure in the new approach to poetry was Charles Baudelaire (1821–67). His first book of poems *Les Fleurs du mal* (*The Flowers of Evil*) appeared the same year as Flaubert's infamous novel and similarly met with a criminal charge. This time the writer was convicted, and Baudelaire had to agree to remove the six most offending poems. The book offers often disturbing views of the depravity and degradation of Parisian life, with a relatively frank avowal of erotic desire. The central motif is the effort to transform unwholesome or disturbing experiences into art marked by such beautiful symbols as the swan. Baudelaire was very active as an art critic, especially championing Delacroix and the first Impressionist artists.

Late in Baudelaire's life two younger authors emerged who enjoy high regard in the annals of literary modernism as much for their brief and controversial lives as for their writings. The fascination with the limited life span seems a holdover from Romanticism, and one can cite Neo-romantic elements in the writings of many authors who emerged much later in the century. Isidore Ducasse (1846–1870), who wrote as the Comte du Lautrámont, died in obscure circumstances in Paris in 1870, perhaps as a victim of the siege that ended the Franco-Prussian War. He is remembered best as the author of a strange and somewhat prophetic book called *Les Chants de Maldoror*, not published until 1890. The book contains bizarre, dreamlike, often violent imagery that helps to explain Lautrámont's adoption by the Surrealists of the following century.

The other younger contemporary of Baudelaire, who enjoys a more prominent place in the canon of modern French poetry, was Arthur Rimbaud (1854–91). Between the ages of 15 and 19 he produced his entire body of written work, including the books *Le Bateau ivre* (*The Drunken Boat*), *Les Illuminations* (*Illuminations*), and *Une Saison en enfer* (*A Season in Hell*). These were poems filled with often long, languid lines that celebrated the vagabond life and what Rimbaud referred to in his letters as the poet's need to be "a seer" (*un voyant*) and to experiment with the extreme limits of sensory experience. As Baudelaire had done, Rimbaud experimented with the so-called prose poem, which has grown into a major subgenre of modern French poetry. The rest of his life Rimbaud devoted to adventure and travel, a process perhaps begun on the barricades of the Paris Commune in 1871. He formed a powerfully erotic and violent relationship with another Symbolist poet named Paul Verlaine (1844–96), who coined the phrase *les poètes maudits* (poets who are damned) to describe his generation. It is a phrase that has come to be applied to a whole series of modern "outlaw" writers. It is noteworthy that French poets beginning with Baudelaire made an icon of Edgar Allen Poe (1809–49), both for his poetry and for his life of extreme intoxication, something Baudelaire had seen as a means to artistic insight, but which led Verlaine to the same kind of alcoholic dissipation that destroyed Poe.

A much more cerebral version of poetic symbolism was found in the poems of Stéphane Mallarmé (1842–98), little recognized during his lifetime outside the circle of fellow poets, painters, and aesthetes who gathered regularly at his home in Paris to hear him hold forth about poetic language and his personal aesthetic. Mallarmé believed that the poet should craft a kind of written language that resembled no other, applicable to the pure realm of the page. To this end, he experimented with unusual typography, creating poems that were visual artifacts in an almost calligraphic way. The most extreme example of this approach is his ambitious poem *Un Coup de dés* (*A Roll of the Dice*). Mallarmé inspired a younger generation of poets led by Paul Valéry (1871–1945) to carry on the Symbolist tradition, and he dabbled in a variety of literary projects, including the brief editorship of a women's fashion magazine.

One of the painters who befriended Mallarmé was Édouard Manet (1832–83), and Baudelaire had also gravitated toward him in earlier years. Manet was associated with the Impressionist movement in painting, although his earliest and most controversial canvases seemed to grow out of a Realist aesthetic. However, if Manet's style could have been seen as close to Realism, his was a highly eccentric and off-center kind of Realism producing works that jolted viewers with their sexual frankness and odd juxtapositions. He first attracted attention for his paintings that were rejected by the Salon exhibitions of the Royal Academy of Painting and Sculpture (again, this was during the Second Empire). One, which he attempted to exhibit in 1863, was his *Le Déjeuner sur l'herbe* (*Lunch on the Grass*), which depicts a trio of picnickers, two men and one young woman – who is nude. Manet further assaulted the artistic conventions of the female nude with his 1867 painting *Olympia*, which presents the viewer with a reclining nude female figure whose piercing gaze meets one head-on. In the painting Manet's white model in the foreground is being attended by a clothed, seemingly shocked black maid in the shadowed background, so that Manet managed

as well to violate the racial codes that intersected with gender (i.e., that white women were chaste and demure while black women were lascivious).

Manet's first critics condemned what they called the flatness of his painting, as if mere surface was all that interested him. Such a charge would come to be leveled even more at the artists who joined Manet in the Impressionist movement. A good example, and someone who has received renewed attention in recent years, was Gustave Caillebotte (1849–1914). Claude Monet (1840–1920) and Pierre-Auguste Renoir (1841–1919) would carry experiments with light and surface to greater extremes, and most today who speak of Impressionism have their works (nudes, flowers, landscapes, river and seascapes) in mind. Berthe Morisot (1841–95), Manet's sister-in-law, and the American expatriate painter Mary Cassatt (1844–1926) produced Impressionist canvases that explored women's domestic world, with scenes of female readers or mothers with children. Somewhat allied with Impressionism, yet known for distinctive, highly personal subject matter (for example, ballet dancers, bathers, thoroughbred horses) often rendered in pastels, was Edgar Degas (1834–1917).

Impressionism gave way to "Post-Impressionism," a term applied to artists who took the Impressionist aesthetic as their point of departure but who moved in idiosyncratic directions that begin to anticipate the early twentieth-century movement known as Expressionism. Such artists certainly include Vincent Van Gogh (1853–90), the Dutch-born painter whose greatest accomplishments took place after he moved to Provence, where he filled his canvases with the shimmering, dazzling light of that region. While in Arles, he spent time with his friend Paul Gauguin (1848–1903), who found his greatest inspiration far from France on the South Pacific island of Tahiti. Often painted on wood and other rough surfaces, Gauguin's late works glorified tropical motifs and especially the beauty of Tahitian women. Meanwhile in Paris, Henri de Toulouse-Lautrec (1864–1901) captured the personalities of performers and café habitués of the bohemian Montmartre district.

The richly detailed interiors depicted in the works of Édouard Vuillard (1868–1940) and Pierre Bonnard (1867–1947) were examples of Post-Impressionist art that contained reminders of the efforts of Impressionists like Monet to register minute details of the play of light on the surfaces represented on the canvas. Georges Seurat (1859–91) and Paul Signac (1863–1935) exaggerated this approach into the style known as *pointillisme*. By the end of the century Post-Impressionism increasingly gave way to examples of painters experimenting with techniques that would anticipate later stages of the avant-garde. The somewhat Symbolist painter Odilon Redon (1840–1916) seemed to illustrate the emergent Freudian fascination with dreams with his haunting improbable images. The isolated self-taught Parisian painter Henri Rousseau (1844–1910) likewise achieved a dreamlike quality in his exotic scenes that would make him an inspiration for Surrealists. Elsewhere in Europe, examples could be found of painters whose bold use of color and very personal subject matter anticipated either Expressionism, as in the case of the Norwegian painter Edvard Munch (1863–1944), or Surrealism, as in the violent imagery produced by Belgian artist James Ensor (1860–1949), whose works almost seemed a throwback to Flemish masters like Bosch or Breughel.

As the example of Redon in the previous paragraph shows, Symbolism continued to thrive in the arts through the end of the nineteenth century. This is especially evident in music. The preeminent Symbolist composer of the era was Claude Debussy (1863–1918), one of whose most celebrated works was the atmospheric *Prélude à l'après-midi d'un faune*, based on a poem by Mallarmé. Debussy's pupil Maurice Ravel (1875–1937) continued the Symbolist tradition, but with an attitude receptive in later years to jazz. Popular musical forms often influenced more elite ones, and certainly the late nineteenth century was a time of enthusiasm for folk genres. In the British Isles, the vogue for folk music was related to the widespread influence of the Arts and Crafts movement in the decorative arts encouraged by the example of the writer William Morris (1834–96). In Ireland writers like Lady Gregory (1852–1932) and William Butler Yeats (1865–1939) sought a nationalist revival, which included recovering traditional poems and songs and even the fading Gaelic language.

The French came to refer to the last years of the nineteenth century as the *fin-de-siècle*, which apart from its literal meaning, connoted a sense of a waning cultural epoch, one filled with worries as well as vitality. Some composers of this period remained unclassifiable in the sense of any musical "school," and a vivid example is provided by the music of the French genius Erik Satie (1866–1925). Satie produced quirky, deliberately humorous or ironic pieces meant to mock the pretensions of the serious music public. He called his music "furniture music," meaning it was not really to be listened to, but simply admitted as part of the atmosphere. Such a concept anticipated the so-called "ambient" music of a century later.

If, in Satie's case, what made him "avant-garde" had nothing to do with some obvious school or movement, his contemporary counterpart in literature was Alfred Jarry, a one-of-a-kind playwright and all-around provocateur who burst upon the Parisian literary scene with his 1896 play *Ubu roi* (*King Ubu*), a play whose mangled syntax and improbable staging outraged and confounded the theatre-going public, exactly as its author intended. He wrote other plays, but became better known for his strange antics. These included speaking loudly and abruptly in the squeaky, mechanical-sounding voice of his famous character Ubu, sitting in bars drinking absinthe colored with ink, and while thus imbibing occasionally firing a loaded pistol into the air. In addition he founded a whimsical institution he called the "College of Pataphysics," over which he presided and on behalf of which he issued occasional proclamations. Jarry died the lonely death of a reclusive and destitute alcoholic, but he served as the harbinger for many radical literary experiments to come.

Nietzsche and Freud

The eccentric and often deliberately shocking artistic examples of the *fin-de-siècle* have been cited often as indications that this was an age of a new irrational cultural spirit. Certainly it was a time in which confidence in the scientific outlook began to wane for many, and disturbing dark new trends – the kind artists are often best positioned to detect – appeared to be emerging. Of all the intellectual figures of the late nineteenth century we might cite as representative of the new sensibility, no two have remained more influential than Friedrich Nietzsche and Sigmund Freud, but neither of them, especially Nietzsche, was to have the kind of impact on the nineteenth century that he would thereafter.

Friedrich Nietzsche (1844–1900) was a brilliant German philosopher who hated being German and radically stood the conventional style of philosophical argument on its head. In such singular works as *The Birth of Tragedy* (1872) and *Thus Spoke Zarathustra* (1892) he denounced his civilization as one in which "God" had been killed, by which he appeared to mean the inspired godlike qualities within each man, by an excessively rational (his term was "Apollonian') civilization. What was needed was for each person to overcome this defeat and to achieve the status of "overman" (*Übermensch*). This was interpreted, with dire consequences for later European history, as an endorsement of a "master race" kind of ideology. In fact, Nietzsche had ended his cherished friendship with the composer Wagner precisely over the latter's virulent antisemitism. Also, it must be pointed out that Nietzsche's writings, since he made expository argument subservient to stylistic experimentation (writing philosophical texts as if they were literary) make it very difficult to impose any kind of systematic order to his work or to say with any finality what he "meant." But clearly generations of modern artists and thinkers have taken inspiration from his uncompromising individualism and questing spirit.

Sigmund Freud (1856–1939) was also someone who offered ideas and writings that, at first, simply could not get a hearing. Despite this, his relentless labors as a theorist for the psychoanalytic enterprise he founded gradually brought him considerable renown. Trained as a physician in his native Vienna, Freud became interested in the problem of hysteria, considered during the 1880s to be exclusively a female malady. Through unsuccessful efforts to treat hysterical patients that briefly included hypnosis, he stumbled upon the so-called "talking cure," which he would designate as psychoanalysis. He first announced this in the book *Studies in Hysteria* (1895), co-authored with his mentor Josef Breuer (1842–1925). Gradually, Freud worked his way toward the theoretical foundations of psychoanalysis that postulated models of human psychological development that had everything to do with childhood experiences and traumas that the psyche has to repress, but which return with great force to interfere with satisfactory adult existence. Freud's analysis of his own dreams in *Die Traumdeutung* (1900, *Interpretation of Dreams*) gave him the insight into these patterns of experience that he was able to bring to bear in his clinical practice. But at the century's end, Freud's reputation was still under attack because of the emphasis he placed on his patients' psychosexuality, or their psychological attempts to deal with their own sexual experiences, fears, or anxieties.

Late Nineteenth-Century Popular Culture

Freud's teachings resonated within a *fin-de-siècle* culture that abounded with at times morbid sexual preoccupations. Syphilis was a common scourge, and a patriarchal culture tended to blame the so-called "New Woman" (i.e., a more emancipated and assertive type of woman) for its spread. Likewise, this was the era during which "homosexuality" came to be a term commonly applied to a new type of person deemed abnormal, and many European countries adopted laws criminalizing homosexual behavior. The celebrated writer Oscar Wilde (1854–1900) was a famous victim of the new aggressive legal climate. In France, still smarting from its 1870 military defeat, a declining birth rate fed sexual fears and gender preoccupations that were all bound up with notions of military readiness and masculine honor. This malaise was exacerbated by the Dreyfus Affair of the 1890s. In such a climate, homosexuality, whether male or female, was viewed as a threat to the nation's very survival.

Such sexual worries were related to the phenomenon of greater available leisure time. Organized sport began to play an important role, especially in England in the late part of the nineteenth century. Beneficial exercise and games were seen as vital to the class interests of the privileged orders, so that English public schools led the way in organized competitions for rowing, track and field, football, and cricket. Even girls' schools began to form athletic teams, as the vogue for sport overcame the legacy of longheld medical opinion that young women were simply too delicate to participate in athletics. Soccer (or football) evolved from the anarchy of earlier decades into leagues and standardized rules that soon spread to other parts of Europe. Finally, the modern Olympic Games began as a result of the founding in 1894 of the International Olympic Committee. Sport as a component of entertainment was well underway.

In *fin-de-siècle* Paris, middle-class audiences flocked to the boulevard theatres for light opera and to the fashionable cafés for the musical entertainments know as *cafés-concerts* – a milieu portrayed memorably by Toulouse-Lautrec. In England, the popular music halls evolved from drinking establishments that offered entertainment. In Vienna, crowds flocked to enjoy the waltzes of Johann Strauss (1804–49), whose wild popularity helps to explain the lack of attention accorded the somber music of Gustav Mahler. One of the responses to popular entertainment was concern about its relationship to alcoholism and drug use. The French were alarmed about the craze for absinthe, a debilitating overly potent beverage, and the use of opiates was widespread in many European cities.

By the very end of the century, especially in Paris, the kind of mass "spectacle" that prefigured the modern mass media had' emerged. Here, entertainment included popular museums such as the Musée Grévin, a wax museum like Madame Tussaud's in London, and even visits to the morgue, to which the tabloid press had alerted curious onlookers. Finally, the origins of what would become the motion picture industry began to appear by the late 1890s. Of course, this technology had evolved out of photography, a nineteenth-century innovation that had evolved from mere curiosity into a more serious art form.

After photography came into its own with the introduction of the photo/negative process in the 1840s, it was not long before various uses and genres emerged, from portraiture (including commemoration of the deceased) to what would become photojournalism and even pornography. Some of the earliest accomplished photographers specialized in portraits, beginning with those practicing the time-consuming method that produced what were called *daguerrotypes*. By the 1860s the photo/negative process had been refined and more easily usable cameras had been introduced. Two of the greatest portrait photographers were Victorian English artists, Julia Margaret Cameron (1815–79) and Charles Lewis Dodgson (1832–98). The former photographed such celebrated neighbors as the poet Alfred, Lord Tennyson (1809–92) and the astronomer Sir John Herschel (1792–1871), the originator of the very term "photography." Dodgson, better known as Lewis Carroll, preferred to photograph his young friend Alice Liddell (the model for *Through the Looking-Glass*) and other girls. Even more than he, Cameron photographed young children in stylized poses that today's viewers might find disturbingly erotic, a reminder that there is much more to Victorian attitudes than we have been led to believe.

The greatest French portrait photographer, whose subjects included Baudelaire, Manet, Delacroix, and Flaubert, was Gaspard-Félix Tournachon, a.k.a. Nadar (1820–1910). He gained great fame for lending his services to the military, going up above Paris during the 1870 siege to photograph troop movements. Not only were photography's military uses apparent to French authorities, but also photography came to be widely used in criminology, with experts often believing that they could recognize criminal "types" from facial characteristics painstakingly recorded by the camera. A pioneer in this regard, toward creating what some have called a "carceral society" of increasing surveillance, was Alphonse Bertillon (1832–98).

By the time the brothers Lumière – Auguste (1862–1954) and Louis-Jean (1864–1948) – invented the motion picture camera and screened the first short films in Paris (in 1895 a film of workers leaving a factory in Lyon, and in 1896 dramatic footage of a railroad train leaving the station – so dramatic that viewers leapt in terror from their seats), the art form and entertainment *par excellence* of the following century had announced itself.

GUIDE TO FURTHER READING

Cranston's *The Romantic Movement* is a very compact and useful overview of a long history. Ellison's *Delicate Subjects* brings recent feminist criticism to bear on standard Romantic authors. Buruma's *Anglomania* examines the love-hate relationship Europeans have had with Great Britain in the modern era. The Romantic period provides some fascinating examples. Paris, as the most significant center of modernism in the arts, figures prominently in the writings of T. J. Clark, of whose many books *The Painting of Modern Life* is an outstanding example. Matsuda's *The Memory of the Modern* devotes early chapters to a similar cultural setting. Schorske's *Fin-de-Siècle Vienna*

remains a crucial study of the remarkable milieu of Freud, Strauss waltzes, and artistic decadence. Gay's *Freud* is one of the many books he has devoted to introducing Freud's significance to historians. Pletsch's *Young Nietzsche* builds upon the enormous explosion of recent reinterpretations to advance a provocative argument. Winders's *Gender, Theory, and the Canon* brings feminist critical perspectives to bear on historical reinterpretations of Flaubert, Nietzsche, Freud, and other writers.

Holt's entertaining and well-researched *Sport and the British* is one of many books he has devoted to this subject. Schwartz's *Spectacular Realities* offers a novel interpretation of *fin-de-siècle* mass entertainment. On the subject of photography, Rosenblum's *A World History of Photography* contains excellent chapters on its nineteenth-century origins. Mavor's *Pleasures Taken* presents a powerful reading of Victorian photography. For more on the role of photography in nineteenth-century Europe, consult "Photography and the Culture of Modernity" in *European Culture Since 1848* by Winders.

CHAPTER TWENTY-THREE

Schooling: Culture and the State

SHARIF GEMIE

During the nineteenth century a new land was discovered. European observers were particularly impressed by the explorers' accounts which spoke of the orderly nature of the inhabitants, the fraternal unity of their society, their enlightened and progressive rulers, their polite children, hard-working adults and dedicated bureaucrats. Scientists and sociologists, novelists and politicians excitedly debated the implications of this discovery. What was the name of this new country? – The School.

In this chapter I will explore some common features of this new land. In particular, I will analyze the political-educational project which I will term "the schooling program." My use of this term is intended to remind readers that when examining the development of schools in nineteenth-century Europe, we are always looking at deeper and wider themes than the simple physical presence of teachers and pupils in schoolrooms. This chapter will also consider the experience of parents, local government officials, bureaucrats, and political activists. It will contrast pupils' actual experience of schooling with the ideals of the schooling program. In summary form, it will note how the chasm between the schooling program's ideals and classroom reality created strains among the teachers themselves and how, on occasion, these contradictions could lead to forms of politicization.

Before turning to these themes, a word or two about method. Put simply, there are two

methods by which to analyze schooling. One may be termed "institutional" and is still the form most commonly used in history of education courses at teacher training colleges. The main aim of this method is to provide would-be teachers with information concerning the background to the pedagogic and administrative framework within which they will be working. Obviously, this is often extremely useful: no one could, for example, understand the ferocity with which the presence of veiled Muslim girls in French state schools is debated today without first knowing something about French state ideals of *laïcité* or "secularism." The institutional approach, however, does have some flaws: at its worst, it is reduced to a simplistic story of progress, in which each minister is more far-sighted than the last, and each law more generous. In particular, the institutional approach is extremely weak in acknowledging the influence of forms of education *outside* the school.

The principal alternative approach is a social history of education, which turns from examining schools as if they were autonomous organisms, and concentrates on the interaction between those involved in schooling (pupils, teachers, local and state bureaucrats, and parents) and wider cultural and social influences.[1] While this form of history is perhaps less effective in demonstrating "why school regulations are the way they are," it is more likely to illuminate critical themes and to provoke a healthy skepticism about the nature of schooling.

Obviously, there is not sufficient space in this short chapter to debate "what is Europe?" One provisional and partial answer, however, does emerge in the pages that follow. When examining the schooling program, we can note immediately that this was a transnational phenomenon. David Vincent even describes it as "a single European project."[2] Governments and bureaucrats were consciously comparing different schooling programs; debates took place within a context of explicit rivalry between nations to implement the schooling program. The schooling program was something that brought together different nations, and which created similarities between them. It therefore played some significant role in encouraging a common European consciousness.

Lastly, in this chapter, I will be drawing evidence from primary and secondary schools, and from universities. This will undoubtedly lead to some oversimplifying of the historical record. Readers should be aware that during the nineteenth century, schooling was rigidly structured along class lines. Peasants' and workers' children went to primary schools, but very rarely progressed to secondary schools. Middle-class families and aristocrats either hired home-based tutors for their children or sent them to exclusive preparatory schools, and then enrolled them in secondary schools. In general, only rich young men were able to enroll in universities, although – across Europe – a tiny number of female students began to enter higher education towards the end of the nineteenth century.

The Schooling Program

Today, there is a common assumption that the acquisition and development of reading, writing, and arithmetic – the 3R's – are central to any school. This is, at best, a misunderstanding of the nature of schooling; at worst, this assumption functions as an ideology to justify or to conceal oppressive and authoritarian practices. As will be shown, pre-industrial peoples had their own forms of education prior to the generalization of mass schooling. These older structures usually interacted with literate and numerate cultures and – when necessary – they were fully capable of generalizing literacy and numeracy among the majority of the population. While nineteenth-century governments normally hoped that the development of mass schooling would encourage the wider spread of literacy and numeracy among their populations, this was never their first priority.

What distinguishes schooling from older educational practices is therefore *not* any specific concentration on learning outcomes, but rather schooling's consciously and deliberately organized nature. David Ortiz may well be right to argue that the nineteenth-century Spanish press functioned as "an informal education system . . . alongside Spain's formal one," but it could hardly be claimed that the structures of newspaper distribution, readership, and reception had been consciously designed to facilitate this educational function.[3] Nineteenth-century people could acquire an education almost anywhere: in fields or in workshops, in cafés or in art galleries. Schools, however, were the only places which – ideally – were specifically designed for this purpose. To this first point, we can add a second qualification to distinguish a school from – for example – the lesson that a governess might provide for an aristocratic child in a domestic setting. The key pedagogic innovation provided by schooling is the class: a collection of children of broadly similar ages and abilities who study, simultaneously, the same topic under the guidance of a trained instructor. Usually, school administrations preferred to separate boys and girls in classes, but states and local authorities often found this requirement too costly.

Schooling's origins are still hotly debated. Contesting historians have respectively proposed Protestant and Catholic beginnings. Perhaps both are right: it seems likely that religious rivalry during the sixteenth century created the first recognizable "classes" in modern Europe, as churchmen on both sides sought to impose rigidly clear theological principles on large sections of their populations.

During the eighteenth century governments and writers debated questions concerning schooling. A number of key attitudes emerged. An elitist current admired the classical, humanist values inspired by texts from Ancient Greece and Rome. For such writers, the acquisition of Latin and Greek was the hallmark of any true education: such requirements meant that, almost by definition, only the privileged few could be properly educated. These humanists were in turn criticized by more modern, scientific or industrial writers, who were beginning to think in terms of mass schooling. Often, they were labeled "utilitarians," by which was meant that they promoted an education that was directly useful to the age in which they were living. Lastly, there were a large number of skeptics, who were concerned that any attempt by government to intervene in popular culture was likely to provoke discontent and even rebellions.

Industrialization and the French Revolution rapidly altered the nature of this debate. Following the mass revolutionary movements of the 1790s, it was difficult for religious or secular conservatives to argue that there was a natural, naive goodness among the masses which should be left unbesmirched by any trace of book learning. Moreover, industrialization was putting a strain on traditional patterns of education: under conditions in which children would be engaged in tasks about which their parents knew almost nothing, how could a responsible government expect families to prepare their children for modern working practices? Furthermore, the immediate cultural consequence of industrialization was often a decline in literacy rates as the first generation of industrial workers lost contact with traditional educational practices and took up deskilled positions in the new industries.[4] Urban explorers like Alban de Villeneuve-Bargemont (1784–1850) in France and Henry Mayhew (1812–87) in Britain brought back terrifying accounts of family life and culture among the new working class. In general, despite the common clichés concerning "Victorian values," the nineteenth century was a period of the loss in confidence in the family to carry out any significant socio-educational role. Such worries even spread to bourgeois parents, who were prepared to invest more and more in their children's schooling.[5]

Another cultural concern also developed during the nineteenth century. Commercial publishers wanted to increase book sales by appealing to new markets, in particular to women. This worried cultural conservatives, who imagined that the female reader was an innocent, falling unthinkingly into an addiction to a new, highly toxic drug. Flaubert's *Madame Bovary* (published in 1857) is probably the most famous literary evocation of this theme, but France was not unique in this respect. In Russia, cultural conservatives were equally concerned by the spread of *Zhorzhzandovshchina*, or George-Sandism, the cult of the unmarried, free-thinking French woman writer who used a masculine pseudonym. Russian conservatives believed that this cult was being spread among young women by their irresponsible reading habits.[6]

Under these circumstances, liberals and conservatives agreed that state action was urgently needed. There was always a nationalist dimension to such debates. As early as the beginning of the eighteenth century, bureaucrats who worked with Peter the Great argued that mass schooling was needed if Russia was to compete with other nations.[7] Spanish liberals in the late nineteenth century argued that through mass schooling, Spain would be Europeanized, and so develop into "a modern nation-state."[8] These types of social, cultural, and economic concerns shaped the schooling program. While one can identify particular conservative, liberal, and humanist strands, governing groups agreed that schooling was at once a vaccine against the unfortunate tendencies of their age (materialism, demoralization, mass politicization) *and* an instrument to allow modernization to evolve in an orderly and responsible manner. Schools aimed to teach pupils to believe in the nation-state, to behave politely, to follow a timetable, to work as a mass, and to respect people in authority even before their teachers began to consider literacy and numeracy.

Such aims led governments into massive reform programs. Even the simple matter of counting the number of schools in a particular region usually involved the creation of specifically trained bureaucracy as – across Europe – it became clear that methods such as relying on the good will of local gentry, or asking mayors and local councilors to carry out this task, were not going to be effective. The notorious "paper schools" of nineteenth-century Russia, which existed only in the imaginations of local government officials, are but one example of the "hall of mirrors" that central government directives could produce.[9]

Pupils' Experiences

We must begin by insisting on one crucial principle: education was bigger than the world of the school, and this observation remains valid even in the twenty-first century, when schooling has been generalized to the majority of European populations.

A glance at a few nineteenth-century autobiographies demonstrates the range of educational influences encountered outside the school. Heinrich Heine (1797–1856), a middle-class German radical who spent much of his life in exile, recalled his mother's worries about the maidservants in their house. "She scolded the maids for telling ghost stories in my presence. In short, she did everything in her power to safeguard me from superstition and poetry."[10] The first memories of Alexander Herzen (1812–70) were of his old nurse telling and retelling him stories of Napoleon's invasion of Moscow.[11] He also recalled how the servants in his house appeared as stable, reliable friends, people whom he could trust, while the series of tutors and governors who taught him at home seemed fickle, capricious, and changing. Frédéric Mistral (1830–1914) was one of the first promoters of a separate, southern French or Provencal identity. In 1855 he helped publish an *Almanach Provençal*, which collected traditional poems, stories, legends, jokes, and riddles. He noted, observantly, that these items contained "all the tradition, all the humor, all the spirit" of his people.[12] In the west of France, Pierre-Jakez Hélias (1914–95) was given an intensive Breton-language education by his grandfather *before* he went to school. It largely consisted of traditional riddles, tongue-twisters, and sayings. Later, Hélias noted how this education had developed his powers of speech, and wondered "how did our illiterate ancestors ever imagine these exercises?"[13] Hélias makes a highly significant observation later in his autobiography. Following his time in primary school, he began work as a peasant. For this, too, he needed to be trained.

> I learnt how to use all the resources of the countryside: the trees, the plants, the water, the stones, the birds and the winds. I learnt to waste nothing which might sooner or later be useful, never to cut two branches from a hedge when only one was needed. This was how I was trained . . . for the peasant's craft.[14]

Those Romantic conservatives who fondly imagined that the unschooled peoples of the villages lived their lives in happy ignorance were making a fundamental error. Forms of education were all around: they could be found around the baby's crib and in the fields, in the workshops and in the cafés, as people talked, argued, listened and, above all, taught themselves in a wide variety of different ways.

Normally, such forms of education did not involve mass literacy, although (as in the example of Mistral's *Almanach*) on occasion they might interact with printed materials. But it was certainly possible to generalize mass literacy without schooling. While any historian of education would wish to be cautious before identifying the first country to have successfully achieved mass literacy, one prominent candidate for this position is eighteenth-century Sweden. A particular mixture of religious and state concerns led to the passing of the Church Law of 1686, according to which an adult would only be accepted for Holy Communion if he or she were capable of reading the Bible. Without such abilities, adults would not be able to become full members of the church, nor would they be able to marry. The Swedish church certainly attempted to encourage literacy by printing a number of cheap, simple collections of psalms, prayers, and catechisms. But the principal vehicle for teaching literacy was not the church, but the family. A supplementary decree of 1723 threatened to fine families who failed to teach their children to read. In this case, adults were only required to read: mass writing came later, with the generalization of schooling in the late nineteenth century. This example from eighteenth-century Sweden, however, remains an intriguing demonstration of the possibility of non-school forms of teaching.[15]

A similar trend can be observed in nineteenth-century Russia. Some peasants grew concerned about levels of illiteracy, and proposed to act against it in a concerted and collective manner. They formed their own "wild" schools, separate from and independent of those encouraged by the state. According to one historian, these informal, unofficial initiatives were probably more effective than the state schools in raising literacy rates.[16]

The dominant trend in nineteenth-century Europe, however, was a move away from traditional educational structures and towards the generalization of mass schooling. Within a traditional context education could occur almost unconsciously and informally: was Herzen's nurse aware that she was beginning the education of the future writer and radical? The school, on the other hand, proclaimed loudly and clearly that it was there to implement and to enforce children's education. Entry into its rooms was a rite of passage, a dividing line marking early infancy off from childhood proper, drawing children out of their homes, families, and workplaces.

Many families disliked this intrusion of the state's demands into their domestic economy: children were often needed by their families as workers, and their absence at school was resented. In some villages in Russia, peasants would even pay money in order to avoid sending their children to school.[17] Throughout the nineteenth century, teachers would complain about children's uneven attendance at classes, particularly in the countryside as peasants would call their children back to help with the harvest and other agricultural tasks.

As they entered the schoolroom, something happened to the children. For some, the school seemed a place of surrealist absurdity: why, wondered the Breton-speaking Hélias, was his Breton-speaking teacher now talking in French? Worse still, why were his Breton-speaking parents now insisting that he imitate the schoolteacher's new language?[18] He and his friends would gather together in miserable little groups during playtime, and complain about their situation.

Elsewhere, however, entry into a classroom could almost produce an opposite effect. Barbara Engel gives a striking description of the day in 1869 on which 200 young women trooped into the newly opened courses at the Alarchin school in St. Petersburg. They came from different backgrounds: they were the daughters of minor nobles, civil servants, merchants, priests, and shopkeepers. But, by and large, they had all spontaneously adopted the informal uniform of the "New Woman": short hair, plain skirts, and – often – blue-tinted glasses. Sitting on the school benches together produced a sudden shock of generational self-recognition: they were not alone, other young women thought like them.[19] Herzen felt something similar as he entered Moscow University in 1825. The university became the

> one common meeting-place, from all parts of the country and all sections of society; there [the students] cast off the prejudices they had acquired at home, reached a common level, formed ties of brotherhood with one another, and then went back to every part of Russia and penetrated every class.[20]

While the schooling program certainly wanted to encourage pupils and students to think as collective teams, this was intended to prepare them for an orderly work discipline. These idealistic, dissident identities were both unexpected and undesirable.

What happened to these new pupils in the school? Did they learn the orderly, progressive morality which the schooling program hoped to generalize? The answer, inevitably, is that there was an extremely wide range of different experiences. While Hélias, our Breton schoolboy, records the deep alienation which he felt within the French-language school system, it should be remembered that he went on to become a lecturer in a teacher training college. In other words, feelings of loneliness, despair, and even rebellion at school are not necessarily signs of a dysfunctional schooling system: they may simply be the inevitable symptoms of a difficult cultural transition.

One common point does emerge, however, as one surveys nineteenth-century autobiographies. Each writer obviously considered that their education was an important part of their life: if nothing else, they needed to explain to their readers how they came to acquire literacy and, on occasion, to apologize for deficiencies in their writing abilities. Each of them also felt that it was important to record the different educational stimuli that they had received. Inevitably, this usually means that they spend several chapters recording their impression of their different schools. These normally take the form, however, of memories of particular teachers. In other words, records of personalized contacts with particular individuals tend to be recalled, whereas the ideals of the schooling program were to encourage a greater, deeper, and wider consciousness, perhaps in the form of some sense of patriotism or political awakening.

While one must be wary about making simplistic generalizations based on a relatively small number of texts, most autobiographers make quite fiercely negative comments about their schooling. Teachers seem to have had little prestige and attracted little respect or affection. In this sense, Herzen's remarks about a relative's new wife can be cited as typical. She was a teacher in Smolny Convent. She resembled

the most typical specimen of a Petersburg governess . . . thin, blonde, and very shortsighted, she looked the teacher and the moralist all over. By no means stupid, she was full of an icy enthusiasm in her talk, she abounded in commonplaces about virtue and devotion, she knew history and geography by heart, spoke French with repulsive correctness, and concealed a high opinion of herself under an artificial and Jesuitical humility. These traits are common to all pedants in petticoats.[21]

Perhaps it is significant that Herzen's taunts are directed at a woman, for female teachers found it particularly difficult to become socially acceptable. The male teacher could be understood as some approximate equivalent to the priest: but the schoolmistress? At the sight of a female teacher, Russian peasants would suck their teeth and quote the old proverb: "the hair is long but the mind is short."[22] From the opposite end of Europe, we can cite a further example which illustrates the difficulties faced by women holding some form of public educational authority. In the 1850s the French state slowly developed a network of female educational inspectors, charged with evaluating nursery schools and primary schools. When one arrived in the village of Malicorne (Sarthe), the mayor ordered her to be arrested on the charge that she must be a prostitute: he had never heard of the post of *inspectrice*.[23]

These examples suggest not only a prejudice against women, but also a deeper hostility on the part of parents against state intervention in local communities. The new teacher was rarely welcomed, whether male or female. Peasants in settled communities had their own forms of education: they tended to resent this intruder. The state-centered ideals of the schooling program meant little to them. These attitudes meant that even before going to school, children were often learning a certain skepticism or hostility toward the new institution from their parents.

This initial hostility was often strengthened by children's classroom experiences. The new teachers had a tough job on their hands: poorly trained (if trained at all), underpaid, resented by villagers and bureaucrats, they were then faced with a class full of ill-disciplined children who – probably – had never before been required to sit quietly and listen. Some of this new generation of teachers, after a few false starts, did discover their talents. A gifted teacher could almost bewitch their pupils with their eloquence and their enthusiasm. One favorable inspector's report from 1902 presents us with a persuasive representation of one such successful teacher.

An intelligent, hardworking, lively schoolmistress whose unique concern is her school . . . Nothing is left to chance here. She prepares her lessons seriously each day. The teaching is varied, lively, clear, well-designed for the level of the children she's teaching. The teacher holds her audience in the palm of her hand. They obey a sign from her hand or a glance from her eye . . . She can do what she likes with children, and it's a real pleasure to watch their development, to hear their precise, well-spoken responses.[24]

But, for every successful teacher, how many others were simply out of their depth, and resentful of their difficult position? Leo Tolstoy (1828–1910) was passionately concerned about the development of peasants' schools in Russia. He traveled widely and wrote a number of thought-provoking studies on schools across Europe. One of his observations rings true: "the teacher, for the greater part, sees in his pupils his natural enemies."[25] Teachers normally could see only one method by which to maintain order and discipline within their classes: intimidation.

The impression that one gains from nineteenth-century autobiographies is that, for most pupils, schools meant violence. One weary comment from Heine speaks volumes: what was the difference between regular Latin verbs and irregular Latin verbs? Irregular verbs required more flogging.[26] Elizabeth Ham's autobiography includes four long chapters concerning her schooling. What is her first sentence about her first school, old Molly Brown's Dame School? "Her instrument of authority was a long black stick with which she could reach the head of any of her pupils."[27] Is it any wonder that Tolstoy noted that schools were built like prisons?[28]

For many pupils, the teacher's physical violence was not an exceptional but a normal part of their schooling. While this regrettable point usually features in their autobiographies, one wonders if it might not hide another more substantial point about the nature of schooling. Aside from the teacher's brutality, we should not forget the effects of schooling on pupil's health. Schools and colleges were often unhealthy places: in boarding schools, underfed, cold pupils easily fell victim to infections in winter. The prestigious college of Saint-Cyr opened in France in 1686. It was designed specifically for an elite, the talented daughters of poor aristocrats, but it soon acquired a reputation as a "death camp" (*mouroir*): almost 4 percent of its pupils died there each year.[29]

Mistral's *Mémoires* also provide some telling examples of similar experiences. He moved from primary school to a secondary school in Avignon. This was a rare privilege, but one that he rarely seemed to appreciate.

When I was about fourteen, my absence from the fields and from those who spoke my Provençale language never left me. [These feelings] finished by throwing me into a deep, melancholy nostalgia . . . My sadness was mixed with a deep disgust for this artificial world within which I was locked, and a profound longing for some vague ideal which I thought I saw, there, on the horizon.[30]

At the end of his secondary schooling he prepared for the exam which would allow him to go to university. On the day he went for his exam, he stopped in a café. One of the serving-girls noticed how ill he looked. "Isn't he pale! It's easy to see that all that reading doesn't do you any good."[31]

Aside from these points about the pupils' physical health, one wonders about their mental health. What was the effect of long hours of compulsory instruction by incompetent and often violent teachers? In particular, one should remember that given the frequent absence of textbooks and writing materials, many lessons amounted to demands by teachers that their pupils memorize never-ending lists. Heine remembered – among others – lists of Roman kings, lists of dates, lists of nouns ending in –*im*, and lists of regular verbs.[32] There was a certain element of continuity here: in earlier centuries, the churches had used catechisms – sets of simple questions and answers concerning basic theological points – as instruments to spread doctrine. As in the nineteenth-century schools, these lessons were often literally beaten into the slower pupils: "blows from the cane led us to Heaven" noted Hélias about his catechism class.[33] R. A. Houston perceptively notes that one can question what exactly was happening here. "What passed for reading was often not what twentieth-century observers would understand by the term."[34] In schools, pupils were treated as mere "absorbers of facts."[35] Although the ideologues of the schooling program often spoke the language of progress and liberalization, the new schools of the early nineteenth century used the same mind-deadening methods as the older church classes. It was not until the various national states had increased their budgets for schooling that, later in the nineteenth century, the use of blackboards, textbooks, and exercise books spread and the possibility of a more active form of learning gradually emerged.

How did pupils react? In general, they hated their schooling. Heine notes that he was happy when a holiday was declared, as it meant no school.[36] As we have seen, Mistral's spontaneous, instinctive rebellion against his schooling led him into a nostalgic romanticization of Provencal culture. Perhaps still more importantly, schooling was usually a boring, meaningless experience. Many years later, Elizabeth Ham tried to remember what they had done at school. "I have no great idea of what we did at Miss Mason's besides learning a dozen words in a spelling-book, reading once in the morning and once in the afternoon, and sitting the remainder of the time . . . sewing."[37] There was little here about which a child could feel proud: most of the skills acquired, with the exception of sewing, were largely irrelevant to the immediate family context. Later, as the process was further bureaucratized, it was possible to feel some sense of achievement at passing an exam or winning a certificate, but often these were remembered with joy because they marked the *end* of schooling. Lastly, children certainly had fond memories of the friends they made at school, but usually these friendships were formed *against* the school's authority structures.[38]

On occasion parents might object to particular teachers. Certainly, most parents had some concept of a necessary limit to teachers' violence, and would object when they thought punishments were excessive or unfair. In general, however, most parents only had the haziest of ideas as to what went on in schools. When they sought to evaluate a school, they looked for simple, easily verifiable signs. A teacher's absence from the classroom would be quickly noted, as would the smell of drink on a teacher's breath. As teachers were often thought of as secular priests, any hint of immoral behavior – being seen in the wrong places, reading the wrong sort of books, associating with the wrong people – could also quickly become part of malicious village gossip. These prescriptions were applied most harshly to female teachers, but – in general – they often constricted all teachers' freedom, and led teachers to feel that they were constantly being watched by hostile spies. Normally, however, parents were simply not capable of evaluating how effective a particular teacher was.[39] Moreover, successful teachers who learnt how to integrate themselves into a village or town community could acquire some authority of their own. The expulsion of a child from the school could be experienced by the parents as a form of public humiliation, and a challenge to their own status as proper parents.

Let us return to what is perhaps the most important question: what did children learn at school? While attendance at school may certainly have accelerated the nineteenth-century rise in literacy rates, it certainly should not be seen as the sole determinant. Ex-pupils' autobiographies are revealing on this point. Ham had been attending school for several years, and had been taught, after a fashion, to decipher the words of the Bible and the Book of Psalms. This experience, however, did not awaken in her any desire to read. Then, one day, a family friend gave her a book "which I kept a long time to look at the pictures and the pretty gilt cover, when at length it suddenly entered my head "what a nice thing it would be if I could but read it myself.'"[40] The implications of this comment are worth considering: even though she had followed the mechanical lessons at school, it never occurred to Ham that she had come away with any particular ability to *do* something. She had to find this out for herself, outside the school. Eklof cites a similarly revealing incident from the Russian state bureaucracy. In those days before photocopiers, gifted primary school pupils were subsequently employed as copywriters: in other words, they had to copy out, by hand, particular texts of which a minister or a bureaucrat required multiple copies. At one point, it was noted that these ex-pupils therefore had access to some quite sensitive political information. Was it wise to allow this practice to continue? Officials concluded that there was no reason to worry: given the manner in which they had been taught, it was extremely unlikely that one of these copywriters would ever understand a word of what they were writing.[41] These points demonstrate some of the limits of the schooling program. The lessons it taught were often shallow, and rarely encouraged any spirit of initiative among pupils.

What of wider cultural goals? Did schooling generalize a sense of patriotism? Here, there is some evidence of success. One could cite the noisy pro-war demonstrations of German students in August 1914 as a memorable example of the clear integration of young people into the state's political culture. In this case, they accepted war as a test of their education.[42] More generally, the willingness of young men across Europe to accept mobilization orders in 1914 is a good demonstration of how ubiquitous patriotism had become.

Despite the rise of the school, despite the drift upwards in school attendance figures and literacy levels, *real* education still mainly took place outside the school. Schooling at best gave pupils a series of mechanically learnt skills; a supplementary stage in their education was needed for pupils to take stock of their skills and to consider what use, if any, they could make of them. An original and imaginative essay by Céline Grasser outlines just such a process. She has studied references to gardens in the diaries kept by middle-class young women in the years before their marriages. Grasser finds that they transformed their family gardens into "places of education." There, young women could be alone, and could make some evaluation of their lives and prospects. They could observe the rhythms of fertility, flowering, and decay – "the birds and the bees" – and consider their own futures as mothers. Above all, they would write their diaries in such places, thus affirming their identities in forms not anticipated by their schools.[43]

Teachers' Experiences

So far in this chapter we have considered two aspects of schooling: the chilly, calculating projects of the schooling program, and the brain-dulling experience of the majority of pupils. Alongside these histories, there was another voice: the experience of the teachers themselves. It is probably in this group that we can note the most dramatic changes. The first and most important transformation is simply that they did slowly become "a group." In early modern Europe, teaching was merely a task that any reasonably well-educated adult might undertake. My favorite example of this attitude comes from Carlo Ginzburg's marvelous *The Cheese and the Worms*: a recreation of the life of Menocchio, a heretic miller in sixteenth-century Italy. At his trial, Menocchio tells his judges: "I have been a sawyer, miller, innkeeper, I have kept a school for children to learn the abacus and reading and writing, and I also play the guitar at festivals."[44]

The ideals of the schooling program rejected the well-meaning amateurism of people like Menocchio, and instead demanded that all teachers should be trained professionals. However, training cost money, and it proved immensely difficult to organize national systems of teacher training. Moreover, governments had a second concern. Training systems potentially established a common base of experience for all teachers, which could then take the form of a common professional consciousness; this in turn might provoke teachers, as a body, to make collective demands on their employers, the state. In the mid-nineteenth century, governments were concerned by the political activism of teachers during the 1848 revolutions; in the late nineteenth century, they were worried by the growth of revolutionary theories among a minority of teachers.[45]

In general, however, few teachers joined trade unions or became revolutionaries. The professional identity which was propagated in teacher training colleges encouraged teachers to think of themselves as separate from and superior to the working class. In many countries – such as France and Prussia – teachers were classified as civil servants, not workers. Moreover, governments called for teachers to become dedicated servants to the state and – in another curious echo of older religious cultures – began to suggest that teachers should be modest, retiring, obedient, and self-sacrificing. Teaching, it was argued, was a vocation, not a trade. At times such ideals could genuinely inspire and unite teachers working in a particular sector: late nineteenth-century German universities can be cited as a prominent example of this type of success. Here, academics accepted and exploited "an apolitical, traditionalistic ethic" of *Bildung* (education or culture), which was explicitly cited in debates between state and university authorities.[46]

Teachers' common experiences did lead to some significant sense of group identity, often initially based on a sense of shared culture with the government and the schooling program. If one imagines the model of a hostile community, in which established local authorities (priests, mayors, aristocrats, notables, and parents) were frequently hostile to the presence of a new teacher, then one can easily understand how teachers could well decide that the forces of the state (the government, educational bureaucrats, other civil servants) were their only allies. Advice from inspectors and ministers that teachers should not join a union was therefore taken seriously.

Teachers' frustrations with the contradictory forces of schooling program ideologies and classroom realities were more likely to be expressed by their adherence to various pedagogic reform movements. Defining these movements politically is a difficult task: they were located in a type of political borderland, and can often be interpreted both as a continuation and development of schooling program ideals, and as a critique of them. They could attract support from idealist liberals, feminists, socialists, and anarchists. At times, they could even sound bizarrely anachronistic, as one detects in their rhetoric an echo of the older classical ideals of eighteenth-century humanists, principally expressed in their concern that education should be about something more than equipping the children of the poor to become factory workers.

There were, however, some common features. Reformers tended to criticize the schooling program for producing a mechanical, over-regulated form of education. At times this could be expressed through the participation of reform-minded teachers in government initiated debates. For example, in France, many teachers sent in critical impressions about the forms of discipline used in secondary schools in a long enquiry of 1853–4.[47] More often, teachers and other concerned people formed non-official pressure groups. Majorie Lamberti has

written a useful study of the German League for School Reform, which attracted the support of about 125,000 teachers in 1912. Her description of the League's ideals sums up some of the common concerns of these reform movements. The League called for a "new pedagogy," which was inspired by "a yearning for the unity of human nature and a desire to overcome an excessive intellectualism and to cultivate the emotional, imaginative, sensory, and creative capacities of the human being."[48] Earlier in the nineteenth century, Germany had also been the site for another reform movement. Liberals had sponsored a wider-ranging campaign for the creation of a network of kindergardens. There was an explicit connection between the radical liberal ideals of the pre-1848 period and these institutions. "Under the non-coercive and reasonable guidance of the teacher, the kindergarten was pictured as a microcosm of the liberal state where order was based not on fear of deference but on freely assumed responsibility."[49]

Some reformers despaired of the possibility of significantly ameliorating the nature of the schooling program. They turned to consider other forms of opposition. Tolstoy, in Russia, set up a model school for peasants in Yasnaya-Polyana. At the opposite end of Europe, Francisco Ferrer y Guardia left republican circles to declare himself an anarchist and to create "the Modern School," an institution which was dedicated to the implementation of non-authoritarian principles in education. Significantly, the same coalition of reforming forces continued to support his initiative: anti-clericals and republicans sent their children to his school.[50] Inevitably, the Spanish state did not allow his initiative to continue for long. Ferrer was arrested in 1909 on trumped-up charges of inciting rebellion, and executed soon after: his death attracted protests from intellectuals, humanitarians, and educationalists across Europe.

Such forms of open opposition only attracted support from a minority of teachers. Nonetheless, it is significant that teachers were beginning to think critically about their profession and their social function and that – more often than not – their debates and proposals were critical of government policy.

Conclusion

To return to the metaphor introduced in our opening paragraph, it makes sense to see schooling as a utopian fable, a promised land, a cause that inspired but which also bewildered. Generations of ministers and civil servants were infatuated with ideals of bringing order and regularity into the lives of the lower classes. The new ranks of trained teachers dedicated themselves in quiet, exhausting work, "at the chalkface," voluntarily taking on extra pupils, giving evening classes to adults, believing that their labors would lead to a more just and more liberal society. Lastly, at least a minority of pupils were infected with this zeal, and came to believe that without a certificate or a qualification, their lives would be worthless. Schooling structured lives; it prepared children for the hierarchies and organizations, the prejudices and myths of the adult world. Perhaps the most troubling aspect of the schooling program was simply the misleading assertion that schooling was somehow separate from society; that exterior forces stopped at the schoolroom doors.[51]

Many of the most important aspects of education continued *outside* the school. Communicative and essential linguistic skills were still largely taught by mothers and fathers to their children; trade skills were still learnt through formal and informal apprenticeships; novelists, cultural activists, artists still needed to look outside the school to find inspiration for cultural productions of any real value. When they came to look back on their school days, most autobiographers recalled a series of humiliations and scenes of violence; few seem to have come away with any real affection for the new institution.

ACKNOWLEDGMENTS

I would like to thank Stefan Berger, Patricia Clark, and Melanie Ilic for their useful comments on previous drafts of this chapter. I also thank Ursula Masson for recommending some key texts.

NOTES

1 The contrast between the two approaches is nicely summarized in the first chapter of Maynes (1985). For a fuller debate, see the exchange between Harrigan (1998) and Gemie (1999b).
2 Vincent (2000: 2).
3 Ortiz (2001).
4 Maynes (1985: 124); Vincent (2000: 67–8).
5 See, for example, Pellissier (2003).
6 Lyons (2001); Engel (1983: 37). For a useful introductory debate on similar concerns in a German context, see Linton (1988).
7 Eklof (1986: 49).
8 Andrés and Braster (1999: 76).
9 Eklof (1986: 34). On this point, see also Gemie (1992).
10 Heine (1948: 68).
11 Herzen (1983: 21).
12 Mistral (1906: 186).
13 Hélias (1975: 73).
14 Ibid: 306.
15 Information taken from Johansson (1988).
16 Eklof (1986: 84).
17 Ibid: 31.
18 Hélias (1975: 205).
19 Engel (1983: 110).
20 Herzen (1983: 109).
21 Ibid: 71.
22 Eklof (1986: 188).
23 Clark (2000: 31–2).
24 Quoted in Gemie (1995: 132–3).
25 Tolstoy (1972: 12).
26 Heine (1948: 59).
27 Ham (1945: 18).
28 Tolstoy (1972: 16).
29 Picco (2003).
30 Mistral (1906: 89).
31 Ibid: 110.
32 Heine (1948: 58).
33 Hélias (1975: 128).
34 Houston (1988: 57).
35 Maynes (1985: 62).
36 Heine (1948: 58).
37 Ham (1945: 24).
38 For a fuller discussion of this point in the context of students at teacher training colleges, see Gemie (1995: ch. 5).
39 For a fuller discussion of parents' attitudes to teachers, see Gemie (1995: ch. 7).

40 Ham (1945: 32).
41 Eklof (1986: 45).
42 Jarausch (1984).
43 Grasser (2003).
44 Ginzburg (1989: 103).
45 Barkin (1983); Feely (1989).
46 O'Boyle (1983: 13).
47 Caron (2003).
48 Lamberti (2000: 35).
49 Allen (1986: 439).
50 On Ferrer, see Bookchin (1976: 129–32).
51 This paragraph is loosely drawn from Bourdieu (2002).

GUIDE TO FURTHER READING

Students of this topic are fortunate that there have been an excellent number of well-researched, well-argued textbooks which present intelligent surveys of issues. Houston's *Literacy in Early Modern Europe* obviously concerns an earlier period, but does provide useful information and clear analyses of the cultural impact of early schools. Maynes's *Schooling in Western Europe* is a thought-provoking and informative survey of the development of schooling. Vincent's *Rise of Mass Literacy* concerns a somewhat separate topic, but includes detailed and well-structured arguments concerning this important theme. Bardet, Luc, Robin-Romero, and Rollet's *Lorsque l'enfant grandit* contains no less than 62 essays. While these vary in quality and relevance, the work is a helpful guide to recent lines of research.

The debate between Harrigan and Gemie presents some good examples of the manner in which methodological topics are being discussed. On this topic, see also my "What is a School?"

The development of schooling in Russia raised many important political and social questions. These are impressively analyzed in Eklof's *Russian Peasant Schools*. To this work can be added Engel's *Mothers and Daughters*, which considers how education affected women's lives.

In France, schooling was central to the construction of a modern, patriotic, republican identity. Bourdieu's "L'idéologie jacobine" is a short, acerbic review of this legacy. In recent years, historians have turned to consider the integration of marginalized social groups into its structures. Feely's *Rebels with Causes* is a useful study of a radical political intervention. Clark's *Rise of Professional Women in France* presents a wider consideration of women's careers and the state. My own *Women and Schooling* is a social and cultural history of women's experiences. Lyons, *Readers and Society*, discusses the allied topic of literacy in France.

Johansson's "Literacy Campaigns in Sweden" is an important study of an early development of mass literacy. Jarausch's "German Students in the First World War" presents a valuable analysis of some of the effects of university education in nineteenth-century Germany. To this can be added the articles by Allen, Barkin, Lamberti, and Linton, which each give useful information about the activities of radical groups.

CHAPTER TWENTY-FOUR

The Age of Historism

MATTHEW JEFFERIES

The Historical Century

On February 20, 1909 the Parisian newspaper *Le Figaro* carried on its front page an explosive manifesto by the Italian writer F. T. Marinetti (1876–1944). Point ten of this "Founding Manifesto of Futurism" proclaimed: "We will destroy the museums, libraries, academies of every kind." "We want to free this land," it continued, "from its smelly gangrene of professors, archeologists, *ciceroni* and antiquarians . . . We mean to free her from the numberless museums that cover her like so many graveyards."[1] Marinetti's vitriol was aimed primarily at his Italian homeland, but avant-garde writers and artists right across the continent shared the iconoclastic conviction that the new century must bring a clean break with the past. Not every modernist went as far as Marinetti in his hatred of museums, but all were aware of the dominant and – from their perspective – malign influence of historist patterns of thought on European life in the nineteenth century. Today, however, while most studies of the Victorian age recognize the era's historical-mindedness, its true significance is often underestimated. This is perhaps not surprising, since a preoccupation with the past may appear out of step with other defining features of the age: the belief in "progress," scientific and technological achievement, and the breathless pace of social and economic change. Yet without the century's distinctive historical consciousness at least two of its most significant movements, evolutionism and Marxism, could scarcely have existed. In fact, while the nineteenth century is often referred to as the Age of the Bourgeoisie, the Age of Nationalism, or the Age of Steam, a strong case can be made for the Age of Historism, too. As the eminent American historian Peter Gay puts it: "The nineteenth century was preeminently the historical century."[2]

"Historism" – a less ideologically laden word than the more familiar "historicism"[3] – stands here for the nineteenth century's preoccupation with the past; its tendency to see everything in historical terms, and to regard historical context as the key to understanding structures of all kinds. One important aspect of this phenomenon was the development of history as a scholarly discipline, with its new-found "scientific" approach and the gradual professionalization of its practitioners. Indeed, it would be possible to document the Age of Historism simply by reference to the opening of archives and museums, the growth of historical journals and associations, the creation of chairs in history at leading universities, and the prominence of historians in public life. Yet there is much more to it than that. The role history played in the consciousness of nineteenth-century Europeans went far beyond History with a capital "H." For a start, it exerted a profound influence on a host of other disciplines, and not just traditional bedfellows like religion and philosophy. As Herbert

Butterfield noted: "There were now two ways in which every branch of science was to be studied: first by its own forms of technical procedure, and secondly by an examination of its history."[4] Thus to study literature or philology meant to study the history of texts or languages; to study architecture meant learning the history of architectural styles, and so on. In short, history became "the guardian discipline of 'truth' in the nineteenth century."[5]

Many branches of the natural and "life" sciences also adopted historical modes of understanding: anthropology, botany, geology, comparative anatomy, and physiology each "sought to explain present form by locating it as an outcome of past development."[6] Charles Darwin's *On the Origin of Species* (1859) and *Descent of Man* (1871) did this and more, redefining what it meant to be human in the process. Towards the end of the century Social Darwinists would attempt to draw conclusions for contemporary society from Darwin's theories, but European politicians were already well accustomed to invoking "the lessons of history." These historical lessons enjoyed what Olive Anderson has described as "a revered and secure place among the household gods of the mid-nineteenth-century governing class,"[7] though they also provided a justification for those such as Karl Marx who wished to see them toppled. The instrumentalization of history in the service of governments and ideologies was, as we shall see, an important aspect of the age. At a time when only a tiny minority of Europeans attended university, one must, however, also look beyond academic and intellectual life to understand the pervasiveness of history in the nineteenth century. Victorians, and their continental equivalents, could call on a colorful picture gallery of history, formed less by the work of professional historians than by the authors and illustrators of school textbooks, historical novels, tourist guides, and reproductions of popular paintings. Although much of this may have been history of the "fancy-dress" variety, a genuine interest in the past was nevertheless a significant feature of popular culture at this time.

The nineteenth century's preoccupation with history was a consequence of the process of historicization or "temporalization" that started in the eighteenth century – with the attempts of Enlightenment thinkers such as Adam Smith to divide mankind's social and economic development into periods or stages – and flourished in the "Age of Revolutions." The historical convulsions of the French Revolution, the Napoleonic Wars, the scientific and industrial revolutions all highlighted the impermanence of political, social, and economic structures. The rapid changes ushered in by these upheavals showed the extent to which life was historically determined, and prompted an upsurge of interest in the past, since "the discovery of one's own historicity is ... the premise for an interest in the past."[8] For the influential French theorist Michel Foucault, this unprecedented interest in the past was also a kind of extreme nostalgia, caused by man's sense of being "dispossessed" of history: his growing awareness that there was "no unified, anthropocentric history, but rather a number of "histories" ... which [did] not place him at their centre."[9] Certainly, many historians have recognized that for all the nineteenth century's optimism and talk of progress, there was a powerful sense of loss as well.

Temporal perceptions were challenged further during the course of the century by the revolution in transport and communications. As Wolfgang Schivelbusch has shown, the coming of the railway, with its "annihilation of space by time" (Marx), was particularly significant.[10] In 1843 the Paris-based German poet Heinrich Heine (1797–1856) observed:

> Space is killed by the railways, and we are left with time alone ... Just imagine what will happen when the lines to Belgium and Germany are completed and connected up to their railways! I feel as if the mountains and forests of all countries were advancing on Paris. Even now, I can smell the German linden trees; the North Sea's breakers are rolling against my door.[11]

The new "industrialized" consciousness of the nineteenth century was also formed by the unprecedented importance of timekeeping in the workplace. Where the working day had previously been shaped by the rising and setting of the sun, now its principal regulator was the clock and the factory bell. It was in this context, Philippa Levine argues, that "history was to acquire powerful human appeal as the intellectual mechanism whereby time could be measured and evaluated."[12]

Secularization also played its part. This was a much slower process, to be sure, but for those who began to doubt the existence of a God or a heavenly afterlife, time and its mysteries became an increasingly pressing concern. The cumulative lessons of geology and archeology ensured that the traditional Christian chronology – which dated the Earth's creation to the year 4004 BC and therefore allowed for a total of less than 6,000 years of history – became ever more difficult to uphold. In 1819, when the director of the National Museum of Denmark, Christian J. Thomsen (1786–1865), first proposed the "Three Age system" – organizing the artifacts in his museum by tracing human development through the successive use of stone, bronze, and iron tools – most Europeans still believed in the literal truth of the Bible's account of creation. Thomsen's successor, J. J. A. Worsaae (1821–85), carried out a series of excavations that not only supported the Three Age theory, but also suggested that the Stone Age was much older than previously imagined. The coining of the term "prehistory" in 1851 and the discovery of Neanderthal man six years later put further pressure on Christian convention. By the time a refined version of Thomsen and Worsaae's periodization, the Montelius system, had gained general acceptance among archeologists in the late nineteenth century, even religious leaders had begun to abandon the concept of the 6,000-year-old planet. The discoveries of geologists and archeologists had effectively elongated the very concept of time itself.[13]

A third explanatory factor for the preoccupation with history was the rise of modern nationalism across Europe after 1789. History provided the means by which nationalists could construct, or affirm, the legitimacy of their nation, producing the collective memories that were needed by all such "imagined" communities. The results – whether based on careful archival research, imaginative use of folk tales, or blatant forgery – were often remarkably similar, with the same tropes reappearing in very different national contexts. Many nations, for instance, claimed a manifest destiny or historic mission, which made them superior to other less fortunate peoples. The "Whig Interpretation of History" in Britain is perhaps the best-known example,[14] but it also informed the sense of cultural mission in Germany and the revolutionary tradition in France. These national teleologies were usually constructed around certain key dates – 1215, 1688, and 1832 in the British case – and implied that history had a detectable sense of direction.[15] They also help to explain the apparent contradiction between the century's preoccupation with the past and its faith in progress. History, it was believed, should provide a usable past, not only to "explain the present" but also to "mould the future."[16] Little wonder, then, that history became a key element of the nineteenth-century school curriculum.

It would be wrong, of course, to suggest that historical consciousness was a purely Victorian invention, or that a sense of the past only began in 1800. The "history plays" of Shakespeare, Marlowe, and others had enjoyed great popularity in Elizabethan England; educated men and women had been fascinated by the relics of antiquity since the early Renaissance; and the Grand Tour of Europe undertaken by wealthy young men in the eighteenth century often took in sites of historical interest, such as the ruins of Pompeii. For hundreds of years, so-called antiquarians had been demonstrating an acquisitive interest in the past by assembling large collections of manuscripts, coins, and other material remains. There was no shortage of history to read before 1800 either. When the first volume of Edward Gibbon's *The History of the Decline and Fall of the Roman Empire* appeared in 1776, approximately one in every nine books published in Britain was a work of history. In the German lands the figure was perhaps as high as one in five.[17] Yet, as J. H. Plumb notes, "this vast extension of historical literature and of historical knowledge did not lead, initially, to the type of historical understanding which we attempt. Its intention was largely to purify and establish the 'how' of history, not the 'why.'"[18]

A short chapter such as this cannot hope to provide a comprehensive explanation of how and why a distinctly different kind of historical-mindedness emerged in nineteenth-century Europe. It will, however, attempt to survey a number of key areas: from the development of history as an academic discipline, through historical novels, paintings, museums, and architecture. It will then consider some of the uses and abuses of history in the nineteenth century, focusing in particular on the involvement of historians in politics and the so-called "invention of tradition."

The Discipline of History

At the start of the nineteenth century, the terms "antiquarianism," "archeology," and "history" were largely synonymous, but well before the century's end they had each become quite separate disciplines, with the latter two characterized by a growing degree of professionalization and specialization, and the former disparaged as the realm of the eccentric amateur.[19] Subsequently, as Stephen Bann notes, it has become "an article of faith" within the historical community that while there were historians before 1800, "only after that date does it become possible and necessary to speak of the *professional* historian."[20] It is generally agreed that this development owed much to historians at German universities such as Göttingen, where history was established as an independent teaching subject in the late eighteenth century. Although history had long been taught in European universities – a *lectio historica* was established at the University of Mainz as early as 1504, the Regius Professorships in Modern History at Oxford and Cambridge date from 1724, while a chair of history and morals was instituted at the Collège de France in 1769 – it was invariably subordinated to the needs of other disciplines, such as theology and law.

Of all the German historians, the most influential was Leopold von Ranke (1795–1886), whose scientific-empirical approach – which required the historian to discriminate between primary and secondary sources, to immerse himself in the former, and to interpret these documents critically but sympathetically, with the aim of understanding "how things actually happened" (*wie es eigentlich gewesen*)[21] – is

invariably singled out as the crucial methodological innovation. Although it can be argued that Ranke's originality has been exaggerated, he undoubtedly became the "mythic repository for the attitudes of the 'new' historiography of the nineteenth century."[22] Ranke's French contemporary Augustin Thierry, whose *History of the Norman Conquest* (1825) was published just months after the German's famous dictum had first appeared in print, also made extensive use of original documents. By comparison, however, Britain was something of a methodological backwater, where the most prominent historians of the day – Thomas Carlyle (1795–1881) and Thomas Babington Macaulay (1800–59) – were "men of letters" of a much more traditional kind,[23] though this did not stop Lord Macaulay's five volume *History of England* selling more than 140,000 sets in Britain alone.[24]

The eventual triumph of the Rankean method was predicated on a major change in the availability of primary source materials. Before the nineteenth century, archives as we understand them today were rare in Europe, and most were in any case barred to researchers until the middle years of the century, although in France a number of archives had been forcibly opened in the wake of 1789. Newly independent Belgium led the way in making its records more freely available in the 1830s. In Britain the Public Record Office Act was passed in 1838, but another twenty years passed before the PRO opened its doors. Many other countries followed suit in the 1850s and 1860s, and for a new generation of historians the dusty archive became something of a sacred space. A frequently retold anecdote from 1851 illustrates this well. The German historian Heinrich Sybel was on a research trip to the National Archives in Paris when he noticed the files of the revolutionary Committee of Public Safety. "What dust!" the historian is supposed to have exclaimed. "Respect it," answered the archivist; "it is the dust of 1795."[25] Interestingly, it was men like this Parisian archivist – civil servants responsible for the classification of national records – who Levine believes "may lay claim to the title of the earliest professional historians," rather than the likes of Ranke or Thierry.[26] One of the consequences of the opening of the archives was "to increase the bias in favour of political history. It released a mass of documentation which, almost by definition, envisaged history in its connection with government."[27] Thus the most popular of all forms of history in the nineteenth century was the multi-volume political narrative of a particular country or epoch. Although these included some of the longest works ever written, often running to a dozen tomes or more, the new "scientific history" at first remained accessible to a general readership: partly because – as Hayden White has shown[28] – it employed many of the same rhetorical structures and "plot" devices as works of fiction in the Western literary tradition; but also because nineteenth-century historians were often powerful poetic talents in their own right.

At the other end of the scale in terms of length, but no less serious in intent, were history's first professional journals, boasting more stringent standards of methodological rigor and critical accuracy than their antiquarian predecessors. Appropriately, the German *Historische Zeitschrift* (1859) came first; followed by the French *Révue historique* (1876), the Italian *Rivista storica italiana* (1884), and the *English Historical Review* (1886). Most of these journals were published under the auspices of national historical associations, which were founded throughout nineteenth-century Europe, and which helped to bind together what Peter Lambert wryly refers to as the "imagined community" of historians.[29] In Britain the most important were the British Archaeological Association (1843), the Royal Historical Society (1868), and the Society of Biblical Archaeology (1870). Predating all of these was the influential Society for the Study of Early German History, which was founded in Frankfurt in 1819. The Society was behind the multi-volume *Monumenta Gemaniae Historica*, described by G. P. Gooch as "the greatest cooperative historical work of the century."[30]

In mid-century the number of university teaching posts in history began to multiply across Western Europe – Manchester's first Chair in Ancient and Modern History, for instance, was created in 1853 – but it was a patchy process, with the German states in the lead (28 professors by 1850, rising to 185 by 1910),[31] and the Netherlands bringing up the rear. It would be wrong, moreover, to imagine that all the new professors of history were "scientists" in the Rankean mold: the Regius Professor of History at Cambridge in the 1860s was none other than Charles Kingsley (1819–75), a much-loved novelist (*The Water Babies*) and one time Anglican vicar, but no historian. Indeed, Kingsley devoted his inaugural lecture as Regius Professor of History to a refutation of "scientific history," a term which he used pejoratively. It is also salutary to note that the Oxford School of Modern History was not created until 1872 and the Cambridge History Tripos until several years later. History was comparatively slow to develop as a university subject in its own right because, as Levine notes, "the acceptance of history as a curricular subject worthy of separate academic attention was attended by a good deal of hostility . . . until the early 1870s it was not deemed a sufficient subject for exclusive study."[32]

Historism in a Wider Context

The development of history as a discipline and profession is often cited as a major reason for the emergence of a new kind of historical consciousness in the first half of the nineteenth century. It can be argued, however, that the historiographical revolution was "a byproduct, rather than the effective cause, of this unprecedented preoccupation with the past."[33] Certainly, Stephen Bann's conviction that Ranke be viewed as part of a much broader cultural change is surely correct. "Scientific history" may have offered a fresh and compelling way of making sense of the past, but so too did the historical novels, paintings, and museums of the period. Each influenced the other. Historians, for instance, were quick to acknowledge the importance of historical novelists – particularly Sir Walter Scott – on the development of their work. Marx, Ranke, and Thierry all commented on Scott's impact. The French historian recalled: "My admiration for this great writer was profound; it grew as I contrasted his wonderful comprehension of the past with the petty erudition of the most celebrated modern historians."[34] Thomas Carlyle was less of an admirer, but nevertheless acknowledged that "these Historical Novels have taught all men this truth . . . that the bygone ages of the world were actually filled by living men, not by protocols, state-papers, controversies and abstractions of men."[35] Carlyle's quote highlights one of the most widely perceived advantages of the historical novel over "scientific history": its capacity to portray private, personal responses to great events. Its other great strength lay in the ability to reconstruct the lives of ordinary people, thereby performing a function similar to that of social history today.[36]

Although Sir Walter Scott has long since fallen out of favor, it should not be forgotten that the influential critic George Lukács saw in Scott's novels – beginning with *Waverly* in 1814 – the first literary expression of a modern historical consciousness. Unlike earlier writers, who had used history merely as a backdrop, Scott was interested in "precisely the specifically historical, that is, derivation of the individuality of character from the historical peculiarity of their age."[37] David Brown points out that unlike many nineteenth-century historians – although like Ranke – "Scott does not attempt to subordinate the past to the present, or seek to produce a story which is the ratification if not the glorification of the present."[38] This was not the case with all historical novelists: the majority wrote with the present very much in mind. In English literature, works such as Edward Bulwer Lytton's *Harold, Last of the Saxon Kings* (1848) or Charles Kingsley's *Hereward the Wake* (1866) went back to the Middle Ages to explore the roots of Victorian Britain's liberty and prosperity, and were therefore a literary expression of the Whig interpretation of history. Similarly informed by present concerns was Benjamin Disraeli's *Sybil, or the Two Nations* (1846), a novel which attempted "to lay claim to the national past and 'wrench' the Middle Ages from Whig historians," by appropriating "the radical rhetoric of the 'Norman Yoke' for Tory propaganda."[39]

Not all historical novelists could go on to become prime minister, of course, but many struck the same patriotic tone. It was to be found, for instance, in the works of the Spaniard Benito Perez Galdos (1843–1920),

who called his 46-novel cycle *Episodios nacionales*, Anders Fryxell (1795–1881), whose *Stories from Swedish History* also ran to 46 volumes; Alexandre Dumas (1802–70) and Victor Hugo (1802–85) in France; the Germans Gustav Freytag (1816–95) and Joseph Victor Scheffel (1826–86), and so on. In Central and Eastern Europe historical novels often contained explicit expressions of nationalist sentiment. This was also the case in pre-unification Piedmont, where the historian Cesare Balbo's novels, such as *Fieramosca* and *Niccolo de Lapi*, did much to stimulate pride and interest in the Italian past.

Compared to the historical novel, the contribution of the visual arts to the new historical consciousness of the nineteenth century is rarely discussed. However, the emergence of "scientific history" coincided with what Bann refers to as a "ferment in representation" across Europe.[40] Joseph Nicéphore Niepce's first photographic image (1822), Louis Daguerre's historical diorama (1823), and the remarkable rise of the lithographic print all fell in the same decade as Ranke's famous dictum. The lithograph, in particular, became "a genuinely new medium in the popularization of history."[41] Illustrated history books could now be mass produced and sold at relatively low prices, allowing ordinary people to "see" the past more directly than ever before. Subsequent innovations in printmaking during the course of the century also made full-color reproductions of popular oil paintings accessible to the general public for the first time. These paintings, "a glittering pageant, full of striking and romantic tableaux, peopled by . . . heroes and heroines,"[42] often portrayed scenes from national history or classical mythology, and were considered to represent the true peak of artistic endeavor. The primacy of history painting over other genres – emphasized by the scale of awards on offer from Royal Academies – was not in itself new. Where late eighteenth and nineteenth-century history paintings differed from earlier works was in the care and attention paid to historical accuracy. Previously, little if any consideration was given to the appropriateness of dress, architectural settings, or physical appearances. By 1840, however, it was seemed quite reasonable for Thackeray to

remark in a review of the Royal Academy exhibition: "A painter should be as careful about
his costumes as an historian about his dates."[43]

In the quest for accuracy the painter was
assisted by the numerous compendiums of historic dress, customs, arms and armor, furniture
and architecture assembled by antiquarians in
the decades either side of 1800. Combined
with the Romantic era's more powerful poetic
vision, it produced a new kind of history painting, exemplified by the work of largely forgotten painters such as R. P. Bonnington
(1802–28) and G. F. Watts (1817–1904) in
Britain, the Frenchman Paul Delaroche
(1797–1856), the German Karl von Piloty
(1826–86), and the Italians Giuseppe Bezzuoli
(1784–1855) and Francesco Hayez
(1791–1882). Such artists had, in Roy Strong's
words, "acquired the almost magical power to
waft the onlooker back in a time machine to
witness the fall of Clarendon or watch Mary
Queen of Scots make her way to the scaffold.
The artist seemed to possess superhuman abilities, as though he alone could make time stand
still."[44]

The golden age of history painting fell in
the middle decades of the century.[45] One of
Germany's leading painters, Wilhelm von
Kaulbach (1804–74), captured the mood of
the time perfectly when he remarked: "It is
history we must paint. History is the religion
of our age; only history is in keeping with the
times."[46] Kaulbach's words echoed those of
Albertine de Broglie, who in a letter to the
French historian Prosper de Barante wrote:
"History is the Muse of our time; we are, I
think, the first who have understood the
past."[47] The didactic and moral qualities of
nineteenth-century history paintings ensured
that they found widespread employment in
schools and textbooks as well as museums and
galleries, and many became lodged in the
popular imagination. That was certainly the
case with the painting which provided Strong
with the title for his book, *And when did you
last see your father?* (1878) by William Frederick Yeames (1835–1915). Set in the English
Civil War, this sentimental image of doomed
cavaliers and stern Puritans became so famous
that it was even recreated as a wax tableau at
Madame Tussaud's in London.[48] Like most
nineteenth-century history paintings, it may
not have been great art, but it made an important contribution to the Age of Historism.

If paintings and illustrated books played a
large part in forming the new historical consciousness, then so too did museums. The
contents of a museum could give body and
substance to history in a way that no book or
painting could match, and the century produced a plethora of new establishments, which
were sometimes grouped together to create
distinctive city districts. There were museums
of national and local history; of archeology,
applied art, science, and natural history; later,
ethnographical and colonial museums, too.
While many of these were based on earlier collections, it was only in the nineteenth century
that they became accessible to a significant
section of the general public. Fundamental
changes also occurred in the way in which items
were displayed. What had formerly been simple
accumulations of objects, in the tradition of the
antiquarian's "cabinet of curiosities," were now
classified and ordered into conscious narratives.
It was a process that has been described as "a
shift from stories to histories, from fragments
to totalities, from cabinets to museums."[49]

Historicized principles of museum display
were first developed in France, at institutions
such as the Musée des monuments français,
which owed its existence to the quick thinking
of the painter Alexandre Lenoir (1761–1839).
At the height of French revolutionary terror,
as radicals like Chaumette, Hébért, and Hariot
tried to preempt the Italian Futurists by
burning down the National Library and
destroying the artistic treasures of France's
past, Lenoir rescued literally hundreds of
threatened objects, hiding them in the former
Convent des Petits-Augustins in Paris. By 1795
it was already safe to put some of them on
show. Significantly, however, he did not simply
present the salvaged items as a treasure trove.
Bann describes how Lenoir "placed the recu-
perated objects on exhibition to the public
within an overall chronological scheme that
appears to have been without precedent."[50]
The objects were set out across five rooms,
with each housing the products of a particular
century. The visitor's route, which led from the
thirteenth to the seventeenth centuries, was

partly determined by the layout of the convent and its succession of vast rooms, but also by Lenoir's own narrative intent. The museum was closed by royal ordinance in 1816, but it provided formative childhood experiences for the painter Eugène Delacroix and the historian Jules Michelet.[51]

Subsequently, some of Lenoir's collection was housed with that of another innovative curator, Alexandre Du Sommerard, in the Musée de Cluny (1832). This collection consisted of valuable treasures from many historical epochs, but also simple utilitarian objects not previously considered worthy of saving. Du Sommerard used the fifteenth-century Hôtel de Cluny's rich historical associations to recreate a series of convincing period rooms, based not on the arbitrary division of centuries, but as they might once have been lived in. These two different strategies of display – Lenoir's *galleria progressiva* and Du Sommerard's period ensembles – were both to prove influential in the nineteenth century, although as Bann notes, "the 'poetics' of the modern museum is not Du Sommerard's system, nor is it that of Lenoir. Instead it lies in the alternation of the two."[52] The Victoria and Albert Museum in London, founded in the 1850s, was one of many to adopt this combination.

For those important historic objects that were too large to accommodate in even the grandest of museums, the nineteenth century saw the rise of preservationism for the first time. The casual indifference with which important architectural and historical structures were regularly removed from the European landscape is hard to comprehend today, but in the 1800s few eyebrows were raised when prehistoric graves or stone circles were broken up for building materials, or when medieval cathedrals and palaces were used as barns. Once again, it took a combination of antiquarian activism and a change in aesthetic sensibilities to trigger a change in attitude. Works such as Goethe's essay on Strasbourg Cathedral (1773), Wordsworth's "A Few Lines Composed Upon Tintern Abbey" (1798), and Arcisse de Caumont's richly illustrated compendium of Normandy's medieval architecture (1830) placed a new value on the previously disparaged Middle Ages. They not only in-spired a Gothic Revival among contemporary architects, but also led to the foundation of the first associations for historic preservation.

The lead was again taken in France, where the historian François Guizot (1787–1874) served as minister for education under the July Monarchy. Guizot, who believed that "the institutions of a people cannot properly be understood without knowledge of its history,"[53] founded both the Société de l'histoire de France and the Commission des Monuments Historiques in the 1830s. Significantly, the commission's general inspector, Prosper Mérimée (1803–70), was a former historical novelist, who had been inspired by Walter Scott and counted the Romantics Delacroix and Victor Hugo among his friends. Mérimée not only spent three decades diligently compiling an official inventory of historic buildings and archeological sites, but he also engaged the brilliant young neo-Gothic architect Viollet-le-Duc (1814–79) to begin restoring some of them. The dangerous liaison between preservation and restoration has been the subject of lively debate ever since. Indeed, few controversies better illustrate the nineteenth century's complex relationship with the past than this one. So extensive were some of these "restoration" projects – including Viollet-le-Duc's own makeover of the Romanesque church at Vézelay in the 1840s, or the contemporaneous restoration of Cologne cathedral (finally completed in 1880) – that many architectural historians today regard these as nineteenth-century rather than medieval buildings. As Jane Fawcett bluntly puts it: "One of the ironies of the Gothic Revival is that it largely destroyed the very buildings from which it drew its inspiration. Considerably more medieval architecture was lost through restoration than through demolition."[54]

When the newly founded National Trust in Britain acquired its first property – Afriston Clergy House in Sussex – for £10 in 1896, it too was confronted with a similar dilemma; if the sagging, half-timbered walls and colander-like thatched roof were completely rebuilt, would the building still be "historic"?[55] There would be no easy answers to such dilemmas. In his study of *English Culture and the Decline of the Industrial Spirit*, Martin Wiener writes:

"Preservationism carried with it two inter-twined attitudes that link the movement to broader currents in later-Victorian culture and society. First, a loss of confidence in the creative powers of one's contemporaries and an eleva-tion of the past over the present; and second, a highly critical view of industrial capitalism."[56] It was not until the very last years of the century, however, that architects and critics began to view the practice of building in his-toric styles as a vote of no confidence in the cre-ative powers of their own age. On the contrary, the desire to design museums and art galleries as classical temples, town halls as Renaissance *palazzi*, or railway stations as Gothic cathedrals, demonstrated a sense of mastery over the past that oozed self-confidence. As the Gothic revivalist architect George Gilbert Scott asserted in 1857: "I want . . . to show to the public that we aim not at a dead antiquarian revival, but at developing upon the basis of the indigenous architecture of our own country, a style which will be preeminently that of our own age."[57] It was the "arrogance" of Gilbert Scott – and in particular his plans for the "restoration" of Tewkesbury Abbey – which led William Morris to establish a forerunner of the National Trust, the Society for the Preser-vation of Ancient Buildings, in 1877. Scott's attitude, however, was more typical of the age. After all, even his celebrated namesake Sir Walter had shamelessly plundered the ruins of another medieval abbey, at Melrose, for pieces of stonework to incorporate into his own fantasy castle at Abbotsford.

The idea that history was a stockyard of motifs and idioms, to be employed at will, was well established among architects and their patrons by the middle years of the century. The diligent research of antiquarians, followed by the rapid expansion of art history as an acade-mic discipline, ensured that all the major Euro-pean styles and epochs had been documented in word and picture, providing architects and designers with an unprecedented wealth of structural and decorative solutions. Combined with the new materials and manufacturing processes offered by technological progress, the possibilities seemed endless. It was hardly sur-prising, therefore, that the "single most domi-nant characteristic of Victorian architecture was its diversity,"[58] or that the nineteenth-century city resembled a living museum of past styles. Later, it would be argued that such architecture debased and de-historified the past, leaving only empty shells, devoid of any meaning. Until then, however, for nineteenth-century archi-tects – as for novelists, painters, and museum curators – the past was of central importance.

The Uses and Abuses of History

J. H. Plumb once wrote: "The more literate and sophisticated the society becomes, the more complex and powerful become the uses to which the past is put."[59] This was all too apparent in the nineteenth century, when history was pressed into service on behalf of nations, ideologies, and causes of all kinds. It would be wrong to imagine, however, that his-torians were in any way unwilling accomplices. On the contrary, historians – including those who claimed an objective, scientific detachment – often led from the front. The aforementioned François Guizot, who went on to become prime minister of France, was by no means the only nineteenth-century figure to combine the roles of historian and politician. The political life of Victorian Britain, for instance, benefited from the insights of a host of parliamentarians who had written about the past: Macaulay, Lord John Russell, Sir George Cornewall Lewis, John McGregor, and William Massey, as well as the historical novelists Disraeli and Bulwer Lytton.[60] It was hardly surprising then, that parliamentary exchanges were frequently full of historical analogies, sometimes of a most arcane kind. Historians in France were even more active in their country's political life: Adolphe Thiers (1797–1877) emulated Guizot in becoming prime minister, and was later pres-ident of the Third Republic; while the great Alexis de Tocqueville (1805–59) was foreign minister for a short period in 1849.

It was in the new, or aspirant, nations of the nineteenth century, however, that historians were most involved in political life. As James Sheehan has observed: "History mattered to everyone, but never as much as to those it had treated badly, people with national aspirations but no national state, people whose hopes for the future depended on their memories of the past."[61] This was particularly apparent in Eastern Europe and the Balkans. In Greece, for example, it was the rediscovery of past glories among a small elite of historians, antiquarians, and Romantics that led to the War of Independence in the 1820s. "Once independence had been achieved," Richard Clogg notes, "the whole cultural orientation of the new state revolved around ancient Greece."[62] This was symbolized by the decision to transfer the capital from Nafplion to Athens, which at that time was little more than a village. Inspired in part by the Greek example, the Czech historian Frantisek Palacky (1798–1876) played a leading role in the revolutions of 1848. According to Richard Plaschka, "the ideal that the young Palacky tried to attain was that of the historian who bears witness for his nation, or rather who acts as his nation's representative, in short the historian who becomes the national and political leader of his people."[63] Although he failed as a revolutionary, he succeeded almost single-handedly in creating a sense of Czech national identity in the Austrian province of Bohemia. As the nineteenth-century historian Pekar put it, Palacky dug up the Czech past from under the dust of archives and libraries: "It was the labour of half a century, it was like excavating a city buried for hundreds of years, the vast Pompeii of a whole people."[64]

The founding of nation-states in Italy (1861) and Germany (1871) provided a further demonstration of the extent to which the historical profession was involved in the construction of national mythologies: historians such as Heinrich von Treitschke and Antonio Cosci sought to legitimize the manner of each nation's unification by emphasizing the historical mission of the House of Hohenzollern and the House of Savoy, respectively. Treitschke even took his vocal support of Bismarck into the newly established *Reichstag*, where he sat on the right wing of the National Liberals. Other men who not only wrote about their nation's past but also helped to shape the course of its development included Mihail Koglniceanu (1817–91), a Moldovan who founded modern historical writing in Romania and became that country's foreign minister in the late 1870s,[65] and Stojan Novakovi (1842–1915), who wrote some fifty books and was president of the Royal Serbian Academy of Sciences, but was also three times minister of education and twice prime minister at the end of the century.[66]

Much has been written in recent years about the integrative function of history and its role in nation building, but few works have been as influential as Eric Hobsbawm and Terence Ranger's 1983 collection, *The Invention of Tradition*. Although some critics have attacked the distinction implicit in the book between the false consciousness of "invented" traditions and the truth of "real" history,[67] it does provide numerous useful examples of how history became a "legitimator of action and cement of group cohesion" in both the new and older states of nineteenth-century Europe. The book highlights countless historical continuities that were invented, "either by semi-fiction (Boadicea, Vercingetorix, Arminius the Cheruscan) or by forgery (Ossian, the Czech medieval manuscripts)," and which endowed a wide range of national groups with a sense of historical legitimacy.[68] Most of these particular "invented traditions" date back to the early years of the Age of Historism, but it is important to stress that "a second efflorescence of invented ritual and tradition" occurred in the later nineteenth century, too.[69] This second wave of "invented traditions" became manifest in the building of monuments, the celebration of historic anniversaries, and the staging of festivals; all of which sought to involve the masses through ritual and symbol rather than a real sharing of power.

As with so much in the nineteenth century, the French Revolutionary period – which had begun with the toppling of a hated symbol, the Bastille – set the tone by producing a new kind of symbolic politics. Jean-Jacques Rousseau (1712–78) had advocated civic festivals on the classical Greek model as a way of raising public morality, but under the Jacobins they gained a more specific national purpose: "to make the people love the Republic and to ensure the maintenance of order and public peace."[70] The revolutionary "tree of liberty" might not have put down particularly deep roots as a symbol, but the idea of uniting a nation through monument and ritual caught on across the continent. National monuments were subsequently erected throughout nineteenth-century Europe, but were particularly numerous in newly founded or recently expanded states, where a sense of identity was still weak and rulers were particularly eager to establish their legitimacy.[71] Such monuments were seen as an important tool in the construction of national identities, providing a focal point for festivals and ceremonies, and standing as symbols of permanence in rapidly changing societies. The extraordinary Vittorio Emmanuele II monument, built provocatively at the ancient heart of Rome, was a particularly grandiose example, taking decades to build. Like many such structures, it became an object of satire as well as a site of national communion, and was soon dubbed "the false teeth." In the German Empire, where there was a veritable monument mania in the last decades of the century, most monuments were dedicated to the first Kaiser Wilhelm or his Chancellor Bismarck, while in France it was the image of Marianne – a female personification of the nation – that became a familiar sight across the republic. It would be wrong, however, to see all such monuments as symbols of authority, imposed from above on unwilling populations. In fact, wherever they were built, "national" monuments tended to be the work of local notables and committees of active citizens, and were motivated by a wide range of considerations, including commerce and tourism. Some – such as the Bismarck monuments erected in Germany after his dismissal in 1890 – can even be regarded as symbols of opposition.[72]

Public festivals in the nineteenth century were invariably based around historic dates, and were either annual events – such as Sedan Day in Germany (from 1873) and Bastille Day in France (from 1880) – or celebrated specific anniversaries. Important examples of the latter included the Schiller centenary in Germany (1859), the centenary of the deaths of Voltaire and Rousseau in France (1878), and anniver-saries for Galileo (1864), Dante (1865), and Machiavelli (1869) in Italy. It seemed, in fact, as if no jubilee was too small to celebrate in nineteenth-century Europe. Appropriately, at the very end of the Age of Historism in 1898, there was even a centennial celebration for a historian: the popular French republican Jules Michelet.[73]

By the 1890s, however, much had changed. As Charles Rearick observes, "historical-mindedness" had become "a sense of over-ripeness, of . . . ageing and even decaying."[74] There were many reasons why history's crown began to slip. In part, it was simply that the new ways of bringing the past to life, which had once appeared so fresh and exciting – the historical novel, history painting, the museum, scientific history itself – had lost their novelty. It was also, however, because historism had become identified with a doomed search to secure an ever more detailed but ultimately meaningless knowledge of the past, with the result that one knew more and more, about less and less. In painting, for instance, "what had begun as a thrilling adventure, an artistic time machine, had by the third quarter of the nine-teenth century become paralysing. A door had been flung open into the past, the artist had entered and had found himself not emanci-pated but imprisoned."[75] The death-knell for the Age of Historism had in fact been sounded some years earlier when the philosopher Friedrich Nietzsche (1844–1900) launched his celebrated attack on the superficiality of the nineteenth century's historical consciousness in the second of his *Untimely Meditations*, enti-tled "On The Uses and Disadvantages of History for Life." Nietzsche's essay posed the question: "Is life to dominate knowledge and science, or is knowledge to dominate life? Which of these two forces is the higher and more decisive?" His own answer was clear: "There can be no doubt: life is the higher."[76] Rather than searching for the fundamental truths of human existence in the random pat-terns of historical development, Nietzsche sug-gested, man should turn to look inside his own mind. This invitation, taken up by Sigmund Freud among others, would help to end the Age of Historism and provide the twentieth century with a new paradigm.

Figure 24.1 Monument to the legendary Germanic tribal leader Arminius (Hermann), who defeated the Roman army in the Battle of the Teutoburg Forest in AD 9 and later became a hero of the German Romantic movement. Conceived and designed by Ernst von Bandel, it was built near Detmold between 1838 and 1875 and originally funded by public subscription, although only completed with Prussian royal funds.

Figure 24.2 Monument to Kaiser Wilhelm I at Koblenz, designed by Bruno Schmitz and built between 1891 and 1897. It was one of around 400 official state funded monuments erected in the 1890s to the memory of modern Germany's first emperor.

Figure 24.3 Monument to Otto von Bismarck in Hamburg, designed by Emil Schaudt and Hugo Lederer, erected between 1901 and 1906. Bismarck monuments were built in great numbers after the Iron Chancellor's death in 1898, mostly paid for by the general public rather than the state.

Figure 24.4 Monument commemorating the Battle of Leipzig ("Battle of the Nations") in 1813, designed by Bruno Schmitz and built between 1900 and 1913. It was financed by a lottery and private donations and was the largest monument in Europe at the time of its construction. Its monumental architecture was designed to make the individual feel small and insignificant, yet at the same time empowered by belonging to a national community of vast potential.

NOTES

1 Apollonio (1973: 22).
2 Gay (1996: 192).
3 Both "historism" and "historicism" are trans-
   lations of *Historismus*, a German word which
   first appeared around 1800. The term "historicism," however, has often been associated
   with a specific philosophical approach that
   attempted to predict the course of human
   history on the basis of past behavior, suggesting that history was developing towards
   a particular end according to predetermined
   laws, whereas historism can be seen as an
   evolutionary concept which understands all
   political order as historically developed. It is
   in this context that the word is used here. See
   Berger (1995: 188, n. 6); also Hamilton
   (1996).
4 Butterfield (1969: 1).
5 Kucich (2000: 17).
6 Campbell, Labbe, and Shuttleworth (2000:
   3).
7 Anderson (1967: 99).
8 Wittkau (1992: 27).
9 Bann (1984: 16).
10 Schivelbusch (1986: 33).
11 Quoted in ibid: 37.
12 Levine (1986: 3–4).
13 Plumb (1969: 131).
14 Butterfield (1931).
15 Berger, Donovan, and Passmore (1999:
   11).
16 The phrases come from Disraeli's *Sybil* and
   are quoted by Melman (1991: 575).
17 Butterfield (1969: 37).
18 Plumb (1969: 125).
19 Levine (1986); also Crane (1999: 194).
20 Bann (1984: 14).
21 This phrase appeared in the preface to
   Ranke's *Histories of the Latin and Teutonic
   Peoples* (1824). Its most appropriate translation into English, and the author's intended
   meaning, have both been subject to much
   debate.
22 Bann (1984: 9).
23 Warren (2003).
24 Stuchtey (1999: 30).
25 Gooch (1913: 141).
26 Levine (1986: 2).
27 Butterfield (1969: 117).
28 White (1973).
29 Lambert (2003: 42).
30 Gooch (1913: 67).
31 Lambert (2003: 45).
32 Levine (1986: 136–7).
33 Bann (1984: 2).
34 Quoted by Gooch (1913: 170).
35 Quoted by Brown (1979: 204).
36 Melman (1991: 581).
37 Quoted by Brown (1979: 195).
38 Ibid: 203.
39 Melman (1991: 579).
40 Bann (1984: 25).
41 Ibid: 60.
42 Strong (1978: 7).
43 Ibid: 60.
44 Ibid: 47.
45 Ibid: 36.
46 Quoted by Brix and Steinhauser (1978:
   272).
47 Quoted by Bann (1984: vi).
48 Strong (1978: 136).
49 Crane (1999: 187).
50 Bann (1984: 83).
51 Bazin (1967: 173–4).
52 Bann (1984: 90–1).
53 Quoted by Crossley (1999: 53).
54 Fawcett (1976: 75).
55 Weideger (1994: 37).
56 Wiener (1981: 69).
57 Quoted in Macleod (1971: 18).
58 Ibid: 123.
59 Plumb (1969: 11).
60 Anderson (1967: 89).
61 Sheehan (2000: 144).
62 Clogg (1988: 24).
63 Plaschka (1974: 94).
64 Quoted in ibid: 96.
65 Jelavich (1988: 87).
66 Djordjevi (1988: 58).
67 Bann in the preface to Myrone and Peltz
   (1999: xix).
68 Hobsbawm and Ranger (1983: 7).
69 Cannadine (1983: 103).
70 Mosse (1971: 170).
71 Jefferies (2003: 57–72).
72 Ibid: 127.
73 Rearick (1974).
74 Rearick (1977: 451).
75 Strong (1978: 72).
76 Nietzsche (1983: 121).

GUIDE TO FURTHER READING

This chapter has been particularly informed by the work of the art historian Stephen Bann, notably *The Clothing of Clio* and his essay collection *The Inventions of History*. Both contain a wealth of intriguing detail, as does Philippa Levine's excellent *The Amateur and the Professional*, and Myrone and Peltz's *Producing the Past*. Arguably, however, the biggest intellectual debt is owed to Hobsbawm and Ranger's *Invention of Tradition*, which remains required reading for anyone interested in the instrumentalization of history in nineteenth-century Europe (and beyond). Although I disagree with many of his interpretations, it would also be churlish not to acknowledge the work of George L. Mosse on national monuments and festivals, best approached through his *Nationalization of the Masses*. Finally, mention must be made of two useful and accessible books put together by the editor of the present volume: Berger, Donovan, and Passmore's, *Writing National Histories* and Berger, Feldner, and Passmore's *Writing History*.

CHAPTER TWENTY-FIVE

The Century of Science

KATHRYN M. OLESKO

Max Weber's master narrative of the nineteenth century, outlined in *The Protestant Ethic and the Spirit of Capitalism* (1904–5) and other works, rested squarely on an understanding of science and the forms of rationality associated with it. In his view the unfolding of the Enlightenment promise of progress and emancipation through the application of reason came to a crashing halt in the years prior to World War I, the *terminus ad quem* of the century. Weber expressed his pessimistic views on modernity in many ways, but none is more memorable than his phrase "the iron cage," a physical and visual metaphor for the perceived separation of reason and values. This indictment of modernity, echoed by scholars since, has been responsible for a separation of another type: the separation of science from a broader historical understanding of the century.

Although historians have paid lip service to Weber's interpretation, few have integrated the salient categories of Weber's analysis – in particular scientific culture and bourgeois rationality – into their interpretations of the nineteenth century. The fault is in part the result of a professional division of labor. Historians generally leave the task of interpreting science to more specialist historians of science, and the task of interpreting rationality either to philosophers or intellectual historians. The result is a bifurcated history that fails to address adequately the complexities of lived historical reality in the nineteenth century, not only of the roles of science and technology in it, but also of the ways social groups appropriated reason, reasonableness, and rationality for their own ends. The story of science *in* nineteenth-century European history thus remains for the most part an unfinished project.

Yet the nineteenth century was a "century of science." From the French Revolution to World War I the scientific disciplines – both natural and social – took shape; the scientific persona in the form of the professional scientist emerged; and scientific institutions in the form of popular clubs, specialized academies and institutes, research laboratories (both pure and applied), technical government agencies, and educational curricula at schools and universities became embedded in European life. The scientific community and its institutional system of support became an integral part of everyday life as well as high politics. Science, its technical practices, and its rational ways of thinking contributed strongly to the shaping of the self, society, and the state – so much so that by the end of the century it was not unusual to find social issues treated as technical problems in the application of rationality. No wonder then that Weber and like-minded social scientists such as Émile Durkheim spoke of modernity in Janus-like terms: condemning it for its emphasis on reason and the sciences, but also supporting its reliance on the social sciences to provide the diagnostics and therapeutics that could lead to reform and betterment.

The Landscape of Science

The emergence of the natural and social sciences in the form of disciplines after 1800 represented a radical intellectual and social departure from earlier conceptions of knowledge. Until the seventeenth century the scholastic curriculum organized knowledge into the seven liberal arts (astronomy, music, geometry, arithmetic, rhetoric, grammar, and dialectic) and philosophy (logic, ethics, and physics). During the eighteenth century, knowledge – including natural philosophy, which embraced most of what became known later as the natural sciences – was regarded in theory as a unity best represented in encyclopedias or compendia. Although specialization occurred in practical areas like astronomy, forestry, and in other domains strategic to the state and the operation of the economy, such fracturing was not ideal, was generally associated with the arts and trades, and was epistemologically inferior to more encompassing forms of knowledge. The court, the state, and the academy were the principal patrons of natural philosophy on the continent, while in Great Britain the natural philosopher found an audience in the public sphere and a patron in the state bureaucracy. All over early modern Europe the Catholic church was exceptional among all institutions in its support of astronomy. Universities, by contrast, had not yet institutionalized intellectual innovation to any great degree. The eighteenth-century belief in the "unity of knowledge" was difficult to eradicate. Even after the emergence of the disciplines with their sharply defined intellectual boundaries, a belief in unity persisted in the German ideal of *Wissenschaft* and in British and continental Romantic science, but both proved incapable of surviving the more thoroughgoing intellectual and social transformations associated with the disciplines.

Historians know more about how rather than why sharply defined areas of knowledge with their own methods, problems, and practitioners took shape after 1800. Specialization in the physical sciences occurred first (due in part to a rapid adaptation of methods from astronomy), in the life sciences around mid-century, and at the end of the century, the social sciences. The process was not merely intellectual. The modern disciplines were also characterized by institutionalized systems of training, recruitment, and professional behavior, as well as specialized forms of association and communication (professional societies and journals). Sociologist Rudolf Stichweh, among others, has drawn connections between the rise of the middle class and the appearance of disciplinary knowledge in the German states: the two developments intersect in the state examination system for credentialing bureaucrats and other functionaries that became a route to social advancement for the educated middle class.[1] Historian R. Steven Turner has called the Prussian examination system, to take one prominent example, a "powerful instrument of modernization within the professions."[2] Similar connections between scientific knowledge, social mobility, and professional careers in both state service and the sciences were also found in the Cambridge Mathematical Tripos in Great Britain[3] and more generally in the French Grandes Écoles. Goethe's *Faust* (1806) projected anxiety about the volatile combination of ambition, power, and knowledge, but in reality all European state examination systems created avenues of upward social mobility based on the free expression of talent, concentrated training, and superior academic achievement.

No factor was more important in the social reproduction of individuals dedicated to knowledge production than the sharpening of the identity of those who studied the natural (and later, social) world. In previous centuries philosophers, academicians, bureaucrats, and others studied nature by avocation. Those who excelled at it were called "geniuses" until the 1830s; but genius by definition was believed to be a personal gift, and so could not be systematically reproduced by institutional means. Debates early in the century over the notion of genius bespoke a deep-seated change in the role of natural knowledge in the public sphere where it was democratized, criticized, but most of all, accessible. Coincident with the emergence of the disciplines and the pedagogical means for teaching them, the scientific persona took shape. A debate in the British Association for the Advancement of Science over who exactly the motley crew of individuals were who purported to study natural philosophy prompted Samuel Coleridge to ask the polymath William Whewell to think of a moniker appropriate for them. He did, and in 1834 coined the word "scientist" for those engaged in the study of nature; by the end of the century it applied to those who studied the body, the mind, and society as well. Within decades thereafter genius became a term of derision, suspicion, and distrust because it connoted privacy and secrecy, rather than public knowledge and openness. Only in undertakings that could not be completely taught or codified – such as art – did the term genius retain currency and respect.[4]

The emergence of science as a vocation in the nineteenth century was thus an affirmation of the social investment in pedagogical systems designed to create types of individuals – experts – whose qualifications were certified by institutional and often state-sanctioned standardized rules of judgment. But the very same educational systems that were responsible for turning out scientists also acted as sieves that allowed only certain types of individuals to do so. For most of the century the gender barriers of higher education prevented women from becoming scientists. *Pace* Max Weber's later contrast between science and politics as vocations, the scientific persona in the nineteenth century took shape within a moral space – as Charles Taylor wrote in general about the modern self – within which certain actions and behaviors were imbued with virtue, such as the open disclosure of sources, the honest reporting of data, and the meticulous calculation of errors of measurement.[5]

A complex system of social reproduction appeared simultaneously with the emergence of the scientific disciplines, especially in universities where the training of the next generation of practitioners took place. German universities took the lead in training natural scientists because they integrated research and teaching early in the century, but by the end of the century nearly all European universities had followed suit. Secondary schools were important partners in sustaining social reproduction in the natural sciences and mathematics through their employment of university-trained teachers and their ambitious efforts in reforming science

pedagogy across the century. The intensification of industrialization in the second half of the century aided the coalescence of two curricular tracks in secondary and tertiary education: classical and "modern." The success of technical education in the sciences and engineering was based in part on its appeal to the middle and lower middle classes.

The scientific disciplines congealed as coherent bodies of knowledge with enough structure to be passed on to the next generation, thereby facilitating social reproduction, but also enough fluidity to allow for modifications through research. The principal site of scientific research was the university-based laboratory or institute, and later in the century, industrial laboratories, state agencies, and privately funded research institutes. The earliest university-based scientific laboratories and institutes were in chemistry, but after about the 1860s specialized facilities for physics grew markedly due to the close ties between industrial culture and measuring practices and the need to train the next generation in techniques of measurement. These physical laboratories and institutes, in which Germany first took the lead, were found primarily in industrializing regions, dedicated themselves primarily to teaching, but also served as important centers of social interaction. With simple origins in glass-walled cases known as cabinets for housing instruments, physical institutes grew to include research and teaching laboratories, lecture rooms, and smaller rooms for individualized study and practice. Some even included apartments for institute directors. Between 1865 and 1914, German universities possessed 21 such institutes. Facilities outside Germany were more modest by comparison. The Cavendish Laboratory of the University of Cambridge, for instance, opened in 1871 under the direction of James Clerk Maxwell; until 1879 its modest research agenda included nothing more interesting than research on electrical units, then a matter of international debate. Women were finally admitted in the early 1880s, a novelty in European higher education. Not until the end of the century did the Cavendish offer degrees (bachelor's and master's) to students who had not matriculated at Cambridge as undergraduates, a condition that had inhibited the types of international visitors that frequented German laboratories and institutes.[6]

These intellectual, social, and institutional changes based largely in European educational systems by no means constituted the entirety of scientific culture. Some traits of eighteenth-century natural knowledge persisted, albeit now absorbed into new administrative and institutional frameworks. Public service work, for instance, still tied science to the state. Astronomers such as George Airy in Great Britain, Friedrich Wilhelm Bessel in Germany, and François Arago in France contributed to projects like weights and measures reform, military and cadastral mapping, meteorological data, and insurance and other practical issues. Outside the university, professional societies like the British Association for the Advancement of Science (founded 1831) and a rich journal culture sustained intellectual communication among scientists, while civic associations dedicated to science and technology promoted exchanges in the public sphere between scientists and society, integrated scientific discourse into daily life, and encouraged rational solutions to agricultural and economic problems.[7] After the mid-century revolutions on the continent a popular journal culture dedicated to nature and the natural world spread the ideas, rational ways of thinking, and ethos of the natural sciences.[8]

By the end of the century the landscape of scientific culture included not only educational institutions, industries, and civic associations, but also industrial laboratories, national laboratories, and privately funded institutions for scientific research. The first industrial laboratories appeared after 1860: outstanding examples include Alfred Krupp's chemistry laboratory at his Essen steel foundry; chemical testing laboratories associated with foundries around Sheffield, England; the organic chemistry laboratories established in Britain, France, Switzerland, and Germany following the discovery of synthetic aniline dyes in 1856; and the laboratories of the burgeoning electrical industry, including Siemens & Halske in Germany and Philipps in the Netherlands, dedicated to research and development in communication (including the telephone), artificial

lighting, and in utility supply and regulation. University laboratories, whose directors had the added responsibility of teaching, proved incapable of both sustaining innovation and handling state responsibilities. As a result, European governments established large-scale national laboratories to handle basic research as well as testing in the name of public safety and consumer protection. The first of these was the Berlin-based Physikalisch-Technische Reichsanstalt (1887), followed by the National Physical Laboratory in Teddington, England (1899). Also inaugurating the era of "big science" was the establishment of private research institutes, such those of the Kaiser-Wilhelm-Gesellschaft in Germany, whose first institute opened in 1911.[9]

The conceptual landscape of the natural and social sciences was by then marked by ideas and theories that were both research subjects for practitioners and a new conceptual framework for interpreting the quotidian. Terms that crossed the divide between science and society included: energy, entropy, electrical current, and electromagnetism from physics; cell and evolution from the biological sciences; probability, uncertainty, and non-Euclidean space from the mathematical sciences; and anomie, ego, and subconscious from the social sciences. The institutionalization and professionalization of science in the nineteenth century thus was not only a sign of the socialization of science, but also the scientific rationalization of society.

Science and the Definition of the Self

Over the course of the nineteenth century the rational discourses of the natural and social sciences as conveyed primarily in medicine and public health redefined the body and mind as entities that could be known through the specialized language of experts rather than through religion as they had been for so long. The growing interest in body types – the result of social change, the photograph, and physical anthropology – destroyed the Enlightenment's belief in natural law with its assumption that the commonalities of humanity were far more important than any environmentally caused differences. Social scientists, physicians, and psychiatrists isolated individual and group differences ostensibly to create classifications, but the inevitable result was the construction of hierarchies cast in the vocabulary of the physical and biological sciences. In England, France, and Germany psychiatry became an important means through which the middle class articulated its own identity by defining normalcy in terms of rationality or the absence of mental illness. The latter was, in any event, easier to define. Race and gender proved to be the most malleable traits in the scientific construction of the self. Paul Broca's Anthropological Society of Paris created a racial typology based on phrenology in the 1850s, while anthropometry served equally well in confirming the inferiority of women or the pathological, atavistic physical type characteristic (in Cesare Lombroso's mind) of the criminal. In the 1890s Jean-Martin Charcot used the camera to document a physiognomy of insanity that became an iconography of mental illness. In all of these examples the sobriety of scientific investigation was compromised by political uses of the aesthetics of objectivity, usually in support of the status quo.[10]

Although the burgeoning reading public of the eighteenth century helped to shift the emphasis from the sense of hearing to that of sight, vision became the key sense of the nineteenth century through science and technology. The transition from an aural culture to a visual one was the result of the massive reorganization of knowledge leading to the formation of the disciplines; of the shift from an *a priori* to an empiricist theory of vision; and of the introduction of several new visual technologies. The first two changes were linked. Older theories of vision, including that of Immanuel Kant, regarded the sense of sight as *a priori* or innate and the eye as a camera obscura. But between 1810 and 1840 a subjective theory of vision grounded in physics and physiology took shape, with elements from the study of color perception, nerve impulses, and after images. A physiological optics that capitalized on the imperfections of the eye replaced the objective geometrical optics of the camera obscura and its mathematical space grounded in perspective.[11]

The transition from an innate to an empiricist theory of vision coincided with the fascination with optical illusions in everyday life, as are found in the stories of E. T. A. Hoffmann wherein new social groups, new urban spaces, and new mechanical devices challenged customary patterns of recognition. The railway journey reorganized space into what Wolfgang Schivelbusch has called "panoramic vision": the view of the landscape from a train window, framed by telegraph poles.[12] The play on visual illusion occurred also in new visual forms like the panorama, introduced by Robert Barker in Edinburgh in 1787, and the diorama, first created in Paris by Charles-Marie Bouton and Louis Daguerre in 1822, as well as in new visual technologies, such as the kaleidoscope (1822), the thaumatrope (1825), the phenakistiscope (1833), and the stereoscope (1838). All became mass produced, commercialized popular toys by mid-century. Especially crucial to the transformation of the visual experience in the nineteenth century was the stereoscope, invented by David Brewster. It highlighted the persistently unstable and subjective nature of vision by playing on binocularity and depth perception. The stereoscope subverted the type of contemplation associated with the camera obscura and perspective. Instead, the new observer had to *learn to see* and could only see within a prescribed set of possibilities. This empiricist theory of vision placed sight within a field of physiological and mental operations that constantly tested and verified experience. At the end of the century mass produced items, the visual array of images, and the frenetic pace of life characteristic of industrial culture (especially in the workplace and the marketplace) led to concerns about visual distractions that caused inattention, lowered productivity, and induced neurasthenia. Hence the attempt not only to stabilize perception through the teaching of precision measurement, perspective, or geometrical drawing, but also to understand the scientific foundation of inattention and exclusions of the visual field by analyzing visual reaction times, a popular subject of psychological investigation.[13]

Numbers also defined the self in the nineteenth century. The Enlightenment had its "reasonable man," but the French Revolution and the terror that followed gave pause to the idea of rationality or reasonableness as necessarily defining the self. Individuals were, in any event, fickle, idiosyncratic, and difficult to pin down precisely. Far more reliable and predictable, the Belgian statistician Adolphe Quetelet argued, was *l'homme moyen*, the average man. Measuring the traits of individuals (height, weight, age at marriage, fertility, mortality, and other traits), Quetelet found that the distribution of measurements followed the same bell curve that Carl Friedrich Gauss had identified as governing the distribution of errors in observational astronomy. In his "social physics" of 1831, Quetelet introduced his average man as the foundation of the broad laws of social behavior that could be incorporated into legislation aimed at reform. Or, more appropriate to his age of revolution, the calculation of averages from year to year could lead to the isolation of perturbations to which an opposing force (reform legislation) could be applied to neutralize potential social uprisings. (Hence, the collection of statistics soared in the mid-century revolutions, 1848–52.) Whether in good times or bad, the average man was the essence of mass society. Embodying the virtue of temperance, he was the moral ideal of an age in constant fear of losing its bearings.[14]

Science and the Construction of Society and Communal Spaces

Although Europeans possessed ways of speaking about society in the eighteenth century, the French Revolution and industrialization spurred new ways of thinking about social groups and of the operation of society as a whole. Both changes separated civil society from the state, and acknowledged the properties of groups of individuals separate from politics. Nonetheless, the politically motivated gathering of statistics by governments after 1800 – in censuses, crime rates, suicide rates, and the like – provided the first inkling that there was an order to individuals gathered together in groups. "Society" emerged as a concept linked to numbers in statistics. Not until the end of the century, though, did a

science of society – sociology – appear as a full-fledged discipline. The numbers that had by then defined social regularities were the foundation for articulating the normal and the pathological in terms of what Émile Durkheim called social facts: institutional norms that prescribed ways of acting within certain limits, thus functioning as behavioral constraints. Hence Durkheim could argue in *Suicide* (1897) that anomie or the absence of communal norms created pathological states such as high suicide rates, which were the manifestation of institutionalized egoism, the opposite of communal norms.

Historians customarily associated the formation of civil society in the eighteenth century with reading clubs, but the transformation of the public sphere in the nineteenth century was due in large part to the integration into it of the rational discourse of communication associated with the natural sciences. During the eighteenth century in Britain chemistry and civil culture developed symbiotically,[15] but it was not until much later that the integration of science and civil society occurred on the continent, where the surge in associational life in the nineteenth century occurred in part as a result of popular interest in science and technology outside the university, the institute, and the academy. Far from being merely a popular exposition of the ideas and theories of the natural sciences, the scientific culture that thrived in civil society was a nursery for the bourgeois virtues of toleration, openness, and rationality.

Science and technology provided the vocabulary and the material means to articulate the finer details of communal spaces, especially urban ones. Artificial light, in particular electric lighting, produced a pluralistic visual environment in Europe's urban areas now subject to the optical control of space. The gas lamp (1810s), and especially electric lamps (1880s), changed street life by facilitating greater surveillance by authorities, by creating night life, and by introducing psychological transformations in the perception of night and day. Paintings like Vincent Van Gogh's *Café Terrace at Place du Forum* (1888) are illustrative of the nocturnal spaces and activities – such as *flânerie* – created by an artificial light that competed with heaven's stars. Dark areas of the city drew the attention of police, for they were associated with criminality. During the revolutions of the 1830s street lanterns were so identified with state authority that lantern smashing became a form of rebellion – as well as a way to reappropriate the street from authorities, as the street urchin Gavroche did in Victor Hugo's *Les Misérables* (1865). Unlit spaces generated nocturnal insecurity, one of the many new psychological feelings spawned by science and technology.[16]

Physiology, chemistry, and biology became municipal sciences that united the laboratory culture of the scientist with the urban environment of water, pollution, epidemiology, and public health. Urban sanitation movements – including sewer systems, water hydraulics, and bathhouses – coincided nearly exactly with the mid-century revolutions as well as with the increase of air pollution caused by factories (especially chemical ones) and the switch from wood to coal as the primary fuel. Edwin Chadwick's sanitary movement in England after 1846 associated communal bathhouses with the mission to civilize the working class; Baron von Haussmann's Parisian sewers of the 1850s were in part intended as a bulwark for the moral order of society; and Hamburg's sewer and bathhouse reform of the same period, inaugurated by the Englishman William Lindley, was built on the belief that dirt and pollution spread disease and disorder while cleanliness promoted public order. The internationally known German chemist Justus Liebig argued in 1844 that soap was the measure of the prosperity and culture of the state (only to be contradicted later by Heinrich von Treitschke, who remarked that the British conflated soap and civilization). The fact of the matter was that most urban cultures vacillated on the issue. In Hamburg, for instance, where public baths had been closed in the eighteenth century in the belief that they were a source of disease, less than half the population regularly took a bath at the end of the nineteenth century. The nineteenth-century public health movement, built on the principles of scientific medicine, mixed politics and scientific rationality in its emphasis on circulation as the guiding metaphor for the "air and light" movement that governed urban planning. But

cleanliness in the second half of the century was more than a matter of health and hygiene: it became a marker of bourgeois distance not only from dirt and pollution, but also from the criminal, the disorderly, and the dangerous. The quotidian appropriation of principles from science and medicine enacted in the use of water technologies thus contributed to bourgeois traits and values.[17]

Yet when the collective health of individuals became the index of the entire social organism, as it did in the second half of the century, the physician, physiologist, chemist, and biologist all became *de facto* agents of the state acting for the social good. Whereas in the 1860s and 1870s liberalism and free trade upheld the non-interventionist state, capitalist cycles and their deleterious consequences later in the century opened the door for interventionist policies guided by experts. The germ theory of disease – supported by the discovery of the bacteria for anthrax in 1876 and for tuberculosis in 1882 – prompted policies to eliminate dirt, both material and social. The growing consensus in the 1880s that chromosomes were the heredity substance in the cell nucleus responsible for passing on traits – a belief reinforced by the rediscovery of Gregor Mendel's laws of inheritance in 1900 – shifted attention away from the environment and toward the biology of reproduction as a way to reduce the occurrence of undesirable social, mental, and physical traits. Taken to the extreme, selective breeding became racial hygiene: a politics of healthcare based on biological heredity as a means of controlling pathological behavior. Racial hygiene was also perceived as an effective antidote to social welfare because rather than protecting the weakest elements of society, it sought to eliminate them. In seeking rational solutions to social problems, scientific medicine and a public health grounded in scientific principles led to the invasion of the vocabulary of the life sciences into politics, economics, and civil society, as well as to the integration of scientific experts into the state bureaucratic apparatus.[18]

Science and the Nation-State

Scholarship since Michel Foucault's *Discipline and Punish* (1977) has supported his thesis that the modern liberal state is in part upheld by the sciences of the body and the mind, especially psychiatry and psychology, scientific medicine, criminology, and pedagogy. A closer examination of the relationship between knowledge and the state demonstrates, however, that nearly all the natural and social sciences were deployed in the construction of the sinews of the types of dispersed power that Foucault believed existed alongside the traditional expressions of state sovereignty, including the military and the police. In the second half of the century most European states used scientific expertise for social welfare, political administration, and economic productivity. By World War I, they had in addition established agencies for uniform weights and measures, health policy, materials testing, industrial codes, and other matters – all in the name of national security, public safety, public health, consumer protection, social welfare, and the overall wellbeing of the state. Regulatory agencies established uniformity in the material world and concepts of "normalcy" for the social world. Indeed, as the century drew to a close, state sponsored social hygiene became closely allied to eugenics as a means to counteract perceived social degeneracy caused by industrialization. The preference for protecting and policing society over preserving individual rights extended to the science of criminology: throughout Europe crime became more a matter of social hygiene than retributive justice.

The state's use of science and technology for its own political ends was not new to the nineteenth century, as several examples from the eighteenth century illustrate. In 1714 when Isaac Newton was himself in state service as warden of the mint, Queen Anne established the Board of Longitude by an Act of Parliament and launched a competition aimed at securing a means for the accurate determination of longitude at sea, a race in which the English cabinet- and clock-maker John Harrison proved victorious over Europe's professional astronomers. Nearly all German-speaking states in Central Europe used cameralism as a way of harnessing the state's considerable resources, from silver mines to the population at large. Embracing both baroque classificatory schemes and the emancipatory goals of Enlightenment

reason, cameralists viewed science and technology as suited for reform, repair, and reinstatement of social order. Science and technology were integrated into the French state like no other. The science of cartography literally defined France from the ground up: four generations of the Cassini family of astronomers created the first accurate national map based on triangulation, published between 1798 and 1812. And when the revolution recreated the state anew, scientists were once again central to the process in the creation of the meter, the new revolutionary unit of length, defined as 1/10,000,000 of the meridian running through Paris, measured from Dunkirk to Barcelona and expressed in the form of a platinum bar cast in 1799.

What continued into the nineteenth century in the relationship between science, power, and the state was the overwhelming reliance upon quantification in the acquisition, interpretation, and representation of knowledge, but now stripped of the Enlightenment's belief in the absolute certainty and objectivity of results. Both numerical tabulation and measurements were subject to the statistical assessments of methods based on probability calculus; even the most exacting of precision measurements (say those taken in triangulation projects) were subject to the method of least squares and its probabilistic determination of the limits of certainty. Despite the uncertainties of quantitative results, most European administrators remained firm in their resolve to continue to use them as a foundation for policy. In their support the Statistical Society of Paris proclaimed in 1860 that statistics was an indispensable science for the liberal state and for good governance of society, and later in the century the French Academy of Sciences admitted that numerical results in any event constituted transparent facts about the world. European nations in essence defined themselves through the tools that became a part of the social sciences. The populace tended to view surveys – such as the compilation of vital statistics in France or taxpayers in Great Britain – as state intrusions into private life, but they became essential information for bettering administrative services, economic productivity, and even physical infrastructure by mid-century. Alexandre Parent-Duchâtelet's statistics on prostitution in Paris of 1836 were, for instance, viewed in conjunction with the planned installation of a new sewer system as a part of the overall effort to institute a culture of cleanliness in service of public health.

The most visible manifestation of the relationship between science and national identity was the construction of state maps based on triangulation, precision measurement, and the surveyors' instrumentarium of theodolites, sextants, calipers, thermometers, telescopes, heliotropes, repetition circles, plumb lines and levels, comparators, and metal bars for laying out baselines. Whereas in the eighteenth century cartography was a military exercise in preparation for war, in the nineteenth century military officers worked side by side with state astronomers to define the geography of the state by geometric means. France took the lead during the Napoleonic period by attempting to extend the Cassini map to newly conquered lands, but Switzerland is perhaps the best example of the union of power, knowledge, and space in mapmaking. The construction of the first trigonometric and topographic map of Switzerland took place under the direction of General Guillaume-Henri Dafour between 1832 and 1865, coinciding with the constructive phase of Swiss liberalism between 1830 and 1848. The map provided not only the first bird's-eye view of the country, but also the physical space of military, transportation, communication, and hydraulic projects. Indeed, it is argued that the idea of "Switzerland" as a cartographic entity preceded the full realization of the definition of the nation.[19]

Even more than cartography, statistics and other sciences defined the nation, and they defined the most unwieldy of nineteenth-century political entities, the empire, and none more than the British Empire, and within it, India. The idea that possession of science and technology was a yardstick of civilization was already centuries old by the time Britain brought irrigation, the railroad, the telegraph, and other technologies to Indian soil. Rather than defining India similar to the way in which they had defined Britain, these technologies instead necessitated administration and governance by the occupying power and those who cooperated with it, and thus consolidated the empire. No printed work shows more clearly the connection between scientific data collection and empire definition than Rudyard Kipling's *Kim* (1901). Throughout the novel, scientific knowledge is used to stress power relations, subject a people and remove agency from them, and illustrate the superiority of Western rationality over Eastern irrationality. Kim himself is a surveyor trained in one of the most disciplined mathematical practices of the nineteenth century, but under the guidance of the obsessive collector of ethnographical data, Colonel Creighton, Kim "surveys" by other means, joining Creighton in a massive spy operation designed to prevent rebellion and maintain the empire. Both of them were agents of the massive deployment of resources to gather scientific data about the empire – so much so that some historians have argued that the empire existed only on paper, in the files of the British Museum. Science and technology thus helped the British to conceive of an empire distant in space and culture; to construct hierarchies based on racial and national stereotyping and on the possession of rational knowledge, and to transform the definition of "classified" from mere organization to secret state knowledge. Whether in British India, German Southwest Africa, or the Belgian Congo, the rational sciences were an important part of the combined European imperial project.[20]

An Example from Physics: Energy and Culture

One concept from the physical sciences that attained cultural currency in all three areas – self, society, and the state – was energy. Although historians hitherto believed that the conservation of energy was an example of a mid-century cluster of discoveries concerning the conservation of force, Crosbie Smith has demonstrated that the central group in the articulation of the concept was found in northern British industrial culture and consisted of the brothers James and William Thomson, James Clerk Maxwell, and others. The concept of energy, linked via the new science of thermodynamics to ideas of work, waste, and (eventually) entropy (the dissipation of energy or the disorder of the universe), decisively shifted interpretations of physical reality away from the French deterministic one with its emphasis upon mechanics and reversibility toward one that understood reality in statistical terms and that posited the irreversibility of complex physical processes. In 1854 William Thomson coined the term "thermodynamics." Ongoing efforts at industrialization provided the cultural context for linking energy to economic concerns, especially the efficient production of power. Because no engine was perfectly efficient, practitioners not only separated the inefficient human world from the (apparently) efficient natural one, but also attributed inefficiencies in the human world to human imperfections, specifically to the lack of skill in the design of engines. Thus, the mere attempt to achieve efficiency was imbued with moral overtones as a step toward improvement, perfection, and the efficient use of resources, while inefficiencies and waste were associated with evil. The belief in irreversibility, furthermore, killed all belief in cyclical cosmologies and so endorsed the doctrine of a specific beginning to the age of the earth consistent with Christian views on time. Energy physics thus became a weapon against anti-Christian materialists and naturalists, but the complete dissipation of energy was believed to represent pessimistic fatalism inconsistent with Christian belief in redemption. Thermodynamics in the northern British experience thus meshed with cultures of industrialization and Presbyterianism through Whig, reforming, and progressive values, which in turn aided the cultural integration of energy into the quotidian.

Energy became a powerful concept for interpreting psychological, social, economic, and political realities. The division of gender activities into productive (male) and reproductive (female) spheres seemed especially illustrative of the conservation of energy and its calculus of input and output. Menstruation was thus viewed as depleting the woman's reservoir of energy, leaving her with less to invest in both physical and intellectual activities; hence her absence from the productive sphere and from intellectual life was merely the result of biolog-ical determinism. Anson Rabinbach has argued that the conservation of energy gave the idea of the "human motor" considerable credence given the central importance of human labor and the working class to industrializing Europe. The working body became one of the many devices that converted energy into work, just like the steam engine. With this image of the body as a source of productive energy in mind, liberal social reformers believed they could craft legislation that would efficiently channel that energy into productive enterprises. But such hopes of harnessing the labor power of the human machine could not overcome one of the persistent disorders of modernity – fatigue – as much a moral as a physical shortcoming, studied by scientists like Etienne-Jules Marey and Angelo Mosso in the laboratory between the 1870s and the 1890s. The socioeconomic problem of human productivity was thus subject to empirical research guided by rational principles in the hopes of producing a calculus of energy and fatigue. So pervasive was the belief in the conservation of energy that Sigmund Freud made it one of the foundations of the dynamics of the human mind: he thought of neuroses and abnormal behaviors as physical manifestations of an imbalance in psychical energies.[21]

Science and Modernity

The cumulative effect of science upon life at the end of the century by all accounts was regarded as ambiguous. Scientists like Rudolf Virchow praised the entry of science into daily life and its role in the rational upbringing of the population, but others regarded that infiltration as suspicious if not destructive of fundamental values. As psychologists everywhere knew, a general nervous temperament seemed to permeate society thanks to precision clocks accurate to one minute in the marketplace and train station, an electrified urban environment, and a pace of life that seemed out of control. National identity itself became a psychic phenomenon. Gestalt psychologists believed that science was incapable of dealing with the problems of daily life and so called for a new way of looking at objective reality. Appropriately, Friedrich Nietzsche – perhaps the harshest critic of progress as historical emplotment – astutely noted that modernity coincided with the collapse of classical theories of vision and that modern objectivity was simply a form of "bad taste."[22]

And yet such criticisms bred their own peculiar forms of optimism similar to what the German philosopher Georg Friedrich Hegel had found when he was among the first to criticize modernity at the beginning of the century. Hegel had been critical of Enlightenment rationality and the hardening of ideas in the disciplines, but he wanted a critical spirit, and identified one way of achieving it in the *Preface to the Phenomenology of the Mind* (1806). So did Nietzsche, who sought to replace the harsh daylight of the Enlightenment with a "twilight," to replace reason with the senses, and to replace science by art. Secularization accompanied modernity, to be sure, yet the issue was not one of a constant conflict with the Bible, but rather of finding substitutes for traditional religion. This search remained high on the list of priorities for scientists. Durkheim believed that a replacement for religion could be found in sociology, for it affirmed the importance of ethical norms in social life. Charcot, Freud's teacher, studied the Marian cult at Lourdes not only in an attempt to explain miraculous cures in rational terms, but also to understand why miracles worked only for those who believed in them. From there he hoped he would then be able to explain why psychiatry, like the miraculous, was effective only where there was belief in its powers.[23] Weber himself admitted that the historical process of rationalization could be countered by personal charisma, a liberal notion based on individual personality, creativity, and idiosyncrasy, all traits the disciplines had buried when they eliminated the possibility of genius. The interpretation of natural processes according to the principles of statistics and probability seemed to remove a purposeful deity from nature, but Albert Einstein, whose revolutionary theories of 1905 on spacetime, the photoelectric effect, and Brownian motion (the latter requiring a foundation in statistics), refused to believe that the universe was governed by chance.

Daily life continued to metamorphose as a result of developments in science and technology, and not everyone greeted the accompanying changes with disdain. A new global chronometric regime was instituted in 1884 with the meridian running through the Greenwich Observatory in Britain as the zero point of 24 equal time zones of 15° each. Aside from a single Russian anarchist immortalized in Joseph Conrad's novel *The Secret Agent* (1907), no one seems to have strongly objected to this universal standard time. Nor were there objections to universal standards for electrical units, established in 1881, which paved the way for the management of the electrical utilities that would power other new inventions such as the telephone, cinema, and radio. The notion of modernity as it took shape in the nineteenth century rested on the roles of science, technology, and reason in the historical process, especially in the unfolding of the Enlightenment promise of progress and emancipation through the application of reason. The turn-of-the-century sentiment against science and technology might itself be interpreted as the continued affirmation of the critical function of reason in the public sphere, a development in which science and scientific culture had played such large parts.

NOTES

1 Stichweh (1992).
2 Turner (1980: 119).
3 Warwick (2003).
4 Schaffer (1990).
5 Taylor (1989); Olesko (1991).
6 Cahan (1985); Kim (2002).
7 Morrel and Thackray (1981); Nyhart and Broman (2002).
8 Cantor et al. (2004).
9 Cahan (1989).
10 Russett (1989); Wetzell (2000); Goldstein (1987).
11 Crary (1992).
12 Schivelbusch (1986).
13 Crary (1999).
14 Porter (1986).
15 Golinski (1992).
16 Schivelbusch (1988); Schlör (1998).
17 Reid (1991); Evans (1987); Ladd (1990); Goubert (1989).

18   Weindling (1989).
19   Gugerli and Speich (2002).
20   Adas (1989); Richards (1993); Prakash
     (1999).
21   Rabinbach (1990).
22   Radkau (1998); Ash (1995).
23   Goldstein (1987).

GUIDE TO FURTHER READING

A lively introduction to the social history of knowledge and attendant practices in late eighteenth-century institutions ranging from the academy to the literary public sphere can be found in Peter Burke's well-written survey, *A Social History of Knowledge from Gutenberg to Diderot*. For an engrossing example of how one state harnessed science and technology as the new century began, see Ken Alder's story of the meter, a project carried out in the heady days after the French Revolution: *The Measure of All Things*. David Cahan's *From Natural Philosophy to the Sciences* is an assessment of the historiography on nineteenth-century science; it also identifies important new directions of research.

Many scientific concepts, including forms of scientific rationality, filtered into daily life. On how probability in the form of risk assessment became a part of everyday thinking, see Gigerenzer et al.'s *Empire of Chance*. Bureaucrats and other public officials clung to the "objectivity" of numbers when trust and power were in short supply, according to Theodore Porter in *Trust in Numbers*. Few scientific concepts entered common parlance as thoroughly as did energy and work; see Smith's *Science of Energy* and Rabinbach's provocative *Human Motor*. On how science and technology changed time-consciousness and the perception of time and space, see Kern's *Culture of Time and Space*. The final chapters in the revised edition of Benedict Anderson's *Imagined Communities* still offer provocative ways of thinking about national identity in terms of the artifacts of science and technology.

The cultural criticism of science, technology, and rationality and their roles in the construction of modernity are best approached through the original writings of major European intellectuals of the period, especially Karl Marx, Friedrich Nietzsche, Émile Durkheim, Sigmund Freud, and especially Max Weber.

CHAPTER TWENTY-SIX

Police and the Law

CHRIS A. WILLIAMS

Introduction

The state is that body which claims a monopoly on the authorization of legitimate force, and the police are the institution entrusted with the exercise of this claim within the state's borders.[1] The very ubiquity of police organizations has prevented them from receiving the kind of historical scrutiny which has been lavished on the more immediately dramatic exercise of state power in war. Yet the development of European police institutions, their expansion, and the first steps leading towards their integration, are matters of great significance for the study of nineteenth-century Europe. Most European regimes of the late eighteenth century claimed many police powers, but had very few policemen. During the nineteenth century, institutions were developed to enforce these claims to power, not usually through the imposition of a new vision for the state, but as a consequence of attempts to solve discrete problems which beset it.[2] Efficient police systems allowed governments a high degree of freedom of action in protecting their subjects from one another, and themselves from their subjects.

Before the 1970s, the historiography of policing was largely dormant, and dominated in the main by the views of "official" historians working from within the perspectives of the institutions that they were studying. They were inclined to look at the development of police

forces from a highly teleological perspective, concentrating on those factors in the past which appeared to presage future developments, or lend prestige to the organization. With the growth of social history, this viewpoint began to be challenged, and the writing of more analytical histories of police institutions is now commonplace in most European countries. While those actions of the police which have immediate impacts on political events have received attention, the social history of the everyday exercise of police power has been less systematically covered. But overall, enough work has been done to allow a tentative attempt at a synthesis, although this will inevitably be provisional and limited in geographical scope and in the institutions towards which it has directed its attention. Innovations such as gendarmeries and "new" uniformed forces have largely been studied at the expense of the traditional, often local, law enforcement bodies, which have not left many easily accessible bodies of sources. This has tended to reinforce the view of contemporary police reformers that the old bodies were ineffectual. Recent work in the UK on various unreformed police institutions has revealed most of these to be far more effective than their successors maintained, and it may well be that a closer look at their counterparts in the rest of Europe will lead to a similar conclusion.

Several theorists have had a major impact on the way that historians have considered this topic – on the types of questions that they have considered it legitimate to ask, and on the terms in which they have presented their answers. The work of Marx and his successors on the role played by class is crucial. In the nineteenth century much of the exercise of police power, and the justification for it, was directed to sustain the rule of groups who defined their own suitability in terms of their control of property, and were engaged against those whose material interests were counter to this. From the imposition of the free market in grain and land, through the clampdown on trade union organization and working-class political parties, to the social disciplining that led to a malleable workforce, police had a place in the front line of the nineteenth century's various "social wars."[3] Marx's theoretical work largely left the state identified in one-dimensional terms. An expansion of these can be found in the work of Max Weber, who at the end of the nineteenth century produced a detailed categorization of various forms of power, authority, and organization in the state. For him, the most efficient form of organization, one that had triumphed, was the bureaucracy. In this system, regular activities are assigned as official duties, authority to give commands is distributed in a stable way, methodical provision is made for the regular fulfillment of duties, and only persons who qualify under general rules are employed.[4] This was the dominant form of authority, but Weber's other two categories – patriarchialism, which is personal authority founded on tradition, and charisma, which is authority deriving from personal characteristics alone – also need to be taken into account.

The most influential theorist of the issue of power has been Michel Foucault. His *Discipline and Punish* painted a graphic picture of the shift in the modern age from punishing the body to controlling the psyche.[5] Subsequent empirical work has cast doubt on the extent to which the "total institution" was ever achieved. Nevertheless, many of Foucault's concepts have a resonance in all aspects of the social history of the state in the nineteenth century: in the disciplining of police institutions themselves, and in the generalized bureaucratic surveillance of the population and other means whereby power pervaded society. He stressed that criminal justice institutions are not merely repressive, but are productive also: they serve to create forms of social relations. Another motor for social change can be found in the work of the increasingly influential historical sociologist Norbert Elias, whose major theoretical contribution was the notion of the "civilizing process" in Western Europe.[6] In centralized states, elites attempt to differentiate their behavior from the ruled by introducing ever greater refinement in personal behavior and manners. This process can be seen in action in the attempts by state authorities to impose these new norms, often against the opposition of many of their subjects.[7] Between them these four offer frameworks that, combined with empirical research, are capable of answering most of the questions currently posed of the subject.

The Impact of the Napoleonic Regime

The starting point for any survey of police systems must be that of the French Empire, since so much of the rest of the century's developments were carried out either in emulation of it or in reaction against it. In France itself, Napoleon inherited a variety of civilian police organizations from the *ancien régime*, the Revolution, and the Directory. The ministry of police was responsible for intelligence gathering and state security, but prefects, mayors, and the Paris *Prefect de Police* also exercised police powers in their areas. There was also the gendarmerie, a military body devoted to maintaining order in the countryside, which had evolved from the old *maréchausée* through the counter-insurgency campaigns of the 1790s. Bonaparte developed these elements into an efficient system, which he attempted to implant not just in France, but elsewhere.

Gendarmeries patrolled main roads, visited fairs and markets, and they were available to accompany civil police officers when necessary. They escorted tax receipts, policed troops on the march, restored order, and helped the populace fight natural disasters. Gendarmeries were set up in the wake of French armies, where they suppressed "brigandage" and smuggling, policed the armies, and attempted to control deserters and stragglers. Their place in the Napoleonic system was a function of their ability to do these tasks effectively, rather than the fruit of any grand plan, but their usefulness as an institution in a threatening environment drew them to the attention of governments across Europe who needed to restore order after the wars were over.

During the wars the Gendarmerie was emulated in Bavaria, Württemberg, and other German states allied with France.[8] France's enemies also turned to it as a model: as a consequence of defeat by the French, the Prussians created a gendarmerie on the French model in 1812.[9] The Napoleonic Gendarmerie of Lombardy was taken over by the returning Habsburg authorities, precisely because it was seen as so efficient.[10] In the Kingdom of Piedmont, the Imperial Gendarmerie had been active for 12 years when King Victor Emmanuel was restored in 1814. His general policy was an attempt to turn the administrative clock back to 1798; yet he recreated an institution to play the role of the Gendarmerie, the *Carabinieri*. In the Papal States, after the war Secretary of State Consalvi dissolved the traditional *sbirri* and substituted a *Carabinieri*, with an attendant system of surveillance and regulation.

In other countries, gendarmeries were often founded initially in disputed districts where there was potential for insurrection or subversion, then extended nationally when it became clear that they were able to perform all manner of useful tasks. This was the model followed in Ireland, the Netherlands, and the Austrian Empire. In Spain, the *Guardia Civil* was created in 1844 by the moderate wing of the liberals, anxious to cement their authority by being seen to be able to control banditry and guarantee freedom of movement in the country. The potential for violent social change gave a new urgency to the state's attempts to monopolize force and police the marginal. As Hughes puts it, after the upheavals of the French Revolution and given the nature of the threat of Jacobinism: "Beggars, vagabonds, and brigands were no longer sad reminders of an imperfect world, but rather problems that had to be eradicated before society came apart at

the seams."[11] By upholding a single common code of law, and providing a ready and available means whereby offenses against it could be stopped and offenders punished, police forces exercised a key centripetal role, clamping down on multifarious local customs and bringing the mores of the towns to the countryside.[12] As well as helping to create a unitary national state in this way, they also often enforced universal male conscription, which was eventually to play its own role in the evolution of a more unified national consciousness.

The suppression of banditry was a key task for the gendarme: military sweeps against bandits were inevitably temporary, but the dispersed barracks of the gendarmerie meant that they could keep the countryside under enduring watch. In Sicily, and the *Mezzogiorno*, where the Bourbons had struggled to suppress open lawlessness which was nodded at by the local magnates, the *Carabinieri* – whose main loyalty was to the state – fought alongside the army in the Brigands' War following unification. The ability to control banditry and other forms of crime could lead to an increase in the legitimacy of the state among those groups most likely to suffer from them. Conversely, the failure to establish an effective rule of law able to protect property and persons could fuel the active opposition of local elites to the regime, as was the case in the Papal States in the 1820s.[13] Although some forces, such as the Irish Constabulary, were wary of allowing men to serve in their district of origin, others, such as Napoleon's, were happy to accommodate this, not least because they needed a certain proportion of locals – in Brittany or the Midi as much as in Flanders or the Rhineland – to speak the regional language or dialect.[14]

By the mid-century much of Europe was covered by a network of gendarmerie-style forces. Most of these were organized in units of four to eight men, quartered in barracks in towns or along main roads. They mounted regular patrols covering their allotted district, and sent voluminous reports – on matters internal, political, and criminal – up the chain of command. The utility of the gendarmeries for state building was important, but it should not be exaggerated: in the German Empire, the exercise of all police powers remained the responsibility of the individual states.[15] Gendarmeries posed a threat to the ability of magnates to exercise influence over their lands and tenants, which could produce opposition, as when Prussian landowners lobbied hard and successfully up until 1848 for that state's gendarmerie to be kept small. As a branch of the regular army, it competed with that body for resources, and the resentment of the army was a reason why the Habsburg Gendarmerie was cut down in the 1860s.[16] Over the century these forces evolved in different ways: in France they lost out to the greater emphasis placed by the Third Republic on an efficient civilian police; in Spain and Italy they grew more independent and prestigious; in Ireland (where after 1867 they were the sole police force outside Dublin) they became "domesticated"; and in Germany and Russia they remained small in numerical terms. Nevertheless, as a legacy of the Napoleonic Wars, they remain one of the most important police innovations of the nineteenth century.

Haute Police

Europe's ruling groups – the vast majority of whom saw in the example of the French Revolution a threat to their position – regarded policing as a political issue as much as an administrative or legal one. They needed the *haute police* function – the protection of the regime – both for self-preservation and because without a stable state, their claim to protect the individual might be compromised. They knew that there was always "more to cops than robbers."[17]

Political policing took many forms. Regimes might need to watch prominent but potentially unruly members of the dynasties and courts on which most relied. In 1836 Bow Street Runner Henry Goddard was paid by the British government to tail the Duke of Brunswick, the unpopular nephew of William IV.[18] After the assassination of Alexander II in 1881, the Russian civil and political police were reorganized under the unified control of the ministry of the interior. Before, the political police had concentrated on the potential threat posed by nobility and other elements at the court; afterwards, they widened their attention, taking in not just the radical intelligentsia but also the "all-sided surveillance" of the Russian people as a whole.[19] Political policing in France was the responsibility of the prefects of departments and of Paris, whose duty of "general police" gave them power over local police *commissaires*, and was normally seen as a higher priority than the control of crime and public order. In practice this was carried out through censorship, payments to informers, and the compilation of police reports on social and political life.[20] Another expression of political concern was border security, and the surveillance of foreigners. This could be given a republican gloss: in 1879 Clemenceau called for the political police of France to be diverted entirely to the surveillance of borders and foreign visitors so the French themselves could be free to enjoy liberty spared from the threat of external subversion.[21] Concern over the movement of foreigners also prompted the German authorities to reintroduce the passport for movement between the German states in the 1880s, moving away from the doctrine of free movement enacted by the North German Confederation in 1867.[22]

Changes of regime, especially in France, posed a problem for the *haute police* function: usually, incoming rulers recognized that they needed the expertise of the police establishment more than they wanted to purge the security apparatus. Thus the first consolidating act of the incoming power was usually to order civilian police functionaries back to their posts. The Bourbons held the Gendarmerie to a higher standard, and its ranks were purged of the most ardent Bonapartists, as well as much "dead wood" after the Hundred Days.[23] One discontinuity in the French methods of political policing was that under the Third Republic officials lost their formal immunity from prosecution for crimes carried out in the service of the state. Political police units were not always high handed. Despite the subsequent smears of the nationalist *leggenda nera* the Habsburgs in Italy were very careful to make sure that every possible legal form was upheld in political prosecutions, and pressed for sentences well below the maximum.

The *haute police* function is also an obvious example of Foucault's maxim that criminal justice institutions do not merely repress: they also create. Secret police – especially in states where censorship was strong and effective – served as one means whereby the authorities could be informed of discontent, its causes, and sometimes even its possible remedies.[24] In addition to their role concerning the surveillance of the marginal and the disaffected, and the production of intelligence on the mood of the population, police also functioned as a feedback mechanism and a general inspectorate. In the Papal States they gathered information on the effectiveness of public administration. In Austrian-administered Venetia, one of the key roles of the police was to monitor the effectiveness and personal morality of public employers, clergy, and teachers. Before any post was filled, the authorities required a report of the candidate's abilities, rectitude, and past career. The Habsburg authorities believed that the chief defense of the legitimacy of their rule in Italy was their ability to govern fairly and according to the law: they were more afraid of scandal than of conspiracy.

The *haute police* function was also present in Britain, a country which prided itself on not having a political police. For the middle fifty years of the century, there was substantial opposition to the idea of political policing, stemming largely from outrage at the use of *agents provocateurs* by the government in the 1810s. Yet both unreformed and new police participated in covert and open surveillance against the Chartist Movement, and in 1839 the central government temporarily set up its own police forces in Birmingham and Manchester, where the local authorities were considered suspect or incompetent, and Chartists were strong. It was the threat from Ireland – where overt political policing had never gone away – that led to the creation of Special Branch in 1883.[25] Protecting the state was always one of the tasks of British police, but the strength of the British regime was such that this role did not assume the prominence it held elsewhere.

Police cooperation, especially over political issues, was used as an important element of foreign policy. Before 1848, Austria devoted much effort to forging police links with other states, concentrating on the German Confed-

eration. The assassination of the Empress Elisabeth in 1898 led to the International Anti-Anarchist Conference in Rome, which became bogged down when an effort to reach a common definition of the legitimate goals of overt political policing left Britain and France resisting demands to harmonize their extradition laws with those of the German, Russian, and Austro-Hungarian empires. Treaties or exchange of information at diplomatic levels, though, neither necessarily produced nor precluded operational integration "on the ground." There are some instances of officially ordained cooperation at local level: for example, in the 1850s, a treaty between Austria and Saxony set up conferences of the gendarmerie units in their border regions.[26] But in the main, the development of effective police cooperation proceeded independently of openly advertised initiatives at central government level and was made possible by the attainment by various national police institutions of a degree of professional independence from their respective "parent" governments.[27] The Russian foreign counter-intelligence service operated throughout Europe to counter the efforts of émigré revolutionaries. Although the governments of the liberal democracies were overtly reluctant to cooperate with them, by the end of the century "the evolving police subculture " allowed them to work closely with the police of Britain, France, Italy, and Switzerland.[28]

The Role of Traditional Justice

The nineteenth century saw the extinction of almost all of the rights of seigniorial justice in Europe, in favor of the jurisdiction of the state. But even before this period, the power of landholders themselves to pronounce justice had been closely trammeled. In Prussia many magnates employed judges on their estates, and owned the right to convene courts therein. The judges, though, needed to be qualified, and had a right of appeal to the state if they were dismissed. They concerned themselves largely with civil law – chiefly because this could be made to pay, unlike criminal law. They generally produced fair verdicts in cases within the peasantry, but in conflicts between these and managers or proprietors, sometimes tended to find in favor of the latter, especially when reinforcing their different status under law as members of different "estates."[29] Over the course of the century, private justice was largely assumed into the state system. In 1816 the Papal government significantly reduced the number of baronial jurisdictions by forcing their owners to underwrite all the attendant policing and judicial costs – a prospect at which most of them balked. In the German states, the rights of magnates over justice ended in 1872, when they passed, not to the empire, but to its various constituent states.

In much of Southeast Europe, the issue of the exercise of state power in rural areas was intimately tied up with the fate of the state itself. Weaker states turned (or were forced to turn) to foreign examples for emulation – after 1878 Montenegro imported Dutch police officers as instructors, while in the Ottoman Empire a group of British army and police officers attempted to fashion a gendarmerie rule book using as models those of the Royal Irish Constabulary, the Indian Police, the South African Police, and the French Gendarmerie.[30] Although the Ottoman Empire progressively centralized its multiple policing agencies, the unstable basis for its political authority, and its inability to exclude external powers from its internal affairs, continually sapped its claim to a monopoly of force.[31] Yet even when the integrity of the state was ensured, attempting to impose the legal and police models developed in the rich, powerful, and urbanized northwest of Europe upon very different societies was not an easy task, as the British discovered in the Ionian Isles.[32]

All over Europe, rural communities tended to have their own codes of acceptable behavior, particularly over the use of shared resources in areas where customary law was important. Often these were enforced with brutal sanctions applied by some members of the community. For example, in Russia, arson was often used again peasants who were perceived as having offended against the community.[33] In Ireland gangs such as the Whiteboys threatened and attacked those who had taken the side of the landowner against the smallholder, or were seen as bettering themselves at the expense of their neighbors. The authorities faced great difficulties in prosecuting this "agrarian crime," although the extent to which these were the product of intimidation or of community solidarity remains debatable. Unwritten law and community sanctions applied also to social transgressors through often-violent shaming ceremonies collectively called by historians "rough music" or "charivari," although in practice they were given many different local names.

Russia in the second half of the nineteenth century offers an example of the counterposing of "community justice" to the state's attempts to enforce a monopoly of law. The Emancipation of 1861 brought with it a series of legal reforms in the court systems, designed to replace the personal jurisdiction of the landlord with a series of peasant courts, which were constituted to apply customary, not state law.[34] By the end of the nineteenth century, these new *volost* courts were being used by peasants in search of justice – but at the same time the imposition of traditional peasant values via the use of retributive measures such as arson attacks was continuing. In the long term, this process demonstrates a move away from a system dominated by the arbitration of the community towards one where the state's courts were being used more often. But the process was highly uneven, and it is difficult to conclude that the "legal consciousness" of Russian peasants had moved in the direction desired by the reformers. Nor did the latter succeed in permanently ejecting the nobility from the judicial process: the reform of 1861 which introduced professional Justices of the Peace was repealed in 1889 by a regime anxious to shore up its support among landowners, and the Land Captains who replaced them were drawn from the ranks of the nobility. In the meantime, the efforts to reinvigorate the chronically underfunded (and hence corrupt) provincial police stalled owing to the unwillingness of the state to foot the bill.[35]

It may be no surprise that in rural areas with very few police, a weak tradition of attachment to formal justice systems, and largely stable populations, the unwritten law of the village was often more important than the written law. The same issues, though, arose in some of the most heavily policed parts of the continent, where the legitimacy of the law was rarely overtly challenged, and where all sections of the population made use of it. In late nineteenth-century London, many working-class people expected the magistrates in the police courts not to deliver abstract justice, but to arbitrate their problems. In London, the community was applying informal sanctions against miscreants until at least 1900, sometimes alongside the official law of police and courts, and sometimes instead of it.[36]

Private interests could also supplant the "official" police in the workplace. The British system of policing could allow employers to exercise wide police powers if they could pass the required legislation: throughout the nineteenth century, discipline in the mills of Yorkshire's West Riding was enforced by inspectors with police powers under the control of the manufacturers themselves organized as the Worsted Committee.[37] German factory owners also organized their own police forces. Centralized state law enforcement had become more dominant, but it was only one element in a wider system.

Policing and Regulation

Even before the French Revolution, under the impact of the desire by the state for increasingly effective powers of surveillance and control, the idea of "police" had expanded from a general term referring to the administration of the internal affairs of a nation to refer to a preventive and repressive arm of the state.[38] A whole raft of police regulations, especially those concerning the detail of economic activity and the registration of the population, had been enacted across Europe. The flexibility of "the police" was often enormous: in France the Paris Prefecture of Police itself could issue and enforce ordinances dealing with public order. In Berlin police could both write and enforce the rules dealing with their own dignity, and defining the penalties for compromising it. In this way, they could justify holding suspects without charge for up to 14 days, despite German law limiting this to 24 hours. A police

with the power to react to preserve the orderly functioning of public life could use that power to bolster its own standing.

The urbanization of much of Europe during the nineteenth century provided an incentive to establish police powers over urban space. To work, the city had not only to be a place where property was secure, but also to be a place where people could move freely, and where the environment was kept habitable. This demand for effective urban governance drove the expansion of police forces, as can be seen from the hundreds of general and local laws and regulations which they had to enforce. The rural context exerted similar demands concerning issues such as the registration and movement of animals; after the 1840s the Royal Irish Constabulary spent far more time checking dog licenses than fighting Fenians.[39]

Regulation increased, as did its enforcement. The reach of the "new" police forces, as measured by the number of people they arrested, was great. This led to the rise of the "policeman-state" as a powerful presence in working-class life.[40] The police used the power of regulation and discretionary enforcement to impose a certain morality on the working classes, especially those engaged in practices which were seen as immoral, politically threatening, or both. Many police agents and bureaucrats interpreted the "common good" as the protection of property, and thus paid little or no attention to the rights of the propertyless.[41] Overstretched and undermanned state machines often resorted to the brutal exercise of arbitrary power to compensate for their lack of depth.[42]

Police forces began to develop a sense of themselves. In Britain, lower-ranking officers, working long hours for low pay and only the possibility of a pension, began to lobby collectively for better working conditions. This agitation bore fruit with the 1890 Police Act, guaranteeing them a pension.[43] In France, civil police began to organize into trade unions, and these were one of the sources of the drive for increased professionalism through better training that began to emerge at the end of the century.[44] Science legitimized policing within society; it also legitimized policing as a profession.

The Civil Model

As well as the "state military" police, the gendarmerie, Europe also extended and developed two other models of police accountability, which Emsley has called "state civil" and "municipal civil."[45] In 1800 it also boasted a plethora of "old police" institutions, whose legal foundation often went back centuries, although their actual organization and composition was generally far more recent. In the UK, parish constables, in Italy *sbirri*, in France *guards champêtre*, in Norway *lensmenn* – all exercised authority in rural areas, with more or less prestige and independence.[46] During the century, the majority (though not all) of these were replaced by new civil police institutions, usually answerable to the national authorities. The British case, where county constabularies were a responsibility of local government, is less of an exception than it appears to be: local government was the bench of Justices of the Peace, led by landowners who were often themselves major players in national politics.[47] When elected county councils arrived in 1888, they did not take over police powers; these were given to a joint committee of councilors and magistrates.

Their urban counterparts in many states retained a higher degree of independence. In France, although the *commissaire de police* of a town was appointed by the state, he was paid by the municipality, which also controlled the size and pay of his force. German practice varied between states: in Prussia all policing was in theory the responsibility of the state, though in practice the cities exercised much immediate authority, whereas in Saxony the big cities were independent. Throughout most of Europe, the authority of state-controlled civil police such as the Italian *Guardia di Publica Sicurezza* was supplemented and in some cases challenged by forces formed and financed locally, such as the *Guardie Municipali* formed in many Italian cities by the 1860s.

The "civil model" appeared to originate in London. In 1800, magistrate Patrick Colquhoun advocated the application of Beccarian principles to the policing of the poor and masterless in London. The police reform project reached a key point in 1829 when the Metropolitan Police took over the patrolling of the London area (outside the historic City of London) from local government. This force was controlled directly from the government's Home Office, it was uniformed and unarmed, and promised a career open to talent; all but the highest ranks were open to those who had risen from the ranks. This reform was Utilitarian in that it cut through the existing local jurisdictions, but the form that the Metropolitan Police took was modeled closely on the best of the "old" watch forces as run by the parishes. Indeed, one of the complaints against the Metropolitan force was that in some parts of the capital it put fewer men on the streets than its predecessors, despite costing more.[48] But until 1839, when the last of the old police offices were closed down, it did not have the city to itself. The model of a uniformed preventive police was subsequently extended to the rest of Great Britain, but it was 1857 before it became compulsory for counties to supersede parish constables with their own "new" police forces. London was not unique: the replacement of both a low-skilled force and a system of householder obligation by a single bureaucratic unit also occurred in Hamburg in 1852. Nor was it first: in the spring of 1829, a few score *serjeants de ville*, a uniformed, unarmed force responsible for preserving order and preventing crime, were sent out onto the streets of Paris.[49]

Despite their theoretical differences, the Common Law of Great Britain, and the Roman Law of the rest of Europe had many similarities on the level of prosecutions of "everyday" crime. Mellaerts has found that in both Britain and France the active cooperation of the wider community was necessary to exercise the police power against miscreants, and in the late nineteenth-century French town, the locally controlled municipal police were prominent in bringing offenders to justice. In theory the victim had no control over the prosecution, which was brought by the state, but in practice, victims had a great deal of influence over what happened. The Netherlands was an "odd man out": there the prosecution of minor crime was far more contained within the structures of officialdom.[50]

The civil model attracted reformers across the continent. Bologna, Stockholm, Turin, and

Berlin all adopted "modern" police forces after 1848. In part this was a reflection of the reputation of London's Metropolitan Police, which was perceived as having been a key player in the peaceful defeat of Chartism in that year. Throughout the second half of the nineteenth century, Germans from across the political spectrum unfavorably contrasted their police with those of Britain; in 1873 even the Prussian minister of the interior joined in the chorus, claiming that the superior development of the British system was due to its earlier foundation.[51] Hamburg's police system in the 1850s and 1860s was also intended to be as overtly unmilitary (and cheap) as possible, and was justified in relation to the English model. In Berlin, though, the *Schutzmannschaft* began in 1848 as a civilian force uniformed in top hats, but by 1851 – the year that it took over the role of the Prussian Gendarmerie within the city – this was replaced by a military-style uniform, and a commentator remarked that the Berlin policeman went on patrol "armed as if for war."[52]

The British police model was invoked by reformers in Italy, who proffered it as a model for the reform of their own institutions. The example of "other countries" had a powerful rhetorical force in the places wherein it was deployed, but it often relied on misrepresentation. In the last decades of the nineteenth century, hundreds of Metropolitan Police routinely carried pistols on patrol, and in many parts of Britain the police were still seen as an alien and unwelcome force by many members of the working class.[53] A uniformed, efficient, non-paramilitary force was not necessarily a locally controlled one. In 1900 the police of London, Paris, Berlin, and almost all the major German cities were controlled independently of municipal government. In Germany the trend was for less, not more, municipal control; Kiel and Saarbrücken ceded control (and expense) of policing to their state governments over the course of the century. The city-states of Hamburg and Bremen provided an exception: in these cases, state control was effectively municipal control. In Hamburg before 1869 the police chief was a senator, who also ruled on thousands of minor criminal and civil cases per year, for which the Senate as a whole was

the court of appeal: municipal control could function as the rule of an elite rather than the rule of law.[54] Nevertheless, the virtue of local control was consistently advanced as one element of the ideal of policing by consent.

Conclusions

It is very difficult to count numbers of policemen, and harder still to assess their "effectiveness." However, we can conclude that overall the nineteenth-century changes in European police systems had led to the continent being more heavily policed, by more centralized bodies, which were more likely to be under the close control of the state. Police were often now supposed to be more separated from the local community, although in practice most had to accommodate to it in some way. Actual police cooperation across borders was often patchy, but by the end of the century the principle that it ought to exist was well established. Internally the "policeman state" had substantially advanced the claims of the authorities to a monopoly of force, and proved a potent means for reassuring those in power that the threats to their position – from rural backwardness, urban chaos, insurgent workers, political opponents, or criminal elements – could be kept under control.

ACKNOWLEDGMENTS

I wish to acknowledge the help of John Carter Wood, Paul Lawrence, Clive Emsley, and Lucy Faire.

NOTES

1   Bittner (1970: 40). Weber posited that the state claims a *Gewaltmonopol*: the "ability to rule" violence, not the more monolithic and unchallenged power suggested by "monopoly." See Spierenburg (2001: 98).
2   Raeff (1975).
3   Neocleous (2000); Storch (1975); Lüdtke (1979); Spencer (1992); Eastwood (1996).
4   Weber (1968: 954–82).
5   Foucault (1977).

6   Mennell (1989).
7   Wood (2004).
8   Emsley (1999b: 173–80).
9   Spencer (1992: 5–6).
10 Laven (1996: 388).
11 Hughes (1994: 257).
12 Weber (1977: 50–66).
13 Hughes (1994: 95)..
14 Emsley (2000).
15 Fosdick (1972: 68).
16 Emsley and Philips (1999: 242).
17 Hughes (1994: 34).
18 Goddard (1956: 35–8).
19 Johnson (1972: 222).
20 Spitzer (1964/5); Payne (1958).
21 Liang (1992: 45).
22 Torpey (2000: 109–10).
23 Emsley (1999b: 84–7).
24 Laven (1996: 395, 401).
25 Porter (1991).
26 Liang (1992: 19–23, 31).
27 Deflem (2002b: 457).
28 Zuckerman (2003: 67).
29 Wienfort (2000).
30 Liang (1992: 153); Coope (1880: 9).
31 Swanson (1972: 255); Karpat (1972: 259).
32 Pratt (1978: 106–10).
33 Frierson (1997: 121).
34 Frierson (1986: 528).
35 Abbott (1973: 299).
36 Davis (1984: 314).
37 Godfrey (2002).
38 Axtmann (1992).
39 Lowe and Malcolm (1992).
40 Gatrell (1990: 259, 281).
41 Lüdtke (1989).
42 Davis (1988: 241).
43 Steedman (1984: 124–30).
44 Berlière (1991: 53).
45 Emsley (1999a: 35–6).
46 Emsley (1983); Næshagen (2000: 188).
47 Storch and Philips (1999: 47).
48 Reynolds (1998: 154).
49 Emsley (1983: 58).
50 Mellaerts (2000: 47).
51 Spencer (1992: 156).
52 Emsley (1983: 101–2); see also Reinke (1991: 55).
53 Emsley (1985: 125–49); Gatrell (1990).
54 Evans (1987: 88).

GUIDE TO FURTHER READING

The best institutional histories of European police systems in general are by Clive Emsley: *Policing and its Context 1750–1870* and *Gendarmes and the State in Nineteenth-Century Europe*. Emsley's *The English Police: A Political and Social History* is a good introduction to this topic, while the connections and contrasts between the British and Irish experiences are featured in Palmer's *Police and Protest in England and Ireland*. Liang's *The Rise of Modern Police and the European State System from Metternich to the Second World War* relates police power and interstate relations. The development of cooperation between European police forces is described in Deflem's *Policing World Society*.

The relationship between police and policy in Italy has been covered by Davis in *Conflict and Control*, and in greater detail in a more limited area by Hughes in *Crime, Disorder and the Risorgimento*. An excellent case study of policing in Germany is Spencer's *Police and Social Order in German Cities*. Neocleous's *Fabrication of Social Order* rethinks the social and political significance of police reform. The rise and significance of techniques of identification are featured in Torpey's *Invention of the Passport*. Ongoing research on the topic of police and the law is usually reviewed in the English/French language journal *Crime, Histoire et Sociétés/Crime, History and Societies*.

CHAPTER TWENTY-SEVEN

The Cultural History of Crime

DANIEL M. VYLETA

Introduction

When I left, Littré's thesis that crime is insanity was raging; I come back – and crime is no longer insanity but precisely common sense itself . . . (Fyodor Dostoevsky, *Demons*)[1]

It has become a matter of historiographic orthodoxy that the nineteenth century invented not only the criminal, but also the degenerate, the sex killer, and the criminologist. There is much truth in this tale of invention, although it has taken on something of the roundness of myth in its many retellings. Only recently have historians begun to focus on the fluctuations, inconsistencies, and tensions within the many narratives nineteenth-century scholars and laymen told about crime, its perpetrators and their adversaries. This chapter provides an introduction to the diverse body of thought – popular, legal, and scientific – that fed into the construction of criminality in a century that saw the rise of the detective novel, underwent a sustained period of prison reform, embraced fingerprinting as a central investigative technology, and ended by raising the specter of eugenic measures as a means of curbing the spread of dangerous delinquents.

From Crimes to Criminals

When the century opened, persons who committed crimes were widely regarded as no different from their fellow men and women, apart from in their decision to break laws that others chose to honor. Cesare Beccaria (1738–94), whose *Dei Delitti e Delle Pene* (*Essay on Crime and Punishment*, first published in 1764) represents one of the most influential Enlightenment statements on the issue, depicted laws as no more than societal norms aimed at social order, and argued, echoing Hobbes, that obedience to these laws involved the loss of some part of one's personal liberty. He freely acknowledged that this trade, in which liberty was exchanged for security, stood in violation of the human passions which urge us to pursue our own interests in the face of such artificial constraints. The legislator – likened by Beccaria to a "skilful architect" who battled the indelible forces of gravity – thus had to design a system of punishments whose severity was precisely sufficient to convince reason that respect for the laws served one's own interests better than their violation, and induce the individual to reign in their passions.

Towards the end of the century many of these insights were under heavy attack. From a vision of criminality that centered on the criminal action, one had moved to focus upon the criminal agent. Many theorists of crime who now often worked within the new science of criminology, or within medical/psychiatric professions, insisted that criminals could be differentiated from the general population by means other than a reference to their criminal acts, though there was significant dispute as to where this deviance could be located (e.g., in criminal bodies, their minds, their hereditary make-up, their upbringing and exposure to alcohol, bad nutrition, etc.).

This shift in perspective is above all associated with the work of the Italian scholar Cesare Lombroso (1835–1909), whose controversial 1876 thesis of the "Born Criminal" (*L'uomo delinquente* – literally "Criminal Man") exercised the minds of scholars throughout Europe.[2] In its original formulation, Lombroso claimed that criminals "proper" were atavisms – evolutionary throwbacks – and hence anthropologically different from the non-criminal population. He further argued that this anthropological difference could be traced upon the bodies of criminals through a series of identifying marks or stigmata. Lombroso had thus found an objective way of revealing a subject's criminal essence, by measuring discrete parts of his or her body. The markers of difference included such items as protruding ears, insensitivity to pain, low hairlines, brachycephalic skulls, asymmetrical gaits, and a proclivity for epilepsy. By the end of the century, Lombrosians, in a tireless search to find a master-clue that would provide reliable identification of born criminals, had added such items as (criminal) hip-bones, palm-lines, levels of blood pressure, the quantity of mucus that collects in the corners of the mouth, the length of the second toe, the sebum-gland located in criminal cheeks, the size of the Adam's apple, and the existence and shape of fingernail lines, all of which received detailed scholarly attention.

These, then, are (to speak with Weber) the two "ideal types" of models of criminality that bracket the century. The following section maps some of the road that links Beccaria to Lombroso, before turning to the challenges mounted against the Lombrosian analysis.

Disciplining the Passions: Towards the Invention of the Criminal

Beccaria's account, which owed much to the Scottish Enlightenment's project of creating a "science of man," happily combined a vision of human beings as rational calculators of self-interest, and as agents in thrall to their passion.[3] Indeed, this dual model provided the starting point for much of early and mid-nineteenth century thought on crime, above all in England. Despite the faith in the rationality of criminals, and hence in their basic anthropologic sameness *vis-à-vis* the wider population, theorists of crime and punishment following Beccaria soon began to stress that there were significant differences in individuals' respective abilities to resist moral temptation. In other words, certain strata within society – and specific individuals within those – were marked not yet as *deviant* in some essentialist sense of the term, but as weak, coarse, and barbaric. They could be reclaimed for civilization through a program of moral habituation.

We find this train of thought in a wide variety of guises: both the early Victorian social novel and Victorian social reformers such as Henry Mayhew (1812–87) conceived of the poor – whom they wished to save – as quasi-savages, whose animal natures easily overpowered their rational parts. Mayhew's *London Labour, and the London Poor* (1861) listed the many forms of "wanderers" whose defective socialization did not allow them to find a stable place within society. His enumeration included pickpockets, beggars, and prostitutes, but also cabmen, coachmen, and sailors: he did not differentiate strictly by the legality of the respective "profession" but rather aimed to establish a social typology that was independent of actual criminal actions. He also introduced the idea that these individuals could be distinguished from the general population by their cheek-bones and protruding jaws, their use of slang, their laziness and cruelty. While one can see the outlines of an anthropologically and socially based knowledge of the criminal as "other" in such observations, it is also clear that redemption of these unfortunates remained an attainable goal in this sort of literature.[4]

A related discourse about criminality can be observed on the continent, for instance in the various German states. Here officials in the early nineteenth century frequently focused on bandit gangs that had operated largely in rural areas for centuries.[5] They cast these offenders as "tribes" or "castes" who formed separate societies within the state, with their own customs, laws, and language. "Criminal" was not the chosen term of designation for the individuals involved in such gangs – they were simply "villains" and "crooks" [*Bösewichter*, *Gauner*], morally reprehensible men who challenged social order. The stress in this literature was upon policing rather than punishment, let alone prison reform; it was interested in how one could improve identification procedures, and was keen to provide biographical and physical descriptions of particularly reprehensible and successful villains. Implicitly, of course, the stress upon the social dimension of criminal tribes acknowledged a similar lack of socialization to that found in Mayhew, while also assuming that they were fully rational actors. Indeed, the drive to gain a biographical access to these "crooks" was linked to the growing desire to find the root of their criminal disposition in a life of dissipation that had been freely embraced. Once again the concepts of rationality and free will were thus married to a narrative of the inexorable logic of habituation. In this narrative, criminal society – whether rural robber bands, or later, as industrialization and urbanization transformed society as a whole, the urban criminal milieu   was conceptualized as an inversion of respectable society, living by their own (corrupt) laws and customs.[6]

The most famous example, perhaps, of the vision of criminals as potentially rational actors whose unbridled passions needed to be disciplined through the educative force of habit was Jeremy Bentham's Panopticon. In this prison design – first conceived in 1791, and privately referred to as a "mill for grinding rogues honest" – individuals were to be totally isolated from the outside world and put into a position, by means of an ingenious rotund design where all cells faced a central guard tower, in which they deemed themselves observed at all times. In time the Panopticon would teach them to observe themselves, and the prison regime of abstinence and order would become internalized.[7]

Indeed, the entire program of prison reform that started in England (taking many a cue from the United States) and swept most of Western Europe in the course of the nineteenth century combined such reformist ideas – reformist in the literal sense as human beings were to be made anew within their sturdy walls – with Beccaria's stress on deterrence. Prisons had to be places both terrible and character building; they presupposed potential criminal actors rational enough to anticipate the consequences of their actions, and actual criminals whose rational faculties were obscured by their lack of civilization. In itself, the idea to utilize imprisonment as punishment was new to the nineteenth century: in 1764 Beccaria could still confidently characterize imprisonment as a state that "precedes conviction." Prisons were used to hold suspects, debtors, and – for brief spells – vagrants; they were unhygienic institutions full of corruption and violence. They were also, however, porous entities into which the outside world could and did spill. Visitors were a regular feature in seventeenth and eighteenth-century prisons, and the incarcerated – who were not yet segregated according to their offense or indeed their gender – continued to be economic actors as they bought food and other items from their jailors, or gambled it away with their friends on the inside and those on the out.[8]

The proposed "new" prison came in various stages, and its penetration of Europe as a whole was a protracted and slow affair. The most emulated model of prison architecture and governance was the Pentonville prison, which opened in London in 1842. Based on the "separate system" first developed in a Philadelphia penal institution, it sought to deprive prisoners of all contact with each other and the outside world and strip them of their former identities in order to enact a rebirth. To this end each prisoner was issued a separate cell; prisoner names were replaced by numbers; guards walked silently on padded shoes, according to an intricate system of time clocks. Even in chapel prisoners found themselves in separate stalls. At the same time forced labor became a staple of prison life, even though whether this should be productive labor or labor for its own sake was subject to much debate: while some reformers upheld an ideal of self-financing prisons, others argued for labor as punishment and favored contraptions such as the treadmill where prisoners were deliberately alienated from their work and forcefully subjugated to the rhythms of a machine that produced precisely nothing.[9]

Pentonville-style prisons, and other prisons designed around solitary confinement, were gradually introduced in much of Western Europe despite their high costs. One should note that these changes did not affect all prisoners, were not uniform across Europe, and that reform was not an entirely systematized process. In England, for instance, a local prison system – with a separate administration and to some degree a separate prison culture – remained in place through most of the nineteenth century. Indeed, only Belgium (and to a lesser degree the Netherlands) managed to impose solitary confinement upon the vast majority of its prisoners. In France only half the prison population was housed in individual cells by 1900; in Prussia perhaps some 60 percent. Indeed, some countries – most notably Russia, Spain, and Italy – lagged far behind in this age of the prison. In Italian *Bagnios* (convict prisons), for instance, prisoners remained chained together in pairs until 1901 and sat in large, open rooms. In Russia reliance on corporal punishment, forced labor, and deportation (to Siberia) continued throughout the century, although there was some push for penal reform late in the century.[10]

One interesting aspect of the new prison was that it in many ways can be said to have accelerated the process of turning "the villain" of old into "the criminal." It not only removed men and women convicted of criminal offenses from the public eye, creating a strict physical separation between deviant and lawful citizen that had not existed previously. It also created a distinct prison culture that set criminals apart in their own identities. It was in prison that criminals, officially stripped of their names and not allowed to communicate with each other, bonded by creating systems of signs and a distinct prison *argot* which could not be understood by outsiders, and by inscribing wishes and memories upon their own bodies in the form of tattoos – the same tattoos that were such a central sign for the born criminal's savage insensibility to pain in Lombroso's theory. Some of these features of a criminal culture had, it is true, preexisted in those

robber bands that had exercised the imaginations of officials and the wider public since the sixteenth century. Here, however, the cultural bond was not forged within the geographic and social context of the "real" world, but in a place apart, subject to its own cultural dynamics.[11]

The prison also provided a place in which "criminals" could be studied by criminologists, and one that already implicitly suggested their coherence as a group. Lombroso measured convicts and collected prison graffiti and other writing; one of his critics, the professor of forensic medicine in Lyon, Alexandre Lacassagne (1843–1924), made a study of some 1,600 prison tattoos only to disprove some of his assertions; a host of medical men measured the skulls and brains of deceased prisoners. Moreover, prison diet and hardship physically normalized the prisoners, giving them the same pale, haggard look that helped convince so many contemporaries that they should be understood as a breed apart.

Lombroso's thesis not only fed on these penological developments, demanding that a convict's degree of criminality and not his or her criminal act should determine punishment. It also drew on a longstanding and disparate tradition within European thought which both identified distinct *types* of human beings and explained human actions by reference to physiological or psychological mechanisms that were organic in nature and hence beyond the individual agent's control. One may cite, for instance, the phrenological ideas formulated by the Austrian Franz Joseph Gall (1758–1828) early in the century. Gall's proposal was that the exterior skull shape betrayed which parts of the brain were strongly developed (or, conversely, atrophied), and that the brain itself could be subdivided into 27 "faculties," each of which could be spatially located. The study of a person's skull, in other words, allowed the assessment of a person's personality traits, which were understood as a function of the individual's physiological make-up. Gall's reception was mixed, but he found some resonance among physicians in France where he worked from 1807. In the 1870s – contemporary with Lombroso's search for the criminal man – French scholars such as Arthur Bordier and Paul Broca drew on Gall's ideas to compile systematic systems of classifications for criminals, based upon their skull anatomies.

Within psychiatry too – a discipline that prior to Freud firmly tied psychological abnormality to physiological causes – theoretical models were developed to explain the actions of seemingly rational, but extremely violent and immoral criminals. In the 1830s the British psychiatrist James Prichard (1786–1848) developed a theory that postulated a form of insanity which incapacitated moral judgment, while in France the concept of "monomania" and more specifically "homicidal monomania" – a type of insanity that left the intellectual powers intact but compulsively led the afflicted person to commit murder – was explored by a string of scholars. Again, such theories served to depict certain criminals as psychologically (and in the final analysis physiologically) abnormal, though none of these scholars sought to use them in order to arrive at a universal definition of criminality.

In the 1840s and 1850s two Frenchmen, Prosper Lucas (1805–85) and Bénédict-Auguste Morel (1809–73), developed the theory of degeneration, which received much attention, and was to become one of the key tropes of criminological discourse at the end of the century. In its most dominant form it once again isolated physiological markers which betrayed the pathological state of an organism, a pathology that could be acquired through a life of alcoholism and sexual dissipation and was then passed on from generation to generation.[12]

These ideas were concurrent – if partially incompatible – with the conception of criminality incarnated in the prison reform movement, and prepared the ground for Lombroso's bold thesis. They circulated primarily among the medical professions, while jurists, magistrates, and "philanthropist" reformers by and large remained married to a vision of crime broadly compatible with Becceria's Enlightenment position. The story of the late nineteenth century is thus also the story of the gradual medicalization of the language about crime (i.e., the growing importance given to medical knowledge about criminals within society). Once again, Cesare Lombroso, who started life as a physician and psychiatrist and ended up as

a professor of criminal anthropology – a subject he himself created – may serve as a convenient cipher for this narrative.

Lombroso's Critics

It would be wrong to conclude from this, however, that Lombroso's conception of criminality was widely accepted, or that it was the only reconceptualization of criminality that emerged in the second half of the nineteenth century. Indeed, the Italian's ideas encountered significant resistance in most European countries, including Italy. In France a distinct criminological tradition came into being whose initial focus was primarily sociological rather than physiological or psychological and which found broad backing among not only sociologists, but also medical doctors, jurists, and moralists. Thus the above-mentioned psychiatrist Alexandre Lacassagne stressed the importance of the criminal milieu (i.e., social pathology) for the creation of criminals. The judge and sociologist Gabriel Tarde (1843–1904) similarly stressed the importance of social factors and proposed that both crime and vice were a matter of imitation – indeed, of fashion – that hardened into habits and became deeply ingrained in certain milieus.[13]

Despite this rejection of Lombroso's ideas it would be a mistake to assume that this "sociological school" ran against the trend of medicalization, or indeed diffused notions of a criminal typology. Lacassagne, for instance, combined the stress on environmental factors with the theory that certain individuals were more easily induced to crime than others, and that this difference was rooted in variations of brain topography. He also acknowledged that many criminals did display physical abnormalities of the sort Lombroso described, but blamed environmental factors for these. In the 1880s and especially the 1890s environmental factors and biological models were more and more superimposed by reference to the theory of degeneration and to neo-Lamarckian models of heredity: the latter allowed for acquired pathologies (e.g., via alcoholism) to be passed on to the next generation. Criminals were thus narrated not as atavistic throwbacks but as the symptoms of a gradual, negative evolution that was fueled by a dangerous and unhealthy social life. As such they could still in some senses be regarded as responsible for their criminal deeds – the justice system after all was rooted in the assumption of free will, and many jurists worried about the implications of determinist models of crime.[14]

In Germany Lombroso's ideas were similarly transformed in their reception. Even those like the psychiatrist Hans Kurella (1858–1916), who hailed *L'uomo delinquente* as a work of genius, rejected the theory of atavism as an explanatory crutch, and preferred to interpret criminal stigmata as signs of degeneration. The claim that criminal difference should be primarily located upon criminal bodies also soon came under attack, and, by the end of the century, criminal anthropology had been supplanted by criminal psychology: deviance was now primarily located in psychological difference. The importance of environmental factors was hotly debated, but as in France these could ultimately be reconciled with medical models by proposing an interaction between hereditary inclination and social pressures upon the "criminal." This compromise was worked out primarily by the criminal jurist and penal reformer Franz von Liszt (1851–1919) and the psychiatrist Gustav Aschaffenburg (1866–1944).

In England the reception of Lombroso's ideas was perhaps the most skeptical. Here administrators within the legal system showed themselves unimpressed by the intellectual "radicalism" that spilled over from the continent, and were more concerned with the efficient governing of crime on all levels. Psychiatrists for the most part also proved themselves resistant to criminological ideas, in part because they were integrated into the pragmatic tasks of giving evidence in court or helping determine degrees of prison regimen, and could not match up this day-to-day experience with Lombroso's bold theoretical claims.[15] That is not to say that Lombroso found no admirers, the most notable of them the sexologist Henry Havelock Ellis (1859–1939). Degeneration theory also attracted a significant following, including the psychiatrist Henry Maudsley (1835–1918), who wrote a series of books on the subject, evaluating its threat to society. The theme of heredity's

impact on crime (and the eugenic conclusions this suggested), however, only entered the mainstream debate about criminality and began to influence penal policy with the advent of the twentieth century.[16]

Lombroso's ideas can therefore hardly be described as representative of nineteenth-century European thought on crime. What his work was symptomatic of, however, was a gradual shift towards a medical model of crime that sought to isolate organic and social factors that made criminals distinct from the population at large. Thus, even though most doctors and jurists rejected the Italian's account, his ideas set the agenda for debate about criminals in most European countries.

One should note that while Lombroso himself was an active proponent of prison reform in Italy (which lagged far behind many Western European countries), arguing that born criminals should be separated from occasional criminals lest the latter be further corrupted, elsewhere in Europe the reception of his anthropological and later medical models of crime coincided with a broad disillusionment with the success of the reformist prison. Recidivism was a primary concern of the age and suggested to many that the dual assumptions underlying the reform efforts – that inmates could be reformed, and that the knowledge of sure punishment would convince them not to commit crimes again – were not working. The explanation that some men and women were constitutionally inclined to be criminals seemed to explain this phenomenon.

Criminalistics, Rational Criminals, and Irrational Masses

It is often ignored in this narrative of criminal "otherness," however, that a conception of criminals as indistinguishable from the general population and as identifiable only through their criminal acts and their prison records survived the rise of criminology proper, whether in its anthropological, sociological, or psychological guise. First of all one should note that even the most enthusiastic of Lombrosians were careful to estimate that only a certain percentage of the criminal population were criminal by constitution, leaving a majority whose criminality had to be explained by other means. Secondly, the inability of criminology to successfully pinpoint stable markers for criminality frustrated those whose concerns were primarily with the practical problem of policing, detection, and convicting criminals in court. After all, the implicit promise of Lombroso's original endeavor had been to identify criminals independently of their crimes, potentially even prior to them. As the search for criminal markers moved inside the criminal psyche, or retreated to once again highlight sociological and biographic details about a criminal that could only be gathered *ex post facto*, this promise became more and more elusive. Indeed, one may explain the enthusiasm for statistical approaches to crime at the end of the century as an implicit dismissal of the hope that the individual criminal could be identified in the abstract. The approach had been pioneered by the Belgian Lambert Adolphe Jacques Quetelet (1796–1874) in the 1830s, but in the decades that followed it more and more turned into a historical and comparative science that attempted to assess the importance of different variables such as religion, profession, and, from the turn of the century onwards, race, upon criminal patterns. While this investigation was broadly compatible with any number of beliefs in the causes of crime, including biological ones, it abstracted individual criminals into aggregate numbers and no longer displayed any of the epistemological ambitions that were central to the initial criminological project.

This feeling that criminology had failed in a central aspect led to the revival and reconfiguration of a distinct and rival approach to criminality, which called itself *criminalistics*. One of its most important advocates, the Austrian Hans Gross (1847–1915), consciously and explicitly rejected criminological assumptions. He maintained that criminal anthropology's key problem was that, from the outset, it had falsely understood itself as "the science of the physical and mental *distinctiveness* of the criminal. One had already included the assumption, *that* such a distinctiveness exists, into the definition [of the criminal]."[17] His *Handbook for Investigative Judges* (1893) and its companion

volume *Criminalpsychology* (1898) sought to sidestep this problem by shifting the emphasis away from the criminal and onto the investigative and judicial processes. He insisted that the study of crime could simply not be divorced from these and called for a dedicated science dealing with all the issues pertaining to this perception. Gross's books and articles thus aimed at serving as training and reference manuals in the detective art, covering both the handling of physical evidence and the psychological side of detection where one dealt with defendants, witnesses, jurors, and the like. Gross's understanding of these "clues" was one that explicitly rejected reductive typologization (a method he christened "phenomenological"). His psychological writings were interested in the "normal" rather than the abnormal psyche and did not differentiate between the population at large and criminals. Indeed, Gross for the most part operated under the assumption of rational criminals.[18]

Gross's and other "criminalistic" treatments of crime drew substantially on mid-nineteenth century primers of crime, such as Friedrich Christian Bendedikt Avé-Lallement's three volume *Das Deutsche Gaunerthum* ("German Villains"), which had similar encyclopedic ambitions in creating lists of criminal vocabulary, criminal tools, and criminal tricks. Gross added his psychological preoccupations to this tradition as well as a technical/scientific rigor, and explicitly placed it into the context of the criminological debate about criminal "difference" in order to propose a rival vision of criminality.

A second important context for the coexistence of various conceptualizations of criminals during the final years of the century was a growing discourse – both within criminology and elsewhere – that focused on the sensory and psychological unreliability of the population at large. There was, for instance, a lively debate surrounding the concept of "suggestibility" that focused on both witnesses and the potential victims of crime. Here the senses and memories of members of the wider public were depicted as extremely malleable: the public became a plaything of external stimuli (novels, newspapers, stories told by their neighbors or maids) that led to false memories. Far from honing in on criminal psychological deficiencies, then, this discourse served to mark the average man or woman as weak willed and unreliable, and implicitly worried about rational criminals who would be able to take advantage of the situation. Indeed, the literature devoted to "modern" types of crime such as stockmarket frauds typically pitted intelligent crooks and their profit-orientated rationality against foolish victims who were ill-adjusted to modernity and hence easy prey.

One should also note that the discussion surrounding "degeneration" was not one limited to criminals. Its tendency was to implicate large strata of society, articulating some of the contemporary bourgeois concern about the rise of "the masses," or, as Robert Nye has argued in the case of *Belle Epoche* France, providing articulation for a feeling of national decline.[19] Prophets of degeneration often argued in terms of a diseased age, highlighting any number of individuals – vagrants, prostitutes, gamblers, suicides. Indeed, among some theorists, degeneration and the disease of "neurasthenia" – caused by the overloading of the nervous system by the frantic, ever-changing stimuli of the modern age – had spread deeply into the general population. This belief destroyed any hope that a clearly delineable group of deviants could be pinpointed, whose excision would restore the health of the body politic. The German psychiatrist Paul Näcke (1851–1913), for instance, argued that the hereditary pool was so contaminated by inferior traits that anyone could potentially turn to criminality or insanity depending on environmental influences. As the century closed, therefore, the narratives of deviant criminals and nervous, degenerate, and/or suggestible masses had become so interlaced that it was possible for various commentators either to argue for criminals as the worst affected by this dynamic of decline (as did the Dutch criminologist van Hamel) or to focus one's concern on the unreliability of the general population in the face of the difficulties of actually identifying and bringing to justice criminal actors.

Technologies and Crime

One aspect of the rise of a criminalistic access to criminality was the emergence of a distinct technology devoted to detection and policing. The most famous examples of this new technology are Bertillon's anthropometric system and the rise of dactyloscopy. Both thought to answer the problem of finding a descriptive system for criminals that would allow the authorities to identify criminals beyond doubt and that could be filed in a systematic manner. Photography, which had suggested itself as a solution by the mid-century, did not answer the second problem – no system could be devised to order the complex visual information found in a photographic picture according to systematic categories.

Alphonse Bertillon's (1853–1914) anthropometric system answered this challenge. It was first developed in 1879, disseminated with his 1885 publication of *Identification anthropométrique*, and introduced across much of Europe in the following decade. The Bertillon system issued each processed individual with a number code, derived from measurements of the offender's height, reach, height when seated, length of head, width of head, length of right ear, width of right ear, size of left foot, length of left middle finger, length of little finger, length of left forearm. After measuring a suspect, their data could be compared to all offenders already processed by the system: if they were a repeat offender, the filing cabinet would soon yield their identity card, which included a photo. Despite Bertillon's interest in "reading" discrete parts of the body to establish identity, the system did not embrace any claim regarding criminal "deviance"; indeed, there was no qualitative difference between data gathered from a criminal or non-criminal.[20]

Fingerprinting, by contrast, did originally hope to chart differences between various population groups and enshrine a racial (if not criminal) typology. It was developed, in part, by Sir William Herschel, an English district commissioner stationed in Bengal, who desired to tell apart the otherwise undifferentiable mass of Indian colonial subjects.[21] Concurrently, a physician serving at a Tokyo hospital, Henry Faulds, devised a rudimentary system of classification for fingerprints and expressed the hope that these arches, whorls, and loops were hereditary in nature and could thus provide insight into human evolution. Francis Galton (1822–1911) took up these ideas and for some years pursued the fruitless dream that racial identity – of Jews, "Negroes," and others – was directly evident in their prints.[22] The hope for racially distinct prints would resurface in Nazi Germany, when various scholars tried to isolate particularities of Gypsy fingerprints.[23] Despite these ambitions, most practitioners within the various justice systems quickly abandoned the idea that fingerprints would provide *referential* identification. Instead, dactyloscopy evolved into a system of classification in which a print communicated nothing at all about the physical, mental, or moral characteristics of the criminal subject. Over the first two decades of the twentieth century, fingerprinting gradually replaced the Bertillon system across Europe: the technology of taking a print was both cheaper and less prone to human error than the eleven anthropometric measurements demanded by the older system.

If these identification systems frustrated attempts to pinpoint the difference between criminals and non-criminals, photography also proved a two-edged sword in the criminological arsenal. In the 1850s and early 1860s photographs of criminals tended, aesthetically, to borrow heavily from portrait photography of "respectable" citizens: they were shot, for the most part, in photographic studios and used similar backdrops and poses. Slowly, a visual language of mug-shots emerged: increasingly, criminals were photographed in front of brick prison walls, framing them in a context that was decidedly non-bourgeois. By the 1890s criminals were often photographed in special chairs to which a mirror had been attached: the resulting image showed the criminal both face on and in profile. Often, the criminals were also asked to raise their hands in front of their chests. Bertillon, Morel, and Lombroso, after all, had all highlighted the importance of discrete parts of the body, if for different reasons: the first sought to establish individuality from a series of fragments, the other two claimed that they could serve as clues that added up to a type of human being. The images that were thus produced showed criminals as two-headed creatures whose hands were awkwardly extended in front of them. Arguably such shots created a visual language that set criminals apart and stressed their "otherness." Indeed, photos were often used as evidence for criminal difference. At the same time photographs implicitly challenged such claims by stressing the criminal's individuality: the spectator was called upon to ignore the many differences between the various depicted subjects and focus upon often ephemeral similarities.[24]

In the mid-1880s attempts were made – once again by Galton – to develop a photographic technique that would overcome this problem and display types rather than individuals. He superimposed a number of portraits – among others those of consumptives, Jews, and criminals – on top of each other, claiming that the blurry result revealed the essence contained in the displayed type. Galton's experiments were widely noted but did not find any consistent implementation.[25] Photography, then, may have dreamed of depicting criminals as distinct others, but as a technology implicitly conspired against easy typologization.

Women and Crime; Race and Crime

It will surprise no one that nineteenth-century narratives of crime were gendered, nor perhaps that the focus of treatments of female deviance fell upon sexuality. Prostitution was commonly treated as the female equivalent of male criminality, and the milieus of pimp, prostitute, and criminal were commonly conflated. Lombroso's *Donna Delinquente* ("Criminal Woman") was paradigmatic in this context, and once again one can observe that the criticism of his methods and explanatory models did not preclude criminologists throughout Europe from adapting many of his ideas.[26]

The interaction of race and crime is a more contested issue. It is complicated by the fact that a variety of usages of the term abounded in the nineteenth century – it could be used virtually synonymously with nation (e.g., we find theorists talking about the Dutch or the German race), to describe ethnic groups within nations, and only gradually was it consistently used to refer to supranational groups whose coherence was biological rather than cultural or historical.

It is against this background of a slowly emerging biological understanding of "race" that one needs to place nineteenth-century narratives of criminalities specific to Jews and Gypsies, the two groups that were most frequently singled out. Early and mid-nineteenth century tales of Jewish crime, such as A. F. Thiele's 1842 *Jewish Crooks in Germany* focused on Jewish criminal bandit gangs. The primary marker of Jewish criminality for Thiele lay in Jewish criminal competence: Jewish crooks were more cunning and skillful than their Christian counterparts, hence more dangerous. While Thiele's assertions were echoed by other nineteenth-century commentators on crime, his views were far from universal. Friedrich Christian Benedikt Avé-Lallement, for instance, explicitly rejected Thiele's idea that there was a specifically Jewish criminality that was distinct from its Christian equivalent. Late in the century, he used skull shapes to argue that there was in fact no racial difference between European Jews and Gentiles.

Cesare Lombroso – himself Jewish – also devoted a special section in his reworking of his original thesis to Jewish criminality. His results were ambiguous. He argued that Jewish criminality was on the whole lower than that of the Gentile population, that Jews were prone to certain types of crime (e.g., forgeries and smuggling), and that the roots of this criminality were historical and could at least be partially explained by reference to the persecution and discrimination they had endured. He thus made no reference to his theory of atavism at all, and rather chose to embrace a socio-historical explanation for Jewish criminal particularities.[27]

At the end of the century Jewish criminality started to become more and more the subject of a statistical debate. No dedicated attempt at overlapping alleged anthropological or psychological markers of Jews and those of criminals was made within criminology, despite a suggestive number of similarities between antisemitic narratives of Jews and criminological narratives of born criminals.[28] Jews were narrated above all as calculating economic criminals who exploited the innocent (e.g., by luring women to South America and elsewhere and enslaving them as prostitutes.)[29]

"Gypsy" criminality was quite a different case. A longstanding tradition marked them as a criminal "race" who were uncivilized, acted by instinct, and indeed were often systematically likened to animals. Commentator after commentator re-rehearsed their supposed racial characteristics, including their pungent, bestial smell, irrespective of whether these prejudices fit in with a given theorist's general analysis of crime.

Finally, one might note that Lombroso's theories interacted with another sort of racism, one which was upheld by many northern Italians, who, in the decades after Italian unification, fretted about the poor, seemingly "primitive" south in which criminal organizations made an explicit challenge to social order. It was easier for some of these observers to explain away the social problems facing the new state with reference to biological factors and invoke an atavistic race unsuited to life in the modern era.[30]

Popular and Literary Perspectives of Crime

Crime was a theme for popular cultural output long before the nineteenth century. Brigands, bandits, and highwaymen popped up – often as heroes, at times as villains – in plays, travelogues, and popular songs; publishers brought out collections of the age's most heinous crimes for the titillation of their readers; individual criminals could be celebrated in the form of romantic adventure stories. The nineteenth century brought new twists to this tradition. It was the century in which the novel triumphed over other forms of popular literature and found large, national audiences. By the mid-century literary realism, with its claim of depicting social or psychological realities of a particular historical moment, came to dominate many national literary cultures. Within these novels – particularly in England and France – crime played the special role. We have already noted the reformist ambitions and moralistic fervor of the early Victorian social novel – one need only think of Oliver Twist's adventures and Bill Sykes's habitual criminal disposition.[31] But the criminal was soon pushed to the edge of the literary stage by the emergence of what is perhaps the most distinct literary archetype dreamed up by the nineteenth century: the detective.

At the start of the century the police detective had not yet been established as a literary commonplace. In his earliest incarnations he was a thoroughly disreputable figure, uncomfortably close indeed to the criminal elements whom he sought to bring to justice. Thus, in the loosely autobiographical *Memoirs* (published 1829–30) of Eugene-François Vidocq, one-time convict and escape artist, later chief of the Parisian *Sûreté*, we find the figure of a sexually amoral spy who infiltrates the underworld with the help of a whole bag of disguises. Far from creating a safe dichotomy between criminal and hero, then, we are introduced into a murky world in which yesterday's crook could be tomorrow's detective without any great moral transformation, whose gift in "thief taking" owes much to the very skills that made him a successful criminal in the first place.[32]

The birth of the modern detective story proper is commonly attributed to Edgar Allen Poe's "Murders in the Rue Morgue" (first published in 1841). Dupin, Poe's detective protagonist in this and a number of other stories, uses discrete details about a murder case which he picks up from a careful perusal of the Parisian papers and through some breathtaking analytical acrobatics conclusively proves the murderer who horribly disfigured two victims to be an escaped orangutan. Dupin has none of Vidocq's unsavory biographical background – indeed, he is a distinctly aristocratic figure – but there is a disconcerting level of distance between him and the world. He encounters the crimes as purely analytical puzzles, with little reference to justice. There is little interest in the criminal at all in these stories, and the victims, too, are reduced largely to their functions within the mystery that demands solution.[33]

While Poe's Dupin found many imitators, initially these were mostly French (e.g., Gobirau's Père Tabaret). In England the freshly established detective force found mid-Victorian literary admirers who did bestow certain moral virtues upon them, and also wrote them into solidly lower middle-class identities. Dickens' Inspector Bucket (*Bleak House*, published

1852–3) deserves a mention here, as does Wilkie Collins' Inspector Cuff (in *The Moonstone*, 1868), whose hatchet-faced countenance and keen eye does something to foreshadow the coming of Holmes. The mysteries these inspectors work on, are not, however, the acts of master criminals, born or otherwise, but rather affairs of missing wills, gambling debts, gentlemen's secret and illegitimate children, mistaken identities, etc. – they have their origins in misunderstandings, mistakes, and the moral failures of those who know better. Interestingly, these detectives more often than not failed to solve the mystery, which was unraveled by the guiding hand of destiny and its co-conspirator, coincidence.[34]

This changed with Arthur Conan Doyle's *A Study in Scarlet* (1887), and the birth of Sherlock Holmes. Holmes, of course, owed much to Dupin, and in his early incarnation displays a similar distance to the world, and similarly reduces crimes to mere scientific puzzles whose solution is satisfying in itself – a shift that harmonizes with the decline of the moralistic treatment of crime in late Victorian society, as Martin Wiener argues.[35] The nature of the detective problems changed in the decades that separate Dupin from Holmes, however: where the earlier breed of detective needed no more than a keen eye for detail, presence, and astonishing powers of induction, with Holmes there emerged a detective type who also had to be a scientifically trained expert. The development in fiction here mirrored the shift from handbooks about villains to criminalistics proper: the former would describe in great detail how a crook might use deceit to sell a lame horse, but it was only with the arrival of Gross and his ilk that one finds descriptions and diagrams on how to interpret blood splatters, or that technical know-how (such as how to draw a crime scene) was discussed.

One also notes that the whole logic of the detective genre was not particularly compatible with a vision of criminals as incarnations of a stable type. While they would regularly invoke racial stereotypes (e.g., Holmes's "Orientals," Collins' savage "Hindoos") and towards the end of the nineteenth century made occasional references to the powers of heredity that predisposed some men to become criminal geniuses (Moriarty is the classic example), the genre in itself relied on an open-ended semiotics of criminality.[36] It would not do to recognize criminal after criminal by a smart look at their ears or skull: cunning criminals well capable of fooling the "unobserving public" and drawing the detective into a game of cat and mouse made better reading fare. Besides, the focus of such books was the detective, and rather than cementing any firm notion of born/degenerate criminals they tended to stress their natural aptitude for their profession and imply a class of men who were "born detectives." Indeed, the decadent aspects of Holmes, including his mood swings, his aloofness, and his cocaine habit – aspects that were muted in later Holmes stories lest it alienate the readership – hint at a conceptualization of him as a "Genius" proper, a status that many nineteenth-century theorists understood to be closely related to degeneracy. One should add that Holmes quickly conquered Europe. In Germany and throughout the Austro-Hungarian Empire he became much more popular than any domestic crime fiction.

This is not to imply that the nineteenth-century novel showed no interest at all in applying the criminological theories bandied about by scholars to criminal actors themselves. Emile Zola's *La Bête Humaine* explicitly explored the powers of heredity over individuals, and drew both on the notion of homicidal monomania and on some of the physical characteristics of the Lombrosian, atavistic criminal in its description of two of the novel's murderers. One should add, however, that it seems equally concerned with exposing the animal slumbering in all men (and women) under a thin varnish of civilization. Bram Stoker's *Dracula* is similarly provided with a list of stigmata of atavism/degeneracy and its hero, van Helsing, didactically rehearses the theory of born criminality. One could argue, however, that the fact that Lombrosian ideas found popular articulation in a gothic tale of supernatural evil precisely points to their lack of attraction for depictions of criminals in a realist mold. At the start of the twentieth century Conrad's *The Secret Agent* has its anarchists both poke fun at Lombroso and yet fall under his theory's explanatory thrall.[37] Dostoevsky and Tolstoy

also both displayed some interest in late nineteenth-century developments within criminology, but their tone was largely dismissive. Tolstoy's *Resurrection* went so far as to depict Lombroso's (and other criminologists') teachings as a shallow sham that served to hide the social injustices that produced criminals who were neither degenerate, nor in fact morally at fault. And while it is true that Dostoevsky's murderers tended to suffer from epilepsy (as he did himself) and that his notes betray a fascination with psychological science, it is still clear that the act of murder is never reduced simply to a function of disease, society, or disposition. Dostoevsky frequently used the term psychology to refer not to the medical study of abnormality, but rather understood it to consist of the close observation of "normal" people. In this his approach to crime shared many a similarity with Gross's phenomenological project.[38]

Of course, there were also many non-fictional popular treatments of crime throughout the nineteenth century. The most important of these, certainly by the end of the century, were newspapers. The triumph of the mass paper – often illustrated – is closely linked to its championing of the topic of crime. It is hard to generalize as to whether or not crime and trial reports in such papers tended to systematically render an image of criminals as belonging to a deviant type. The infamous London "Ripper" for instance, was routinely identified as "mad," a "Man Monster," "savage," or "vampire"; Stevenson's image of Jekyll and Hyde was equally ubiquitous.[39] The example of trial reporting in the Austrian press just after the end of the century, by contrast, shows the papers little concerned to narrate criminals as born or bred deviants, even in cases of violent crimes. Here a criminalistic access to crime dominated, which cast the reader into the role of armchair detective, and the language of pathology was more likely to surface in connection to witnesses or indeed victims than in connection to the defendants.

Conclusions

The present survey is by no means complete. I have not mentioned, for instance, the nineteenth century's inheritance of the early British

Romantic tradition that depicted criminals as the victims of social injustice, honest men turning to theft or murder due to the betrayal of a society that sent them to war, denied them an education, or stripped them of their property. Coleridge's criminal wasting away in *The Dungeon* ("Each pore and natural outlet shrivell'd up / By ignorance and parching poverty / His energies roll back upon the heart, / And stagnate and corrupt; till changed to poison") or Wordsworth's good sailor who is left hanging on a gibbet in his *Adventures on Salisbury Plain* may serve as examples.[40] It has also glossed over similar sentiments articulated in a longstanding socialist tradition of narrating crime as a function of social injustice that can trace its roots back to Thomas Moore's *Utopia* and survived the above-discussed medicalization of criminality more or less intact; in its Marxist articulation it stressed the moral corruption intrinsic to a capitalist social order, which tempted both the poor and the rich into crime. I have also said too little about the perception of southern Italian and Mediterranean bandits and pirates who were glamorized both in Byron's *The Corsair* (1814) and in English "Captivity Narratives" of the 1860s, in which the released victims of kidnappings often upheld their captors' nobility. Much could also be said about the changing functions of deportation, which was used first (e.g., in England and some German states) to deal with the overflow in prisons, then, in 1848, to rid oneself of dangerous political criminals (primarily in France, though also, in the form of "internal" deportation, in the Austro-Hungarian Empire), and finally became a method (proposed or real, depending on the country) of ridding oneself of so-called degenerate elements.

The point of such a list is to drive home the chapter's central argument that the cultural history of nineteenth-century crime is not only a tale of change but also one of variety and contradiction. The medicalization of criminological discourse in the last quarter of the century was also accompanied by the (re-) emergence of a specific kind of criminalistic discourse; the pathologization of the criminal was often accompanied by the pathologization of large parts of the population (and at times, through the tale of genius, that of the detective). The

new prison came, and fell from grace, in the course of the century, forged out of the messy amalgam of reformist, utilitarian, and retributive thought. Perpetrators of crime at the beginning of the century could be conceptualized as heroes and adventurers, or immoral men unsuited for civilization; at the end of the century they were narrated alternatively as victims of hereditary and/or social forces, as rational professionals, or as public actors in court dramas.

Many of these narratives persist at the beginning of the twenty-first century, as does the conceptual confusion surrounding them: we continue to formulate versions of born or bred criminality alongside tales of criminal heroes; we expect and accept that "cop" shows provides different "perps" than mass-murderer films; we identify with the heisters of *Oceans Eleven*, read about O. J. Simpson's DNA fingerprints, and argue whether or not our personalities are genetically determined. The nineteenth century remains alive in us, as do the stories it told about crime.

NOTES

1 Dostoevsky (1994: 420). The slogan "crime is insanity" is wrongly attributed to Littré, and may refer to Georget, Esquirol, or possibly Quetelet. Cf. ibid (728, n. 2).
2 On Lombroso and the various incarnations of his theory, see Gibson (2002).
3 Beirne (1994).
4 Wiener (1990: 31ff.); Garland (1994: 33).
5 Danker (1988).
6 Becker (2002: 43–57, 177ff.); Evans (1998: 151–8).
7 Semple (1993: 152–5 and *passim*); also Foucault (1977).
8 McGowen (1995: 80ff.).
9 Ibid; McConville (1995).
10 Davis (1988: 216); O'Brian (1995); Scheerer (1996); Berger (1974: 270ff.); Adams (1996).
11 O'Brian (1995); Caplan (2000).
12 For a comparable summary of influences on Lombroso, see Wetzell (2000: 15ff.).
13 Nye (1984: 98ff.).
14 Ibid (124–6).

15 Garland (1994: 44 and *passim*).

16 Ibid: 50–3.

17 Gross (1898: 1–2).

18 Gross's status within criminology remains controversial; his theoretical contribution and originality tend to be downplayed. For an alternative account, see Becker (1998). One should also note that attempts to bridge the conceptual differences between criminology and criminalistics were made within Italy, above all by Salvatore Ottolenghi. See Gibson (2002: 135ff.).

19 Nye (1984: xi–xiii).

20 Regener (1999).

21 Cole (2001: 63ff.); Sengoopta (2003).

22 Cole (2001: 103ff.); Gillham (2001: 242–3).

23 Schenk (1994: 201–3).

24 Regener (1999) stresses more than I the power of photography to demark criminals as "others."

25 Sekula (1989).

26 Gibson (1982; 2002: 175–208).

27 Vyleta (2004, 2005); Gibson (2002: 97–126).

28 For an argument that criminological and antisemitic narratives *were* superimposed, see Gilman (1991).

29 Bristow (1982) perhaps overstates the narrative of degeneracy as applied to Jews.

30 Davis (1988: 335).

31 Pykett (2003).

32 Ousby (1976: 44–55).

33 Thomas (2002).

34 Ousby (1976: 115–26).

35 Wiener (1990: 224).

36 For a list of references to degeneracy in Sherlock Holmes stories, see Greenslade (1994: 100–5).

37 For further links between degeneration theory and fiction, see Pick (1989).

38 Belknap (2002) stresses Dostoevsky's interest in the findings of contemporary (abnormal) psychological *science* more than I do.

39 Curtis (2001: 119ff.).

40 Roe (1988: 132 and *passim*).

GUIDE TO FURTHER READING

The best places to start reading about the emergence of criminology in the nineteenth century in various national contexts are the first two chapters of Wetzell's *Inventing the Criminal*, Wiener's *Reconstructing the Criminal*, and Nye's *Crime, Madness and Politics in Modern France*. Evans's *Tales from the German Underworld* provides a good introduction to the changing understanding of crime earlier in the century, within a German context. Davis's *Conflict and Control* and Gibson's *Born to Crime* explore the Italian situation post-unification and place Lombroso's thought in its context.

For the prison reform movement, Foucault's groundbreaking *Discipline and Punish* is indispensable, if best read in conjunction with more recent literature. Morris and Rothman's *Oxford History of the Prison* provides a solid introduction and helpful bibliographic guidance. Garland's *Punishment and Modern Society* applies a broadly Foucauldian model to the English prison reform movement.

For fiction, Priestman's *Cambridge Companion to Crime Fiction* is an excellent starting place, as is Ousby's fascinating *Bloodhounds in Heaven*. Greenslade's *Degeneration, Culture and the Novel 1880–1940* is the most complete guide to treatment of degeneration theory in late nineteenth-century fiction; Pick also provides valuable insights in his *Faces of Degeneration*.

No monograph dedicated to nineteenth-century criminalistic thought and its theoretical implications exists at present. The best starting point may be Sekula's excellent article "The Body and the Archive" and Cole's more recent monograph on identification procedures *Suspect Identities*. Those interested in the relationship of photography and crime should also consult Tagg's *Burden of Representation*.

CHAPTER TWENTY-EIGHT

Medical Discourses

JOHN C. WALLER

For all the self-confidence of Europe's medical profession on the eve of the twentieth century, the previous 100 years had certainly not seen a revolution in curative medicine. Throughout the nineteenth century, doctors had been able to do little for patients suffering from the majority of chronic maladies or from those struck down by infectious killers like tuberculosis, typhoid, typhus, cholera, diphtheria, or scarlet fever. The number of lives destroyed by epidemic disease did decline significantly in the closing years of the century, but the biomedical paradigm could take only limited credit for this achievement.

In terms of healing the sick, the art of medicine was yet to reach maturity. And, to their credit, elite physicians of the later 1800s were often candid in acknowledging the dubiousness of the remedies they prescribed.[1] Nevertheless, the 1800s did witness a considerable increase in the medical profession's knowledge of the nature and causes of ill health. With the proliferation of new diagnostic tools, a more rigorous approach to the study of disease involving systematic quantification, post mortem and chemical analysis, combined with the advent of the germ theory of disease, the practice of medicine by the year 1900 had progressed in fundamental ways. This chapter surveys some of these developments as well as the social and epidemiological shifts by which they were underpinned.

Background: Medicine in the 1700s

The eighteenth century was a period for medical system building.[2] A number of different conceptual frameworks competed for ascendancy. Many physicians remained wedded to elaborated versions of the ancient humoural conception of disease, ascribing maladies to an excess or deficiency of one or other bodily fluid or to the corruption of these fluids. For others, malady arose from some kind of pathology involving the solid parts of the body: muscle fibers rendered too lax or too taut, or nerves under-excited or over-stimulated. But for all their many differences, medical discourses had shared several key features. Many of these themes would persist well into the following century.

First, ailments were seldom associated with the idea of necessary causes. In time-honored fashion, practitioners saw most maladies as a result of a discordance between an individual's lifestyle and their constitutional make-up. Physicians reasoned that a change in weather, a bout of mental anguish, a deficient or overly rich diet, or an over-indulgence in venous spirits might induce a general organismic imbalance and thereby cause disease. The precise form an illness took was said to depend as much upon the individual's particular susceptibilities and humoural state as upon extraneous factors.

Second, treatment regimes for each of the rival medical systems overlapped. The rationales for use might have differed, but regulating the patient's secretions, whether using enemas, bloodletting, purges, or cupping, was the staple therapeutic strategy. Accordingly, whether a physician emphasized the role of nerves, muscles, or humours, his therapeutic regime was nearly always designed to assist the body's natural healing properties: restoring balance and harmony.

Third, physicians tended to invoke a totality of causal factors: physical, psychological, social, and moral. Causal explanations also discriminated between "proximate" and "remote" causes. Proximate causes were usually synonymous with the disease process itself, be it excess blood, occluded arteries, inadequate nervous stimulation, and so forth. Remote causes were further subdivided into "predisposing" and "exciting" factors, the former referring to aspects of the individual's constitution that rendered it susceptible to malady of a particular kind, and the latter denoting the factor that triggered its onset. As this implies, medical theory was largely geared to explaining why certain individuals succumbed to maladies where others did not, and why some people suffered from one disease and others from quite different afflictions.

Views of illness were in this sense highly individualized. This is not to say, however, that epidemiological perspectives did not exist. Some English physicians of the later 1600s and the 1700s sought to explain the manifestation of infectious disease in terms of environmental determinants, harking back to the Hippocratic concern with airs, waters, and places. To many of these physicians it seemed obvious that insalubrious surroundings gave rise to high levels of fever. This population perspective was encouraged by the increasing involvement of physicians in hospitals and infirmaries for the sick poor. The trend towards population health as the level of analysis and intervention was more visible on the continent. The Bavarian-born Johann Peter Frank introduced the notion of medical police in 1779, an imagined body of physicians responsible for the health and wellbeing of the entire population. In France, state appointed physiocrats assumed

responsibility for investigating the environmental causes of maladies and trying to prevent cattle diseases.

This notwithstanding, most influential physicians of the 1800s still spent most of their time ministering to their elite patients in a face-to-face manner. Indeed, some have argued that the fact that the physician's gaze tended to be focused on the individual fee-paying patient influenced how sickness was characterized. Relying heavily on the patient's narrative and, hence, on their subjective experience of disease, the doctor thus attached inordinate importance to the patient's symptoms and in doing so confused these for the malady itself.[3] But this preoccupation with what we now know to be merely symptoms was only to be expected where physicians had limited access to cadavers for post mortem dissection and knew nothing of disease-causing microbes. The eighteenth-century physician had little else to go on aside from the patient's testimony and his observations of their pulse, the color and taste of their urine, the dryness of their tongue, and the quantity and texture of their stools.

In addition, eighteenth-century medical theories, drawing as they did on ancient doctrines of balance and the body's capacity for self-healing, were not only intellectually reputable, but also provided a coherent and easy-to-visualize explanation for most aspects of health and disease.[4] Medical progress, however, required the demise of ancient humouralism and its many variants. And this is one reason why the medical reforms of post-1789 France were so crucially important to the advent of modern medicine.

Paris Medicine

Following the revolution, the French government set about overhauling the way physicians were educated.[5] In the reformed system, elite physicians were made into civil servants and spent much of their time treating hospital patients and training new generations of physicians on the wards of Paris's vast municipal hospitals. "Read little, see much, do much" was the motto of the reformist Antoine Fourcroy. And he ensured that students no longer spent their university years pouring over ancient texts and hardly seeing a patient until they qualified.

Perhaps the most significant feature of these reforms was the considerable emphasis placed upon internal bodily investigations. In part due to the insatiable demand of the imperial army for trained physicians with a knowledge of how to treat wounds, physic and surgery were deliberately sutured together. "Medicine and surgery are two branches of the same science," Fourcroy declared. The cavities of the body became the primary sites for analysis among the new generations of elite Paris physicians. These clinicians devoted themselves to correlating the external signs of disease with underlying lesions (tumors, inflammation, and gangrene) that could often be detected during post mortem. In doing so, they hoped to discern fundamental patterns to sickness, to reveal that beneath the bewildering array of individual symptoms there lay a narrow range of distinct clinical entities.

Of equal importance, Paris medicine helped undermine the remnants of ancient humouralism by focusing attention on the solid components of the body. One of the luminaries of Paris medicine was René Théophile Hyacinthe Laennec (1781–1826), author of several brilliant studies on the thoracic cavity and its ailments. The key to Laennec's success was his invention in 1816 of the stethoscope. This simple instrument provided a powerful means of exploring the body's cavities. Learning to distinguish subtly different chest sounds, Laennec showed that it was possible to diagnose accurately bronchitis, pneumonia, and tuberculosis. Following the protocol of Paris medicine, he also conducted large numbers of post mortem examinations upon the corpses of those who had died of tuberculosis. Laennec consistently found distinctive nodules in the organs of its victims from which he deduced that tuberculosis is a specific malady, whether it affects the brain, lungs, liver, or gut. Gaspard Laurent Bayle (1774–1816) furnished complementary evidence. He revealed that tuberculosis begins with the appearance of localized tissue pathologies and only subsequently gives rise to the disease's characteristic symptoms of wasting, shortness of breath, and bloody sputum.

The achievements of Laennec, Bayle, and many others were made possible by the concentration of large numbers of poor patients in Parisian hospitals. Since those who could not pay for their care forfeited any rights over their corpses, clinicians enjoyed unrivaled opportunities for post mortem dissection. The presence of hundreds of patients on hospital wards allowed for the effective application of quantitative methods to medicine. Pierre Louis pioneered this development by systematically evaluating the efficacy of particular treatments. Louis never doubted that interventions like bleeding actually worked, but his studies reinforced the French school's general skepticism about the value of standard remedies. Lastly, the congregation of the sick in wards may have helped divert the physician's gaze away from the idiosyncrasies of the individual towards the common features of disease.

The search for clinico-pathological correlations extended to the nascent discipline of psychiatry. The physician had not traditionally been the most obvious candidate for asylum master: this was a role more typically assumed by laymen, often those with clerical training. But by the fourth decade of the nineteenth century, psychiatrists had emerged as the leading carers for the insane in Europe and America. The alienist's ability to usurp the lay asylum manager had depended in part on his ability to define mental disorder as an essentially medical problem. Determined that insanity should be seen as affecting the material brain, the province of medicine, many European psychiatrists embraced phrenology during the early 1800s. By the 1820s psychiatrists had also adopted the methods and theories of the Paris medical schools, and were actively seeking to correlate the symptoms of various kinds of madness with lesions to the brain and other organs. In this manner, Parisian pathological anatomy infused psychiatry. To such "moral" causes of mental alienation as failed love affairs, bereavement, disastrous business ventures, and religious fanaticism, psychiatrists added "physical" causes such as brain lesions. Both were said to contribute to nervous collapse or to the adoption of false ideas. Ergo, only the medically trained were qualified to help.[6]

The significance of Paris medicine, however, is often overstated. A number of eighteenth-century physicians had anticipated its dual emphasis on autopsy and the localization of disease in the solid components of the body. In addition, several French clinicians repudiated the growing emphasis on disease specificity. F. J. V. Broussais (1772–1838) attacked the "localists" for representing disease as being somehow qualitatively different from health. Instead, Broussais argued, ill health involves a deviation from normality caused when regular physiological processes go awry. Perhaps more importantly, in many ways the actual practice of medicine did not change much at all. Plenty of physicians spurned the stethoscope. Many more recoiled at the imperious attitude some Paris clinicians adopted towards their patients. Critics also scorned a therapeutic nihilism that not only seemed defeatist but was almost guaranteed to alienate private patients. Thus, in the wake of Paris medicine, an increasing gap opened up between the advocates of heroic medical intervention and those who argued that the physician could do nothing but provide a strengthening diet and prescribe plenty of rest.

Yet even if Paris medicine was contested and only modestly innovative, there was something significant about what happened in French hospitals following the convulsions of political revolution. The sheer scale and intensity of the research effort, and the magnetic attraction Paris had for students from America and other parts of Europe, made it a vital center for medical advance and the propagation of new ideas.[7] This is indicated by the successes of those who were influenced by the trends of Paris medicine. Inspired by the French example, Thomas Hodgkin (1798–1866), a clinician at Guy's Hospital in London, described the malignant disease of the lymph glands later called Hodgkin's disease. His colleague, Thomas Addison (1793–1860), distinguished two kinds of anemia, one of them involving lesions in the suprarenals (Addison's disease). And Richard Bright (1789–1858), also of Guy's Hospital, showed that dropsy is caused by renal disease. These achievements were matched by discoveries in the hospitals of Vienna, Dublin, and elsewhere. In major hospitals throughout Europe, the divide between physic and surgery was becoming indistinct.

The Rise of Laboratory Medicine

Medicine done Paris style did not for long remain at the leading edge of medical science. By the 1830s a new and ultimately extremely fertile site for investigation had emerged. In purpose-built laboratories in German-speaking Europe, scientists applied the methods of natural science to the living body, searching for general laws of health and disease. Laboratory medical science was not new: there were plenty of ancient and modern precursors. But beginning with the inception of Justus von Liebig's (1803–73) Institute of Chemistry at the University of Giessen in 1824, unprecedented time and resources were allowed for basic research. Liebig's chief contribution to medicine was to insist on the close relationship between physiology and chemistry.

He and his students set to work on understanding the chemical processes of the body by analyzing its intakes and outflows. Liebig's approach was emphatically experimental and quantitative. Johannes Müller (1800–58) followed the same route. The professor of anatomy and physiology at the recently founded University of Berlin, Müller performed cutting-edge research into neurophysiology. He also trained a generation of physiologists expert in the procedures of medical science: animal experimentation, the recording of physiological events, and the careful design of experiments. One of Müller's students, Carl Ludwig (1816–95), introduced the kymograph in 1847, an instrument for measuring the blood pressure and pulse of animals. It exemplified the new drive to reduce the complexity of physiological action into a numerical form that could be compared with results obtained elsewhere.

At the same time the reliability of the thermometer was dramatically improved. For generations, doctors and scientists had been unable to agree on a single scale or the most appropriate fluid to use. After decades of technological improvement, in 1868 the German medical scientist Carl Wunderlich (1815–77) established the thermometer's credentials in his treatise *On the Temperature in Diseases*. By taking patients' temperatures at different times and with different maladies Wunderlich demonstrated the tight relationship that often holds between temperature and disease condition. On this basis he provided an effective means of distinguishing typhus from typhoid fever.

Wielded by German laboratory scientists like Rudolf Virchow (1821–1902), much-improved microscopes also allowed significant advances to be made. "Learn to see microscopically," he famously implored his students. And it was as a result of doing so that Virchow, Theodore Schwann (1810–82) and Matthias Schleiden (1804–81) established the cell as the basic unit of animal and plant life. Virchow took the significance of the cell a step further and argued that disease is the result of disturbances in the structure and the function of the body's cells. In 1847, simultaneously with Edinburgh's John Hughes Bennett (1812–75), Virchow described the condition of leukemia.

The study of the mind was also advanced in the new scientific laboratories. French and German experimental physiologists localized different forms of aphasia to discrete sections of the brain. Wilhelm Griesinger (1817–68) inspired psychiatrists in Germany to see that "mental diseases are brain diseases." In addition, German psychiatrists significantly advanced the study of psychosis. Emil Kraepelin (1856–1926) carefully subdivided these disorders and established the differences in prognosis for different conditions.

Medical students flocked to Berlin, Munich, and Giessen to learn from the new masters of experiment. Paris, too, had its attractions. Among the most accomplished physiologists of the 1800s was the Frenchman Claude Bernard (1813–78). He carried out vivisection experiments which revealed, among many other things, the role of the liver in synthesizing glycogen and maintaining appropriate glucose levels, the digestive functions of the pancreas, the role of nerves in controlling blood flow, and the actions of poisons on particular parts of the neuromuscular system. His experiments advanced knowledge of how the body maintains a balance of sugars, salts, and oxygen –

later called homeostasis. Reflecting on the importance of experiment in his 1865 *An Introduction to the Study of Experimental Medicine*, Bernard insisted that doctors at the bedside could never tame the complexity of the environment in which disease occurred. Only through carefully controlled and designed vivisection experiments, he stressed, could medicine advance.

The rise of physiological science eventually transformed clinical practice. Medical knowledge of digestive, neurological, neuromuscular and nutritional disorders dramatically increased. And in addition to the stethoscope, by the late 1800s the clinician or hospital orderly could employ any of a fast growing battery of diagnostic instruments: the thermometer, the sphygmomanometer for measuring blood pressure, the sphymograph for gauging the pulse, the spirometer for measuring the lungs' vital capacity, and, by the early 1900s, electrocardiographs for monitoring heart function. Illness was measurable and disease routinely expressed in terms of millimeters or milliliters and precise deviations from the normal. Medical scientists also developed straightforward diagnostic tests involving red or white blood cell counts for identifying leukemia. In 1841 France's Alfred Becquerel (1814–62) had revealed the quantities of water, urea, uric acid, lactic acid, albumin, and inorganic salts present in urine in health and different states of disease. This finding gave rise to simple chemical tests for Bright's disease and for gout.

The introduction of new diagnostic equipment was often resisted, in part due to a fear on the part of hospital clinicians that their roles were being deskilled. But by the late 1800s, larger European hospitals were acquiring diagnostic laboratories staffed by trained technicians.[8] The vague practices of uroscopy and pulse lore were fast being replaced by exact, quantitative tests.

Contagion and Infection

European cities of the early 1800s grew with deadly rapidity. Sanitary provisions were nearly always *ad hoc* and inadequate. The dirty, hastily constructed and poorly ventilated tenement districts inhabited by the new industrial proletariat were incubators for infectious disease. Measles, diphtheria, chickenpox and scarlet fever, typhus and typhoid, tuberculosis and, from the 1830s, cholera, destroyed hundreds of thousands of lives. In the process, medical discourses became focused more on the environmental determinants of ill health.

In the earlier decades of the century, occasional recourse was made to providentialism. But of all the *exciting* causes of infectious disease, the poisonous miasma was the most commonly invoked in the first three quarters of the century. Miasmas were pathogenic conditions of the atmosphere said to arise from rotting flesh, vegetable matter, rancid pools of water, and excrement-clogged drains. By and large, the presence of a miasma was indicated by its foul odor.

It was largely on the basis of the miasma theories that European states initiated the slow process of sanitary reform. At first there were doubts as to whether miasmatic particles could infect drinking water. Even as late as 1854, when the English doctor John Snow (1813–58) claimed to have proven that a cholera epidemic in London arose from water drawn from a single infected pump reservoir, many doctors were dismissive. But by mid-century the importance of clean drinking water was fast on the way to achieving general acceptance.[9]

Yet if infection via the inhalation or ingestion of miasmatic particles was a staple of medical discourse, the notion of direct person to person transmission, or contagion, was highly controversial. Some doctors simply refuted the idea of contagion, emphatically denying that the seeds of disease could be conveyed on their hands, breath, or bodily fluids. There are several reasons why medical personnel refused to accept that disease could be passed from person to person. Infectious maladies disproportionately hit the poorer and hence most malodorous areas of habitation, so that it often seemed unnecessary to impute anything other than miasmas inhaled directly from source, be it a stinking drain, a rotting carcass, or a stagnant, fetid pool. Moreover, the evidence for contagionism was highly ambiguous. All doctors could point to scores of cases where

those who had nursed people dying from cholera, typhoid, or tuberculosis never themselves showed a trace of the disease.

But there were also political dimensions to this debate. For many medical writers, adopting the theory of contagion gave the authorities an excuse to make no effort to clean up the physical environment of towns and cities on the basis that it was enough to impose quarantine regulations whenever disease struck. Anti-contagionism, in contrast, suggested the need for a proactive, managerial social policy involving routine street cleaning, sanitary reform, the disinfecting of drains, and tight restrictions on the location of abattoirs and graveyards. Anti-contagionists, though ultimately proven incorrect, can therefore be seen as the more socially and politically progressive wing of medical opinion in the first two-thirds of the nineteenth century: they pushed the hardest for governments to get involved in promoting public health.

There is also evidence that anti-contagionism had a strong appeal to those who had most to lose from the sudden imposition of quarantine restrictions: merchants and traders. Some scholars argue that doctors sympathetic to liberal economic ideologies were predisposed to cast doubt on contagionism.[10] Self-interest of a different kind has been implicated in the hostility of hospital staff to the concept of contagion. Europe's larger hospitals, several of them established in the late 1700s, were notorious for their high rates of post-operative mortality. The 1840s did see some attempts to clean up the surgical detritus of wards and operating theatres. But many surgeons continued to operate in clothing stained with the blood and pus of previous patients; few washed their hands before operations or their instruments after; some recycled the same plasters and dressings; and nearly all reused the leeches employed to draw blood. Consistent with this, most surgeons, nurses, and midwives adamantly denied that infection was transmissible from patient to patient.

One reason for this aversion to contagionism is suggested by the experiences of those who did speculate about contagion. In 1795 the Scot Alexander Gordon (1752–99) wrote a treatise accusing the midwives in a neighborhood of Aberdeen of spreading puerperal fever, more commonly known as childbed fever, from mother to mother upon their persons. During the 1840s, the American poet and physician Oliver Wendell Holmes (1809–94) also implicated doctors and midwives in a series of fatalities among mothers. And in 1847 the Hungarian Ignaz Semmelweis (1818–65), working in a maternity ward of the Vienna General Hospital, instituted a regime of handwashing in chloride of lime among students and doctors who were in the practice of assisting in the delivery of babies having taken part in the autopsies of women who had died of childbed fever. Semmelweis argued, on the basis of hospital mortality data, that childbed fever was caused by the transfer of "morbid particles" from the bodies of the dead to the living in an ongoing cycle. His introduction of handwashing led to a dramatic decline in deaths to childbed fever.[11]

Gordon, Holmes, and Semmelweis, however, were subject to stinging rebukes from many of their colleagues. All three were faced by the difficulty of convincing midwives and other hospital staff that they were directly responsible for an inadvertent holocaust of mothers. This possibility was perhaps too much for most to contemplate, at least until the contagionist case became irresistible with the advent of germ theory. Into the 1880s some surgeons still operated in soiled garments and with hands that seldom came into contact with disinfectant.

But the dichotomy between contagionists and anti-contagionists has often been drawn too boldly. In reality, few doctors rejected the idea outright. A large proportion assumed that although airborne miasmas were required to start epidemics, thereafter the seeds of infection could be conveyed from person to person. Nevertheless, contagionism did not become an axiom of medical theory until the later acceptance of germ theory.

The Public's Health

Eighteenth-century physicians developed a relatively sophisticated social epidemiology that emphasized both environmental and personal factors in predisposing individuals and communities to epidemic disease. Accordingly, in the 1800s numerous doctors identified poverty as a major predisposing cause of epidemics. For instance, during the late 1840s Rudolf Virchow was sent to identify the causes of a severe typhus epidemic in Upper Silesia, a province of Prussia. The disease had hit the politically suppressed Polish minority hardest of all, and Virchow argued that the most rational response would be to help alleviate the social conditions of the Polish inhabitants. In a similar vein, in 1821 the French doctor Rene Louis Villermé published his study *Recherches statistiques sur la ville de Paris* which demonstrated a close correlation between the poor arrondissements of the city and the incidence of fatal disease.

Yet there was no systematic attempt to tackle poverty itself in France, Germany, or Britain. In fact, most English sanitarians played down the importance of predisposing factors like poverty and stressed instead the exciting cause or miasma.[12] On this basis they campaigned hard for large-scale sanitation reform: the cleaning of refuse from streets and houses, the regulation of "offensive trades" (such as tanning and slaughtering), and the construction of vast new networks of drains, together with complementary systems to bring clean water into towns for drinking and for flushing away the effluence. In Britain, Edwin Chadwick enjoyed a measure of success, though large-scale sanitation reform did not begin in London until after the 1858 Great Stink, when the stench from the Thames became so overpoweringly foul that it permeated the chambers of the new Houses of Parliament, then in session. The result was the construction of London's elaborate network of sewers.

In France, public health reformers achieved far less than their British counterparts. Local health officers, appointed after legislation of 1848, were equipped with only advisory powers. And sanitary reform came so slowly that there were still an estimated 85,000 cesspools in Paris in 1870.[13] Greater progress was made in Germany, where large cities like Munich began pumping in fresh water from regions far upstream and then piping polluted water into the river downstream of the city. Hamburg was exceptional in that as late as 1892 it lacked a sand filtration plant for purifying its drinking water. Many of Hamburg's privies were also unconnected to the main sewer pipes and there remained large numbers of undrained alleys and courtyards. When cholera struck in 1892, Hamburg was hit far harder than any other European city.[14]

The governing authorities of Hamburg had resented the public expenditure involved in proper sanitary reform. In their parsimony they were not alone. Ratepayers across Europe, extolling the virtues of retrenchment and individual responsibility, had vigorously fought the public health campaigners. But by the early 1900s, public health campaigns had scored a number of important victories. Even if most sanitary reforms were guided by a false belief in a miasmatic cause of epidemics, the results were nearly always salutary.

Medicine in the Community

For all the many advances in the diagnosis and understanding of malady, there were many continuities between medical theory and practice in the eighteenth and nineteenth centuries. Bleeding remained a staple remedy into the 1850s and beyond. As this implies, the rationale of therapeutics still rested on the need either to regulate intakes and outgos or restore the patient's vitality. In addition, few doctors during the first two thirds of the 1800s imagined that diseases like tuberculosis, typhoid, or cholera were caused by specific causative agents. With the exception of smallpox and cowpox, and a few fungal infections, diseases were seldom associated with necessary causes.

Just as strikingly, the idea of the individual constitution continued to play a central role in medical discourse. Whether a person had developed a chronic condition or succumbed to an infectious malady, most practitioners sought to explain how their constitution had been compromised and why they were suffering from one malady instead of another. Ill health took on a specific form in accordance with the particular susceptibilities of the sick person. Gender was also deemed significant: men and women were said to fall sick for different reasons. And even the major epidemic killers were typically associated with exciting factors no more specific than generic gases released by rotting matter.

Within this framework of ideas, health was increasingly said to constitute a state of adequate bodily or constitutional vitality. Disease ensued when this vitality was somehow dissipated or drained away. Poor heredity, inadequate nutrition, lives of unremitting labor, or the routine inhalation of vitiated air containing too little oxygen or carrying asphyxiating gases like carbonic acid or carbureted hydrogen were deemed capable of causing a dangerous weakening of the vital powers. Dramatic changes in an individual's state of being were also considered perilous: adolescence, menarche, menstruation, pregnancy, and menopause were seen as risky disruptions to the body's physiological rhythms. The same understanding of health as requiring internal balance and vitality also underpinned the period's marked enthusiasm for alternative therapies, not least hydropathy and naturopathy.

This paradigm was also highly conducive to medical moralizing. Far from replacing religious moral authority, many doctors instead usurped it by framing traditional moral injunctions in medical terms. Sickness became the wages of sin and robust health the fitting reward of the virtuous.[15] The rich genre of medical advice literature contained a myriad homiletic warnings against sexual excess, gluttony, poor personal hygiene, opium eating and, above all, the consumption of excess alcohol.[16] By transgressing the boundaries of moral behavior, it was said that individuals weakened their constitutions. And disease, essentially a proxy for divine justice, then appropriately ensued.

The higher social classes were not always exempt from this kind of medical moralism. From the early 1800s, alienists were warning of the dangers of over-exertion, mental and physical. Doctors and alienists also marshaled medical arguments against the emergent feminist movement. Mind-work, leading alienists explained, diverted essential supplies of blood, nervous energy, and nutriment from the ovaries to the brain.[17] In addition, medical discourses often reinforced taboos against unbridled sexuality. Doctors sought to cool the ardor of courting couples and they condemned sex unredeemed by matrimony.

The clear relationship between poverty and disease reinforced the paradigm of medical moralism. It was relatively easy for cultures avowing rugged individualism to interpret poverty as the result of immoral behavior. Thus, the French hygienist Villermé argued that in order to ameliorate the impact of epidemic disease on the poorer quarters, the lower classes had to be morally regenerated, encouraged through a combination of example, persuasion, and propaganda to live sober, decent, and industrious lives. Once they had been subjected to the civilizing efforts of their social superiors, Villermé insisted, the poor would be able to escape the constricting coils of poverty and disease. The idea that the poor brought sickness upon themselves was widely held.

Fears concerning the *nation's* health intensified during the nineteenth century as urban underclasses grew in size and volatility and evidence accrued suggesting that the lower orders were breeding more rapidly than their social superiors. As attitudes towards the poor among medical scientists hardened, a variety of pessimistic hereditarian social philosophies gained credibility. Most nineteenth century doctors and scientists assumed that life events shaped one's heredity, that a parent who slipped into insanity would tend to pass on to their children an increased susceptibility to do the same.[18] Around mid-century, ideas about the depletion of nervous powers and of the danger of ruining one's heredity coalesced in the theory of degeneration. According to this idea, entire lineages, potentially even whole nations, were doomed by poor conditions and immorality to hereditary moral and physical degeneracy.[19]

The hereditarian turn also infused psychiatry. The relative optimism of the early 1800s eventually gave way to a feeling that few forms of mental malady were actually curable. And as asylum medical superintendents assumed more custodial functions, a rival professional trend saw alienists begin to treat the "neuroses" (neurasthenia and hysteria in particular) in out-patient settings employing therapies like rest, milk diets, hypnosis and, increasingly, talk therapy.

But if medical moralism was a powerful force in the 1800s, not all were considered blameworthy when they were struck down with serious mental or physical illness. In particular, "respectable" victims of tuberculosis were often characterized as delicate, refined, even angelic.[20] When applied to women, the framing of consumption often encapsulated the ideal of respectable womanhood, of tender emotions easily jarred, causing a fatal weakening of the vital spirits. Extreme emotional sensitivity was also said to render the artist of genius vulnerable, a claim seemingly supported by the names of some of its most famous victims: Keats, Chopin, Chekov, R. L. Stevenson, and Emily Brontë.

Not until the 1880s was it proven that consumption is a bacterial infection that can be passed from person to person. This realization that the condition is contagious undermined any attempt to characterize it as an emblem of personal refinement.

The Germ Revolution

By the middle of the nineteenth century, the idea that specific germs might cause infectious disease was still marginal. During the 1840s, the German pathologist Jacob Henle (1809–85) suggested that living micro-organisms may cause certain maladies. But his evidence was too incomplete and the conceptual hurdles too high for mainstream medicine to take much notice. Then again, enough was known about the ubiquity of microbes for germ theory to have at least some credibility. Moreover, ideas of poisonous miasmas had prepared the minds of doctors for the possibility that tiny particles might cause disease.

Bacteria had first been seen in the seventeenth century. Few writers, however, had implicated them in the onset of disease. When it was found that germs were always present in rotting tissue and putrefying filth, most assumed that they were formed spontaneously during the process of rotting. In any case, rival miasma theories appeared to work perfectly well. The small cadre of germ theorists seemed to most doctors to be trying to introduce into the debate unnecessary theoretical complexity. In addition, there appeared to be no evidence that disease germs actually existed. A major problem here was the obvious technical difficulty that bacteria are hard to see. The myriad different species of microbe are also exceptionally difficult to tell apart. The discovery that germs cause disease was therefore dependent upon advances in the quality of microscopes and upon the availability of synthetic dyes, most of which were produced by the fast-expanding German textile industry of the later 1800s.

But the first real successes for the germ theorists were achieved by the French chemist Louis Pasteur (1822–95). During the 1850s he was able to show that wines, beers, and vinegars contain micro-organisms that vary in appearance. In a superb series of experiments he then demonstrated that different bacteria cause different reactions. In the same decade, by way of further and no less elegant experiments, Pasteur even managed to persuade the majority of French scientists that germs do not arise spontaneously in putrefying matter, but that they are the *causes* of processes like putrefaction and fermentation.

Anthrax was the first major bacterial infection to come under close scrutiny. Most veterinarians in France and elsewhere had decided that some combination of soil and humidity must be to blame for this disease. Yet a number of nineteenth-century microscopists, not least the Frenchman Casimir Joseph Davaine (1812–82), identified in the bloodstream of anthracic rodents and sheep distinctive rod-shaped corpuscles. Inspired by Pasteur's work on fermentation, Davaine tried to prove that these microbial entities were the real cause of anthrax.

But it was left to the German bacteriologist Robert Koch (1843–1910), in the 1870s still a struggling general practitioner, to lend Davaine's studies real credibility. Having maintained an anthracic infection through dozens of generations of mice, this master microscopist then revealed that the rod-shaped corpuscles have a life cycle fully compatible with their being the cause of anthrax. The *coup de grâce* was delivered to the remaining doubters at a public trial of Pasteur's long-awaited anthrax vaccine in mid-1881 in the small town of Pouilly-le-Fort. Fifty sheep were injected with

a virulent strain of anthrax, only 25 of which had previously received "protective injections" of attenuated anthrax bacilli. As Pasteur had boldly prophesied weeks before, only the vaccinated sheep survived. The trial was an unmitigated success for Pasteur and for the germ theory.

Bacteriologists still had to prove that the big epidemic killers were caused by germs. In preparation for doing just this, in 1881 Robert Koch publicly set out what was required in order to prove once and for all the role of specific germs in causing specific diseases. The criteria he set became famous as Koch's four postulates. First, the bacterium must be present in every case of the disease. Second, it must be isolated from the diseased host and grown in pure culture. Third, the specific disease must be reproduced when a pure culture of the bacterium is inoculated into a healthy, susceptible host. Fourth, the bacterium must be recoverable from experimentally infected hosts.

As Koch realized, the key problem in satisfying these postulates was the extreme difficulty of telling apart different species of microbe. The germ theorist's task was made still trickier because he could never be sure that he was using pure cultures of the specific microbes he wished to study. Part of the solution came with the introduction of solid media on which to grow bacteria: first, the humble potato, and subsequently, agar jelly grown on Petri dishes. With solid media and the availability of a growing range of textile dyes, Koch turned to the study of tuberculosis, the single biggest killer of the nineteenth century. And, on March 24, 1882, having identified a distinctive germ and satisfied his four postulates, Robert Koch was finally able to announce publicly: "In the bacillus we have, therefore, the actual tubercle virus."

Only a year later, Koch and his team reported from Alexandria and then Calcutta that they had identified the bacteria responsible for cholera. In fact, Koch failed to satisfy all his postulates in this case since experimental animals are not usually susceptible to the bacillus. This gave considerable credence to the rival germ theory expounded by the German chemist and public health reformer Max von Pettenkofer (1818–1901). He argued that germs only become dangerous once they have spent time "germinating" in moist soil containing plenty of rotting organic matter, such as human or animal effluence. Having passed through a victim's body, Pettenkofer insisted, a germ has to spend time in an appropriate soil medium before it can become infectious again. Versions of Pettenkofer's germ-soil theory made considerable sense to British doctors working in India.[21] It was only properly invalidated during the 1890s by the Russian-born scientist Waldemar Haffkine (1860–1930). Working in Pasteur's lab, he was able to produce a strain of cholera bacteria so potent that it did manage to kill laboratory animals. Haffkine went on to develop an effective anti-cholera vaccine which he tested successfully in India in 1894. This breakthrough established the germ theory of cholera.

During the 1880s and 1890s, medical scientists in Europe managed to identify the bacterial culprits of most of the major epidemic killers. Proof that diphtheria is caused by specific bacteria required the combined (and intensely competitive) efforts of both Koch's and Pasteur's laboratories. In 1884 a characteristic germ was identified in smears and tissue fragments from the tonsils of several children killed by diphtheria. Pasteur's team soon after established that this diphtheria bacillus produces a deadly poison that causes major organ damage. And Emil Behring (1854–1917), another of Koch's assistants, found that organisms rendered immune to the toxin produced antitoxin sera. On Christmas Day 1891, samples of this antitoxin were used for the first time on a human patient. The trial was an emphatic success. With help from Behring's antitoxin, by the early 1900s mortality from diphtheria had dropped by more than 50 percent.

George Gaffky (1850–1918), yet another member of Robert Koch's team, was the first to identify the typhoid bacterium. Then in 1897 the British military scientist Almroth Wright (1861–1947) developed the first viable vaccine. It was employed to considerable success during the Boer War. The plague bacillus was isolated independently by Alexandre Yersin (1863–1943) and Shibasaburo Kitasato (1852–1931) during the Hong Kong epidemic

of 1894. Shortly after, the vital role played by the flea in plague transmission was finally elucidated. By this stage, the germ theory of disease had truly arrived. The germs responsible for anthrax, cholera, diphtheria, and tuberculosis, as well as leprosy and gangrene, had been found by the late 1880s. The next ten years saw the discovery of the microbial causes of pneumonia, gonorrhea, and cerebrospinal meningitis in addition to plague, tetanus, typhoid, and undulant fever. Virtually every year between 1879 and 1899 scientists unlocked the secret of another important infectious disease.

Alongside these advances, medical scientists acquired a stronger grasp of the mechanics of immunity. Many bacteriologists believed that the bactericidal property was present within blood serum, hence the capacity for organisms to acquire immunity and produce antitoxins. This "humoural" form of immunity was most strongly associated with the tiny white cells known as lymphocytes. A rival theory ascribed immunity to phagocytes, relatively large cells that could be seen in certain species to ingest invading pathogens.[22] By the late 1890s, the view was emerging that the cellular and humoural forms of immunity worked in unison to protect the body's integrity from invading bacteria.

The implications of the discovery that germs cause disease were many and varied. At the theoretical level germ theory was highly innovative. It was now recognized that specific infectious diseases have specific causes: that the same species of germ will nearly always induce the identical condition in susceptible hosts. Knowledge of germs also improved diagnostics: blood tests could be performed to see if patients had antibodies for specific conditions. Germ theory did not, however, immediately translate into massive health benefits. In the Western world, civilian deaths from big epidemic killers were already in decline as a result of vast improvements in sanitation, drainage, and water quality, as well as rising standards of nutrition. But germ theory revealed that mankind is continually being threatened by disease agents invisible to the naked eye. This realization drove the advent of scrupulously aseptic surgery, strict hygienic reforms in catering and food production, the chlorination of mains water, and the pasteurization of dairy products.

A recognition of the deadly threat posed by unseen germs also had a profound public impact. Many people were shocked, or in some cases forced, into adopting new attitudes about the prevention of sickness. Handwashing using powerful disinfectants became routine. Listerine appeared on the chemist's shelf. And for those who could afford it, the ornate Victorian water closet gave way to the Spartan, almost puritanical, modern bathroom. The white china toilet surrounded with smooth, tiled walls and floors became the new sanitary ideal.

Germ theory brought with it a sudden rise in the credibility of contagionism. News that tuberculosis was spread by germs contained in, among other things, exhaled water droplets generated considerable anxiety. Some reactions bordered on the hysterical: numbers of writers, including physicians, warned against kissing and shaking hands. More sober reactions to the invisible germ included large-scale public campaigns to persuade those with infectious diseases to avoid coughing and sneezing in others' faces and to dispose of contaminated material in responsible ways. After Koch's discoveries, spitting was seen as the chief cause of the spread of tuberculosis. Several countries installed spittoons in popular meeting places and in stations. The French and British governments also set up dispensaries to track down cases of tuberculosis and offered the victim's family advice and disinfectant.[23]

The fear of contagion increased the stigmatization of the sick, especially the tuberculous. Some states passed legislation allowing for the quarantining of those who did not observe the new hygiene regulations borne of germ theory. And hundreds of essentially custodial sanatoria were established. These more draconian policies were combined with aggressive public health campaigns designed to teach people the new laws of health. These efforts were in part inspired by an atmosphere of intense national rivalry as European states became more interested in the health and fighting fitness of their peoples.

Yet in many ways the new discoveries were rapidly incorporated into preexisting medical frameworks. In particular, germ theory did not eclipse the traditional division of the causes of malady into both exciting and predisposing causes. Many doctors continued to focus on the bodily weaknesses and inherited predispositions that left the victim susceptible to the invasion and multiplication of potentially deadly germs. This emphasis on predisposing factors also meshed with the late nineteenth-century fascination for race and allowed bacteriology to be formulated in explicitly racialist terms.[24] Links were often made between microbes or their vectors and alleged racial types. The idea of the silent carrier, a concept popularized through the plight of America's "Typhoid Mary," exacerbated suspicion directed at outsiders.

The Balance Sheet

Medical knowledge had grown during the 1800s faster than in any previous hundred year period. Doctors now saw far beyond the symptom complexes that virtually filled the medical gaze of the eighteenth century. Grand speculative frameworks had given way to laboratory diagnostics and empirical, laboratory research involving carefully controlled vivisection experiments. Medicine was vastly more scientific and doctors knew it. They could now see themselves as the custodians of esoteric knowledge, far beyond the competency of most of their patients. And the patient's subjective experience of illness was rapidly receding from view. Already, in fact, doctors were having to implore their colleagues to treat whole patients, not just malfunctioning organs.

Yet the paradox of all this scientific advance was that few tangible health benefits had so far accrued. Anti-typhoid vaccinations would prove highly significant during World War I. Diphtheria and tetanus antitoxins also saved many lives. And advances in medical chemistry, exemplified in the availability of reliable concoctions of morphine and laudanum, brought many people relief from anxiety and sleeplessness (at the risk of addiction in some cases). But most of the time doctors in late century were still relying on either depletive medicines (emetics and purges) or, more commonly, restoratives, in the form of carefully managed diets. The hospital physician was justifying his status in terms of his ability to diagnose accurately, not his capacity to cure.

Nevertheless, medical discourses, in particular miasma theory, had led to major improvements in public health. And it was on the basis of the achievements of Pasteur, Koch, and their contemporary bacteriologists that medicine would experience its "golden age" of the mid-1900s, marked by the advent of a medicine that could cure disease, and not only prevent its onset.

NOTES

1 Porter (1999), esp. ch. 21.
2 Risse (1992: 149–71).
3 Jewson (1974).
4 Rosenberg (1985). See also Waller (2003).
5 Ackerknecht (1967); Gelfand (1980).
6 Scull (1993); Goldstein (1987).
7 Weisz (1995).
8 Reiser (1978).
9 Smith (1979); Hardy (1993); Wohl (1984).
10 Ackerknecht (1987); Evans (1987).
11 Loudon (2000).
12 Hamlin (1992).
13 Porter (1999).
14 Evans (1987).
15 Rosenberg (1969).
16 Allen (2000).
17 Oppenheim (1991).
18 Rosenberg (1969).
19 Pick (1989).
20 Barnes (1995).
21 Worboys (2000).
22 Silverstein (1989).
23 Tomes (1998); Barnes (1995).
24 Kraut (1995).

GUIDE TO FURTHER READING

The best general accounts of nineteenth-century medicine are Rosenberg's "Therapeutic Revolution," Bynum's *Science and the Practice of Medicine in the Nineteenth Century*, and Porter's *Greatest Benefit to Mankind*. For the controversy about the nature and significance of Paris medicine, see Hannaway and La Berge, *Constructing Paris Medicine*. There is currently considerable disagreement over why psychiatry emerged as a major medical specialty in the 1800s: whose interests were being served and how much influence the psychiatrists had. Porter and Wright's *Confinement of the Insane, 1800–1965* provides a nice summary of recent historiographical trends and developments. Also useful is Micale and Porter's *Discovering the History of Psychiatry*. For the conflicts among localists and contagionists in the sphere of public health, see in particular Hamlin's "Predisposing Causes" and Evans's *Death in Hamburg*. See also Rosenberg's *Explaining Epidemics*. Worboys' *Spreading Germs* usefully reveals the complexity of germ theories in the later 1800s and the variety of germ theories that arose in this period. Debate still continues over the amount of credit owed to medical professionals for the health transition of the late 1800s and early 1900s. For this contentious area, see McKeown's *Role of Medicine*, and, for criticism of the McKeown thesis, Szreter's "Importance of Social Intervention in Britain's Mortality Decline."

CHAPTER TWENTY-NINE

Sexuality

IVAN CROZIER

The nineteenth century was a time of fundamental shifts with regard to conceptions of sexuality in Europe. During this century concepts of perversion were formalized within medical discourses, prostitution was studied from a variety of medical, social, and legal perspectives, the "sexual double standard" was challenged as well as reified by different groups in society, birth control became an issue of political importance as well as a social problem, and general moral attitudes towards sexuality were in great flux, which figured in new conceptions of the self in relation to religion, society, and gender as well as individual psychology. The legacy of these developments for the twentieth century included reconceptualized gender relations with regard to sexual issues, knowledge about birth control and sexuality that was far more "respectable" than it had been in earlier times, a variety of scientific discourses that placed sexuality at the very center of the concept of what it meant to be human, and a cornucopia of perspectives on issues such as homosexuality, marriage, masturbation, child sexuality, and sexual education.

This chapter is a schematic overview of the discourses about sexuality that were significant in nineteenth-century Europe (including the United Kingdom). It shows how many of these discourses were related to one another, and also serves to illustrate how the types of sexual issues that predominated in the period were often reformulated into other issues. It also illustrates

the common themes that dominated discussions of sexuality – most notably gender, but also conceptions of the normal and pathological, and ideas about social position that fed into discussions of sexuality throughout the period. Further, it draws special attention to the important role that medicine had in the formation of ideas of sexuality in the nineteenth century. Issues that are covered in this chapter include public attitudes towards sexuality, including artistic and literary representations of sex, homosexuality, pornography, masturbation, contraception, venereal disease, prostitution, forensic science and sexuality, the medicalization of sexuality, and developments within sex education. This chapter is not intended to isolate all of the local nuances of different sexual themes in various cultural settings, but rather introduces the main issues that the historian of sexuality should look out for.

Common to European countries was an increasing anxiety about sexuality deriving in part from concerns about the changing demographies of all countries in the nineteenth century, with a vast growth in city populations, ideas of danger and a reconceptualization of personal interactions associated with these changes, as well as the visible signs of degeneration and destitution, a growth in prostitution, and an expanding of possible sexual opportunities that city life entails.[1] These changes, while not necessarily sexual issues in themselves, were often exacerbating factors of the sexual anxieties of the time. They capture the real flavor of sexual possibilities in the period; these nineteenth-century sexual anxieties were not entirely discursive, but were based on actual sexual practices and sexual problems.

The sexual anxieties of the nineteenth century were often drawn out over issues of public and private activities. During this century, significant changes in family and social life meant a policing of new boundaries concerned with appropriate behaviors. We find that sexuality was especially affected, with private ideals of selfhood being constructed over issues such as masturbation, romantic love, perversions, etc., while public sexuality was controlled over issues such as indecent behaviors, prostitution, homosexuality, marriage and divorce laws, and public health. Displays of sexuality were both formalized and subverted in artistic and pornographic forms, and pertinent social reactions to the increased sexualization over the century were manifest in both public opinion and in legal censure. Key issues included who had access to sexual material as well as what was being represented.

It is important when writing about the history of sexuality to pay some debt to other historians who have worked in the field. The most eminent of these is French theorist Michel Foucault, who argued that rather than being a time of sexual repression, the nineteenth century was a time of proliferation of sexual discourses and a panoply of control measures were put in place to isolate, study, exalt and challenge the sexual status quo. Far from being sex-free, the nineteenth century was an age obsessed with sexuality. Foucault's work has been the central theoretical commitment to many working on the history of sexuality, and many nuanced histories have shown how sexual discourses have provided the means of policing the population, but also have given the potential for new forms of (sexual) existence. By allying themselves with Foucault's work, many historians have investigated issues of power and control as they surround the construction of sexuality. Topics such as sexual science, birth control, gender, and the construction of sexual identities have drawn in one way or another from Foucault's writing. Foucault's influence has been felt in all areas of the discipline, and

he is still the starting point for many new works.[2]

Public Attitudes Towards Sexuality

The most important aspect of sexuality that has come to typify the nineteenth century is a sense that there was a different moral attitude towards sexual issues. More than any other period, the Victorian period is held up as a time of sexual repression, of a moral distaste in sexual matters. Even the English adjective of "Victorian" is pejorative where sexual attitudes are concerned. This standard view is based on the evangelical image of family life, where sexual issues were held to be base compared with higher moral concerns such as faith, charity, intellectual pursuit, and civic duty. Central to this conception of society was the father figure, who led his family in prayer, who loved his wife and children, and protected them from baser influences. Deriving from, and supporting, this conception was the ideology that respectable women did not enjoy sex, and that children were normally sexless beings. Further, traditional ideals of marriage in the period were also being challenged. Many countries changed their divorce laws during the nineteenth century, reflecting ideals of romantic attachment as well as an altered view of property rights and gender relations. Although there was a disparity between the genders with regard to sexual issues, discourses of romantic ideals – as well as popular representations of these ideals – dramatically increased during the century.

These images of the Christian family are best located in responses to the anxieties that sexuality produced. Sexual education was not a matter for schoolteachers or even doctors in this period, but was rather the province of the father and the church preacher and characteristically they had little to add to the topic of a factual nature. The kinds of advice that was to be given, according to sexual advice manuals, was that sexual purity was central to maintaining respectability and control over oneself. Sex was – according to this treatment – not a topic of polite conversation, a point that cannot be separated from the notion that the working classes were more sexualized, and the middle classes adopted an evangelical stance towards sexual matters. Furthermore, a proliferation of protection leagues to prevent young girls becoming prostitutes, societies for the suppression of vice to cut down on the spread of pornography and tasteless art, and such like support this view that there was a decided war against sexuality in the period. It was even formalized in biological thought by the advent of eugenics in order to control the ramifications of sexual intercourse for the "good" of the race: sex was to be productive and for social benefit, not a mere pleasure, in these discourses.

The standard argument about sexuality in the nineteenth century relied on concepts of the sexual double standard: men were naturally sexual beings, and could not help the occasional indiscretion, while women were naturally passive and pure. The main outlet – according to this conception – was prostitution, which both maintained the moral code of "normal" women being sexless and held above base instinct, while allowing men to indulge themselves physically with "fallen women" who were either atavistically or morally disposed towards selling their sex. These kinds of ideas were formalized in medical literature as well as in other popular forms, with some especially strong lines of argument coming from the Italian positivist school in anthropology, as well as from sundry doctors who studied prostitution.[3] These ideas about prostitution and the double standard were challenged by feminists involved in the purity movement, and were celebrated by the artists and poets of the demimonde.[4]

This view of sexual morality, while partially sustainable by addressing certain texts, has undergone a number of fairly substantial criticisms by historians. The most significant contribution to these revisions was the challenge to the "repression hypothesis" by Foucault, mentioned above. Also of particular import is the recent attention historians have paid to what the Victorians actually did in bed, rather than what they wrote about the evils of lust. Detailed views of the changing patterns of birth rates, especially out of wedlock, certainly suggest that people were having sex for the "wrong" reasons (i.e., non-married). The archives at the Foundling Hospital in London are one such source to suggest that some women were prepared to have sex outside of the sanctity of marriage. In her detailed study *Love in the Time of Victoria*, Françoise Barret-Ducrocq has shown that women who left their newborn infants at the Foundling Hospital were often duped into having sex before wedlock on the promise that they would later be "made respectable."[5] Many of these women, according to the records that they left with the hospital, felt that they would otherwise lose their beaux if they did not succumb to the sexual opportunities provided by dark alleyways or public parks. Contemporary evidence of the numbers of infanticides also supports the view that women were having pregnancies out of wedlock, with the mid-1870s discussions in the *British Medical Journal* emphasizing many of the germane issues surrounding birth out of wedlock, and the repercussions of breaches of promise by men who were callously impregnating otherwise respectable women.

Not all women were tricked into giving up their virginities to unscrupulous men against the wall of a darkened alley or in a field. Much attention has been given to cases of women explicitly enjoying sex, in which the passionate lives of various nineteenth-century women are documented.[6] Furthermore, cases in sexological studies amply evidence the fact that both men and women were capable of indulging their erotic lives regardless of social opprobrium. Needless to say, many of these options were more available to men, as they were less constrained socially by the problems of childbirth, as well as having many more opportunities to indulge their passions outside respectable family life.

Sexuality in Art and Literature

Representations of sexuality in both art and literature changed dramatically over the nineteenth century, in keeping both with social developments and as specific developments within these creative fields. These sources reflect the interests in sexual topics in the period while also providing a broader base for sexual consumerism by the readers and buyers of such creations. The proliferation of sexual imagery in this material can be used to understand the kinds of sexual issues that were at stake, as well as considering more aesthetic issues, such as the variety of sexual experiences and the notions of sex that were held by various artists, as well as the political and polemical uses of sexual imagery in art and literature.[7]

In literary terms, French literature has been occasionally used as a synonym for sexually explicit material. There has in Britain been a euphemistic sense that French novels were somehow sexually explicit, unlike the treatment of such topics on the other side of the Channel. For instance, the novels of Emile Zola, such as *Nana* (1880) and especially *Therese Raquin* (1867), rely upon the sexual activities of the characters for their central plot development. Zola used explicit discussion of sexuality as a way of illustrating the real lives of the lower orders in France. His concern with issues such as prostitution, female arousal, and sexual passion allowed him to explore character according to the Naturalist manifesto that he developed during this period. Gustave Flaubert's *Madame Bovary* (1856), while not as explicitly sexual as Zola, also portrays the downfall of a married woman who acted upon her sensual desires. While the same kinds of behavior had been exhibited in other texts – for example, Stendhal's *The Red and The Black* (1830) told of the protagonist, Julian Sorel, leaving Madame Renal, the wife of his employer, with "nothing left to desire" – the treatment of infidelity by Flaubert and Zola linked it to the downfall of the adulterous woman, and as such used sex as a means for delineating "appropriate" behavior, but on the other hand also illustrating the realization that women were sexual beings, even if it killed them.

Other sexualities were also explored in European literature during the nineteenth century. The eponymous Viennese author of *Venus in Furs* (1870), Baron Leopold von Sacher-Masoch – after whom masochism was named by the Austrian sexologist Richard von Krafft-Ebing – told the story of the sexual subjugation of the main character by a fur-clad diva. Not only was a reversal of gendered sexual stereotypes achieved in this text, but also the protagonist uses his subjugation in order to control his mistress, Wanda, by contractually binding her to perform tasks of humiliation and general wickedness. The same cannot be said of the rather more sensual erotic poetry of Charles Baudelaire. Baudelaire's poems, such as "Afternoon Song," "Hymn to Beauty," and "The Jewels," emphasize submission, feminine power, and a celebration of the female form in erotic encounters. In both instances, however, there is a celebration of the sexually liberated female – able to be engaged by the less aggressive male who does not have to stoop to the use of prostitutes and other "immoral" women in order to achieve sexual satisfaction. This situation suggests a challenge to the widely perceived sexual double standard, although one must also remain aware of the use of such images as a subversion of social norms for artistic effect.

Another area of sexual fascination for nineteenth-century writers was lesbianism. This interest took many forms. *Mademoiselle de Maupin* (1835), by Théophile Gautier, was not explicitly lesbian, but used a transvestite female character, with whom the female character Rosette falls in love and lures to bed, not minding when she discovers the misunderstanding. More literary options became available with George Augustus Sala's translation of *Index Expurgatorius of Martial, literally translated, comprising all of the Epigrams hitherto omitted by English translators* (1868), which contained graphic descriptions of lesbianism, including the practice of cunnilingus, under the guise of respectability of a classical work, but really sold for its titillating value. More subtle discussions of lesbianism, nevertheless highly eroticized, can be found in vampire stories such as Bram Stoker's *Dracula* (1897), and Sheridan Le Fanu's *Carmilla* (1872). In these texts, a heavily sexual undercurrent is portrayed through the erotic (and Sapphic) encounters of the female protagonists. The effect of these depictions of lesbianism was both to emphasize female sexuality while also placing it on a footing with the more actively conceived male counterpart by portraying it as secretive, intimate, and lavish, at the same time objectifying it for the reader's erotic pleasure, however subtly masked as a horror story.

There also existed a subtle use of the sexual topic of masturbation for literary purposes. Charles Dickens' *David Copperfield* (1850) used this trope in his portrayal of Uriah Heep, with his sunken eyes, clammy handshake, and general nervousness and guilt displaying his habitual masturbation (according to the medical authors of the time). Robert Louis Stevenson's *Strange Case of Dr. Jekyll and Mr. Hyde* (1887) also touches on this sexualized reading, with hints about masturbation (secret, private vices that change the character in both mood and appearance) barely disguised in the text. In both instances, the uses of accepted representations of masturbators was used as an illustration of the downwards spiral on which the boy who played with himself or the adolescent unable to control himself might find himself, although codified to fit Victorian sensibilities.

Written against the grain of sexual moralizing at the end of the century, the literary decadent movement, including Edmond and Jules Goncourt, J.-K. Huysmans, Paul Verlaine, and Oscar Wilde, aimed to celebrate sexual immorality in all of its perversity – often deliberately so for literary effect. An example such as Huysmans' *A Rebours* portrays the corruption of a youth into depravity by Des Esseintes. Paris, the corrupt city of seductions, is proudly displayed in the journals of the Brothers Goncourt. These literary representations fit into the burgeoning literature associated with decadence, and its medicalized form, degeneration. The city as a sexual space is not portrayed as something to be afraid of while pining for the pastoral solace of the country, but as an exciting series of possibilities and erotic encounters.

Not all representations of sexuality in nineteenth-century literature were found in novels or "highbrow" literature; pornography flourished in the period, as in all others. Print pornography was not a nineteenth-century invention. Long lineages of pornographic writings have been traced. There were, however, some new developments in this genre that are worth considering. While seventeenth and eighteenth-century pornography was much more political – showing the corruption of the church, or in some examples such as the Marquis de Sade's *Philosophy in the Bedroom*,

the reading of revolutionary pamphlets as a supplement to the sexual acts themselves – works produced in the nineteenth century, in contrast, were more "pornotopian."[8] Without giving too much attention to the topic, sexual issues in Victorian pornography included sexual intercourse, birching and whipping, sodomy, domination, oral sex, and lesbianism. The main emphasis was upon insatiable women (often portrayed as innocent virgins awoken to libertinism by various means) and indefatigable men, for whom satisfying multiple sexual partners with several orgasms back-to-back posed no real problem. Notable examples of such pornotopia include "Walter's" *My Secret Life* (published in multiple volumes in the 1890s), which enrolled many of the tropes of Victorian morality, and subverted them. One of the more interesting French examples was George Sand's lover, Alfred de Musset's, *Gamiani, ou Une Nuit d'Excès* (1835). This text follows the insatiable sexual appetite of the female protagonist through her relationship with the voyeur, Alçide, as well as her amorous adventures with depraved monks, innumerable nuns, an innocent virgin, and a donkey of prodigious endowment. The emphasis in this text is on the unnatural nature of Gamiani's desires and her unquenchable lust.

Turning to sexuality in nineteenth-century visual art, we find that an emphasis on the classical allowed for artistic representations of sexuality and nudity that were within the bounds of public acceptability. The neo-classical nudes of Jean-Auguste-Dominique Ingres, such as his 1814 *Le Grand Odalisque*, and Eugène Delacroix's *Odalisque Reclining on a Divan* (ca. 1827–8), show an emphasis on female sexuality exposed for the viewer under the guise of classical respectability. On the other side of the Channel, Augustus Leopold Egg painted his triptych *Past and Present* (1859) as a morality play dealing with the downfall of an adulterous woman to a life of prostitution. These kind of salutary messages fitted with other Victorian ideals of female chastity and sexual control. In contrast, the Pre-Raphaelite depictions of female sexual desire celebrated feminine sexuality. William Holman Hunt's *The Hireling Shepherd* (1851) shows a female shepherdess in an accessible position with her lover as an interpretation of Longus' *Daphnis and Chloe*. This theme of female sensuality made respectable through interpreting classical stories was taken further by one of the successors to the Pre-Raphaelite tradition, John William Waterhouse, whose *Hylas and the Nymphs* (ca. 1896) puts female desire in predatory mode, with numerous stunning nude beauties awaiting Hylas' dip into the water – a sexual suicide that would have appealed to numerous anxious Victorian young men.

At the middle of the century in France, a move towards realism allowed for more graphic depictions of the demimonde. Examples of the many works include Gustave Courbet's precursor to the modern-day "beaver shot," *L'Origin du Monde* (1866); Edgar Degas' ballerinas and especially his bathing women; Eduard Manet's *Dejeuner sur l'Herbe* (1863); and Henri de Toulouse-Lautrec's numerous paintings of vivid prostitutes. Of course, in private, artists had indulged their interests in the erotic; for example, J. M. W. Turner's sketchbooks contained many graphic drawings and water colors of coupling scenes with all of the graphic exposure of a Brett Whiteley or an Egon Schiele, but were mostly destroyed by the sensible and susceptible art critic, John Ruskin. These sexual representations were meant for the artist, not the public, and celebrated his affair with the enigmatic Mrs. Booth.

A move towards realism allowed for sexual subject matter to be displayed in galleries that reworked the classical nude into a writhing sexual being. The boudoir paintings of Manet, Renoir, and Degas were significant contributions to this modernization of the sexualized subject, and were emulated by others such as Walter Sickert and J. M. Whistler. A highly homoeroticized side to this turn came from Simeon Solomon and H. S. Tuke, both of whom arc famed for their gorgeous boy nudes. All over Europe, a variety of erotic artworks emerged. The Belgian Fernand Khnopff's *Istar* (1888) influenced Gustave Klimt and Alphonse Mucha in the Successionist and Art Nouveau tradition of the 1890s–1910s. Other examples in this illustrative tradition include the sexualized pictures of Aubrey Beardsley. Sexually explicit or enticing works proliferated in the later part of the century.

In a different medium, sculptor Auguste Rodin's famous *The Kiss* (1886–98) developed Neo-Classical ideals after Michelangelo. The sensual subject matter of this famous piece – the story of Paolo and Francesca from Dante's *Divine Comedy* – captures the image of female lust in Francesca's infidelity. Rather than focusing on the punishment of the adulterous couple, as Dante did by emphasizing their punishment, Rodin's work is significantly modern in that it shows the first unchaste kiss that began the couple's undoing. A version of this work, one of the most famed sculptures of the nineteenth century, caused such a stir in the Sussex town of Lewes in the early twentieth century that it was draped with cloth so as not to incite the passions of the young men and women in the town. Lewesian Pauls and Franceses were too much at risk in the South Downs even in the next century.

One of the key nineteenth-century advancements in capturing images was of course photography. Photography allowed for a sexualization of the gaze; it gave the photographer the ability to objectify, the ability to select the desired object through mechanically reproduced choices. While this is a general trend in photographic art, it was taken up in the production of pornography almost as soon as photography was invented. There is much evidence that pornographic photographic images went on sale in order to fill the demand for sexually explicit material, but with the added benefit of replication for the producer who had hitherto required etching techniques. Examples of erotic photography produced in France of nude women in a variety of poses – from lesbian couples to Swedish women bound up in postures of eroticized slaves – flooded the pornographic market, and held this position until the development of internet pornography.

With slightly more artistic pretensions, Baron Wilhelm von Gloeden in Sicily and Wilhelm von Plüschow in Naples were soon providing photographs of naked youths and children to homosexual men such as John Addington Symonds and Edmund Gosse. These images were often extensions of the classical ideal that many of the buyers had come to appreciate while studying in the great universities; stunning naked youths adopting classical poses and using motifs from the Greek and Roman worlds were captured in the glorious Italian sunshine. Not all such pictures were produced by homosexual men living in Italy, making use of the freedom to indulge their (artistic) desires provided by the *Code Napoléon*. Edward Sambourne, the Chelsea-dwelling illustrator for *Punch*, became a member of the Camera Club (a male-only photographic club with facilities in Charing Cross Road, founded in 1887). As a member of this club, Sambourne took numerous nude and compromising photos of various women and girls, not always including images of the upper body in his work. These nude studies blur the boundary between explicit pornographic photography and erotic artworks in their own right; they are not quite the same as French photographs of women spreading their legs, but nor are they classical portraiture.

Aside from these artistic developments, a more typical pornographic industry producing photographs of people copulating and fellating was soon widely available, especially being imported from France and Belgium to other parts of Europe. At the end of the century, erotic film emerged almost contemporaneously with the development of cinema. These were short, such as the 45-second *A Victorian Lady in Her Boudoir* (British, 1896), showing a naked matron parading around the room, or the one minute *Peintre Facétieaux* (France, 1899), in which a young model strips for the artist. Both capture the "Peeping Tom" side to sexual voyeurism, where the wonder of what other people behind closed doors were doing became a suitable pornographic trope. This was heightened by the fact that the early viewing spaces for such erotic film were in male public conveniences.

In artistic and literary depictions of sexuality in the nineteenth century we see various changes in the increasingly explicit sexual nature of many representations. This is less the case with pornographic representations – which were explicit by definition – although even in this field there was a move from the politically motivated erotica of the eighteenth century to more purely libertarian pursuits. The development of new media, such as photography and film, allowed for more varied pornographic representations. Nevertheless, throughout this period, a more general development of sexually explicit subject matter – from stories with a central reliance on sexual material, to intimate depictions in artistic images – suggests that along with the changing attitudes to sexual morality that can be shown to have developed over the nineteenth century, art and literature also adopted sex as a favorable, or at least useful, subject matter, reflecting the social changes that were occurring.

Contraception

The issue of contraception in the nineteenth century requires attention to a number of themes, including class issues, gender issues, political issues, and medical issues. Argument as to whether contraception increased during the nineteenth century, and if so, what brought this change about, has to address these various elements. Evidence for the decline in birth rates during the period per capita certainly suggest that something was being done to curb the incidence of pregnancy.[9] This would have had all manner of appeal, from those using restraint to follow the frugal directives of the Rev. Thomas Malthus's *Principle of Population* (1798), through to those who were keen to avoid the risks of childbirth.

Another interest in birth control came from a variety of radical secularists, who picked up on Malthus's writings in a number of ways of which the Reverend would not have approved. James Mill, in the Supplement to *Encyclopaedia Britannica*, Francis Place, in his "Diabolical Handbills," and Richard Carlile in *Every Woman's Book* (1826) – the first full-length book in which prevention was openly advocated – all began promulgating various ideas about contraception. Others in Paris were also advocating birth control based on scientific and political premises: Joseph Garnier, professor of political economy at Paris and editor of *Journal des Economistes*, and Adam Raciborski, who drew attention to the monthly period as a method for birth control (confining intercourse to 8 days after and 3 days before the menstrual epoch). Other texts that soon flooded the secularist radical birth control market included

Robert Dale Owen's *Moral Physiology* (1830), Charles Knowlton's *Fruits of Philosophy* (1832), and George Drysdale's *Elements of Social Science* (first published 1854, but continuously updated until the author's death in 1900). A variety of methods for controlling birth were advocated in these various texts, including Drysdale's reliance upon withdrawal, Carlile suggesting the sponge, and Knowlton prescribing a chemical injection of a caustic solution of zinc sulphate, or alum.

The fact that a number of people faced trial over the spreading of birth control literature illustrates the perceived risks that contraceptive knowledge was supposed to have for society. Annie Besant, champion of female sexual knowledge, was arrested in 1877 (with accomplice Charles Bradlaugh) for distributing Knowlton's *Fruits of Philosophy* (and her defense brief was later published as the *Law of Population*, which was itself considered an obscene publication in Sydney, Australia). What was at stake in these arrests was sexual knowledge, and the control of who got it. Doctors were considered suitable; women, children, and the working classes were not. And it was access to women and the working classes in particular that many birth-control advocates were struggling to attain. Their writings were perceived as (and in many cases were) championing sexual freedom, and the wholesale separation of sexual pleasure from reproduction. It was against this imagined threat to society that many reactionaries rallied. And it was the embodiment of these doctrines that all sex should not lead to children that eventually led to the decline in birth rates and widespread changes in sexual experience.

Masturbation

Many of the anxieties surrounding sexuality in the nineteenth century focused specifically upon pleasuring the self. Despite being nowadays considered as practically universal (at least among males), masturbation was the topic of much medical discussion in the nineteenth century. Since the middle of the eighteenth century, a variety of ever-increasing study was given to the topic, including the attendant moral, physical, and sexual evils of masturbation, and the modes of controlling it. This focus was not initially confined to medical work. Since Saint Augustine's *Confessions*, strictures had been placed on masturbation within the Christian framework. These fears became medicalized with the anonymous early eighteenth-century pamphlet *Onania; or the Heinous Sin of Self-Pollution, and all its Frightful Consequences, in both Sexes, Considered. With Spiritual and Physical Advice to Those, who have already injur'd themselves by this Abominable Practice. And Seasonable Admonition to the Youth (of both SEXES) and those whose Tuition they are under, whether Parents, Guardians, Masters, or Mistresses. To which is Added, A Letter from a Lady Concerning the Use and Abuse of the Marriage-Bed. With the Author's Answer thereto*, and especially with Swiss doctor S. A. A. D. Tissot's *L'Onanisme* (1760).

One interesting correlation concerning the marked increase in anti-masturbation literature was the contemporary increase in pornography. Another correlation was the growth of pedagogical texts that sought to describe the best ways of bringing up children. Control of auto-erotic desires was one such way. Masturbation was primarily conceived of as a male problem during the nineteenth century, despite the fact that many of the early Swiss and German texts on the problem contained wood cuts of young girls masturbating themselves with objects such as hair pins, or by rubbing themselves against the bed frame.[10]

The most significant nineteenth-century text on masturbation and its problems was by French doctor Claude-François Lallemand, whose *Des Pertes seminales involontaires* (1842) popularized a new disease entity: spermatorrhoea. This disorder was the involuntary leaking of semen, most usually associated with too much masturbation (although it is still a symptom of the long-term use of the East African stimulant *Khat* or *Miraa*, and not purely a medical fiction). Spermatorrhoea led to a variety of disorders, from clammy hands and rings under the eyes to hair loss, sapped strength, and in extreme cases, death. The cure for spermatorrhoea suggested by Lallemand, and adopted by his followers, was the prevention of masturbation by means of cauterizing the penis with a caustic substance after a bougie had been passed down the urethra to clear it of any blockages.

A number of British doctors reacted to Lallemand's text. George Drysdale's main reason for writing birth control tracts was to encourage free sexual unions without fear of pregnancy rather than resorting to masturbation, primarily as a result of his painful penile cauterization by Lallemand in Montpellier. Several other doctors, such as J. L. Milton, John Skelton, and especially William Acton, have come to be associated with writing on the problem. Acton's *Functions and Disorders of the Reproductive Organs* (1857), while most cited for its scant reference to females not requiring sexual satisfaction, was primarily aimed at alleviating other causes of male anxiety – predominantly masturbation. Acton's text, typically for the genre, argued that the way to avoid the misfortunes of self-pleasure was through other, more "wholesome" pursuits, such as rowing, cricket, and rugby. These sports were institutionalized within the British public school system as one means of controlling boys and dissuading them from playing with themselves in the evenings through sheer exhaustion.

Discussion of female masturbation, although prevalent in eighteenth-century literature, was largely missing from the texts of the following century. Female masturbation did not lead to spermatorrhoea. A spate of attention was given to the problem after Isaac Baker Brown was struck off the British Medical Register for performing clitoridectomies on numerous women in 1866. The perceived benefits of this intervention were described in his On the Curability of Certain Forms of Insanity, Epilepsy, Catalepsy and Hysteria in Females (1866). While the practice did not gain a stronghold in Europe or Britain, it was much more widely accepted in America. Nevertheless, there were nowhere near the same anxieties of women touching themselves as with boys doing the same.

One key aspect of masturbation was its general conception as both a cause and symptom of insanity. Numerous nineteenth-century psychiatrists, including Jean-Etienne-Dominique Esquirol, J. C. Prichard, Wilhelm Griesinger, Henry Maudsley, and Richard von Krafft-Ebing, discussed masturbation in rela-

tion to moral insanity, degeneration, and hysteria. Its role in the formation of perversions was addressed by French psychologist Alfred Binet and Munich physician Albert von Schrenck-Notzing, among others (to be discussed below). Admissions to asylums during the nineteenth century for moral insanity as demonstrated by "self-abuse" were high; psychiatric cases of the period also draw special attention to the fact of a patient masturbating.

Masturbation in many ways captures the essence of nineteenth-century anxieties about sexuality. While the practice had not received much attention in the preceding centuries, a combination of the growth of medicine and particularly the focus upon sexuality as an area worthy of medical attention, as well as the expanded understanding of psychiatry, led to the problematization of masturbation as a sexual practice that failed to fit the criteria of sex-for-reproduction that had been the assumption of much conceptualization of sexuality. The breaking of this connection, through work on birth control as well as new scientific theories of sexual behavior, led eventually to a change in ideas about the problems of masturbation – and indeed of sexuality in general.

Homosexuality

One of the key aspects for understanding nineteenth-century attitudes towards homosexuality is the separation of private and public ideas of sexuality. Fears about masturbation were also linked to such ideas about the control of private sexual experience. In some jurisdictions in Europe, especially those with the *Code Napoléon*, homosexual behavior was not legally problematic, provided it was carried out between consenting adults (although it continued to have a less than ideal social and moral outlook). In other countries, for example England and the German states that adopted the Prussian legal code, homosexuality was illegal. In Britain, until 1861, sodomy carried a death penalty (and had done so since 1538), regardless of whether it was a private or public act. After this time, it was commuted to ten years' hard labor. This punishment was often carried out even in cases of anal rape, as the common belief was that a struggling victim could overcome the assailant, unless they were first rendered unconscious.

A number of prominent homosexual rights activists emerged during the nineteenth century in order to challenge these laws. The most significant was Karl Heinrich Ulrichs, a Bavarian lawyer who stood to lose much if the Prussian code was adopted in the new, unified Germany. Ulrichs' response during the 1850s and 1860s to the proposed change in law was to propose a model for a "third sex": a "male soul in a female body" and vice versa, which was used to both explain and naturalize homosexuality (thus making it something that should not be criminal, but simply a part of nature). This move was one of the first steps towards discussing homosexuality as a type and not an act. Ulrichs proposed the name Urning (Uranian) for a male who loved men, and Dioninge for lesbians. These models, which would be the basis for later sexological ideas about the causes of homosexuality, were widely disseminated in Ulrichs' vast body of writings, and were broadly adopted and adapted by other homosexuals around Europe, such as John Addington Symonds and Edward Carpenter.

The link between the law and homosexuality is demonstrated by a number of prominent nineteenth-century trials. In Germany, these involved Baron von Malzahn (a.k.a. Count Cajus) and Prince Philipp of Eulenburg; in France, Baron Jacques d'Adelswärd-Fersen. In England the 1871 trial of homosexual transvestites Boulton and Park included reference to a Lord Arthur Clinton, MP, son of the Duke of Newcastle, who committed suicide rather than face trial; the Cleveland Street Scandal, which implicated Lord Arthur Somerset, head of the Prince of Wales' stables, and two other prominent men, the Earl of Euston and an army colonel. Hints were also dropped that the scandal included Edward, Prince of Wales. Most well known of all is the trial of Oscar Wilde, precipitated after his involvement with Bosie, the son of the Marquis of Queensbury. These high-profile trials, well researched because so widely publicized due to the important people involved, were not the extent of homosexual activity in Europe in the 1800s, however. A growing body of work is uncovering details of gay subcultures, based on trial transcripts, police reports, and other documents. The mapping of homosexuality in urban spaces has proved to be a research area that has usefully shown the ways in which homosexuals (often men) could form networks of erotic contacts.

Likewise, a number of works have appeared examining lesbian lives through letter writing and journals. These texts show how lesbians were able to act within society, often as "passing women," women who dressed as men and "married" their lovers so as to live together without arousing suspicion or censure. A further source that has been given much attention for the purpose of uncovering sex in history has been the case reports in medical literature. These cases, which are often condemned by historians as pathologizing past desires, have allowed deep insight into all manner of sexual behaviors, including homosexuality. The implication has been that sexual subcultures have been located in various ways, from the famed "Woman Haters Balls" in Germany to various flagellation brothels of London, particularly an establishment named Verbena Lodge that was frequented by poet Charles Algernon Swinburne.

Homosexuality became a topic of great interest in the nineteenth century, due to legal changes as well as to the development of a "gay liberation" movement. Medical attention also did much to raise the profile of homosexuality, although not always in positive ways. It is difficult to assess the incidence of homosexuality in the period, but one thing that the nineteenth century did foster was a strong development of homosexual subcultures, which although not unique to the century, do seem to have been more prevalent.

Venereal Disease

One of the main medical interests in sexuality comes from the control of venereal disease. The importance for such control stems largely from military concerns, as in Europe and in Britain, many soldiers and sailors were suffering from syphilis and other venereal diseases, and thus were unable to take part in active service. As a direct result, the nineteenth century saw a number of aspects of medical progress in the understanding and treatments of venereal diseases. They include establishing the separation between gonorrhea and syphilis (for some time considered to be the same disease) and the categorization of primary, secondary, and tertiary stages of syphilis by Philippe Ricord in the 1830s; and the isolation of the causative agents *Neisseria gonorrhoeae* (1879) and *Treponema pallidum* (1905).

Treatment of venereal diseases since the Renaissance relied heavily on the systemic use of mercury, as well as on more localized treatments, such as cauterization of the infected parts with a caustic solution such as silver nitrate. Mercury was given to the patient to the point were they salivated in the hope that the systemic poison would also manage to bring the disease under control – effectively by "cooking" it out (this was before germ theory). In the early years of the twentieth century, Salversan – the first synthetic antibiotic, designed specifically to cure syphilis – was developed by a German doctor, Paul Erlich (1909). Other means for combating venereal diseases included condom use in Europe as a prophylactic against venereal disease. Some doctors, such as English surgeon William Acton, also advocated a simple washing of the penis after potentially infected sexual intercourse.

As mentioned above, the significance of venereal disease for the state and the military was crucial to nineteenth-century policies. The ravages of syphilis on the soldiering populations of many European countries have been addressed by scholars. At some periods, as many as a quarter of a brigade could be affected by venereal infection. As a direct response to this problem, military and government officials attended to what was widely perceived to be the main vector for infection: prostitutes.

Prostitution

To the casual observer, prostitution seems to have thrived in the nineteenth century. One of the reasons for this was the sexual double standard, which sanctioned and even encouraged men to seek their pleasures outside of the sanctity of marriage. Another reason is that the regulation of prostitution by the Contagious Diseases Acts in Britain has been famously studied by historians, and this has attracted a lot of attention to the problem. Prostitution was not, however, an indigenous British problem. Other European countries also had implemented various systems of control or licensing of prostitutes in order to keep the problem under control. For instance, Belgium and France maintained the importance of the registration of prostitutes, where women were registered and submitted to regular health check in specialist facilities in order to try to control the spread of syphilis. Non-registered women could be punished if they were found working without proper registration papers, or if they failed to show up for compulsory genital inspections to establish their "health" for the male clientele; women who were infected with syphilis were detained until the symptoms – especially the weeping chancres that spread the disease – had passed. Other countries, such as Germany and Austria, had so-called "Eros centers," equivalents to modern-day "red-light" districts where prostitution was concentrated. London, too, had a number of areas that were chiefly haunted by "women of the night." Soho, Kings Cross, Waterloo, etc. were areas that have been associated with women for hire – reasons for these areas being heavily prostituted have to do with the cheapness of housing, the proximity to major railway stations and theatres, and the centrality of these regions.

The study of prostitution since the mid-nineteenth century has included reference to class issues and gender issues – especially the sexual double standard. Prostitutes were seen as being forced into selling sex because of the limited occupations available to women, the worse conditions found in poorly paid factory work, and the fact that there was a veritable army of men willing to pay for pleasures with prostitutes. Although a number of people made feminist and political criticisms of these problems, the main attention to prostitution came from the medical profession, as they were most strongly involved with issues of regulation.

The first great ethnological work dealing with prostitution was A.-J.-B. Parent-

Duchâtelet's 1836 *De la prostitution dans la ville de Paris*. This text gives vast detail of the kinds of women who were working in the sex trade. Points that have often been cited by later doctors, as well as historians, have included the penchant for lesbian activity among prostitutes. Further attention to prostitutes was proffered by St. Petersburg physician Pauline Tarnowski, who focused on details such as the ear shape of women sex workers. In the 1850s, other studies of prostitution came from English doctor William Acton (1813–75), whose detailed studies of prostitutes included those of Brussels and Paris as well as a comparison of the different boroughs of London. Acton is also famous for his support of the Contagious Diseases Acts, the system of regulation of prostitution between 1864–9 in garrison towns, whereby women suspected of being prostitutes would be forcibly examined for venereal infection (although no such examination was made of the clients). Although Acton widely supported these Acts, giving evidence to the Select Committee investigating them, stressing that they should be more widely adopted, and championing a Parisian system of regulation though registration which he believed should be brought to Britain, enough criticism of the Acts from perspectives that highlighted gender inequality and of the morals of prostitute usage (famously by Josephine Baker, but also by other activists operating in societies interested in the suppression of vice) led to the lifting of these statutes. Prostitution in Britain has since been an ill-regulated affair.

Some of the most intense attention was given to prostitution in the late 1880s, after a number of prostitutes were brutally murdered and mutilated in East London. These murders, by the un-arrested Jack the Ripper, became a scandal that rocked London and the rest of the world. Psychiatrists in America wrote theories about these murders and related them to sexual sadism – a concept that was being developed. Continental sexologists also wrote about the Ripper murders as examples of *lustmord*. Other cases of prostitute murder and mutilation, such as those of Franziska Hofer on December 26, 1898 and Anna Spilka on December 31, 1898, both in Vienna by different killers, did not attract the same sustained attention.[11]

Prostitution in many ways captures many of the problems of nineteenth-century sexuality. In this topic, we see the struggle for reorganizing gender relations, responses to few sanctioned sexual outlets, concerns about public health and medical problems, strictures of female sexual choice, responses to the lack of suitable controls of sexual behavior, and moral outrage. It was seen by many as the flip-side to masturbation, the other sexual bugbear of the period. Many sexual radicals of the period believed that both problems, masturbation and prostitution, would disappear once more liberal attitudes to sex had been accepted by society.

Forensic Science and Sexuality

One of the medical specialisms apart from venerealogy that paid attention to sexuality was forensic medicine. Medical jurisprudence was a new area of growth in the nineteenth century. Sexual issues addressed by forensic specialists included proofs of sexual crimes such as rape, sodomy, bestiality, etc. There were a number of differences in approach to sexual knowledge in Germany, France, and the UK, the dominant centers of forensic research at the time. In Prussian law it was held that any crime that focused on the body would require a medical examination to show that the body displayed signs that were fitting with the alleged crime. This meant that there was much need for doctors to be explicit about sexual crime. The opposite held true in Britain, where there was a significant struggle for doctors to have their knowledge accepted in court. Addressing sexual problems was usually an incidental part of other medical forensic interests, even though German court physician Johann Casper noted that one in ten crimes had a sexual element.

For these reasons, a number of important doctors wrote about sexual crimes in their texts. Johann Casper (Germany), Ambroise Tardieu (France), Philippe Ricord (France), and Alfred Swaine Taylor (Britain) all addressed the specifics of crimes such as rape and sodomy in their texts, specifying the physical signs that would be left by these crimes on both the victim and (if any) upon the accused. In these texts, the specific state of the anus of the habitual sodomite, the state of the vagina of a recent defloration, and the shape of the penis of the active bugger were all detailed for use in the courtroom, as were issues such as the detection of venereal disease, the correct identification of semen stains on underclothing, and the interpretation of wounds, scratches, bite marks, and other incidental damage on either the victim or the perpetrator of sexual assaults. The effect that this detailed knowledge had was to position certain doctors as experts in medical jurisprudence. Such expertise entered the legal narratives insofar as it could be used to support a verdict. It also grew significantly, as there was an increase in policing during the nineteenth century. Police surgeons further formalized this relationship between the law and medicine.[12]

One interesting offshoot of the growth of forensic medicine in the nineteenth century was that it became a starting point for sexual science. While many doctors were only interested in the detection of sexual crimes, a number of practitioners, especially in Germany, started to muse about the causes of particular crimes. The main topic of this attention was homosexuality, for particularly Johann Casper noted that it was often of congenital origin, that the perpetrators of such crimes had always felt attracted to people of the same sex. These kinds of statement about the nature of the issue, rather than a strict adherence to evidence, encouraged other doctors to treat the problem of sexuality in a new way.

Medicalization of Sexuality

Apart from the issues of venereal diseases and medical opinion on the problem of prostitution, and apart from forensic evidence about sexual crimes, there was a great deal of other attention to other aspects of the medicalization of sexuality that deserve mention. Psychiatrists had paid attention to sexual issues for a number of years, particularly as certain psychological problems such as hysteria, chlorosis, and "moral insanity" were often believed to have a sexual component. Further, many of the medical treatments of homosexuality were in relation to the law. But psychiatrists were increasingly finding that individuals may be sexually attracted to members of the same sex, but were not consummating these desires. By

treating these unrequited homoerotic lustings as indicative of psychiatric problems, a "turf war" between psychiatrists and other medical professionals ensued, with struggles to reclassify homosexuality in particular as a mental rather than criminal issue. The way that psychiatrists proceeded was to attend to the problem of the sexual impulse in general. This attention was the foundation of the new medical specialism of sexology.[13]

The development of sexology in Europe stemmed from the need by psychiatrists to understand sexual perversions. In particular, there was the need to understand why some forms of behavior, although illegal, were still widely practiced. What followed was a drive to categorize all manner of the so-called perverse behaviors into new "types" of individual. This started with startled doctors reporting cases of homosexuality, but soon snow-balled into detailed descriptions of sexual types. The premier example of this was Austrian psychiatrist Richard von Krafft-Ebing, whose 1886 *Psychopathia sexualis* was continually updated from a short work of a little over a hundred pages, to a massive tome containing descriptions of very many "perverted" acts and types of individual. Some of these included lust murderers, homosexuals, lesbians, zoophiles, sadists, masochists, and fetishists of sundry persuasions. These categories were developed over time.

Having categorized the types of sexual perversion in the 1870–80 period, there was much interest in describing exactly what was going on in the minds of the perpetrators of these acts. Attention to the sexual impulse had of course been a problem for other fields, such as Darwinian biology, which relied on the concept of sexual selection. Work by French psychologist Alfred Binet utilized the concept of the fetish to explain the specificity of sexual desire. The sexual object, be it a silk handkerchief, red hair, a body part such as firm buttocks, or a particular person, aroused feelings that had come to be associated with sexual desire. The fetish was explained as a part of a model for all behavior, which sought to explain why individuals are turned on by one thing in particular, rather than – to use heterosexuality as an example – all members of the opposite sex. Fetishes, for

Binet and the many who read him, were able to explain love psychologically. Binet and followers such as Charles Féré developed this model to explain all manner of sexual "perversions" as simply variations on the same basic impulse. These ideas were taken up by a number of sexologists who were predominantly interested in explaining perversions as acquired individual psychological manifestations. Other variations of the model came from those interested in hypnotism. Munich physician Albert von Schrenck-Notzing suggested that homosexuality, for example, was caused by young boys thinking about other naked youths while they masturbated, thus creating a psychic link between voluptuous feelings and the bodies of their contemporaries. These habits were particularly enforced in boarding schools, where boys often masturbated in groups.

On the other side of this sexological debate were those who, following Casper and Carl Westphal, stressed the congenital aspects of sexual "perversions." A strong contingent of doctors noted that their patients came to them suggesting that they had always felt attracted to people of the same sex. This evidence was used by a number of sexologists to emphasize that sexual feelings were not able to be controlled by individuals, and (in some cases) that they further could not be held criminally responsible for their desires. Such ideas utilized the growing body of evidence of anthropologists and historians that all varieties of sexual "perversion" could be found in other cultures, and in different epochs. Congenitalist sexologists used these arguments to further suggest that these acts were universal and natural. The same sexologists were occasionally prone to use this evidence to argue that certain sexual crimes, such as homosexuality, were not unnatural, and therefore should not be illegal.

One feature of sexological writing that has been used by many historians as evidence of past sexual lives has been the case histories that were included in sexological discourses. Case histories played a number of functions. They were presented as a form of description for a new perversion for the benefit of other doctors who had not come across such behaviors; they were held up as examples of varieties of sexual practices; they were used to challenge other theories; they were used as evidence for sexological claims. Another aspect of sexual case histories is that they were read by other "patients," who often gained some solace from the fact that they were not "alone." Many of the cases of English sexologist Havelock Ellis were gathered by individuals writing to him after reading his works, encouraged by the liberal message that he was promulgating. Some of these letters were converted into new cases in Ellis's later editions. All of them indicate the kinds of sex that people were having in this period.

Although neo-Foucauldian historians have often criticized nineteenth-century sexologists for their writings about sexual "perversions," it must be remembered that many of the sexologists in question were trying to achieve better knowledge of human sexuality, not merely to label and pathologize individuals, but to better understand human experiences. While it is not to be expected that these psychiatrists were in a position to formulate arguments that would meet today's political criteria, and while a number of the treatments of the individuals by sexologists were outrageous, there remains a sense that many sexologists were actually trying to use sexual science for the benefit of those who were suffering legal and social opprobrium because of their desires. German doctor Magnus Hirschfeld and English sex psychologist Havelock Ellis were two of the more active sexologists who tried to bring about changes in the social conditions of those with "alternative" sexual desires. The fact that other homosexuals, such as Edward Carpenter and John Addington Symonds (as well as Hirschfeld himself), gave support to this use of sexual science strongly suggests that sexology was seen in part as a progressive movement for social reform. This is not to deny that there was also a struggle for sexologists to set up psychiatric and behavioral criteria for studying individual desires, but it must be remembered that sexologists engaged with these problems not for explicitly homophobic reasons, but for professional ones. Sexology's prime aim was to educate other doctors, lawyers, and eventually the public at large about different forms of sexual behavior. In order to do so, these doctors had to develop appropriate criteria among themselves with which to understand the problem.

Educating the general public about sexuality was something that had begun in the nineteenth century with anti-masturbation texts, birth control tracts, and sexological ideas. It was also a part of a longer tradition of advice for conception.[14] But organized sex education, designed explicitly for school children and young adults, was not something that was properly organized until the twentieth century. While numerous sexual radicals (e.g., George Drysdale) shared this aim with some sexologists such as Havelock Ellis and Magnus Hirschfeld, the bulk of sexual knowledge in the nineteenth century was maintained within strict boundaries. In many ways, sex education was more of a twentieth-century legacy to nineteenth-century sexual discourses, including the way that sexual reform pushed a sexual education agenda in various European countries.

Conclusion

What can be said about sexuality in the nineteenth century other than that there was a lot of it, and that it had a variety of different modes of existence? Certain discursive forms that culminated in the centralization of sexuality as an issue of individuality – the making of the sexual self – while not being a purely nineteenth-century exercise, certainly developed in this period. The culmination of this in Freudian or libido psychoanalysis also had its roots in the last years of the nineteenth century, when sexologists were working on individual sexual desires. But more importantly, individuals – particularly feminists and homosexual rights activists, as well as sexologists and anthropologists – did much to destabilize the notion of a single, heteronormative mode of sexuality. These challenges reflect the growth of sexual variability, both in terms of practice and representation, throughout the nineteenth century. It is important to realize that while "alternative" forms of sexual expression existed well before the nineteenth century, the meaning of these alternative desires and practices was wholly recast due to the political agitations of artists, authors, scientists, and social critics. Sexuality in the nineteenth century made the

transition from a religiously dominated moral issue to an issue of concern to scientific naturalists who were simply describing what happens, and used these observations to argue for a change in sexual policies and attitudes. Artists and authors too used naturalistic depictions of sexual activity in order to conform to modernist standards and to illustrate better their characters' lives and psyches. One of the major legacies of nineteenth-century sexual thought was the separation of sex from reproduction, by reorganizing the place sex occupied in society and in conceptions of individuality.

A survey chapter of this type cannot deal with all aspects of sexuality, or with all of the various local or even national cultures and interests. While there is a sense of sexual differences between various European countries, many of the issues – from fears about masturbation, anxieties about sodomy, concerns about female propriety, controls of prostitution, and a growing interest in children's sexuality – were shared, even if they surfaced in different ways in specific contexts and in various texts. A great many topics have also been passed over quickly or ignored. Attention deserves to be paid to several areas: to the issues of sexuality raised by European anthropological work that grew over the nineteenth century; the relationship between mental illness and sexuality, particularly considering the work that has been done on hysteria and neuroses in relation to sexuality; the nascent concern with childhood sexuality and puberty that was attended to by doctors and pedagogues in the period; the formalization of heterosexual categories such as nymphomania and satyriasis, and the way that these categories reflect gendered norms in medical and social discourses; detailed examination of the sexual laws of specific jurisdictions, focusing upon legal controls of pornography, homosexuality, and other sexual crimes; the stigmatization of incest; illegitimacy rates in various contexts and the social reactions to these cases of children born out of wedlock. All of the topics of this list would also be able to be addressed in specific local detail. It is worth knowing about Polish pornography, Swedish sodomy, Italian moral insanity, and Spanish spanking, and the ways that these sexual topics differed between national cultures. Some of this comparative work is being done, but much more attention is necessary.

NOTES

1 See chapter 5, this volume.
2 Foucault (1984).
3 See below and chapter 27, this volume.
4 See chapter 15, this volume.
5 Barret-Ducrocq (1991).
6 Gay (1985).
7 See chapter 22, this volume.
8 Marcus (1966).
9 Szreter (1996).
10 Laqueur (2003).
11 See chapter 27, this volume. Thanks to Dan Vyleta for these references.
12 See chapter 26, this volume.
13 See chapter 28, this volume.
14 Porter and Hall (1995).

GUIDE TO FURTHER READING

The history of sexuality is a thriving field with its own *Journal of the History of Sexuality*, an email list (H-Histsex@h-net.msu.edu), and a great number of books and articles. Many of the historians in the field are greatly indebted to Foucault's *History of Sexuality* (the first volume, *The Will to Know*, is relevant to this chapter). Since Foucault, scholars have picked up a number of issues, including prostitution (Walkowitz, *City of Dreadful Delight*; Corbin, *Women for Hire*), birth control (McLaren, Birth Control in Nineteenth Century England; Porter and Hall, *The Facts of Life*), sexology (Oosterhuis, *Stepchildren of Nature*; Crozier, "The Medical Construction of Homosexuality and its Relation to the Law in Nineteenth-Century England"), and homosexuality (Healy, *Homosexual Desire in Revolutionary Russia*; Cocks, *Nameless Offences*) as important topics for historical focus. This list is far from exhaustive, both in terms of authors and subjects. New areas of work are continually expanding, such as sexual space in cities (Cook, "A New City of Friends"). Also, much comparative work between different contexts is being done. Special attention should be drawn to the edited collections by Eder, Hall, and Hekma, *Sexual Cultures in Europe, Vol. 1: National Histories*, and *vol. 2: Themes in Sexuality*, which was one of the first collections to try to draw together a comparative approach to sexuality in different European national contexts.

Part VI

The International System, Colonialism, and War

CHAPTER VI

The International System,
Colonialism, and War

CHAPTER THIRTY

Restrained Competition: International Relations

WILLIAM MULLIGAN

International relations in the nineteenth century were stable, yet flexible, and peaceful, yet competitive. The five great powers – Austria, Britain, France, Prussia (later Germany), and Russia – maintained their position as the dominant states in European politics, though their relative positions changed. For the most part, small states were not extinguished, with the notable exception of the German and Italian states after the wars of unification. Yet the system was flexible enough to accommodate the formation of new states such as Belgium, Serbia, and Greece. There were no general wars between 1815 and 1914, and the most extensive conflict, the Crimean War, was limited in its scope and aims. Wars tended to modify the international system, not overturn it. While there were numerous crises, it is striking that they were resolved on a regular basis without the resort to war. States tended to engage in restrained competition, rather than violent confrontation, as was the case in the eighteenth and first half of the twentieth century.

The reasons for this comparative success in managing international relations have been long debated by historians and no single cause can explain the largely peaceful annals of the nineteenth century or the occasional outbreak of wars. One school of historians, the most notable of whom is Hans Ulrich Wehler, argues that domestic policy concerns dominate the formulation of foreign policy.[1] This can explain both the outbreak of wars and the maintenance of peace. For instance, conservative statesmen feared that revolution would follow war, so they avoided confrontational foreign policies. The link – made evident in the French revolutionary and Napoleonic wars – was further illustrated by the 1905 revolution in Russia after defeat against Japan in the Far East. Yet that same war had been fought, according to some historians, because the tsar believed a victorious war would bolster the prestige of the Romanov dynasty. Similarly, some have argued that Germany's leaders went to war in 1914 to escape from a domestic political crisis. A further illustration of the primacy of domestic politics in the explanation of foreign policy is the argument that figures such as Napoleon III and Palmerston courted popularity at home by pursuing aggressive policies abroad. Another approach identifies ideologies such as pan-Slavism, nationalism, and liberalism as fundamental determinants of foreign policy.[2]

Other scholars have turned their attention to the international system. States' primary concerns were security, survival, influence, and perhaps territorial expansion. They reacted to pressures within the system rather than within the domestic policy arena – a primacy of foreign, as opposed to domestic, policy. On this reading, Napoleon III's policies aimed to overturn the Vienna settlement and assert French leadership within Europe, while Palmerston defended legitimate British interests, particularly against France and Russia in the Ottoman Empire. Germany went to war in 1914 to prevent a further deterioration in its position, squeezed by growing Russian power. The balance of power and its shifts serve to explain war and peace in the nineteenth century, and for the most part the balance favored the status quo great powers – all but France until 1853, and Germany after 1870.[3] Recent studies, especially by Paul Schroeder, have argued that a simple balance of power model is an insufficient explanation for the stability of the European states system. The 1815 settlement also introduced a new set of values to international relations. Alliances were no longer formed for temporary advantage and as a prelude to war; instead, they were largely defensive. Indeed, powers tended to "group together" to restrain any aggression. The institutions and practice of diplomacy became more sophisticated and strengthened peace. A greater respect for international law and treaties than existed in the eighteenth century became evident, while 18 conferences and congresses were held between 1830 and 1878 to resolve international disputes.[4] These features were strongest between 1815 and 1848, and existed in modified form after 1871, but were undermined by national *Realpolitik* in the 1850s and 1860s, represented by figures such as Cavour and Bismarck.

A Revolution in International Politics, 1789–1815

Before the new era came the transition. The French revolutionary and Napoleonic wars transformed European politics but the origins of the wars lay in eighteenth century power politics rather than an ideological clash between *ancien régime* Europe and the universalism of the French Revolution. Ideology was an instrument, not a determinant, of policy, easily subordinated to the national interest. The international crisis which led to the outbreak of the French revolutionary wars began in 1787 with Austrian and Russian attempts to dismember the Ottoman Empire in Europe.[5] Although this failed, it set off a search for territorial compensation. By the time the French revolutionary wars ended at the Peace of

Amiens in 1802, territory had changed hands on a much more extensive scale than ever before. The state of Poland was partitioned between the three eastern great powers, France annexed the Rhineland and Belgium, and Britain had overrun most of France's colonies. The geopolitical transformation continued in the Napoleonic period with the end of the Holy Roman Empire, the growth of medium German states, the brief eclipse of Austria and Prussia as great powers, and the creation of the Kingdom of Italy.[6] The rapidity and scale of change was the result of the power of the modern state. Taming the modern state, especially the great powers, in the sphere of international relations, was one of the principal achievements of the nineteenth century.[7] The power of the modern state made power politics an unwise course of action for nineteenth-century statesmen who, by and large, were restrained in the conduct of diplomacy.

A highly destructive war is not a sufficient precondition for changes in the conduct of international relations. *Forces profondes* can play an important role in international affairs, but the choices of statesmen in any given situation determine the outcome. New ideas and suggestions about the international order emerged. Gentz, an adviser to Metternich, advocated a system of public law to protect states, though he acknowledged that it had to be based on the realities of power within the states system. The British prime minister, Pitt, outlined a plan in 1805 for the balance of power in Europe which depended on the creation of buffer states to France. Although this was not implemented it was the basis, along with the creation of intermediary bodies, for Castlereagh's policy at Vienna. The policies of other states also indicated elements of continuity and change. France interfered in German affairs, but broke with its traditional policy of supporting the Holy Roman Empire and instead weakened Central Europe by promoting the interests of the medium German states. The principle of the balance of power was modified, rather than discarded, by statesmen searching for a new European order.[8]

The disruption of traditional patterns of authority throughout Europe during the French revolutionary and Napoleonic wars left a legacy of unresolved social and political problems which fueled international crises after 1815. Changes of regime in small and medium states were the cause of anxious moments in the chancelleries of the great powers. The revolt in Spain in 1820, which stimulated revolts in the Italian states, was largely due to the disastrous consequences of the fighting in the Iberian peninsula. Calls for constitutional change in Germany after 1815 were often related to promises given during the Wars of Liberation. Metternich kept a watchful eye over would-be generous rulers who threatened the post-1815 settlement by giving their subjects representative government. Expectations of political change, either caused by Napoleonic dispensations or dubious proclamations as the French lost their grip over the continent, produced what at first sight seemed to be largely domestic political crises, but which were deeply affected by great power intervention. Along with a new respect for the power of the modern state and new ideas about the international system, the social and political legacies of the revolutionary and Napoleonic period were the signposts on the way towards nineteenth-century diplomacy.

The Vienna Order, 1815–1848

The Congress of Vienna of 1814–15 inaugurated the Vienna System. This, and the subsequent Vienna Order, is closely associated with the Concert of Europe, a notoriously slippery concept much disputed by historians and political scientists. There is not even agreement on how long the era lasted, with a variety of plausible dates: 1821, when Britain refused to support Austria in suppressing revolts against conservative regimes in Italy; 1848, when the revolutions destroyed the Restoration regimes upon which the Concert depended; or 1854, when the Crimean War began, the first great power war since 1815. A study on détente before 1914 argues that the Concert remained an element of the international system until World War I.[9] Neither is there agreement about why it came about. The failure of eighteenth-century power politics, some historians argue,

was clear after 25 years of war, while the idea of a higher European interest, above the national interest, led to more harmonious relations. Others have stressed the conservative solidarity of Austria, Britain, Prussia, and Russia. Finally, there is little agreement about what constituted the values and practices of the Concert of Europe. The most parsimonious would only note an acceptance of the balance of power and a rejection of territorial aggrandizement, a system of restrained competition. Others would include the regular conferences and close consultation which built up trust, preferring to speak of an equilibrium of rights and interests among the great powers. A further element was the sacrosanct nature of the 1815 treaties and a consequent respect for international law.[10] Even contemporaries disagreed about the function of the Concert. For Metternich, with whom the system is most closely associated, the Concert preserved the domestic, as well as the international, settlement of 1815. For Canning and Palmerston, it was a flexible instrument which allowed for political change as long as this did not disturb the territorial balance of power.[11]

Given such a disparity of views, it is appropriate to start with a minimalist definition of the characteristics of the international system after 1815. First and foremost, an era of restrained competition between the great powers, focusing on increasing and maintaining influence in small states and peripheral areas, dominated European politics in this period. The Treaty of Chaumont (March 1814) sought to make the balance of power more durable. It gave the four victor powers a common interest in the preservation of the status quo, and France under the Bourbons seemed unlikely to challenge this settlement. Each of the great powers emerged relatively satisfied by the 1815 settlement. Russia, along with Britain the strongest power, extended its Polish possessions, allowing it to exert massive strategic influence over Prussia. Russia was the dominant power in the Balkans, which was not subject to the 1815 treaties, a significant omission.

In Central Europe, Prussia had wanted Saxony, but instead received the Rhineland. This, as Brendan Simms notes, was a hugely

significant, if unwanted, geopolitical revolution.[12] It reoriented the Prussian monarchy
towards the west and gave it the leading role in
the defense of Germany against France. The
German states, including Prussia and Austria,
were formed into the German Confederation,
a defensively oriented organization. It acted as
a barrier to Russian and French domination
of the continent, fitting into the system of
restrained competition. It provided territorial
security for states of the Third Germany,
notably Bavaria, Baden, and Württemberg.
Austria became the president of the German
Confederation. The rivalry of Austria and
Prussia ensured a balance of power within
Germany, which the smaller states used to
maintain their independence. In general Austrian interests turned towards the Balkans and
Italy where it gained Lombardy-Venetia, balancing Russian and French ambitions. While
this gave Austria a pivotal place in the European balance of power, it would overstretch its
resources unless other European powers took
account of Austria's vital interests.

France was surrounded by buffer zones. As
well as the Rhineland where Prussia and Bavaria
stood guard, Piedmont-Sardinia watched
over the Franco-Italian border. Italy, unlike
Germany, was not formed into a Confederation. The Papal States, Kingdom of the Two
Sicilies, and various duchies enjoyed independence under the watchful eye of Metternich.
Finally, in Northwest Europe, the Netherlands
combined the former United Provinces with
Belgium to create a buffer against France. This
satisfied British continental security. Statesmen
recognized that France was an important
element of the balance of power. Even in
January 1815, there had been an Anglo-
Franco-Austrian alliance against Russian-
backed Prussian designs on Saxony. France was
quickly restored to the Concert (albeit on trial
as Reiner Marcowitz remarks) at the 1818
Congress of Aachen, which sanctioned the
withdrawal of Allied troops.[13]

This provoked a brief crisis of confidence in
the Prussian government, fearful of renewed
French expansionism. Yet the major crises until
1848 were not caused by direct great power
rivalry but by changes in the domestic politics
of the small – all the other – states and great

power efforts to control and influence these
changes. These raised questions about the formation of new governments and states, the
rights of the great powers to intervene, and the
nature of the 1815 treaties. In the decade
between 1819 and 1829 crises occurred in
Germany, Spain, Italy, and the Balkans. During
these crises there was little evidence of a higher
European interest; great powers acted in their
own interest. The vulnerability of small states
to the great powers and their wishes was particularly evident in the German, Italian, and
Spanish crises.[14] Nor is a broad thesis of conservative solidarity overly persuasive. Metternich was the only leader to pursue a rigorous
conservative, legitimist policy, but one which
also happened to serve Austria's interest;
Alexander I and Nicholas I supported the
Greek and Serbian revolts against the
Ottomans.[15] Domestic political pressures
played little role in the formulation of great
power foreign policy. Even in Britain, Canning
and Castlereagh tried to ensure parliamentary
and popular support for a policy already
decided upon, and if this was not possible, to
ensure that public opinion did not push British
policy along dangerous lines. The great powers
were concerned to maintain and possibly
extend their influence in particular spheres
while ensuring that rivals did not encroach. Yet
this competition was restrained because the
great powers were not prepared to use military
force against each other, even if they did against
other states, and because the balance of
power system established in 1815 enjoyed
legitimacy.[16]

The German and Italian crises were easily
managed by Prussia and Austria. The constitutional aspirations of the South German
states were crushed, showing the vulnerability
of small states. Britain's doctrine of nonintervention and Castlereagh's absence from
the Troppau Congress in late 1820 marked the
end of regular formal meetings of the five great
powers leaders. In Spain and the Balkans the
nature of restrained competition was most
evident. In Spain a military revolt had forced
the reintroduction of the liberal 1812 constitution. For three years the great powers
jockeyed for position. Then, in 1823, France
marched in to restore Ferdinand VII's autoc-

racy and forestall Russian intervention. The French did not seek territory, merely influence, but as it happened Ferdinand VII tended to rely more on Russian, than French, support. Small and medium states could be fickle. The Russians lent wavering support to the Greek revolt of the 1820s against Ottoman rule, eventually declaring war against the Ottomans in 1828. Britain and France intervened to aid the Greeks and to control Russian policy in the Balkans. All three powers guaranteed Greek independence in 1830, leading to the independent kingdom of Greece in 1832. Ultimately, Britain and France became the influential voices in Greece, not Russia. It is notable that the great powers tried to act multilaterally, or at the minimum to ensure that there was no significant opposition. Yet this was not due to a sense of European solidarity, but rather an acknowledgment that unilateral action could provoke a coalition. Within these limits, each power tried to extend its influence, though outcomes, as events in Spain and Greece demonstrated, were not always predictable and could be dependent on the foreign policy interests of those states.

The revolutions of 1830 showed the flexibility of the system. The new French regime was accepted, with Palmerston leading the way. The British doctrine that the territorial status quo, and not the domestic regime, mattered was accepted by the other powers. But the revolt in Belgium in the same year against William I, king of the Netherlands, showed that even the territorial status quo could alter. His appeals to the sanctity of the 1815 treaties went unheeded, an illustration of the primacy of power over law in international relations, and the vulnerability of small states in nineteenth-century diplomacy. Belgium's creation in 1831, bolstered by a guarantee of its neutrality by the great powers, was the destruction of one state (the Netherlands), as much as the formation of a new one. Belgian security was only important to the great powers because they feared that the Belgian revolutionaries might unite with France, damaging the territorial buffers of 1815. If the Concert of Europe was sufficiently flexible to accommodate Belgian independence, the new state proved a model of restraint, eschewing any aspirations towards union with France which would have meant

war. Belgian independence was preserved by the constellations of great power politics, rather than the flimsy treaty guarantees of 1831 to which no great power felt bound.[17]

Security concerns rather than ideological principles had dictated the policy of the three eastern and conservative great powers. Austria's and Russia's repression of revolts in Italy in 1830 and Poland in 1831 respectively showed that the spheres of influence marked out in 1815 were broadly respected. Prussia also fulfilled its role as guardian of the Rhineland against any possible French invasion in 1830, underlining the geopolitical shift of its priorities towards western Germany, which had taken place in 1815. The German Confederation could not play the defensive role assigned to it by the 1815 settlement. Military mobilization was dependent on the initiative of individual states, most notably Prussia. That state confirmed itself as the leading German power, while Austria had non-German commitments in Italy. The Third Germany looked to Prussia for protection against the potential French menace – the rights enshrined in treaties still depended on military force. It remained a balance of power system, not an equilibrium of rights and interests. Restraint was induced by calculations of power, spheres of influence, and grouping rather than an automatic respect for international treaties.

The 1830 revolutions appeared at first glance to have opened an ideological rift within Europe with three conservative eastern great powers facing liberal France and Britain. In 1833 Austria, Prussia, and Russia concluded a treaty allowing intervention in aid of any legitimate ruler against revolution. In 1834 France, Britain, Spain, and Portugal concluded the Quadruple Alliance. Yet ideology played little role in diplomacy in the 1830s.[18] Rather, what sparked this bout of alliance formation was a crisis in the Ottoman Empire when Russia supported the sultan against Mehmet Ali, the Egyptian leader. Austria, therefore, was more concerned with propping up the Ottoman Empire and the treaty was designed to control Russia. France and Austria flirted with each other, while Britain saw the Quadruple Alliance as a momentary agreement to restrain Russian policy towards the Ottoman Empire.

No great power wanted war, though one nearly did occur in 1840, again due to a Turkish–Egyptian crisis. While France was backing Mehmet Ali who was in a position to destroy the Ottoman Empire, the other four powers forced the Egyptians to surrender gains in Syria and Crete. The other powers faced down French threats and in July 1841 the great powers concluded the Straits Convention which closed the Black Sea to naval vessels in peacetime. Restraint characterized Russian, and eventually French, policy. The Vienna System had survived its final crisis before the 1848 revolutions. There had been no sustained evidence of respect for the 1815 treaties. Changes took place or did not take place because of power political relations. Power politics was also more important than ideological predispositions in the formation of foreign policy. There was, however, significant restraint in the foreign policies of the great powers. This was principally due to the practice of grouping which isolated disruptive states. Moreover, no state wanted war, since the domestic political risks were too great and the potential foreign policy gains were minimal. Finally, the spheres of influence were well drawn at Vienna, which meant that the only major area of friction was the Ottoman Empire. The stability of the Vienna System was guaranteed by the British and Russian preponderance of power, though it was power which could not easily be mobilized for aggressive purposes, since Russia lacked the financial strength and Britain had no standing army; if this was disrupted, it would open new political possibilities.

The Crimean Moment, 1848–1871

Between 1848 and 1871, five major wars occurred involving the great powers and two major new states, Italy and Germany, were created. This marked a radical change in the conduct of international relations. The relative weight of the great powers constantly shifted throughout this period, with France regaining a central role. The decline of British and Russian influence was the crucial systemic change. The subsequent disaggregation of

power in the international system enabled states to achieve revisionist goals. During this period, there were various versions of a new international system – a free trade order, pursued by Britain, which would have ensured its hegemony; a liberal order, based on nation-states and free trade, which Britain and France could have imposed after the Crimean War, but did not have sufficient interest in; and an order based on power politics and the *Machtstaat*, pursued by France, Prussia, and Piedmont-Sardinia.[19]

The 1848 revolutions represented a massive challenge to the territorial settlement of 1815, particularly in Central Europe where the formation of German, Hungarian, and Italian states became possible. The Concert of Europe demonstrated its continued strength in preventing any territorial change and averting a war between the great powers. This was partly due to the monarchical solidarity of the three eastern powers, though calculations of power relations played the decisive role. For the most part, the habits of grouping and restraint informed the foreign policies of the great powers, despite nationalist pressures.[20] Small states, such as Piedmont-Sardinia in Italy, which challenged the territorial order were left to pay the price, while those, like Belgium and Denmark, which sought the maintenance of the status quo were supported. The incentives during the international crisis were for restraint. Yet there was also evidence of flexibility. Statesmen were wiling to countenance change – such as the unification of Germany under Prussia – as long as it did not disrupt the balance of power. To this extent, the Concert system survived 1848 in terms of the principles of the behavior of the great powers.

Britain and Russia played a particularly important role in controlling the international consequences of the revolutions in their particular spheres of influence. Britain recognized another new French regime which signaled its conservative foreign policy by assuring Spain and Belgium of its peaceful intentions. Russia played a much more dramatic role in Central Europe where it suppressed a Hungarian revolt which threatened the Habsburg Empire. Austria was active in Italy, defeating Piedmont-Sardinia in 1848 and 1849. The most revisionist great power was Prussia. Prussia could have united Germany in 1848–9, had Frederick William IV shown more decisive leadership. While the great powers forced Prussia to back down after its invasion of Denmark in the summer of 1848, there was no active opposition to the proposals of the Frankfurt parliament to create a new *kleindeutsch* (small German) state. France looked on with some apprehension, but Britain would have seen a Prussian led, liberal Germany as a secure buffer between France and Russia. This was in keeping with the principle of non-interference in German affairs. However, Prussia failed to take the opportunity. On the other hand, the plans of the Austrian Chancellor Schwarzenberg for a Reich with a population of 70 million – it would have included the German Confederation and the non-German territories of Prussia and Austria – were opposed by France, Britain, and Russia as a violation of the balance of power. Therefore the spheres of influence and balance, created in 1815, were maintained.[21]

Historians have, however, argued that the 1848 revolutions marked the collapse of the Concert of Europe. A generation of hard-nosed realists, bent on national prestige and aggrandizement, came to the fore. They were willing to appeal to liberal and national sentiment to serve their own ends. Palmerston, Napoleon III, Schwarzenberg, and Bismarck are the principal examples. Alexander Cuza, the Romanian statesman, and Cavour, the prime minister of Piedmont-Sardinia, showed small states could also pursue *Realpolitik*.[22] Yet, as has been argued, states had continually pursued their own national interest since 1815. War once again became an instrument of policy, though why this was so remains an area for research. There had been mobilizations, war scares, and wars before 1848, so the reemergence of war as an instrument of policy was a gradual process. Issues such as German and Italian nationalism had been on the agenda since the 1820s, while none of the rivalries – Austro-French in Italy, Austro-Prussian in Germany, and Anglo-French in Belgium – were new. Equally, Napoleon III was one in a succession of French revisionist statesmen since 1815.

What was new was the radical transformation of the international system during the Crimean War, the central event of European diplomatic history in the nineteenth century. It resulted from blunder and miscalculation, a "somewhat bizarre" war, according to David Goldfrank, which saw France and Britain defeat Russia, and Napoleon III, a revisionist, emerge as the arbiter of European politics.[23] The initial crisis centered on the rights of Catholics and Orthodox Christians in the Ottoman Empire, rights which were represented by France and Russia, respectively. The crisis escalated, Russia occupied the Danubian Principalities, the Ottomans declared war on Russia in 1853, and in March 1854 France and Britain followed. There was more at stake than religious rights. The three great powers were most concerned about their influence in the Ottoman Empire, where they had economic, strategic, and ideological interests. Russia, reluctantly, believed that the collapse of the Ottoman Empire was imminent and was staking out its claim. Britain and France feared the dissolution of the Ottoman Empire and the growth of Russian influence, and this was more important than any domestic political pressure on Palmerston or Napoleon. Napoleon had an additional agenda; the destruction of the Holy Alliance between the three eastern great powers. While Prussian neutrality leaned towards Russia, Austria, fearful of the Russian occupation of the Danubian Principalities and growing influence in the Balkans, maintained a pro-western neutrality despite Nicholas I's rescue of the Habsburg monarchy in 1849. The competition for influence on the periphery of Europe, which had been restrained before 1854, was now decided by military force.

The war aims of the great powers were restrained, as the 1856 Peace of Paris demonstrated. Russia remained a great power, even if the Black Sea was demilitarized, making the Crimea vulnerable to further attack. The terms which ended the war were restrained, but the consequences were far-reaching and revolutionary. First, Russia lost its role as the arbiter of European politics, and like France, became a revisionist power. Britain had contained the Russian threat, but due to increased French power, was less influential in continental affairs.

Second, Napoleon had succeeded in ending the anti-French constellation in Europe.[24] Third, Austria now found itself isolated, and hence much more vulnerable in the Hungarian, Italian, and German questions. Fourth, Prussia was almost forced out of the Concert system in 1856, but it, like Piedmont-Sardinia which entered the Concert in 1856, profited most from the disaggregation of power in Europe. This was the final and most important consequence. The great powers had such a varied range of interests, and only Austria was unequivocally in favor of the status quo, that a reordering of Europe was highly probable. The grouping which had taken place in previous crises and had maintained peace could no longer take place. Restrained competition now extended to limited wars.

Napoleon III advocated the reorganization of Europe along nationalist lines, a position which he maintained despite the evident damage it would do to French security.[25] Neither a united Italy nor a united Germany could benefit France. Napoleon III concluded a secret treaty with Cavour, who sought to exploit Italian nationalist feeling to extend Piedmontese power against Austria in Lombardy-Venetia. Austria stumbled into war in the summer of 1859 and after two defeats by French forces arrived at a truce. The peace settlement saw France gain Savoy and Nice, and transfer Lombardy to Piedmont, which also gained Tuscany, Parma, Modena, and the Papal Marches in plebiscites. The proclamation of the Kingdom of Italy only occurred in 1861 after Garibaldi had invaded the Kingdom of Naples. Cavour used this opportunity, citing unrest, to invade the Papal States and then the Kingdom of Naples, both of which, with the exception of Rome, were amalgamated into the Kingdom of Italy. Yet France did not benefit from the unification of Italy. Napoleon III confirmed his reputation as an unreliable partner, leading to French isolation in the late 1860s. The disintegration of the Concert, the exposure of Austrian weaknesses, and the Piedmontese example put Prussia, despite its constitutional crisis, in a position to assume leadership within Germany.

Bismarck was appointed minister president in September 1862 at the height of the consti-

tutional crisis in Prussia. His foreign policy, however, was dictated by the international system and Prussia's search for security, not domestic political concerns. Too much focus on Bismarck does an injustice to the complexities of the 1860s. Europe was occupied with a series of crises and questions throughout the 1860s which opened the space for the unification of Germany under Prussian leadership.[26] Britain and France were distracted by the American Civil War and the Mexican Revolution, respectively. Closer to home, Napoleon's dependency on Catholic support prevented an alliance with Italy, while his interference in Polish revolt in Russia in 1863 increased his isolation. For the most part Russia concentrated on internal consolidation and modernization, and its primary foreign policy interest was in the Balkans. It slowly regained some of its influence there. In 1859 Cuza had united the Danubian Principalities in the *de facto* independent state of Romania, while in 1867 Turkish troops withdrew from Serbia. A lengthy crisis in Crete between 1866 and 1869 caused further friction between the great powers.

There were half-hearted attempts to prevent the three wars of German unification, but grouping strategies no longer worked. Constitutional reforms in Denmark sparked the first crisis over the position of Schleswig-Holstein. In 1848 Russia and Britain had supported the Danes, but in 1864 Prussia and Austria invaded Denmark unopposed. This was but momentary cooperation between the two German rivals and indeed their dual control over the two duchies was the excuse for conflict in 1866. The real issue, of course, was dominance in Germany. Bismarck was no doctrinaire warmonger; rather, he sought a diplomatic victory, but was prepared to use military force if necessary. In 1866 Austria either had to back down and effectively surrender its claim to parity with Prussia in Germany, or fight to retain the position. Bismarck had prepared for a military struggle by forging an alliance with Italy which would gain Venetia in the event of an Austrian defeat. Without French support, neither Britain nor Russia could intervene. To ensure nonintervention after victory in July 1866, Bismarck pursued limited aims, forming the North German Confederation under Prussian leadership. The Habsburgs lost Venetia, and the following year the Dual Monarchy, known as Austria-Hungary, was established when Hungary was given autonomy.

A number of historians have suggested that the 1866 settlement was more stable than that of 1871.[27] A stable balance of power existed within Europe, particularly between Prussia and France. The two wing powers, Britain and Russia, could tolerate the increase in Prussian power, and with Europe quiet, pursue domestic reforms and imperial expansion outside of Europe. The loss of overburdening responsibilities in Italy and Germany, and the internal domestic reforms, stabilized the Habsburg monarchy. Yet there were structural pressures, pointing towards conflict. France had not been compensated for the rapid increase in Prussian power. Moreover, the "Liberal Empire" made Napoleon's rule susceptible to domestic political pressure and prestige politics. Prussia's foreign policy situation had deteriorated with the recovery of Austria and increasing anti-Prussianism in southern Germany, while a potential constitutional crisis loomed.[28] Bismarck sought to use the Hohenzollern candidature for the Spanish throne as a means of forcing France into a diplomatic capitulation which would revive Prussia's international standing, or more likely a war which would decide which of the great powers was *primus inter pares*. The plan nearly misfired, but Bismarck's edited version of the Ems telegram sparked nationalist fury in France and a declaration of war. By September the Second Empire had collapsed. In January 1871 the German Reich, now including Bavaria, Baden, and Württemberg, was founded. Instead of great power intervention, Russia took the opportunity to revise the Black Sea clauses and Italy seized Rome to complete unification.

The New Stability, 1871–1890

In 1871 it was not clear that the great powers had fought their final conflict until 1914. Bismarck instigated a war scare in 1875 to thwart French recovery. He received an important rebuke from Russia and Britain, which acted as a guarantee of France's post-1871 position. This marked the stabilization of the international order.[29] With the exception of France, all the great powers accepted their position after 1871. The international order enjoyed a legitimacy, not evident since 1854, and the status quo was maintained by German power and French isolation. Arguably the balance of power was destroyed by Germany's absorption of the South German states and consequent semi-hegemonic position, but the threat to the order could only come from a weakened France. This was the most important feature of the international system until the early 1890s, when Germany's position among the great powers began to deteriorate. The basis of the new system was *Machtpolitik*. After 1815 calculations of power had been fundamental to international politics, but this was made much more explicit in the 1850s and 1860s. Military power acted as a deterrent and induced restraint, rather than provoking war.

Despite the war scare of 1875, Bismarck pursued a peace policy throughout his two decades as chancellor. Rainer Lahme suggested Bismarck changed from a Cavour into a Metternich, though without the same legitimizing mission as the Austrian statesman.[30] He realized that the maintenance of the European balance of power and German security were two sides of the same coin. This was similar to the Vienna order when national interest and European stability were overlapping concerns. However, Bismarck's Germany was far more powerful than Metternich's Austria, and therefore better equipped to maintain stability. Against that, Bismarck's room for diplomatic maneuver was considerably more limited. French antagonism was a given, and he struggled to control latent Austro-Russian antagonism in the Balkans. In addition to Bismarck's central role after 1870, it should be noted that the history of international relations in this period did not begin and end with the German chancellor. Other states had important interests which limited Bismarck's options. The influence of the wing powers, decisive up to 1848 but dormant since the end of the Crimean War, had revived. There may have been six great powers, but three of these – Britain, Russia, and Germany – were genuinely independent.

The limits of Bismarck's control were amply illustrated in the Eastern crisis which began in 1875 with a revolt against Ottoman rule in Bosnia-Herzegovina. This spread quickly, but the Ottomans were able to suppress it. Yet old questions about the stability of Ottoman rule had resurfaced and created the conditions for a crisis. The question of Europe's duty to defend Christians in the Ottoman Empire, enshrined in the 1856 Peace of Paris, gave them an opportunity to intervene. This was related to competition for influence at the court of the Pforte, notably between Russia and Britain. Attempts to reach an agreed European settlement by imposing reforms on the Ottomans failed, with Britain opposing any settlement which would restore Russian influence in the region. Russia, following agreement with Austria, declared war on Turkey. Although the war did not run smoothly, Russia imposed the Treaty of San Stefano on Turkey in March 1878, but its terms violated the Austro-Russian understanding of the previous year – the creation of a large, independent Bulgaria, effectively a Russian satellite state. Neither Austria nor Britain was prepared to tolerate independent Russian solutions to the Eastern Question. A show of British naval force and the exhaustion of the Russian military forced new negotiations which took place at the Congress of Berlin in 1878. Bulgaria was greatly reduced, diminishing Russia's influence in the Balkans. Austria, on the other hand, occupied Bosnia-Herzegovina, though these provinces remained under the sultan's sovereignty, while Britain secured its position in the eastern Mediterranean with Cyprus. The settlement satisfied everyone, save Russia and Bulgaria. This put enormous pressure on Bismarck's position. He believed that the diversion of conflict to the periphery, as happened in the Eastern crisis where Germany had no vital interests, would increase German security. It had not, Russia felt it had been betrayed, and the contradictions in Germany's efforts to maintain good relations simultaneously with Russia and Austria were exposed.

Bismarck tried to improve Germany's position by establishing a network of defensive alliances. In 1879 he concluded the Dual Alliance with Austria, in 1881 the League of the Three Emperors was revived, and in 1882 Italy joined Germany and Austria in the Triple Alliance. However, it was the emergence of imperial rivalries which eased the pressure on Germany. The Mediterranean was the site of early imperial rivalries between Italy, France, and Britain. In 1881 France occupied Tunis, a blow to Italian prestige. The following year a nationalist crisis in Egypt threatened British and French interests in the Suez Canal. Plans for a joint intervention broke down, and without the sanction of the Concert of Europe, Gladstone ordered the occupation of Egypt. Strategic interests, as well as the investments of the City of London, influenced the British decision.[31] Yet the improvement in Britain's strategic position was outweighed by its reduced room for maneuver. Egypt clouded Anglo-French relations for two decades, and made Britain more dependent on German goodwill. In addition to imperial rivalries with France, Britain faced an expanding Russia in Central Asia. Imperial rivalries were not separate from the European balance of power; rather, they were an accretion to it.[32] France, in particular, could only pursue an expansive imperial strategy, largely in the service of national prestige, if it was freed from fear of German attack. France also faced a European and imperial rival in Italy. Smaller imperial powers, notably Belgium and the Netherlands, also had interconnected European and imperial interests, keenly watching the development of Anglo-German relations.[33]

Bismarck viewed imperial projects in a strategic, not an economic, light. He made a second attempt to divert European rivalries to the periphery and create more room for maneuver. Anglo-French rivalry would lead both powers to seek German friendship. Bismarck approached Jules Ferry, French prime minister, on the basis of opposition to Britain's annexation of land without any effective occupying power. This led to a conference at Berlin in 1884–5 where France, Britain, and Germany were the main actors. The conference sanctioned the two contradictory principles of free trade and effective administration. Ultimately, paying for administration led to special trading rights for the country doing the administering. By the end of the conference, the

Franco-German détente, built on colonial matters, collapsed. However, it was replaced by an increasingly close Anglo-German relationship, which was reinforced by the Mediterranean Agreements of 1887 when Austria and Italy, Germany's two main allies, agreed with Britain to maintain the status quo in the Balkans.

Stability in the Balkans was threatened by the Bulgarian crisis, which was part of a major systemic crisis between 1885 and 1887.[34] French and Russian rivalry with Britain in the imperial sphere remained serious, while Franco-German antagonism flared up in a brief war scare in 1887. However, the most important crisis arose in Bulgaria, where Russia had lost control over its client state, a demonstration of the independence of small states if the balance of power favored them. Alexander of Battenburg, Prince of Bulgaria, sought to unite the two parts of Bulgaria separated in 1878 and received British and Austrian support. This provoked a crisis within the Balkans, where Serbia mobilized, fearing that its position within the local balance of power would be undermined. Within the general European balance of power there was a small state balance in the Balkans. With British and Austrian support, Bulgaria managed to avoid Russian occupation. British support for Austria did not save Bismarck from Russian accusations that Germany had let their old ally down for a second time in a major crisis in the Balkans. Within Russia there was a debate over whether to seek an alliance with France, or continue with Germany. This was Bismarck's nightmare. He rejected arguments in favor of a preventive war in 1887 against either France or Russia, and he also warned Austria that the Dual Alliance was defensive. Instead, he concluded the Reinsurance Treaty with Russia in late 1887, which supported Russian influence at Constantinople. It did not contradict his other alliances and it perpetuated the isolation of France. The resolution of the multiple crises of 1885–7 has been called a "triumph of diplomacy" by A. J. P. Taylor. There had been a real possibility of war – war scares and mobilizations peppered the crises. While war was avoided, none of the sources of conflict had been resolved. Nor did Bismarck's diplomatic strategy of diverting conflict to the periphery have any long-term prospects of success. It had worked in the imperialist case, but not in the Balkan one.

By the end of Bismarck's reign as chancellor, potential new power blocs were emerging and military power was playing an increasingly important role in deterrence. Britain was now associated with Germany through the Mediterranean Agreements with Italy and Austria. Russia and France had Britain as a common rival, and at times of isolation, Russian leaders considered the possibility of an alliance with France. Critics have charged that Bismarck resorted to a system of stopgap measures which were increasingly tortuous. Klaus Hildebrand has accepted that Bismarck's room for maneuver had reduced since 1871, but noted that contradictions are evident in any foreign policy system.[35] The strengths and weaknesses of the international system were one and the same by the late 1880s. Military force could lead to a massive conflagration, but because of this, the great powers were less likely to risk it. Bismarck prevailed over his general staff, while Boulanger was forced out by realistic French leaders. New conflicts emerged, especially in the imperial sphere, while the Balkans had been the site of the two major crises of the period. Yet the multiple conflicts paradoxically increased the flexibility of the system. For instance, Anglo-French antagonism in the imperial sphere was balanced by British support for French great power status in Europe.

The Maintenance of Peace, the Origins of War, 1890–1914

Imperialist expansion and crises have long been cited as a major cause of World War I.[36] Anglo-German competition resulted from imperial and naval expansion, while other rivalries were exacerbated. Yet imperial policies could also stabilize the European states system. First, it provided an outlet for expansion. France used its empire, much of which was useless in economic terms, to buttress its great power position within Europe. Smaller powers could also develop large empires, though the loss of empire in the case of Spain at the end of the

1890s could provoke a crisis of confidence. Second, overseas crises were never likely to provoke a European war. Only Russia went to war over colonies and that was against Japan, not believed to be a great power. To a certain extent, overseas crises such as the Anglo-French crisis at Fashoda in 1898 provided a school for conflict resolution. Third, ententes could be formed on the back of resolved crises. Imperial security was based on compromise, flexibility, and mutual concessions, all ingredients of a stable international system.

Aggressive nationalism is associated with imperialist expansion and rivalry. It has been argued that governments, looking for domestic political approval, followed excessively aggressive policies. However, the evidence for this is limited. First, some statesmen shared the assumptions of pressure groups such as the navy, imperial and army leagues which emerged in European states before 1914. British leaders could spot the German naval threat without the Navy League's helpful advice. Second, statesmen rarely started from the domestic political point of view when making foreign policy. The conditions of the international system, rather than domestic political pressures, dominated the memoranda of the foreign offices of the era. Third, statesmen were far more conciliatory than the pressure groups. Fourth, statesmen did not adopt a consistent ideological approach to foreign policy. Pan-Slavism only featured on the tsarist agenda when it suited Russia's geopolitical needs. The problem with occasionally playing to the gallery was that it could feed popular appetite for a more aggressive policy. The way in which popular opinion contributed to frictions in the international system was more subtle than a direct impact on the formulation of foreign policy. Governments paid close attention to press campaigns in rival states and assumed that aggressive press opinion did reflect the foreign policies of other states. In this way, popular opinion shaped foreign perceptions of a country's policy, feeding, for example, beliefs that Germany was an inveterately aggressive military state.[37]

Peripheral conflicts had been the central element of European politics until 1908. At first glance the major characteristic of the international system since 1890 was the creation of two power blocs, the Triple Alliance between Austria, Germany, and Italy and the Dual Alliance between France and Russia. The latter was reinforced by ententes with Britain in 1904 and 1907. This threatened to establish a bipolar system, reducing the flexibility of the international system and making general conflict more likely. It also made life very uncomfortable for small powers caught between the great powers, such as Serbia, Denmark, and Belgium. The major crises between 1908 and 1914 turned into ritual and dangerous confrontations between each bloc. However, recent research qualifies this picture in important ways. First, the two blocs made each great power more secure. Poincaré believed that any perceived disintegration of either bloc might lead one power to strike out of fear for its deteriorating position. Second, within each bloc, states could act to restrain their partners. In particular, Germany and Britain performed this function by restraining weaker partners. Third, there was cooperation across blocs, and they were far more permeable than their critics recognized. There were Franco-German, Anglo-German, and Austro-Russian détentes, to name but some developments before 1914. Secure within their own bloc, powers could cooperate with potential enemies. This was a difficult balance to strike, because if there was too much cooperation, it could lead to Poincaré's feared disintegration of the blocs.[38]

The militarization of international relations was another feature which allegedly caused the outbreak of war. Military leaders were too influential, overruling their diplomatic counterparts. However, this did not happen on a regular basis. The July crisis of 1914 was the sole occasion. Wolfgang Mommsen has pointed to a "topos of inevitable war" in the years before 1914. Yet the grave predictions about the nature of the next war – vast loss of life, revolution, the end of civilization – made statesmen extremely reluctant to resort to military force. The "myth of the short war" was not widely shared before 1914. In the light of the resolved crises before 1914, Friedrich Kießling has identified a "topos of the avoided war." Military power could act as a deterrent, as it had done with relative effectiveness since 1815. The decisive factors in the explanation of crises outcomes were the interaction between the behavior of the blocs and the respective weight given to diplomatic and military crisis management.

The Russo-Japanese war of 1904–5 produced a major change in the international system. First, Britain and France feared getting dragged into war on behalf of their allies, and concluded an entente which also removed the major points of friction between these two states in Morocco and Egypt. Second, Russia was temporarily removed as a power factor, increasing French insecurity. When Russia returned to international politics, it pursued a conciliatory policy, concluding an entente with Britain in 1907 to resolve differences in Central Asia. It also cooperated with Austria over Balkan policy, at least initially. Third, Germany's efforts to exploit the momentary weakness of the Dual Alliance by threatening France in Morocco backfired and gave the Anglo-French entente a continental dimension. Fourth, the gravity of international politics returned to the European continent, ending the safety valve of imperialist expansion. The Bosnian crisis of 1908–9 demonstrates the contingent nature of international politics. It stemmed from an Austro-Russian deal to cooperate in the Balkans. Austria could annex Bosnia and Herzegovina, which it had occupied since 1878, and in return it would support Russian policy on the Straits. The deal was botched, due to the incompetence and bad faith of both parties. After Austria had annexed the provinces, Russia decided to call for an international conference. Germany sensed Russia's military weakness and the reluctance of her two allies to fight over the Balkans. Germany supported Austria's actions and promised to back its diplomatic stance with military power. This proved a decisive deterrent. Compromise was not necessary in this dispute because the military preponderance of one bloc was so overwhelming. Although it did leave Russia bitter, it did not predetermine policy in any future crisis. Indeed, in 1910, William II and Nicholas II met at Potsdam, causing a flurry of speculation that the Three Emperors' League was about to be revived and it was only at the last moment that Russia failed to ratify the agreement.

If it is possible to date the start of the French revolutionary wars to 1787 because it produced the systemic crisis which culminated in war in 1792, then a case could be made that the systemic crisis which led to World War I originated with a revolt against the sultan of Morocco and French military intervention to protect him in May 1911. Germany, fearing that meek acceptance of this violation of the 1906 Algeciras agreements which had ended the first Moroccan crisis would be a major blow to its prestige, banked on a demonstration of strength. Germany did not want war, but it did adopt a warlike stance. Britain signaled its support for France. Historians have questioned whether Britain's interests were served by a balance of power policy, or indeed whether this was its real interest, noting that Britain had to constantly appease its major imperial rivals, France and Russia. Yet the trend of British foreign policy since 1870 had been to oppose any changes in the European balance of power. Nor can the imperial and continental elements of British policy be easily disentangled. Because the continent was the fulcrum of the global balance of power, power shifts there would automatically affect the security of the British Empire.[39] Germany was forced to accept meager compensation in the French Congo in return for French control of Morocco.

French gains in Morocco triggered Italy's decision to seize Tripoli, which led to war with the Ottoman Empire. There was a certain feeling of recklessness as Italy, the least of the great powers, desperately sought to maintain that status with a prestige policy. There was also genuine rivalry with France in the Mediterranean. Italy's action endangered the Ottoman Empire. This confounded the other great powers who, aware of potential unrest in the Balkans, had a tacit understanding to prop up the "sick man of Europe." Italy did not achieve a decisive victory in North Africa and the war spread. The weakening position of the Ottoman Empire led to the creation of the Balkan League, supported by Russia, in the summer of 1912. Bulgaria, Greece, Montenegro, and Serbia conducted a successful war against the Ottomans in autumn 1912 and were only restrained by united great power action. A second war between the Balkan states in 1913 left Bulgaria considerably weakened, while Serbia had doubled its territory and population within two years. The shift within the Balkan balance of power damaged the position of the Triple Alliance. Italy was regarded as an unstable partner by Austria and Germany and both of these were beginning to entertain doubts about the other's support. Austria, now behaving like a Balkan state rather than a great power, was forced to shift its military focus to Serbia. Germany, however, had been relying on a significant Austrian contribution to hold off any Russian attack while the German army dealt with France. Austria also felt that Germany had been too ready to compromise Austrian interests in the Balkans. Therefore, the series of crises after 1911 caused a feeling of vulnerability in Berlin and Vienna, and encouraged a belief that it would be best to strike before any further deterioration. On this reading the July crisis was seized upon as the last chance.

A study of 33 crises between 1856 and 1914 argues that the increasingly crisis-ridden international system was almost bound to end in general war.[40] Yet an examination of the period 1911–14 can lead to a very different conclusion. A new system, based on détente, was emerging. The significance of the crises in this period is that they did *not* lead to war, that the international system had developed mechanisms to resolve crises. In the late 1780s this had not been the case. Even before the Moroccan crisis there had been talk of a Franco-German détente. Before 1914 diplomats emphasized improving relations between Germany and Britain, Austria and Russia, and France and Germany. Agreements were reached on questions such as the Portuguese Empire between Germany and Britain. The First Balkan War saw cooperation across the blocs and the return of the Concert mechanism. A conference of ambassadors met in London to resolve the borders of the new Serbia which was pushing towards the Adriatic Sea. Austria opposed this, and the great powers, with the exception of Russia, sent ships to the Adriatic to force the Serbs to back down. Russia advised Serbia to do so through diplomatic channels. Although the Concert was not used to resolve the Second Balkan War, Austria was again able to prevent Serbian access to the sea. All the major diplomatic crises within Europe since 1878 had been resolved without war. The resolution of crises is as significant as their occurrence.

The questions about the July crisis must focus on the differences from previous crises resolution. The impact of domestic political crisis has been vastly exaggerated. Britain, rather than Germany, the oft-cited example of the crisis-ridden domestic polity seeking refuge in war, was facing considerably greater constitutional issues, possibly even civil war and mutiny over the Irish question. The first crucial difference in 1914 was the failure of Germany to restrain Austria, and of Britain to restrain Russia and France. In other words, there was a return to bloc confrontations. In 1909 and 1911 one side had been forced to back down, not wanting to risk war. In 1914 military measures on both sides, particularly in Germany and Russia, placed too much pressure on possible diplomatic resolutions. There were voices urging negotiation and a return to the Concert methods, but brinksmanship, especially in Berlin, where it was believed until July 29 that the Russians would back down due to the lack of British, and hence French, support, put paid to those hopes. Having seen their positions deteriorate in the first half of 1914 and mistakenly fearing further decline, Germany and Austria sought a diplomatic victory against Russia and the defeat of Serbia, rather than compromise. Miscalculation, based on an optimistic overestimation of one's own resources, had led to war in 1792; in 1914, it was a pessimistic miscalculation about the future that informed policy decisions.

New Directions in the Study of International History

Although diplomatic history is the oldest form of historical writing, important areas of research remain. New questions have been posed, and venerable methodologies revived. Three in particular come to mind. Probably the most significant publication on international history in recent times is Paul Schroeder's *The Transformation of European Politics*.[41] He argues that international history has to take account of "systemic rules" and "structural limits." The understandings which underpinned statesmen's policies in the nineteenth century, according to Schroeder, were radically transformed at the Congress of Vienna, and a far greater respect for treaties and international law predominated. This has been the starting point for numerous studies on the Concert period up to 1848. Kießling's work examines the systemic rules and statesmen's perceptions of détente before 1914 in a similar vein.[42] Yet with some exceptions the period between the Crimean War and World War I has not received the same attention given to the Concert era.

A second, and related, area of research is into the mentalities which informed statesmen's approaches to foreign policy. For example, the "topos of inevitable war" has received considerable attention. Sönke Neitzel has written on the idea of "world empires" – that the international system would be dominated by three or four global empires – Russia, the United States, Britain, and possibly Germany – in the twentieth century.[43] Further research will lead to a better understanding of the "hidden assumptions" of statesmen, such as peace, the nature of prestige, and the fear of revolution. There is greater cross-pollination between diplomatic historians and their colleagues in other areas, such as cultural and social history, which has benefited diplomatic history. Equally, international history can be brought back into the state and society.

Third, an older methodology, the primacy of foreign policy, can show how international politics affected the development of societies and domestic politics.[44] Issues such as state formation, national identity, and the modernization process could all benefit from an acquaintance with the international context. The primacy of foreign versus domestic politics continues to inform many studies of international relations. They offer a starting point for research into the foreign policies of individual states. Although the use of the primacy of foreign policy is most prevalent in German historiography, it can be applied to other states.

If the history of international relations has long lost its dominant place in the profession, it has experienced a revival in recent times. A number of series, such as *Origins of Modern Wars*, *Krieg in der Geschichte*, and *Studien zur internationalen Geschichte*, bear witness to this renewed interest. There remain important areas for primary source research, particularly the foreign policies of the small states and their place in the international system. Research on nineteenth-century international relations will be informed by the new work on the international system and its rules, an interest in the mentalities of the decision makers, and the continuing debate between advocates of the primacy of foreign and domestic politics. As well as seeking out the origins of wars, historians need to examine the construction and maintenance of the largely peaceful nineteenth-century international system.

NOTES

1   Wehler (1985).
2   Jelavich (1991); Heydemann (1995).
3   Bartlett (1996).
4   Schroeder (1994); see also Baumgart (1999).
5   Blanning (1986).
6   Dufraisse and Kerautret (1999); Dwyer (2001b).
7   Kruger (1991).
8   Wentker (2002); Neri (1997); Dülffer (2002a).
9   Krüger (1991); Albrecht-Carrié (1968); Langhorne (1981); Doering-Manteuffel (1991).
10 Schroeder (1994: 575–82); Soutou (2000); Conze (2001); Pyta (1996).
11 Heydemann (1995: 348–59); Holbraad (1970).
12 Simms (1998: 108).
13 Marcowitz (2001).
14 Gruner (1992); Schroeder (1986).
15 Hartley (1994: 132–6, 156–9); Jelavich (1991: 27–41).
16 Angelow (1996: 26–32).
17 Lademacher (1973, 1974).
18 Schroeder (1986: 712).
19 Doering-Manteuffel (2000).
20 Schulz (2003).
21 Mosse (1958: 13–50).
22 Baumgart (1999: 156–7); Doering-Manteuffel (1991: 8–10); Conze (2001: 235–41).

23 Goldfrank (1999); see also Baumgart (2000).
24 Stauch (1996).
25 Echard (1984).
26 Mosse (1958); Kolb (1987).
27 Hildebrand (1995: 13–24); Schroeder (2000).
28 Becker (2003); Wetzel (2001).
29 Hillgruber (1979: 35–52).
30 Lahme (1990: 13–14).
31 Robinson and Gallagher (1968).
32 Dülffer (2002b); Wesseling (1988); Langhorne (1981: 21–8).
33 See the contributions to Förster, Mommsen, and Robinson (1988).
34 Dülffer, Kröger, and Wippich (1997: 369–407).
35 Hildebrand (1990).
36 Joll (1992: 174–96).
37 Rosenberger (1998); Mommsen (1973).
38 Keiger (1983).
39 Wilson (1985).
40 Dülffer, Kröger, and Wippich (1997).
41 Schroeder (1994).
42 Kießling (2002).
43 Neitzel (2000).
44 For a review of recent literature, see Simms (2003).

GUIDE TO FURTHER READING

Taylor's *Struggle for Mastery in Europe, 1848–1918* and Schroeder's *Transformation of European Politics, 1763–1848*, both part of the Oxford History of Modern Europe series, provide excellent and detailed introductions, though they are separated by forty years, style, and most importantly, approach. The Concert of Europe, and debates about its nature, is one of the central themes of the nineteenth century. It is well covered by Albrecht-Carrié, *The Concert of Europe* and Holbraad, *The Concert of Europe*. Two contrasting views on the impulses behind foreign policy are offered by Wehler, *The German Empire* and Simms, *Struggle for Mastery in Germany*. Renouvin and Duroselle have written on the structures of international relations in *Introduction to the History of International Relations*. Excellent surveys of individual countries include Jelavich's *Russia's Balkan Entanglements*, Chamberlain's *Pax Britannica?*, Keiger's *France and the Origins of the First World War*, Lowe and Marzari's *Italian Foreign Policy, 1870–1940*, and Sked's *Decline and Fall of the Habsburg Empire*.

CHAPTER THIRTY-ONE

War

UTE FREVERT

The long nineteenth century began and ended in conflict. The wars that marked its beginning and end were both modern conflicts. Compared to their forerunners they followed a different logic and were fought by different types of soldiers. More importantly they breached the traditional boundary between military and civilian society. In effect, the nineteenth century saw a modernization of warfare, both in theory and in practice.

This modernization of war was a multidimensional phenomenon which affected the ideological interpretation and political legitimation of military conflicts as well as their social contexts, their economic and technical preparation, and their execution. The nineteenth century set new standards and introduced changes which had repercussions right into the late twentieth century. In one sense, however, the nineteenth century was consistent with the traditions of the early modern period: war was carried out then, as before, as the preserve of state powers. This continuity is more apparent when compared to recent events. The emergence of new military protagonists since September 11, 2001 has weakened the importance of states as primary military opponents. New players have emerged, both internal – one thinks of the role of rival warlords in Afghanistan and Somalia – and external – such as Al Qaieda.

The Nationalization of War

Since the early modern period the sovereignty of states had been based upon their rulers' ability to declare war and to mount military operations against other states. The early modern state, which, on the European continent, was often absolutist, had acquired the "monopoly of legitimate physical violence" in a long and conflict-ridden process.[1] A standing army allowed a state to exercise this authority both externally and internally against its own population. The military was the instrument of domination for absolutist princes. The prince set the army in motion, defined its goals, and ended its actions. Wars were planned in cabinet by the closest circle of advisors to the ruler. The majority of soldiers who fought them were mercenaries, often recruited from abroad. The indigenous population were neither asked for its opinion nor informed of the progress of these conflicts; its taxes merely flowed into the war chests and financed the war effort.

By the end of the eighteenth century this style of cabinet war came to an end, at least in France. The French Revolution destroyed not only the political system of the *ancien régime*, but also the traditional logic of warfare. The nation was appointed as the highest sovereign power and the decision over war and peace was placed in the hands of the people and their elected representatives. Coupled to these momentous changes was the hope that war would henceforth be conducted less arbitrarily. It was believed that wars of aggression would be consigned to the past and that wars would be fought for defensive purposes alone. The German philosopher Immanuel Kant allowed himself the "sweet dream" of eternal peace in 1795. Republican, constitutional states, in which citizens themselves were allowed to decide between war and peace, would *per se* be more peaceful than despotic regimes, whose rulers chose war "as a form of entertainment." Out of rational individual interest citizens would naturally opt for peaceful settlement over conflict. Above all their "commercial spirit" would inescapably lead them to renounce war.[2]

Yet even during Kant's lifetime this reasoning was shown to have shaky foundations. Since 1792, the Paris National Assembly had voted for war on numerous occasions. Although this could still be legitimized as defensive in view of neighboring states' fierce opposition, the situation changed dramatically once Napoleon gained control of France's foreign policy. His plan for Europe, garnished with the revolutionary rhetoric of emancipation, was based on conquest, not defense. All of Europe, from Spain to Russia, was to be subject to French hegemony. Hundreds of thousands of soldiers willingly followed their charismatic commander to increase France's glory and to spread the blessings of the Revolution to all European peoples – with or against their will.

Both officially and in retrospect, Napoleon justified this ambitious campaign as France's mission to establish the idea of national self-determination on the European continent. Just as the French nation had declared its sovereignty, so too should the Spaniards, Italians, Germans, and Poles have the chance to liberate themselves from absolutist rule and to regulate their political affairs according to their own discretion. Thus, Napoleon counted on the support of social groups and movements, which had worked toward a strengthening of national interests and identities since the middle of the eighteenth century. "Nation" here took on a double meaning. It meant not only a community of free citizens, but also the solidarity of people who felt bound through a common language, customs, and traditions.

The latter meaning applied above all to Italy and Germany, where state and national borders did not correspond. Also Poland, which had altogether lost its statehood in the late eighteenth century, suited the Napoleonic project of national rebirth and self-determination. Every nation, so the promise went, possessed the right to its own state and this right would be granted with the help of French soldiers.

Yet, as events in Italy were soon to show, Napoleon's troops primarily aimed to establish either direct or indirect rule over the conquered and occupied regions rather than founding independent nation-states. Some regions were simply annexed and directly absorbed into the French state. Others, such as the German states of the Confederation of the Rhine, remained formally independent and were allowed to enrich and expand themselves at the cost of weaker neighbors. At the same time, though, they enjoyed the "protection" of France, were bound to its domestic and foreign policy, and had to raise soldiers and revenue for Napoleon's wars of conquest.

For the general population this appeared at first to repeat a familiar pattern. Once again they were involuntarily involved in warfare, had to accommodate and feed foreign troops, pay contributions, raise soldiers, and pledge allegiance to a new ruler. However, Napoleon had more in store: constitutional proposals, administrative reforms, and a new Civil Code. In some areas, his armies were thus initially feted as liberators. Silesian farmers hoped for an end to feudalism, while the citizens of Berlin observed with malicious glee the humiliation of the much-hated Prussian officer corps. Generally, however, this positive mood of expectation did not last long. The national rhetoric pedaled by the French forces of occupation was soon turned against them. Native politicians and officials seized upon it and, supported by a corona of intellectuals and journalists, mobilized the people for an insurrection against the "foreigners."[3]

This was now indeed a revolutionary project, devised and led by declared anti-revolutionaries. In order to drive the French from the country every means was justified, even when this meant imitating them. European dynastic rulers had been deeply skeptical and distrustful of national slogans, tainted as they were with the scent of civil participation and critique of absolutism. Ambitious reformers, however, now convinced the monarchs to make these slogans their own in an effort to rally the people against the enemy. The Prussian king even promised a constitution, and the notion of "subjects" disappeared to make room for that of "citizens." Simultaneously, the concept of the "nation" considerably broadened to encompass not merely the immediate homeland, such as Prussia, Bavaria, or Hamburg, but also all those who spoke the same language and shared a common cultural canon (history, literature, music, architecture, art, Christian religion). In this interpretation the war of liberation against Napoleon had at least two goals. The first was to reestablish the sovereign rights of formerly occupied or "protected" states. The second was to unite the whole "nation" and to overcome its fragmentation.

In the view of Italian and German "patriots" this fragmentation was territorial in nature, while the British saw it as predominantly social and confessional. In Britain, which was successfully defended from the Napoleonic land-grab, the long, drawn-out conflict was likewise conducted under national banners. The rhetoric of national unity, which sought to bridge political, social, religious, and gender differences, was strong and influential. Although it was initially supported and developed, above all, by middle-class and aristocratic circles, it increasingly included people from the lower orders. Patriotic songs, pamphlets, and poems were widely circulated and evoked feelings of solidarity that had an intensity not hitherto seen.[4]

Another new phenomenon was the visible manner in which the concept of dynastic patriotism was widened and democratized. While the Fatherland had been congruent with the dominion of the ruler as *pater patriae* in the early modern period, it now developed into the property of the population. It belonged to all, and therefore expected from all, the same devotion, love, and passion. Patriotism was elevated at the same time to a political duty, to a passport to citizenship, and was staged through a variety of symbolic and rhetorical means. The borderlines between "fatherland" and "nation"

were therefore fluid; already by the early nineteenth century both terms were often used synonymously.

Patriotic-national emotions appeared for the first time with widespread and excessive force within the context of the revolutionary wars as well as their Napoleonic and anti-Napoleonic sequels. Not only were French soldiers guided by nationalist slogans; the counter-mobilization also occurred through recourse to tropes of the love for the Fatherland and national unity. When the nation or Fatherland encompassed all citizens, it was obvious that all would be intoxicated by its greatness, its strength, and its dignity. The national project was a common one, from which no one was to be excluded – especially not when the nation found itself at war. This demand for inclusion was expressed, most compellingly, in the famous law of August 1793 which called all French people to the *levée en masse*: "Young men will go off to fight; married men will forge weapons and transport food supplies; women will make tents and clothing and will provide the service in hospitals; children will shred old linen; old men will be taken to the public squares to offer encouragement to the warriors and to preach the hatred of kings and the unity of the Republic."[5]

Such fervent rhetoric, modeled on classical examples, was based as much on exclusion as inclusion. The appeal to republican unity was accompanied by a hatred of anyone who tried to disturb it. In 1793 it was the monarchies of the First Coalition and their aristocratic sympathizers in France itself that threatened to upset this unity. The greater the real or supposed threat was, the stronger the emotions and the closer the national bond among those who felt threatened. A similar tendency was visible two decades later east of the Rhine. The speeches, leaflets, and pamphlets that agitators such as Ernst Moritz Arndt and others used to call for struggle against Napoleon were permeated with hate. Every form of invective was available to describe the French, from "vain" and "slavish" to "thieving," "debauched," and "cruel." They were fiends, who were not only to be fought, but were also to be hated and despised. In contrast, "Teutonic men" were to bear themselves "honestly," "honorably," and "free" and stand side by side as "brothers" in the struggle for the common Fatherland.[6]

This new language of the nation not only bound its members together; it also distinguished them from enemies, who were likewise "nationalized" and grouped into stereotyped collectives. This construction of identity was formulated with utmost clarity in Arndt's famous poem "The German Fatherland." Arndt wrote: "There is the German Fatherland / Where fury exterminates French trash / Where every Frenchman is called foe / Where every German is called friend."[7] Fraternal friendship within; hostile, fury-filled demarcation without: this was the recipe for national self-discovery as it was praised and practiced between 1792 and 1815 in many European countries. The war would become doubly nationalized: it was an expression of international enmity and a form of national self-attestation. In the "people's war" (Arndt) the nation found itself united. It was through warfare that the territorial, political, and cultural identity of the nation would be asserted and sometimes created for the very first time.

This close association between the nation and war, established in the late eighteenth and early nineteenth centuries, remained characteristic of future developments. Admittedly, the anti-Napoleonic wars did not fill all the high-flying expectations attached to them as projects of national unity and self-determination. Neither Polish and German, nor Italian patriots received a nation-state, since the Holy Alliance of conservative monarchs, which reordered Europe's power system after 1815, pronounced themselves decisively against nationalist enthusiasm. For many reasons they regarded the growing nationalist movements as a danger to the political stability of the continent and sought to banish them by force.

The events of 1848, however, showed that these attempts at repression had failed. In Italy, Germany, and the Habsburg Empire movements for social, political, and national emancipation merged to form an explosive mix. The revolutions in Vienna, Prague, Budapest, Milan, and Berlin all contained a national message which threatened domestic political arrangements and added to their militancy. During the process of radicalization, all hopes that nation-states could develop peacefully and consensually were shattered. Too many different interests collided for this to become a reality. Wherever national movements were directed against foreign occupation, violent action virtually appeared the only solution. The 1820s and 1830s had already provided Europe with a foretaste of things to come. In Greece, then a part of the Ottoman Empire, rebels had been fighting since 1821 for national independence. Not only did volunteers from all over Europe hurry to help them, so too did warships from France, Britain, and Russia. They were instrumental in deciding the outcome of the conflict, which culminated in the foundation of a sovereign Greek state in 1830. Polish officers who rebelled against Russian rule in Warsaw in the same year were less successful. Although they managed to put the Russian prince to flight and establish a national government, it was dissolved a year later by tsarist troops. The latter were supported by the monarchs in Vienna and Berlin, for whom an independent Poland was a thorn in their conservative sides.

Although the Poles, despite repeated rebellions, were unable to free themselves from Russian, Prussian, and Austrian rule, the Greek victory served as a bright example for national movements in other European countries. That wars must be accepted as part of the struggle for national independence was scarcely disputed. Such wars were regarded as legitimate and just, ennobled by the political goal. This interpretation even accommodated military intervention by third parties, notwithstanding the fact that they mostly followed different motives. When the Russian tsar militarily supported the Serbian rebellion against the Ottoman Empire and the foundation of the Greek state, he was not primarily concerned with national demands for independence. Instead, Russia wanted to control the straits between the Black and Mediterranean seas and therefore sought every imaginable opportunity to weaken the Ottoman Empire. The invasion of the Moldavian and Walachian ports by Russian troops in 1853, which provoked a declaration of war by Turkey, was part of a strategic calculation designed to extend Russian power in Southeast Europe and the Caucasus. On the other hand, this, unlike the Greek secession, did not suit French and British interests. They sided with Turkey in 1854 and dealt Russia a decisive military defeat in the Crimea.

Classic power politics were likewise at work when France supported the Italian war against Austria in 1859. Napoleon III upheld the tradition of his uncle insofar as he tried to renew France's role as the foremost power in Europe. Therefore, when he promised the Piedmont government military and political aid against the Habsburg presence in upper and central Italy, he was optimistic of weakening the Danubian monarchy and increasing the influence of his own country. Apart from this, he looked for direct territorial gain: after the victory over Austria, Piedmont gratefully and obediently transferred Savoy and Nice to France.

Still, following the spirit of the times, war had to be legitimized by national motives. Piedmont thus fought for Italy's national independence, while France hurried to help its brave neighbor throw off the foreign yoke out of a sense of fraternal solidarity. Piquantly, on this occasion propaganda and underlying goals became entangled. The national idea developed an explosive strength that the French emperor had not reckoned with and upset his calculations. Instead of being content with the liberation of Lombardy, the national movement spread beyond the north and initiated a chain of rebellions and demonstrations in central and southern Italy, which concluded in the birth of an Italian national state. The limited war against Austria, which France had foreseen, therefore set in motion an uncontrollable development. This clearly changed the European balance of power and was not at all in the interests of France.

Napoleon's political ambitions also came undone in Central Europe. After repeatedly courting conflict through renewed claims to the left bank of the Rhine, he allowed himself to be led into a declaration of war against Prussia in 1870 in a deft maneuver by Bismarck. Once again, he had underestimated the national dimension. By portraying the war as a struggle for unification against a longstanding resentful enemy, Bismarck was successful in securing both the support of a broad liberal movement and the cooperation of the anti-Prussian southern German states. In his ability to couple national interests and state-power considerations, Bismarck was not just the French emperor's equal, but, as the events of 1870–1 showed, his superior. For the deeply conservative Prussian monarchy the wartime alliance with liberal nationalism paid off. Prussia-Germany could enlarge and stabilize its power to the detriment of France. Moreover, the national movement, which had long been convinced that its goal was unachievable without war, adopted Bismarck and his chief of staff, Moltke, as its new heroes. Through their courage and determination, so it seemed, the national project, begun in 1813, had come to a successful conclusion.

The Democratization of War

The nationalization of war in the course of the nineteenth century was accompanied by its democratization, which created the social base for the new legitimation of war. Without this broad social support for warfare the nationalistic rationale for and justification of war would have been rootless. The democratization of war secured an empathic resonance and a willingness to participate which distinguished modern wars from premodern conflicts.

This "democratization" meant nothing less than that the group conducting war was quantitatively expanded until it potentially encompassed the whole population. Once again the French Revolution was the godfather of this process. As much as a declaration of war, so went its Credo, should follow national interests and goals, its consequences, too, should be borne by the whole nation. The mobilization ordinance of 1793 quoted above thus listed each individual social group – young and old men, children, and women – and assigned to each special tasks. In this manner, the French National Assembly went far beyond previous definitions of who was liable for war service. Under the *ancien régime* the circle of soldiers had been narrow. Of the 102 infantry regiments raised by the French army in 1789, 23 were composed of foreign mercenaries. In Prussia half the army was made up of foreigners. The rest were recruited from the natives seduced by the promises of recruiting sergeants or, as in Prussia, subjected to a selective conscription system. The latter affected the rural population almost exclusively, especially its poorer sections.[8]

Many military experts of the late eighteenth century criticized this recruiting system as much too limited and socially unjust. Moreover, they condemned the brutal disciplinary measures endured by the soldiers of the *ancien régime*. Beatings were as common as offensive abuse by officers and sergeants. No room was to be left for this type of behavior in the new armies, formed according to revolutionary principles. These principles not only placed high value on equality and fair treatment. They also believed the defense of the nation had to be an affair for the whole nation, not delegated to an exclusive section of the population. Every citizen was by definition also a soldier – and every soldier a citizen.

This axiom implied serious structural change. It confronted the *citoyen* with the task of defending his nation through arms and participating in war. On the other hand, it placed upon the army the obligation to afford its citizen-soldiers legal rights and humane treatment. New military regulations were therefore as necessary as a reformed system of recruitment that would expand and generalize the pool of soldiers.

In this way the maxim of *égalité* and *fraternité* could be served. But the principle of *liberté* was necessarily damaged when all citizens were compelled to enlist and defend the nation by force of arms. How was this contradiction to be solved? At first, it was believed that the citizen, convinced of the need to protect the achievements of the revolution and the territorial integrity of the nation, would join the army of his own volition. Many did just that, but not enough by far for the increasing expansion of the hyperactive French armies. The National Assembly, therefore, had no choice but to introduce conscription: compulsory military service for all young men.

Why was conscription introduced for men alone and why only for the young? Such questions emerge not only in modern perspectives; contemporaries also posed them. The age regulation met with general approval. Young men, roughly between 20 and 24, were regarded as the best soldiers. It was believed that adoles-

cents would not meet the physical requirements in terms of height and strength. Older men would probably experience tension between their military service and their "civil obligations," above all their family duties. It was feared that married men would not make good soldiers because concern for wife and children would negatively affect their military performance. Furthermore, their absence from home and hearth would cause grave economic problems, something the state was unable and unwilling to deal with. In contrast to the armies of the eighteenth century, which were largely composed of married soldiers, the military administration of the nineteenth century wanted single, childless recruits. As a result financial privileges, such as those provided by the *ancien régime* for fathers, were abolished.

Consequently, the new people's or national wars were meant to be fought by young, single men. Only when their number and supply was inadequate were older, married men to be mobilized. Younger recruits were not only presumed to be healthy, strong, and independent; they were also expected to be adventurous and have gung-ho attitudes. In 1808 the Prussian civil servant and historian Barthold Niebuhr praised military service at "around the age of 20, when your heart and soul is fully in it" as a manly rite of passage "because it steels the character, making you manly and complete as a human being." Songs and poems also portrayed war as a great adventure that demanded young men of courage and valor. They would be richly compensated through manly camaraderie and the admiration of the female public, as well as the thanks of the Fatherland.[9]

The call did not go unanswered. The Prussian governor Vincke observed in 1815 that young men in particular, hastened "to the colors most willingly and joyfully." In contrast, when Vincke himself, as a 40-year-old husband, father, and senior official, toyed with the idea of volunteering, he met at best with a lack of understanding, at worst outright mockery. His wife, friends, and peers shared the view that the Fatherland had greater need for men like him in civil posts than in the military. War service was left to "the young," who, as Friedrich Schiller wrote in his much-quoted *Reiterlied* of 1797, risked their lives in order to win life.[10]

This, however, was far too self-interested a reason for military engagement as far as the propagandists of the new people's war were concerned. In their view, one went to war to save the nation. One risked one's life for higher collective goals, not for one's personal gain. This abstract and generalized interpretation of war leant it nobility, which was passed on to those who fought it. The citizen-soldier of the people's war was not simply a mercenary intent on lining his own pocket. Instead, he protected the honor and integrity of the nation.

Both revolutionary France and absolutist Prussia sought to mobilize their young men for war by using this same rhetoric of national and personal honor. But even additional financial inducements and the possibility of a career were not sufficient to recruit enough volunteers. Prussia therefore followed the French example and in 1813–14 enacted ordinances and laws which obligated men to perform war service. It not only drafted young men when there was the threat of war or hostilities had been declared. It also drafted them during times of peace. It was argued that, in order to be prepared for the eventuality of war, soldiers had to be trained beforehand. All young men were therefore liable for military service and were to be familiarized with the necessities of war.

This was *the* real revolutionary measure of the Napoleonic era, one that enduringly and deeply changed the relationship between civil society, the military, and war. In order to conduct the new national wars the military required a large number of well-trained, combat-ready men. Instead of recruiting men to become professional soldiers and maintaining them as a permanent force, the modern armies of the nineteenth and twentieth centuries drafted and trained them only temporarily. In this way, if war broke out, they could not only fall back on those currently being trained. They could also draw upon a large reservoir of older cohorts, whose period of training was already a couple of years old. Consequently, the army, led by professional officers and sergeants, had a manly "people in arms" at its disposal, which could be set in motion to replenish huge land forces.

Almost all continental European armies adopted this form of recruitment in the course of the nineteenth century. France and Prussia took the lead, Austria followed in 1868, tsarist Russia in 1874.[11] All, with the exception of Great Britain, sooner or later became convinced of the advantages of the new system and learnt from its successes. Why the British state took a different path is easily explained. Great Britain could afford a small army because of its geography. It depended completely on the navy to protect its coastline. When threatened with invasion, paramilitary formations were mobilized, which were in the main only temporarily active. Even the security needs of a vastly expanding colonial empire were met without deploying a large territorial army. Only when the numbers volunteering to fight in World War I proved inadequate to cover the losses sustained on the Western Front did the British government introduce conscription in 1916, only to abolish it again in 1921.[12]

Great Britain therefore established itself as the most liberal country in Europe in that it extended the greatest respect to the freedom of its citizens and to their right to choose. Everywhere, military service was distinctly unpopular, and its introduction on the continent was generally met with vocal protests. The middle class in particular opposed its imposition vehemently. To many it appeared both an outrageous state intervention into civil liberties and an economic catastrophe when young men had their education and professional careers disrupted for several years. Less elaborate and fewer objections came from the lower classes. Instead, men voted with their feet and sought to avoid conscription through a variety of tricks.

In any case, it soon became apparent after the end of the Napoleonic Wars that the conscript armies were unable to take in as many soldiers as were *de jure* at their disposal. In Prussia in the 1830s and 1840s only between 10 and 15 percent of mustered men were actually drafted into the army. Even after 1871 the figure for the whole German Empire was never more than a quarter. That meant that the great majority of those liable for conscription never saw barracks from the inside. In fact, the majority of men were discharged on medical grounds since the military wanted only the healthiest soldiers and applied the strictest standards.[13]

De facto, then, the "democratization" of military service was not as all embracing as originally planned. Limited budgets restricted the extensive mobilization of the male population. Furthermore, in many continental states the pool of soldiers, following the French model, was socially and economically limited. According to this system, every young man who could pay a certain amount of money was freed from the obligation of military service. The proceeds were distributed among the soldiers that had been drafted in for extended service. This mode of *remplacement* had several advantages for all involved. The civil rights of the individual were protected, while soldiers received extra pay, which smoothed their transition into civilian life. Meanwhile, the army was able to retain a core of long-service units and sergeants who were better trained and could be employed long term.

These pragmatic arguments met massive criticism in Prussia. There it had already been decided at the beginning of the nineteenth century – albeit in the face of administrative, military, and civil resistance – not to use a system of substitutes. Two motives were given for this. First, it was believed necessary ideologically to raise the value of military service to a "holy duty" and honor. Secondly, it was hoped that broader social participation would lead to a qualitative improvement of military culture and efficiency. If young, middle-class men had to serve in the army, this would inevitably contribute to civilizing military procedures. At the same time, young men from good homes could form a core of efficient reserve officers, who would be of great use in case of war. It also appeared a striking and embarrassing contradiction if, on the one hand, military service was declared a civil duty and, on the other, men could buy their way out. If this were so the army would remain what it had always been under the *ancien régime*, "a bunch of mercenaries." Conversely, civil society would persist, as Freiherr vom Stein complained, in an "un-warlike and cowardly attitude." In other words only a general service could "build a noble, martial national character."[14]

The introduction and enforcement of general military service was therefore bound together by the desire to civilize the military,

increase its efficiency, and militarize the nation. Admittedly, the generality of this service only existed on paper due to the limited recruiting quotas. Furthermore, middle-class recruits held privileges not available to their comrades from both the rural and urban lower classes. Nevertheless, the Prussian recruitment system proved its worth, so that, from the 1860s, it was adopted by most other European states. Even France converted to it in 1872 following the lost war against Germany.[15]

Had general military service fulfilled the hopes of the military reformers of the late eighteenth and nineteenth centuries? As far as the civilizing of the military was concerned, there were indeed positive developments. Demeaning corporal punishment was abolished and soldiers gained the right to complain to higher authorities if they were not treated respectfully by their superiors. The soldiers' living conditions and medical care were similarly improved. Increasingly, meritocratic principles gained the upper hand, while officers had to comply with higher educational standards. A career as a professional officer was no longer reserved for men of noble birth, but became available to those from the middle classes. By the outbreak of World War I, three out of four lieutenants in the German army were of middle-class origins.

Yet despite such positive approaches, the limits of civilizing warfare remained obvious. The military formed its own culture which was far from compatible with civil ideas and practices. Its procedures were raw, the tone harsh, and orders could not be debated. What was demanded of soldiers was obedience, not negotiation or reasoned objection. Disciplinary regulations were correspondingly strict; many countries even introduced an independent military law. The political rights of soldiers were limited. Generally, soldiers were not meant to engage in politics and were disenfranchised on the grounds of age anyway. Furthermore, life in the army differed markedly from civilian patterns. In the second half of the nineteenth century the increasing accommodation of soldiers in barracks was accompanied by an extreme group orientation. A soldier served, but also lived, slept, ate, and washed in the masculine environment of the barrack community. Camaraderie was writ large, even when the grinding routine led to sadistic acts and could drive more sensitive recruits to suicide.

Moreover, what of the other purpose assigned to military service by Freiherr vom Stein (and others)? Did it really make the nation more "warlike"? The answer is not simple. On the one hand, the systematic and continued military training of young men undoubtedly had profound implications. Even if only a portion of the male population was affected, they made up substantial numbers. In Germany alone between 200,000 and 300,000 men were drafted annually in the decades before World War I. The greater number of those remained with the colors for three years. During this time they not only learnt "civil" virtues such as order, cleanliness, and thrift. They also learnt how to follow orders, to march in line and column, to fire a gun, and to use a bayonet. They heard lectures about past wars and prepared for the coming ones. After their active service, they often joined a local veterans' association to maintain the company of ex-servicemen and march in national celebrations. A belligerent, martial habit consequently flowered in civil life, although it often took on a folkloristic character.[16]

On the other hand, it can hardly be argued that such a habit was only to be found in countries that had introduced conscription. Bellicose sentiments were also evident in Great Britain, which had no compulsory military service, before the Great War. There, many youths joined the Boy Scout movement, which mixed military forms with leisure activities and focused on camaraderie, patriotism, and lust for adventure. A chauvinistic press placed the government under pressure not to back down in international conflicts, but to go on the offensive. Finally, more than 2 million young men volunteered to join the army in 1914/15, despite the fact that there was no threat of invasion and that the island state was not protecting its own borders, but those of France and Belgium.[17]

A "warlike national character" was therefore not exclusively bound up with the personal experience of military service – just as not every young man who performed service left the barrack a militarist. Yet military service undoubtedly contributed to spreading accep-

tance of the reality of and potentiality for war in civil society. Year after year millions of young men prepared to kill and be killed. Meanwhile, millions of older men reminisced about their own service and past wars were extravagantly glorified and imbued with nationalist meaning.

What role did women play in this scenario? Were they also to cultivate warlike sentiments? Were they too "born defenders" of their Fatherland? We have already seen how the French Revolution only considered men when it spoke of *soldats-citoyens*. When women petitioned in 1790–1 to enter the National Guard and bear arms they were met with scorn and derision. With verve, the male parliamentarians rejected the request in the name of the "natural order": nature had not meant women to give death, but life.[18]

This argument was repeatedly used throughout the nineteenth and twentieth centuries to justify men's exclusive right to bear arms as well as the exclusion of all women from the military. In modern civil society, which ordered the relationship between the sexes according to clear, well-defined principles, the handiwork of war belonged unambiguously to men. This was based on tradition and history, but above all on the unchangeable laws of nature.[19] Whoever questioned those laws, like the female Jacobins, threatened to undermine the social order and caused general chaos.

Closer analysis reveals an interesting differentiation in this rhetoric of gender differences. When war should be made palatable to men, the talk was of honor and civil duty. An emphasis was placed upon sacrifice. Men risked and gave up their lives and health to protect the home country. Central to this discourse was heroic death, not the act of killing. That men would have to kill other men was left unspoken – in the appeals for mobilization as well as in the military histories, regulations, and field manuals, which were meant to prepare soldiers for their mission. In contrast, when women were being excluded from the military, the negative aspects of destruction and annihilation were stressed. Instead of personal heroism and honor, it was the brutal act of killing, rehearsed during service and the daily reality of war, that received ample coverage. The intention was to shock – and it achieved this end. The majority of women agreed with the female author who, in 1826, declared war and the army as "unnatural" and completely opposed to the "natural profession of women to be mothers." Only in case of emergency and when no male protector was around, were women permitted to grab a weapon. War and active killing, however, were thoroughly male issues – just as politics was.[20]

At this point the debate over the gender of war received a new political color. For nineteenth-century contemporaries, war and politics were closely connected. Since politics involved the regulation of international relations, it was intimately linked with the decision of war and peace. Only men, however, could make such a decision. Conservatives and liberals were absolutely united on this point: the right to participate in the politics of civil society belonged exclusively to those prepared to defend that society with their "life and death." Since women were freed from this obligation due to their "natural calling," they were not permitted any political rights either.[21]

The democratization of war, which followed from generalized military service, was a key argument in the nineteenth-century franchise campaigns and for the expansion of access to the political sphere. Consequently, when women began to think of themselves as citizens too, this liaison was vehemently turned against them. How could they break it off? Hardly anyone wanted to question the male monopoly on war and military service. Few wished to join the radical group of pacifists, who strove to give up war completely and abolish the military. Instead, most women chose to reject the narrow identification of politics, foreign affairs, and war. For them, politics and active citizenship encompassed many more issues and concerns, such as education and social welfare where women were heavily involved. But even wars, as they were eager to point out, were by no means a purely male affair. Women, after all, brought the soldiers of the future into the world (often losing their own lives in doing so). Furthermore, women played a vital role in military hospitals, where they accomplished "a patriotic feat equal to the achievement of men in military service."[22]

Women had indeed contributed in their own way to the democratization of war. They had been included in the French *levée en masse* of 1793 as producers of clothing and tents as well as nurses for wounded soldiers. During the Napoleonic Wars, women from the upper and middle classes came together in associations across Europe to collect money for the troops and to organize support services. In 1854 Florence Nightingale and 38 other ladies hastened to help British soldiers wounded in the Crimea. Although it was not until World War I that women were first employed in large numbers as military nurses, since the second half of the nineteenth century the figure of the angelic nurse standing at the side of the male soldier was a role model of female patriotism. Hundreds of thousands of (mostly young) women took nursing courses in order to make themselves useful in case of war. Many joined the nursing corps of the Red Cross, an international organization founded in 1863 that aimed to improve the lot of wounded soldiers.[23]

It was through this engagement, which was compatible with their female-motherly "calling," that women contributed to making modern warfare that inclusive, "democratic" event it was supposed to be since 1793. Women were anything but "born" pacifists. If they seldom wanted or were allowed to fight wars, they took active part in their preparation, execution, and aftermath. They belonged to organizations that demanded the expansion of colonies, thereby placing their trust in military power. They raised funds for the construction of warships and let their daughters join girls' movements that adopted the military nurse as role model. Clearly, women felt as patriotic and nationalistic as men, and when war came, were ready to play their part.

Absolute War and the Increasing Violence of Warfare

Both the democratization and nationalization of warfare in the nineteenth century meant that military conflict began to loom large in the minds of contemporaries. Allusions to it, both direct and indirect, occurred everywhere and at all levels. Memories of war were passed from generation to generation. War stories had their place in school and youth books. Photographs taken during military service hung in living rooms. Veterans' associations staged anniversary celebrations in which whole villages and towns would participate. Finally, commemorative monuments remembered the fallen and honored them as heroes. War, so it appeared, was adopted by society as an extraordinary, but nevertheless, recurrent state.

Yet, at the same time, the reality of modern warfare eluded such easy replication. The more brutal and violent a war, the more difficult it became to report those experiences. The gulf between the homefront and the frontline became ever greater, the divergent experiences of civil life and war ever more incommunicable. Modern war, which depended so heavily on civil resources in the form of men, weapons, and munitions, created conditions that left civilian ideas, standards, and expectations far behind. There opened an abyss that reached its deepest point in the two world wars of the twentieth century. The way was prepared, however, by the innovations in military technology and tactics developed during the late eighteenth and nineteenth centuries.

The French, under their extremely gifted commander, Napoleon, were again in the vanguard of these developments. Napoleon revolutionized warfare, especially for the infantry and artillery, and introduced more flexible and unconventional forms of fighting. Moreover, he was a great believer in the decisive battle, by which all forces were concentrated on one point. As 1806 showed, winning the upper hand had major consequences for the whole campaign. Once victory over the Prussian troops at Jena and Auerstädt was secured, the rest of Napoleon's campaign was comparatively easy. The majority of forts still held by the enemy simply surrendered without a fight.

For Napoleon's contemporaries this was a mind-blowing experience. It represented a completely new form of warfare. Officers and politicians quickly drew their conclusions and copied the French model as closely as possible. It proved enough to drive back the French troops and vanquish them in decisive battles with enormous casualties on both sides. At Wagram in 1809, 70,000 dead and wounded were left on the field. At the Leipzig "Völkerschlacht," in which over half a million soldiers

fought, the number was more than 100,000. Out of the 600,000 soldiers of Napoleon's Grand Army who marched into Russia in 1812, only a few thousand returned. Altogether, the belligerent states lost almost 4 million men between 1792 and 1815.[24]

Scarcely anyone was prepared for this magnitude of conflict. The war had not merely become more "absolute." It had also, as noted by the Prussian officer and military theoretician Carl von Clausewitz, become more deadly. For Clausewitz, war had therefore "come closer to its true nature, its absolute perfection." Yet he did not attach any value judgment to his observation. Instead, he regarded it as confirmation of a general principle. Modern war, as initiated by Napoleon, had shed its political shackles. Its driving force was the will to annihilation – although annihilation was not synonymous with physical liquidation. However, for both adversaries the "defeat of the opponent" became the "natural goal" of war and had to be energetically and ruthlessly pursued. That this would result in great bloodshed and "bloody slaughter" was logical. In the face of this logic, it was absurd "little by little to blunt the swords one wields out of consideration of making war more humane."[25]

Of this absolute or "natural" form of war, not much had remained in the eighteenth century, observed Clausewitz. Instead, war had been reined in and developed into the "mere business of governments," into a "game" of limited risks. "To gain a moderate advantage in order to make use of it when it came to forging the peace was the goal even of the most ambitious." The methods were also moderate, far removed from the brutality and savagery that had accompanied the Thirty Years' War. Pillaging and attacks on the civilian population rarely occurred and, when they did, they were seen as "pointless" and counterproductive. Since the French Revolution, however, any restrictions on military violence had been swept away. The nationalization of war released an energy and potential for violence that sought its like. Goals became as extreme as the means with which they were to be achieved. Clausewitz did not dare to predict with any certainty as to whether this "absolute violence" could again be tamed and whether future wars would be fought with the same existential fervor. He was, however, skeptical over whether the barriers "once torn-down" could be "built again."[26]

Helmuth von Moltke, the Prussian chief of staff since 1857, had a clearer view – and he himself contributed further to the growing violence of war. Apart from glorifying war as the father of "mankind's most noble virtues," he developed an efficient and pathbreaking concept of warfare that built on Napoleon's and Clausewitz's lessons. He too supported the idea of the decisive battle – not least because it shortened wars. In the era of mass armies wars were not meant to last long, otherwise the military would face almost irresolvable logistical and supply problems. The provisioning of soldiers alone caused great problems, even when commanders fell back on the Napoleonic principle of exploiting the resources of conquered countries. Moreover, the national economy suffered during long wars, to say nothing of personal losses endured by soldiers and their families.

These logistical and economic problems made it imperative to achieve "a great and quick decision," to seek a battle in which as much as possible of the opposing force could be destroyed, thereby hindering it to array and rearrange its troops. Consequently, the role of the artillery became increasingly important and technology, supported by spreading industrialization, made important advances in this area. European countries competed with each other to possess the largest cannon, the deadliest missile, and the most accurate gun. The armaments industries produced them in ever growing numbers, constantly adjusting their design, and they promised fast delivery. As early as 1869 Moltke spoke admiringly of the "ever enhanced fire power of our time." This improvement continued unabated in the following decades and reached its high point during World War I. In that conflict artillery fire accounted for three out of four casualties. In 1814 the number had been a mere 20 percent.[27]

However, it was not only artillery guns that increased in strength and accuracy. Infantry arms also developed into ever more deadly weapons. Even before the machine gun revolutionized ballistic technology and rapidity of fire in 1885, the new breech-loading rifle, such as the Prussian needle rifle and the French Chassepot, allowed faster loading and hit their target at a greater distance. Prussian mission tactics also enhanced the fighting capability of the infantry. Instead of squeezing men into compact linear formations or dense columns, Moltke allowed his soldiers to spread out, thereby increasing their range of fire and accuracy.

By applying these vastly more mobile tactics, the Prussian-German troops gained victory over the French army, which surrendered at Sedan in 1870. Quick deployment coupled with an excellent mobilization plan contributed to their success. Moltke's ability to use the rail network procured for his army immense initial success. Its positive effect on the morale of the soldiers – and demoralization of the enemy – can scarcely be underrated. The duration of the campaign also corresponded to Moltke's principles. The war lasted about a month and appeared to be complete following the capture of the French emperor and his army. Politics, however, saw it otherwise. The new republican government in Paris rejected a general capitulation and called upon the people to begin a *guerre à outrance* instead.

As in 1793, this war was defined as a struggle for existence, a conflict for national survival. The *levée en masse* was renewed. The French interior minister, Léon Gambetta, announced it with great pathos: all citizens were summoned to resist the German invaders. The figure of the *franc-tireur*, the partisan, was born.[28] What appeared as justified from the perspective of national defense turned out to be a dangerous blurring of boundaries that had serious implications for future conflicts. The international law of war had hitherto clearly distinguished between combatants and non-combatants. Now this separation was abrogated. If civilians were allowed, indeed obliged, to fire upon enemy soldiers, they lost the protection of international conventions. This entailed incalculable consequences for warfare and the relationship between invading troops and the civil population. Moltke, who observed these developments at first hand, commented on them with great concern: "The nagging of the franc-tireurs has to be paid for by bloody reprisals, and the war puts on a more violent character. It is bad enough that armies have sometimes to be set to butcher one another; there is no necessity for setting whole nations against each other – that is not progress, but rather a return to barbarism."[29]

This and other signs of "barbarization" invoked increasing resistance to the idea of war in the second half of the nineteenth century. The most radical opponents were pacifist groups that wished to abolish the military altogether and outlaw war. Their numbers, however, were extremely small and only where they were closely involved with other political movements, as in France and Great Britain, did they find a public voice. More pragmatic and moderate were organizations like the International Red Cross, founded at the instigation of the Swiss Henri Dunant in 1863. Dunant had become interested in the fate of wounded soldiers and their lack of adequate medical aid at the battle of Solferino. He supported the establishment of voluntary relief societies, which assisted the medical orderlies during war and prepared for their task in peacetime. Moreover, he untiringly advocated securing medical personnel on the battlefield. In 1864, the Geneva Convention was signed by 12 governments. It was the first example of a treaty of international humanitarian law in history.[30]

Following their success in having the wounded and their helpers protected by international agreement, Dunant and his fellow campaigners turned their attention to the lot of prisoners of war, whom they wanted placed under a neutral authority. However, this initiative met with strong opposition, and not just by the German general staff. There was general skepticism over whether international appointments or the intervention of neutral states could humanize warfare. In the naked struggle for power and in the alliance system that dominated Europe in the latter half of the nineteenth century, the seat of "earthly judgment" had to remain empty.[31]

This, however, did not prevent the architects of international law from making further efforts to codify the conduct of war. What Hugo Grotius had begun in the early seventeenth century became even more urgent in the era of mass armies, citizen-soldiers, and ever more destructive weapons. In all countries, there was an attempt to bind warfare to generalized principles. From 1856 diplomats, lawyers, and political leaders met to reinforce these principles through international agreement. The Hague Land and Sea Ordinances of 1899 were the first binding regulations affirmed by all the signatory states, from Spain to Japan. They banned poison gas and those weapons that caused "superfluous injury." They prohibited looting and the killing of soldiers who had already surrendered. They demanded the humane treatment of POWs and the exemption of churches, hospitals, museums, and schools from attack. Furthermore, they regulated the status of combatants and the protection of the civilian population.[32]

At the same time, though, they employed the extremely elastic concept of the "necessities of war," thereby offering states the opportunity to get around the precept of humane warfare under certain circumstances.[33] This played into the hands of those who planned modern war as total war. Moltke, for example, consistently argued that war must not only be waged against an enemy army, but also against an enemy government and their resources. He also believed that all means that were not "clearly reprehensible" should be used to achieve a quick victory. Moreover, one could not expect soldiers to be super-heroes in the "abnormal conditions of war." Of course, everything should be done to ensure discipline among the troops. In this matter, the conduct of the commander was decisive. His "sense of honor and righteousness" necessarily had to be strengthened. In the long run, Moltke was convinced that the "gradual progress of civilization" would lead to a general humanizing of war. In his view it was scarcely conceivable that modern Europeans would perpetrate the same horrors that had accompanied the Thirty Years' War or the "current oriental struggles" (meaning the Russian–Turkish War of 1877–8).[34]

Had Moltke, who died in 1891, lived to see World War I he would have been rudely awakened from his sweet dream and taught a painful lesson. The dreadful destructive power of the weapons, the seemingly never-ending supply of material and men, and the extreme (and unusually long) strain borne by the fighting troops led to an explosion of violence that surpassed all precedents. The death toll was immense. On the first day of the Somme (July 1, 1916) alone, more soldiers fell than during the whole of the Franco-German War of 1870. The unceasing artillery salvos caused immense losses, but close combat in this static war also took its toll. Under these circumstances excessive brutality by individuals was not unusual. In fact, it became an integral part of warfare under the rubric of "the necessities of war" and led to the use of poison gas, the systematic devastation of occupied land, the shooting of suspicious civilians, the deliberate razing of buildings, and the deportation of able-bodied men.[35]

The outbreak of war in 1914 also steamrollered those initiatives for international mediation and arbitration intended to solve conflicts peacefully. Steps for de-escalation through the intervention of neutral states, and the establishment of a commission of inquiry and a court of law that had been agreed on in The Hague in 1899 were not taken. In a sense, the text of the treaty had already foreseen this. It was to apply only to those "differences of an international nature involving neither honor nor vital interests."[36] When hostilities were declared in 1914, however, honor was omnipresent and all powers were convinced that the war was a struggle for national existence. There was no room for mediation and restraint, politics abdicated, and the war would indeed be absolute and total.

ACKNOWLEDGMENTS

This chapter was translated from German by Leighton James.

NOTES

1   Weber (1993: 8); see also Finer (1975: 84–163).
2   Kant (1968).
3   Woolf (1991); Hagemann (2002).
4   Colley (1992).
5   Forrest (1990: 75).
6   Arndt (1988: 15, 29); see also Jeismann (1992: part 1).
7   Ibid: 82.
8   Forrest (1990: 27–38); Frevert (2004: 11–14).
9   Frevert (2004: 29); see also Schmidt (1976); Hagemann (2002: 135–43).
10 Frevert (2004: 31); Schiller (1967: 52).
11 Jansen (2004); Moran and Waldron (2003); Sanborn (2003).
12 Colley (1992: 283–319); Best (1986: 231–43); Adams and Poirier (1987).
13 Frevert (2004: 49, 55, 90, 153, 200).
14 Ibid: 19.
15 Mitchell (1979).
16 Vogel (1997: esp. pp. 275–8).
17 Summers (1976, 1981); MacKenzie (1992).
18 Duhet (1977: 117).
19 Frevert (1995: 31–50, 119–24).
20 Woltmann (1826: 183–7).
21 Frevert (2004: 118, 208–11).
22 Dohm (1982: 171–3).
23 Summers (1988); Quartaert (2001: esp. ch. 5).
24 Best (1986: 114); Wawro (2000: 16–23).
25 Clausewitz (1993: 280, 319, 339).
26 Ibid: 333, 334, 336, 340.
27 Moltke, "Auswahl aus seinen Schriften," in Stumpf (1993: 487, 436, 449); see also Wawro (2000: 9).
28 Howard (1961); Audoin-Rouzeau (1989: 210–19).
29 Moltke's letter to his brother Adolf, October 27, 1870 (Moltke 1896: 231).
30 Riesenberger (1992: 15–32).
31 Stumpf (1993: 476, 487).
32 Best (1980: ch. 3); Friedman (1972: 149–416, esp. 224–35).
33 Ibid: 229.
34 Stumpf (1993: 482, 487–9).
35 Ferro (1969); Keegan (1975, 2000).
36 Friedman (1972: 209); see also Dülffer (1981).

GUIDE TO FURTHER READING

Whoever is interested in military theory and strategy should consult Paret et al.'s *Makers of Modern Strategy from Machiavelli to the Nuclear Age* and Paret's *Understanding War*. John Keegan's books on modern warfare – *A History of Warfare, The Face of Battle, The First World War* – attempt very successfully to connect operational history with diplomatic relations and the mentality of those who do the planning and fighting. A highly elucidating investigation into the mindsets of German military administrators during the imperial period (1870–1914) is presented by Hull, *Absolute Destruction*. Comparative studies are rare, but badly needed. A broad overview on European developments during the nineteenth century is provided by Wawro's *Warfare and Society in Europe, 1792–1914*, which covers the same period as Best's *War and Society in Revolu-* *tionary Europe*, and Bond's *War and Society in Europe*, chs. 1–4. Best's *Humanity in Warfare* is a helpful examination of the attempts to control, contain, and "humanize" wars. As for military–civil relations and the history of conscription in nineteenth-century Europe, see the articles in Moran and Waldron's *People in Arms* and, for Germany, Frevert's *A Nation in Barracks*. A gendered view of war is presented by Melman, *Borderlines*.

CHAPTER THIRTY-TWO

Colonialism

TRUTZ VON TROTHA

"Globalization" is undisputedly the key concept of the present. The term implies the view that we have only recently entered the "Age of Globalization," with its worldwide networks, concentration, and dynamism of politics, economy, and culture. From the perspective of contemporaries of the turn of the sixteenth century, however, things look quite different. For them, the beginning of globalization was marked by two precise dates: October 12, 1492 and May 18, 1498. On that date in October, Christopher Columbus came ashore on an island in the West Indies that its inhabitants called Guanahaní and which he promptly renamed as San Salvador, claiming it for Spain. And the May date marks the day when Vasco da Gama reached Calicut, ten months and ten days after he had set sail from Lisbon and crossed the Indian Ocean, guided by an Arab pilot. Contemporaries of the European Renaissance were correct in believing that on these two days the European horizon was extended infinitely and previously undreamed of possibilities became conceivable. Between these two dates lies the signing of the Treaty of Tordesillas on June 7, 1494, in which Spain and Portugal divided up the world among themselves. Cast into the form of an international treaty, this took the notion that the world as a whole lay within the grasp of Europe and added to it a missionary claim of domination and civilization that encompassed the entire world. All three dates emphasize the fact that the history

of globalization traces back much further than often assumed today and is primarily a history of European expansion, colonialism, and imperialism. A "global history" perspective moves colonialism into the center of historiography, out of its marginal existence within the history of international relations and historiography focused primarily on individual nations.

What is Colonialism?

Colonialism is a process of establishing and exercising power and authority at a supraregional level. Based on war and violence or the threat of it, a state or an organized group of people tied directly to the state establishes control over a society in a territory that is typically separated from the imperial, land-seizing power by an ocean. This society differs substantially from the society of the imperial country at least in its sociocultural order and it has its own history. The rule over the subdued society is determined territorially. The subjugated society loses, more or less completely, its political and diplomatic autonomy under international law and enters into a direct, formal dependence on the colonial power or its representatives. The goals of colonial rule have a markedly one-sided orientation toward the political, economic, and social interests and the culture of the colonial power. Those in power and the vast majority of the colonized population remain more or less strangers to each other in the face of the political, economic, social, and cultural antagonism of the "colonial situation" and its consequences.

Colonialism as a means of domination through force is a reiteration of events that have continually repeated over history: wars of conquest, tribute relations between orders of different magnitudes of power, empires of European or non-European antiquity and the Middle Ages or of the modern territorial state itself. It is all too easily forgotten that the modern territorial state is closely related to colonial rule with respect to its use of violence and the methods and conditions of power and domination in its incipient stages. Colonialism is one form of seizing land by force, which is a basic manifestation in world history. The violence involved in setting up colonial rule as well as the violence that existed especially in the settlement colonies toward the end of colonial domination make colonialism a part of the history of war and genocide, above and beyond all destruction of the natural environment in the colonial robber, mining, and plantation economies, and the "export" of epidemics and disease, which reached a genocidal magnitude, especially in Latin America. We will never know how many people died in these wars and genocides and in their aftermath. Colonialism marked the establishment and decline of rule on smoldering fields of rubble piled high with corpses. A cruel paradox of the colonial violence is the key role played by local forces and "ethnic soldiers." According to the politics of *divide et impera* – divide and rule – colonial conquerors recruiting soldiers took advantage of local oppositions and hostilities and, in Africa for instance, deployed soldiers from other, non-African colonies.

Among the forms of violent land seizure, colonialism is unique in history with respect to its conditions, actors, the changing hegemony of the actors throughout its roughly 500–year history, its system of domination, effects, the extent of land seized and its range, which spanned oceans. Almost two-thirds of humanity were dominated in the period from 1880 to 1940 through imperious claims by the British, French, Belgians, Dutch, Germans, Danes, Spaniards, Portuguese, Italians, Russians,

Japanese, and US-Americans. Britain alone, which was the leading colonial power during the Age of Imperialism – that is, the final phase of overseas expansion coming forth from Europe – ruled over almost one-fourth of the land area of the earth and about one-third of the world's population at the time.

Colonialism is part of the history of colonization. Under constitutional and international law, three basic types of dependent territories can be distinguished during the period of high colonialism. There were "colonies," "protectorates," and "mandates," classified according to type of possession and degree to which the conquered societies lost their sovereignty, but these distinctions were relatively meaningless for the reality of the rule that was exercised, as the subjugated populations had no voice in any of these constructions. More important are distinctions based on the form of expansion and the goals set by the colonial power with respect to each individual colony.

The forms of colonial expansion extended from the "construction of naval networks," "overseas settlement colonization," and "empire-building wars of conquest" to the transitions to "border colonization," which played a substantial role in the beginnings of non-maritime – that is, atypical – colonialism, by which Russia moved out to Siberia and the Pacific in the sixteenth and seventeenth centuries.[1] Trade colonies predominated in the tropics, corresponding to the goals set by the colonial power, the social structure of the conquerors, and the situation and nature of the colony. Here the focus was economic, to find new markets, and the group of European administrative officials, missionaries, and employees of overseas trading posts was extraordinarily small. As the property interests of the settlers and their need for workers grew, the conflict potential between colonizers and colonized in the settlement colonies increased and the position of the colonial administration became more precarious. Both were reflected in bloody colonial wars, such as in German Southwest Africa, as well as in the fact that the "classical" settlement colonies in North America and South Africa brought forth the first successful decolonization movements and wars of independence of European settlers. The same was true for the plantation colonies. Conflicts over land, displacement of indigenous populations, and ruthless treatment of the "labor issue," which also characterized the mining colonies, became cause for ruinous and genocidal wars.

These types of colonies defined by the conquerors were confronted by the virtually boundless diversity of natural conditions and political, economic, social, and cultural orders of the conquered countries. In 1914 these countries made up almost three-quarters of the surface of the earth (excluding Antarctica). They were home to societies and cultures that ranged from hunters and gatherers with totemism and shamanism and relatively far-reaching social equality to highly complex states with monotheistic religions. The diversity of colonialism shows that it cannot be reduced to simple patterns that characterize anticolonialist theories, from those of John Atkinson Hobson or Lenin, to André Gunder Frank and Samir Amin, and especially the "victims' discourse" of anticolonialist activism and *tiers mondisme*. Colonialism is a phenomenon of colossal diversity that encompassed a multitude of colonialisms.

Establishing colonial rule was a drawn-out process in which the competing actors were not all on the side of the conquerors. There were just as many on the side of those who had been conquered. The formation of colonial power structures took place within the framework of a deeply entangled, multi-layered and inter-related competition between and among conquerors and conquered, which brought about diverse forms of resistance against – as well as arrangement and co-operation with – colonialism. Much depended on the respective internal interests and lines of conflict of the affected societies and groups. Colonial rule was the outcome of a painful and arduous learning process for both conquerors and conquered, in the course of which new problems continually arose and had to be resolved. For the conquerors these problems were primarily technical, economic, organizational, and related to power strategies. The problems of the colonized groups resulted from the special situations of their respective domestic and external

relations at the time the Europeans arrived and from the establishment of the conquerors' authority and their influence on local conditions.

With the age of imperialism came a fundamentally new inequality to this struggle. Since this time the overseas countries were confronted with a problem of adaptation to the European "revolution in power," that is, modern statehood, industrialization, and the mechanization of war.[2] With few exceptions, such as Japan, they failed to resolve this problem. What was a problem of adaptation and forced subjugation for the people in the colonies was a problem of rule for the colonial conquerors. They were unsuccessful in finding a lasting solution with respect to both the economic interests of the European metropoles and the effectiveness of the colonial rule. Colonial domination remained precarious from the outset.

The early Spanish and Portuguese colonial empires gained untold wealth from their colonial possessions by means of a robber economy and monopolistic profits within the scope of the mercantile system. In the end, however, this wealth brought their demise. The drain of wealth bled white the Dutch East Indies economically between 1830 and 1860. But even the British Empire was economically meaningful only for short periods, such as between 1945 and 1951. All in all, since the phase of high imperialism, colonialism had not satisfied the self-interested expectations of the colonial powers. Apart from considerable profits of individual branches, companies, and speculators, in the end the colonies remained economically marginal and brought undesirable burdens to state coffers. Expectations with regard to demography and social policy were disappointed or irrelevant. And with respect to domestic and foreign policy, colonial possessions became increasingly a burden.

The problem of rule was the crux of colonialism's economically doubtful balance sheet; this involved establishing an effective state administration and reorganizing the economy, society and culture of the colonies in the interests of the colonial power.[3] The colonial state remained a weak state, and the society of the conquerors a "colonial society." The economy did not become a "national" economy, but instead remained a "colonial economy." In spite of the innumerable effects that missionaries, schools, colonial lingua franca, science, and technology had on the colonies, the colonized insisted on the autonomy of their cultures, which consequently became pitfalls for the conquerors' arrogant, civilizational claims of superiority. Cultural tough-mindedness and localization of Western culture accompanied colonialistic globalization from the very beginning, by both the conquered and the conqueror. The "exporter" of cultural patterns and political, social, and economic institutions participated in the process of localization just as much as did the "importer." That is one reason why reference to the "Europeanization of the world" is misleading in the context of European expansion. Europe's utopias of rule, economy, and culture were drawn into the whirlpool of localization everywhere. Localization is at the core of the process of globalization.

Colonial Expansion between Commerce and Conquest

When Columbus set off westward and Vasco da Gama found a sea route to India around the Cape of Good Hope, they were ringing in the process of European expansion. This process was not unique to Europe in the century from 1450 to 1550. It was the "Age of Gunpowder Empires," a century of expansionist processes throughout all of Eurasia. If anything should be considered unique about the beginning of the European process of expansion, it was its unwavering urge toward economic expansion in the face of the political and military blockade by the expanding Ottoman Empire. The maritime character of the expansion allowed the modern scientific and technological revolution to develop fields such as cartography, navigation, logistics, shipbuilding, and military technology. The Atlantic Ocean undisputedly became the "European Sea." The sheer range of the expansion and the diverse forms of domination with which Europe actually carried out the expansion can also be seen as unique. It began with Portuguese "naval network colo-

nialism" of "armed traders" who worked their way into the existing trade networks; its counterpart was Spanish "subjugation colonialism" of conquerors who destroyed the existing political structures and set about the arduous task of establishing a colonial regime. Colonialism became a "project of commerce" in the Indian Ocean and a "project of conquest" in the Americas, as Adam Smith noted.[4] This polarity between trade and conquest carried through the entire history of colonialism like a recurring theme. It was still determinant in the nineteenth century, when colonialism assumed the forms of "informal" and "formal imperialism," "free trade imperialism," and colonial rule.

"Informal imperialism" is understood as a form of control of foreign policy and economy of a polity which does not affect the formal political autonomy of the political order.[5] The controlled polity can, within certain limits, implement its own foreign policy and regulate its own internal affairs. There is no colonial administration. The imperial goal is economic control and penetration of the region, the opening of its market for foreign investments and products of the imperial power, unhindered or privileged trade, the *de jure* and *de facto* guarantee of foreign property, and immunity of foreign citizens *vis à vis* local laws and courts. Techniques for maintaining this informal imperialism are diplomatic pressure, military threats with occasional military interventions, the right to station foreign troops, unbalanced treaties, free trade regimes, extraterritoriality, and consular jurisdiction. Informal imperialism comes in the form of diplomats, consuls, maritime officers, military and political "advisors" and, above all, "residents." A prime example for the diversity of power forms that were used in informal imperialism was the Opium War from 1840 to 1842 and its aftermath. Up to the late nineteenth century, virtually all Western colonial powers, including the United States, and Japan, had gained a foothold in China, making it into a semicolonial country. In the first half of the nineteenth century – with a certain peak in the 1850s and 1860s – almost all colonial powers practiced a juxtaposition of informal and formal imperialism. Primarily the United States and Japan made use of informal imperialism, the former, for example, in republican Cuba from 1902 to 1959 and the latter for the step by step expansion of the Japanese sphere of influence in China. In connection with naval network colonialism, for which the Portuguese were a model, informal imperialism determined Britain's beginnings on the Indian subcontinent and the power position of Britain in South America, Thailand, Persia, and in the Ottoman Empire. However, the connection between economic interests and political power was more vulnerable in informal imperialism than the term or political events suggest. South America is an example that shows that British traders or investors could not count on political assistance from the state in critical situations, and that governments showed great reserve toward the ideas of traders, bankers, or bondholders in promoting and supporting economic interests through political means.[6]

"Formal imperialism," or "colonialism," describes the seizure of political and administrative control in a polity by the imperial powers. It involves conquest, taking possession of the conquered territories, and the establishment and exercise of colonial rule. Colonialism dominated British policies in India from the mid-eighteenth century, when Britain and the East India Company adopted the idea of Richard Clive, the later conqueror of Bengal. Clive had declared in 1755: "We must indeed become the Nabobs ourselves,"[7] in which he was referring to the regional deputies, or viceroys, of the Mughal rulers. With the brutal suppression of the bloody "Indian Mutiny" of 1857–8, Clive's program had become reality within a century. English rule in India turned into English rule over India and India became the Crown Jewel of the British Empire. The British viceroy ruled with Asian pomp and ceremony and in 1876 Queen Victoria was proclaimed Empress of India (Kaisar-I-Hind). French policies followed the principles of formal imperialism after the collapse of the French positions in India and Canada. Charles X sent out a naval expedition in 1830 that occupied Algiers. Saigon followed in 1859. Starting in 1854 France resumed its activities in Senegal. The settlement of Australia starting in 1788 was an example of formal imperialism, as was the conquest and settlement of New

Zealand from 1840. In 1830 the Dutch began intervening directly into land use on Java, the main island of Dutch India, and subjugating the outer Indonesian islands. Between the 1840s and 1870 Russia practically concluded its conquest of Central Asia. Russia pursued only limited goals there, such as securing the Siberian border and providing some opposition to Britain's penetration of India; it was satisfied with protectorates, as was possible in the case of Bukhara (southwest-central Uzbekistan) and Khiva (west-central Uzbekistan). But Russia largely failed in its attempts to rule according to patterns of informal imperialism. In 1898 it divided Central Asia into two provinces, each with a governor-general, and put it under colonial rule.

Formal imperialism was not totally unleashed until the "partition of Africa." The Berlin conference on West Africa in the winter of 1884–5, often erroneously referred to as the Congo Conference, sealed this partition and was the starting gun for the final lap in the "race for Africa." Representatives from 13 European countries, the United States and the Ottoman Empire came together at this conference of *partage sans parti*[8] presided over by the chancellor of the German Reich, Otto von Bismarck. Negotiations still conducted in the spirit of informal imperialism sought to secure for all countries free access and "nondiscriminatory" trade for the region of the "Congo basin" and to declare free navigation on the Congo and Niger rivers. In the spirit of formal imperialism, the conference aimed to fix and stake out the possessions up to that point along the African coast and to tie further territorial claims to proof of actual possession. Historians accurately view the decade before and after the Berlin conference as a turning point in the development of colonialism and imperialism, separating high imperialism from early imperialism and the colonial history of early modern times and pre-revolutionary Europe.

From the time of the transatlantic slave trade, which presumably shipped 12–15 million Africans to the Caribbean and American coasts between 1450 and 1870, Africa became caught in the pull of global networks of unprecedented magnitude and intensity. High imperialism and its accompanying "scramble" made Africa into a focal point of politicizing globality. It represented the epitome of what had been a foundation of European expansion since the Spanish–Portuguese competition, that is, competition among European nation-states. The dynamics of European expansion were always part of the dynamics through which the European nation-states emerged, consolidated, and competed among one another. In the Age of Imperialism this force assumed a new quality. Imperialism was the will and ability of the nation-states – especially those in Europe – to define national interests within the international system as world policy interests and to view the colonies as a pledge within global power politics. It was a view of European power politics as world politics, and imperialistic colonial policies were seen as global power policies by means of colonies.

The unleashing of formal imperialism also meant that colonialism was "democratized" in the Age of High Imperialism. Imperialism and colonialism became caught in the maelstrom of nationalistically charged public opinion. Colonial policies and jingoism joined forces and could thus help decide elections, as was the case in the so-called "Hottentot elections" of 1907 in the German Empire.

A "project" of conquest, as Adam Smith subtly phrased it, is one thing; conquest and domination of the "periphery" and the establishment and implementation of colonial rule is something else. Looking back on the history of colonialism as a project of conquest, it is obvious that the establishment and maintenance of colonial rule was less a "project" than it was "muddling through," in which colonialist dreams and utopias of domination broke down, the arrogant sense of superiority of the colonial lords confronted the diversity of strategies of defiance among the conquered, and the ethnocentric sense of a civilizing mission got caught in the snares of the colonial situation and localization.

Colonial Rule

Nineteenth-century colonialism and imperialism were many things at once. But above all they were a utopia of domination – the utopia of implementing state rule in the conquered territories. In the history of colonialism, utopia at first almost always took the form of colonial companies, the most famous of which was certainly the British East India Company with its modern administrative structures. In the course of the development of colonial rule, colonial companies were put increasingly under the firm control of parliaments or governments of the "mother countries." Models for this kind of state rule were the European mother countries. With respect to these models, a "state" is consequently to be understood as a centralized territorial regime whose central power rather successfully claims the monopoly on legitimate use of physical force. The central authority has the resources of force more or less at its disposal, monopolizes the justification for use of force, and claims for itself monopolies in the normative order, that is, in setting norms, sanctioning violations of those norms, and enforcing the sanctions. In addition, the central power has access to a bureaucratic apparatus of rule and, accordingly, it claims direct exercise of power over the subjects, and is able at least in part to achieve this claim.

Setting up a colonial state was a revolutionary endeavor and amounted to radically changing the conquered society. It thus provoked virtually all possible serious conflicts that could emerge from human encounters. Also, during the period of High Imperialism and the scramble for colonial possessions in Africa, the utopia of the occidental state had been stripped of the civic, democratic, and constitutional aspects of the European process of nation building that it had in the second half of the eighteenth and all of the nineteenth centuries, and there was no basis for fundamental cultural common ground. Colonial law was the "law" of the conquerors. It strictly distinguished between "natives' rights" and rights that applied to the colonizers, and emphasized the executive primacy of the colonial government and administration *vis-à-vis* even the "white" population, which, in the German colonies for example, was subject to consular jurisdiction. The much-studied legal pluralism of the colonies underlines how deep the cleft extended between conqueror and conquered. The violent invaders were, and remained, foreign conquerors, even in their own view.

All the differences in types of colonialism notwithstanding, it is important not to lose sight of fundamental common ground. This includes the precarious nature of colonial rule through despotism, indirect rule, the limits of basic legitimacy, and the ever-present strategies of defiance.[9]

Despotism and the Limited Range of Colonial Rule

The colonial state was without a doubt a violent one. This was true both for its beginnings, in more or less bloody campaigns of conquest that fancied themselves as "expeditions," and for the many forms of violence with which the members of colonial society treated the subjugated populations. Both instances of this violence became a catalyst, mobilizing "twofold anticolonialism," the anticolonialism of the colonized and the anticolonialist critique and movements in Europe. The colonial state was violent above all in its everyday, routinized exercise of authority, that is, in the colonial administration. Its administrative actions were constitutively despotic.

We can distinguish three basic forms of state administrations in the colonies: despotic, intermediary rule, and bureaucratic. A despotic administration is characterized by arbitrary and violent action and threats of violence. Intermediary administrative action makes use of local agents and brokers – of which chiefs, interpreters, and local police were most important in West Africa – to implement administrative decisions. Bureaucratic administrations have direct access to their subjects, thus do not need intermediaries, and are based on abstract and general regulations. These abstract rules, to the extent that they concern the residents, are made known to the public or to representatives of the population and are commonly laid down in writing. The empirical relationships among the individual administration types were as diverse as the local conditions or the personalities of the local officials.

More significant with regard to routinized despotism is that the entire administration stood in the shadow of arbitrary and violent actions. Arbitrariness and violence are expansive. With respect to the state, this means that,

under conditions that lacked any effective institutional and normative means of keeping the force in check, the arbitrary and violent actions extended to all interactions between the people and the state administration. Georges Balandier spoke fittingly of the "colonial situation,"[10] in which contact between colonizers and the colonized necessarily resulted in mutual antagonisms. This corresponded to the situation of routinized despotic administrative actions. Colonial rule was a "despotic situation" for the colonized. The despotic situation was a social order without any basic trust, one of generalized suspicion in which all communication between administration and representatives of the central state authority, on the one hand, and the colonized, on the other, took place within the expectations of arbitrary and violent actions. The flip side of the despotic nature of colonial rule was, however, the *pax colonialis*. The more or less effective claim to a state monopoly on the use of force and the threat of force by the colonial power was imposed on the peoples and population groups of the colonial states with relative success.

Montesquieu's rigorous analysis of despotism also applied for the colonial regime: the scope of the colonial state and its ability to assert its decisions faced very strict limitations.[11] This refers not only to the diverse and continual challenges to the colonial claim to power by violent resistance and other forms of political opposition that culminated in movements for independence; it also applies to the degree of institutionalization of state rule itself. The colonial state was a precarious form of statehood. It is one of the forms of a weak state. Signs of this weakness are the key role that violence and force played in the administration of the colonial territories, the outstanding significance of intermediary administrative action, and the strict limits imposed on actions of the bureaucratic administration.

"Indirect Rule"

There are two sides to the intermediacy of colonial rule: internal and external. Internal intermediacy refers to the relatively great independence of the local administrative civil servants *vis-à-vis* the power centers. At the level of colonial administration it was the equivalent to what was referred to as "subimperialism" in periphery-oriented imperialism theories, in other words the fact that "expeditions," adventurers, business people, the military, or diplomats often – if not usually – furthered the acquisition of colonial land on their own and even against the declared will of their governments in Europe. Cecil Rhodes in South Africa exemplified subimperialism on a large scale, as did Gustav Nachtigal on the West African coast on a small scale. The impressive French colonial officer Robert Delavignette hit the mark in describing internal intermediacy in *Les Vrais chefs de l'empire*, choosing his title to refer to the "district officers" or "Commandants de cercle." The widespread internal intermediacy in the colonies came as a result of the localization of cultural and political patterns and institutions by the conquerors.

Under conditions of external intermediacy, the administration had to make use of intermediaries and brokers who had access to the local conditions and typically came from those local situations. They could be powerful, such as the Nabobs of the Moghul rulers in India or the *Fulani* emirates in northern Nigeria, or they could lack power, such as the *Ewe* chiefs in the German colony of Togo. External intermediators have also been referred to by Henri Brunschwig as "collaborators": the local police, interpreters, administrative or trading post employees, schoolteachers, or catechists.[12]

Colonial empires, worldviews, and cultures differed according to the respective system of authorities and figures of intermediary administration. We can distinguish in particular the British colonial policies of indirect rule from the direct rule *à la française*. But the practice of the conquerors reflected a less drastic opposition.[13] French direct rule remained by and large a chimera. But British indirect rule could not prevent the local rulers and leadership figures from becoming integrated into the hierarchical order of the colonial administration, especially in Africa.[14]

The colonial state reserved the right to make the final decision on appointment or hiring procedures and on who held which positions. To differing degrees the colonial conquerors changed the traditional rules of investiture.

They always attempted to control them and claimed the right to appoint, name, and remove someone from office. The colonial governments followed the hierarchical principle when inventing or reinforcing hierarchical relations between chiefs or when creating the position and role of the chief in the first place as a link between local administrators and the populace. Consequently, the modern, contemporary chieftainship is neo-traditional in every way. In many cases the colonial administration tried to make the chiefs economically dependent on the administration by letting income flow to them in different ways, typically in the form of appanages. It was an agency of domestication by the central authority that tried to make economically independent intermediaries into dependent brokers, in terms of both economics and social prestige.

The colonial state divided the colonial territories into administrative districts and erected outside borders. Both measures revolutionized the foundations of precolonial rule and leadership. Instead of ruling over people they established rule over territories. The colonial administrations paid careful attention to the borders of the administrative districts and even the outside boundaries did attempt not to violate what colonial officials viewed as tribal boundaries. Yet, despite their best efforts, the so-called "artificial" colonial borders remained a problem for the colonial administrations, for example as regards labor migration or smuggling. The greater the land area to be unified, the more difficult it was to achieve unity and integration.

Despite the different thrusts of bureaucratization, loss of power, and changes in chiefdom since the beginning of European colonial rule, intermediary power by local rulers or chiefs was maintained. The chiefs' most important protection against the power claims of the colonial government was their position in the judiciary, which they managed to defend successfully against all attacks.

Limits of the "Basic Legitimacy"

Despite the attempts of the conquerors to legitimate their rule, the colonized challenged the claims of the colonizers to legitimacy. But no ruler can survive long term without some basic legitimation. It is possible to distinguish several forms of basic legitimacy, but only two are relevant here: organizational power and cultural membership.

The "organizational power" of the rulers is their ability to know how to plan, coordinate, and utilize the members of a society or of large, individual groups in a society to implement and achieve goals that are important for society as a whole. Thus, the elderly Yao Tchedre Kpeo of Lama Kara noted in an interview with Dadja Halla-Kawa Simtaro about the German colonial period: "It was very difficult during the German period. They [the Germans] did not waste time. With them, you always had to be working. They were very strict. And still, people liked them. I liked them then and I still do. They got me to work hard."[15] The organizational power of the rulers was understandably assessed with mixed feelings. The suffering, the harshness of the work, and the cruelty with which the rulers pursued their goals compromised their aim to achieve more legitimacy through demonstrating their "organizational power." And yet the latter undeniably produced results: the trees that were planted, the buildings, streets, bridges, and railroad lines that were built. By securing results that are visible, tangible, and lasting, the rulers proved that their requirements and demands *vis-à-vis* those over whom they ruled were not merely lip service. They showed everyone that the arrogant and overbearing words were followed up with actions. Therefore, the organizational power of colonial rule was among the fundamental sources of their basic legitimacy.

The basic legitimacy of cultural membership worked in just the opposite way. The system of affiliation, determining who belongs and who does not, is constitutive for society. Society is a delimitation separating people and "barbarians," members and non-members, "natives" and foreigners, "us" and "them." However, the criteria that determine membership are by no means clearcut and easily decided. Membership denotes a social, cultural, and historical relationship and thus an extremely variable system. No matter what kind of criteria are used, it is

decisive for the question of basic legitimation that the rulers claim affiliation with those who are ruled and that this claim is confirmed.

European colonial rulers did not achieve such affiliation legitimacy among the vast majority of the colonized population, much less among the indigenous, oppositional elite. That was an insurmountable obstacle. European conquerors remained "the whites" in contrast to "the blacks" or "natives" or whatever the antagonistic stereotypes were. Domination by Europeans remained foreign rule, rule without the basic legitimacy of cultural membership, and this limit in the process of accumulating basic legitimation was used by the resistance movements and the later decolonization movements to their advantage.

Strategies of Defiance

In addition to violent resistance, which accompanied the colonial period from beginning to end, the most important strategies of defiance included movement, disobedience, and defensive communication. "The 'free' man is not the man who rids himself of commands after he has received them, but the man who knows how to evade them in the first place," declared Elias Canetti correctly.[16] Freedom is achieved primarily when commands do not reach the people they are targeting. Accordingly, movement is one of the indispensable principles in the construction of freedom. Free systems are those of movement. Fetters are the sign of being unfree. In the despotic situation of colonial rule, signs of fetters could be found everywhere. People wore chains, were chained together, and wore irons around their necks. Forced laborers slaved away on the roads and buildings that the colonial administration had them build. Soldiers surrounded villages for the purpose of levying taxes. People and livestock were herded together. But common to both despotism and colonial rule were that the commands typically did not reach the people beyond the palace of the governor, the capital, the provincial centers, and the personal presence of the governor or his officials and soldiers. People in the colonial order could and knew how to evade commands by escaping or fleeing. Flight existed in many forms and can be distinguished by the degrees of freedom and powerlessness expressed therein.

The most important form of flight was leaving the colony. In the Western regions of the German colony of Togo, people moving to English territory was a constant administrative problem. The 1913–14 annual report of the station in Ho mentions that there were times when 75–90 percent of the male population had left the villages and moved to the British Gold Coast. A second form of escape was desertion of soldiers, porters, and forced laborers. A third form of flight was hiding. This always existed as soon as forced labor, collection of taxes, vaccinations, or porter services became imminent, often even every time administrative staff or members of the colonial society arrived. Powerlessness was most obvious in the fourth form of escape. It was apparent whenever people left everything and simply got up and ran when police, soldiers, and administrative officials approached. Flight was prevalent in the years of violent subjugation, which is often described euphemistically in colonial historiography as the "pacification phase."

People knew how to evade commands. Nevertheless, the commands of the local administration generally reached the people they were meant for. All in all, a majority of the indigenous population did not leave. Those who hid eventually abandoned their hiding places, and those who fled returned. Consequently, these subjects had to answer to the suggestions and commands of the administration. One way of circumventing the unreasonable demands of the administration was to disobey. Similar to the strategy of flight, disobedience hit the central areas of the system that was restructured by the administration: labor, services for the rulers, trade, agriculture, law, and the manners of subjugation. There were many forms of disobedience – violent and non-violent ones. Lying became a significant form of communication of the colonized. Next to lying stood communicative strategies of "excuses," feigning ignorance, supposed agreement and hiding the truth by silence or by offering random false information. The communication forms of the colonized were marked by an attempt to defend themselves against the questions, suggestions, and demands of the rulers. They were "defen-

sive" in that they were reactions to actions by the state administration or other members of ruling colonial society. They were defensive because they were marked by a single intention: to rid themselves of the rulers with all their questions, suggestions, and commands as quickly as possible and to keep them away. "Defensive communication" aimed to create distance between the colonized and the rulers in a situation in which the colonized were typically no longer in a position to break off the communication and take to their heels. It was also a form of communication in which actors tried to protect their agency in a situation in which they were being forced into the object status of the subjugated in a more or less pronounced way. These various strategies of defiance made life difficult for the colonial administration, which faced obstacles and remained permanently vulnerable, even at times of peaceful administrative routine.

Colonial Society

In line with Robert Delavignette, "colonial society" can be understood as the sociocultural system of groups of the ruling minority of colonial conquerors and their relations with the subjugated population.[17] Depending on the type of colony, a majority of the conquerors was comprised of settlers or of civilian and military officials, administrative employees, missionaries, merchants, and businessmen, either with or without wives and families. The trade colonies especially were societies of bachelors before 1914. Initially, and most importantly, colonial society was small. The ratio of white intruders to subjugated people was tiny. Conquerors and rulers acted from a feeling of superiority. Their belief in their essential superiority was anchored in different ideological currents that prevailed at the time, from Darwinism, Social Darwinism, racism, imperialism, and eugenics to educational policies with their theories of reeducating the colonized. In their contacts with the colonized, members of colonial society forced the "uncivilized" underlings to live in the mimicry of subjugation. But the colonizers themselves were subject to the principle of non-authenticity in colonial society. Members of colonial society lived "in comparison." The measuring stick of the mother country was ever present. Colonial living conditions were measured by it, and many lived with only the necessities – settlers and officials alike, except for a few, such as the privileged "gentlemen" in British India or Southeast Asia. Colonial society was also confronted with localization processes in which the colonized took on elements from the culture of the colonial conquerors. In the German colonies, for instance, members of colonial society never tired of their amused arrogance as expressed by seeing German artifacts or symbols in the hands of African kings, chiefs, or elders. Members of colonial society were wanderers between two worlds. They were homeless. Their society, in comparison, was captive; it was staged, a culture of recreation and reproduction. The colonists tried to recreate that which was authentic – which is how they viewed the homeland – and thus they experienced their own lives as inauthentic. Rulers and indigents alike were caught in the vicious cycle of non-authenticity.

Legally, politically, and economically privileged, and separated from the colonized, members of colonial society lived in a world of and for whites – in the European district, in clubs, in everyday social relations, celebrations, and public events. The unity of colonial society was a dominating, antagonistic, and segregationist unity against the colonized. Death, mostly through disease, was part of it. Death in colonial society was ubiquitous; it brought people together, spared no one, and thus created bonds and solidarity.

The existential solidarity within colonial society led to the fact that it too was subject to localization processes or responded to these with strategies of exclusion. The latter was the uncompromising stigmatization of "going native," which some took the liberty to do. The former was the epitome of the sense of superiority, turning against not only the colonized, but the world of the mother country as well. Localization in many places showed aspects of a conservative anti-modernism. It meant rejecting the industrial civilization and society that was developing, even though these were among the essential preconditions for nineteenth-century colonialism and made the technologies of control available in the first place, from the gunboat and machine gun to the railroad and telegraph.

The separation that emerged in colonial society was predominantly due to the colonizers not knowing the language of the colonized. Rulers and ruled faced each other in silence. Interpreters helped to some extent, as did the use of a mishmash of pidgin or "coastal English" that was common in German colonies which bordered on British ones. But the inadequacy of these linguistic crutches became clear early on. Christian missionaries, aside from scientists on expeditions and some research officials, were usually the only ones to take the effort to learn the so-called "languages of the natives." Many of them were among the most renowned researchers of indigenous languages. The issue of which language should be taught in school was longstanding. Most settlers tended to limit their communication with the indigenous population to the absolute minimum and supported the view that only local languages should be taught in school. There was the widespread fear that the languages of the rulers from the Western world would make emancipatory and anticolonial ideas accessible to the colonized. In Indonesia during the Dutch colonial period, the indigenous population was "forbidden to use the Dutch language whenever colonial rulers wished to underscore the racist caste system symbolically."[18]

Sexual relations between male members of the conqueror class and local women were firmly established in all colonies. Missionaries continually filed charges and there was much heated debate about the "unworthy conduct" of the Europeans, about "half-breeds" and "mixed marriages," to name some but certainly not all of the expressions used in this lascivious debate. In conspicuous opposition to this controversy was the naturalness with which the male members of the colonial privileged class continued, despite such denunciations, to have such sexual relations. Sexual relations were one example of the juxtaposition of separation and connection in relationships between conqueror and conquered. One end of the spectrum of forms of sexual relations between the conqueror class and the subjugated showed characteristics of arbitrariness, lawlessness, humiliation, and violence. They were an expression of the deep chasm separating the two groups. At the other end were forms of sexual relations in which members of colonial society gained limited access to the realities of the colonized. An extreme example of this type is that of the experienced district officer in the initial decades of the colonial period. A district officer typically lived alone in the bush, that is, away from any other Europeans. He was quite familiar with African customs and local life, and part of his way of relating to the community included one or more African mistresses. Sometimes, depending on local customs, the district officer even married a local woman and after leaving the colony made provisions for the support of his indigenous wife and children. However, the vast majority of sexual relationships were between employer and employee in which the unbridgeable gap between master and servant corresponded to an indifferent aristocratic or middle-class employer morality.

Cultural Conquest I: Christian Mission and Schools

From the very beginning the Christian mission was an integral element of European expansion and colonialism, from the Spanish mission in Latin America and the Jesuit mission in the Far East or Canada to the London Missionary Society (founded 1795) and all the other missions that were founded during the period of European expansion and colonialism. Especially in the fifteenth and sixteenth centuries, the efforts of the "heathen mission" finally offered a justification for conquering a foreign country, taking it as a possession and laying claims to power. In the early nineteenth century thousands of Catholic and Protestant missionaries from Europe, North America, and the West Indies set off to spread Christianity in Africa. The missionaries followed the routes of the traders, expedition corps, and explorers, or preceded them. Their stations served the expansive undertakings of unscrupulous traders and presumptuous conquerors and the thirst for knowledge of researching adventurers. An expression of Zulu chief Cetshwayo became famous: "First a missionary, then a consul, and

then come army."[19] If, based on absolute numbers, Christianity is today the world's largest religion, then this is evidence of the most lasting impact of European expansion and Christian missionizing, especially in nineteenth and twentieth-century Africa. Cultural globalization and colonialism in the nineteenth century were – and still are – essentially processes of Christian missionizing. Aggressive colonization and Christian mission were closely connected from the outset. Perhaps the best symbol of this link are a few extant Christian crosses that certainly did not add all that much weight to the hand luggage of travelers and which are part of the inventory in the Museo de Oro in Lima, Peru. With a simple spring mechanism these crosses become sharp daggers.

Christian missionaries expressly shared the feeling of cultural superiority that united colonial society and they were among its most significant sources. As in the colonial civil service, part of this sense of superiority was the patriarchal concept in which the indigenous people held the status of children. That idea was, however, less colonialist than it was Christian, corporative, and in agreement with a missionary culture that viewed the "heathen mission," poor relief, and efforts for the spiritual "betterment" of the European underclasses as different aspects of one and the same religious and missionary responsibility. The close personal, official, protocol-defined, and ceremonial contact between missionaries and colonial administration, which could go so far as the same person serving as messenger of both the faith and the colonial officers, demonstrated to the colonized the unity of missionary and administrative claims to power. This included brusque and intolerant attitudes towards the local cultures. Thus, missionaries everywhere strictly rejected religious or "magical" rituals and polygamy.

From the beginning, the missions had, however, also become a thorn in the side of diverse groups of colonial conquerors by opposing the despotic colonial administration, the genocidal hunger for land of self-satisfying colonists, and the enslavement of indigenous populations as "workhorses" by plantation and mine owners. In connection with the colonized population's acceptance of Christianity, with its individualizing and emancipatory elements and natural rights aspects, the missionary opposition (especially in sub-Saharan Africa) became the social, normative, and cultural gathering ground for resistance to colonial rule and later decolonization movements. These movements first started among Christians and to a considerable extent the movement leaders had been missionary students, catechists, pastors, or priests. In this sense there is a direct link from the famous efforts of the Dominican friars Antonio Montesino and Bartolomé de Las Casas against the genocide of the Indios and their lack of rights in the *encomienda* system, to the missionary opposition to slavery and colonial violence in the nineteenth century, to present-day Latin American liberation theology. Mission and the message of Christianity were the social and cultural spheres of localization and resistance, as well as being sites and objects of the cultural awakening of the colonized.

What applied to colonial society also applied to the mission. The goal of the missionary cultural policies in Africa was to achieve "a Western civilization purified of the political and social 'damage.' "[20] Localization by the conquered was manifested in a variety of syncretic forms between Christian religion and local systems of belief, between local rituals and the rites of the churches of the European missionaries. The competing pluralism of the Christian missions in the nineteenth century led to the founding of new Christian churches as well as the emergence of prophetic and millenarian movements. These churches represented a connection between the localization of Christian religions and resistance to a mission that was experienced as part of colonial rule. Elements of resistance to missionizing and Christianity became obvious within the Hindu and Islamic spheres. "Many varieties of anticolonial solidarity" emerged, which were based on neo-Hinduism and led from "arbitrarily or non-arbitrarily 'invented' religious and cultural traditions" to "a new emphasis on autochthonous and particular traditions, sometimes in a radical fundamentalist shape."[21] Islam differed from all other religions the missionaries encountered in that it was itself a missionary religion with a long, intensive history of con-

frontation with Christianity and it remained largely resistant to Christian missionizing efforts. Islam maintained its integrity and reinforced local culture (in Malaysia for example) through cooperation between the local elites and the British colonial administration, which in the system of indirect rule appreciated cooperation with Islamic rulers and elites in Malaya as much as in India or Central Africa.

Missionizing was not least an "elevator" of social upward mobility, in which the close ties between mission and schools played a major role. Many leadership figures in the decolonization movements, such as Jawaharal Nehru and Kwame Nkrumah, received their secondary schooling at public schools and colleges of the British aristocracy, at the universities of Paris, Leiden, Lisbon, or Moscow, or at Lincoln University in Pennsylvania. But such educational options were reserved during the entire colonial period to a minute upper class in the colonies and did not become relevant until the time of the colonies' pending independence and afterwards. They were insignificant prior to World War I and never affected the schooling of the broad base of the colonial population. German missionary schools prior to 1914 are especially suited to outline the range of schooling in quantitative terms, because "other European powers had nothing even vaguely comparable in the colonies before 1914."[22] Shortly before the war, 5.3 percent of the population in Southwest Africa attended German missionary schools, 1.3 percent in Cameroon, 0.9 percent in German East Africa, 3.2 percent in New Guinea, 0.8 percent in Kiaochow (Jiao Xian), and, notably, 29.4 percent of the total population of roughly 40,000 in Samoa. As an admittedly very general comparison, 86.3 percent of the Prussian population aged ten and older had completed elementary school in 1871.

Unlike France, which in Jacobinic tradition preferred public education, Germany, Britain, and Belgium put education in the hands of the missionaries and at most subsidized it with extremely modest funding. A majority of the mission schools were basically "bush schools" that taught reading, writing, and arithmetic, but concentrated mostly on religious instruction. The missionaries were primarily interested in making holy scripture accessible to the girls and boys, and it was soon translated into indigenous languages. Training as assistants and for subordinate functions in the administration and colonial economy tended to be a supplementary responsibility. "Upbringing" was given greater priority than "education" and the "education" that was acquired – especially in the emerging secondary schools at the turn of the twentieth century – was often rather bizarre. Students learned the names of English rivers and British monarchs; they could recite the classics of French literature or the victories of the Prussian armies against France, but they learned nothing about their own country and their own history. At the same time, what applied to the constant fight over the language of instruction applied no less to education in general. Most probably shared the view of the German Benedictine friar Cyrillus Wehrmeister, whose formula was short and to the point: "Too much is unhealthy."[23]

But school was also the sphere of a new social mobility. Children of slaves and other groups with dependent status were admitted as students. Girls were taught and the schools became the social forge of a new lower middle class of interpreters, police, soldiers, catechists, teachers, and office workers. As brokers and intermediaries they became key figures in the intermediate order of the colonial hierarchy. Quite a few leaders of the resistance to colonial rule and the later protagonists of efforts for independence had previously been students at the colonial and (especially) the missionary schools. For both the powerless and those with high status and authority in the indigenous societies, schools became the measure of reference and the screen on which to project their political or religious ideas and social utopia, which either challenged colonial rule or would challenge it later in the history of colonialism.

Cultural Conquest II: Knowledge between Power, Monologue, and Ethnographic *Rapprochement*

The colonial mission was an undertaking to explore the "natives," and many missionaries were often the first ethnographers. If they wanted to preach to the people, live with them, and win over their spirits and their souls, then it was a good idea to develop an understanding of these people and to be understood by them. One can thus imagine how the missionaries' examination of the indigenous languages represented an enormous step along the path not only to the "others," but generally to the "Other." It must also be kept in mind that, unlike colonial society in the major cities and provincial towns, missionaries and colonial officials "in the bush" lived, if not together, then in close contact with the colonized population. On top of that, the mission as a colonial institution was one thing, but the interest of many missionaries in the living conditions, society, and culture of the conquered people was something else entirely. Individual missionaries continually made an effort systematically to research and document the traditions of the conquered peoples and tribes and their social, cultural, political, and economic institutions and ideas – from the Spanish Franciscan monk Bernardino de Sahagún in the sixteenth century, without whose magnificent work we would know far less today about the Aztec culture; to James Chalmers, the "Livingston of New Guinea," who paid for his missionary work with his life in the second half of the nineteenth century; to Diedrich Westermann, a distinguished African scholar and missionary in the North German Mission Society.

Missionaries were not the only group to compile knowledge about the conquered peoples and their living conditions; colonial civil servants also did so. The bureaucratic administration, with its goal of gaining direct access to the colonized, had an unquenchable thirst for knowledge. The officials counted humans and animals and measured, charted, and prospected; they compiled extensive statistics on weather and climate, disease and labor migrants. This brought a rapid increase in knowledge, at least as regards the natural sciences and medicine. If through all those efforts they still knew so little about the conditions of the colonized, then it was only because they were caught in a dungeon of ignorance through despotic and intermediary rule. Not unlike the situation of the mission, albeit to a far more limited extent, there were quite a few colonial civil servants who pursued research of their environment above and beyond the framework of their official tasks. If colonial civil servants became local historians or ethnologists, it was, however, due to the efforts of individuals. The professionalization of colonial training, as through the Indian Civil Service or the Dutch colonial administration as early as the first half of the nineteenth century, greatly influenced the colonial administrations in sub-Saharan Africa, especially after World War I, and served to increase the significance of the model of the researching colonial civil servant. This model applied only to a very few, all the more impressive personalities, in the colonial civil service as a whole.

Up until the early decades of the twentieth century, research of colonial regions in Africa was based also on the institutions of research trips and expeditions, from Mungo Park to René Caillé, and Heinrich Barth – who to this day is the most important of all research travelers – to Henry Morton Stanley. Scientific "experts," led by linguists, geographers, and doctors, continued to gain importance, especially from the second half of the nineteenth century. They were joined by ethnologists as the distinction between academic researchers and colonial ethnographers became ever more clearcut. The process of institutionalizing ethnology as an independent discipline got off the ground, with the Netherlands leading the way with the first departmental chair in ethnology at the University of Leiden. "Colonial ethnology" and "applied ethnology" emerged, in which ethnology was declared the prerequisite for the development of colonized societies and their cultures.

The relationship between ethnology and colonialism has been heavily criticized.[24] Edward Said's work was especially important in claiming that the discourse between the West and the non-Western world was a Western monologue about the colonial and postcolonial world. Said held that this monologue served to define and essentialize the non-occidental world as the radical Other and the reversal of all that constitutes and is held sacred by the West. In discourse on *the* Orient, he continued, the West defines itself, justifying and legitimizing its claim of cultural hegemony and political domination over the East: "The West is the actor, the Orient a passive reactor. The West is the spectator, the judge, and the jury of every facet of Oriental behavior."[25]

Said's work and the long and ongoing debate that it engendered has directly led to an increase in the research on the image that the colonized had of the conquerors. It is emphasized that Western Orientalism corresponds to an "Occidentalism" in the non-Western world and that at the same time both discourses remain closely interrelated. More important is that ethnographic knowledge comes out of interactions in a competitive network of actors who are members of societies and cultures that are themselves socially differentiated, diverse, and conflict laden. The "informant" in the India of the Orientalists was a scholarly Brahman with his own interests and relations to the less privileged in his society, just as the ignorance of the colonial civil servant was partly a product of strategies of defiance of the subjugated population against the knowledge of the rulers. The monologue that protagonists of postcolonial studies believe they can identify between the Western and the non-Western worlds has many voices, including those at whom the supposed monologue was directed. Often, it is precisely the latter's silence that might be an effective power strategy and the monologue, the torrent of words of the powerful, might be nothing more than helpless chatter hiding fear by whistling in the dark. The "periphery" is more present in the texts that the "anti-Orientalists" deconstruct than even the deconstructed monologue of colonial ethnology seems to suggest.

ACKNOWLEDGMENTS

I am very grateful for the competent and sensitive translation from German into English by Allison Brown.

NOTES

1   Osterhammel (1997: 4–10).
2   Lonsdale (1985: 694).
3   Balandier (1966: 34–61).

4   A. Smith (1994: bk. 4, ch. 7, pt. 1).
5   Gallagher and Robinson (1953: 1–15).
6   Curtin (2002: 42).
7   Osterhammel (1997: 32).
8   Piault (1987).
9   Trotha (1994).
10 Balandier (1966).
11 Montesquieu (2002).
12 Brunschwig (1983).
13 Crowder (1963).
14 Beck (1989).
15 Simtaro (1982: 745).
16 Canetti (1981: 306).
17 Delavignette (1950: 31–63).
18 Osterhammel (1997: 101).
19 Gründer (1992: 569).
20 Gründer (1982: 576).
21 Osterhammel (1997: 99).
22 Gründer (1982: 365).
23 Ibid: 366.
24 Leclerc (1972); Asad (1973).
25 Said (1978: 109).

GUIDE TO FURTHER READING

In addition to Osterhammel's marvelous little book *Colonialism*, which reveals a sound and scholarly judgment and an admirable grasp of all the actual scientific debates covering different disciplines, those readers who are interested in a more detailed treatment of the subject will still find a balanced view and a masterpiece of historical scholarship and erudition in Albertini and Wirz's *European Colonial rule, 1880–1940*. The same can be said for Fieldhouse's *Economics and Empire 1830–1914*, which deals with the important economic side of colonialism and develops some *caveat* against rash conclusions about the relationships between colonialism and economic profitability. Based on case studies reaching from Mexico to Japan and emphasizing the interactional nature of the confrontation between colonizers and colonized, Curtin's *The World and the West* highlights the ways the colonized dealt with the colonial conquest and how colonial conquest often changed societies and cultures through its unintentional consequences. For a succinct, elegant, and masterly summary of the older but still important theoretical debates about colonialism and imperialism, the student of colonialism should read Mommsen's *Theories of Imperialism*. The recent debate about Orientalism, based on Edward Said's book of the same title, which reactivates in cultural terms many of the arguments dealt with in the book by Mommsen, is well documented in Harlow and Carter's *Imperialism and Orientalism*.

Bibliography

Abbott, R., "Police Reform in the Russian Province of Iaroslavl, 1856–1876," *Slavic Review*, 32:2 (1973), pp. 292–302.

Abrams, L., *The Making of Modern Woman: Europe 1789–1918* (London, 2002).

Accampo, E. A., *Industrialization, Family Life and Class Relations: Saint Chamond, 1815–1914* (Berkeley, CA, 1984).

Aceña, P. M., "Development and Modernization of the Financial System, 1844–1935," in N. Sánchez-Albornoz (ed.), *The Economic Modernization of Spain, 1830–1930* (New York, 1987).

Ackerknecht, E. H., *Medicine at the Paris Hospital, 1794–1848* (Baltimore, MD, 1967).

Ackerknecht, E. H., "Anticontagionism between 1821 and 1867," *Bulletin of the History of Medicine* 22 (1987), pp. 562–93.

Adams, B. F., *The Politics of Punishment: Prison Reform in Russia 1863–1917* (DeKalb, IL, 1996).

Adams, R. J. Q. and P. P. Poirier, *The Conscription Controversy in Great Britain, 1900–18* (Basingstoke, 1987).

Adas, M., *Machines as the Measure of Men: Science, Technology, and Ideologies of Western Dominance* (Ithaca, NY, 1989).

Agulhon, M., *Marianne into Battle: Republican Imagery and Symbolism in France, 1789–1880* (Cambridge, 1981).

Agulhon, M. and P. Bonte, *Marianne: les visages de la république* (Paris, 1992).

Åkerman, S., U. Högberg, and M. Danielson, "Height, Health and Nutrition in Early Modern Sweden," in A. Brändström and L.-G. Tedebrand (eds.), *Society, Health and Population During the Demographic Transition* (Stockholm, 1986), pp. 413–28.

Albertini, R. von and A. Wirz, *European Colonial Rule, 1880–1940: The Impact of the West on India, Southeast Asia, and Africa* (Westport, CT, 1982).

Albrecht-Carrié, R., *The Concert of Europe* (London, 1968).

Aldcroft, D. H. and S. P. Ville, *The European Economy 1750–1914: A Thematic Approach* (Manchester, 1994).

Alder, K., *The Measure of All Things* (New York, 2002).

Alexander, S., *Women's Work in Nineteenth-Century London: A Study of the Years 1820–50* (London, 1983).

Allen, A. T., "Gardens of Children, Gardens of God: Kindergartens and Day Care Centers in Nineteenth-Century Germany," *Journal of Social History* 19 (1986), pp. 433–50.

Allen, P. L., "The Wages of Sin: Sex and Disease," *Past and Present* (Chicago, 2000).

Allen, R. C. and C. Ó Gráda, "On the Road Again with Arthur Young: English, Irish and French Agriculture During the Industrial Revolution," *Journal of Economic History* 48 (1988).

Almog, S., *Nationalism and Antisemitism in Modern Europe 1815–1945* (Jerusalem, 1990).

Alter, G., "Theories of Fertility Decline: A Nonspecialist's Guide to the Current Debate," in J. Gillis, L. A. Tilly, and D. Levine (eds.), *The European Experience of Declining Fertility, 1850–1970: The Quiet Revolution* (Oxford, 1992), pp. 13–27.

Alter, P., *Nationalism*, 2nd edn. (London, 1994).

Alter, P., *The German Question and Europe: A History* (London, 2000).

Altermatt, U., *Der Weg der Schweizer Katholiken ins Ghetto* (Zurich, 1972).

Altermatt, U., *Katholizismus und Moderne. Zur Sozial- und Mentalitätsgeschichte der Schweizer Katholiken im 19. und 20. Jahrhundert* (Zurich, 1989).

Ambjörnson, R., *Öst och Väst. Tankar om Europa mellan Asien och Amerika* (Stockholm, 1994).

Amdam, R. P., "Industrial Espionage and the Transfer of Technology to the Early Norwegian Glass Industry," in K. Bruland (ed.), *Technology Transfer and Scandinavian Industrialisation* (Oxford, 1991), pp. 73–94.

Amin, S., *Domination et sous-développement* (Montréal, 1974).

Aminzade, R., *Ballots and Barricades: Class Formation and Republican Politics in France 1830–1871* (Princeton, NJ, 1993).

Amman, P. H., *Revolution and Mass Democracy: The Paris Club Movement in 1848* (Princeton, NJ, 1975).

Anderson, B., *Imagined Communities: Reflections on the Origins and Spread of Nationalism*, 2nd edn. (London 1991).

Anderson, J. L., *Explaining Long-Term Economic Change* (Cambridge, 1995).

Anderson, M., *Family Structure in Nineteenth Century Lancashire* (Cambridge, 1971).

Anderson, M., *Population Change in North-Western Europe, 1750–1850* (Basingstoke, 1988).

Anderson, M. L., "The Kulturkampf and the Course of German History," *Central European History* 19 (1986), pp. 82–115.

Anderson, M. L., "Voter, Junker, Landrat, Priest: The Old Authorities and the New Franchise in Imperial Germany," *American Historical Review* 5 (1993), pp. 1448–74.

Anderson, M. L., "The Limits of Secularization: On the Problem of the Catholic Revival in Nineteenth-Century Germany," *Historical Journal* 38:3 (1995), pp. 647–70.

Anderson, M. L., *Practising Democracy: Elections and Political Culture in Imperial Germany* (Princeton, NJ, 2000).

Anderson, M. L., "Living Apart and Together in Germany," in H. W. Smith (ed.), *Protestants, Catholics and Jews in Germany, 1800–1914* (Oxford, 2001), pp. 317–32.

Anderson, M. S., *The Eastern Question, 1774–1923: A Study in International Relations* (London, 1966).

Anderson, O., "The Political Uses of History in Mid Nineteenth-Century England," *Past and Present* 36 (1967), pp. 87–105.

Angelow, J., *Von Wien nach Königgrätz. Die Sicherheitspolitik des Deutschen Bundes im europäischen Gleichgewicht (1815–1866)* (Munich, 1996).

Ansley J. and S. C. Watkins (eds.), *The Decline of Fertility in Europe* (Princeton, NJ, 1986).

Apollonio, U. (ed.), *Futurist Manifestos* (London, 1973).

Applegate, C., "A Europe of Regions: Reflections on the Historiography of Sub-National Places in Modern Times," *American Historical Review* 104 (1999), pp. 1157–82.

Applegate, C., "Democracy or Reaction? The Political Implications of Localist Ideas in Wilhelmine and Weimar Germany," in L. E. Jones and J. Retallack (eds.), *Elections, Mass Politics and Social Change* (Cambridge, 1992), p. 256.

Applewhite, H. B. and D. G. Levy, "Women, Radicalization, and the Fall of the French Monarchy," in H. B. Applewhite and D. G. Levy (eds.), *Women and Politics in the Age of Democratic Revolution* (Ann Arbor, MI, 1993), pp. 81–108.

Armstrong, J. A., *Nations before Nationalism* (Chapel Hill, NC, 1982).

Arndt, E. M., "Kurzer Katechismus für teutsche Soldaten (1812)," in E. M. Arndt, *Drei Flugschriften* (Berlin, 1988).

Aronsson, P., "Swedish Rural Society and Political Culture: The Eighteenth- and Nineteenth-Century Experience," *Rural History* 3:1 (1992), pp. 41–57.

Asad, T. (ed.), *Anthropology and the Colonial Encounter* (London, 1973).

Ash, M., *Gestalt Psychology in German Culture, 1890–1967: Holism and the Quest for Objectivity* (Cambridge, 1995).

Audoin-Rouzeau, S., *1870: La France dans la guerre* (Paris, 1989).

Avineri, S., *The Social and Political Thought of Karl Marx* (Cambridge, 1968).

Avineri, S., *Hegel's Theory of the Modern State* (Cambridge, 1972).

Avineri, S., *The Making of Modern Zionism: The Intellectual Origins of the Jewish State* (New York, 1981).

Axtmann, R., " 'Police' and the Formation of the Modern State," *German History* 10:1 (1992), pp. 39–61.

Bailey, P., *Leisure and Class in Victorian England* (London, 1978).

Baines, D., *Emigration from Europe 1815–1930* (Houndmills, 1991).

Bairoch, P., "Agriculture and the Industrial Revolution, 1700–1914," trans. M. Grindrod, in C. Cipolla (ed.), *Fontana Economic History of Europe, Vol. 3: The Industrial Revolution* (London, 1973), pp. 452–506.

Baker, A., "Deterioration or Development?: The Peasant Economy of Moscow Province Prior to 1914," *Russian History/Histoire Russe* 5:1 (1978), pp. 1–23.

Baker, A. R. H., *Ideology and Landscape in Historical Perspective* (Cambridge, 1992).

Baker, A. R. H., "Farm Schools in Nineteenth Century France and the Case of La Charmoise, 1847–1865," *Agricultural History Review*, 44:1 (1996), pp. 47–62.

Baker, K. M. (ed.), *The French Revolution and the Creation of Modern Political Culture* (Oxford, 1987).

Bakounine, M., *Confession* (Paris, 1974) [1851].

Balandier, G., "The Colonial Situation: A Theoretical Approach," in I. Wallerstein (ed.), *Social Change and the Colonial Situation* (New York, 1966), pp. 34–61.

Banac, I. and P. A. Bushkovitch (eds.), *The Nobility in Russia and Eastern Europe* (New Haven, CT, 1983).

Bank, J., *Het roemrijk vaderland: cultureel nationalisme in Nederland in de negentiende eeuw* (The Hague, 1990).

Banks, J. A., *Victorian Values: Secularism and the Size of Families* (London, 1981).

Bann, S., *The Clothing of Clio* (Cambridge, 1984).

Bann, S., *The Inventions of History* (Manchester, 1990).

Banton, M., *Racial Theories* (Cambridge, 1987).

Barber, P. and C. Board, *Tales from the Map Room: Fact and Fiction about Maps and their Makers* (London, 1993).

Bardet, J. P., J. N. Luc, I. Robin-Romero and C. Rollett (eds.), *Lorsque l'enfant grandit* (Paris, 2003).

Barkan, E., *The Retreat of Scientific Racism: Changing Concepts of Race in Britain and the United States Between the World Wars* (Cambridge, 1992).

Barker, E., *The Development of Public Services in Western Europe: 1660–1930* (London, 1944).

Barkin, K., "Social Control and the Volksschule in Vormärz Prussia," *Central European History* 61:1 (1983), pp. 31–52.

Barnard, F. M., *Herder's Social and Political Thought: From Enlightenment to Nationalism* (Oxford, 1965).

Barnes, D., *Making of a Social Disease: Tuberculosis in Nineteenth-Century France* (Berkeley, CA, 1995).

Baron, S. W., *The Russian Jew under Tsars and Soviets*, 2nd edn. (New York, 1987).

Barret-Ducrocq, F., *Love in the Time of Victoria: Sexuality, Class and Gender in Nineteenth-Century London*, trans. J. Howe (New York, 1991).

Barrow, L. and I. Bullock, *Democratic Ideas and the British Labour Movement 1880–1914* (Cambridge, 1996).

Bartlett, C. J., *Peace, War and the European Powers, 1814–1914* (London, 1996).

Baten, J., "Heights and Real Wages in the 18th and 19th Centuries: An International Overview," *Jahrbuch für Wirtschaftsgeschichte* (2000/1), pp. 61–76.

Baumgart, W., *Europäisches Konzert und nationale Bewegung. Internationale Beziehungen 1830–1878* (Paderborn, 1999).

Baumgart, W., "Der Krimkrieg, 1853–56," in B. Wegner (ed.), *Wie Kriege entstehen. Zum historischen Hintergrund von Staatenkonflikten* (Paderborn, 2000), pp. 191–209.

Bayley, D., "The Police and Political Change in Comparative Perspective," *Law and Society Review* 6:1 (1971), pp. 91–112.

Bazin, G., *The Museum Age* (Brussels, 1967).

Beaver, M. W., "Population, Infant Mortality and Milk," *Population Studies* 27 (1973), pp. 243–54.

Bebel, A., *Woman under Socialism*, trans. D. De Leon (New York, 1971).

Beck, K., "Stämme im Schatten des Flugs: Zur Entstehung administrativer Häuptlingstümer im nördlichen Sudan," *Sociologicus* 39 (1989), pp. 19–35.

Becker, J. (ed.), *Bismarcks "Spanische Diversion" 1870 und der preußisch-deutsche Reichsgründungskrieg. Quellen zur Vor- und Nachgeschichte der Hohenzollern-Kandidatur für den Thron in Madrid 1866–1932*, Vol. 1 (Paderborn, 2003).

Becker, P., "Die Rezeption der Physiologie in Kriminalistik und Kriminologie: Variationen über Norm und Ausgrenzung," in P. Sarasin and J. Tanner (eds.), *Physiologie und industrielle Gesellschaft. Studien zur Verwissenschaftlichung des Körpers im 19. und 20. Jahrhundert* (Frankfurt am Main, 1998), pp. 453–90.

Becker, P., *Verderbnis und Entartung, Eine Geschichte der Kriminologie des 19. Jahrhunderts als Diskurs und Praxis* (Göttingen, 2002).

Becker, W., "Der Kulturkampf als europäisches und als deutsches Phänomen," *Historisches Jahrbuch* 101 (1984), pp. 422–46.

Beckett, J. V. and M. Turner, "Taxation and Economic Growth in Eighteenth-Century England," *Economic History Review* 43:3 (1990), pp. 377–403.

Beer, G., *Darwin's Plots: Evolutionary Narrative in Darwin, George Eliot and Nineteenth Century Fiction* (London, 1985).

Beetham, D., *Max Weber and the Theory of Modern Politics*, 2nd edn. (Cambridge, 1985).

Behagg, C., "Masters and Manufacturers: Social Values and the Smaller Unit of Production in Birmingham, 1800–1850," in G. Crossick and H.-G. Haupt (eds.), *Shopkeepers and Master Artisans in Nineteenth-Century Europe* (London, 1984).

Behagg, C., *Politics and Production in the Early Nineteenth Century* (London, 1990).

Beirne, P., "Inventing Criminology: The 'Science of Man' in Cesare Beccaria's Dei Delitti e Della Pene," in P. Beirne (ed.), *The Origins and Growth of Criminology: Essays on Intellectual History 1760–1945* (Dartmouth 1994), pp. 777–820.

Belchem, J., "Charity, Ethnicity and the Catholic Parish," in J. Belchem (ed.), *Merseypride: Essays in Liverpool Exceptionalism* (Liverpool, 2000), pp. 101–27.

Belknap, R. L., "Dostoevskii and Psychology," in W. J. Leatherbarrow (ed.), *The Cambridge Companion to Dostoevskii* (Cambridge, 2002), pp. 131–47.

Bell, D., "Lingua Populi, Lingua Dei: Language, Religion and the Origins of French Revolutionary Nationalism," *American Historical Review* 5 (1995), pp. 1403–37.

Bell, D., *The Cult of the Nation in France: Inventing Nationalism 1680–1800* (Cambridge, MA, 2001).

Bell, H. D., *Sesto San Giovanni: Workers, Culture and Politics in an Italian Town 1880–1922* (New Brunswick, NJ, 1986).

Belliustin, I. *Description of the Parish Clergy in Rural Russia: The Memoir of a Nineteenth Century Parish Priest* (New York, 1985).

Benbassa, E. and A. Rodrigue, *The Jews of the Balkans: The Judeo-Spanish Community, 15th to 20th Centuries* (Oxford, 1995).

Bengtsson, T. and M. Lindström, "Childhood Misery and Disease in Later Life: The Effects of Mortality in Old Age of Hazards Experienced in Early Life, Southern Sweden, 1760–1894," *Population Studies* 54 (2000), pp. 263–77.

Bentham, J., *Constitutional Code: Volume I*, ed. F. Rosen and J. H. Burns (Oxford, 1983).

Berdahl, R. M., *The Politics of the Prussian Nobility: The Development of a Conservative Ideology, 1770–1848* (Princeton, NJ, 1988).

Berend, I. T., *History Derailed: Central and Eastern Europe in the Long Nineteenth Century* (Berkeley, CA, 2003).

Berenson, E., *Populist Religion and Left-Wing Politics in France 1830–1852* (London, 1984).

Berezin, M. and M. Schain, *Europe without Borders: Remapping Territory, Citizenship and Identity in a Transnational Age* (Baltimore, MD, 2003).

Berg, H. v. d., "'Free Love' in Imperial Germany: Anarchism and Patriarchy, 1870–1918," *Anarchist Studies* 4:1 (1996), pp. 3–27.

Berg, M., *The Age of Manufactures: Industry, Innovation and Work in Britain, 1700–1820* (Oxford, 1986).

Berg, M., "What Difference did Women's Work Make to the Industrial Revolution?" *History Workshop Journal* 35 (1993), pp. 22–44.

Berger, S., "Historians and Nation-Building in Germany after Reunification," *Past and Present* 148 (1995).

Berger, S., *Social Democracy and the Working Class in Nineteenth and Twentieth Century Germany* (Harlow, 2000).

Berger, S. and A. Smith (eds.), *Nationalism, Labour and Ethnicity, c. 1870–1939* (Manchester, 1999).

Berger, S., M. Donovan, and K. Passmore (eds.), *Writing National Histories: Western Europe since 1800* (London, 1999).

Berger, S., H. Feldner, and K. Passmore (eds.), *Writing History: Theory and Practice* (London, 2003).

Berger, T., *Die konstante Repression* (Frankfurt am Main, 1974).

Berlanstein, L. R. (ed.), *The Industrial Revolution and Work in Nineteenth-Century Europe* (London, 1992).

Berlière, J.-M., "The Professionalization of the Police Under the Third Republic in France, 1875–1914," in C. Emsley and B. Weinberger (eds.), *Policing Western Europe: Politics, Professionalism, and Public Order, 1850–1940* (London, 1991), pp. 36–54.

Berlin, I., *Russian Thinkers* (London, 1978).

Bernstein, E., *Evolutionary Socialism: A Criticism and Affirmation* (New York, 1961).

Besier, G., *Religion Nation Kultur: Die Geschichte der christlichen Kirchen in den gesellschaftlichen Umbrüchen des 19. Jahrhunderts* (Neukirchen-Vluyn, 1994).

Best, G., *Humanity in Warfare* (New York, 1980).

Best, G., *War and Society in Revolutionary Europe, 1770–1870* (Oxford, 1986).

Bhaba, H. K. (ed.), *Nation and Narration* (London, 1991).

Biagini, E., *Liberty, Retrenchment and Reform: Popular Liberalism in the Age of Gladstone* (Cambridge, 1992).

Biernacki, R., *The Fabrication of Labor: Germany and Britain, 1640–1914* (Berkeley, CA, 1995).

Billig, M., *Banal Nationalism* (London, 1995).

Birnbaum, P. and I. Katznelson (eds.), *Paths of Emancipation: Jews, States and Citizenship* (Princeton, NJ, 1995).

Bischoff, V. and Marino, M., "Melting Pot-Mythen als Szenarien amerikanischer Identität zur Zeit der New Immigration," in B. Giesen (ed.), *Nationale und kulturelle Identität. Studien zur Entwicklung des kollektiven Bewußtseins in der Neuzeit* (Frankfurt am Main, 1991).

Bittner, E., *The Functions of Police in Modern Society* (Washington, DC, 1970).

Black, C. E. (ed.), *The Transformation of Russian Society* (Cambridge, MA, 1960).

Blackbourn, D., *Class, Religion and Local Politics in Wilhelmine Germany: The Centre Party in Wurttemberg* (London, 1980).

Blackbourn, D., "The Politics of Demagogy in Imperial Germany," *Past and Present* 113 (1986), pp. 152–84.

Blackbourn, D., "The Catholic Church in Europe since the French Revolution: A Review Article," *Comparative Studies in Society and History* 4 (1991), pp. 777–88.

Blackbourn, D., "New Legislatures: Germany 1871–1914," *Historical Research* (1992).

Blackbourn, D., *Marpingen: Apparitions of the Virgin Mary in Bismarckian Germany* (Oxford, 1993).

Blackbourn, D., *History of Germany 1780–1918* (Oxford, 2003).

Blackbourn, D. and G. Eley, *The Peculiarities of German History: Bourgeois Society and Politics in Nineteenth-Century Germany* (Oxford, 1985).

Blackbourn, D. and R. J. Evans (eds.), *The German Bourgeoisie: Essays on the Social History of the German Middle Class from the Late Eighteenth Century to the Early Twentieth Century* (London, 1991).

Blanning, T. C. W., *The Origins of the French Revolutionary Wars* (London, 1986).

Blaschke, O., "Die Kolonialisierung der Laienwelt. Priester als Milieumanager und die Kanäle klerikaler Kuratel," in O. Blaschke and F. M. Kuhlemann (eds.), *Religion im Kaiserreich. Milieus-Mentalitäten-Krisen* (Gütersloh, 1996), pp. 93–135.

Blaschke, O., "Das 19. Jahrhundert: Ein Zweites Konfessionelles Zeitalter?" *Geschichte und Gesellschaft* 26 (2000), pp. 38–75.

Blaschke, O. and F.-M. Kuhlemann, "Religion in Geschichte und Gesellschaft. Sozialhistorische Perspektiven für die vergleichende Erforschung religiöser Mentalitäten und Milieus," in O. Blaschke and F. M. Kuhlemann (eds.), *Religion im Kaiserreich. Milieus-Mentalitäten-Krisen* (Gütersloh, 1996), pp. 7–56.

Blom, I., K. Hagemann, and C. Hall (eds.), *Gendered Nations: Nationalisms and Gender Order in the Long Nineteenth Century* (Oxford, 2000).

Blom, J. C. H. and E. Lamberts (eds.), *History of the Low Countries* (Oxford, 1999).

Blum, J., *The End of the Old Order in Rural Europe* (Princeton, NJ, 1978).

Bock, G., *Women in European History* (London, 2001).

Bock, G. and P. Thane (eds.), *Maternity and Gender Policies: Women and the Rise of the European Welfare State* (London, 1991).

Boer, P. Den et al., *The History of the Idea of Europe* (London, 1995).

Bond, B., *War and Society in Europe, 1870–1970* (Leicester, 1983).

Bonnell, V., *Roots of Rebellion: Workers, Politics and Organizations in St. Petersburg and Moscow 1900–1914* (Berkeley, CA, 1983).

Bookchin, M., *The Spanish Anarchists: The Heroic Years, 1868–1936* (New York, 1976).

Bourdieu, P., "L'idéologie jacobine," in P. Bourdieu, *Interventions, 1961–2001* (Marseille, 2002), pp. 55–61.

Bourke, J., "Dairywomen and Affectionate Wives: Women in the Irish Dairy Industry, 1890–1914," *Agricultural History Review* 38 (1990), pp. 149–64.

Bourke, J., *Husbandry to Housewifery: Women, Economic Change and Housework in Ireland, 1890–1914* (Oxford, 1993).

Bowler, P., *The Eclipse of Darwin: Anti-Darwinian Evolution Theories in the Decades Around 1900* (Baltimore, MD, 1983).

Boxer, M. and J. Quartaert (eds.), *Socialist Women* (New York, 1978).

Boyce, D. G., *Nationalism in Ireland* (London, 1995).

Brabander, G. L. de, *Regional Specialization, Employment and Economic Growth in Belgium between 1846 and 1970* (New York, 1981).

Bradley, F. H., "Some Remarks on Punishment," *International Journal of Ethics* 4 (1894), pp. 269–84.

Brague, R., *Europe, la voie romaine* (Paris, 1999).

Brändström, A. and L.-G. Tedebrand (eds.), *Society, Health and Population During the Demographic Transition* (Stockholm, 1988).

Brändström, A. and L.-G. Tedebrand (eds.), *Population Dynamics During Industrialization* (Umeå, 2000).

Breuilly, J., *Labour and Liberalism in Nineteenth-Century Europe: Essays in Comparative History* (Manchester, 1992).

Breuilly, J., *Nationalism and the State*, 2nd edn. (Manchester, 1993).

Breuilly, J. (ed.), *Nineteenth-Century Germany: Politics, Culture and Society, 1780–1918* (London, 2001).

Breuilly, J., "Nationalismus als kulturelle Konstruktion: einige Überlegungen," in J. Echternkamp and S. O. Müller (eds.), *Die Politik der Nation: Deutscher Nationalismus in Krieg und Krisen 1760–1960* (Munich, 2002).

Brewer, J., *The Sinews of Power: War, Money and the English State, 1688–1783* (London, 1989).

Brewer, J., "The Eighteenth-Century British State: Contexts and Issues," in L. Stone (ed.), *An Imperial State at War: Britain from 1689 to 1815* (London, 1994), pp. 52–71.

Bristow, E. J, *Prostitution and Prejudice: The Jewish Fight against White Slavery 1870–1939* (Oxford, 1982).

Brix, M. and M. Steinhauser, *Geschichte allein ist zeitgemäß. Historismus in Deutschland* (Lahn, 1978).

Brockliss, L. W., *Calver's Web: Enlightenment and the Republic of Letters in Eighteenth Century France* (Oxford, 2002).

Brose, E. D., *The Politics of Technological Change in Prussia* (Princeton, NJ, 1993).

Brown, C., *Religion and Society in Scotland since 1707* (Edinburgh, 1997).

Brown, C., *The Death of Christian Britain* (London, 2001).

Brown, D., *Walter Scott and the Historical Imagination* (London, 1979).

Bruland, K. (ed.), *Technology Transfer and Scandinavian Industrialization* (Providence, RI, 1991).

Brunschwig, H., *Noirs et blancs dans l'Afrique noire française où comment le colonisé devient colonisateur (1870–1914)* (Paris, 1983).

Buchinsky, M. and B. Polak, "The Emergence of a National Capital Market in England, 1710–1880," *Journal of Economic History* 53:1 (1993), pp. 1–24.

Büchner, L., *Man in the Past, Present and Future: A Popular Account of Recent Scientific Research as Regards the Origins, Position and Prospects of the Human Race* (London, 1872) [1869].

Bucur, M. and N. M. Wingfield (eds.), *Staging the Past: The Politics of Commemoration in Habsburg Central Europe 1848 to the Present* (West Lafayette, LA, 2001).

Bugge, P., "Central Europe: A Tool for Historians or a Political Concept?" *European Review of History* 6:1 (1999).

Bull, A. C. and P. Corner, *From Peasant to Entrepreneur: The Survival of the Family Economy in Italy* (Oxford, 1993).

Bull, P., *Land, Politics and Nationalism: A Study of the Irish Land Question* (Dublin, 1996).

Burke, E., *The Works of the Rt. Hon. Edmund Burke* (London, 1826).

Burke, P., *A Social History of Knowledge from Gutenberg to Diderot* (Cambridge, 2000).

Burke, P., *Eyewitnessing: The Use of Images as Historical Evidence* (London, 2001).

Burrow, J., *A Liberal Descent* (Cambridge, 1981).

Burrow, J., *The Crisis of Reason* (New Haven, CT, 2000).

Burton, A., *Burdens of History: British Feminists, Indian Women, and Imperial Culture* (Chapel Hill, NC, 1994).

Buruma, I., *Anglomania: A European Love Affair* (New York, 1998).

Bush, M. L. (ed.), *Social Orders and Social Classes in Europe since 1500* (Longman, 1992).

Bush, M. L. (ed.), *Serfdom and Slavery: Studies in Legal Bondage* (London, 1996).

Bush, M. L., *Servitude in Modern Times* (Cambridge, 2000).

Butterfield, H., *The Whig Interpretation of History* (London, 1931).

Butterfield, H., *Man on his Past* (Cambridge, 1969).

Buyst, E., J. P. Smits, J. L. v. Zanden, and Jan Luiten, "National Accounts for the Low Countries, 1800–1990," *Scandinavian Economic History Review* 43:1 (1995), pp. 53–76.

Bynum, W. F. *Science and the Practice of Medicine in the Nineteenth Century* (Cambridge, 1994).

Byres, T. J., *Capitalism from Above and Capitalism from Below: An Essay in Comparative Political Economy* (Basingstoke, 1996).

Cacciari, M., *Geo-filosofia dell'Europa* (Milan, 1994).

Cahan, D., "The Institutional Revolution in German Physics, 1865–1914," *Historical Studies in the Physical Sciences* 15 (1985), pp. 1–65.

Cahan, D., *An Institute for an Empire: The Physikalisch-Technische Reichsanstalt 1871–1918* (Cambridge, 1989).

Cahan, D. (ed.), *From Natural Philosophy to the Sciences: Writing the History of Nineteenth-Century Science* (Chicago, 2003).

Cameron, R. (ed.), *Banking in the Early Stages of Industrialization* (Oxford, 1967).

Campbell, B. M. S. and M. Overton (eds.), *Land, Labour and Livestock: Historical Studies in European Agricultural Productivity* (Manchester, 1991).

Campbell, M., J. Labbe, and S. Shuttleworth (eds.), *Memory and Memorials, 1789–1914* (London, 2000).

Campbell, P., *French Electoral Systems and Elections since 1789* (London, 1958).

Canetti, E., *Crowds and Power* (New York, 1981) [1960].

Cannadine, D., "The Context, Performance and Meaning of Ritual," in E. Hobsbawm and T. Ranger (eds.), *The Invention of Tradition* (Cambridge, 1983).

Cannadine, D., *The Decline and Fall of the British Aristocracy* (New Haven, CT, 1990).

Cannadine, D., "The Making of the British Upper Classes," in D. Cannadine, *Aspects of Aristocracy: Grandeur and Decline in Modern Britain* (New Haven, CT, 1994), pp. 9–36.

Canning, K., "Gender and the Politics of Class Formation: Rethinking German Labor History," *American Historical Review* 97:3 (1992), pp. 736–68.

Canning, K., *Languages of Labor and Gender: Female Factory Work in Germany, 1850–1914* (Ithaca, NY, 1996a).

Canning, K., "Social Policy, Body Politics: Recasting the Social Question in Germany, 1875–1900," in L. L. Frader and S. O. Rose (eds.), *Gender and Class in Modern Europe* (Ithaca, NY, 1996b), pp. 211–37.

Canning, K., "'The Man Transformed into a Maiden?' Languages of Grievance and the Politics of Class in Germany, 1850–1914," *International Labor and Working Class History* 49:1 (1996c), pp. 47–72.

Cantor, G. et al., *Science in the Nineteenth-Century Periodical* (Cambridge, 2004).

Caplan, J., "National Tattooing: Traditions of Tattooing in Nineteenth Century Europe," in J. Caplan (ed.), *Written on the Body: The Tattoo in European and American History* (London, 2000), pp. 156–73.

Caplan, J. (ed.), *Written on the Body: The Tattoo in European and American History* (London, 2000).

Cardoza, A. L., *Aristocrats in Bourgeois Italy: The Piedmontese Nobility, 1861–1930* (Cambridge, 1997).

Caron, J.-C., "Maintenir l'ordre dans les collèges et les lycées: théories et pratiques disciplinaires dans l'enseignement français (1815–1870)," in J.-P. Bardet, J.-N. Luc, I. Robin-Romero, and C. Rollett (eds.), *Lorsque l'enfant grandit* (Paris, 2003), pp. 605–17.

Carver, T., *Marx and Engels* (Brighton, 1983).

Cassis, Y., "Banks and the Rise of Capitalism in Switzerland, Fifteenth to Twentieth Century," in A. Teichova, K. v. Hentenryk, and D. Ziegler (eds.), *Banking, Trade and Industry: Europe, America and Asia from the Thirteenth to the Twentieth Century* (Cambridge, 1997), pp. 157–72.

Castoriadis, C., *Le Monde morcélé* (Paris, 1990).

Cecil, H., *Liberty and Authority* (London, 1910).

Cell, J. W., *British Colonial Administration in the Mid-Nineteenth Century: The Policy Making Process* (New Haven, CT, 1970).

Chadwick, O., *The Secularisation of the European Mind in the Nineteenth Century* (Cambridge, 1975).

Chadwick, O., *The Popes and European Revolution* (Oxford, 1981).

Chamberlain, M., *"Pax Britannica?" British Foreign Policy, 1789–1914* (London, 1988).

Chamberlin, J. and S. Gilman (eds.), *Degeneration: The Dark Side of Progress* (New York, 1985).

Charle, C., *Les Hauts fonctionnaires en France au XIXe siècle* (Paris, 1980).

Charle, C., *A Social History of France in the Nineteenth Century* (Oxford, 1994).

Chase, M., *"The People's Farm": English Agrarianism, 1775–1840* (Oxford, 1988).

Chaudhuri, N. and M. Strobel (eds.), *Western Women and Imperialism: Complicity and Resistance* (Bloomington, IN, 1992).

Cherry, S., "The Role of a Provincial Hospital: The Norfolk and Norwich Hospital, 1771–1880," *Population Studies* 26 (1972), pp. 291–306.

Chesnais, J.-C., *La Transition démographique. Etapes, formes, implications économiques* (Paris, 1986).

Chester, N., *The English Administrative System: 1780–1870* (Oxford, 1981).

Chirot, D. (ed.), *The Origins of Backwardness in Eastern Europe: Economics and Politics from the Middle Ages Until the Early Twentieth Century* (Berkeley, CA, 1989).

Choay, F., *The Invention of the Historic Monument* (Cambridge, 2001).

Christensen, J. P., R. Hjerppe, O. Krantz, and C.-A. Nilsson, "Nordic Historical National Accounts since the 1880s," *Scandinavian Economic History Review* 43:1 (1995), pp. 30–52.

Church, C. H., *Revolution and Red Tape: The French Ministerial Bureaucracy 1770–1860* (Oxford, 1981).

Church, C. H., *Europe in 1830: Revolution and Political Change* (London, 1983).

Cipolla, C., *The Fontana Economic History of Europe*, vols. 3 and 4 (London, 1973).

Clark, A., "The Rhetoric of Chartist Domesticity: Gender, Language, and Class in the 1830s and 1840s," *Journal of British Studies* (1992).

Clark, A., *The Struggle for the Breeches: Gender and the Making of the British Working Class* (Berkeley, CA, 1995).

Clark, C. and W. Kaiser (eds.), *Culture Wars: Secular-Catholic Conflict in Nineteenth Century Europe* (Cambridge, 2003).

Clark, G., M. Huberman, and P. Lindert, "A British Food Puzzle, 1770–1850: Evidence from Labour Inputs," *Economic History Review* 48:2 (1995), pp. 215–37.

Clark, L. L., *The Rise of Professional Women in France: Gender and Public Administration since 1830* (Cambridge, 2000).

Clark, M., *Modern Italy 1871–1995* (London, 1996).

Clark, S. (ed.), *The Annales School: Critical Assessments*, 4 vols (London, 1999).

Clark, T. J. *The Painting of Modern Life: Paris in the Age of Manet and His Followers*, revd. edn. (Princeton, NJ, 1999).

Clarkson, L. A., *Proto-Industrialization: The First Phase of Industrialization? Class in Germany before the First World War* (London, 1990).

Clausewitz, C. von, *Vom Kriege* [1832–4], in R. Stumpf (ed.), *Kriegstheorie und Kriegsgeschichte* (Frankfurt, 1993).

Clemens, A., P. Groote, and R. Albers, "The Contribution of Physical and Human Capital to Economic Growth in the Netherlands, 1850–1913," *Economic and Social History in the Netherlands* 7 (1996), pp. 181–98.

Clements, B., B. A. Engel, and C. D. Wrobobec (eds.), *Russian Women: Accommodation, Resistance, Transformation* (Berkeley, CA, 1991).

Clements, H., *Alfred Russel Wallace: Biologist and Social Reformer* (London, 1983).

Clifford, J., *The Predicament of Culture: Twentieth-Century Ethnography* (Cambridge, MA, 1988).

Clifford, J. and G. Marcus (eds.), *Writing Culture: The Politics and Poetry of Ethnography* (Berkeley, CA, 1986).

Clogg, R., "The Greeks and their Past," in D. Deletant and H. Hanak (eds.), *Historians and Nation-Builders* (Basingstoke, 1988).

Clogg, R., *A Concise History of Greece* (Cambridge, 1992).

Coale, A. J., S. Watkins, and S. Cotts (eds.), *The Decline of Fertility in Europe* (Princeton, NJ, 1986).

Cobban A., *The Social Interpretation of the French Revolution* (Cambridge, 1964).

Cocks, H., *Nameless Offences: Homosexual Desire in the Nineteenth Century* (London, 2003).

Cohen, J. S., *Finance and Industrialization in Italy, 1894–1914* (New York, 1977).

Cole, G. D. H., *A Century of Co-Operation* (Manchester, 1944).

Cole, J., *The Power of Large Numbers: Population, Politics and Gender in Nineteenth-Century France* (Ithaca, NY, 2000).

Cole, S. A., *Suspect Identities: A History of Fingerprinting and Criminal Identification* (Cambridge, MA, 2001).

Coleman, J. A., *The Evolution of Dutch Catholicism 1958–1974* (Los Angeles, 1978).

Colley, L., *Britons: Forging the Nation 1707–1837* (New Haven, CT, 1992).

Collins, M., "English Bank Development within a European Context, 1850–1939," *Economic History Review* 51:1 (1998), pp. 1–24.

Conrad, C., "National Historiography as a Transnational Object," in S. Berger (ed.), *Representations of the Past: The Writing of National Histories in Europe*, newsletter 1 (Strasbourg, 2004), pp. 3–5.

Conroy, M. S. (ed.), *Emerging Democracy in Late-Imperial Russia: Case Studies on Local Self-Government (The Zemstvos) State Duma Elections, The Tsarist Government and the State Council Before and During World War I* (Colorado, 1998).

Constant, B., *Political Writings*, ed. B. Fontana (Cambridge, 1988).

Conversi, D., *The Basques, the Catalans and Spain* (London, 1997).

Conze, E., " 'Wer von Europa spricht, hat Unrecht' – Aufstieg und Verfall des vertraglichen Multilateralismus im europäischen Staatensystem des 19. Jahrhunderts," *Historisches Jahrbuch* (2001), pp. 214–41.

Cook, M., "A New City of Friends: London and Homosexuality in the 1890s," *History Workshop Journal* 56 (2003), pp. 33–58.

Coope, W. J., *The History of the Imperial Ottoman Gendarmerie* (London, 1880).

Corbin, A., *Women for Hire: Prostitution and Sexuality in France after 1850* (Cambridge, MA, 1996).

Corbin, A., *Village Bells: Sound and Meaning in the Nineteenth-Century French Countryside* (New York, 1998).

Corbin, A., *The Life of an Unknown: The Rediscovered World of a Clog Maker in Nineteenth-Century France* (New York, 2001).

Corrigan, P. and D. Sayer, *The Great Arch: English State Formation as Cultural Revolution* (Oxford, 1985).

Corsi, P. and P. Weindling, "Darwinism in Germany, France and Italy," in D. Kohn (ed.), *The Darwinian Heritage* (Princeton, NJ, 1985), pp. 683–729.

Corsini, C. A. and P. P. Viazzo (eds.), *The Decline of Infant Mortality in Europe, 1800–1950: Four National Case Studies* (Florence, 1993).

Cowling, M. and J. Martin (eds.), *Marx's Eighteenth Brumaire: (Post)Modern Interpretations* (London, 2002).

Cracraft, J., *The Church Reform of Peter the Great* (London, 1971).

Crafts, N., "Exogenous or Endogenous Growth? The Industrial Revolution Reconsidered," *Journal of Economic History* 55:4 (1995a), pp. 745–72.

Crafts, N., "Recent Research on the National Accounts of the UK, 1700–1939," *Scandinavian Economic History Review* 43:1 (1995b), pp. 17–29.

Crampton, R. J., *A Concise History of Bulgaria* (Cambridge, 1997).

Crane, S., "Story, History and the Passionate Collector," in M. Myrone and L. Peltz (eds.), *Producing the Past: Aspects of Antiquarian Culture and Practice, 1700–1850* (Aldershot, 1999).

Cranston, M., *The Romantic Movement* (Oxford, 1994).

Crary, J., *Techniques of the Observer: On Vision and Modernity in the Nineteenth Century* (Cambridge, 1992).

Crary, J., *Suspensions of Perception: Attention, Spectacle, and Modern Culture* (Cambridge, 1999).

Crook, P., *Darwinism, War and History* (Cambridge, 1994).

Crook, P., "American Eugenics and the Nazis: Recent Historiography," *The European Legacy* 7 (2002), pp. 363–81.

Cross, G., *Immigrant Workers in Industrial France: The Making of a New Labouring Class* (Philadelphia, PA, 1983).

Crossick, G., *An Artisan Elite in Victorian Society: Kentish London, 1840–1880* (London, 1978).

Crossick, G. (ed.), *The Artisan and the European Town, 1500–1900* (London, 1997).

Crossick, G. and H.-G. Haupt (eds.), *Shopkeepers and Master Artisans in Nineteenth-Century Europe* (London, 1984).

Crossick, G. and S. Jaumain (eds.), *Cathedrals of Consumption: The European Department Store 1850–1939* (Aldershot, 1999).

Crossley, C., "History as a Principle of Legitimation in France (1820–48)," in S. Berger, M. Donovan, and K. Passmore (eds.), *Writing National Histories: Western Europe since 1800* (London, 1999).

Crowder, M., "Indirect Rule – French and British Style," *Africa* 34 (1963), pp. 293–305.

Crozier, I., "William Acton and the History of Sexuality: The Professional and Medical Contexts," *Journal of Victorian Culture* 5 (2000), pp. 1–27.

Crozier, I., "The Medical Construction of Homosexuality and its Relation to the Law in Nineteenth-Century England," *Medical History* 45 (2001), pp. 61–82.

Crozier, I., "La sexologie et la définition du 'normal' entre 1860 et 1900," *Cahiers du genre*, La distinction entre sexe et genre. Une histoire entre biologie et culture, special volume edited by I. Löwy and H. Rouch, 34 (2003).

Cueva, J. de la, "The Assault on the City of Levites: Spain," in C. Clark and W. Kaiser (eds.), *Culture Wars: Secular–Catholic Conflict in Nineteenth-Century Europe* (Cambridge, 2004), pp. 183–4.

Curtin, P. D., *The World and the West: The European Challenge and the Overseas Response in the Age of Empire* (Cambridge, 2002).

Curtis, Jr., L. P., *Jack the Ripper and the London Press* (New Haven, CT, 2001).

Dahrendorf, R., *Society and Politics in Germany* (London, 1968).

Danker, U., *Räuberbanden im Alten Reich um 1700, Ein Beitrag zur Geschichte von Herrschaft und Kriminalität in der Frühen Neuzeit* (Frankfurt am Main, 1988).

Darwin, C., *The Descent of Man and Selection in Relation to Sex*, 2nd revd. edn. (London, 1906) [1871].

Darwin, C., *On the Origin of Species by Means of Natural Selection, or the Preservation of Favoured Races in the Struggle for Life* (Harmondsworth, 1968) [1859].

Darwin, C. and T. H. Huxley, *Autobiographies* (Oxford, 1983).

Daunton, M. J. (ed.), *Housing the Worker, 1850–1914: A Comparative Perspective* (London, 1983).

Daunton, M. J., *Progress and Poverty: An Economic and Social History of Britain 1700–1850* (Oxford, 1995).

Davidoff, L. and C. Hall, *Family Fortunes: Men and Women of the English Middle Class, 1780–1950* (Chicago, 1987).

Davin, A., "Imperialism and Motherhood," *History Workshop Journal* 5 (1978), pp. 9–65.

Davies, N., *Europe: A History* (Oxford, 1996).

Davis, J., "A Poor Man's System of Justice: The London Police Courts in the Second Half of the Nineteenth Century," *Historical Journal* 27:2 (1984), pp. 309–35.

Davis, J. A, *Conflict and Control: Law and Order in Nineteenth Century Italy* (Basingstoke, 1988).

Davis, J. A. (ed.), *The Short Oxford History of Italy: Italy in the Nineteenth Century 1796–1900* (Oxford, 2000).

De la Motte, D. and J. M. Przblyski (eds.), *Making the News: Modernity and the Mass Press in Nineteenth-Century France* (Amherst, MA, 1989).

Deák, I., *Beyond Nationalism: A Social and Political History of the Habsburg Officer Corps, 1848–1918* (Oxford, 1990).

Deflem, M., *Policing World Society: Historical Foundations of International Police Cooperation* (Oxford, 2002a).

Deflem, M., "Technology and the Internationalization of Policing: A Comparative-Historical Perspective," *Justice Quarterly* 19:3 (2002b), pp. 453–75.

Delanty, G., "Conceptions of Europe: A Review of Recent Trends," *European Journal of Social Theory* 6:4 (2003).

Delavignette, R., *Freedom and Authority in French West Africa* (Oxford, 1950).

Deletant, D. and H. Hanak (eds.), *Historians as Nation-Builders* (Basingstoke, 1988).

Dennison, T. K. and A. W. Carus, "The Invention of the Russian Rural Commune: Haxthausen and the Evidence," *Historical Journal* 46:3 (2003), pp. 561–82.

Desan, S., *Reclaiming the Sacred: Lay Religion and Politics in Revolutionary France* (Ithaca, NY, 1990).

Deschamps, H., "Et maintenant, Lord Lugard?" *Africa* 33 (1963), pp. 293–305.

Desmond, A., *Huxley* (Harmondsworth, 1998).

Desmond, A. and J. Moore, *Darwin* (London, 1991).

Djordjevi, D., "Stojan Novakovi: Historian, Politician, Diplomat," in D. Deletant and H. Hanak (eds.), *Historians and Nation-Builders* (Basingstoke, 1988).

Doering-Manteuffel, A., *Vom Wiener Kongreß zur Pariser Konferenz. England, die deutsche Frage und das Mächtesystem 1815–1856* (Göttingen, 1991).

Doering-Manteuffel, A., "Internationale Geschichte als Systemgeschichte. Strukturen und Handlungsmuster im europäischen Staatensystem des 19. und 20. Jahrhunderts," in W. Loth and J. Osterhammel (eds.), *Internationale Geschichte. Themen – Ergebnisse – Aussichten* (Munich, 2000), pp. 97–100.

Dohm, H., *Die wissenschaftliche Emancipation der Frau* (Zürich, 1982) [1874].

Donnan, H. and T. Wilson, *Borders: Frontiers of Identity, Nation and State* (Oxford, 1999).

Dostoevsky, F., *Demons*, trans. R. Pevear and L. Volokhonsky (London, 1994) [1871].

Douglas, R., *"Great Nations Still Enchained": The Cartoonists' Vision of Empire 1848–1914* (London, 1994).

Dowe, D., H.-G. Haupt, D. Langewiesche, and J. Sperber (eds.), *Europe in 1848: Revolution and Reform* (Oxford, 2000).

Downs, L. L., *Writing Gender History* (London, 2004).

Doyle, W., *The Oxford History of the French Revolution* (Oxford, 1989).

Droz, J., *L'Europe centrale* (Paris, 1960).

Duffy, M., *The Englishman and the Foreigner: The English Satirical Print 1600–1832* (Cambridge, 1986).

Dufraisse, R. and M. Kerautret, *La France napoléonienne. Aspects extérieurs, 1799–1815* (Paris, 1999).

Duhet, P. M., *Les Femmes et la révolution 1789–1794* (Paris, 1977).

Dülffer, J., *Regeln gegen den Krieg? Die Haager Friedenskonferenzen von 1899 und 1907 in der internationalen Politik* (Berlin, 1981).

Dülffer, J., "Modelle der Friedenssicherung in Deutschland seit der Französischen Revolution – Joseph Görres, Friedrich Gentz und die Entwicklung seither," in M. Kröger, U. S. Soenius, and S. Wunsch (eds.), *Im Zeichen der Gewalt. Frieden und Krieg im 19. und 20. Jahrhundert* (Cologne, 2002a), pp. 8–25.

Dülffer, J., "Vom europäischen Mächtesystem zum Weltstaatensystem um die Jahrhundertwende," in M. Kröger, U. S. Soenius, and S. Wunsch (eds.), *Im Zeichen der Gewalt. Frieden und Krieg im 19. und 20. Jahrhundert* (Cologne, 2002b), pp. 49–65.

Dülffer, J., M. Kröger, and R.-H. Wippich, *Vermiedene Kriege. Deeskalation und Konflikte der Großmächte zwischen Krimkrieg und Erstem Weltkrieg (1856–1914)* (Munich, 1997).

Dunbabin, J. P. D., *Rural Discontent in Nineteenth-Century Britian* (London, 1974).

Durkheim, E., *Professional Ethics and Civic Morals* (London, 1957).

Duroselle, J.-B., *Europe: A History of its Peoples* (London, 1990).

Dwyer, P. G. (ed.), *The Rise of Prussia 1700–1830* (Harlow, 2000).

Dwyer, P. G. (ed.), *Conquest and Assimilation: Rethinking Prussian History 1830–1947* (Harlow, 2001a).

Dwyer, P. G. (ed.), *Napoleon and Europe* (London, 2001b).

Dyhouse, C., "Working-Class Mothers and Infant Mortality in England, 1895–1914," *Journal of Social History* 12 (1987), pp. 248–67.

Dyson, K., *The State Tradition in Western Europe* (Oxford, 1980).

Eastwood, D., *Governing Rural England: Traditions and Transformation in Local Government 1780–1840* (Oxford, 1994).

Eastwood, D., "Communities, Protest and Police in Early Nineteenth-Century Oxfordshire: The Enclosure of Otmoor Reconsidered," *Agricultural History Review* 44:1 (1996), pp. 35–46.

Eccleshall, R. and O'Sullivan, N. (eds.), *The Nature of the Right* (London, 1989).

Echard, W. E., *Napoleon III and the Concert of Europe* (Baton Rouge, LA, 1984).

Echternkamp, J., *Der Aufstieg des deutschen Nationalismus (1770–1840)* (Frankfurt am Main, 1998).

Eder, F. X., L. Hall, and G. Hekma (eds.), *Sexual Cultures in Europe, Vol. 1: National Histories* (Manchester, 1999a).

Eder, F. X., L. Hall, and G. Hekma (eds.), *Sexual Cultures in Europe, Vol. 2: Themes in Sexuality* (Manchester, 1999b).

Edvinsson, S. and H. Nilsson, "Urban Mortality in Sweden during the 19th Century," in A. Brändström and L.-G. Tedebrand (eds.), *Population Dynamics During Industrialization* (Umeå, 2000), pp. 39–82.

Edwards, S., *The Paris Commune, 1871* (London, 1971).

Ehmer, J., *Bevölkerungsgeschichte und Historische Demographie 1800–2000* (Munich, 2004).

Eisenstadt, S., *Fundamentalism, Sectarianism, Revolution* (Cambridge, 1999).

Eklof, B., *Russian Peasant Schools: Officialdom, Village Culture and Popular Pedagogy, 1861–1914* (Berkeley, CA, 1986).

Eley, G., *Reshaping the German Right: Radical Nationalism and Political Change after Bismark* (New Haven, CT, 1980).

Eley, G. (ed.), *Society, Culture and the State in Germany 1870–1939* (Ann Arbor, MI, 1996).

Eley, G., *Forging Democracy: The History of the Left in Europe, 1850–2000* (Oxford, 2002).

Elias, N., *The Court Society* (New York, 1983) [1969].

Elliott, J., "A Europe of Composite Monarchies," *Past and Present* 137 (1992), pp. 48–71.

Ellis, J., *The Georgian Town, 1680–1840* (Basingstoke, 2001).

Ellison, J., *Delicate Subjects: Romanticism, Gender, and the Ethics of Understanding* (Ithaca, NY, 1990).

Emmons, T., *The Formation of Political Parties and the First National Elections in Russia* (Cambridge, MA, 1983).

Emsley, C., *Policing and Its Context 1750–1870* (London, 1983).

Emsley, C., "'The Thump of Wood on a Swede Turnip': Police Violence in Nineteenth-Century England," *Criminal Justice History* 6 (1985), pp. 125–49.

Emsley, C., *The English Police: A Political and Social History* (London, 1996).

Emsley, C., "A Typology of Nineteenth-Century Police," *Crime, Histoire & Sociétés/Crime, History and Societies* 3:1 (1999a), pp. 29–44.

Emsley, C., *Gendarmes and the State in Nineteenth-Century Europe* (Oxford, 1999b).

Emsley, C., "'The Best Way to Keep the Peace in a Country': Napoleon's Gendarmes and their legacy," in D. Laven and L. Riall (eds.), *Napoleon's Legacy: Problems of Government in Restoration Europe* (Oxford, 2000).

Emsley, C. and S. Philips, "The Habsburg Gendarmerie: A Research Agenda," *German History* 17:2 (1999), pp. 241–50.

Encrevé, A., *Les Protestants en France de 1800 à nos jours* (Paris, 1985).

Endelman, T. M., *The Jews of Britain 1656–2000* (Berkeley, CA, 2002).

Engel, B. A., *Mothers and Daughters: Women of the Intelligentsia in Nineteenth-Century Russia* (Cambridge, 1983).

Engel, B. A. and C. N. Rosenthal (eds.), *Five Sisters: Women against the Tsar* (New York, 1975).

Engels, F., *The Condition of the Working Class in England* (Oxford, 1971).

Engelstein, J., *Moscow 1905: Working Class Organization and Political Conflict* (Stanford, CA, 1982).

Entrèves, A. P., *The Notion of the State* (Oxford, 1967).

Epstein, J. and D. Thompson (eds.), *The Chartist Experience* (London, 1982).

Eriksonas, L., *National Heroes and National Identities: Scotland, Norway and Lithuania* (Brussels, 2004).

Evans, E., *The Forging of the Modern State: Early Industrial Britain 1783–1870* (London, 1983).

Evans, E. L., "Catholic Political Movements in Germany, Switzerland and the Netherlands: Note for a Comparative Approach," *Central European History* 17 (1984), pp. 92–119.

Evans, E. L. *The Cross and the Ballot: Catholic Political Parties in Germany, Switzerland, Austria, Belgium and the Netherlands, 1785–1985* (Boston, MA, 1999).

Evans, R. J., "Prostitution, State and Society in Imperial Germany," *Past and Present* 70 (1976), pp. 106–29.

Evans, R. J. (ed.), *Society and Politics in Wilhelmine Germany* (London, 1978).

Evans, R. J., *Death in Hamburg: Society and Politics in the Cholera Years 1830–1910* (Oxford, 1987).

Evans, R. J., *Proletarians and Politics: Socialism, Protest and the Working Class in Germany before the First World War* (London, 1990).

Evans, R. J, *Tales from the German Underworld: Crime and Punishment in the Nineteenth Century* (New Haven, CT, 1998).

Evans, R. J. and W. R. Lee (eds.), *The German Peasantry: Conflict and Community in Rural Society from the Eighteenth to the Twentieth Centuries* (London, 1986).

Fanon, F., *The Damned*, foreword by J.-P. Sartre (Paris, 1963).

Farr, J. R., *Artisans in Europe, 1300–1914* (Cambridge, 2000).

Fawcett, J. (ed.), *The Future of the Past: Attitudes to Conservation* (London, 1976).

Feely, F. M., *Rebels with Causes: A Study of Revolutionary Syndicalist Culture among French Primary School Teachers between 1880 and 1919* (Cambridge, 1989).

Feinstein, C. H., "Capital Accumulation and the Industrial Revolution," in R. Floud and D. McCloskey (eds.), *The Economic History of Britain since 1700*, Vol. 1 (Cambridge, 1981), pp. 128–42.

Ferguson, N., "The European Economy, 1815–1914," in T. C. W. Blanning (ed.), *Short Oxford History of Europe: The Nineteenth Century* (Oxford, 2000), pp. 78–125.

Fernández Pérez, P., "Tolerance and Endogamy: Entrepreneurial Strategies in Eighteenth-Century Spain," *Journal of European Economic History* 29:2/3 (2000), pp. 271–93.

Ferri, E., *Socialism and Positive Science (Darwin – Spencer – Marx)* (London, 1905) [1894].

Ferro, M., *La Grande guerre, 1914–1918* (Paris, 1969).

Fevert, U., "Honour and Middle-Class Cultures: The History of the Duel in England and Germany," in J. Kocka and A. Mitchell (eds.), *Bourgeois Society in Nineteenth-Century Europe* (Oxford, 1993), pp. 179–207.

Fieldhouse, D. K., *Economics and Empire 1830–1914* (London, 1973).

Figes, O., *A People's Tragedy: The Russian Revolution 1891–1924* (London, 1997).

Figes, O., *Nastasha's Dance: A Cultural History of Russia* (Harmondsworth, 2002).

Finer, S. E., "State- and Nation-Building in Europe: The Role of the Military," in C. Tilly (ed.), *The Formation of National States in Western Europe* (Princeton, NJ, 1975), pp. 84–163.

Finzsch, N. and R. Jütte (eds.), *Institutions of Confinement: Hospitals, Asylums, and Prisons in Western Europe and North America, 1500–1950* (Cambridge, 1996).

Flacke, M. (ed.), *Mythen der Nationen: ein europäisches Panorama* (Berlin, 1998).

Fletcher, I., L. E. Nym Mayhall, and P. Levine (eds.), *Women's Suffrage in the British Empire: Citizenship, Nation and Race* (London, 2000).

Flinn, M. W., *British Population Growth 1700–1850* (Basingstoke, 1970).

Flora, P. and A. J. Heidenheimer (eds.), *The Development of Welfare States in Europe and America* (New Brunswick, NJ, 1982).

Floud, R., K. W. Wachter, and A. Gregory, *Height, Health and History: Nutritional Status in the United Kingdom, 1750–1980* (Cambridge, 1990).

Fogel, R. W., "Economic Growth, Population Theory, and Physiology: The Bearing of Long-Term Processes on the Making of Economic Policy," *American Economic Review*, 84:3 (1994), pp. 369–95.

Fonseca, H. A., "Agrarian Elites and Economic Growth in Nineteenth-Century Portugal: The Example of the Alentejo in the Liberal Era (1850–1910)," *Social History* 28 (2003), pp. 202–26.

Ford, C., "Religion and the Politics of Cultural Change in Provincial France: The Resistance of 1902 in Lower Brittany," *Journal of Modern History* 62:1 (1990), pp. 1–33.

Ford, C., "Religion and Popular Culture in Modern Europe," *Journal of Modern History* 65:1 (1993), pp. 152–75.

Forrest, A., *The Soldiers of the French Revolution* (Durham, 1990).

Förster, S., W. Mommsen, and R. Robinson (eds.), *Bismarck, Europe and Africa: The Berlin West Africa Conference and the Onset of Partition* (Oxford, 1988).

Fosdick, R. B., *European Police Systems* (Montclair, NJ, 1972) [1915].

Foucault, M., *Discipline and Punish: The Birth of the Prison* (New York, 1977).

Foucault, M., *History of Sexuality* (New York, 1984).

Fourier, C., *The Utopian Vision of Charles Fourier: Selected Texts on Work, Love, and Passionate Attraction*, ed. and trans. J. Beecher and R. Bienvenu (London, 1971).

Fox, R. and A. Guagnini (eds.), *Education, Technology and Industrial Performance in Europe, 1850–1939* (Cambridge, 1993).

Frader, L. L. and S. O. Rose (eds.), *Gender and Class in Modern Europe* (Ithaca, NY, 1996).

Fraile, P., "Putting Order Into the Cities: The Evolution of 'Policy Science' in Eighteenth-Century Spain," *Urban History* 25:1 (1998), pp. 22–35.

Fraisse, G. and M. Perrot (eds.), *A History of Women in the West, Vol. 4: Emerging Feminism from Revolution to World War* (Cambridge, MA, 1993).

Frank, A. G., "The Development of Underdevelopment," *Monthly Review* 18:4 (1966), pp. 23–8.

Frank, S. P., *Crime, Cultural Conflict and Justice in Rural Russia, 1856–1914* (Berkeley, CA, 1999).

Frankel, J. and S. J. Zipperstein (eds.), *Assimilation and Community: The Jews in Nineteenth-Century Europe* (Cambridge, 1992).

Franzoi, B., *At the Very Least She Pays the Rent: Women and German Industrialization, 1871–1914* (Westport, CT, 1985).

Fraser, D., *Urban Politics in Victorian England* (Leicester, 1976).

Frazee, C. A. *The Orthodox Church and Independent Greece 1821–1852* (Cambridge, 1969).

Freeden, M., *The New Liberalism* (Oxford, 1978).

Freeden, M., *Ideologies and Political Theory* (Oxford, 1996).

Freeze, G., "Case of Stunted Anticlericalism: Clergy and Society in Imperial Russia," *European Studies Review* 13 (1983a), pp. 177–200.

Freeze, G., *The Parish Clergy in Nineteenth Century Russia: Crisis, Reform, Counter-Reform* (Princeton, NJ, 1983b).

Freeze, G., "Subversive Piety: Religion and the Political Crisis in Late Imperial History," *Journal of Modern History* 68 (1996), pp. 308–50.

Freifeld, A., *Nationalism and the Crowd in Liberal Hungary 1848–1914* (Washington, DC, 2000).

Freifeld, M., "Technological Change and the 'Self-Acting' Mule: A Study of Skill and the Sexual Division of Labor," *Social History* 11:3 (1986), pp. 319–43.

Fremdling, R., "Foreign Competition and Technological Change: British Exports and the Modernization of the German Iron Industry from the 1820s to the 1860s," in W. R. Lee (ed.), *German Industry and German Industrialization: Essays in German Economic and Business History in the Nineteenth and Twentieth Centuries* (London, 1991a), pp. 47–76.

Fremdling, R., "Productivity Comparison between Great Britain and Germany, 1855–1915," *Scandinavian Economic History Review*, 39:1 (1991b), pp. 28–42.

Fremdling, R. and G. Knieps, "Competitive Regulation and Nationalization: The Prussian Railway System in the Nineteenth Century," *Scandinavian Economic History Review* 41:2 (1993), pp. 129–54.

Frevert, U., *Women in German History: From Bourgeois Emancipation to Sexual Liberation* (Oxford, 1989).

Frevert, U., "Honour and Middle-Class Cultures: The History of the Duel in England and Germany," in J. Kocka and A. Mitchell (eds.), *Bourgeois Society in Nineteenth-Century Europe* (Oxford, 1993), pp. 207–40.

Frevert, U., *"Mann und Weib, und Weib und Mann": Geschlechter-Differenzen in der Moderne* (Munich, 1995).

Frevert, U., *A Nation in Barracks: Modern Germany, Military Conscription and Civil Society* (Oxford, 2004), pp. 11–14.

Fridlizius, G., "The Deformation of Cohorts: Nineteenth Century Mortality in a Generational Perspective," *Scandinavian Economic History Review*, 37:3 (1989), pp. 3–17.

Fried, R. C., *The Italian Prefects: A Study in Administrative Politics* (New Haven, CT, 1963).

Friedman, L. (ed.), *The Law of War: A Documentary History*, Vol. 1 (New York, 1972).

Frierson, C. A., "Rural Justice in Public Opinion: The Volost Court Debate 1861–1912," *Slavonic and East European Review* 64:4 (1986), pp. 526–45.

Frierson, C. A., *Peasant Icons: Representations of Rural People in Late Nineteenth-Century Russia* (Oxford, 1993).

Frierson, C. A., "Of Red Roosters, Revenge and the Search for Justice: Rural Arson in European Russia in the Late Imperial Era," in P. Solomon (ed.) *Reforming Justice in Russia, 1864–1996: Power, Culture and the Limits of Legal Order* (London, 1997), pp. 107–30.

Friesel, E., *Atlas of Modern Jewish History* (New York, 1990).

Fukuyama, F., *The End of History and the Last Man* (London, 1992).

Funkenstein, A., *Perceptions of Jewish History* (Berkeley, CA, 1993).

Furet, F., *Interpreting the French Revolution* (Cambridge, 1981).

Furst, L. B., *The Contours of European Romanticism* (London, 1979).

Galemma, A. et al. (eds.), *Images of the Nation: Different Meanings of Dutchness 1870–1940* (Amsterdam, 1993).

Gallagher, J. and R. Robinson, "The Imperialism of Free Trade," *Economic History Review* 2nd ser., 6:1 (1953), pp. 1–15.

Gallant, T. W., *Experiencing Dominion: Culture, Identity and Power in the British Mediterranean* (Notre Dame, IN, 2002).

Gantet, C., *Guerre, paix et construction des États, 1618–1714* (Paris, 2003).

Garland, D., *Punishment and Modern Society: a Study in Social Theory* (Chicago, 1990).

Garland, D., "Of Crimes and Criminals: The Development of Criminology in Britain," in M. Maguire, R. Morgan, and R. Reiner (eds.), *The Oxford Handbook of Criminology* (Oxford, 1994), pp. 17–68.

Garrard, J., *Leadership and Power in Northern Industrial Towns 1830–1880* (Manchester, 1983).

Garrard, J., "Parties, Members and Voters after 1867," in T. R. Gourvish and A. O'Day (eds.), *Later Victorian Britain 1867–1900* (Basingstoke, 1988).

Garrard, J., *Democratisation in Britain's Elites: Civil Society and Reform since 1800* (Basingstoke, 2002).

Garrard, J., V. Tolz, and R. White (eds.), *European Democratisation since 1800* (Basingstoke, 1999).

Garrett, E. M., "The Trials of Labour: Motherhood versus Employment in a Nineteenth-Century Textile Centre," *Continuity and Change* 5:1 (1990), pp. 121–54.

Garrett, E. M., A. Reid, K. Schürer, and S. Szreter, *Changing Family Size in England and Wales: Place, Class and Demography, 1891–1911* (Cambridge, 2001).

Garscha, W. and C. Schindler (eds.), *Labour Movement and National Identity* (Vienna, 1994).

Gartner, L. P., *History of the Jews in Modern Times* (Oxford, 2001).

Gash, N., *Politics in the Age of Peel* (London, 1969).

Gash, N., *Aristocracy and People: Britain 1815–1865* (Cambridge, MA, 1979).

Gates, D., *The Napoleonic Wars, 1803–1815* (London, 1997).

Gatrell, V. A. C., "Crime, Authority and the Policeman-State," in F. M. L. Thompson (ed.), *The Cambridge Social History of Britain*, Vol. 3 (Cambridge, 1990), pp. 243–310.

Gatz, E. (ed.), *Geschichte des kirchlichen Lebens in den deutschsprachigen Ländern seit dem Ende des 18. Jh. Bd. 1 Die Bistümer und ihre Pfarreien* (Freiburg, 1990).

Gay, P., *Education of the Senses: The Bourgeois Experience, Victoria to Freud*, Vol. 1 (Oxford, 1985).

Gay, P., *Freud: A Life for Our Time* (New York, 1988).

Gay, P., *The Naked Heart* (London, 1996).

Geary, D., *European Labour Protest* (London, 1981).

Geary, D. (ed.), *Labour and Socialist Movements in Europe Before 1914* (Oxford, 1989).

Gelfand, T., *Professionalizing Modern Medicine: Paris Surgeons and Medical Science and Institutions in the Eighteenth Century* (Westport, CT, 1980).

Gellner, E., *Nations and Nationalism* (Oxford, 1983).

Gemie, S., "What is a School? Defining and Controlling Primary Schooling in Early Nineteenth Century France," *History of Education* 21:2 (1992), pp. 129–47.

Gemie, S., "Counter-Community: An Aspect of Anarchist Political Culture," *Journal of Contemporary History* 29 (1994), pp. 349–67.

Gemie, S., *Women and Schooling: Gender, Authority and Identity in the Female Schooling Sector, France, 1815–1914* (Keele, 1995).

Gemie, S., "Anarchism and Feminism: A Historical Survey," *Women's History Review* 5:3 (1996), pp. 417–44.

Gemie, S., *French Revolutions, 1815–1914: An Introduction* (Edinburgh, 1999a).

Gemie, S., "Institutional History, Social History, Women's History: A Comment on Patrick Harrigan's 'Women Teachers and the Schooling of Girls in France,'" *French Historical Studies* 22:4 (1999b), pp. 613–23.

Genet, J.-P. (ed.), *L'État moderne: Genèse. Bilans et Perspectives. Actes du Colloque tenu au CNRS à Paris les 19–20 Septembre 1989* (Paris, 1990).

Gerhard, U., *Debating Women's Equality: Toward a Feminist Theory of Law from a European Perspective* (New Brunswick, NJ, 2001).

Gerschenkron, A., *Economic Backwardness in Historical Perspective* (Cambridge, MA, 1966).

Gerschenkron, A., *Continuity in History and Other Essays* (Princeton, NJ, 1968).

Gerth, H. H. and C. Wright Mills (eds.), *From Max Weber* (London, 1948).

Gibson, M. S, "The 'Female Offender' and the Italian School of Criminal Anthropology," *European Studies* 12 (1982), pp. 155–65.

Gibson, M. S., *Born to Crime: Cesare Lombroso and the Origins of Biological Criminality* (Westport, CT, 2002).

Gibson, R., *The Social History of French Catholicism, 1789–1914* (London, 1989).

Gibson, R. and M. Blinkhorn (eds.), *Landownership and Power in Modern Europe* (London, 1991).

Gigerenzer, G. et al. (eds.), *The Empire of Chance: How Probability Changed Science and Everyday Life* (Cambridge, 1989).

Gilbert, S. M. and S. Gubar, *The Madwoman in the Attic: The Woman Writer and the Nineteenth-Century Literary Imagination* (New Haven, CT, 1979).

Gildea, R., *Barricades and Borders: Europe 1800–1914*, 3rd edn. (Oxford, 2003).

Gillham, N. W., *A Life of Sir Francis Galton, From African Exploration to the Birth of Eugenics* (Oxford, 2001).

Gillis, J. R., *The Prussian Bureaucracy in Crisis 1840–1860: Origins of an Administrative Ethos* (Stanford, CA, 1971).

Gillis, J. R., *Commemorations: The Politics of National Identity* (Princeton, NJ, 1994).

Gilman, S., *The Jew's Body* (New York, 1991).

Ginzburg, C., *The Cheese and the Worms: The Cosmos of a Sixteenth Century Miller* (New York, 1989).

Goddard, H., *Memoirs of a Bow Street Runner* (London, 1956).

Godfrey, B., "Private Policing and the Workplace: The Worsted Committee and the Policing of Labor in Northern England, 1840–1880," in *Criminal Justice History, Vol. 16: Policing and War in Europe* (Westport, CT, 2002), pp. 87–106.

Godineau, D., *The Women of Paris and their French Revolution* (Berkeley, CA, 1998).

Goldby, J. M. and A. W. Purdue, *The Civilization of the Crowd: Popular Culture in England, 1750–1900* (New York, 1985).

Goldfrank, D. M., *The Origins of the Crimean War* (London, 1999).

Goldstein, J., *Console and Classify: The French Psychiatric Profession in the Nineteenth Century* (Cambridge, 1987).

Golinski, J., *Science as Popular Culture: Chemistry and Enlightenment in Britain 1760–1820* (Cambridge, 1992).

Gooch, G. P., *History and Historians in the Nineteenth Century* (London, 1913).

Good, D. F. and M. Tongshu, "The Economic Growth of Central and Eastern Europe in Comparative Perspective, 1870–1989," *European Review of Economic History* 2 (1999), pp. 103–37.

Goose, N., *Population, Economy and Family Structure in Hertfordshire in 1851, Vol. 1: The Berkhamstead Region* (Hatfield, 1996).

Gorski, P., "The Mosaic Moment: An Early Modernist Critique of Modernist Theories of Nationalism," *American Journal of Sociology* 105 (2000), pp. 1428–68.

Goss, J., *The Mapmaker's Art: A History of Cartography* (London, 1993).

Goubert, J.-P., *The Conquest of Water* (Princeton, NJ, 1989).

Graf, F., "Alter Geist und neuer Mensch. Religiöse Zukunftserwartungen um 1900," in U. Frevert (ed.), *Das neue Jahrhundert. Europäische Zeitdiagnosen und Zukunftsentwürfe um 1900* (Göttingen, 2000), pp. 85–228.

Grasser, C., " 'Jeune fille en fleur' contre 'good girl': la construction d'identités féminines bourgeoises au jardin, France et Angleterre 1820–1870," in J.-P. Bardet, J.-N. Luc, I. Robin-Romero, and C. Rollett (eds.), *Lorsque l'enfant grandit* (Paris, 2003), pp. 257–68.

Gray, R., *The Factory Question and Industrial England, 1830–1860* (Cambridge, 1996).

Green, A., *Fatherlands: State-Building and Nationhood in Nineteenth Century Germany* (Cambridge, 2001).

Greenfeld, L., *Nationalism: Five Roads to Modernity* (Cambridge, MA, 1992).

Greenslade, W., *Degeneration, Culture and the Novel 1880–1940* (Cambridge, 1994).

Greg, W. R., "On the Failure of 'Natural Selection' in the Case of Man," *Frazer's Magazine* 78 (1868).

Griffiths, R. T. and J. de Meere, "The Growth of the Dutch Economy in the Nineteenth Century: Back to Basics?" *Tijdschrift voor Geschiedenis* 96 (1983), pp. 563–72.

Gross, H., "Aufgabe und Ziele," in *Archiv für Kriminalanthropologie und Kriminalistik* 1 (1898).

Gründer, H., *Christliche Mission und deutscher Imperialismus. Eine politische Geschichte ihrer Beziehungen wähend der deutschen Kolonialzeit (1884–1914) unter besonderer Berücksichtigung Afrikas und Chinas* (Paderborn, 1982).

Gründer, H., *Welteroberung und Christentum. Ein Handbuch zur Geschichte der Neuzeit* (Gütersloh, 1992).

Gruner, W. D., "Die Rolle und Funktion von 'Kleinstaaten' im internationalen System, 1815–1914. Die Bedeutung des Endes der Deutschen Klein- und Mittelstaaten für die Europäische Ordnung," in W. D. Gruner, *Deutschland mitten in Europa* (Hamburg, 1992).

Gugerli, D. and D. Speich, *Topographien der Nation: Politik, kartographische Ordnung und Landschaft im 19. Jahrhundert* (Zurich, 2002).

Guha, S., "The Importance of Social Intervention in England's Mortality Decline: The Evidence Reviewed," *Social History of Medicine* 7:1 (1994), pp. 89–113.

Gullickson, G., *Unruly Women of Paris: Images of the Commune* (Ithaca, NY, 1996).

Gumplowicz, L., *Outlines of Sociology* (New York, 1963) [1885].

Gumplowicz, L., *Sociologie et politique* (Paris, 1898) [1892].

Guttsman, W. L., *The British Political Elite* (London, 1963).

Guttsman, W. L., *The German Social Democratic Party* (London, 1981).

Habermas, J., *The Structural Transformation of the Public Sphere: An Inquiry into a Category of Bourgeois Culture* (Cambridge, 1992).

Haeckel, E., *The History of Creation, or the Development of the Earth and its Inhabitants by the Action of Natural Causes*, 2 vols. (London, 1876) [1868].

Hagemann, K., "Of 'Manly Valor' and 'German Honour': Nation, War and Masculinity in the Age of the Prussian Uprising against Napoleon," *Central European History* 30 (1997), pp. 187–220.

Hagemann, K., *"Männlicher Muth und Teutsche Ehre": Nation, Militär und Geschlecht zur Zeit der Antinapoleonischen Kriege Preußens* (Paderborn, 2002).

Hagemann, K., "Female Patriots: Women, War and the Nation in the Period of the Prussian-German Anti-Napoleonic Wars," *Gender and History* 16:2 (2004), pp. 397–424.

Hagen, W. W., *Ordinary Prussians: Brandenburg Junkers and Villagers, 1500–1840* (Cambridge, 2002).

Haines, M. R., "Socio-Economic Differences in Infant Mortality during Mortality Decline: England and Wales, 1890–1911," *Population Studies* 49:2 (1995), pp. 297–315.

Hajnal, J., "European Marriage Patterns in Perspective," in D. V. Glass and D. E. Eversley (eds.), *Population and History* (London, 1965), pp. 101–43.

Hajnal, J., "Two Kinds of Pre-Industrial Household Formation Systems," *Population and Development Review* 8 (1982), pp. 449–94.

Hale, J., *The Civilization of Europe in the Renaissance* (London, 1993).

Hale, J., "The Renaissance Idea of Europe," in S. García (ed.), *European Identity and the Search for Legitimacy* (London, 1993), pp. 46–63.

Hall, C., "The Rule of Difference: Gender, Class and Empire in the Making of the 1832 Reform Act," in I. Blom, K. Hagemann, and C. Hall (eds.), *Gendered Nations: Nationalisms and Gender Order in the Long Nineteenth Century* (Oxford, 2000), pp. 10–35.

Hall, C., *Civilizing Subjects: Metropole and Colony in the English Imagination, 1830–1867* (Cambridge, 2002).

Ham, E., *By Herself, 1783–1820* (London, 1945).

Hamilton, P., *Historicism* (London, 1996).

Hamlin, C., "Predisposing Causes and Public Health in Early Nineteenth Century Medical Thought," *Social History of Medicine* 5 (1992), pp. 43–70.

Hanham, H. J., *Elections and Party Management: Politics in the Times of Disraeli and Gladstone* (London, 1959).

Hannaford, I., *Race: The History of an Idea in the West* (Washington, DC, 1996).

Hannam, J. and K. Hunt, *Socialist Women: Britain, 1880s to 1920s* (London, 2000).

Hannaway, C. and A. La Berge (eds.), *Constructing Paris Medicine* (Amsterdam, 1998).

Hardy, A., *The Epidemic Streets: Infectious Disease and the Rise of Preventive Medicine, 1856–1900* (Oxford, 1993).

Harley, C. K., "Reassessing the Industrial Revolution: A Macro View," in J. Mokyr (ed.), *The British Industrial Revolution: An Economic Perspective* (Boulder, CO, 1993), pp. 171–226.

Harley, J. B., "Meaning and Ambiguity in Tudor Cartography," in S. Tyacke (ed.), *English Map-Making 1500–1650: Historical Essays* (London, 1983), pp. 22–45.

Harling, P., *The Waning of "Old Corruption": The Politics of Economic Reform in Britain, 1779–1846* (Oxford, 1996).

Harlow, B. and M. Carter, *Imperialism and Orientalism: A Documentary Sourcebook* (Oxford, 1999).

Harrigan, P., "Women Teachers and the Schooling of Girls in France: Recent Historiographical Trends," *French Historical Studies* 21:4 (1998), pp. 593–610.

Harrington, J. and H. W. Smith, "Confessionalization, Community and State Building in Germany 1555–1870," *Journal of Modern History* 69:1 (1997), pp. 77–101.

Harris, J. and P. Thane, "British and European Bankers, 1880–1914: An 'Aristocratic Bourgeoisie'?" in P. Thane, G. Crossick, and R. Floud (eds.), *The Power of the Past: Essays for Eric Hobsbawm* (Cambridge, 1984), pp. 215–34.

Harris, R., "Political Economy, Interest Groups, Legal Institutions, and the Repeal of the Bubble Act in 1825," *Economic History Review* 50:4 (1997), pp. 675–96.

Harrison, C., *The Bourgeois Citizen in Nineteenth-Century France: Gender, Sociability and the Uses of Emulation* (Oxford, 1999).

Harrison, J., "The Agrarian History of Spain, 1800–1960," *Agricultural History Review* 37 (1989), pp. 180–7.

Harrison, J. F. C., *Robert Owen and the Owenites in Britain and America* (London, 1969).

Harsin, J., *Policing Prostitution in 19th Century Paris* (Princeton, NJ, 1985).

Hart, N., "Beyond Infant Mortality: Gender and Stillbirth in Reproductive Mortality before the Twentieth Century," *Population Studies* 52:2 (1998), pp. 215–30.

Hartley, J. M., *Alexander I* (London, 1994).

Hassan, J. A., "The Growth and Impact of the British Water Industry in the Nineteenth Century," *Economic History Review* 38 (1985), pp. 531–47.

Hau, M., "Industrialization and Culture: The Case of Alsace," *Journal of European Economic History* 29:2/3 (2000), pp. 295–306.

Haug, C. J., *Leisure and Urbanism in Nineteenth-Century Nice* (Lawrence, KS, 1982).

Haupt, G., *Socialism and the Great War* (Oxford, 1972).

Hause, S. C. and A. R. Kenney, *Women's Suffrage and Social Politics in the French Third Republic* (Princeton, NJ, 1984).

Hausen, K., "Family and Role-Division: The Polarization of Sexual Stereotypes in the Nineteenth Century – An Aspect of the Dissociation of Work and Family Life," in R. J. Evans and W. R. Lee (eds.), *The German Family* (London, 1981), pp. 5–57.

Hawkins, M., *Social Darwinism in European and American Thought, 1860–1945: Nature as Model and Nature as Threat* (Cambridge, 1997).

Hay, D., *Europe: The Emergence of an Idea*, 2nd edn. (Edinburgh, 1968).

Haycraft, J. B., *Darwinism and Race Progress* (London, 1895).

Hazaresingh, S., "Religion and Politics in the Saint-Napoleon Festivity 1852–70: Anti-Clericalism, Local Patriotism and Modernity," *English Historical Review* 119 (2004), pp. 614–49.

Healy, D., *Homosexual Desire in Revolutionary Russia: The Regulation of Sexual and Gender Dissent* (Chicago, 2001).

Hearder, H., *Italy in the Age of the Risorgimento 1790–1870* (London, 1988).

Heerma van Voss, L. and M. van der Linden (eds.), *Class and Other Identities: Gender, Religion and Ethnicity in the Writing of European Labour History* (Oxford, 2002).

Hegel, G. W. F., *The Philosophy of Right*, trans. T. M. Knox (Oxford, 1952).

Heikkinen, S., *Labour and the Market: Workers, Wages and Living Standards in Finland, 1850–1913* (Helsinki, 1997).

Heilbronner, O., "In Search of the Catholic (rural) Bourgeoisie: The Peculiarities of the South German *Bürgertum*," *Central European History* 29:2 (1996), pp. 175–200.

Heilbronner, O., "From Ghetto to Ghetto: The Place of German Catholic Society in Recent Historiography," *Journal of Modern History* 72 (2000), pp. 453–95.

Heine, H., *Self Portrait and Other Prose Writings* (Secancus, NJ, 1948).

Hélias, P.-J., *Le Cheval d'Orgeuil: mémoires d'un Breton du pays bigouden* (Paris, 1975).

Hempton, D., "Religious Life in Industrial Britain, 1830–1914," in S. Gilley and W. I. Sheils (eds.), *A History of Religion in Britain* (Oxford, 1994), pp. 308–12.

Henriksen, I., "The Transformation of Danish Agriculture 1870–1914," in K. G. Persson (ed.), *The Economic Development of Denmark and Norway since 1870* (Aldershot, 1993), pp. 153–80.

Hentenryk, G. Kurgan-Van, "A Forgotten Class: The Petite Bourgeoisie in Belgium, 1850–1914," in G. Crossick and H.-G. Haupt (eds.), *Shopkeepers and Master Artisans in Nineteenth-Century Europe* (London, 1984), p. 126.

Herbert, R., *Jean-François Millet* (London, 1976).

Herzen, A., *From the Other Shore* (London, 1956).

Herzen, A., *Childhood, Youth and Exile*, trans. J. D. Duff (London, 1983).

Herzog, D., *Intimacy and Exclusion: Religious Politics in Pre-Revolutionary Baden* (Princeton, NJ, 1996).

Hewittson, M. and T. Baycroft (eds.), *Nationalism in Europe, 1789–1914* (Oxford, 2006).

Heydemann, G., *Konstitution gegen Revolution. Die britische Deutschland- und Italienpolitik 1815–1848* (Göttingen, 1995).

Heywood, C., "The Growth of Population," in P. M. Pilbeam (ed.), *Themes in Modern European History 1780–1830* (London, 1995), pp. 177–203.

Higgs, D. C., *Nobles in Nineteenth-Century France* (Baltimore, MD, 1987).

Hilden, P., *Working Women and Socialist Politics in France 1880–1914: A Regional Study* (Oxford, 1986).

Hilden, P., *Women, Work, and Politics: Belgium, 1830–1914* (Oxford, 1993).

Hildebrand, K., "Bismarck's Foreign Policy: A System of Stopgaps?" in G. Schöllgen (ed.), *Escape into War? The Foreign Policy of Imperial Germany* (Oxford, 1990).

Hildebrand, K., *Das vergangene Reich. Deutsche Außenpolitik von Bismarck bis Hitler 1871–1945* (Stuttgart, 1995), pp. 13–24.

Hillgruber, A., *Deutsche Großmacht- und Weltpolitik im 19. und 20. Jahrhundert* (Düsseldorf, 1979).

Hillyar, A. and J. McDermid, *Revolutionary Women in Russia, 1870–1917* (Manchester, 2000).

Hitchens, K. *The Romanians, 1774–1866* (Oxford, 1996).

Hobhouse, L. T., *Liberalism* (London, 1911).

Hobsbawm, E., *The Age of Revolution, 1789–1848* (London, 1962).

Hobsbawm, E., *Labouring Men* (London, 1964).

Hobsbawm, E., *The Age of Capital, 1848–1875* (London, 1975a).

Hobsbawm, E., *Industry and Empire* (London, 1975b).

Hobsbawm, E., *Worlds of Labour* (London, 1984).

Hobsbawm, E., *The Age of Empire 1875–1914* (London, 1987).

Hobsbawm, E., *Nations and Nationalism since 1780: Programme, Myth, Reality* (Cambridge, 1997).

Hobsbawm, E. and T. Ranger (eds.), *The Invention of Tradition* (Cambridge, 1983).

Hobson, J. A., *Imperialism: A Study* (London, 1902).

Hobson, J. A., *The Crisis of Liberalism*, ed. P. F. Clarke (Brighton, 1974).

Hochedlinger, M., *Austria's Wars of Emergence: War, State and Society in the Hapsburg Monarchy 1683–1797* (Harlow, 2003).

Hochstadt, S., "Migration in Preindustrial Germany," *Central European History* 16 (1983), pp. 195–224.

Hoerder, D. and L. P. Moch (eds.), *European Migrants: Global and Local Perspectives* (Boston, MA, 1996).

Höfert, A., "Wissen und Türkengefahr. Die Formierung des ethnografischen Wissenskorpus über die Osmanen in Europa (15.–16. Jahrhundert)." PhD thesis, European University Institute (Florence, 2001).

Hoffman, P. T., D. S. Jacks, P. Levin, and P. H. Lindert, "Real Inequality in Europe since 1500," *Journal of Economic History* 62:2 (2002), pp. 322–55.

Holbraad, C., *The Concert of Europe* (London, 1970).

Hollingsworth, T. H., "Mortality in the British Peerage Families since 1600," *Population*, special number (1977), pp. 323–51.

Holmes, S., *Benjamin Constant and the Making of Modern Liberalism* (New Haven, CT, 1984).

Holt, R., *Sport and the British: A Modern History* (Oxford, 1993).

Honegger, C., *Die Ordnung der Geschlechter. Die Wissenschaften vom Menschen und das Weib 1750–1850* (Frankfurt am Main, 1991).

Honeyman, K., *Gender and Industrialization* (Basingstoke, 2000).

Honour, H., *The European Vision of America: A Special Exhibition* (Cleveland, OH, 1975).

Hope, N., *German and Scandinavian Protestantism 1700–1918* (Oxford, 1995).

Hoppe, G. and J. Langton, *Peasantry to Capitalism: Western Östergötland in the Nineteenth Century* (Cambridge, 1994).

Hoppit, J., "Counting the Industrial Revolution," *Economic History Review* 43:2 (1990), pp. 173–93.

Horley, G. P. H., "The Agricultural Revolution in Northern England, 1750–1880: Nitrogen, Legumes and Crop Productivity," *Economic History Review* 2nd ser., 34 (1981), pp. 71–93.

Horowitz, D. L., *The Italian Labour Movement* (Cambridge, MA, 1963).

Horrell, S. and J. Humphries, "Old questions, New Data and Alternative Perspectives: Families' Living Standards in the Industrial Revolution," *Journal of Economic History* 52 (1992), pp. 849–80.

Hosking, G. A., *The Russian Constitutional Experiment: Government and Duma 1907–1914* (Cambridge, 1973).

Hosking, G. A. and R. Service (eds.), *Reinterpreting Russia* (London, 1999).

Hostetter, R., *The Italian Socialist Movement: Origins 1862–82* (Princeton, NJ, 1958).

Houston, R. A., *Literacy in Early Modern Europe: Culture and Education, 1500–1800* (Burnt Mill, 1988).

Houston, R. A., "Mortality in Early Modern Scotland: The Life Expectancy of Advocates," *Continuity and Change* 7:1 (1992), pp. 47–70.

Houston, R. A. and W. A. Prest, " 'To Die in the Term': The Mortality of English Barristers," *Journal of Interdisciplinary History* 26:2 (1995), pp. 233–49.

Howard, J. J., "Patriot Mothers in the Post-Risorgimento: Women After the Italian Revolution," in C. Berkin and C. Lovett (eds.), *Women, War, and Revolution* (New York, 1980), pp. 237–58.

Howard, M., *The Franco-Prussian War: The German Invasion of France, 1870–1871* (London, 1961).

Howarth, J. and P. G. Cerny, *Elites in France: Origins, Reproduction and Power* (London, 1981).

Howkins, A., "Labour History and the Rural Poor, 1850–1980," *Rural History* 1:1 (1990), pp. 113–22.

Hroch, M., *Social Preconditions of National Revival in Europe* (Cambridge, 1985).

Huberman, M., *Escape from the Market: Negotiating Work in Lancashire* (Cambridge, 1996).

Hübinger, G., *Kulturprotestantismus und Politik* (Tübingen, 1994).

Hubner, E.-R., *Dokumente zur Deutschen Verfassungsgeschichte, Vol. 1: Deutsche Verfassungsdokumente, 1815–1850* (Stuttgart, 1954).

Huck, P., "Infant Mortality in Nine Industrial Parishes in Northern England 1813–1836," *Population Studies* 48:3 (1994), pp. 513–26.

Hudson, P. (ed.), *Regions and Industries: A Perspective on the Industrial Revolution in Britain* (Cambridge, 1989).

Hudson, P., *The Industrial Revolution* (London, 1992).

Hufton, O., "Women Without Men: Widows and Spinsters in Britain and France in the Eighteenth Century," *Journal of Family History* 9 (1984), pp. 355–76.

Hughes, S., *Crime, Disorder and the Risorgimento: The Politics of Policing in Bologna* (Cambridge, 1994).

Hull, I. V., *Absolute Destruction: Military Culture and the Practices of War in Imperial Germany* (Ithaca, NY, 2004).

Humboldt, W. von, *The Limits of State Action*, ed. and trans. J. W. Burrow (Cambridge, 1969).

Hunt, J. C., "The 'Egalitarianism' of the Right: The Agrarian Leagues in South-West Germany, 1893–1914," *Journal of Contemporary History* 10 (1975), pp. 513–30.

Hutchinson, J., *The Dynamics of Cultural Nationalism: The Gaelic Revival and the Creation of the Irish Nation State* (London, 1987).

Hutchison, W. R. and H. Lehmann (eds.), *Many Are Chosen: Divine Election and Western Nationalism* (Minneapolis, MN, 1994).

Hutton, P., *The Cult of Revolutionary Tradition: The Blanquists in French Politics* (Berkeley, CA, 1981).

Huxley, T. H., *Evolution and Ethics* (London, 1894).

Hyman, P. E., *The Jews of Modern France* (Berkeley, CA, 1998).

Iggers, G. G., *The German Conception of History* (Middletown, OH, 1968).

Ionescu, G. (ed.), *The Political Thought of Saint-Simon* (London, 1976).

Jackson, Jr., G. D., "Peasant Political Movements in Eastern Europe," in H. A. Landsberger (ed.), *Rural Protest: Peasant Movements and Social Change* (Basingstoke, 1974), pp. 259–315.

James, H., *A German Identity 1770–1990*, revd. edn. (London, 1990).

Jansen, C. (ed.), *Der Bürger als Soldat: Die Militarisierung europäischer Gesellschaften im langen 19. Jahrhundert* (Essen, 2004).

Janssens, A. (ed.), "The Rise and Decline of the Male Breadwinner Family?" *International Review of Social History*, Supplement 5 (Cambridge, 1998).

Jarausch, K. H., "German Students in the First World War," *Central European History* 17 (1984), pp. 310–29.

Jarrick, A., *Back to Modern Reason: Johan Hjerpe and Other Petit Bourgeois in Stockholm in the Age of Enlightenment* (Liverpool, 1999).

Jedin, H. (ed.), *History of the Church: Vol. 7: The Church between Revolution and Restoration*; *Vol. 8: The Church in the Age of Liberalism*; *Vol. 9: The Church in the Industrial Age* (London, 1981).

Jefferies, M., *Imperial Culture in Germany, 1871–1918* (Basingstoke, 2003).

Jeismann, M., *Das Vaterland der Feinde: Studien zum nationalen Feindbegriff und Selbstverständnis in Deutschland und Frankreich 1792–1918* (Stuttgart, 1992).

Jelavich, B., "Mihail Koglniceanu: Historian as Foreign Minister, 1876–8," in D. Deletant and H. Hanak (eds.), *Historians and Nation-Builders* (Basingstoke, 1988).

Jelavich, B., *Russia's Balkan Entanglements, 1806–1914* (Cambridge, 1991).

Jelavich, C., *South Slav Nationalisms: Textbooks and Yugoslav Union before 1914* (Columbus, OH, 1990).

Jennings, J., *Georges Sorel* (London, 1985).

Jewson, N., "Medical Knowledge and the Patronage System in 18th Century England," *Sociology* 8 (1974), pp. 369–85.

Johansson, E., "Literacy Campaigns in Sweden," *Interchange* 19:3/4 (1988), pp. 135–62.

Johansson, K., *Child Mortality during the Demographic Transition: A Longitudinal Analysis of a Rural Population in Southern Sweden, 1766–1894* (Lund, 2004).

Johansson, S. R., "Welfare, Mortality and Gender Over Three Centuries," *Continuity and Change* 6:2 (1991), pp. 135–78.

Johnson, C., *Utopian Communism in France: Cabet and the Icarians, 1839–1851* (Ithaca, NY, 1974).

Johnson, C., "Economic Change and Artisan Discontent: The Tailors' History, 1800–1848," in R. Price (ed.), *Revolution and Reaction: 1848 and the Second French Republic* (London, 1975), pp. 87–114.

Johnson, R., "Zagranichnaia Agentura: The Tsarist Political Police in Europe," *Journal of Contemporary History* 7:1/2 (1972), pp. 221–42.

Joll, J., *The Second International* (London, 1955).

Joll, J., *The Anarchists*, 2nd edn. (London, 1979).

Joll, J., *The Origins of the First World War*, 2nd edn. (London, 1992).

Jones, E., *Growth: Recurring Economic Change in World History* (Oxford, 1988).

Jones, L. E. and J. Retalluck (eds.), *Elections, Mass Politics and Social Change in Modern Germany* (Cambridge, 1992).

Jonsson, U., "The Paradox of Share Tenancy Under Capitalism: A Comparative Perspective on Late Nineteenth- and Early Twentieth-Century French and Italian Sharecropping," *Rural History* 3:2 (1992), pp. 191–217.

Jordanova, L., *Sexual Visions: Images of Gender in Science and Medicine between the 18th and the 20th Centuries* (Madison, WI, 1989).

Joyce, P., *Work, Society and Politics: The Culture of the Factory in Later Victorian England* (Brighton, 1980).

Joyce, P., *Visions of the People: Industrial England and the Question of Class, 1848–1914* (Cambridge, 1991).

Judson, P., *Exclusive Revolutionaries: Liberal Politics, Social Experience, and National Identity in the Austrian Empire, 1848–1914* (Ann Arbor, MI, 1996).

Judt, T., *Marxism and the French Left* (Oxford, 1986).

Kaa, D. J. van de, "Anchored Narratives: The Story and Findings of Half a Century of Research into the Determinants of Fertility," *Population Studies* 50:3 (1996), pp. 389–432.

Kaelble, H., "French Bourgeoisie and German Bürgertum, 1870–1914," in S. N. Kalyvas (ed.), *The Rise of Christian Democracy in Europe* (Ithaca, NY, 1996).

Kaminsky, A. P., *The India Office, 1880–1910* (London, 1986).

Kant, I., "Zum ewigen Frieden. Ein philosophischer Entwurf," in *Kants Werke: Akademie Textausgabe*, Vol. 8 (Berlin, 1968), pp. 341–86.

Kaplan, T., *Anarchists of Andalusia 1868–1903* (Princeton, NJ, 1977).

Karpat, K., "The Transformation of the Ottoman State, 1789–1908," *International Journal of Middle East Studies* 3:3 (1972), pp. 243–81.

Katz, J., *From Prejudice to Destruction: Antisemitism 1700–1933* (Cambridge, MA, 1980).

Katz, J. (ed.), *Toward Modernity: The European Jewish Model* (New Brunswick, NJ, 1987).

Kautsky, K., *Selected Political Writings*, ed. P. Goode (London, 1983).

Keane, J., "Despotism and Democracy: The Origins and Development of the Distinction Between Civil Society and the State," in J. Keane (ed.), *Civil Society and the State: New European Perspectives* (New York, 1988).

Kearns, G., "The Urban Penalty and the Population History of England," in A. Brändström and L.-G. Tedebrand (eds.), *Society, Health and Population during the Demographic Transition* (Stockholm, 1988), pp. 213–36.

Kearns, G., "Demography and Urbanization: A Geographic Overview," in A. Brändström and L.-G. Tedebrand (eds.), *Population Dynamics During Industrialization* (Umeå, 2000).

Kearns, G., W. R. Lee, and J. Rogers, "The Interaction of Political and Economic Factors in the Management of Urban Public Health," in M. C. Nelson and J. Rogers (eds.), *Urbanisation and the Epidemiologic Transition* (Uppsala, 1989), pp. 9–82.

Kedourie, E., *Nationalism* (London, 1960).

Keegan, J., *The Face of Battle* (London, 1975).

Keegan, J., *A History of Warfare* (London, 1993).

Keegan, J., *The First World War* (New York, 2000).

Keiger, J., *France and the Origins of the First World War* (London, 1983).

Kelly, A. (ed. and trans.), *The German Worker: Working Class Autobiographies from the Age of Industrialization* (Berkeley, CA, 1987).

Kennedy, P., *The Rise of Anglo-German Antagonism, 1860–1914* (London, 1980).

Kern, S., *The Culture of Time and Space, 1880–1918* (Cambridge, 1983).

Kidd, B., *Social Evolution* (London, 1895) [1894].

Kiernan, V. G., "State and Nation in Western Europe," *Past and Present* 31 (1965).

Kießling, F., *Gegen den "großen Krieg"? Entspannung in den internationalen Beziehungen 1911–1914* (Munich, 2002).

Kieval, H. J., *The Making of Czech Jewry: National Conflict and Jewish Society in Bohemia, 1870–1918* (New York, 1988).

Kieval, H. J., *Languages of Community: The Jewish Experience in the Czech Lands* (Berkeley, CA, 2000).

Kim, D., *Leadership and Creativity: A History of the Cavendish Laboratory, 1871–1919* (Dordrecht, 2002).

King, S., "Migrants on the Margin? Mobility, Integration and Occupation in the West Riding, 1650–1820," *Journal of Historical Geography* 23 (1997), pp. 284–303.

Kintner, H. J., "Trends and Regional Differences in Breastfeeding in Germany from 1871 to 1937," *Journal of Family History* (1985), pp. 163–82.

Kirby, D., *The Baltic World 1772–1993: Europe's Northern Periphery in an Age of Change* (London, 1995).

Kirk, D., "Demographic Transition Theory," *Population Studies* 50 (1996), pp. 361–88.

Kirk, N., *The Growth of Working-Class Reformism in Mid-Victorian England* (London, 1985).

Kitchen, M., *The Political Economy of Germany, 1815–1914* (London, 1978).

Kizenko, N., *A Prodigal Saint: Father John of Kronstadt and the Russian People* (Philadelphia, PA, 2000).

Klier, J. D., *Imperial Russia's Jewish Question, 1855–1881* (Cambridge, 1995).

Klier, J. D., *Russia Gathers Her Jews: The Origins of the "Jewish Question" in Russia, 1772–1825* (Dekalb, IL, 1986).

Knipping, J. B., *Iconography of the Counter Reformation in the Netherlands: Heaven on Earth*, 2 vols. (Leiden, 1974).

Knodel, J. E., *The Decline of Fertility in Germany, 1871–1939* (Princeton, NJ, 1974).

Knodel, J. E, *Demographic Behavior in the Past: A Study of Fourteen German Village Populations in the Eighteenth and Nineteenth Centuries* (Cambridge, 1988).

Kocka, J., "Craft Traditions and the Labor Movement in 19th Century Germany," in P. Thane, G. Grossick, and R. Floud (eds.), *The Power of the Past: Essays for Eric Hobsbawm* (Cambridge, 1989), pp. 95–117.

Kocka, J., "The Middle Classes in Europe," *Journal of Modern History* 65 (1995), pp. 703–800.

Kocka, J. and A. Mitchell (eds.), *Bourgeois Society in Nineteenth-Century Europe* (Oxford, 1993), pp. 273–301.

Koergård, N., "The Industrial Development of Denmark 1840–1914," *Journal of European Economic History* 19:2 (1990), pp. 271–91.

Kohn, H., *Nationalism: Its Meaning and History* (London, 1955).

Kolb, E. (ed.), *Europa vor dem Krieg von 1870. Mächtekonstellation – Konfliktfelder – Kriegsausbruch* (Munich, 1987).

Kolchin, P., *Unfree Labor: American Slavery and Russian Serfdom* (Cambridge, MA, 1987).

Kolchin, P., "After Serfdom: Russian Emancipation in Comparative Perspective," in S. L. Engerman (ed.), *Terms of Labor: Slavery, Serfdom, and Free Labor* (Stanford, CA., 1999).

Koliopoulos, G., *Brigands without a Cause: Brigandage and Irredentism in Modern Greece, 1821–1912* (Oxford, 1987).

Komlos, J., *Biological Standard of Living* (London, 1995).

Koning, N., *The Failure of Agrarian Capitalism: Agrarian Politics in the UK, Germany, the Netherlands and the USA, 1846–1919* (London, 1994).

Körner, A. (ed.), *1848: A European Revolution? International Ideas and National Memories of 1848* (Basingstoke, 2000).

Koselleck, R., *Critique and Crisis: Enlightenment and the Pathogenesis of Modern Society* (Oxford, 1988) [1954].

Koselleck, R., "Volk, Nation," in O. Brunner, W. Conze, and R. Koselleck (eds.), *Geschichtliche Grundbegriffe*, Vol. 7 (Stuttgart, 1992).

Koselleck, R., "The Eighteenth Century as the Beginning of Modernity," in *The Practice of Conceptual History: Timing History, Spacing Concepts* (Stanford, CA, 2002), pp. 154–69.

Koshar, R., *German Travel Cultures* (Oxford, 2000).

Kotsonis, Y., *Making Peasants Backward: Managing Populations in Russian Agricultural Cooperatives, 1861–1914* (New York, 1999).

Koven, S. and S. Michel (eds.), *Mothers of a New World: Maternalist Policies and the Origins of the Welfare States* (London, 1993).

Krause, W. and D. J. Puffert, "Chemicals, Strategy and Tariffs: Tariff Policy and the Soda Industry in Imperial Germany," *European Review of Economic History* 4 (2000), pp. 285–309.

Kraut, A. M., *Silent Travellers: Germs, Genes and the "Immigrant Menace"* (Baltimore, MD, 1995).

Kretschmann, C. and H. Pahl, "Ein 'Zweites Konfessionelles Zeitalter'? Vom Nutzen und Nachteil einer neuen Epochensignatur," *Historische Zeitschrift* 276:2 (2003), pp. 369–91.

Kriedte, P., H. Medick, and J. Schlumbohm, *Industrialisation before Industrialisation: Rural Industry in the Genesis of Capitalism* (Cambridge, 1981).

Kropotkin, P., *Fields, Factories and Workshops* (London, 1899).

Krüger, P., "'Von Bismarck zu Hitler'? – Die Agonie des europäischen Staatensystems 1938/39," in P. Krüger (ed.), *Kontinuität und Wandel in der Staatenordnung der Neuzeit. Beiträge zur Geschichte des internationalen Systems* (Marburg, 1991).

Kucich, G., "Romanticism and the Re-engendering of Historical Memory," in M. Campbell, J. Labbe, and S. Shuttleworth (eds.), *Memory and Memorials, 1789–1914* (London, 2000).

Kunitz, S. J., "Speculations on the European Mortality Decline," *Economic History Review* 36 (1983), pp. 349–64.

Kunitz, S. J., "Mortality since Malthus," in D. Coleman and R. Schofield (eds.), *The State of Population Theory: Forward from Malthus* (Oxford, 1986), pp. 278–300.

Kytir, J. and R. Münz, "Infant Mortality in Austria 1820–1950: Trends and Regional Patterns," in C. A. Corsini and P. P. Viazzo (eds.), *The Decline of Infant Mortality in Europe 1800–1950: Four National Case Studies* (Florence, 1993), pp. 71–86.

Ladd, B., *Urban Planning and Civic Order in Germany, 1860–1914* (Cambridge, 1990).

Lademacher, H., "Frankreich, Preußen und die belgische Frage in der Juli-Monarchie," in R. Poidevin and H.-O. Sieburg (eds.), *Aspects des relations franco-allemandes, 1830–1848* (Metz, 1973), pp. 47–62.

Lademacher, H., *Die belgische Neutralität als Problem der europäischen Politik* (Bonn, 1974).

Lahme, R., *Deutsche Aussenpolitik 1890–1894. Von der Gleichgewichtspolitik Bismarcks zur Allianzstrategie Caprivis* (Göttingen, 1990).

Lains, P., "Southern European Economic Backwardness Revisited: The Role of Open Economy Forces in Portugal and the Balkans, 1870–1913," *Scandinavian Economic History Review* 50:1 (2002), pp. 24–43.

Lambert, P., "The Professionalization and Institutionalization of History," in S. Berger, H. Feldner, and K. Passmore (eds.), *Writing History: Theory and Practice* (London, 2003).

Lamberti, M., *State, Society and the Elementary School in Imperial Germany* (New York, 1989).

Lamberti, M., "Radical Schoolteachers and the Progressive Education Movement in Germany 1900–1914," *History of Education Quarterly* 40:1 (2000), pp. 22–48.

Landers, J., "Mortality and Metropolis: The Case of London 1675–1825," *Population Studies*, 41:1 (1987), pp. 59–76.

Landes, J., *Women and the Public Sphere in the Age of the French Revolution* (Ithaca, NY, 1988).

Landry, A., *La Révolution démographique. Etudes et essais sur les problèmes de la population* (Paris, 1934).

Lane, B. M., "Government Buildings in European Capitals 1870–1914," in H.-J. Teuteberg (ed.), *Urbanisierung im 19. und 20. Jahrhundert* (Cologne, 1983).

Lane, T., *Liverpool: Gateway of Empire* (London, 1987).

Langford, P., *Englishness Identified: Manners and Character 1650–1850* (Oxford, 2000).

Langhorne, R., *The Collapse of the Concert of Europe: International Politics, 1890–1914* (London, 1981).

Lankester, E. R., *Degeneration: A Chapter in Darwinism* (London, 1880).

Lannon, F., *Privilege, Persecution and Prophecy: The Catholic Church in Spain, 1875–1975* (Oxford, 1987).

Lapouge, G. V. de, *Les Sélections sociales* (Paris, 1896).

Lapouge, G. V. de, *L'Aryen: son role social* (Paris, 1899).

Laqueur, T., *Solitary Sex: A Cultural History of Masturbation* (New York, 2003).

Laqueur, W. and G. L. Mosse (eds.), *Historians in Politics* (London, 1974).

Latourette, K. S., *Christianity in a Revolutionary Age, Vol. 2: The Nineteenth Century in Europe: The Protestant and Eastern Churches* (New York, 1959).

Laven, D., "Law and Order in Habsburg Venetia 1814–1835," *Historical Journal* 39:2 (1996), pp. 383–403.

Laven, D. and L. Riall (eds.), *Napoleon's Legacy: Problems of Government in Restoration Europe* (Oxford, 2000).

Lawrence, P., *Nationalism in Europe, 1780–1850* (London, 2004).

Lawton, R. and R. Lee (eds.), *Urban Population Development in Western Europe from the Late Eighteenth to the Early Twentieth Century* (Liverpool, 1989).

Lawton, R. and R. Lee (eds.), *Population and Society in Western European Port-Cities, c.1650–1939* (Liverpool, 2001).

Le Corbeiller, C., "Miss America and her Sisters: Personification of the Four Parts of the World," *Metropolitan Museum Bulletin* 19 (1960), pp. 209–23.

Le Rider, J., *La Mitteleuropa* (Paris, 1994).

Lebrun, R., *Throne and Altar: The Political and Religious Thought of Joseph de Maistre* (Ottawa, 1965).

Leclerc, G., *Anthropologie et colonialisme. Essai sur l'histoire de l'africanisme* (Paris, 1972).

Lee, C. H., "Regional Inequalities in Infant Mortality in Britain, 1861–1971: Patterns and Hypotheses," *Population Studies* 45:1 (1991), pp. 55–65.

Lee, R., "The Socio-Economic and Demographic Characteristics of Port Cities: A Typology for Comparative Analysis?" *Urban History* 25:2 (1998), pp. 147–72.

Lee, R., "Urban Labor Markets, In-Migration, and Demographic Growth: Bremen, 1815–1914," *Journal of Interdisciplinary History* 33 (1999), pp. 437–73.

Lee, R., "'Relative Backwardness' and Long-Run Development: Economic, Demographic and Social Changes," in J. Breuilly (ed.), *Nineteenth Century Germany Politics, Culture, and Society 1780–1918* (London, 2001), p. 86.

Lee, W. R., "Bastardy and the Socioeconomic Structure of South Germany," *Journal of Interdisciplinary History* 7:3 (1977a), pp. 403–25.

Lee, W. R., *Population Growth, Economic Development and Social Change in Bavaria 1750–1850* (New York, 1977b).

Lee, W. R. (ed.), *European Demography and Economic Growth* (London, 1979).

Lee, W. R., "Women's Work and the Family: Some Demographic Implications of Gender-Specific Rural Work Patterns in Nineteenth-Century Germany," in P. Hudson and W. R. Lee (eds.), *Women's Work and the Family Economy in Historical Perspective* (Manchester 1990), pp. 50–75.

Lee, W. R. and P. Marschalck, "Infant Mortality in Bremen in the 19th Century," *History of the Family* 7 (2002), pp. 557–83.

Leerssen, J. T., *Nationaal denken in Europa: een cultuurhistorisch schets* (Amsterdam, 1999).

Leerssen, J. T. and M. van Montfrans (eds.), *Borders and Territories: Yearbook of European Studies* 6 (Amsterdam, 1993).

Lehmann, H. and H. Wellenreuther (eds.), *German and American Nationalism: A Comparative Perspective* (Oxford, 1999).

Lehning, J. R., *Peasant and French: Cultural Contact in Rural France during the Nineteenth Century* (Cambridge, 1995).

Lenin, V. I., *Collected Works*, Vol. 22 (Moscow, 1982).

Lenin, V. I., *Imperialism: The Highest Stage of Capitalism: A Popular Outline*, intro. P. Patnaik (New Delhi, 2000) [1917].

Levin, A., *The Second Duma: A Study of the Social Democratic Party and the Russian Constitutional Experiment* (Hamden, CT, 1966).

Levin, A., *The Third Duma: Election and Profile* (Hamden, CT, 1973).

Levine, D., "Sampling History: The English Population," *Journal of Interdisciplinary History* 28:4 (1998), pp. 605–32.

Levine, P., *The Amateur and the Professional: Antiquarians, Historians and Archaeologists in Victorian England* (Cambridge, 1986).

Levinger, M., *Enlightened Nationalism: The Transformation of Prussian Political Culture 1806–1848* (Oxford, 2000).

Levy, C., "Fascism, National Socialism and Conservatives in Europe, 1914–1945: Issues for Comparativists," *Contemporary European History* 8:1 (1999), pp. 97–126.

Levy, C., "Currents of Italian Syndicalism before 1926," *International Review of Social History* 45 (2000), pp. 209–50.

Lewenhak, S., *Women and Trade Unions* (London, 1977).

Lewis, G., "The Peasantry, Rural Change and Conservative Agrarianism: Lower Austria at the Turn of the Century," *Past and Present* 81 (1978), pp. 119–43.

Lewis, J., (ed.), *Labour and Love: Women's Experience of Home and Family, 1850–1940* (Oxford, 1986).

Lewis, J., "Gender, the Family and Women's Agency in the Building of 'Welfare States': The British Case," *Social History* 19 (1994), pp. 37–55.

Liang, H.-H., *The Rise of Modern Police and the European State System from Metternich to the Second World War* (Cambridge, 1992).

Lichtheim, G., *A Short History of Socialism* (London, 1970).

Lidtke, V., *The Alternative Culture* (Oxford, 1985).

Lieven D., *The Aristocracy in Europe, 1815–1914* (London, 1992).

Lieven, D., "Dilemmas of Empire 1850–1918: Power, Territory, Identity," *Journal of Contemporary History* 34 (1999), pp. 163–200.

Lieven, D. (ed.), *Empire: The Russian Empire and Its Rivals* (London, 2003).

Lincoln, B. W., *The Great Reforms: Autocracy, Bureaucracy and Politics of Change in Imperial Russia* (Dekalb, IL, 1990).

Lindemann, A., *A History of European Socialism* (New Haven, CT, 1983).

Linden, M. van der and W. Thorpe (eds.), *Revolutionary Syndicalism: An International Perspective* (Aldershot, 1990).

Lindert, P. and J. G. Williamson, "English Workers' Living Standards during the Industrial Revolution: A New Look," *Economic History Review* 36:1 (1983), pp. 1–25.

Lindhart, P. G., *Kirchengeschichte Skandinaviens* (Göttingen, 1983).

Linton, D. S., "Between School and Marriage, Workshop and Household: Young Working Women as a Social Problem in Late Imperial Germany," *European History Quarterly* 18:4 (1988), pp. 387–408.

Lipset, S. M., "Radicalism or Reformism: The Sources of Working-Class Politics," *American Political Science Review* 77 (1983), pp. 1–18.

Lis, C., *Social Change and the Labouring Poor: Antwerp, 1770–1860* (New Haven, CT, 1986).

Litvak, L., *Musa Libertaria: Arte, Literatura y vida cultural del anarquismo espanol (1880–1913)* (Barcelona, 1981).

Livesey, J., *Making Democracy in the French Revolution* (Cambridge, MA, 2001).

Livi-Bacci, M., "Socio-Group Forerunners of Fertility Control in Europe," in A. J. Coale and S. C. Watkins (eds.), *The Decline of Fertility in Europe* (Princeton, NJ, 1986), pp. 182–200.

Lonsdale, J., "The European Scramble and Conquest in African History," in R. Olivier and G. N. Sanderson (eds.), *The Cambridge History of Africa, Vol. 6: From 1870 to 1905* (Cambridge, 1985), pp. 680–766.

Lorenz, C., "Beyond Good and Evil? The German Empire of 1871 and Modern German Historiography," *Journal of Contemporary History* 30 (1995), pp. 729–65.

Lorimer, D. A., *Colour, Class and the Victorians: English Attitudes to the Negro in the Mid-Nineteenth Century* (Leicester, 1978).

Loth, W., "Soziale Bewegungen im Katholizismus des Kaiserreches," *Geschichte und Gesellschaft* 17 (1991), pp. 279–310.

Loudon, I., *The Tragedy of Childbed Fever* (Oxford, 2000).

Lowe, C. J. and F. Marzari, *Italian Foreign Policy, 1870–1940* (London, 1975).

Lowe, W. J. and E. L. Malcolm, "The Domestication of the Royal Irish Constabulary, 1836–1922," *Irish Economic and Social History* 19 (1992), pp. 27–48.

Lüdtke, A., "The Role of State Violence in the Period of Transition to Industrial Capitalism: The Example of Prussia from 1815 to 1848," *Social History* 4:2 (1979), pp. 175–221.

Lüdtke, A., *Police and State in Prussia, 1815–1850* (Cambridge, 1989).

Lukes, S., *Emile Durkheim* (London, 1992).

Lumley, R. and J. Morris (eds.), *The New History of the Italian South: The Mezzogiorno Revisited* (Exeter, 1997).

Lundgreen, P., "Educational Opportunity and Status Attainment: Two Different Cities in 19th-Century Germany," *Journal of Social History* 22:2 (1988/9), pp. 328–38.

Lupo, S., "I Proprietari Terrieri nel Mezzogiorno," in P. Bevilacqua (ed.), *Storia Dell'Agrcicoltura Italiana in Età Contemporanea, II. Unomini e Classi* (Venice, 1990).

Lyons, M., *Readers and Society in Nineteenth-Century France: Workers, Women, Peasants* (Houndmills, 2001).

Lyttelton, A., "Landlords, Peasants and the Limits of Liberalism," in J. A. Davis (ed.), *Gramsci and Italy's Passive Revolution* (London, 1979).

McBriar, A., *Fabian Socialism and English Politics* (Cambridge, 1966).

McCahill, M. and E. A. Wasson, "The New Peerage: Recruitment to the House of Lords, 1704–1847," *Historical Journal* 46:1 (2003), pp. 1–38.

McCloskey, D. N., "The Industrial Revolution 1780–1860: A Survey," in R. Floud and D. N. McCloskey (eds.), *The Economic History of Britain since 1700* (Cambridge, 1981), pp. 103–27.

McConville, S., "The Victorian Prison, England 1865–1965," in N. Morris and D. J. Rothman (eds.), *The Oxford History of the Prison: The Practice of Punishment in Western Society* (Oxford, 1995), pp. 131–67.

MacDermot, M., *A History of Bulgaria 1393–1885* (London, 1962).

Macey, D. A. J., *Government and Peasant in Russia, 1861–1906: The Prehistory of the Stolypin Reforms* (De Kalb, IL, 1987).

McGowen, R., "The Well-Ordered Prison: England 1780–1865," in N. Morris and D. J. Rothman (eds.), *The Oxford History of the Prison: The Practice of Punishment in Western Society* (Oxford, 1995).

Mack Smith, D., *Italy and Its Monarchy* (New Haven, CT, 1989).

MacKenzie, J. M., *Popular Imperialism and the Military 1850–1950* (Manchester, 1992).

McKeown, T., *The Modern Rise of Population* (New York, 1976).

McKeown, T., *The Role of Medicine: Dream, Mirage, or Nemesis?* (London, 1976b).

McKeown, T. and R. G. Record, "Reasons for the Decline of Mortality in England and Wales during the 19th Century," *Population Studies* 16 (1962), pp. 92–122.

McKeown, T., R. G. Brown, and R. G. Record, "An Interpretation of the Modern Rise of Population," *Population Studies* 26 (1972), pp. 345–82.

Mackie, T. T. and R. Rose, *The International Almanac of Electoral History* (Basingstoke, 1974).

Mackinnon, A., "Were Women Present at the Demographic Transition? Questions from a Feminist Historian to Historical Demographers," *Gender and History* 7:2 (1995), pp. 222–40.

McLaren, A., *Birth Control in Nineteenth Century England* (New York, 1978).

McLellan, D., *Marxism After Marx* (Basingstoke, 1998).

McLeod, H., "Building the 'Catholic Ghetto': Catholic Organisations 1870–1914," in W. J. Sheils and D. Wood (eds.), *Voluntary Religion: Studies in Church History*, Vol. 23 (Oxford, 1986), pp. 411–44.

McLeod, H., "Weibliche Frömmigkeit–männlicher Unglaube? Religion und Kirchen im bürgerlichen 19. Jahrhundert," in U. Frevert (ed.), *Bürgerinnen und Bürger* (Göttingen, 1988), pp. 134–56.

McLeod, H., *Piety and Poverty: Working-Class Religion in Berlin, London and New York, 1870–1914* (New York, 1996).

McLeod, H., *Religion and the People of Western Europe, 1789–1989* (Oxford, 1997).

McLeod, H., *Secularisation in Western Europe 1848–1914* (New York, 2000).

Macleod, R., *Style and Society: Architectural Ideology in Britain 1835–1914* (London, 1971).

McMillan, J., "'Priest Hits Girl': On the Front Line in the 'War of the Two Frances'," in C. Clark and W. Kaiser (eds.), *Culture Wars: Secular–Catholic Conflict in Nineteenth Century Europe* (Cambridge, 2003), pp. 77–101.

McPhee, P., *The Politics of Rural Life: Political Mobilisation in the French Countryside 1846–52* (Oxford, 1992).

McPhee, P., *Revolution and Environment in Southern France: Peasants, Lords and Murder in the Corbières, 1780–1830* (Oxford, 1999).

McPhee, P., *A Social History of France, 1789–1914*, 2nd edn. (Basingstoke, 2004).

Maddison, A., *Monitoring the World Economy 1820–1992* (Paris, 1995).

Mager, W., *Die Entstehung des modernen Staatsbegriffs* (Wiesbaden, 1968).

Magnusson, L., *An Economic History of Sweden* (London, 2000).

Maistre, J. de, *The Works of Joseph de Maistre*, selected and trans. J. Lively (London, 1965).

Malatesta, M., "The Landed Aristocracy During the Nineteenth and Early Twentieth Centuries," in *The European Way: European Societies During the Nineteenth and Twentieth Centuries* (New York, 2004), pp. 68–88.

Malcolmson, R., *Popular Recreations in English Society, 1700–1850* (Cambridge, 1973).

Maleová, J., "The Emancipation of Women for the Benefit of the Nation: The Czech Women's Movement," in S. Paletschek and B. Pietrow-Ennker (eds.), *Women's Emancipation Movements in the Nineteenth Century* (Stanford, 2004), pp. 17–71.

Malmborg, M. af and B. Stråth (eds.), *The Meaning of Europe: Variety and Contention Within and Among Nations* (Oxford, 2002).

Malthus, T. R., *An Essay on the Principle of Population* (Cambridge, 1992) [1798].

Mann, M., *The Sources of Social Power, Vol. 2: The Rise of Classes and Nation States 1760–1914* (Cambridge, 1993).

Mantl, E., *Heirat als Privileg. Obrigkeitliche Heiratsbeschränkungen in Tirol und Vorarlberg 1820 bis 1920* (Vienna, 1997).

Mar del Pozo Andrés, M. del, and J. F. A. Braster, "The Rebirth of the 'Spanish Race': The State, Nationalism and Education in Spain, 1875–1931," *European History Quarterly* 29:1 (1999), pp. 75–107.

Marcowitz, R., *Die Interdependenz französischer Innen- und Außenpolitik 1814/15–1851/52* (Stuttgart, 2001).

Marcus, S., *The Other Victorians: A Study of Sexuality and Pornography in Mid-Nineteenth-Century England* (New York, 1966).

Margry, P. J. and H. te Velde, "Contested Rituals and the Battle for Public Space: The Netherlands," in C. Clark and W. Kaiser (eds.), *Culture Wars: Secular–Catholic Conflict in Nineteenth-Century Europe* (Cambridge, 2004), pp. 129–51.

Marshall, P., *Demanding the Impossible: A History of Anarchism* (London, 1993).

Martin, B., *The Agony of Modernization: Labor and Industrialization in Spain* (Ithaca, NY, 1990).

Marx, K., *The Eighteenth Brumaire of Louis Bonaparte* (London, 1852).

Marx, K., *Karl Marx: Selected Writings*, ed. D. McLellan (Oxford, 1977).

Marx, K. and F. Engels, *The Communist Manifesto*, in K. Marx and F. Engels, *Collected Works*, Vol. 6 (New York, 1975), pp. 477–517.

Mathias, P., *The First Industrial Nation: An Economic History of Britain 1700–1914* (London, 1969).

Mathias, P. and J. A. Davis (eds.), *The Nature of Industrialization, Vol. 4: Agriculture and Industrialization from the Eighteenth Century to the Present Day* (Oxford, 1996).

Matsuda, M. K. *The Memory of the Modern* (Oxford, 1996).

Mavor, C., *Pleasures Taken: Performances of Sexuality and Loss in Victorian Photographs* (Durham, 1995).

Mayer, A. J., *The Persistence of the Old Regime: Europe to the Great War* (London, 1981).

Mayhall, L. E. N., "The Rhetorics of Slavery and Citizenship: Suffragist Discourse and Canonical Texts in Britain, 1880–1914," in K. Canning and S. O. Rose (eds.), *Gender, Citizenship and Subjectivities* (London, 2002).

Maynes, M. J., *Schooling in Western Europe: A Social History* (Albany, NY, 1985).

Maza, S., *The Myth of the French Bourgeoisie* (Cambridge, MA, 2003).

Mazower, M., *Dark Continent: Europe's Twentieth Century* (New York, 1998).

Mazower, M., *The Balkans* (London, 2001).

Meinecke, F., *Cosmopolitanism and the National State* (Princeton, NJ, 1970) [1907].

Mellaerts, W., "Criminal Justice in Provincial England, France and the Netherlands, c. 1880–1950: Some Comparative Perspectives," *Crime, Histoire & Sociétés/Crime, History and Societies* 4:2 (2000), pp. 19–52.

Melman, B., "Claiming the Nation's Past: The Invention of an Anglo-Saxon Tradition," *Journal of Contemporary History* 26 (1991), pp. 575–95.

Melman, B. (ed.), *Borderlines: Genders and Identities in War and Peace 1870–1930* (London, 1998).

Mendelsohn, E., *On Modern Jewish Politics* (New York, 1993).

Mendes-Flohr, P. and J. Reinharz (eds.), *The Jew in the Modern World: A Documentary History*, 2nd edn. (New York, 1995).

Mennell, S., *Norbert Elias: An Introduction* (Oxford, 1989).

Mercer, A. J., "Smallpox and Epidemiological-Demographic Change in Europe: The Role of Vaccination," *Population Studies* 39:2 (1985), pp. 287–307.

Mergel, T., *Zwischen Klasse und Konfession. Katholisches Bürgertum im Rheinland 1790–1914* (Göttingen, 1994).

Mergel, T., "Die subtile Macht der Liebe: Geschlecht, Erziehung und Frömmigkeit in Katholischen Rheinischen Bürgerfamlilien 1830–1910," in I. G. von Olenhusen, *Frauen unter dem Patriarchat der Kirchen. Katholikinnen und Protestantinnen im 19. und 20.Jh* (Stuttgart, 1995), pp. 22–47.

Merriman, J., *The Red City: Limoges and the French Nineteenth Century* (Oxford, 1985).

Meyer, A. J., *The Persistence of the Old Regime in Europe* (London, 1981).

Meyer, M. A. (ed.), *German-Jewish History in Modern Times*, 4 vols (New York, 1996–8).

Micale, M. S. and R. Porter (eds.), *Discovering the History of Psychiatry* (Oxford, 1994).

Michelet, J., *Histoire de la révolution française*, 2 vols. (Paris, 1979).

Midgely, C., *Women Against Slavery: The British Campaigns 1780–1870* (London, 1995).

Miles, A., *Social Mobility in Nineteenth- and Early Twentieth-Century England* (New York, 1999).

Miliukov, P., *Outlines of Russian Culture: Religion and the Church in Russia* (Philadelphia, PA, 1942).

Mill, J. S., *On the Subjection of Women* (Arlington Heights, IL, 1980).

Millar, J., *An Historical View of the English Government from the Settlement of the Saxons in Britain*, Vol. 1 (London, 1818).

Miller, J. A., *Mastering the Market: The State and the Grain Trade in Northern France, 1700–1860s* (Cambridge, 1991).

Miller, M. B., *The Bon Marché: Bourgeois Culture and the Department Store, 1869–1920* (London, 1981).

Mills, D. and R. Tinley, "Population Turnover in an Eighteenth-Century Lincolnshire Parish in a Comparative Context," *Local Population Studies* 52 (1994), pp. 30–8.

Milward, A. S. and S. B. Saul, *The Development of the Economies of Continental Europe, 1850–1914* (Cambridge, MA, 1977).

Mingay, G. E. (ed.), *Arthur Young and His Times* (London, 1975).

Mironov, B. N., "New Approaches to Old Problems: The Well-Being of the Population of Russia from 1821 to 1910 as Measured by Physical Stature," *Slavic Review* 58:1 (1999), pp. 1–26.

Mistral, F., *Mémoires et récits: mes origines* (Paris; Plon, 1906).

Mitchell, A., *Victors and Vanquished: The German Influence on the Army and the Navy in France* (Chapel Hill, NC, 1979).

Mitchell, B. R., *International Historical Statistics: Europe, 1750–1988*, 3rd edn. (London, 1992).

Moch, L. P., *Moving Europeans: Migration in Western Europe since 1650*, 2nd edn. (Bloomington, IN, 2003).

Moeller, R. G. (ed.), *Peasants and Lords in Modern Germany: Recent Studies in Agricultural History* (Boston, MA, 1986).

Mokyr, J., "Editor's Introduction: The New Economic History and the Industrial Revolution," in J. Mokyr (ed.), *The British Industrial Revolution: An Economic Perspective* (Oxford, 1993), pp. 1–31.

Molinas, C. and L. Prados de la Escosura, "Was Spain Different? Spanish Historical Backwardness Revisited," *Explorations in Economic History* 26 (1989), pp. 385–402.

Moltke, H. von, *Moltke's Letters to his Wife*, Vol. 2 (London, 1896).

Mommsen, W. J., "Domestic Factors in German Foreign Policy before 1914," *Central European History* 6 (1973), pp. 3–43.

Mommsen, W. J., *Theories of Imperialism* (New York, 1980).

Mommsen, W. J. and H.-G. Husung, *The Development of Trade Unionism in Great Britain and Germany 1880–1914* (London, 1985).

Mommsen, W. J. and W. Mock (eds.), *The Emergence of the Welfare State in Britain and Germany, 1850–1950* (London, 1981).

Monmonier, M., *How to Lie with Maps*, 2nd edn. (Chicago, 1996).

Montesquieu, *The Spirits of the Laws* (Cambridge, 2002) [1748].

Mooers, C., *The Making of Bourgeois Europe: Absolutism, Revolution, and the Rise of Capitalism in England, France and Germany* (London, 1991).

Moon, D., "Peasants into Russian Citizens? A Comparative Perspective," *Revolutionary Russia* 9:1 (1996), pp. 43–81.

Moon, D., *The Russian Peasantry 1600–1930: The World the Peasants Made* (Harlow, 1999).

Moon, D., *The Abolition of Serfdom in Russia, 1762–1907* (Harlow, 2001).

Moore, B., *Social Origins of Dictatorship and Democracy: Lord and Peasant in the Making of the Modern World* (Boston, MA, 1966).

Moore, D. C., *The Politics of Deference* (Brighton, 1976).

Mooser, J., "Property and Wood Theft: Agrarian Capitalism and Social Conflict in Rural Society, 1800–50: A Westphalian Case Study," in R. G. Moeller (ed.), *Peasants and Lords in Modern Germany: Recent Studies in Agricultural History* (Boston, MA, 1986).

Moran, D. and A. Waldron (eds.), *The People in Arms: Military Myth and National Mobilization since the French Revolution* (Cambridge, 2003).

Morrel, J. and A. Thackray, *Gentlemen of Science: Early Years of the British Association for the Advancement of Science* (Oxford, 1981).

Morris, N. and D. J. Rothman (eds.), *The Oxford History of the Prison: The Practice of Punishment in Western Society* (Oxford, 1995).

Moses, C. G., *French Feminism in the Nineteenth Century* (Albany, NY, 1984).

Moses, J., *Trade Unionism in Germany* (London, 1982).

Mosse, G. L., "Caesarism, Circuses and Monuments," *Journal of Contemporary History* 6 (1971), pp. 167–82.

Mosse, G. L., *The Nationalization of the Masses* (New York, 1975).

Mosse, W., "Nobility and Middle Classes in Nineteenth-Century Europe: A Comparative Study," in J. Kocka and A. Mitchell (eds.), *Bourgeois Society in Nineteenth-Century Europe* (Oxford, 1993), pp. 70–102.

Mosse, W., *The European Powers and the German Question, 1848–71, with Special Reference to England and Russia* (Cambridge, 1958).

Mueller, H.-E., *Bureaucracy, Education, and Monopoly: Civil Service Reforms in Prussia and England* (Berkeley, CA, 1984).

Mueller, T., "Empowering Anarchy: Power, Hegemony and Anarchist Strategy," *Anarchist Studies* 11:2 (2003), pp. 122–49

Muir, E. and G. Ruggiero (eds.), *History From Crime* (Baltimore, MD, 1994).

Myrone, M. and L. Peltz (eds.), *Producing the Past: Aspects of Antiquarian Culture and Practice 1700–1850* (Aldershot, 1999).

Naarden, B., *Socialist Europe and Revolutionary Russia: Perception and Prejudice, 1848–1923* (Cambridge, 1992).

Næshagen, F., "Norway's Democratic and Conservative Tradition in Policing," *Scandinavian Journal of History* 25:3 (2000), pp. 177–95.

Nathans, B., *Beyond the Pale: The Jewish Encounter with Late Imperial Russia* (Berkeley, CA, 2001).

Naumann, F., "Die Entwicklung des Christentums im 19. Jahrhundert," in G. Wolf (ed.), *Das 19. Jahrhundert. 24 Aufsätze zur Jahrhundertwende* (Strasbourg, 1900).

Nederveen Pieterse, J., *White on Black: Images of Africa and Blacks in Western Popular Culture* (New Haven, CT, 1992).

Neitzel, S., *Weltmacht oder Untergang. Die Weltreichslehre im Zeitalter des Imperialismus* (Paderborn, 2000).

Neocleous, M., *The Fabrication of Social Order: A Critical Theory of Police Power* (London, 2000).

Neri, D., "Frankreichs Reichspolitik auf dem Rastatter Kongress, 1797–1799," *Francia*, 24:2 (1997), pp. 137–57.

Netting, R., *Balancing on an Alp: Ecological Change and Continuity in a Swiss Mountain Community* (Cambridge, 1981).

Nettl, J. P., "The German Social Democratic Party as a Political Model," *Past and Present* 30 (1965), pp. 65–95.

Nicholas, S. and D. Oxley, "The Living Standards of Women during the Industrial Revolution, 1795–1820," *Economic History Review* 46:4 (1993), pp. 723–49.

Nicholls, D., *The Pluralist State* (Basingstoke, 1994).

Nichols, R. L. and T. G. Stavrou (eds.), *Russian Orthodoxy Under the Old Regime* (Minneapolis, MN, 1978).

Nietzsche, F., "On the Uses and Disadvantages of History for Life," in *Untimely Meditations*, trans. R. J. Hollingdale (Cambridge, 1983).

Nietzsche, F., *On the Genealogy of Morality*, ed. K. Ansell-Pearson, trans. C. Diethe (Cambridge, 1994).

Nipperdey, T., *Religion im Umbruch. Deutschland 1870–1918* (Munich, 1988).

Noiriel, G., *Workers in French Society in the 19th and 20th Centuries* (Oxford, 1990).

Noiriel, G., *La Tyrannie du national. Le droit d'asile en Europe 1793–1993* (Paris, 1991).

Nora, P. (ed.), *Les Lieux de mémoire*, 7 vols. (Paris, 1997).

Nordstrom, B. J., *Scandinavia since 1500* (Minneapolis, MN, 2000).

Norman, H. and J. Rogers, "Marriage and Reproduction in a Changing Society: Sweden 1750–1950," in J. Rogers and H. Norman (eds.), *The Nordic Family: Perspectives on Family Research* (Uppsala, 1985), pp. 43–59.

Norman, H. and H. Runblom, *Transatlantic Connections: Nordic Migration to the New World after 1800* (Oslo, 1988).

Nossiter, T., *Influence, Opinion and Political Idioms in Reformed England* (Brighton, 1975).

Notestein, F. W., "Population – the Long View," in T. W. Schulz (ed.), *Food for the World* (Chicago, 1945), pp. 37–57.

Nowak, K., *Geschichte des Christentums in Deutschland* (Munich, 1995).

Noyes, P. H., *Organization and Revolution: Working-Class Associations in the German Revolutions of 1848–49* (Princeton, NJ, 1966).

Nye, R. A, *Crime, Madness and Politics in Modern France: The Medical Concept of National Decline* (Princeton, NJ, 1984).

Nyhart, L. and T. Broman (eds.), *Science and Civil Society, Vol. 17: Osiris* (Chicago, 2002).

O'Boyle, L., "The Problem of an Excess of Educated Men in Western Europe, 1800–1850," *Journal of Modern History* 42 (1970), pp. 472–95.

O'Boyle, L., "Learning for Its Own Sake: The German University as Nineteenth-Century Model," *Comparative Studies in Society and History* 25 (1983), pp. 3–25.

O'Brian, P., "The Prison on the Continent: Europe 1865–1965," in N. Morris and D. J. Rothman (eds.), *The Oxford History of the Prison: The Practice of Punishment in Western Society* (Oxford, 1995).

O'Brien, P. K. (ed.), *Railways and the Economic Development of Western Europe 1830–1914* (London, 1983).

O'Brien, P. K., "Path Dependency, or Why Britain became an Industrialized and Urbanized Economy long before France," *Economic History Review* 49:2 (1996), pp. 213–49.

O'Brien, P. K., T. Griffiths, and P. Hunt, "Political Components of the Industrial Revolution: Parliament and the English Cotton Textile Industry, 1660–1774," *Economic History Review* 44:3 (1991), pp. 395–423.

O'Gorman, F., *Edmund Burke* (London, 1973).

O'Gorman, F., *Voters, Patrons and Parties: The Unreformed Electorate of Hanoverian England 1734–1832* (Oxford, 1990).

O'Gorman, F., "Campaign Rituals and Ceremonies: The Social Meaning of Elections 1780–1860," *Past and Present* 135 (1992).

O'Meara, T., *Church and Culture: German Catholic Theology 1860–1914* (Notre Dame, IN, 1991).

O'Rourke, K. H. and J. G. Williamson, "Education, Globalization and Catch-Up: Scandinavia in the Swedish Mirror," *Scandinavian Economic History Review* 43:3 (1995), pp. 287–309.

Obelkevich, J., "Religion," in F. L. Thompson (ed.), *The Cambridge Social History of Britain 1750–1950*, Vol. 3 (Cambridge, 1990), pp. 311–57.

Obolensky, D., *The Byzantine Commonwealth: Eastern Europe 500–1453* (London, 1974).

Ockman, C., *Ingres's Eroticized Bodies: Retracing the Serpentine Line* (New Haven, CT, 1995).

Offen, K., "Depopulation, Nationalism and Feminism in Fin-de-Siècle France," *American Historical Review* 9:3 (1984), pp. 648–76.

Offen, K., "Contextualizing the Theory and Practice of Feminism in Nineteenth-Century Europe (1789–1914)," in R. Bridenthal, S. Stuard, and M. Wiesner (eds.), *Becoming Visible: Women in European History*, 3rd edn. (Boston, MA, 1998), pp. 327–55.

Offen, K., *European Feminisms, 1700–1950: A Political History* (Stanford, CA, 2000).

Ogé, F., "Héritage Révolutionnaire: Les Forêts Pyrénéennes, Enjeux des Conflits État-Communautés," in A. Corvol (ed.), *La Nature en révolution, 1750–1800* (Paris, 1993).

Ogilvie, S. C. and M. Cerman (eds.), *European Proto-Industrialization* (Cambridge, 1996).

Olenhusen, I. G. von, *Frauen unter dem Patriarchat der Kirchen. Katholikinnen und Protestantinnen im 19. und 20. Jahrhundert* (Stuttgart, 1995).

Olesko, K., *Physics as a Calling: Discipline and Practice in the Königsberg Seminar for Physics* (Ithaca, NY, 1991).

Omran, A. R., "The Epidemiological Transition: A Theory of the Epidemiology of Population Change," *Milbank Memorial Fund Quarterly* 49 (1971), pp. 509–38.

Oosterhuis, H., *Stepchildren of Nature: Krafft-Ebing, Psychiatry, and the Making of Sexual Identity* (Chicago, 2000).

Oppenheim, J., *"Shattered Nerves": Doctors, Patients, and Depression in Victorian England* (Oxford, 1991).

Oppenheimer, F., *The State* (Montreal, 1975).

Oram, G., *Worthless Men: Race, Eugenics and the Death Penalty in the British Army During the First World War* (London, 1998).

Ortiz, D., "Redefining Public Education: Contestation, the Press and Education in Regency Spain, 1885–1902," *Journal of Social History* 35:1 (2001), pp. 73–94.

Osborne, L. B., *Geographical Fun: Humorous Maps of Serious Countries* (Rohnert Park, CA, 1999).

Osterhammel, J., *Colonialism: A Theoretical Overview* (Princeton, NJ, 1997).

Osterhammel, J. and N. P. Petersson, *Geschichte der Globalisierung. Dimensionen, Prozesse, Epochen* (Munich, 2003).

Ostrogorski, M., *Democracy and the Organization of Political Parties* (New York, 1970) [1902].

Ousby, I., *Bloodhounds in Heaven: The Detective in English Fiction from Godwin to Doyle* (Cambridge, MA, 1976).

Overton, M., *Agricultural Revolution in England: The Transformation of the Agrarian Economy, 1500–1850* (Cambridge, 1996a).

Overton, M., "Re-establishing the English Agricultural Revolution," *Agricultural History Review* 44 (1996b), pp. 1–20.

Owen, R., *A New View of Society and Other Writings* (London, 1927).

Özmurur, S. and Pamuk, S., "Real Wages and Standards of Living in the Ottoman Empire, 1489–1914," *Journal of Economic History* 62:2 (2002), pp. 293–321.

Palairet, M., *The Balkan Economies c. 1800–1914: Evolution without Development* (Cambridge, 1997).

Paletschek, S., *Frauen und Dissens. Frauen im Deutschkatholizmus und in den freien Gemeinden 1841–1852* (Göttingen, 1990).

Paletschek, S. and B. Pietrow-Ennker (eds.), *Women's Emancipation Movements in the Nineteenth Century: A European Perspective* (Stanford, CA, 2004).

Palmer, R. R., *The Age of Democratic Revolution*, 2 vols (Princeton, NJ, 1959–64).

Palmer, S., *Police and Protest in England and Ireland, 1780–1850* (Cambridge, 1988).

Paret, P., *Art as History* (Princeton, NJ, 1988).

Paret, P., *Understanding War: Essays on Clausewitz and the History of Military Power* (Princeton, NJ, 1992).

Paret, P., with G. A. Craig and F. Gilbert (eds.), *Makers of Modern Strategy from Machiavelli to the Nuclear Age* (Princeton, NJ, 1986).

Parker, G., *The Military Revolution: Military Innovation and the Rise of the West, 1500–1800* (Cambridge, 1988).

Parr, J., "Disaggregating the Sexual Division of Labour: A Transatlantic Case Study," *Comparative Studies in Society and History* 30:2 (1988), pp. 511–33.

Parry, J. P., "Nonconformity, Clericalism and 'Englishness': The United Kingdom," in C. Clark and W. Kaiser (eds.), *Culture Wars: Secular–Catholic Conflict in Nineteenth-Century Europe* (Cambridge, 2004), p. 154.

Parsons, G. (ed.), *Religion in Victorian Britain*, 4 vols. (Manchester, 1988).

Pastoreau, M. and J. C. Schmitt, *Europe: mémoire et emblèmes* (Paris, 1990).

Patriarca, S., *Numbers and Nationhood: Writing Statistics in Nineteenth-Century Italy* (Cambridge, 1996).

Paxton, R., *French Peasant Fascism: Henry Dorgère's Greenshirts and the Crises of French Agriculture* (Oxford, 1997).

Payne, H. C., "Theory and Practice of Political Police During the Second Empire in France," *Journal of Modern History* 30:1 (1958), pp. 14–23.

Payne, H. C., *The Police State of Louis Napoleon Bonaparte, 1851–1860* (Seattle, 1966).

Pearson, R., *European Nationalism 1789–1920* (London, 1994).

Pedersen, S., *Family, Dependence and the Origins of the Welfare State: Britain and France, 1914–1945* (Cambridge, 1993).

Pellew, J., *The Home Office 1848–1914: From Clerks to Bureaucrats* (London, 1982).

Pellissier, C., "Loisirs et sociabilités juveniles au sein du patriciat lyonnais (1848–1914)," in J.-P. Bardet, J.-N. Luc, I. Robin-Romero, and C. Rollett (eds.), *Lorsque l'enfant grandit* (Paris, 2003), pp. 471–86.

Pels, P. and O. Salemink (eds.), *Colonial Subjects: Essays on the Practical History of Anthropology* (Ann Arbor, MI, 2000).

Pérez Moreda, V., "Spain's Demographic Modernization, 1800–1930," in N. Sánchez-Albornoz (ed.), *The Economic Modernization of Spain, 1830–1930* (New York, 1987), pp. 13–41.

Perrot, J.-C. and S. Woolf, *State and Statistics in France, 1789–1815* (Harwood, 1984).

Petruscewicz, M., *Latifundium: Moral Economy and Material Life in a European Periphery* (Ann Arbor, MI, 1996).

Petruscewicz, M., "Land-Based Modernization and the Culture of Landed Elites in the Nineteenth-Century Mezzogiorno," in E. Dal Lago and R. Halpern (eds.), *The American South and the Italian Mezzogiorno: Essays in Comparative History* (Basingstoke, 2002), pp. 95–111.

Pfister, R., *Kirchengeschichte der Schweiz*, Vol. 3 (Zurich, 1984).

Phillips, A. and B. Taylor, "Sex and Skill: Notes Towards a Feminist Economics," *Feminist Review* 6 (1980), pp. 79–88.

Phillips, J., *The Great Reform Bill in the Boroughs: English Electoral Behaviour 1818–41* (Oxford, 1992).

Piault, M. H., "Avant-propos. L'effect colonial: pour une revision des faits!," in M. H. Piault, *La Colonization: rupture ou parenthèse* (Paris, 1987), pp. 9–12.

Picco, D., "Vivre et mourir à Saint-Cyr, entre 1686 at 1793," in J.-P. Bardet, J.-N. Luc, I. Robin-Romero, and C. Rollett (eds.), *Lorsque l'enfant grandit* (Paris, 2003), pp. 144–5.

Pick, D., *Faces of Degeneration: A European Disorder, c. 1848–c. 1918* (Cambridge, 1989).

Pierenkemper, T. and R. Tilly, *The German Economy During the Nineteenth Century* (Oxford, 2004).

Pilbeam, P., *The Middle Classes in Europe 1789–1914: France, Germany, Italy and Russia* (London, 1990).

Pilbeam, P., "From Orders to Classes," in T. C. W. Blanning (ed.), *The Oxford Illustrated History of Modern Europe* (Oxford, 1996), pp. 94–120.

Pilbeam, P., *French Socialists Before Marx: Workers, Women and the Social Question in France* (Teddington, 2000).

Pilbeam, P., *Madame Tussaud and the History of Waxworks* (Hambledon, 2003).

Pinter, W. M., "The Evolution of Civil Officialdom 1755–1855," in W. M. Pinter and D. K. Rowney (eds.), *Russian Officialdom: The Bureaucratization of Russian Society from the Seventeenth to the Twentieth Century* (London, 1980).

Pipes, R., *Russia Under the Old Regime* (Harmondsworth, 1974).

Pipes, R., *The Russian Revolution 1899–1919* (London, 1990).

Plaschka, R. G., "The Political Significance of Frantisek Palacky," in W. Laqueur and G. L. Mosse (eds.), *Historians in Politics* (London, 1974).

Pletsch, C., *Young Nietzsche: Becoming a Genius* (New York, 1991).

Plumb, J. H., *The Death of the Past* (London, 1969).

Poggi, G., *The Development of the Modern State* (London, 1978).

Pohle, M., "Risk, Information and Noise: Risk Perception and Risk Management of French and German Banks during the Nineteenth Century," *Financial History Review* 2:1 (1995), pp. 25–40.

Polasky, J., "Women in Revolutionary Brussels: 'The Source of Our Greatest Strength'," in H. B. Applewhite and D. G. Levy (eds.), *Women and Politics in the Age of Democratic Revolution* (Ann Arbor, MI, 1993) pp. 14–62.

Pollard, S., *Peaceful Conquest: The Industrialization of Europe 1760–1970* (Oxford, 1981).

Pollard, S. and J. Salt (eds.), *Robert Owen* (London, 1971).

Ponteil, F., *Les Institutions de la France de 1814 à 1870* (Paris, 1966).

Pooley, C. G. (ed.), *Housing Strategies in Europe, 1880–1930* (Leicester, 1992).

Poovey, M., *Uneven Developments: The Ideological Work of Gender* (Chicago, 1988).

Porter, B., *The Origins of the Vigilant State: The London Metropolitan Police Special Branch before the First World War* (Woodbridge, 1991).

Porter, R., *The Greatest Benefit to Mankind: A Medical History of Humanity* (New York, 1999).

Porter, R. and L. Hall, *The Facts of Life: The Creation of Sexual Knowledge in Britain, 1650–1950* (New Haven, CT, 1995).

Porter, R. and D. Wright (eds.), *The Confinement of the Insane, 1800–1965: International Perspectives* (Cambridge, 2003).

Porter, R. S., "Seeing the Past," *Past and Present* 118 (1988), pp. 186–205.

Porter, T., *The Zemstvos and the Emergence of Russian Civil Society in Late-Imperial Russia 1864–1917* (San Francisco, 1991).

Porter, T. M., *The Rise of Statistical Thinking, 1820–1900* (Princeton, NJ, 1986).

Porter, T. M., *Trust in Numbers: The Pursuit of Objectivity in Science and Public Life* (Princeton, NJ, 1995).

Pounds, N. J. G., *An Historical Geography of Europe, 1800–1914* (Cambridge, 1985).

Powelson, J. P., *The Story of Land: A World History of Land Tenure and Agrarian Reform* (Cambridge, MA, 1988).

Prados de la Escosura, L., "Foreign Trade and the Spanish Economy during the Nineteenth Century," in N. Sánchez-Albornoz (ed.), *The Economic Modernization of Spain, 1830–1930* (New York, 1987), pp. 128–50.

Prakash, G., *Another Reason: Science and the Imagination of Modern India* (Princeton, NJ, 1999).

Pratt, M., *Britain's Greek Empire: Reflections on the History of the Ionian Islands from the Fall of Byzantium* (London, 1978).

Preston, S. H. and E. van de Walle, "Urban French Mortality in the Nineteenth Century," *Population Studies* 32 (1978), pp. 275–97.

Price, R., *A Social History of Nineteenth-Century France* (London, 1987).

Priestman, M. (ed.), *The Cambridge Companion to Crime Fiction* (Cambridge, 2003).

Prince, M., *The History of Mary Prince, A West Indian Slave, Related by Herself* (Ann Arbor, MI, 1993).

Prinz, M., *Brot und Dividende. Konsumvereine in Deutschland und England vor 1914* (Göttingen, 1996).

Prothero, I., *Artisans and Politics in Early Nineteenth-Century London: John Gast and his Times* (Folkestone, 1979).

Pugh, M., *The Tories and the People* (Oxford, 1985).

Pykett, L., "The Newgate Novel and Sensation Fiction 1830–1868," in M. Priestman (ed.), *The Cambridge Companion to Crime Fiction* (Cambridge, 2003), pp. 19–39.

Pyta, W., "Konzert der Mächte und kollektives Sicherheitssystem. Neue Wege zwischenstaatlicher Friedenswahrung in Europa nach dem Wiener Kongreß 1815," *Jahrbuch des Historischen Kollegs* (1996), pp. 133–72.

Quartaert, J. H., *Staging Philanthropy: Patriotic Women and the National Imagination in Dynastic Germany, 1813–1916* (Ann Arbor, MI, 2001).

Quinn, D., *Patronage and Piety: The Politics of English Roman Catholicism 1850–1900* (London, 1993).

Rabinbach, A., *The Human Motor: Energy, Fatigue, and the Origins of Modernity* (Berkeley, CA, 1990).

Radcliff, P. B., *From Mobilization to Civil War: The Politics of Polarization in the Spanish City of Gijón, 1900–1937* (Cambridge, 1996).

Radkau, J., *Zeitalter der Nervosität* (Munich, 1998).

Raeff, M., "The Well-Ordered Police State and the Development of Modernity in Seventeenth- and Eighteenth-Century Europe: An Attempt at a Comparative Approach," *American Historical Review* 80:5 (1975), pp. 1221–43.

Raeff, M., "The Russian Nobility in the Eighteenth and Nineteenth Centuries: Trends and Comparisons," in I. Banac and P. A. Bushkovitch (eds.), *The Nobility in Russia and Eastern Europe* (New Haven, CT, 1983), pp. 99–121.

Raeff, M., *Understanding Imperial Russia: State and Society in the Ancien Regime* (New York, 1984).

Ramaswamy, S., "Maps and Mother Goddesses in Modern India," *Imago Mundi* 53 (2001), pp. 97–114.

Randall, A. J., "Industrial Conflict and Economic Change: The Regional Context of the Industrial Revolution," *Southern History* 14 (1992), pp. 74–92.

Raphael, L., *Recht und Ordnung. Herrschaft durch Verwaltung im 19. Jahrhundert* (Frankfurt am Main, 2000).

Rearick, C., "Festivals and Politics: The Michelet Centennial of 1898," in W. Laqueur and G. L. Mosse (eds.), *Historians in Politics* (London, 1974).

Rearick, C., "Festivals in Modern France," *Journal of Contemporary History* 12 (1977), pp. 435–60.

Reay, B., "Before the Fertility Transition: Fertility in English Villages, 1800–1880," *Continuity and Change* 9:1 (1994), pp. 91–120.

Rebérioux, M., "Le Mur des fédérés: rouge, 'sang craché'," in P. Nora (ed.), *Les Lieux de mémoire*, Vol. 1 (Paris, 1997).

Reeken, D. von, *Kirchen im Umbruch zur Moderne. Milieubildungsprozesse im nordwestdeutschen Protestantismus 1849–1914* (Gütersloh, 1999).

Regener, S., *Fotografische Erfassung. Zur Geschichte medialer Konstruktionen des Kriminellen* (Munich, 1999), pp. 131–67.

Reid, D., *Paris Sewers and Sewermen: Realities and Representation* (Cambridge, MA, 1991).

Reif, H., "Der katholische Adel Westfalens und die Spaltung des Adelkonservatismus in Preussen während des 19. Jahrhunderts," in K. Teppe and M. Epkenhans (eds.), *Westfalen und Preussen. Integration und Regionalismus* (Paderborn, 1991), pp. 107–24.

Reinhard, W., "Reformation, Counter-Reformation and the Early Modern State: A Reassessment," *Catholic Historical Review* 75 (1989), pp. 383–404.

Reinhard, W., *Geschichte der Staatsgewalt. Eine vergleichende Verfassungsgeschichte Europas von den Anfängen bis zur Gegenwart* (Munich, 1999).

Reinhard, W. and H. Schilling (eds.), *Die katholische Konfessionalisierung* (Gütersloh, 1995).

Reinke, H., " 'Armed as if for war': The State, the Military, and the Professionalisation of the Prussian Police in Imperial Germany," in C. Emsley and B. Weinberger (eds.), *Policing Western Europe: Politics, Professionalism, and Public Order, 1850–1940* (London, 1991), pp. 55–73.

Reiser, S. J., *Medicine and the Reign of Technology* (Cambridge, 1978).

Rémond, R., *Religion and Society in Modern Europe* (Oxford, 1999).

Renan, E., "Qu'est-ce qu' une nation?" in J. Hutchinson and A. D. Smith (eds.), *Nationalism* (Oxford, 1994).

Rendall, J., *The Origins of Modern Feminism: Women in Britain, France, and the United States, 1780–1860* (New York, 1984).

Renouvin, P. and J.-B. Duroselle, *Introduction to the History of International Relations* (London, 1968).

Renton, D., "The Agrarian Roots of Fascism: German Exceptionalism Revisited," *Journal of Peasant Studies* 28:4 (2001), pp. 127–48.

Reynolds, E., *Before the Bobbies: The Night Watch and Police Reform in Metropolitan London, 1720–1830* (Basingstoke, 1998).

Riall, L., "Elite Resistance to State Formation: The Case of Italy," in M. Fulbrook (ed.), *National Histories and European History* (London, 1993).

Riall, L., *The Italian Risorgimento: State, Society and National Unification* (London, 1994).

Riall, L., " 'Ill-Contrived, Badly Executed [and] . . . of no Avail'? Reform and its Impact in the Sicilian *Latifondo* (c. 1770–1910)," in E. Dal Lago and R. Halpern (eds.), *The American South and the Italian Mezzogiorno: Essays in Comparative History* (Basingstoke, 2002), pp. 132–52.

Riall, L., "Elites in Search of Authority: Political Power and Social Order in Nineteenth-Century Sicily," *History Workshop Journal* 55 (2003), pp. 25–46.

Ribalta, P. M., "The Industrial Policy of the Board of Trade in Spain," *Journal of European Economic History* 26:2 (1997), pp. 269–93.

Richards, J. R., *Human Nature after Darwin: A Philosophical Introduction* (London, 2000).

Richards, J. R., *Darwin and the Emergence of Evolutionary Theories of Mind and Behavior* (Chicago, 1987).

Richards, T., *The Imperial Archive: Knowledge and the Fantasy of Empire* (New York, 1993).

Rieber, A. J., *Merchants and Entrepreneurs in Imperial Russia* (Chapel Hill, NC, 1992).

Riesenberger, D., *Für Humanität in Krieg und Frieden: Das Internationale Rote Kreuz 1863–1977* (Göttingen, 1992).

Riley, J. C., "Height, Nutrition and Mortality Risks Reconsidered," *Journal of Interdisciplinary History* 24:3 (1994), pp. 465–92.

Riley, J. C., *Rising Life Expectancy. A Global History* (Cambridge, 2001).

Ringer, F., *Education and Society in Modern Europe* (London, 1979).

Ringrose, D. R., *Spain, Europe, and the "Spanish Miracle," 1700–1900* (Cambridge, 1996).

Ripa, C., *Iconologia, of uytbeeldingen des verstands*, trans. D. P. Pers (Amsterdam, 1644).

Risse, G., "Medicine in the Age of Enlightenment," in A. Wear (ed.) *Medicine in Society: Historical Essays* (Cambridge, 1992), pp. 149–71.

Roberts, M. L., *Disruptive Acts: The New Woman in Fin-de-Siècle France* (Chicago, 2002).

Robinson, R. and J. Gallagher, *Africa and the Victorians: The Official Mind of Imperialism* (London, 1968).

Roe, N., *Wordsworth and Coleridge: The Radical Years* (Oxford, 1988).

Rogers, N., *Whigs, Cities and Popular Politics in the Age of Walpole and Pitt* (Oxford, 1989).

Rolle, F., *Der Mensch. Seine Abstammung und Gesittung im Lichte der Darwinschen Lehre* (Frankfurt am Main, 1866).

Rosanvallon, P., *L'Etat en France de 1789 à nos jours* (Paris, 1990).

Rose, S. O., "Proto-Industry, Women's Work and the Household Economy in the Transition to Industrial Capitalism," *Journal of Family History* 13 (1988), pp. 181–93.

Rose, S. O., *Limited Livelihoods: Gender and Class in Nineteenth-Century England* (Berkeley, CA, 1992).

Rosen, F., *Jeremy Bentham and Representative Democracy* (Oxford, 1983).

Rosenberg, C. E., "The Bitter Fruit: Heredity, Disease, and Social Thought in Nineteenth-Century America," in D. Fleming and B. Bailyn (eds.), *Perspectives in American History*, Vol. 3 (Cambridge, MA, 1969).

Rosenberg, C. E., "The Therapeutic Revolution: Medicine, Meaning, and Social Change in 19th-Century America," in *Sickness and Health in America: Readings in the History of Medicine and Public Health*, 2nd edn. (Madison, WI, 1985).

Rosenberg, C. E., *Explaining Epidemics: And Other Studies in the History of Medicine* (Cambridge, 1991).

Rosenberg, H., *Bureaucracy, Aristocracy and Autocracy: The Prussian Experience 1660–1815* (Cambridge, MA, 1958).

Rosenberger, B., *Zeitungen als Kriegstreiber? Die Rolle der Presse im Vorfeld des Ersten Weltkrieges* (Cologne, 1998).

Rosenblum, N., *A World History of Photography*, 3rd edn. (New York, 1997).

Rösener, W., *The Peasantry in Europe* (Oxford, 1994).

Rostow, W. W., *The Stages of Economic Growth: A Non-Communist Manifesto* (Cambridge, 1960).

Rostow, W. W. (ed.), *The Economics of Take-Off into Sustained Growth* (London, 1963).

Roth, G., *Social Democrats in Imperial Germany* (Totowa, NY, 1963).

Row, M., *From Reich to State: The Rhineland in the Revolutionary Age 1780–1830* (Cambridge, 2004).

Royer, C., "Préface," to C. Darwin, *De L'origine des espèces par selection naturelle, ou des lois de transformation des êtres organises*, 2nd edn. (Paris, 1866).

Royer, C., *Origine de l'homme et des sociétés* (Paris, 1870).

Rubinstein, W. D., *Capitalism, Culture, and Decline in Britain 1750–1990* (London, 1993).

Ruggiero, G. de, *The History of European Liberalism* (Boston, MA, 1959).

Ruggles, S., "The Limitations of English Family Reconstitution: English Population History from 1580–1837," *Continuity and Change* 14:1 (1999), pp. 105–30.

Runciman, S., *The Great Church in Captivity: A Study of the Patriarchate of Constantinople from the Eve of the Turkish Conquest to the Greek War of Independence* (Cambridge, 1968).

Russett, C., *Sexual Science: The Victorian Construction of Womanhood* (Cambridge, MA, 1989).

Rustow, D. A., "Transitions to Democracy," *Comparative Politics* April (1970), p. 337.

Ryan, A., *The Philosophy of John Stuart Mill* (Basingstoke, 1998).

Ryan, W. F., *The Bathhouse at Midnight: Magic in Russia* (Stroud, 1999).

Sagarra, E., *A Social History of Germany, 1648–1914* (New York, 1977).

Said, E., *Orientalism: Western Conceptions of the Orient* (London, 1978).

Saint-Simon, C.-H. de, *Selected Writings on Science, Industry and Social Organisation*, ed. and trans. K. Taylor (London, 1975).

Sala, P., "Modern Forestry and Enclosure: Elitist State Science against Communal Management and Unrestricted Privatisation in Spain, 1855–1900," *Environment and History*, 6 (2000), pp. 151–68.

Salzmann, S. (ed.), *Mythos Europa: Europa und der Stier im Zeitalter der industriellen Zivilisation* (Hamburg, 1988).

Sanborn, J. A., *Drafting the Russian Nation: Military Conscription, Total War, and Mass Politics, 1905–1925* (Dekalb, IL, 2003).

Saunders, D., *Russia in the Age of Reaction and Reform 1801–1881* (London, 1992).

Sayer, K., *Women of the Fields: Representations of Rural Women in the Nineteenth Century* (Manchester, 1995).

Schaffer, S., "Genius in Romantic Natural Philosophy," in A. Cunningham and N. Jardine (eds.), *Romanticism and the Sciences* (Cambridge, 1990), pp. 82–100.

Scheerer, S., "Beyond Confinement: Notes on the History and Possible Future of Solitary Confinement in Germany," in N. Finzsch and R. Jütte (eds.), *Institutions of Confinement: Hospitals, Asylums, and Prisons in Western Europe and North America, 1500–1950* (Cambridge, 1996), pp. 351–8.

Schenk, M., *Rassismus gegen Sinti und Roma. Zur Kontinuität der Zigeunerverfolgung innerhalb der deutschen Gesellschaft von der Weimarer Republik bis in die Gegenwart* (Frankfurt am Main, 1994).

Schieder, T. (ed.), *Sozialstruktur und Organisation europäischer Nationalbewegungen* (Munich, 1971).

Schieder, T., *Nationalismus und Nationalstaat*, 2nd edn. (Göttingen, 1992).

Schieder, W., "Kirche und Revolution: Sozialgeschichtliche Aspekte der Trierer Wallfahrt von 1844," *Archiv für Sozialgeschichte* 14 (1974), pp. 419–54.

Schieder, W. (ed.), *Säkularisation und Mediatisierung. Die Veräusserung der Nationalgüter im Rhein-Mosel-Department 1803–1813* (Boppard, 1987).

Schiller, F., *Schillers Werke*, Vol. 4 (Berlin, 1967).

Schivelbusch, W., *The Railway Journey: The Industrialization of Time and Space in the Nineteenth Century* (Leamington Spa, 1986).

Schivelbusch, W., *Disenchanted Night: The Industrialization of Light in the Nineteenth Century* (Berkeley, CA, 1988).

Schloegl, R., *Glaube und Religion in der Säkularisierung. Die katholische Stadt Köln Aachen, Münster 1700–1840* (Munich, 1995).

Schlör, J., *Nights in the Big City: Paris, Berlin, London 1840–1930* (London, 1998).

Schlumbohm, J., "Social Differences in Age at Marriage: Examples from Rural Germany during the 18th and 19th Centuries," in M. Poulain, R. Leboutte, H. Damas, and E. Vilquin (eds.), *Historiens et Populations. Liber Amicorum Étienne Hélin* (Louvain-la-Neuve, 1991), pp. 593–607.

Schmidt, M., "Die Apotheose des Krieges im 18. und frühen 19. Jahrhundert im deutschen Dichten und Denken," in W. Huber and J. Schwerdtfeger (eds.), *Kirche zwischen Krieg und Frieden* (Stuttgart, 1976).

Schöllgen, G. (ed.), *Escape into War? The Foreign Policy of Imperial Germany* (Oxford, 1990).

Scholliers, P. (ed.), *Real Wages in Nineteenth and Twentieth Century Europe: Historical and Comparative Perspectives* (New York, 1989).

Scholliers, P. and V. Zamagni (eds.), *Labour's Reward: Real Wages and Economic Change in Nineteenth and Twentieth Century Europe* (Aldershot, 1995).

Schorske, C. E., *Fin-de-Siècle Vienna: Politics and Culture* (New York, 1981).

Schroeder, P., "The Nineteenth Century International System: Changes in Structure," *World Politics*, 39 (1986), pp. 1–26.

Schroeder, P., *The Transformation of European Politics, 1763–1848* (Oxford, 1994).

Schroeder, P., "International Politics, Peace and War, 1815–1914," in T. C. W. Blanning (ed.), *The Nineteenth Century* (Oxford, 2000).

Schubert, A., *A Social History of Modern Spain* (London, 1990).

Schulte, R., *The Village in Court: Arson, Infanticide and Poaching in the Court Records of Upper Bavaria, 1848–1910*, trans. B. Selman (Cambridge, 1994).

Schultz, H.-D., "Fantasies of *Mitte*: *Mittellage* and *Mitteleuropa* in German Geographical Discussion in the 19th and 20th Centuries," *Political Geography Quarterly* 8 (1989).

Schulz, M., "A Balancing Act: Domestic Pressures and International Systemic Constraints in the Foreign Policies of the Great Powers, 1848–51," *German History*, 21:3 (2003), pp. 319–46.

Schulze, H., *Staat und Nation in der europäischen Geschichte* (Munich, 1995).

Schulze, H., *States, Nations and Nationalism* (Oxford, 1996).

Schulze, M.-S., "Patterns of Growth and Stagnation in the Late Nineteenth Century Habsburg Economy," *European Review of Economic History* 4 (2000), pp. 311–40.

Schwartz, L. D., *London in the Age of Industrialization: Entrepreneurs, Labour Force, and Living Conditions, 1700–1850* (Cambridge, 1992).

Schwartz, V., *Spectacular Realities: Early Mass Culture in Fin de siècle Paris* (Berkeley, CA, 1998).

Schwarzkopf, J., *Women in the Chartist Movement* (London, 1991).

Schwarzmantel, J., *Socialism and the Idea of the Nation* (London, 1991).

Scott, F. D., *Sweden: The Nation's History* (Carbondale, IL, 1988).

Scott, G., *Feminism and the Politics of Working Women: The Women's Co-operative Guild 1880 to the Second World War* (London, 1998).

Scott, J. C., *Seeing Like a State: How Certain Schemes to Improve the Human Condition Have Failed* (New Haven, CT, 1998).

Scott, J. W., *The Glassmakers of Carmaux* (Cambridge, MA, 1979).

Scott, J. W. "'L'ouvrière! Mot impie, sordide . . .' Women Workers in the Discourse of French Political Economy, 1840–1860," in J. W. Scott (ed.), *Gender and the Politics of History* (New York, 1986), pp. 139–63.

Scott, J. W., *Only Paradoxes to Offer: French Feminists and the Rights of Man* (Cambridge, MA, 1996).

Scott, J. W. and L. A. Tilly, *Women, Work and Family* (New York, 1978).

Scull, A., *The Most Solitary of Afflictions: Madness and Society in Britain, 1700–1900* (New Haven, CT, 1993).

Seccombe, W., "Starting to Stop: Working-Class Fertility Decline in Britain," *Past and Present* 126 (1990), pp. 151–88.

Seccombe, W., "Men's 'Marital Rights' amd Women's 'Wifely Duties': Changing Conjugal Relations in the Fertility Decline," in J. R. Gillis, L. A. Tilly, and D. Levine (eds.), *The European Experience of Declining Fertility, 1850–1970: The Quiet Revolution* (Oxford, 1992), pp. 66–84.

Segalen, M., *Love and Power in the Peasant Family: Rural France in the Nineteenth Century*, trans. S. Matthews (Oxford, 1983).

Seigel, J. E., *Bohemian Paris: Culture, Politics, and the Boundaries of Bourgeois Life, 1830–1930* (New York, 1987).

Sekula, A., "The Body and the Archive," in R. Bolton (ed.), *The Contest of Meaning: Critical Histories of Photography* (Cambridge, MA, 1989), pp. 343–88.

Seltzer, R. M., *Jewish People, Jewish Thought: The Jewish Experience in History* (New York, 1976).

Semple, J., *Bentham's Prison: A Study of the Panopticon Penitentiary* (Oxford, 1993).

Senghaas, D., *The European Experience: A Historical Critique of Development Theory* (Leamington Spa, 1985).

Sengoopta, C., *Imprint of the Raj: How Fingerprinting Was Born in Colonial India* (London, 2003).

Sewell, W. H., *Work and Revolution in France: The Language of Labour from Ancien Régime to Revolution* (Cambridge, 1980).

Sewell, W. H., "Le citoyen/la citoyenne: Activity, Passivity, and the Revolutionary Concept of Citizenship," in C. Lucas (ed.), *The French Revolution and the Creation of Modern Political Culture, Vol. 2: Political Culture of the French Revolution* (Oxford, 1988).

Shanley, M. L., *Feminism, Marriage, and the Law in Victorian England* (Princeton, NJ, 1989).

Sharlin, A., "Natural Decrease in Early Modern Cities: A Reconstruction," *Past and Present* 79 (1978), pp. 126–38.

Shaw, G. B., *Back to Methuselah: A Metabiological Pentateuch* (London, 1931) [1921].

Sheehan, J., "Culture," in T. C. W. Blanning (ed.), *The Nineteenth Century* (Oxford, 2000).

Shevzov, V., *Russian Orthodoxy on the Eve of Revolution* (Oxford, 2004).

Shevzov, V., "Chapels and the Ecclesial World of Prerevolutionary Russian Peasants," *Slavic Review* 55:3 (1996), pp. 585–613.

Shore, C., *Building Europe: The Cultural Policies of European Integration* (London, 2000).

Showalter, E., *Sexual Anarchy: Gender and Culture at the Fin-de-Siècle* (New York, 1990).

Shubert, A., *The Road to Revolution in Spain: The Coal Miners of Asturias 1860–1934* (Chicago, 1987).

Shubert, A., *A Social History of Modern Spain* (London, 1990).

Silber, M. K., "The Emergence of Ultra-Orthodoxy: The Invention of a Tradition," in J. Wertheimer (ed.), *The Uses of Tradition: Jewish Continuity in the Modern Era* (New York, 1992), pp. 23–84.

Silverstein, A. M., *A History of Immunology* (San Diego, CA, 1989).

Simms, B., *The Struggle for Mastery in Germany, 1779–1850* (London, 1998).

Simms, B., "The Return of the Primacy of Foreign Policy," *German History*, 21:3 (2003), pp. 319–46.

Simonton, D., *A History of European Women's Work: 1700 to the Present* (London, 1998).

Simpson, J., *Spanish Agriculture: The Long Siesta, 1765–1965* (Cambridge, 1995).

Simtaro, D. H.-K., *Le Togo "musterkolonie." Souvenirs de l'Allemagne dans la société Togolaise*, 2 vols. (Aix-en-Provence, 1982).

Singer, B., *Village Notables in Nineteenth-Century France: Priests, Mayors, Schoolmasters* (Albany, NY, 1983).

Sked, A., *The Decline and Fall of the Habsburg Empire, 1815–1914* (London, 1989).

Sköld, P., "From Inoculation to Vaccination: Smallpox in Sweden in the Eighteenth and Nineteenth Centuries," *Population Studies* 50:2 (1996), pp. 247–62.

Slack, P., *The English Poor Law 1531–1792* (Basingstoke, 1990).

Sledziewski, E., "The French Revolution as the Turning Point," in G. Fraisse and M. Perrot (eds.), *A History of Women, Vol. 4: Emerging Feminism from Revolution to World War* (Cambridge, MA, 1993), pp. 4–43.

Smith, A., *An Inquiry into the Nature and Causes of the Wealth of Nations* (New York, 1994) [1776].

Smith, A., *The Ethnic Origins of Nations* (Oxford, 1986).

Smith, A., *The Nation in History: Historiographical Debates about Ethnicity and Nationalism* (Cambridge, 2000).

Smith, B., *Ladies of the Leisure Class: The Bourgeoisie of Northern France in the Nineteenth Century* (Princeton, NJ, 1981).

Smith, B., *Changing Lives: Women in European History since 1700* (Lexington, MA, 1989).

Smith, C., *The Science of Energy: A Cultural History of Energy in Victorian Britain* (Chicago, 1998).

Smith, D., "Tonypandy 1910: Definitions of Community," *Past and Present* 87 (1980), pp. 158–84.

Smith, F. B., *The People's Health, 1830–1910* (London, 1979).

Smith, H. W., "The Learned and the Popular Discourse of Anti-Semitism in the Catholic Milieu of the Kaiserreich," *Central European History* 27 (1994), pp. 315–29.

Smith, H. W., *German Nationalism and Religious Conflict: Culture, Ideology, Politics, 1870–1914* (Princeton, NJ, 1995).

Smith, M. S., *Tariff Reform in France 1860–1900: The Politics of Economic Interest* (London, 1980).

Snowden, F., *Violence and Great Estates in the South of Italy: Violence and Great Estates in Apulia: 1900–1922* (Cambridge, 1986).

Snowden, F., "Mosquitoes, Quinine and the Socialism of Italian Women 1900–1914," *Past and Present* 178 (2003), pp. 175–209.

Sørensen, Øystein (ed.), *Nordic Paths to National Identity in the Nineteenth Century* (Oslo, 1994).

Sorkin, D., *The Transformation of German Jewry* (New York, 1987).

Soutou, G.-H., "Was There a European Order in the Twentieth Century? From the Concert of Europe to the End of the Cold War," *Contemporary European History* 9 (2000), pp. 329–53.

Sowerwine, C., *Sisters or Citizens? Women and Socialism in France since 1876* (New York, 1982).

Spencer, E., *Police and Social Order in German Cities: The Düsseldorf District, 1848–1914* (De Kalb, IL, 1992).

Spencer, H., *The Man Versus the State* (London, 1909).

Sperber, J., "The Shaping of Political Catholicism in the Ruhr Basin 1848–1881," *Central European History* 4 (1983), pp. 346–64.

Sperber, J., *Popular Catholicism in 19th-Century Germany* (Princeton, NJ, 1984).

Sperber, J., *The Kaiser's Voters: Electors and Elections in Imperial Germany* (Cambridge, 1997).

Sperber, J., *Revolutionary Europe, 1780–1850* (Harlow, 2000).

Spierenburg, P., "Violence and the Civilising Process: Does it Work?" *Crime, Histoire & Sociétés* 5:2 (2001), pp. 87–105.

Spitzer, A., "The Bureaucrat as Proconsul: The Restoration Prefect and the Police Générale," *Comparative Studies in Society and History* 7 (1964/5), pp. 371–92.

Spohn, W. and A. Triandafyllidou (eds.), *Europeanisation, National Identities and Migration: Changes in Boundary Constructions between Western and Eastern Europe* (London, 2003).

Spring, D. (ed.), *European Landed Elites in the Nineteenth Century* (Baltimore, MD, 1977).

Spulber, N., *Russia's Economic Transitions: From Late Tsarism to the New Millennium* (Cambridge, 2003).

Stanislawski, M., *Tsar Nicholas I and the Jews: The Transformation of Jewish Society in Russia, 1825–1855* (Philadelphia, PA, 1983).

Starr, F. S., *Decentralization and Self-Government in Russia, 1830–1870* (Princeton, NJ, 1972).

Stauch, M., *Im Schatten der Heiligen Allianz. Frankreichs Preußenpolitik von 1848–57* (Frankfurt, 1996).

Stearns, P., *European Society in Upheaval* (New York, 1967).

Stearns, P., *Revolutionary Syndicalism and French Labour* (New Brunswick, NJ, 1981).

Stearns, P. and H. Mitchell, *Workers and Protest 1880–1914* (Ithaca, NY, 1981).

Steedman, C., *Policing the Victorian Community: The Formation of English Provincial Police Forces, 1856–1880* (London, 1984).

Steenson, G. P., "*Not a Penny! Not a Man!*" *German Social Democracy, 1863–1914* (Pittsburgh, PA, 1981).

Steenson, G. P., *After Marx, Before Lenin: Marxism and Socialist Working-Class Parties in Europe, 1884–1914* (Pittsburgh, PA, 1991).

Steger, M. B., *The Quest for Evolutionary Socialism: Eduard Bernstein and Social Democracy* (Cambridge, 1997).

Steinbach, P., "Reichstag Elections in the Kaiserreich," in L. E. Jones and J. Retallack (eds.), *Elections, Mass Politics and Social Change in Modern Germany* (Cambridge, 1992).

Steinhoff, A., "Building Religious Community: Worship Space and Experience in Strasbourg after the Franco-Prussian War," in H. W. Smith (ed.), *Protestants, Catholics and Jews, Vol. 1: Germany, 1800–1914* (Oxford, 2002), pp. 267–96.

Stewart, M. L., *Women, Work, and the French State: Labour Protection and Social Patriarchy, 1879–1919* (Montreal, 1989).

Stichweh, R., "The Sociology of Scientific Disciplines: On the Genesis and Stability of the Disciplinary Structure of Modern Science," *Science in Context* 5 (1992), pp. 3–15.

Stites, R., *The Women's Liberation Movement in Russia: Feminism, Nihilism and Bolshevism, 1860–1930* (Princeton, NJ, 1978).

Stone, N., *Europe Transformed 1878–1919*, 2nd edn. (Oxford, 1999).

Storch, R., "The Plague of Blue Locusts: Police Reform and Popular Resistance in Northern England 1840–57," *International Review of Social History* 20 (1975), pp. 61–90.

Storch, R. and D. Philips, *Policing Provincial England 1829–1856: The Politics of Reform* (London, 1999).

Stråth, B. (ed.), *Europe and the Other and Europe as the Other* (Brussels, 2000a).

Stråth, B. (ed.), *Myth and Memory in the Construction of Community: Historical Patterns in Europe and Beyond* (Brussels, 2000b).

Stråth, B., "A European Identity: To the Historical Limits of a Concept," in G. Delanty (ed.), *European Journal of Social Theory* 5:4 (2002).

Strikwerda, C., "A Resurgent Religion: The Rise of Catholic Movements in Nineteenth-Century Belgian Cities," in H. McLeod (ed.), *European Religion in the Age of Great Cities* (London, 1995), pp. 61–89.

Strømstad, P., "Artisan Travel and Technology Transfer to Denmark, 1750–1900," in K. Bruland (ed.), *Technology Transfer and Scandinavian Industrialisation* (Oxford, 1991), pp. 135–56.

Strong, R., *And When Did You Last See your Father? The Victorian Painter and British History* (London, 1978).

Strong, T., *Friedrich Nietzsche and the Politics of Transformation* (Urbana, IL, 2000).

Strumingher, L. S., *Women and the Making of the Working Class: Lyon 1830–1870* (St Alban's, VT, 1979).

Struve, W., *Elites Against Democracy* (Princeton, NJ, 1973).

Stuchtey, B., "Literature, Liberty and Life of the Nation," in S. Berger, M. Donovan, and K. Passmore (eds.), *Writing National Histories: Western Europe since 1800* (London, 1999).

Stuchtey, B. and P. Wende (eds.), *British and German Historiography 1750–1950* (Oxford, 2000).

Stumpf, R. (ed.), *Kriegstheorie und Kriegsgeschichte* (Frankfurt/Main, 1993).

Sugar, P. F. and I. J. Lederer (eds.), *Nationalism in Eastern Europe* (London, 1969).

Sullivan, R., "England's 'Age of Invention': The Acceleration of Patents and Patentable Invention during the Industrial Revolution," *Explorations in Economic History* 26 (1989), pp. 424–52.

Summers, A., "Militarism in Britain before the Great War," *History Workshop Journal* 2 (1976), pp. 104–23.

Summers, A., "The Character of Edwardian Nationalism," in P. Kennedy and A. Nicholls (eds.), *Nationalist and Racialist Movements in Britain and Germany before 1914* (London, 1981), pp. 68–87.

Summers, A., *Angels and Citizens: British Women as Military Nurses 1854–1914* (London, 1988).

Sun, R., *"Before the Enemy is Within Our Walls": Catholic Workers in Cologne, 1885–1912* (Boston, MA, 1999).

Supple, F. J., "Ultramontanism in Yorkshire 1850–1900," in G. Parsons (ed.), *Religion in Victorian Britain*, Vol. 4 (Manchester, 1993), pp. 135–49.

Sutherland, D. M. G., "Peasants, Lords, and Leviathan: Winners and Losers from the Abolition of French Feudalism, 1780–1820," *Journal of Economic History* 62:1 (2002), pp. 1–24.

Sutherland D. M. G., *The French Revolution and Empire: The Quest for a Civic Order* (Oxford, 2003).

Suval, S., *Electoral Politics in Wilhelmine Germany* (Chapel Hill, NC, 1985).

Swain, G., *Russian Social Democracy and the Legal Labour Movement 1906–1914* (London, 1983).

Swanson, G., "The Ottoman Police," *Journal of Contemporary History* 7:1/2 (1972), pp. 243–60.

Sylla, R. E. and G. Toniolo (eds.), *Patterns of European Industrialization: The Nineteenth Century* (London, 1991).

Szostack, R., "The Organization of Work: The Emergence of the Factory Revisited," *Journal of Economic Behaviour and Organization* 11 (1989), pp. 343–58.

Szreter, S., "The Importance of Social Intervention in Britain's Mortality Decline c. 1850–1914: A Reinterpretation of the Role of Public Health," *Social History of Medicine* 1 (1988), pp. 1–37.

Szreter, S., "Mortality in England in the Eighteenth and Nineteenth Centuries: A Reply to Sumit Guha," *Social History of Medicine* 7:2 (1994), pp. 269–82.

Szreter, S., *Fertility, Class and Gender in Britain 1860–1940* (Cambridge, 1996).

Tackett, T., *Religion, Revolution and Regional Culture in 18th-Century France: The Ecclesiastical Oath of 1791* (Princeton, NJ, 1986).

Tagg, J., *The Burden of Representation: Essays on Photographies and Histories* (Basingstoke, 1988).

Tallet, F. and N. Atkin (eds.), *Religion, Society and Politics in France since 1789* (London, 1991).

Tallet, F. and N. Atkin (eds.), *Catholicism in Britain and France since 1789* (London, 1996).

Tallet, F. and N. Atkin (eds.), *Priests, Prelates and People: A History of European Catholicism since 1750* (London, 2003).

Taylor, A., *The Struggle for Mastery in Europe, 1848–1918* (Oxford, 1954).

Taylor, B., "'The Men are as Bad as Their Masters . . .' Socialism, Feminism, and Sexual Antagonism in the London Tailoring Trade in the Early 1830s," *Feminist Studies* 5 (1979), pp. 7–40.

Taylor, B., *Eve and the New Jerusalem: Socialism and Feminism in the Nineteenth Century* (New York, 1983).

Taylor, B., *Mary Wollstonecraft and the Feminist Imagination* (Cambridge, 2003).

Taylor, C., *Sources of Self: The Making of Modern Identity* (Cambridge, MA, 1989).

Taylor, K., *The Political Ideas of the Utopian Socialists* (London, 1982).

Taylor, M. W., *The Men Versus the State* (Oxford, 1992).

Temin, P., "Two Views of the British Industrial Revolution," *Journal of Economic History* 57:1 (1997), pp. 63–82.

Thane, P., G. Crossick, and R. Floud (eds.), *The Power of the Past: Essays for Eric Hobsbawm* (Cambridge, 1984).

Therborn, G., *European Modernity and Beyond* (London, 1995).

Thomas, K., *Religion and the Decline of Magic* (London, 1983).

Thomas, P., "Poe's Dupin and the Power of Detection," in K. J Hayes (ed.), *The Cambridge Companion to Edgar Allan Poe* (Cambridge, 2002).

Thompson, D., *Europe since Napoleon* (London, 1966).

Thompson, D., "Women and Nineteenth Century Radical Politics," in J. Mitchell and A. Oakley (eds.), *The Rights and Wrongs of Women* (Harmondsworth, 1976).

Thompson, E. P., *The Making of the English Working Class* (London, 1963).

Thompson, E. P., "The Moral Economy of the English Crowd in the Eighteenth Century," *Past and Present* 50 (1971), pp. 76–136.

Thompson, E. P., *Customs in Common* (Harmondsworth, 1993).

Thompson, F. M. L., *English Landed Society in the Nineteenth Century* (London, 1963).

Thompson, F. M. L., "The Second Agricultural Revolution, 1815–1880," *Economic History Review*, 2nd series, 21 (1968), pp. 62–77.

Thompson, F. M. L., *Gentrification and the Enterprise Culture: Britain 1780–1980* (Oxford, 2001).

Thompson, I. A. A., *War and Government in Habsburg Spain 1560–1620* (London, 1976).

Thompson, W. S., "Population," *American Journal of Sociology* 34:6 (1929), pp. 959–75.

Thomson, M., *The Problem of Mental Deficiency: Eugenics, Democracy and Social Policy in Britain, c. 1870–1959* (Oxford, 1998).

Thönessen, W., *The Emancipation of Women: The Rise and Decline of the Women's Movement in German Social Democracy, 1863–1933* (London, 1973).

Tilly, C. (ed.), *The Formation of Nation States in Western Europe* (Princeton, NJ, 1975).

Tilly, C., *Contention and Democracy in Europe, 1650–2000* (Cambridge, 2004).

Tilly, C. and L. A. Tilly (eds.), *Class Conflict and Collective Action* (London, 1981).

Tilly, L. A., J. W. Scott, and M. Cohen, "Women's Work and European Fertility Patterns," *Journal of Interdisciplinary History* 6:3 (1976), pp. 447–76.

Tilly, R., "German Banking, 1850–1914: Development Assistance for the Strong," *Journal of European Economic History* 15 (1986), pp. 113–52.

Tocqueville, A. de, *Memoir, Letters, and Remains of Alexis de Tocqueville*, Vol. 1 (Cambridge, 1861).

Todorova, M., *Imagining the Balkans* (Oxford, 1997).

Tokmakoff, G., *P. A. Stolypin and the Third Duma: An Appraisal of Three Major Issues* (Langham, MD, 1981).

Tollener, J., "Gymnastics and Religion in Belgium 1892–1914," *International Journal of the History of Sport* 7:3 (1990), pp. 335–45.

Tolstoy, L., *On Education* (Chicago, 1972).

Tolz, V., *Inventing the Nation: Russia* (London, 2001).

Tombs, R., *France 1814–1914* (London, 1996).

Tombs, R., "Politics," in T. C. W. Blanning (ed.), *The Nineteenth Century: Europe 1789–1914* (Oxford, 2000).

Tomes, N., *The Gospel of Germs: Men, Women, and the Microbe in American Life* (Cambridge, MA, 1998).

Tomory, P., *The Life and Art of Henry Fuseli* (London, 1972).

Tönnies, F., *Community and Association* (London, 1974) [1887].

Tooley, R. V., *Leo Belgicus: An Illustrated List of Variants* (London, 1963).

Torpey, J., *The Invention of the Passport. Surveillance, Citizenship, and the State* (Cambridge, 2000).

Townson, N. (ed.), *El Republicanismo en España* (Madrid, 1994).

Trentmann, F. (ed.), *Paradoxes of Civil Society: New Perspectives on Modern German and British History* (Oxford, 2000).

Troebst, S. (ed.), "*Geschichtsregionen*: Concept and Critique," *European Review of History* special issue 10 (2003).

Trotha, T. von, *Koloniale Herrschaft. Zur soziologischen Theorie der Staatsentstehung am Beispiel des "Schutzgebietes Togo"* (Tübingen, 1994).

Trotsky, L., *The History of the Russian Revolution* (London, 1977).

Truant, C., *The Rites of Labor: Brotherhoods of Compagnonnage in Old and New Regime France* (Ithaca, NY, 1994).

Turner, H. A., *Trade Union Growth, Structure and Policy: A Comparative Study of the Cotton Unions* (London, 1962).

Turner, R. S., "The *Bildungsbürgertum* and the Learned Professions in Prussia, 1770–1830: The Origins of a Class," *Histoire Sociale-Social History* 13 (1980), pp. 105–35.

Umbach, M. (ed.), *German Federalism: Past, Present, Future* (London, 2002).

Valenze, D., *The First Industrial Woman* (Oxford, 1995).

Vanvugt, E., *De maagd en de soldaat: koloniale monumenten in Amsterdam en elders* (Amsterdam, 1998).

Vasary, I., "The One-Child System in Rural Hungary," *Continuity and Change* 4:3 (1989), pp. 429–68.

Veer, P. van der and H. Lehmann (eds.), *Nation and Religion: Perspectives on Europe and Asia* (Princeton, NJ, 1999).

Venturi, F., *Roots of Revolution: A History of the Populist and Socialist Movements in Nineteenth-Century Russia* (London, 2001).

Vicinus, M., *Independent Women: Work and Community for Single Women, 1850–1920* (Chicago, 1988).

Vicinus, M., *Intimate Friends: Women Who Loved Women, 1778–1928* (Chicago, 2004).

Vick, B., *Defining Germany: The 1848 Frankfurt Parliamentarians and the National Question* (Cambridge, MA, 2002).

Vickery, A., "Golden Age to Separate Spheres? A Review of the Categories and Chronology of English Women's History," *Historical Journal* 36 (1993), pp. 383–414.

Vidler, A. R., *The Church in an Age of Revolution* (London, 1974).

Vincent, D., *Literacy and Popular Culture: England, 1750–1914* (Cambridge, 1989).

Vincent, D., *The Rise of Mass Literacy: Reading and Writing in Modern Europe* (Cambridge, 2000).

Vital, D., *A People Apart: The Jews in Europe 1789–1939* (Oxford, 1999).

Vogel, J., *Nationen im Gleichschritt: Der Kult der "Nation in Waffen" in Deutschland und Frankreich, 1871–1914* (Göttingen, 1997).

Vogel, U., "Liberty is Beautiful: Von Humboldt's Gift to Liberalism," *History of Political Thought* 3/1 (1982).

Vögele, J., *Urban Mortality Change in England and Germany, 1870–1913* (Liverpool, 1998).

Vögele, J. and W. Woelk, "Public Health and the Development of Infant Mortality in Germany, 1875–1930," *History of the Family* 7:4 (2002), pp. 585–600.

Volkov, S., "Antisemitism as a Cultural Code," *Leo Baeck Institute Year Book*, Vol. 23 (1978a), pp. 25–46.

Volkov, S., *The Rise of Popular Antimodernism in Germany: The Urban Master Artisans, 1873–1896* (Princeton, NJ, 1978b).

Voth, H.-J. and T. Leunig, "Did Smallpox Reduce Height? Stature and the Standard of Living in London, 1770–1873," *Economic History Review* 49:4 (1996), pp. 541–60.

Vries, J. de, *The Economy of Europe in an Age of Crisis* (Cambridge, 1976).

Vries, J. de, *European Urbanization 1500–1800* (London, 1984).

Vries, J. de, "Between Purchasing Power and the World of Goods: Understanding the Household Economy in Early Modern Europe," in J. Brewer and R. Porter (eds.), *Consumption and the World of Goods* (London, 1993), pp. 85–132.

Vyleta, D. M., "Jewish Crimes and Misdemeanours: In Search of Jewish Criminality," *European History Quarterly* (2004).

Vyleta, D. M., *Crime, News and Jews: Vienna 1890–1914* (Oxford, 2005).

Waechter, M., "Mythen-Mächte im amerikanischen Geschichtsbewusstsein. Der Frontier-Mythos," *Geschichte als Argument* 41. Deutscher Historikertag in München 1996 (Munich, 1997).

Wagner, P., *A Sociology of Modernity: Liberty and Discipline* (London, 1994).

Wagner, P., "La forma politica dell'Europa – Europa come forma politica," in G. Bronzini, H. Friese, A. Negri, and P. Wagner (eds.), *Europa, costituzione e movimenti sociali* (Rome, 2003).

Wagner, P., "Palomar's Questions: The Axial Age Hypothesis, European Modernity and Historical Contingency," in J. Arnason et al. (eds.), *Axial Transformations* (Leiden, 2004).

Wagner, P., "Europe," in A. Harrington, B. Marshall, and H.-P. Müller (eds.), *Routledge Encyclopedia of Social Theory* (London, 2006).

Wagner, P. and B. Zimmermann, "Citizenship and Collective Responsibility: On the Political Philosophy of the Nation-Based Welfare State," in L. Magnusson and B. Stråth (eds.), *A European Social Citizenship?* (Brussels, 2004).

Wahl, A., *Confession et comportement dans le campagnes d'Alsace et de Baden*, 2 vols. (Metz, 1980).

Wahrman, D., *Imagining the Middle Class: The Political Representation of Class in Britain, c. 1780–1840* (Cambridge, 1995).

Walicki, A., *A History of Russian Thought* (Oxford, 1980).

Walkowitz, J. R., *Prostitution and Victorian Society: Women, Class, and the State* (Cambridge, 1980).

Walkowitz, J. R., *City of Dreadful Delight: Narratives of Sexual Danger in Late-Victorian London* (Chicago, 1992).

Wall, R., "European Family and Household Systems," in M. Poulain, R. Leboutte, H. Damas, and E. Vilquin (eds.), *Historiens et populations. Liber amicorum Étienne Hélin* (Louvain-la-Neuve, 1991), pp. 617–36.

Wallace, A. R., "The Origin of Human Races and the Antiquity of Man Deduced from the Theory of 'Natural Selection,'" in M. Biddiss (ed.), *Images of Race* (Leicester, 1979).

Walle, E. van de, "France," in W. R. Lee (ed.), *European Demography and Economic Growth* (London, 1979), p. 128.

Waller, B. (ed.), *Themes in Modern European History 1830–1890* (London, 1995).

Waller, J., *The Discovery of the Germ* (New York, 2003).

Waller, P. J., *Town, City and Nation: England 1850–1914* (Oxford, 1983).

Ware, T. *The Orthodox Church* (Harmondsworth, 1963).

Warren, J., "The Rankean Tradition in British Historiography," in S. Berger, H. Feldner, and K. Passmore (eds.), *Writing History: Theory and Practice* (London, 2003).

Warwick, A., *Masters of Theory: Cambridge and the Rise of Mathematical Physics* (Chicago, 2003).

Wawro, G., *Warfare and Society in Europe, 1792–1914* (London, 2000).

Wearmouth, R. F., *Methodism and the Struggle of the Working Classes* (Leicester, 1954).

Webb, S. and B. Webb, *Industrial Democracy* (London, 1897).

Weber, E., *Peasants into Frenchmen: The Modernization of Rural France 1870–1914* (London, 1977).

Weber, M., *Economy and Society: An Outline of Interpretative Sociology* (New York, 1968).

Weber, M., *Politik als Beruf*, 10th edn. (Berlin, 1993).

Weber, M., *Political Writings*, ed. P. Lassman and R. Speirs (Cambridge, 1994).

Webster, R., *Christian Democracy in Italy 1860–1960* (London, 1961).

Wehler, H. U., *The German Empire, 1871–1918* (Leamington Spa, 1985).

Weideger, P., *Gilding the Acorn: Behind the Facade of the National Trust* (London, 1994).

Weikart, R., "Laissez-Faire Social Darwinism and Individualist Competition in Darwin and Huxley," in *The European Legacy* 3 (1998), pp. 17–30.

Weindling, P., *Health, Race, and German Politics between National Unification and Nazism* (Cambridge, 1989).

Weir, D., "Life Under Pressure: France and England, 1670–1870," *Journal of Economic History* 44 (1984), pp. 27–47.

Weiss, O., "Seherinnen und Stigmatisierte," in I. G. von Olenhusen (ed.), *Wunderbare Erscheinungen. Frauen und katholische Frömmigkeit im 19. und 20 Jahrhundert* (Paderborn, 1995), pp. 51–82.

Weisz, G., *The Medical Mandarins: The French Academy of Medicine in the Nineteenth and Early Twentieth Centuries* (Oxford, 1995).

Welch, C., *De Tocqueville* (Oxford, 2001).

Welskopp, T., "Social History," in S. Berger, H. Feldner, and K. Passmore (eds), *Writing History: Theory and Practice* (London, 2003), pp. 203–22.

Wendland, A. V., "Volksgeschichte im Baltikum? Historiographien zwischen nationaler Mobilisierung und wissenschaftlicher Innovation in Estland, Lettland und Litauen (1919–1939)," in M. Hettling (ed.), *Volksgeschichten im Europa der Zwischenkriegszeit* (Göttingen, 2003), pp. 205–38.

Wentker, H., "Der 'Pitt Plan' von 1805 in Krieg und Frieden. Zum Kontinuitätsproblem der britischen Europapolitik in der Ära der Napoleonischen Kriege," *Francia*, 29:2 (2002), pp. 129–45.

Wesseling, H. L., "The Berlin Conference and the Expansion of Europe: A Conclusion," in S. Förster, W. Mommsen, and R. Robinson (eds.), *Bismarck, Europe and Africa: The Berlin West Africa Conference and the Onset of Partition* (Oxford, 1988), pp. 538–9.

Wetzel, D., *A Duel of Giants: Bismarck, Napoleon III and the Origins of the Franco-Prussian War* (Madison, WI, 2001).

Wetzell, R., *Inventing the Criminal: A History of German Criminology 1880–1945* (Chapel Hill, NC, 2000).

White, H., *Metahistory: The Historical Imagination in Nineteenth-Century Europe* (Baltimore, MD, 1973).

Whited, T. L., *Forests and Peasant Politics in Modern France* (New Haven, CT, 2000).

Whitfield, P., *The Image of the World: Twenty Centuries of World Maps* (London, 1994).

Whyte, J., *Catholics in Western Democracies: A Study in Political Behaviour* (Dublin, 1981).

Wiener, M. J., *English Culture and the Decline of the Industrial Spirit, 1850–1980* (Cambridge, 1981).

Wiener, M. J., *Reconstructing the Criminal: Culture, Law and Policy in England 1830–1914* (Cambridge, 1990).

Wienfort, M., "Administration of Private Law or Private Jurisdiction? The Prussian Patrimonial Courts 1820–48," in W. Steinmetz (ed.), *Private Law and Social Inequality in the Industrial Age: Comparing Legal Cultures in Britain, France, Germany and the United States* (Oxford, 2000), pp. 69–88.

Wikander, U. et al. (eds.), *Comparative Studies in Protective Labor Legislation for Women: Europe, the United States and Australia* (Champaign, IL, 1994).

Wikander, U., A. Kessler-Harris, and J. Lewis (eds.), *Protecting Women: Labor Legislation in Europe, United States and Australia, 1880–1920* (Urbana, IL, 1995).

Wildenthal, L. J., *German Women for Empire, 1884–1945* (Durham, 2001).

Williams, N., "Death in its Season: Class, Environment and the Mortality of Infants in Nineteenth-Century Sheffield," *Social History of Medicine* 5:1 (1992), pp. 71–94.

Williams, R. H., *Dream Worlds: Mass Consumption in Late Nineteenth-Century France* (Berkeley, CA, 1982).

Williamson, J. G., "Was the Industrial Revolution Worth it? Disamenities and Death in 19th Century British Towns," *Explorations in Economic History* 19 (1982), pp. 221–45.

Wilson, C. and R. I. Woods, "Fertility in England: A Long-Term Perspective," *Population Studies* 45:3 (1991), pp. 399–417.

Wilson, K., *The Policy of the Entente: Essays on the Determinants of British Foreign Policy, 1904–1914* (Cambridge, 1985).

Winders, J. A., *Gender, Theory, and the Canon* (Madison, WI, 1991).

Winders, J. A., *European Culture Since 1848: From Modern to Postmodern and Beyond* (New York, 2001).

Winnock, M., *Nationalism, Anti-Semitism and Fascism in France* (Stanford, CA, 1998).

Wintle, M. J., *Pillars of Piety: Religion in the Netherlands in the Nineteenth Century 1813–1901* (Hull, 1987).

Wintle, M. J. (ed.), *Culture and Identity in Europe: Perceptions of Diversity and Unity in Past and Present* (Aldershot, 1996).

Wintle, M. J., "Renaissance Maps and the Construction of the Idea of Europe," *Journal of Historical Geography* 25:2 (1999), pp. 137–65.

Wintle, M. J., *An Economic and Social History of the Netherlands, 1800–1920: Demographic, Economic and Social Transition* (Cambridge, 2000).

Wintle, M. J., "Representations of Europe in Cartography and Iconography from the Low Countries," in L. Hellinga et al. (eds.), *The Bookshop of the World: The Role of the Low Countries in the Book-Trade, 1473–1941* ('t Goy-Houten, 2001), pp. 191–206.

Wintle, M. J., "Europe on Parade: World War I and the Changing Visual Representations of the Continent in the Twentieth Century," in M. J. Wintle and M. Spiering (eds.), *Ideas of Europe since 1914: The Legacy of the First World War* (London, 2002), pp. 205–29.

Witt, P. C., "The Prussian Landrat as Tax Official: Some Observations of the Political and Social Functions of the German Civil Service During the Wilhelmine Empire," in G. Iggers (ed.), *The Social History of Politics: Critical Perspectives in West German Historical Writing since 1945* (Leamington Spa, 1985).

Wittkau, A., *Historismus. Zur Geschichte des Begriffs und des Problems* (Göttingen, 1992).

Wixforth, H. and D. Ziegler, "The Niche in the Universal Banking System: The Role and Significance of Private Bankers within German Industry, 1900–1933," *Financial History Review* 1:2 (1994), pp. 99–120.

Wohl, A. S., *Endangered Lives: Public Health in Victorian Britain* (London, 1984).

Wolf, E. R., *Peasant Wars of the Twentieth Century* (New York, 1969).

Wolff, J. and C. Arscott, "'Cultivated Capital': Patronage and Art in Nineteenth-Century Manchester and Leeds," in G. Marsden (ed.), *Victorian Values: Personalities and Perspectives in Nineteenth-Century Society* (London, 1990).

Wolff, L., *Inventing Eastern Europe: The Map of Civilization on the Mind of the Enlightenment* (Stanford, CA, 1994).

Wolffe, J., *God and Greater Britain, 1843–1945* (London, 1994).

Woltmann, K. von, *Über Natur, Bestimmung, Tugend und Bildung der Frauen* (Vienna, 1826).

Wood, A. and R. A. French (eds.), *The Development of Silesia: People and Resources* (Houndmills, 1989).

Wood, J. C., *Violence and Crime in Nineteenth-Century England: The Shadow of Our Refinement* (London, 2004).

Woodhouse, J., "Tales from Another Country: Fictional Treatments of the Russian Peasantry, 1847–1861," *Rural History* 2 (1991), pp. 171–86.

Woods, R. I., *The Population of Britain in the Nineteenth Century* (Basingstoke, 1992).

Woods, R. I., *The Demography of Victorian England and Wales* (Cambridge, 2000).

Woods, R. I., "Urban-Rural Mortality Differentials: An Unresolved Debate," *Population and Development Review* 29 (2003), pp. 29–46.

Woods, R. I., P. A. Watterson, and J. H. Woodward, "The Causes of Rapid Infant Mortality Decline in England and Wales, 1861–1921," Parts I and II, *Population Studies* 42:3 (1988), pp. 343–66 and 43:1 (1989), pp. 113–32.

Woolf, S., "Statistics and the Modern State," *Comparative Studies in Society and History* 31 (1989), pp. 588–603.

Woolf, S., *Napoleon's Integration of Europe* (London, 1991).

Woolf, S., "The Constitution of a European World View in the Revolutionary-Napoleonic Years," *Past and Present* 137 (1992), pp. 72–101.

Woolf, S., "Europe and its Historians," *Contemporary European History* 12 (2003).

Worboys, M., *Spreading Germs: Disease Theories and Medical Practice in Britain, 1865–1900* (Cambridge, 2000).

Wright, G. N., *A Life of Sir Francis Galton, From African Exploration to the Birth of Eugenics* (Oxford, 2001).

Wrigley, E. A., "A Simple Model of London's Importance in Changing English Society and Economy, 1650–1750," *Past and Present* 37 (1967), pp. 44–70.

Wrigley, E. A., *Continuity and Change: The Character of the Industrial Revolution in England* (Cambridge, 1988).

Wrigley, E. A., "Society and Economy in the Eighteenth Century," in L. Stone (ed.), *An Imperial State at War: Britain from 1689 to 1815* (London, 1994), pp. 72–95.

Wrigley, E. A., "Explaining the Rise in Marital Fertility in the 'Long' Eighteenth Century," *Economic History Review* 51:3 (1998), pp. 435–64.

Wrigley, E. A. and R. S. Schofield, *The Population History of England, 1541–1871: A Reconstruction* (Cambridge, 1981).

Wrigley, E. A., R. S. Davies, J. E. Oeppen, and R. S. Schofield, *English Population History from Family Reconstitution 1580–1837* (Cambridge, 1997).

Young, D. M., *The Colonial Office in the Early Nineteenth Century* (London, 1961).

Zamagni, V., *The Economic History of Italy 1860–1990: From the Periphery to the Centre* (Oxford, 1993).

Zanden, J. L. van, "The First Green Revolution: The Growth of Production and Productivity in European Agriculture, 1870–1914," *Economic History Review* 44 (1991), pp. 215–39.

Zanden, J. L. van, "Wages and the Standard of Living in Europe, 1500–1800," *European Review of Economic History* 2 (1999), pp. 175–97.

Zeldin, T., *The Political System of Louis-Napoleon Bonaparte* (London, 1958).

Zerubavel, E., *Terra Cognita: The Mental Discovery of America* (New Brunswick, NJ, 1992).

Ziegler, D., "The Influence of Banking on the Rise and Expansion of Industrial Capitalism in Germany," in A. Teichova, K. van Henenryk, and D. Ziegler (eds.), *Banking, Trade and Industry: Europe, America and Asia from the Thirteenth to the Twentieth Century* (Cambridge, 1997), pp. 131–56.

Zimmer, O., *A Contested Nation: History, Memory and Nationalism in Switzerland 1761–1891* (Cambridge, 2003a).

Zimmer, O., *Nationalism in Europe, 1890–1940* (Basingstoke, 2003b).

Zuckerman, F., *The Tsarist Secret Police Abroad: Policing Europe in a Modernising World* (Basingstoke, 2003).

Index